READINGS ON
READING INSTRUCTION

READINGS ON READING INSTRUCTION

EDITED BY

Albert J. Harris

DIRECTOR, OFFICE OF RESEARCH AND EVALUATION
DIVISION OF TEACHER EDUCATION
CITY UNIVERSITY OF NEW YORK

DAVID McKAY COMPANY, INC.
NEW YORK

READINGS ON READING INSTRUCTION

COPYRIGHT © 1963 BY

DAVID MC KAY COMPANY, INC.

FIRST EDITION MAY 1963
REPRINTED SEPTEMBER 1964

LIBRARY OF CONGRESS CATALOG CARD NUMBER: 63-13176
MANUFACTURED IN THE UNITED STATES OF AMERICA

AS AN advocate of wide reading in varied sources for teachers as well as for children, I have tried to get my students taking courses about reading to become acquainted with the contents of educational periodicals, and with pamphlets, yearbooks, curriculum guides, and proceedings of reading conferences. Even with a well-stocked library, this has proven to be difficult. Aside from the gaps caused when particular articles and issues disappear, there is the very real problem that many students have very little time for reference reading in the library. This is particularly true of those who work, part-time or full-time, while going to school. For many students, extensive reading is impossible if it has to be done in the library.

Readings on Reading Instruction is a collection of selections chosen to provide a varied and nutritious diet of supplementary reading. The sixteen chapters have been chosen so as to resemble the chapter organization of most textbooks on reading instruction, while not duplicating the organization of any one textbook. Within each chapter there is variety. Scholarly summaries of research in a particular area are balanced by lively contributions of the "how to do it" type. Original research papers have generally been included only when the major part of the paper is a description of an interesting teaching procedure. An occasional paper presents a point of view that differs considerably from majority opinion. The list of authors includes most of the recognized American authorities in the field of reading, as well as some writers who are not yet well known. In point of time the papers cover a period of twenty-one years, the earliest having appeared in 1941 and the latest in May, 1962.

Preference has generally been given

to contributions of less than 3,000 words, in order to have variety and balance within each chapter and yet stay within a previously agreed number of pages. This policy has allowed the inclusion of nearly 100 different selections. Some excellent papers that ranged in length between 4,000 and 8,000 words regretfully had to be omitted. In a small number of cases a condensed version from *Education Digest* has been used instead of the original longer paper. In other cases, only part of a longer selection has been used. When that is the case, a line of four dots indicates that some of the original material has been omitted at that point.

References were given in many different ways in the original selections. Some used footnotes, while others referred by number to a list of references at the end. The style of citation differed considerably on such matters as the use of Roman numerals, whether to put date before or after volume, etc. In order to leave the selections intact, references are given exactly as in the original publications. In most selections the original references are given in full; in a few cases, in which the references were not specifically referred to in the article, they have been omitted.

I am very grateful to the many publishers and authors who have graciously given permission to reprint their selections. The authors are identified in the list of Contributors. In addition to the authors, my thanks go to: *Child-hood Education, Education, Educational Administration and Supervision, Education Digest, Elementary English, Elementary School Journal, Exceptional Children, Grade Teacher, Journal of Educational Research, N.E.A. Journal, National Elementary Principal, Phi Delta Kappan, The Reading Teacher,* and *Teachers College Record;* also to Bobbs-Merrill Co.; Bureau of Publications, Teachers College, Columbia University; Educational Testing Service; Ginn and Company; Harper and Row; the Macmillan Company; Metropolitan School Study Council; National Society for the Study of Education; New York State Department of Education; University of Chicago Press; University of Delaware; University of Florida; and University of Pittsburgh; and to Emmett Albert Betts, Donald L. Cleland, George D. Spache, and Russell G. Stauffer.

The many tasks involved in reproducing and arranging the materials and in writing for the necessary permissions were performed mainly by two very capable assistants, my secretary, Mrs. Minnie Graff, and my daughter Charlotte, to both of whom I wish to express my gratitude. The responsibility for choosing the selections and deciding their order and sequence is entirely my own.

ALBERT J. HARRIS
Mount Vernon, N.Y.
July 2, 1962

C O N T R I B U T O R S[1]

HELEN B. AASEN, Elementary School Teacher, Public Schools of Minneapolis, Minnesota

R. VAN ALLEN, Director of Curriculum Coordination, Department of Education, San Diego County, San Diego, California

MAUREE APPLEGATE, Associate Professor of Education, Wisconsin State College, La Crosse, Wisconsin

MARGUERITE P. ARCHER, Reading Consultant, Public Schools, Pelham, New York

EMMETT ALBERT BETTS, Research Professor of Reading, University of Miami, Coral Gables, Florida

EMERY P. BLIESMER, Director, McGuffey Reading Clinic, University of Virginia, Charlottesville, Virginia

HELEN BOWYER, Contributing Editor, *Spelling Progress Bulletin*, 5848 Alcove Ave., North Hollywood, California

BEATRICE E. BRADLEY, Principal, Mayfair School, Philadelphia, Pennsylvania

JAMES I. BROWN, Professor of Rhetoric, University of Minnesota, Minneapolis, Minnesota

JEANNE CHALL, Associate Professor of Education, The City College of the City University of New York, New York, New York

MARIE B. CLARK, Elementary Principal and Teacher of Grade 6, Washington School, Vincennes, Indiana

THEODORE CLYMER, Professor of Education, University of Minnesota, Minneapolis, Minnesota

WILLIAM S. CORLISS, Director of Elementary Curriculum, Birmingham Public Schools, Birmingham, Michigan

MARTHA DALLMANN, Professor of Education, Ohio Wesleyan University, Delaware, Ohio

MARY ANN DANIEL, Reading Consultant, Huntingdon Junior High School, Abington, Pennsylvania

AMO DE BERNARDIS, Assistant Superintendent, Public Schools, Portland, Oregon

LEE C. DEIGHTON, President, The Macmillan Company, New York, New York

EDWARD W. DOLCH, Late Professor Emeritus of Education, University of Illinois, Champaign, Illinois

DOLORES DURKIN, Associate Professor of Education, Teachers College, Columbia University, New York, New York

MURIEL FISCH, Teacher of Sixth Grade, Board of Education, New York, New York

MARGARET FISHBACK, Author, New York, New York

CECIL FLOYD, Assistant Superintendent of Schools, Joplin, Missouri

EDWARD FRY, Director, Reading Clinic, Loyola University, Los Angeles, California

ROMA GANS, Professor Emeritus of Education, Teachers College, Columbia University, New York, New York

HELEN GARRETT, New York State Education Department, Albany, New York

ARTHUR I. GATES, Professor Emeritus of Education and Supervisor of Research, Institute of Language Arts, Teachers College, Columbia University, New York, New York

JOHN I. GOODLAD, Professor of Education, University of California, Los Angeles, California

J. C. GOWAN, Professor of Education and Chairman of Guidance, San Fernando Valley State College, Northridge, California

WILLIAM S. GRAY, Late Profesor Emeritus of Education and Director of Research in Reading, University of Chicago, Chicago, Illinois

PATRICK J. GROFF, Associate Professor of Education, San Diego State College, San Diego, California

RICHARD S. HAMPLEMAN, Associate Professor of Education, North Texas State University, Denton, Texas

ALBERT J. HARRIS, Director of the Educational Clinic and Professor of Education, Queens College of the City University of New York, Flushing, New York

KATHLEEN B. HESTER, Professor of Education, Eastern Michigan University, Ypsilanti, Michigan

GERTRUDE HILDRETH, Professor of Education, Brooklyn College of the City University of New York, Brooklyn, New York

J. KENDALL HOGGARD, Director of Instruction, City Schools, El Dorado, Arkansas

LELAND B. JACOBS, Professor of Education, Teachers College, Columbia University, New York, New York

NANCY LARRICK, Author and Editor, Quakertown, Pennsylvania

MAY LAZAR, Assistant Director (Retired), Bureau of Instructional Research, Board of Education, New York, New York

LUCILE LINDBERG, Professor of Education, Queens College of the City University of New York, Flushing, New York

[1] Only the senior author is listed here for articles with two or more authors.

VIVIAN L. LOVELESS, Teacher of Grade 3, Silverside School, Mount Pleasant Special School District, Wilmington, Delaware

GLENN MCCRACKEN, Director, Department of Audio-Visual Services, New Castle Public Schools, New Castle, Pennsylvania

ROBERT A. MCCRACKEN, Reading Consultant, Fulton Consolidated Schools, Fulton, New York

RUTH V. MCCREARY, Reading Supervisor, Public Schools, Wooster, Ohio

CONSTANCE M. MCCULLOUGH, Professor of Education, San Francisco State College, San Francisco, California

JOHN E. MARTIN, Assistant Professor of Education, Fresno State College, Fresno, California

ALBERT J. MAZURKIEWICZ, Associate Professor of Education and Director, Reading and Study Clinic, Lehigh University, Bethlehem, Pennsylvania

EDITH F. MILLER, Teacher of Grade 5, Central School, Glen Ridge, New Jersey

ANN ESS MORROW, Teacher of English and Counselor, Pontiac Northern High School, Pontiac, Michigan

LILLIAN ORME, Principal, Charles Sumner School, Kansas City, Missouri

ODILLE OUSLEY, Author of Basal Readers, Ginn and Company, Boston, Massachusetts; formerly Professor of Education, University of Georgia, Athens, Georgia

DON H. PARKER, Senior Author, The SRA Multilevel Learning Laboratories, and Multilevel Consultant, Science Research Associates, Chicago, Illinois

HAZEL S. RENCH, Associate Professor of Education, State University of New York, Brockport, New York

HELEN ROCHE, Psychologist and Reading Consultant, Van Dyke Schools, Warren, Michigan

DAVID H. RUSSELL, Professor of Education, University of California, Berkeley, California

HARRY W. SARTAIN, Professor of Education and Director of Falk Laboratory School, University of Pittsburgh, Pittsburgh, Pennsylvania

MARY C. SERRA, Director of the Reading Laboratory, Illinois State Normal University, Normal, Illinois

NILA BANTON SMITH, Professor of Education, New York University, New York, New York

GEORGE D. SPACHE, Head, Reading Laboratory and Clinic, University of Florida, Gainesville, Florida

RUSSELL G. STAUFFER, Director, Reading-Study Center, University of Delaware, Newark, Delaware

DAVID K. STEWART, Director of Elementary Education, Kenosha Public Schools, Kenosha, Wisconsin

EARL K. STOCK, Assistant County Superintendent (Retired), Centre County, Pennsylvania

MARTHA THOMPSON, Elementary Supervisor, Avonworth Union School District, Ben Avon, Pittsburgh 2, Pennsylvania

ROBERT L. THORNDIKE, Professor of Educational Psychology, Teachers College, Columbia University, New York, New York

MILES A. TINKER, Consulting Psychologist, Santa Barbara, California; Professor Emeritus of Psychology, University of Minnesota, Minneapolis, Minnesota

LLOYD S. TIREMAN, Late Professor of Education, University of New Mexico, Albuquerque, New Mexico

GUY W. WAGNER, Director, Curriculum Laboratory, State College of Iowa, Cedar Falls, Iowa

CARLETON WASHBURNE, Distinguished Professor of Education, Michigan State University, Lansing, Michigan; Emeritus Director of Teacher Education, Brooklyn College of the City University of New York, Brooklyn, New York

MARTHA GESLING WEBER, Professor of Education and Director of Reading Center, Bowling Green State University, Bowling Green, Ohio

LESTER R. WHEELER, Director of Reading Clinic and Professor of Education, University of Miami, Coral Gables, Florida

GERTRUDE WHIPPLE, Supervisor of Language Arts, Detroit Public Schools, Detroit, Michigan

MILDRED WIERSEMA, Head of English Department, Pontiac Northern High School, Pontiac, Michigan

PAUL A. WITTY, Professor of Education, Northwestern University, Evanston, Illinois

MARY H. B. WOLLNER, Professor of Education and Parent Consultant to the Reading Clinic, Rockford College, Rockford, Illinois

LOUISE WILLSON WORTHINGTON, Elementary School Consultant, Ginn and Company, Boston, Massachusetts

GRETCHEN WULFING, Director of Elementary School Education (Retired), Oakland Public Schools, Oakland, California

WILLA T. WYNN, Supervisor of Elementary Education, Pittsburgh Public Schools, Pittsburgh, Pennsylvania

CONTENTS

CONTENTS   xiii

CHAPTER I

PERSPECTIVES ON READING

1. CURRENT READING PROBLEMS A WORLD VIEW*

William S. Gray

THE schools of this country are in no sense unique because they face challenging reading problems. Reports from abroad show that every country, language, and culture faces many such problems, which are in need of intensive study. This situation is due to two closely related facts: first, a clear recognition by all nations of the tremendous role that world literacy might play in promoting individual welfare, group progress, international understanding, and world peace; and second, the many challenging problems faced everywhere in efforts to help both children and adults to acquire sufficient competence in reading to use it effectively in promoting personal development and group progress.

Recently a world-wide study was made for the United Nations Educational, Scientific, and Cultural Organization of methods being used in teaching both children and adults to read and write. There follows a discussion of some of the reading problems which, it was found, are being faced in one form or another throughout the world.

Without doubt the most dramatic reading problem which the world now faces relates to the elimination of illiteracy among adults as easily and quickly as possible. Since World War II keen interest in this problem has swept throughout the world like a tidal wave. As the war came to an end, the plight of many people, particularly in underdeveloped areas, stood out in tragic relief. These people had seen

* From William S. Gray, "Current Reading Problems: A World View," *Education Digest,* XXI, No. 4 (December, 1955), 28–31. Reported from *Elementary School Journal, LVI* (September, 1955), 11–17. Reprinted by permission of Mrs. William S. Gray, *Elementary School Journal,* and *Education Digest.*

enough during the war period to know that better conditions existed elsewhere. They were eager to improve their status but lacked the essential knowledge and skills.

Constructive work in many of these areas begins with efforts to solve the most urgent problems faced by a group. The immediate purpose may be to improve sanitation, to eliminate contagious diseases, to improve child care, or to raise better crops. As these steps go forward, it soon becomes apparent that an understanding of improved ways of doing things, of the duties and responsibilities of a good citizen, and of the characteristics, ways of life, attitudes, and ideals of other people is essential to progress. As a result, a burning desire develops on the part of adults to learn to read and to have access to the knowledge and pleasure which printed materials afford.

Attempts to meet this demand bring up pointed questions concerning the level of literacy that is required to insure both individual and group progress. "Functional literacy" has been discussed. This was defined in the Unesco study as that level of ability to read and write which is normally expected of literate people in the area or culture involved. When this requirement was translated into terms of school achievement, it was found that the minimum level of reading ability needed is that normally attained by children completing the fourth grade. But many agencies both in this country and abroad maintain that the standard adopted should be at least one or two grades higher.

A Huge Task

The task involved in achieving world literacy among adults is a tremendous one. About two-thirds of the adult population of the world need some training in reading. Unfortunately, the supply of trained teachers and instructional materials is very limited in a surprisingly large number of areas. But through the cooperation of many agencies, such as Unesco, progress is being made. Fortunately the responsibilities involved are being assumed rapidly by governmental agencies. If the present effort does not diminish, it is safe to predict that within two decades the percentage of functionally literate adults in the world will be double what it is today. It is very stimulating, indeed, to contemplate the tremendous influence of such an achievement on individual development, group progress, and world understanding.

But the hope of a literate world tomorrow lies in the attainment of a relatively high level of literacy on the part of the present generation of boys and girls. The size of the task which the world faces in this connection is indicated by the following statements taken from one of the monographs prepared by Unesco, based on an extended study of children of school age: "Of every ten children in the world, five go to school." Of those in school, "four are in the primary school, and one is receiving post-primary education." These data show that schools are now available for only half of the children in the world. Furthermore, four-fifths of those attending school are in the primary schools, which barely carry the child to the level of functional literacy. Obviously, governmental and other agencies face the responsibility of greatly extending current educational facilities in terms of the number of children served and the length of the schooling provided. They also face the need of finding adequate solutions to several closely related teaching problems.

Among these, and of primary importance, is the choice of methods which should be used in developing the initial attitudes and skills involved in learning to read. This, as in the past, continues to be a subject of controversy. And what of the nature of help needed by retarded or seriously handicapped readers? Evidence secured in the Unesco study showed that poor readers are found in all countries.

Closely paralleling the need of selecting valid methods of teaching reading is the urgent demand for reading materials adapted to the interests, needs, and reading ability of the respective age groups taught. The English-speaking countries, as a whole, are indeed fortunate in respect to the amount of children's literature now available. They have also made some progress in providing interesting books for older children and adults with limited reading ability. However, many countries have done little, if anything, to meet the need for reading materials suited to various age groups. The situation at the adult level is equally serious. As a result the reading skills acquired in literacy classes often disintegrate through disuse. During recent years, however, these needs are being recognized and steps taken to provide suitable materials. Various agencies are also striving to provide so-called "follow-up," or library, material which is related to adult interests.

Why They Read

The problem involved in supplying this need is a tremendous one. This fact was emphasized by the finding in the Unesco study of the reasons why those who have recently attained literacy want to read. They include: to keep posted concerning current events; to secure information relating to health, sanitation, child care, and the raising of crops; to learn of available jobs and to increase one's economic efficiency; to acquire social recognition and prestige; and to increase one's social awareness by learning about community activities and the forces that promote or retard progress; to meet one's civic obligations effectively; to extend knowledge of the world in which one lives by learning about things and events both near and far, about other people and their way of life, and about the natural and social forces that influence the reader; to broaden one's cultural background through access to his literary heritage, thus contributing to a fuller and richer life; and to satisfy religious aspirations and to build a philosophy of life that satisfies one's spiritual needs.

This list of reasons is indeed impressive. The purposes named are comparable in scope to those which prompt people in this country to read. Unfortunately, reading instruction in the past has usually been discontinued for most children and adults as soon as they have learned to read very simple material. Experience shows that, if reading is to serve the broader purposes named, both children and adults must acquire far greater ability to understand and interpret what is read than they have generally acquired in the past. The development of the attitudes and skills involved is without doubt one of the most challenging reading problems which the world faces.

The importance of this problem has been recognized in this country for more than a quarter-century. Accordingly, vigorous effort has been made to promote growth, from the earliest school days, in both breadth and depth of interpretation. Furthermore, the period of systematic training in reading has been extended into high school and college, and guidance has been provided in reading in the various curriculum fields. Although the methods used in Europe in promoting breadth and depth of interpretation differ in many respects from those used here, the importance of the problem is recognized with equal clarity. Many other countries, such as India, which are attempting to train their citizens to assume intelligently the obligations of free men and to engage in social reconstruction, are beginning to provide added training in ability to interpret what is read.

As implied earlier, little more than a foundation for reading has been established when children or adults are able to recognize words independently and accurately and to grasp the sense-meaning of passages. In addition, growth is needed in capacity to read between the lines, to infer what is implied but not stated, and to grasp accurately the meanings conveyed by new language forms and figures of speech. Growth is needed also in ability to recognize parallels in one's own experience and to interpret the ideas acquired in the light of all one knows or can find out. Equally important is ability to think clearly about the accuracy, value, and significance of what is read; to identify the use of loaded words and propaganda; and to evaluate critically the ideas read. Finally, the reader must fuse the ideas read with previous experience so that new understandings are acquired, thinking is clarified, rational attitudes are developed, and improved thinking and behavior patterns are established. Such problems challenge teachers in every part of the world as they attempt to meet reading problems and to make their teaching so effective that it will contribute to the maximum in enriching the lives of their pupils and in helping them to meet their own and their own country's obligations and contributions to culture.

2. WHAT HAVE WE ACCOMPLISHED IN READING?
—A REVIEW OF THE PAST FIFTY YEARS*

Nila Banton Smith

THIS last half-century stands out as a truly golden period in the progress of reading instruction. More innovations have been effected in reading during the last fifty years than during the entire three hundred years antedating this period of American history. I am sure that progress has been equally notable in the other phases of the language arts constellation. It is most appropriate that accomplishments in all of the language arts areas be reviewed upon this momentous occasion —the Golden Anniversary of The National Council of Teachers of English!

Progress in reading instruction has been marked by a succession of turning points. For a period of years reading methods and materials all over the country are quite similar—so similar, in fact, that an unbiased examiner might arrive at the conclusion that all had been turned out of the same mold, with just a slightly different crimp here and there in the contour of the pan. Then, rather suddenly, a new plan becomes popular, and we teach reading in this manner until another turning point arrives. Thus, epoch after epoch of reading instruction passes (26).

* From Nila Banton Smith, "What Have We Accomplished in Reading?—a Review of the Past Fifty Years," *Elementary English*, XXXVIII (March, 1961), 141–50. Reprinted by permission of the author and the National Council of Teachers of English.

Fortunately printed records are available to which we can turn in delineating these epochs and ascertaining their characteristics. In attempting to obtain information to bring to you about reading epochs during our recent half century the following source materials, published between 1910 and 1960, were explored: prominent educational magazines that usually contain reading articles, yearbooks of learned societies, summaries of published investigations in reading, lists of unpublished master's and doctoral researches completed or under way. More than 300 pieces of materials were surveyed for the purpose of picking up the sequence of events and trends which marked the pilgrimage of reading in its upward march from 1910 to the present time. This information will be presented to you by decades.

Accomplishments from 1910 to 1920

The dramatic decade beginning with 1910 ushered in the first truly great breakthrough in reading progress. This was the birth of the scientific movement in education. In 1909 Thorndike made the initial presentation of his handwriting scale before a meeting of the American Association for the Advancement of Science, and in 1910 it was published (29). Generally speaking, the publication of the Thorndike scale has been recognized as the beginning of the contemporary movement for measuring educational products scientifically. In the immediately ensuing years scales and tests appeared rapidly: Courtis arithmetic tests, Hilligas' Composition Scale, Buckingham Spelling Scale—and then a reading test —The Gray Standardized Oral Reading Paragraphs (13). This test was published in 1915. Other reading tests followed shortly.

As a result of the strong new surge of interest in placing education on a scientific basis together with its correlative motives for developing instruments of measurement, we would naturally expect that the scientific study of reading problems would take a vigorous spurt. And this it did.

Through all the years up to 1910 only 34 studies had been reported in reading. During the 1910-20 decade, 200 accounts appeared, about six times as many as had been reported during the entire history of reading preceding this time. These studies had to do mostly with tests and school surveys, as would be expected.

As for method: the most revolutionary thing happened that had happened since clergy began to teach reading in churches, and dames began to teach reading in kitchens. "For hundreds of years oral reading had maintained a supreme and undisputed claim on teaching methods" (25). During this decade, however, the concept of teaching *silent* reading burst into our slumbering complacency like a bombshell. It came suddenly and in the midst of a period in which school people were serenely content in the use of sentence-story methods applied to the oral reading of selections in literary readers. For the most part they continued to use these practices to the end of the decade but the startling new idea was at least launched. Discussions of the advantages of silent reading appeared for the first time in the Sixteenth (16) and in the Eighteenth (17) Yearbooks of the National Society for the Study of Education. Speakers at educational conventions began to talk about it, magazine articles began to discuss it. The idea had been born.

To sum up: developing the concept of applying scientific techniques to the study of reading, devising standardized instruments to measure reading achievement, increasing the number of studies tremendously, initiating the silent reading idea. These seem to have been the major accomplishments from 1910 to 1920.

Accomplishments from 1920 to 1930

The period extending from 1920 to 1930 is perhaps the most golden decade in this golden era of progress in so far as fundamental changes in reading practices are concerned. These changes were largely due to the scientific movement which had shaped up during the preceding period and which now was opening up fresh wells of information with improved and extended applications.

The new studies conducted during this decade carried with them three distinct earmarks of progress: the number increased tremendously; they covered a wider scope of problems; many of them were conducted in classrooms by teachers and other school personnel, rather than being confined to the laboratory.

As to the number of investigations: Gray's summaries reveal that 763 were reported as compared with 200 during the preceding decade. This unprecedented increase reflected the zeal and enthusiasm with which school people were searching for more information about the important subject of reading.

The studies of this period probed a variety of problems, but there were three problem areas which were most highly significant. They were significant because they resulted in sweeping changes in practice. These three areas were: (1) silent reading, (2) individual differences, and (3) remedial reading.

The first half of this decade might well be called "The Age of Silent Reading." "These years were marked with an exaggerated, often exclusive emphasis on silent reading as opposed to the traditional oral reading techniques" (25). As previously mentioned, the concept of teaching silent reading was initiated during the latter part of the preceding period, but it didn't really take hold as a nation-wide classroom practice until the years of 1920 to 1925. This sudden and widespread reversal in practice was largely due to two influences: the development of tests which revealed that silent reading was superior to oral reading in speed and comprehension; and the publication of The Yearbooks of the National Society for the Study of Education. As already indicated, one article each appeared in the Sixteenth (16) and the Eighteenth (17) Yearbooks. The climax, however, came with the publication of the Twentieth Yearbook, Part II (19) of which was devoted entirely to the report of the "Society's Committee on Silent Reading." Following the appearance of this Yearbook, "textbook writers began to produce readers based on silent reading procedures; other authors prepared professional books on silent reading; teachers busied themselves in preparing exercises that would check comprehension of silent reading by means of drawings, true-false statements or completion sentences and so forth. The whole country for a time seemed to be obsessed with the idea of teaching silent reading" (25).

This extreme emphasis, however, was soon balanced with other factors. By 1925 the novelty of the new idea had worn off, somewhat; investigations revealed some unique uses of oral reading, school people discovered that there still were some special needs for oral reading in the school program. Perhaps, the culminating influence came with the publication of the Twenty-Fourth Yearbook, Part I (20), which appeared in 1925. This Yearbook advocated a broader program of reading instruction which among other things recognized both oral and silent reading. New courses of study, professional books and readers immediately reflected the broadened objectives of this Yearbook and methods during the years 1925–1930 were shaped largely by its contents. So during the first two decades of the last fifty years we progressed from extreme oral reading to extreme silent reading to a broader program which recognized both. In my opinion, this was an indication of real accomplishment.

As for individual differences: with the administration of the newly developed tests, a very great fundamental truth became apparent with a violent impact—the realization that there were wide individual differences in the reading achievement of children, in the same grade and in the same classroom. This discovery spurred school people to experiment with a variety of adjustments in classroom organization and instruction, designed to cope with this newly revealed variation in the learning rate of children.

There were reports of adjustments made in classrooms which maintained the regular organization such as ability grouping, flexible promotions, and differentiated assignments. But the pulsating new idea was that of breaking up class organization entirely to permit of individual progression. This plan of organization received as much attention at this time as it is receiving at the present moment. Speeches, articles, and yearbooks dealt with the subject. San Francisco, Los Angeles, Detroit, Winnetka, Madison, Wisconsin and other school systems reported (21) results they had obtained by individual instruction. The states of Connecticut and Illinois reported (21) experiments in individualizing instruction in rural schools.

The various plans, on the whole, were patterned after the Winnetka or the Dalton ideas, in both of which individual progression in reading and other subjects was made possible by means of assignments in which the child worked through subject material that increased in small increments of difficulty. The important point to note is that attention to individual differ-

ences in reading received its first great impetus during this decade of remarkable progress.

The concept of *remedial* reading was launched from its small island of study during this period and sent out over unexplored seas in quest of answers to disability problems. The movement was spurred on by the use of standardized tests. These tests revealed that thousands of boys and girls were failing each year to make normal progress in reading. Published reports of work in the reading disability field indicate that the chief interest at this time was in diagnosing individual cases. As for method, it was during this period that Fernald evolved her kinesthetic method, and that Orton expounded his theory on mixed dominance and the treatment that accompanied it. Remedial reading did get under way during this period.

In beginning reading there also were innovations. Experience charts first came into use. The Nineteenth Yearbook (18), published in 1920, dealt with reading materials. In it examples were given of charts based on children's experiences, and the practice of introducing children to beginning reading through the use of such material was advocated. This practice was not widely accepted until much later, but progress had been made in evolving the idea.

And last but not least, mention must be made of another mark of progress which clearly stamped itself into the later annals of this decade. The reading readiness concept began to take shape at this time.

In 1926 the International Kindergarten Union in cooperation with the

United States Bureau of Education conducted an investigation on "Pupils' Readiness for Reading Instruction upon Entrance to First Grade." The first articles on this subject were published in Childhood Education in January, 1927. Two of these articles used the term "reading readiness." In so far as I am aware, this was the first time that this phrase crept into our reading vocabulary (27). In Gray's summaries published in 1928, he reported for the first time three studies on reading readiness. A few master's theses and a trickling of articles on this subject also appeared before the close of the decade. The new concept, however, was still in the formative stage, and little was done about it in a practical way until the following period, but the movement was on its way.

Much more could be said about the accomplishments made during this unprecedented period. I should like to dwell longer on the accumulation of information gathered about reading and the auspicious innovations in classroom practice that were inaugurated at this time, but I must pass on to other conquests and other days.

Accomplishments from 1930 to 1940

This period may be characterized largely as one of extension and application rather than one of revelation and initiation.

Investigations continued at an accelerated pace. In round figures about 1200 studies were reported between 1930 and 1940. Not only were these studies greater in number, but they were superior in isolation of problems, in designs, and in controls.

Some of the embryo ideas that had sprouted in the preceding decade came into full bloom and fruited profusely at this time. For example: the reading readiness interest reached its zenith in this period (27). Published investigations on this topic increased steadily during each successive year of this decade (9), reaching their climax of frequency in 1940 when Gray reported 22 studies relating to this topic in one year. Since that time the number has decreased steadily.

Turning to unpublished research, this was the heyday of aspiring masters and doctors in finding problems for research in the readiness area. The first doctoral dissertation on readiness was reported in 1927. From that time on, the number of master and doctoral studies increased, reaching its peak in the years 1937 to 1940. Fourteen such studies were completed in 1937, 15 in 1938, 14 in 1939, and 12 in 1940. Since that time only 2 or 3 academic studies on readiness have been reported each year.

A similar trend is seen in published articles on reading readiness. Periodicals abounded with discussions on readiness topics from 1930 to 1940. Articles on this subject rarely appear in present-day literature.

In the light of this evidence, it may be concluded that this was the period of most vigorous emphasis, both on investigations of reading readiness and applications of the readiness theory. The concept has been accepted now and we hear little about it at the present time.

Remedial reading, which had experienced a touch-and-go recognition during the preceding period, now became established and gained stature. Many significant studies were conducted in the remedial reading areas: causes of difficulties, diagnosis, and corrective procedures. Professional books devoted exclusively to remedial reading were first published. Some laboratory studies were still made but the majority of studies now were conducted in schools. Remedial reading, which had started in laboratories, now became a topic for practical experimentation in the public schools themselves.

A new trend that began to emerge was that of giving beginning attention to high school, college, and adult reading. Studies made at these levels, however, were mostly concerned with interests in and uses of reading rather than with reading achievement and teaching procedure.

Every decade reviewed so far has been characterized by one or two events of great distinction. In the 1910–20 decade, it was the application of scientific measurement and investigation to reading, in the 1920–30 era, it was the startling innovations of silent reading and of individual progression. What was the spectacular event in the nineteen-thirties?

The Activity Movement swept the country during these years, and the startling new idea in reading was to teach this skill as a part of the Activity Program. In such a program children worked freely and spontaneously and actively in following their own interests; and teachers were intrigued with the new "game" of trying to get all of their subject matter across through "Units of Work."

In so far as reading was concerned, pupils had access to a considerable number of books bearing largely on the topic of their "Unit of Work." This was the first big impetus for bringing a quantity of books into the classroom for reading. There was a profusion of charts and school-made booklets growing out of children's interests. Pupils read functionally from their co-operatively prepared materials and out of many books in doing research in connection with their Units. In a word, this was how reading proceeded in the Activity Program in the thirties.

We no longer hear of the Activity Program at this time nor of the teaching of reading in connection with this program. The Activity Movement, however, made a vigorous impact on the teaching of reading and other subjects at this time—an impact so strong that its influence still continues. The Activity Movement distracted the school public from its age-old concept of schools centered almost exclusively on subject-matter goals to schools in which consideration is given to the child, himself, his stage of development, his interests, his activities, his choices and his decisions.

In summary, we may say that progress in this decade was characterized by continuing investigations, greater in number, higher in quality than in the preceding decade; intensive application of the readiness concept; transfer of remedial activities from laboratory to classroom; beginning attention to reading at higher levels; and widespread interest in teaching reading as an integral part of the Activity Program.

Accomplishments from 1940 to 1950

An event resulting from progress in science overshadowed all other indications of progress during this period. The "birthday of the atomic age" is officially set as December 2, 1942, when Dr. Enrico Fermi turned on the first successful nuclear energy machine in Chicago. The first atomic bomb destroyed Hiroshima on August 6, 1945. On the face of things this terrifying discovery with its possibilities for good or for evil reduced to comparative insignificance our little scientific achievements in reading. Yet, could this achievement have been possible without reading? Can we cope adequately with its future destructive or beneficent effects, as the case may be, without more efficient reading skill and a wider reading citizenry? The atomic age and reading immediately become interactive.

But we didn't realize this at the time. We were too close to this earth-shaking event to sense its import for reading instruction. The war probably only had two *immediate* effects on reading. One of these was a diminution in the number of reading investigations. This was probably due to the fact that many of the psychologists and educators who conducted research in reading, or stimulated others to do so, were in the armed services.

The other major effect of the war was the shocking discovery that at this day and age thousands of young men in the military service could not read well enough to follow the simple printed instructions for camp life. Coupled with this discovery was the revelation that reading could be taught to these young men in army camps in an amazingly short time. Concurrently, several new investigations disclosed reading deficiencies in large numbers of high school and college students. These several influences combined to produce a spurt in attention to reading at these higher levels. Immediately following the war, a great deal of professional literature on reading emerged and among these publications several bulletins and one Yearbook appeared dealing with high school and college reading. Chief among these publications was a bulletin of the National Education Association titled *Reading Instruction in Secondary Schools* (15), and the Forty-Eighth Yearbook, Part II of The National Society for the Study of Reading, titled *Reading in High School and College* (24). The actual teaching of reading at these levels had not progressed far at this time but the idea was vigorously expanding.

During this period, reading in the content subjects also became a matter of wide discussion and the subject of a few investigations. The studies at this time pointed to the general conclusion that while good readers can read well in all subject fields, special practice in reading in particular subject areas is helpful to average and poor readers.

In the forties, wide recognition was given to the interrelationships amongst the language arts. Studies, articles, speeches were concerned with the relationship of reading to spelling, handwriting, vocabulary, and composition. As a result we came to recognize that reading was not an isolated skill independent of other skills used in the interchange of ideas, but that it was just one aspect of the total language arts constellation mutually dependent upon and interactive with all other skills in the communication dimension.

A strong new concern also sprang up in regard to the effects of three of the newer media for mass communication: comics, movies, and radio. Television did not come in for much attention until the next decade but during this period wide dissemination of entertainment through the first named agencies stirred up worry on the part of school people and parents. They feared that interest in listening to radio, looking at comics, viewing movies would reduce interest in reading and thus decrease the amount of reading done. Numerous popular articles bemoaned the situation and pointed out its dangers. Several studies were conducted directed toward the exploration of students' interests in this area and finding out how much time they devoted to the offerings of these types. Thus initial steps were taken in obtaining information to combat what was thought to be the first threat to reading.

Remedial diagnosis and treatment continued to claim a large segment of the spotlight. Mechanical instruments and devices which had been introduced during the preceding period increased in numbers and use. There were fewer studies reported on psychological factors such as dominance, handedness, eyedness, and reversals. An increasing number were devoted to

personal factors as related to reading: personal interests and attitudes, personal status in social, emotional, and experiential maturity. This attention to other growth and development factors as related to reading was certainly one of the most notable advances made during this period.

To sum up: the chief points of progress during this decade were: increased attention to teaching reading at the higher levels; growing attention to reading in the content subjects; concerns about mass communications; attempts to find relationships between reading and handwriting, spelling, vocabulary and composition; and perhaps, most important of all, a growing consciousness of the profound truth that reading doesn't develop in a vacuum by itself, but that it is part and parcel of general child development and is affected by all other aspects of child growth.

Accomplishments from 1950 to 1960

A most exciting decade! For one thing, interest in reading instruction became almost universal during this period. There was a time when primary teachers were the only people interested in the teaching of reading. Now teachers of all subjects and at all levels want to know more about reading. Parents are asking questions, pursuing books and articles on reading. Students at high-school and college levels and adults beyond college are flocking to reading centers. Slick magazines and laymen are discussing reading freely. A great conflagration of interest has been ignited amongst eachers and students, and more espe-cially amongst the lay public. And this is good.

During this period, however, for the first time in history, reading instruction in American schools underwent harsh and severe criticism by laymen. School people maintained that the criticisms were unfair and rose to the defense of their methods through articles, speeches, discussions, and investiga-tions. Several comparative studies of "Then and Now" were made. These studies, on the whole, showed that we were teaching reading as well as or better than in preceding years.

In so far as progress is concerned the criticism by laymen probably had three good effects: it caused school people to examine their present meth-ods more carefully; it stimulated the interest of parents and other laymen in reading instruction; it offered mo-tives and opportunities to school people to explain the research, psychology, and philosophy on which present meth-ods are based. So in this situation, as is often the case in other situations, even criticism caused reading to move forward.

Perhaps as an off-shoot of interest and criticism, coupled with a growing awareness of the complexity of the reading process, there has been a spurt of activity in the re-instatement and increase of reading courses in the cur-riculums of teacher-training institu-tions. Concurrently with this interest in adding more courses, standards are being raised in regard to the quali-fications of teachers of reading and of reading specialists. This movement toward better-trained teachers in read-ing is a big step forward.

As for the number of investigations: studies during this period reached in-credible proportions. Gray reported over 1,000 studies in his 1960 sum-mary, but in his introduction he said for the first time in his thirty-five years of annual summarizing, "The number of studies are increasing so rapidly that it is no longer possible to report all of them in this annual summary. Those referred to this year represent either a new or distinctive approach to a prob-lem or suggest significant issues in need of further study." Not only was this increase apparent in the published reports of reading investigations, but it also was reflected in the reports of dissertations completed or in progress which soared to new numerical heights, the number reported averaging about 90 per year as compared with about 50 in the preceding decade.

Advance is shown in the subjects of investigation. Reading in the con-tent fields, adult reading deficiencies, and television as related to reading came in for strong additional attention. The most gratifying trend revealed, however, is that we are at present delving more deeply into the reading process and more broadly into the factors that affect it. The former popu-lar topic of phonics now seems to have been replaced with studies of percep-tion. Comprehension is no longer treated as a lump sum; the emphasis at present is upon the higher thinking processes of interpretation and critical reading. The old readiness studies are replaced with investigations of predic-tion and expectancy. Remedial reading is not so much concerned now with studies of gadgets and specific teach-ing remedies as it is with organismic and personality factors. Parental personality, attitudes, and interactions with the child as related to reading entered the research scene for the first time during this period, and many reading investigations concerned with parents and their children are now being reported. Studies are made in regard to the climate of the classroom and its effect on reading. This mere glimpse at some of the subjects of the most recent studies is indicative of a trend toward probing to greater depths and in wider breadths than was evident in most of the studies preceding this period.

Special mention should be made of a clearly discernible advance in regard to reading and the other language arts. In the preceding decade we became strongly concerned about the relationships of reading to the subjects of spelling, handwriting, vocabulary, and composition. During this decade we have moved on to a concern about aspects of the language arts which perhaps are less tangible than the subject matter areas but more inclusive in their application to the entire block of communication skills. Listening studies have increased by leaps and bounds. Some of the most recent dissertation topics have to do with semantic studies of reading content, multiple meanings, figures of speech in reading, and the linguistic approach to reading. Is it not an accomplishment to have moved on from subject interrelationships to relationships dealing with listening and the various aspects of linguistics?

The innovation in reading method which has loomed large on the horizon of late is the plan known as *individualized instruction*. The amount of atten-

tion given to this plan in this decade is comparable to that given to individual instruction in the nineteen-twenties. It probably is the most popular topic of discussion at present in educational magazines and often at teacher gatherings.

This individualized plan of the present is different from individual instruction which was popular in the twenties. The earlier plan was subject-matter oriented. Each child was given subject-matter assignments divided into small increments of difficulty and he was permitted to progress as fast as he, personally, could complete each successive increment. The present plan is child-psychology oriented utilizing particularly Dr. Willard Olson's theory of *seeking, self-selection,* and *pacing* in that the child seeks that which stimulates him, selects the book he desires to read, and proceeds at his own rate.

This plan has been used too recently for research reports to have crept into published summaries of investigations. Most of the research on this topic at present falls into the unpublished category of theses, dissertations, or mimeographed reports of experiments carried on in certain school systems. An examination of the most recent sources listing dissertations completed or under way indicates that a quantity of research is now taking place in regard to this topic. Much of it will undoubtedly find its way into print in the near future.

Much more could be said about this period, but because of lack of time we now shall let the curtain fall over the last scene in fifty years of reading accomplishment. As we review the stirring events of the past, we have a ight to feel cheered, grateful, proud. In looking back in retrospect we might wonder whether another fifty years could possibly bring about so many changes. This was the first period in which experimentation could be conducted scientifically. In consideration of the newly developed tools, our eagerness to learn, and studies conducted, we might reason that practically all facets of reading instruction have been explored and thus another era could never be so great as this.

If we do reason to this conclusion, we probably are wrong. We pioneered during this period in unexplored territory. We chopped down and cleared away the large virgin trees, but perhaps some of the humble shrubs or creeping vines or fragile mosses may hold even more significance for us than the strikingly obvious, first-sight timbers. But these more obscure growths won't yield their significance with the use of heavy saws and axes. We shall need fresh, piercing insights in choosing which of these to select for dislodgment, and then we shall need unique, delicate tools to pry them loose from their tangled environment and to test the potency of their effect.

What I am trying to say is that while our accomplishments have been very great, indeed, it may be that we have only penetrated the first layer, the troposphere, so to speak. Undoubtedly, brilliant new insights will be revealed, ingenious new techniques of experimentation will be evolved. Possibilities of such developments portend opportunities for unlimited achievement in the future.

Most assuredly, we shall not rest complacently in the glory of achievement during this past golden age. Rather shall we look forward to still greater accomplishments in reading. Let us push on and on with more and more vigor in the next decade and the next decade, and in all of the other decades ahead!

REFERENCES

This bibliography would be too voluminous if each separate piece of material examined were listed. In case of educational journals, yearbooks, and summaries of investigations, each successive issue or publication was examined during the period of years indicated by dates accompanying the general reference. In cases in which a specific reference was made, or a quotation was stated from one particular publication, that publication is listed. Professional books on reading were examined but the titles are too numerous to include in this list.

1. BETTS, EMMETT ALBERT, and BETTS, THELMA MARSHALL. *An Index of Professional Literature on Reading and Topics.* New York: American Book Company, 1945.
2. *Childhood Education,* 1–37, 1924–60.
3. *College English,* 1–22, 1939–60.
4. *Doctoral Dissertations Accepted by American Universities.* New York: H. W. Wilson Co., 1934, 1955.
5. *Educational Index,* 1–31. New York: H. W. Wilson Co., 1930–60.
6. *Elementary School Journal,* 10–60, 1910–60.
7. *Elementary English,* 1–37, 1924–60.
8. *English Journal,* 1–49, 1911–60.
9. GOOD, CARTER V. "Doctoral Studies Completed or Under Way," *Phi Delta Kappan,* 1923–53; (Separate publications) Lyda, Mary Louise; Jenson, Glenn; Brown, Stanley; Anderson, Harold, Phi Delta Kappa, Bloomington, Ind., 1954–59.

10. GRAY, WILLIAM S. *Summary of Investigations Relating to Reading.* Supplementary Monograph, No. 28. Chicago: University of Chicago, 1925.

11. ———. "Summary of Investigations Relating to Reading," *Elementary School Journal,* 26–32, 1925–32.

12. ———. "Summary of Investigations Relating to Reading," *Journal of Educational Research,* 5–54, 1932–60.

13. ———. *Oral Reading Paragraphs Test.* Bloomington, Indiana: Public School Publishing Co., 1915.

14. NATIONAL EDUCATION ASSOCIATION, "Newer Practices in Reading in the Elementary School," *The National Elementary Principal,* Seventeenth Yearbook, 1938.

15. NATIONAL EDUCATION ASSOCIATION, *Reading Instruction in Secondary Schools,* Research Bulletin, Vol. 22, No. 1, 1942.

16. NATIONAL SOCIETY FOR THE STUDY OF EDUCATION: *Sixteenth Yearbook, Part I,* 1917.

17. *Eighteenth Yearbook, Part II,* 1919.

18. *Nineteenth Yearbook, Part I,* 1920.

19. *Twentieth Yearbook, Part II,* 1921.

20. *Twenty-Fourth Yearbook, Part I,* 1925.

21. *Twenty-Fourth Yearbook, Part II,* 1925.

22. *Thirty-Sixth Yearbook, Part I,* 1937.

23. *Forty-Eighth Yearbook, Part I,* 1949.

24. *Forty-Eighth Yearbook, Part II,* 1949.

25. SMITH, NILA BANTON. *American Reading Instruction.* New York: Silver Burdett, 1937.

26. ———. "Historical Turning Points in Reading," *National Education Association Journal* (May, 1952), 280–82.

27. ———. *Readiness for Reading and Related Language Arts,* National Council of Teachers of English, 1950.

28. *The Reading Teacher,* International Reading Association, 1–14, 1947–60.

29. THORNDIKE, E. L. *The Thorndike Scale for Handwriting of Children.* New York: Bureau of Publications, Teachers College, Columbia University, 1910.

30. TRAXLER, ARTHUR E. New York: Educational Records Bureau. *Ten Years of Research in Reading* (with Seder, Margaret), 1941. *Another Five Years of Research in Reading* (with Townsend), 1946. *Eight More Years of Research in Reading* (with Townsend), 1955. *Research in Reading During Another Four Years* (with Jungeblut), 1960.

31. U. S. LIBRARY OF CONGRESS, CATALOG DIVISION. *American Doctoral Dissertations Lists.* Washington: Government Printing Office, 1913–40.

3. WHAT IS A GOOD READING PROGRAM?*

Gertrude Whipple

THE eight criteria outlined below are based on publications in the field of reading and are supported by the consensus of judgments of the yearbook committee and its advisers for this chapter. Under each criterion are listed several clues which aid in determining whether a given reading program meets the standard. A good reading program in an elementary school:

1. Is consciously directed toward specific, valid ends which have been agreed upon by the entire school staff. Widely accepted ends are: rich and varied experiences through reading; broadening interests and improved tastes in reading; enjoyment through reading; increased personal and social adjustment; curiosity concerning the ideas given in the reading material; resourcefulness in using reading to satisfy one's purposes; and growth in the fundamental reading abilities, such as ability to recognize the words, to understand the meanings of words, to comprehend and interpret what is read, to locate references bearing on a problem, and to organize ideas gathered from different sources.

   a. The reading activities in the classroom are guided from day to day by the teacher's long-range purposes rather than being allowed to develop in a whimsical manner.

   b. The emphasis in the program is consistent from grade to grade and is directed to different phases of reading rather than to a single phase or a few phases to the neglect of other important goals.

   c. The aims agreed upon are used by the staff as the basis for regular appraisals of their reading program.

2. Co-ordinates reading activities with other aids to child development.

   a. Knowledge of each child's home conditions and his community relationships is sought by the teacher in order to supplement his understanding of the child's classroom behavior (e.g., the teacher confers with parents, visits the home when there is real need, welcomes the child's confidences, knows the school neighborhood, and is acquainted with personal information on school records).

   b. An adequate experiential background is provided for the daily

* From Gertrude Whipple, "Characteristics of a Sound Reading Program," in N. B. Henry (ed.), *Reading in the Elementary School,* Ch. II, Forty-eighth Yearbook of the National Society for the Study of Education, Part II (Chicago: Univ. of Chicago Press, 1949), pp. 34–38. Reprinted by permission of the author, the National Society for the Study of Education, and The University of Chicago Press.

reading (e.g., teachers recognize the building of background as an important phase of reading guidance; before the pupils read, teachers employ discussion, encourage questions, anticipate difficulties, and help pupils to approach the reading with a purpose).

c. Firsthand experiences that illuminate what is read are reported in the class (e.g., telling about a *combine* one has seen in action so that other pupils will understand the reference to a *combine* in the story).

d. Auditory and visual aids are used to stimulate interest in reading, to help explain word meanings, to test the pupil's ability to interpret what is read, and for other important purposes. (Types of aids used are: maps, diagrams, models, exhibits, study prints which are displayed or handed about among the pupils, stereoscopic slides, projected slides which are exhibited on the wall, filmstrips, motion pictures, sound movies, phonograph records, and the radio.)

e. Ideas obtained from the reading are used by the children in a variety of ways (e.g., oral discussion, written composition, pictorial art, dramatization, dance and dramatic rhythms).

f. Listening experiences are related to reading activities, and vice versa (e.g., utilizing in reading the habits which the pupils have acquired in learning to understand spoken language such as the habit of figuring out auditory word forms and their meanings from the clues provided by the statement as a whole; providing opportunity for the child to acquire ideas by listening to oral reading).

g. Parents are kept informed of what the school is doing for the child and what can be done at home to supplement the school experiences.

3. Recognizes that the child's development in reading is closely associated with his development in other language arts.

a. The teacher's survey of the child's abilities and needs is concerned with his progress in various methods of communication—speaking, listening, writing, spelling—not in reading only; the child's language habits and his ability to think are especially studied as indicative of his reading needs.

b. The elements of English are integrated in the classroom schedule (e.g., aspects of reading and expression are taught by the same teacher rather than presented as totally separate learnings).

c. Reading is so taught as to shape the child's thinking, his conversation, and his behavior (e.g., he is encouraged to avoid repeating words of a book without complete understanding; he has higher standards of living because of what he has read; he adopts good health habits learned through reading).

d. Written activities based on reading activities are so guided as to encourage growth in variety and quality of ideas, in ability to organize ideas, in richness of vocabulary, in clarity of expression, in legibility of handwriting, and in accuracy of spelling (e.g., the types of writing undertaken are suited to the individual child's abilities; they are carried out for purposes that appeal to the child; the written materials prepared are appraised so that the child makes steady growth in expression and does not repeat his errors).

4. At any given level, is part of a well-worked-out larger reading program extending through all the elementary- and secondary-school grades.

a. Guidance of reading pervades the whole structure of the school program at each level.

b. Desirable materials, facilities, and resources for reading are provided in all grades.

c. Cumulative record cards in reading are kept and passed on with the pupil to the next teacher in order to provide information about his previous growth in reading. (Teachers do not expect a required degree of reading ability on the part of every pupil.)

d. From one grade to the next the program advances gradually in difficulty for the individual child and, at each stage, is in harmony with his interests and characteristics (e.g., no single program for all the pupils of a class).

e. At each level the reading demands in the different curriculum fields are harmonized; in departmentalized schools all teachers are informed of the pupils' reading abilities and needs and make use of this information in guiding reading; most of the books provided in the content fields should not show a greater degree of difficulty than those provided for basic reading. (This provision is essential in order that the child's thought can be directed to the problem at hand rather than confused by the problem of reading.)

5. Provides varied instruction and flexible requirements as a means of making adequate adjustments to the widely different reading needs of the pupils.

a. The administrative provisions made in the school encourage proper adjustments:

(1) Sufficient time is allowed on the program for study of the needs of pupils and for the guidance of each child in light of his needs.

(2) Wide latitude in interpreting bulletins and courses of study is allowed the teacher in order that he may adapt the program to the interests, abilities, and aptitudes of the pupils.

b. The grouping of the pupils for reading within the classroom is flexible, in accord with the varied and changing needs of the individual child.

c. The reading opportunities provided in the classroom are designed to meet specific needs:

(1) At the beginning of the term and regularly throughout the semester the teacher studies each child's reading needs.

(2) The teacher leads the individual child to adopt purposes for reading which will promote his growth and is versatile in the use of a variety of teaching methods.

(3) The teacher maintains conditions favorable to learning and free from those that confuse or frustrate the individual (e.g., when a child does not respond to the reading instruction, the teacher seeks the causes of his difficulties instead of concluding that the child is a nonreader or has failed to put forth effort).

d. The reading materials provided are sufficient in quantity, in variety of types, and in range of reading difficulty to permit the teacher to make necessary adjustments; teachers are familiar with the content of their reading materials and choose in terms of group and individual needs.

6. Affords, at each level of advancement, adequate guidance of reading in all the various aspects of a broad program of instruction: basic instruction in reading, reading in the content fields, literature, and recreational or free reading.

a. Pupils are given definite instruction in reading (e.g. interpretational, oral reading, meaning vocabulary, word recognition, use of reference books, skimming for main points, careful reading for details, co-ordinated reading of text and illustrative material) as opposed to the provision of mere test exercises in reading; reading activities follow different patterns from day to day.

b. The pupils are guided in reading a variety of material—periodicals, textbooks, supplementary books, reference books in different fields, and books of library type—in the light of their different purposes.

c. Guidance is given to all pupils, the good readers as well as the poor readers (i.e., no group of pupils is left to its own devices in order that the teacher may secure time to teach other pupils).

d. The pupils become increasingly skillful in formulating purposes for reading and in choosing materials and methods of reading that will satisfy these purposes.

e. The pupils engage in abundant voluntary reading outside of school, find intensified satisfactions in such reading, and increasingly apply critical thinking and evaluation to current ideas and points of view.

7. Makes special provisions for supplying the reading needs of cases of extreme reading disability, in

other words, the small proportion of pupils whose needs cannot be satisfied through a strong developmental program.

a. The classroom teacher identifies cases of retardation through regural surveys of pupils' reading needs.

b. Specialized diagnosis of needs is provided by a child study center, or a reading clinic, or a remedial-reading specialist, or, if such services cannot be secured, by a regular teacher who makes a careful study of the child in the light of a knowledge of the professional literature on remedial reading.

c. The teacher builds the reading morale of the failing pupil, helps the sensitive, uneasy, embarrassed, or tense child to relax before attempting to teach him to read.

d. The physical and emotional defects of the failing child are corrected as far as possible; specialized training suited to his individual needs is provided by a skilled regular teacher or a remedial-reading agency.

8. Provides for frequent evaluation of the outcomes of the program and for such revisions as will strengthen the weaknesses discovered.

a. Regular use of appraisal techniques.

b. Consideration of the findings by all those concerned (the teachers, the principal, the supervisors, other adminstrators, and the parents) in relation to the entire school curriculum and determination of needed changes.

c. Gradual revision of the program in the direction of the standards applied.

4. GREATER READING POWER NEEDED TODAY*

Roma Gans

ANYONE who has even a slight acquaintance with today's children notices how up-to-date their interests

* From Roma Gans, "Greater Reading Power Needed Today," *Childhood Education*, XXXVIII, No. 3 (November, 1961), 104–7. Reprinted by permission of the author and the Association for Childhood Education International, 3615 Wisconsin Ave., N.W., Washington 16, D.C.

are. Penetration of space, changing of car patterns, and packaging of foods are topics with which they are at home. They are eager to explore new ideas and, if encouraged, ask for more. Many educators, parents, and producers of materials for children recognize this learning readiness. As a result good schools are continually altering their programs to include more study of the fascinating world about us and are providing books, pamphlets, films, and filmstrips which help the child to grow as an informed individual and as one who is motivated to keep up-to-date.

Emphasis is on continuing one's quest for information and pursuing reading as a regular way of learning. This emphasis is relatively new and absolutely essential if a child is to acquire reading habits and powers which will fit him for constructive living. According to test results of the past several decades, we have produced readers who do well on comprehension and relevant skills. But polls examining adult reading habits reveal the disturbing fact that we have failed to produce a truly reading public, adults who keep up with current affairs via newspapers and magazines and who read books of any kind. *Obviously we produce readers who can read, but too many who don't.* Therefore, along with a concern for developing real powers in reading must be a direct effort to create a continuing, self-propelling reader.

Whetting Appetite to Read Carefully

Many promising efforts in developing such readers can be found in schools. Carefully planned studies of problems and topics in science and social studies—through which children even in primary grades help select reference books, collect pertinent articles from books, papers, and magazines, and stay with one such study for several days and often for weeks—start many a youngster on the path of his continuing reading. He also discovers how much there is to know on almost every topic, a discovery which he might not make if taught in the short lesson-by-the-day manner. A reader whose appetite gets whetted to read about dinosaurs, the Lewis and Clark expedition, or space explorations is tooling himself for perpetuating his education. Teachers and parents who help a child capture this eagerness to read have started him on a promising road of intelligent living.

There are other essential goals in today's reading programs which are proper for these times. In general, schools are eager to teach children to become comprehending critical and selective readers. The "reading-to-give-back" emphasis common in schools thirty or forty years ago may still be the major emphasis in some isolated spots, but in general schools have demonstrated genuine competence in giving broader and more adequate focus to reading programs. The expansion of library facilities in elementary and secondary schools is one form of evidence to support this observation. However, when we examine practices and materials now frequently determined in central administration or curriculum leaders' offices another question presents itself: Are the practices and materials we recommend consistent with our goals? In some (perhaps many) classrooms, yes. In thousands, no. The problem of unraveling the meaning of broadly stated goals in terms of what they imply in day-to-day classroom life has not been adequately met in either large or small school systems.

Reading for Decision-Making

A sketchy look at *power-in-reading* reveals that a reader must develop the abilities necessary to recognize words, to get at the author's meanings, to see the interrelationship of ideas from beginning to end of the story or article, to recall essential points, and to make some personal reactions to them, such as "I like this," "Don't like this," "I believe it," "This is important," or "I am not sure of this." These aspects of power have been widely recognized and taught in our schools. With the provisions of new texts and materials and some changes in method, these reading competencies have been developed. They go considerably beyond the reading-to-recall emphasis of earlier teaching.

However, the power which today's child needs must go beyond this stage. Its development cannot be achieved merely by purchasing new materials and altering some methods. Today's child faces a world in deep controversy. Most important matters on the international and national front are at issue. Not only are there pro and con positions but many variations in between. A conscientious citizen, the type we hope to be developing, takes decision-making seriously. Before he takes a stand on water chloridation, increase in sales taxes, the school bond issue, and increased aid to South America, he tries to gather data, weighs different points of view, and finally relates various proposals to his basic philosophy. To be unable to follow a process similar to this or to be unwilling to makes him either a pawn in the hands of others or an opinionated non-thinker.

The use of reading in the decision-making process demands the application of abilities to think effectively. Schools in stressing critical reading have recognized the involvement of thinking, but proper help to teachers and leaders in the field on developing thinking is only beginning.

Atmosphere Conducive to Thinking

The critical reader who will be able to meet his desire to make competent choices in important matters must be schooled in the ability to think—not only to recognize and recall what he reads but also to grow in his ability to unravel complicated ideas, to analyze them in terms of relevance to the issue at point, to synthesize, to appreciate adequacy and inadequacy of data, and ultimately to evaluate and come to a tentative or final conclusion. Such intellectual powers cannot be confined to a child's reading only but must be a part of the child's whole everyday environment. The classroom atmosphere must be conducive to thinking. It must be an atmosphere in which all youngsters feel at ease, are encouraged to think for themselves and to express their ideas even if divergent from others including the teacher's, and are able to accept correction and help in thinking better.

Central to the creation of such a thinking classroom is a thinking teacher —one who is free, encouraged, and helped to develop a challenging intellectual classroom atmosphere. However, this is a professional need crying for attention. Crowded classrooms, congested time schedules, and "required achievements" all too often minimize or blot out a teacher's concern for *time to think*. This observation alone should cause us to give serious attention to the quality of life which goes on in far too many schools today. Helpful books, pamphlets, and reports of research on thinking are becoming increasingly available to reading program planners; and curriculum and reading specialists, along with teachers and school leaders, must face all changes in common procedures which will help meet this crucial need.

Along with the importance of the classroom atmosphere and the competence of the teacher is the quality of the curriculum with its implicit materials. Content areas that include both current and past important phases open up the interests and encourage the inquiries that aid the child in becoming an informed student. They also acquaint him with materials, various forms of writing, varied ways of presenting data as well as the substance out of which thought-provoking questions arise.

Techniques of discussion and skill in using them are also a part of the teacher's concern.

Well-guided discussion is an essential part of a program geared to develop high-powered reading. The hurried short-answer oral or written comprehension check meets many a classroom need; but its use to the exclusion of thoughtful discussion, sharing of divergent views, pausing to consider and reconsider the use of all the other ways of getting into the deeper understanding of an important learning will deny a child the right to develop as a thinker.

If one accepts points thus far presented, many common assumptions and practices need to be examined. Children need more opportunity and guidance in the selection of materials in school and public libraries. They also need to become selective buyers so that they continue as adults to be competent purchasers and subscribers. Much more opportunity is needed to discuss materials than the crowded schedule of today permits. More attention to authorship is long overdue, and for intermediate and upper grades such problems as ghost-writing, editorialized news, and slanted writing are properly included to increase the child's competence in working his way through today's materials.

Changes in Evaluating Growth

The enhancement of reading power of the kind presented here will demand material changes in evaluating reading growth. Some essential reading skills can be assessed by current tests. Others, however, will require new tests and even year-round observations. Such questions as: Are youngsters growing in ability to act independently to material read? Are they selecting materials for a study with concern for relevance, date of publication, authorship, and all the rest? Are they becoming more sensitive to subtle meanings? Do they ask about the author's purpose or motive? Answers to such questions and others must become a part of the assessment of reading growth.

Children are ready for this deeper concept of reading. It remains for administrators, teachers, curriculum and reading specialists to aid the steady progress toward the development of such reading power. To stop short of the inclusive changes required is to short-change today's child.

5. ARE WE TEACHING READING?*

George D. Spache

THE critics of public education find that the average parent listens with a ready ear. Parents are concerned about the quality of public education and what it does for their children. When asked what they think is the most important thing for children to get from their education in school, 34 per cent of the public says that they consider a mastery of regular school subjects, the fundamentals or Three R's, the most important outcome. This is as important to many parents as character education or preparation for earning a living.

Because of the criticisms and the concern they arouse in the minds of parents, every effort should be made to secure and reveal the results of comparative studies which may indicate the success of present-day schools.

In 1919, New York City conducted a city-wide testing of its pupils using

tests devised and used in 1845. The comparison of the results for several thousand children showed that the pupils of 1919 were superior in spelling and in answering thought questions based on reading materials. The pupils of 1845 were better in answering questions requiring rote learning or sheer memorization.

In 1929, Fish gave the high school entrance test of 1853 to pupils of New York City. The results in 1853 had indicated that eighteen out of twenty students who took the test had qualified for entrance to the high school. The sample of the 1929 pupils included two hundred drawn from ten different sections of the city. Every one of these pupils qualified for entrance to high school when measured by the same standards used in 1853.

Comparison of the reading of sixth-grade pupils of Los Angeles of 1923 and 1933 showed that the later children tested higher by six months above the earlier pupils.

From his survey of the pupils in the

* From *Are We Teaching Reading?*, a 31-page pamphlet (Gainesville, Fla.: University of Florida, 1956), pp. 11–15. Reprinted by permission of the author.

Grand Rapids, Michigan, schools in 1948, Dr. William S. Gray made comparisons with the earlier pupils of 1916. He concluded, "The data show that notable progress has been made in comprehension but that little or no progress has been made in oral reading or speed of silent reading." In 1938, Dr. Charles H. Judd compared the current pupils of St. Louis, Missouri, in grades two to eight with those attending school in 1916. He found that the average scores in oral reading were higher in 1916. These two studies are more readily interpreted if we are familiar with the school's objectives in the teaching of reading in 1916 and in 1938 or 1948. In the 1920's and 30's, American teachers shifted their emphasis from skill in oral reading to stress upon comprehension in silent reading. This change in emphasis was based upon the belief that comprehension in silent reading was a more practical, long-range goal than mere facility in pronouncing words. The results of these two surveys show that modern schools are accomplishing their aims of producing better comprehension of materials read silently, and of de-emphasizing skill in oral reading.

In 1945, Dr. Ernest W. Tiegs studied the educational achievement of 230,000 students in 60 communities in 7 states. He compared these results with the testing records available from previous years. His results, in part, indicate, "the achievement of public school pupils is not falling; in fact the data show a slight though probably not statistically significant gain in achievement." This study included not only reading but also all other fundamental subjects.

In 1941, over 2,500 high school seniors of Indianapolis, Indiana, were given the same test formerly employed in 1919. Eighty per cent of the seniors of 1941 scored higher than the median scores of the seniors in 1919.

A comparison of the achievement of 1921 and 1947 was made in Lincoln, Nebraska, for over five thousand children in grades four to seven. The 1947 pupils were found to be far better in speed and comprehension in reading despite the fact that they were six to eight months younger, on the average, than those attending school in 1921.

A contrast of the achievements of 1948 with those of 1931 was made in Springfield, Illinois, with sixth-grade pupils. The reading accomplishments of the 1948 pupils were found to be superior in every respect.

In 1948, a report comparing the accomplishments of pupils of Springfield, Missouri, with those of 1931 in six schools concluded, ". . . there is reasonably good evidence that the teaching of reading in Springfield is now more successful in producing the outcome we have measured than it was seventeen years ago." A repetition of this study in 1949, contrasting achievement with that of pupils of 1932, again showed the superiority of the later pupils.

The most recent study of comparative achievement of elementary school pupils is that made in 1955 in Evanston, Illinois. The eighth-grade pupils were found to be three months better, on the average, in spelling, and six months superior in reading, to the pupils of twenty years before. The third- and fifth-grade pupils were two and one-half months better on the average in reading, and one month superior in spelling.

Other facts supporting the belief that the American public school is continuing to promote reading growth may be found in the contrast of the scholastic attainments of draftees in World Wars I and II. The achievement of soldiers of World War II was extensively tested and found much higher than that of the soldiers of World War I. As Sloan Wilson says, ". . . More education is being passed on to more children than ever before in history, as well as more health care, entertainment, and all the rest of it." It is obvious from the results of

THEN AND NOW IN READING ACHIEVEMENT

Time	Place	Results
1845–1919	New York City	1919 pupils better in spelling and thought questions, 1845 pupils better in rote learning.
1853–1929	New York City	1929 students superior on high school entrance test.
1923–1933	Los Angeles, California	1933 sixth-grade pupils superior in reading by six months.
1916–1938	St. Louis, Missouri	1916 pupils in grades 2–8 made higher average scores in oral reading.
1919–1941	Indianapolis, Indiana	80% of 1941 seniors higher than average score of 1919.
1945	California, New York, Pennsylvania, Wisconsin, etc. ...	Pupils of 1945 show slight gains in achievement.
1921–1947	Lincoln, Nebraska	1947 pupils of grades 4–7 better in speed and comprehension.
1916–1948	Grand Rapids, Michigan	1948 group superior in comprehension but not in oral or speed of silent reading.
1931–1948	Springfield, Illinois	1948 pupils of sixth grade superior.
1931–1948	Springfield, Missouri	Reading in 1948 superior to that in 1931.
1932–1949	Springfield, Missouri	1949 pupils superior in reading.
1935–1955	Evanston, Illinois	1955 third, fifth, and eighth graders better in spelling and reading.

these studies that the achievement of elementary and secondary pupils has not declined. Present-day pupils are found to be superior in many characteristics to the pupils of earlier years. Thus it appears that it is *not* true that children of today are reading more poorly than those of earlier generations. In fact, the studies make it apparent that there has been a constant, progressive improvement in the quality of American public education.

These various comparative studies that have been cited are arranged below in tabular form to permit quick review of the pertinent facts.

These studies cover a span of more than the last one hundred years. In every comparison except one, the later pupils are shown to be superior in many aspects of their reading achievement. The quality of American public education has continually improved during the latter part of the last century and the first half of this century. This improvement is all the more remarkable when we consider the increase in the number of subjects now taught in the public school, the tremendous growth in the school population, and the shift in emphasis from sheer memorization to intelligent, critical reading to prepare for the demands of present-day life.

6. READING RESEARCH THAT MAKES A DIFFERENCE*

David H. Russell

IT IS a peculiarly American custom to select "the best ten" or "one hundred best" individuals or products. This article selects the "best ten" examples of reading research, not because they are most valuable in all

* From David H. Russell, "Reading Research That Makes a Difference, *"Education Digest,* XXVI (April, 1961), 28–31; reported from *Elementary English,* XXXVIII (February, 1961), 74–78. Reprinted by permission of the author, *Education Digest,* and the National Council of Teachers of English.

situations, but in response to the challenge of a superintendent of schools who said to me, "You university people are always talking about ways research should influence teaching. . . . When did research ever influence the teaching of reading?"

At the time, my answer to the skeptical superintendent was not as complete as I should have liked, so as a result of thinking over his challenge, I list here more fully ten studies which have widely influenced reading instruction over the years. Because most of the researches are well known, I describe their methods and results only briefly.

The first of the classic studies is the series of investigations by G. T. Buswell and C. H. Judd, made at the University of Chicago around 1920. These are examples of "basic" research in education—studies which may be regarded as "pure," as discovery of knowledge for its own sake, but studies which had great influence in showing the advantages of silent over oral reading and which illustrated the differential nature of the reading act.

The analyses destroyed the notion that reading is a unitary activity. Instead, they suggested that reading skills differ with different purposes and materials. Accordingly, wise teachers began to help the child learn to read for a variety of purposes and to use different kinds of printed matter.

A second memorable study was the investigation of errors in paragraph comprehension made by E. L. Thorndike in 1917. This was an example of applied research. In an area which took oral teaching of reading for granted, Thorndike clearly showed differences between mouthing words and understanding meaning. He likened the process of reading a paragraph to that of solving a problem or combining dispersed ideas into a related whole.

By illustrating the wide variety of errors children made in the comprehension of a relatively simple paragraph, Thorndike demonstrated the need for instruction in getting meaning from the printed page. He also raised the issue of causes of misunderstanding and attributed it in part to the overpotency of certain words, thus foreshadowing some recent psychological work on individual perceptions.

A third classic publication, related to Thorndike's study, was a teaching study which helped provide teachers with concrete materials they could use in place of the common oral attack of that day. This was the investigation described in A. I. Gates's *New Methods in Primary Reading.*

In this study, Gates did not toss phonics out the window, as sometimes claimed, but he did show the importance of visual techniques and a method he called "intrinsic" in getting meanings of words and sentences. Such a study led directly to a revolution in teaching materials and in methods which combined a variety of ways for children to recognize words.

Like his study of primary methods and materials, Gates's *The Improvement of Reading* is a report of a number of experiments with diagnostic material. It represents not only a fresh concept in the scientific study of reading but was among the first major investigations in a long list of researches on diagnostic and remedial activities.

The point of view in *The Improvement of Reading* is that most reading retardation and disability are not explained by vague, blanket terms, such as "laziness" or "low intelligence" or "bad attitude," but are the result of a group or syndrome of specific, related factors which must be diagnosed exactly.

The Improvement of Reading contained a battery of diagnostic tests which have been extended by different authors in numerous books and articles on diagnostic and remedial activities. The present-day reading clinic is one example of the diagnostic approach to educational problems, a concept exemplified in Gates's pioneer work.

Reading Interests

A fifth classic in the field of reading investigation was the book on children's reading interests prepared by L. M. Terman and Margaret Lima. *Children's Reading,* reinforced by some of the educational theories of the day, helped provide a basis for the concept of developmental reading. Terman and Lima discovered the typical interests of boys and girls at various age levels and showed how these changed from preschool through early adolescent years. Accordingly, they not only provided some basis for the selection of children's literature at various ages, but they also helped evolve a dynamic concept of children's reading.

The sixth study is an example of the historical method of research. Nila B. Smith's *American Reading Instruction* illustrates the long gradual development of methods and practice which are a basis for what teachers do in classrooms today.

For nearly 300 years, and dating back at least to the alphabet method and theological content of the *New England Primer,* devoted teachers have worked to help their students read accurately and efficiently. Smith's historical survey has given considerable confidence to all persons concerned with reading instruction in what they do and what they advocate.

The methods and materials in use today are not based on the personal opinion of some textbook author or school principal, nor on the whim of an individual teacher. Rather, they are the result of generations of trial in classrooms from colonial to modern times. Smith's study, which should be extended into the last 25 years, can and does provide a background against which current criticisms of teaching can be measured and a basis established for continued research in methods and materials.

A seventh study opened up a new field for evaluation of reading materials rather than influencing classroom teaching methods. This was W. S. Gray and Bernice Leary's *What Makes a Book Readable.* Their formula for measuring the level of difficulty of printed materials has since been simplified by Lorge and other useful formulas developed by Dale-Chall, Flesch, and Spache. Such work still requires extension into measures of concept difficulty and density. It is influencing the writing of textbooks and other materials and makes possible some matching of pupil ability and reading materials to challenge it.

Phonics Research

The role of phonics in reading instruction suggests that research on the topic should be included in any list of "best ten." Unfortunately, no investigation in this area can be labeled "definitive." One of several worthy of mention is the D. C. Agnew study made in 1939, not because it answered all questions about phonics, but because it combined several methods of attack and because it attempted to solve a complex instructional problem, one that some researchers, prophets, and charlatans have attempted to over-simplify ever since.

In general, the Agnew study suggests that there are both advantages and disadvantages in emphasizing phonics methods. It is included as a representative of a group of studies which gave careful leads to the use of phonics.

The ninth study on the list was selected only after much difficult deliberation. In terms of impact, however, the vote goes to Ruth Strang for a series of studies and publications which clearly pointed to the need for developmental reading instruction in secondary schools and colleges. The first edition of *Problems in the Improvement of Reading in High School and College* collated the scattered work in the field up to 1937 and *Explorations in Reading Patterns* extended the interest in reading habits from adolescence into adulthood.

Strang's work helped develop the strong current interest in reading in the post-elementary years and began some study of the relationships of reading interest to other patterns of response to reading materials, an area in which the research is only beginning.

The last study in the "ten best" list is easy to select, not because its impact has yet been great, but because it points the way to important future developments. It is W. S. Gray's *The Teaching of Reading and Writing*. This is a survey done for Unesco in 1956 of methods of instruction in reading and writing around the world. Our methods of study in comparative education are not well developed, but the Gray description points to world-wide problems in literacy, in types of language, and in adaptation of instruction to the nature of the language.

It is worth noting that each of the mentioned studies was closely connected to the problems of its day. For example, the laboratory studies by Buswell and Judd gave basic data about a little-known process in the days psychology was beginning as a science. The impact of the Thorndike and Gates studies can be understood only when one realizes that reading instruction of that day was almost completely oral. The Terman study coincided with some phases of the Progressive Education movement. The Agnew study dealt with a problem which is still concerning primary and intermediate-grade teachers; and the Gray survey, whose impact is still to be felt, came in a day when the United States was beginning to take an interest in the social and educational walfare of the under-developed nations of the world.

Each of these ten studies had impact because they were closely related to the context in which they were made. As we look to the future we must also ask: What is relevant and pressing?

Research in reading has influenced, and will influence, practice. Research can "make a difference."

CHAPTER II

THE PSYCHOLOGY OF READING

7. SOME PRINCIPLES OF LEARNING APPLIED TO READING*

Gertrude Hildreth

EVERY teacher is concerned about giving children the tool of reading which will unlock for them a wide world of new experience. Whether the children learn this tool easily, or slowly and ineffectively will depend in large part upon the teacher's understanding of the learning process as it relates to reading instruction.

This article will summarize the basic principles of learning applied to reading and show how they relate to teaching. These principles give clues to techniques of instruction, to classroom management of learners, to the use and construction of appropriate reading materials. Violation of any of the basic learning principles usually results

* From Gertrude Hildreth, "Some Principles of Learning Applied to Reading," *Education*, LXXIV, No. 9 (May, 1954), 544–49. Reprinted by permission of the author and The Bobbs-Merrill Co., Inc., Indianapolis, Ind.

in ineffective learning if not outright failure. These principles have application to other skills learned at school as well as to symbol learning and habit formation in general.

The reading process is highly complex because it requires discrimination of word forms both visually and with the ear, the two processes operating simultaneously. At the same time reading requires thinking and anticipating meanings expressed in words, essentially a puzzle-solving process.

Purposing and Motivation

It is a well-known fact that you cannot teach a child anything that he does not want to learn. If he genuinely wants to learn he is halfway there before he starts. What a child is forced to learn as a school task won't help the learning process along very much. Children show different degrees of interest in beginning reading. As one teacher commented about a slow learner, "His self-starter seemed to be missing." In both the beginning stages and later on, a genuine interest in learning helps to make reading achievement possible. The teacher must be careful not to confuse lack of interest in learning or will to learn with lack of ability or immaturity that inhibits learning. Lack of interest contributes to lack of attention, a condition that lies at the root of the slow progress made by restless children.

Too often the anxious parent demands of the teacher, "You've got to make my boy learn." "Leave it to me," replies the teacher. "We'll see that he does." But high pressuring an unready or reluctant learner is apt to have the opposite effect. Instead of becoming interested, the child "goes sour" and refuses even to try. Furthermore, he not only comes to hate reading but to dislike the teacher.

The teacher who understands this fundamental learning principle makes certain that at all times the pupils, whether reading alone or to an audience, read for genuine purposes related to their own concerns. At the same time that children are learning to read we want them to learn to love to read. It is short-sighted for the teacher to try to teach reading without considering whether the materials used for instruction interest the pupils.

One slow boy's chief interest was in raising pigeons. The teacher suggested that he go to the library and inquire whether the librarian had anything easy to read on this subject. Sure enough, a book was found for him

that he read, though not too easily. But he kept on trying and was soon back demanding more material on his hobby.

Learning with Understanding: Reading for Meaning

In reading, getting the meaning is all that counts. Everything in the learning process must contribute to eventual grasp of meanings, to reading with full understanding. This principle has a number of important implications for learning and instruction. Every exercise in which a child engages, e.g., matching words, seeing the separate parts in words, saying the words on sight of the flash cards, must lead to comprehension of the printed page. All that counts in learning the ABC's or phonics as aids to reading is the *application* of word recognition skills to the interpretation of print.

As a matter of fact children of even ordinary caliber use all the intelligence they have to make sense out of what they are learning. After drilling on the ABC's for days on end, one beginner finally asked at home, "Mother, what's an L–M–N–O–P?" There are some children who have gone along learning to read even as far as fourth grade without realizing that there is more to reading than word calling.

One reason that readiness is so important is because it insures sufficient maturity for beginners to learn meaningfully from the outset of school instruction. Reading is always easier for the beginner or for the advanced student if he has learned to think meanings on sight of the context and has learned to derive meanings of puzzling words through context clues, so far as possible, e.g., "The word must be *mosquito* because that's probably what the man was bitten by." Reading is easier if you can think what comes next. This principle explains why extensive practice in reading silently to get meanings or to find answers to questions is desirable at all grade levels.

Experiential Background Basic to Learning to Read

A principle related to the foregoing is that for the learner to have a background of experience which ties in with reading context helps to insure learning with understanding. The child is most apt to learn to read with understanding who has had a rich background of relevant experience, whereas the child from an impoverished background may lack experiences that would aid interpretation of context.

Strange as it may seem, free play activities in kindergarten and the primary grades build and sustain reading readiness because they bring the child into intimate contact with his environment, broadening and sharpening his perceptions, and developing his use of language. Children who lack this experiental readiness must be given experiences related to the context used in teaching reading.

A good rule is always to start reading with the things the child knows about, talks and asks about, with material that is related to things he can actually pick up, touch and examine; things he likes to work with, situations that interest him here and now because they are within his level of understanding.

A slow learning class had a rabbit presented to them which they kept for a time in the classroom. They were excited over this event and every day told stories and wrote down things about their new pet. They put him in numerous stories; even wrote him a letter. Net result: before long all the children, even the slowest, were catching on to the reading trick, seeing the relation between talk and writing and reading, learning to absorb a growing vocabulary of common, everyday words.

A slow boy who was keen about sports made better progress when his reading lessons centered about his hobby. Here is one story he learned to read easily.

> We play baseball.
> Bob bats the ball
> I am the catcher.
> We play ball in the park.

Reading and Spoken Language

Because reading deals entirely with spoken word symbols recorded in graphic form, the skill is properly classified as but one phase of the language arts. As one child expressed it, "Readin's just talk wrote down." Language is the tool through which ideas are stored in memory. For these reasons oral language is the basis of interpreting print. As a general rule, anything children have difficulty saying cannot be easily read. There is usually a close relationship between a child's growth in oral language and his progress in reading. It is a wise precaution for the teacher to check each child's "linguability" before predicting the rate at which he will probably learn to read and before planning lessons for the pupils.

The Child Must Do His Own Learning

Learning to read is no exception to the general rule that the best learners always show active effort to learn: they stay with the task until it is accomplished. The child must do his own learning. No one can do it for him. Too often teaching is considered an external process, something done to the child to "make him learn," instead of the mental reactions the child must make on his own account. The child who learns best experiments with the print before him. He asks and responds to questions; he works as hard as he would in trying to solve a puzzle. The good teacher demands that the child think for himself, and works at the task as his own responsibility.

Learning to Read Requires Forming Habits

Catching on to the reading trick, the essential technique the adult uses whenever he wants to get the latest news from the evening paper, is a matter of forming habits which result in synchronizing a set of regimented, arbitrary eye movements (the motor part of the task), with perception and interpretation (the thinking part). This requires hours of practice over a period of years, first to "catch the trick," then to perfect it. The reading technique, like piano playing or certain workbench skills, isn't of much use unless it functions swiftly and smoothly when a new task confronts the performer. Some

children never do get off the plateau where their reading skills have become fixed at a low level of performance, a level too low to be of any practical use in school or life. All of the basic principles of habit formation apply to the task of learning to read.

Learning by Association

Learning to read requires essentially learning to attach meanings already known through conversation to groups of arbitrary letters representing words. The task of the child is first to realize that every word is composed of a relatively small number of letters (the alphabet); then to learn to recognize at sight (spot recognition) as many of these commoner recurring words as possible; and finally to become skillful in using techniques that aid in distinguishing between confusing word forms. The process is not unlike the teacher's task of learning to connect the name of each new student with his face in a class of 30.

How do children learn to fix words in mind? How do mature readers recognize familiar words, and the less familiar or unknown word symbols? We know that children and adults alike have learned to respond to clues of many sorts, features of word structure, visual-sound associations, and others that help to recall the meaning of the observed words. A general rule is that a word is easier to recall when some meaningful association can be established between the word, its form or sound, and the ideas it represents. It is harder to remember words, that is, to build meaningful associations that serve as clues to recognition, if the words stand for abstract ideas rather than for concrete objects. This explains why such words as *which, because, these, outside, every* are difficult for children to learn in any language. When teachers appreciate these facts, they have more patience with children's difficulties in word recognition.

The Role of Perception in Learning to Read

Perception is the mind's response to sensations received from the outside world. Without the capacity to perceive, the human mind would be unable to form associations with symbols and their meanings or to store up memories of word forms, to discover similarities and differences in word forms, a skill that is fundamental in reading and in learning to read. In reading, the visual and auditory perception of word forms must operate smoothly, swiftly, simultaneously. Since all the words printed in English are but longer or shorter combinations of only 26 different letter forms (actually only about 22 of these are frequently used, and several of these are confusing, e.g., "a," "e," "o," "c,"), learning to distinguish among confusing word symbols becomes a formidable task for any child.

Many a child's troubles with reading stem from the inevitable confusions he experiences because many words which look alike mean quite different things, e.g., *quick* and *quit, bright* and *brick,* and so on. Furthermore, the very same word can have different meanings in sentences. One reason slow learners fail to get off a low level plateau is that they are unable to advance in word

discrimination because of the rush of new words that soon surrounds them. The implication of this principle for teaching is that plenty of practice should be given in distinguishing word forms visually and aurally. Children must be trained to look and listen with the intent of learning the distinctions in word forms. Learning to see and hear the distinctions between confusing common words should occupy a considerable part of a child's reading practice time. The teacher should be cautious about keeping the vocabulary simple enough to insure steady growth in word perception and avoid introducing confusing words too near together in the child's reading experience.

The Role of Practice

No one ever did learn anything so complex as the English reading without steady practice extending over a period of years. Practice can be mechanical or it can be productive. In the first case, it may result merely in stamping in errors; in the latter, practice is meaningful. As a result there is steady gain in speed and efficiency because errors are eliminated and correct responses take their place. Trial and error is still a usable concept in considering childhood learning of language skills if we mean by this term that the child, through his continual experimental trials in attacking reading materials, solves his reading puzzles correctly, with the teacher's aid, and on that account is more successful the next time he tries. Under conditions of effective practice there is steady improvement in word recognition and in grasp of the ideas back of the words. Eventually, as a result of fruitful practice, the child reads with a feeling of familiarity and comparative ease.

The fact that words are of unequal difficulty was pointed out above. The teacher who recognizes which words are relatively difficult for most children as well as for an individual pupil makes sure that more practice is given to the "demon items." At times there should be reading practice with material for beginners or slow learners that contain no new word difficulties, an assimilation period so that children can feel fully at home with the words they are learning. There should be frequent vocabulary review (1) with words in normal reading context and (2) words separately out of context.

The Role of Attitudes and the Emotions in Learning to Read

Extensive research has shown that children often have difficulty in learning when disturbing emotional conditions and unfavorable attitudes stand in their way. Children with behavior problems, those who show poor control, are overactive, distractable, unusually aggressive and destructive, babyish and irresponsible, usually have trouble learning to read. There is evidence that the child's fantasies, obsessions, and inhibitions may make it difficult for him to learn certain words.

Discouragement from failure in the early learning stages is apt to have disastrous consequences, because fear and anxiety tend to inhibit efforts to learn. The slow child, particularly, falls a prey to fear and anxiety when he sees those around him making better progress than himself, or when an unsympathetic teacher scolds, shames, or ridicules his efforts before others. What can be this child's feelings when he hears his mother say to the teacher, "He's pretty dumb, but you've got to make him learn, or what will the neighbors think?" Threats and sarcasm slow a child down by causing him to stumble and make errors. Feelings of success are essential to motivate any child to keep on trying. He must see that his efforts count for something; he must have the teacher's approval if he has honestly tried. He should feel happy as the result of his effort to learn. This doesn't mean that teachers should avoid telling a child when he has made an error, but rather that unreasoned punishment of errors may stop the learning process altogether. The teacher's attitude of encouragement, helpfulness, patience, understanding of the child's feelings will accomplish far more than harsh discipline.

Individual Differences

Individual differences show up whenever human beings at any stage of maturity set out to learn the same thing. These differences in learning merely reflect the biological law of human variability. Teachers must recognize differences in the capacities of children the same age and of similar background in learning to read. Where one repetition of a word will suffice for a certain child, another pupil may require ten repetitions and still be uncertain of the word. In general there is a tendency on the part of teachers to underestimate the amount of repetition required by slow learners to fix facts in mind.

Day in, day out the workers in reading clinics hear the same plea, "Can't you bring my child up to grade so he can pass?" Now what would we rather have the child do, waste his valuable time in a vain effort to "come up to grade" or receive some well-planned instruction that will keep him progressing steadily? Once more we must remind ourselves that trying to keep all the children up to some arbitrary, uniform grade standard is wholly unrealistic, even more so today than formerly when "straight promotions" were not so much in vogue. Let our slogan be: each child progressing at his level, with feelings of accomplishment and satisfaction with his efforts.

To adjust the program to individual differences we must ask with respect to every pupil, 1.) What is his readability level, in other words, how well can he now read? 2.) What is the readability level of the material we have here for him to read? Now let's try the books on for size and make sure of a good fit.

Providing for individual differences in ability to read becomes particularly serious in today's crowded classrooms. In a group larger than 25 pupils, slow learners cannot receive the amount of individual attention they need for building good reading habits. There should be much more experimentation with multiple group work, with subgroups no larger than 6 to 10 slow learners.

The transition points from the end of Grade 1 and Grade 2 to the beginning of the next grade offer hazards for many young children because they usually pass to a new teacher who assumes that most of the class have made standard progress during the preceding year. To obviate this hazard two procedures are recommended. 1.) Every teacher should pass on to the next teacher an individual report for each child indicating exactly how far he has progressed during the past year, and 2.) in some cases it is wise for the teacher to go ahead with the group for another year so that no sharp breaks in learning will occur.

There is no question that the best learners of reading had good teachers who patiently helped them over the hurdles and obstacles, who demonstrated efficient techniques, and at the same time helped the children keep up their interest in getting ahead with the task.

8. ANOTHER LOOK AT THE THREE R'S*

Leland B. Jacobs

THE Three R's" is an educational catch phrase that rolls easily off the tongues of citizens, parents, and professional educators when the matter of schooling is under consideration. But it is a rather difficult phrase to encompass realistically; to define. "The Three R's" often seems to be an inflammable topic which is quick to burst into open conflagration. It is a linguistic invention which lends itself conveniently to diverse individual manipulations while seeming to be an orderly device. "The Three R's" is a metaphor, a neat verbalism. "The Three R's" exists in the minds of men as an educational abstraction, connoting the fundamentals in the skills learnings of those being educated in schools. It might be called a pedagogical stereotype that has garnered status on the grounds of longevity and propriety. Because "The Three R's" is an elusive and quixotic phrase, it needs frequent critical re-examination in order that constructive teaching for abundant learning may take place in every classroom in the land.

Modern teachers accept willingly the belief that the school is responsible for providing children and youth with tools of learning and for teaching skill in using those tools, thus aiding the young to become mature, capable individuals

and worthy, well-informed citizens. They know that children and youth seek to reach satisfying levels of accomplishment in the various skills of language, mathematics, and science; of the arts and crafts and physical education; of human relations. They believe that the ability to read, to write, to speak, to listen contributes to fuller personal living and to social effectualness. They would not question that the ability to count, to measure, to use basal arithmetic processes makes personal and vocational achievements possible. They respect childen's skillful symbolization in various types of artistic endeavor. They presume, too, that children will need help in acquiring skills that affect their contacts with other human beings. And because their beliefs in helping children develop competence in the tools of their culture are so deep, they presume that an appropriate amount of school time will be devoted to children's experiences with skills learnings.

Modern teachers also believe that part and parcel of the acceptance of this responsibility is their use in teaching of the best that is known about the growth and development of the young, about learning theory, about mental hygiene, about methods and materials appropriate to helping children comprehend the skills taught. As professional people they are obligated to use the findings of research in improving school practices. Knowing full

* From Leland B. Jacobs, "Another Look at the Three R's," *Teachers College Record*, LV, No. 6 (March, 1954), 308–12. Reprinted by permission of the author and *Teachers College Record*.

well that they will be challenged and questioned by individuals and groups whose viewpoints, for one reason or another, differ from their own, they strive to be true to the best interests of the children whom they teach. This is their first concern in the role of teacher.

⌊Modern teachers believe that the skills are best learned in situations in which they are taught functionally rather than formally or incidentally.⌉In practice, this may mean several things. It means, for instance, that children learn most successfully those skills that they recognize as most needful in carrying on enterprises important to them. It means that the skills taught are put immediately to use, that in use in various differing situations further evaluation of the comprehension and manipulation of the skill takes place as well as further practice for retention and refinement. It means that the child takes personal responsibility for the degree of mastery acquired, and that he both learns the skill itself and acquires certain general know-how concerning ways to master a skill economically and effectively.

From the standpoint of the teacher, to teach skills functionally means to value results other than those achieved by teaching formally or incidentally. In the formal teaching of skills, logic is ascertained and prescribed by experts. The child is expected to accept the prescription without experiencing the process of becoming logical or without relating conclusions to experimental procedures. The learner's role is to acquiesce and comply, to routinize the logic, even if it is disorganizing or illogical to him. In incidental teaching of the skills, seemingly no particular logic is sought. If a particular skill seems to strike the children's or the teacher's fancy, if a child happens to take an interest in it, the teacher gives attention to that skill. But the procedure is catch as catch can, and meaning emerges the child achieves it by accident.

In functional teaching, the teacher believes that skills do not make real sense if they are conceived to be prescribed logical arrangements or sporadic forays. Rather, skill is achieved when the child works to make sense of a tool that, if used appropriately and masterfully, makes a difference in his accomplishments. In functional teaching, not only the particular skill must make sense, but the whole system of skills of which this new acquisition is a part must take on a new, more precise meaning. The cause for learning a skill, the skill itself, and how to design the pattern within which the skill is one thread are all learned concomitantly and thus make the learner more effectual skill-wise. The child understands the logic because he has been involved in re-creating it, and because what might otherwise remain abstract becomes concrete. In the functional teaching of skills, then, children are neither unnaturally forced nor neglected or delayed. For the teacher always works within a framework which, because of the children's previous experiences, already has some formalized dimensions. He also capitalizes upon the unexpected, the interesting, or the incidental. But he does not rely basically on either a rigid or a haphazard approach. Instead, he teaches children those skills that raise their potentialities for further learnings at the strategic time when fullest learning would be blocked if some facility in these skills were not achieved. He also teaches that the children pace their learning at their growing edges.

Modern teachers believe that the skills which children learn should be mid-century modern. They recognize that the skills involved in new media of mass communication—radio, picture magazines, television, for example —cannot be ignored even if they are neglected at school. They know that time tables, new computing devices, and various forms of charts and graphs affect the lives of many children and youths. To read the new types of mappings that the air age has brought into existence calls for the knowledge of new skills. To work in such art forms as wire sculpture or mobiles requires developing skills not necessary in copybook exercises in drawing. Successful interaction with other human beings necessitates developing significant skills in social relationships. Skills related to playing games, using tools, carrying on science experiments, doing research, collecting data, discussing, playing musical instruments: all these and many more at mid-century are accepted as being vital to the all-around development of the child at school. Surely the skills of the original "Three R's" are important. But even the dimensions of reading, writing, and arithmetic are different in current times. And the modern teacher knows that the mid-century child must be competent in more skills than those involved in reading, writing, and arithmetic if he is to use his school experience to help him adapt successfully to and live richly in his home, his neighborhood, and his world.

Modern teachers believe that children learn most thoroughly if concepts are well developed as the ground in which specific skills find their bearings. First-hand sensory experiences—time for the individual to "play with," "muddle through," "feel out"—are of prime import if skill is to be accomplished. Some children need less time in concept-building than do others, but the opportunity to try out the skill must be offered to all of them. In this way the individual comes to understand the potentialities of the general dimensions of the skill within which an accurate response must ultimately be made. The process of learning how to attack a skill learning is significant as well as the achievement of satisfying products. The child scribbles before he writes; he reads pictures before he reads print; he calls out numbers in jumbled sequences before he counts. But from such generalized beginnings come the precisions necessary for true mastery in skills. Teachers see that time spent in converting random experimentation into concept-building is time saved in the long run. When children find the roots of their skills learnings in concepts, they put experience to work to help them perceive identical features and to test these identical features in further activities. Once children have developed adequate concepts of what a particular skill is, they can be intelligent about their practice of that skill. They can probably cut down on the time spent in practice, since they are insightful about what they are doing.

Modern teachers believe in practice

that is purposeful. They know that for the mastery of a skill, time must be provided for testing meanings, for perfecting responses, for using the skill in a variety of functional situations. What they eschew are mass practice for which children may see no need and specific practices which make children abhor or fear tackling further skills learnings. They try to avoid waste of precious school time on skills which, if more neatly gauged to children's developmental potentialities, could be mastered much more economically. They try to remember that command of skills may be several years agrowing, that refinement in command of a specific skill will probably not be achieved at one fell swoop. If high-level refinement of the skills learnings is to be achieved, practice under varied conditions in functional situations at different stages of maturity will have to be provided at various grade levels. Moreover, since random repetition does not assure skillfulness, modern teachers help the child to diagnose and to overcome his specific types of errors in skills learnings so that his practice is constructively aimed toward rapid success and proficiency. In providing for practice in skills, then, the teacher provides various types of practice situations: practice in concept-building, in beginning stages of mastery, in evaluating results, in diagnosing weaknesses or errors, in relating specific skills to the general structure of which the one skill is a part, in using skills functionally, and so on. He also seeks a neat balance between the child's own experimentation and direct assistance when the child can use a lift over a particular hurdle. He is concerned both with

functional proficiency in the skill and with the child's attitudes toward further exploration of skills learnings.

Modern teachers believe that feeling learnings accompany skills learnings. As the child works on the skills fundamental to his further education, his intelligence undergoes emotional as well as intellectual reactions. As he works to achieve skill, he also develops feelings about himself as a person, about his peers and the adults who are working with him, about tasks to be done, about further experiences in learning. While working on a skill, a child may learn to hate, to reject, to avoid, to proliferate, for example, instead of "feeling good" about gaining command of the tools of his culture. Because the modern teacher knows this truth, he tries to create the conditions that genuinely release children to do their best. He aims to make the skills learnings neither easy nor hard but, rather, useful, for he knows that children will work hard if the outcome of the hard work is worth the effort. He creates conditions in which the child does not have to feel very proud of himself or very guilty, but rather can honestly and confidently face up to accomplishments and lacks. The modern teacher provides an atmosphere in which verbal skills, manipulative skills, human relations skills are all prized, and in which giftedness in all such areas is put to work for the best interests of the group and of the individual. He encourages rather than prescribes experimentation; he helps children intellectualize their learnings and their lacks; he gives direct assistance to individuals or groups when they show that they can profit from it, to the end that children continue to believe that they can succeed, that they can count on other people to help them succeed, that others are glad to see them progress, that sticking at a job does pay off even if the results are less than perfect. He guides children in such ways that they are not afraid to be somewhat confused in a learning situation, since out of such confusion problems take shape, work is done, new meanings emerge, and learning eventuates. He plans with them in such ways that they understand the job to be done, map out some ways of accomplishing it, and proceed with freedom, flexibility, and adaptability to accomplish the task undertaken. He teaches them clues for handling tensions and pressures in mastering a skill. He creates a school climate that is secure but not complacent, humane but not overindulgent, problematic but not frustrating, experimental but not faddy, designed but not constrictive. The modern teacher wants children to want greater skill expertness, but not to be ice-bound in a mass of skills. His task is so to keep channels open that children will chart their way, with precise instruments, into further explorations in this important area of school work.

The modern teacher believes that evidence in increasing quantity is accumulating to substantiate the conviction that today's children do succeed adequately in their acquisition of skills. But he also clearly sees certain conditions that affect the work which he is doing in teaching the skills. He recognizes that the children and youth of this country remain in school for more education than in any time in the past, which means wider ranges in abilities and greater difficulties in developing each child's capacities. He recognizes that the great bulge in school population is currently making class sizes so large that the individual does not get some of the attention he deserves. He further realizes that current political, economic, and social pressures and threats in the world are disturbing and disruptive in the lives of children and young people, and do, of course, affect their accomplishments at school. He expects some criticism to be leveled at the schools concerning the teaching of "The Three R's," since down through the history of public education there have been certain complaints and dissatisfactions with the procedures currently in vogue. He is earnest about considering critical differences thoughtfully and professionally. He believes that present practices need continuous evaluation in the light of reliable new evidence concerning the purposes of education, the observable behavior of the learners, and pertinent long-range results and effects. He works to communicate openly with all concerned in relation to the teaching practices he uses, the objectives behind these practices, the outcomes to be achieved. But he tenaciously resists crystallization, or retrogression, or maintaining the *status quo* for the sake of accord and harmony at the price of denying children the best teaching which he is currently capable of doing.

And when new knowledge is available, when new ideas are proposed, when new frontiers of teaching are opened up, the modern teacher will again take another look at "The Three R's."

9. LEARNING THROUGH SEARCHING*

Lucile Lindberg

HOW can I add one more thing to the curriculum? We already have more in the program than we can get done!"

This is a refrain often heard when discussion turns to the need for preparing boys and girls more adequately for today's world. Inferences are made that attention must be given to new areas of thought if children are to be ready for rapidly changing situations.

What are we really saying? Are we saying that what is studied in school is all that will be known and that children learn only what is examined point by point in class? If we are saying this then ours is a hopeless task. Even if we were to persist in it day and night and a child were to learn amazingly fast, we could never include in a school curriculum all the knowledge the child will need in the years ahead.

Because we do have such concern that boys and girls will be well prepared, with the best of intentions we cripple them instead of strengthening them as we try to cover more and more material. It is our responsibility to make certain that children become aware of the great amount of knowledge which already exists and continues to be amassed at a rapid rate,

* From Lucile Lindberg, "Learning through Searching," *Childhood Education*, XXXVIII (October, 1961), 58–60. Reprinted by permission of the author and the Association for Childhood Education International, 3615 Wisconsin Ave., N.W., Washington 16, D.C.

that they develop their power to pursue it and discover still more, and that they become steadily more able to develop evaluative criteria of high quality. They must leave us saying: "There is much still to learn but I am capable of pursuing truth and shall continue to do so the rest of my life. It will be a privilege to be learning always."

There are vast and complicated problems all about; there will always be problems. Our children must not feel, "Oh, dear, why must this be?" but rather, "I am capable of living in the midst of crisis."

Discovering New Learnings

Our responsibility to insure maximal learning is greater than ever before, but we fail in this if we make of the education of our boys and girls a "pouring in" process. Whether or not they achieve according to their potential will depend upon the extent to which each child gains within himself the power to discover new learnings. This does not suggest that children should be left on their own with the hope that they will stumble upon skills and ideas but rather that our focus be placed on helping them develop sound processes of exploration.

When a child has made a discovery the learning involved becomes his own. It is his forever. Even though he may forget it temporarily it is still his, for he can again search for it. What he has discovered he can see in context and understand its relationship to other learnings, sensing many shades of meaning involved. Because he has developed a learning he feels a sense of power over it; he can control it instead of it controlling him and so is spurred on to further learning.

Often a teacher is thought of as one who stands before a group of children and tells or demonstrates, or at least suggests, the experiments or raises the questions. Each of these approaches has a place, but much of teaching must go beyond such procedures if we are to fulfill our obligations. It is possible for a child to have much information and yet not be the master, to develop many skills and yet not know how to use them or realize what they are capable of accomplishing, to work on problems which have been defined by someone else and yet not be able to define them for himself.

Developing Self-Propelled Power

How can we help boys and girls to develop this power over the processes which make it possible for them to learn through searching?

In the tools and knowledges needed in everyday living lies the content needed. No two persons will approach it in exactly the same way. Almost every teacher is already engaged in some activities which encourage the development of these processes. For example, there is the weekly spelling. What power a child can gain as he is helped to study words! Why let him struggle over twenty-five words a week,

thus limiting his opportunity, when by encouraging processes of discovery he can be the master of hundreds? When he knows how to spell even one word he can quickly use this learning to spell many others, checking each one to see if he is correct. If he can spell *habit* he probably can quickly discover how to spell *habits, inhabit, inhabits, inhabiting, inhabited, habitual,* and so on.

If someone shows him how language is developed he gains strength, but if he himself explores and discovers how it is put together he can build his own set of rules which can be checked against those which have already been developed by authorities in the field. Then with eagerness he can probe theirs to find out what they have found that he hasn't and assess whether he likes his own way of organizing as well as theirs.

With pronunciation, too, this applies and he learns the many variations of sound which a letter can have. Instead of being confused by this he thrills to the intricacies of it as he pushes to unearth more and more of them thus becoming a master of his own language and so can look with understanding at the language of others.

Becoming a Part of the Child

He can be helped to enjoy the flow of language as others have put it together, rhythmically expressing ideas and feelings in many ways. He feels the power of the language and grasps the deep significance of a poem, not through dissecting it, but through hearing it again and again until it becomes a part of him. He discovers differences in pattern and ultimately seeks to know the technicalities involved. Hence, it becomes a part of his life to be used always instead of something he once studied.

As he reads we encourage him to talk back to the author, questioning what he finds on the printed page, trying to capture the deeper meanings in what is being said. This implies that what he reads must be worth reading. We cannot afford to take his time for words put together as an exercise. Even in the beginning stages he should read material written well because someone cared to be understood, words so delightfully chosen that he can linger over them. We cannot afford to dictate what shall be read or that all shall read the same. Instead we help him to become increasingly aware of his own feelings about what is read so that he discovers what constitutes quality in written material.

Many Approaches to Problems

In mathematics it is possible to demonstrate the steps in exchange or in long division and ask a child to follow them exactly and so develop techniques. But how much more he can get if we help him to discover mathematical relationships and encourage him to find many ways of approaching problems! As he makes discoveries he is developing power with yet another language, the language of mathematics. He can seek for precision in its use just as he does with words.

A child can learn to search as he studies his own county or state. What crops are raised here? Where else are these crops raised? Which conditions are alike? Which are different? Are there other places in the world where these crops could be raised? Why aren't they?

Discoveries about climate begin to take form. Differences in altitude come into focus. The effect of mountains or ocean on rainfall is noted. Numbers of inhabitants and their needs provide other areas of investigation, as do lines of transportation. Conditions under which settlements were made and by whom make possible still other insights. As each one searches for reasons, shares and checks with others and with authorities, he accumulates vast amounts of knowledge which he is able to use because he has discovered many relationships. He develops the ability to use it to probe the reasons for many other things.

In science he can follow directions for an experiment and take pride in the results and learn as he does this. How much more he can learn and open the way for still further learning if he is guided to do his own searching! "The outside of the pitcher is wet. How could this be? In what ways could you test your hunches? What else did you discover while you were testing them?"

As a child searches and makes discoveries he becomes aware of his developing power. It is exciting and wonderful to him. With this awareness comes the desire to push himself still further, a self-propelling excitement which keeps him perpetually studying. As he senses his growth he values himself more as a human being.

If we help boys and girls to learn the processes of discovering knowledge and ways of working for themselves we need not give our energies to finding fascinating ways to hold their interest or whip up their enthusiasm. The strong urge to pursue learning comes from within.

When we read biographies we often find the phrase *self-made* man—a man who proceeded to study, to discover many truths for himself and, marvelling at them, to use them. The age of the self-made man is not past as has sometimes been implied. It is only beginning. We need parents, teachers, religious educators, and community workers whose purpose in working with children is to help them understand and use every process of exploration available so that they will in truth grow into self-made men who search for truths and finding them move on to ever-deeper understanding.

Knowledge is accumulating at so rapid a rate that no one can absorb as much as he would wish. As man becomes more adept in his searching, both the rate and quality of his learning will soar. The achievement of such quality is an important discipline of democracy.

10. INTELLECTUAL AND PERCEPTUAL DEVELOPMENT*

Albert J. Harris

Intellectual Development

The meaning of intelligence. Although psychologists have not been able to agree on a definition of intelligence, the three ideas that occur most frequently in definitions are that it involves ability to deal effectively with abstractions, to learn, and to respond appropriately in new situations.[1]

Whether intelligence is essentially unitary or is better conceived as a composite of interrelated but separate primary abilities is still in dispute. Most intelligence tests are based on the unitary concept, but tests of "primary abilities" are available from the primary

* From Albert J. Harris, "Reading and Human Development," Chap. II in *Development in and through Reading*, Sixtieth Yearbook, Part I, of the National Society for the Study of Education (Chicago: Univ. of Chicago Press, 1961), pp. 22–25, 27–30. Reprinted by permission of the National Society for the Study of Education.

[1] Horace B. English and Ava C. English, *A Comprehensive Dictionary of Psychological and Psychoanalytical Terms* (New York: David McKay Co., Inc., 1958), p. 268.

grades up. Interrelations of different abilities tend to be high in early childhood and to decrease as adolescence is approached. During the teens, differences in verbal, numerical, spatial, and reasoning abilities are significant for guidance.[2]

The intelligence tests which correlate substantially with progress in reading and other school work have been shown to be weighted with cultural factors. On the other hand, tests which come closer to being culture-free have such low correlations with scholastic success as to be of little use for academic prediction.[3] There is an increasing tendency to use the term "scholastic aptitude tests" for those commonly used in schools, avoiding the implication of measuring native abilities.

The nature of mental growth. Mental growth, as measured by intelligence tests, tends to increase steadily from birth to maturity. The rate of growth during early childhood is generally thought to be more rapid than that attained during the elementary-school years, and the beginning reader, aged six, probably has completed at least half of his total mental growth. The exact shape of the average mental growth curve has not been established. During middle and late childhood, mental growth tends to proceed at a fairly steady rate, begins to slow down as adolescence is reached, and on

Binet-type tests reaches adult status between the ages of sixteen and nineteen.

Most intelligence tests are scored in terms of mental age (M.A.) and intelligence quotient (I.Q.). The M.A. is a measure of the level of mental maturity achieved at a particular time; it, therefore, increases fairly steadily as the child gets older. The I.Q. is a measure of rate of mental development, with the average rate set at the value of 100, and tends on the average to remain fairly constant as the child gets older. The meaning of both measures varies somewhat according to the test used. Intelligence quotients computed by the "deviation" method tend to vary less from year to year than those computed by the older method of dividing mental age by chronological age.[4]

Intelligence and reading. The degree of correlation between measured intelligence and reading performance varies with the tests used as well as with the ages of the children. Individual verbal tests, such as the *Stanford-Binet,* tend to correlate with reading success in the neighborhood of .60 to .70. The primary-grade I.Q. tests, which utilize oral directions and have a high verbal content but use pictures in order to avoid reading, tend to have correlations with reading scores about like those of the Binet. Verbal group mental ability tests from the fourth grade up tend to have higher correlations with reading scores, ranging from .70 to about .85, while the so-called nonverbal or nonlanguage group tests have much lower correlations with reading tests, generally ranging between .20 and .40.[5]

[2] Florence L. Goodenough, "The Measurement of Mental Growth in Childhood," in Leonard Carmichael (ed.), *Manual of Child Psychology* (2d ed.; New York: John Wiley & Sons, Inc., 1954), chap. viii.

[3] Kenneth W. Eells, *Intelligence and Cultural Differences* (Chicago: University of Chicago Press, 1951).

[4] Goodenough, *op. cit.,* pp. 470–77.

Obviously, the verbal group tests have much in common with reading tests; not only the linguistic and reasoning skills necessary for solving the problems but also the reading skills needed to find out what the questions ask. For this reason, verbal group tests above the primary grades do not distinguish between mentally slow children and those with reading disabilities; often the latter are mistakenly categorized as intellectually retarded.

In estimating the potential reading capacity of a child, one compares his measured potentiality (mental ability or listening comprehension) with his present attainment in reading; if the former is significantly higher, a reading disability may exist. The methods of estimating a reading disability range from the simple or direct comparison of reading age with mental age to the use of formulas in which mental age is combined with chronological age (or with chronological and arithmetic ages) or in which I.Q. is combined with the number of years of instruction. The comparison is facilitated when the tests for potentiality and present attainment have been standardized on the same population.

The fact that beginning reading is successfully taught at the age of five in Great Britain, age six in the United States, and age seven in certain other countries was noted in the discussion of reading readiness. The association of the visual perception of a word symbol with its heard and spoken equivalents is a relatively simple form of

associative learning and may not require much intelligence. As the reader progresses, recognition becomes a prerequisite to understanding and reasoning about the content. As understanding and reasoning become increasingly complex and difficult, the significance of intelligence in determining the child's optimum level of reading becomes greater.

Individual differences in intelligence and reading. The closer schools come to helping each child read in accordance with his mental ability, the wider become the differences in reading achievement. If we consider only the middle 80 per cent of the child population (those with I.Q's from 80 to 120), at the beginning of the second grade the expected reading range is from beginning first grade to third grade; at the beginning of sixth grade, from third to eighth grade.[6] If the school is one in which the child who does poorly is not promoted, there will be fewer pupils with low reading scores in each grade but a corresponding number of over-age pupils. Effective reading instruction does not produce more uniform achievement but, rather, helps the very bright to achieve at a superior level and aids the slow to progress successfully but slowly.

Adapting reading instruction to this wide range of normal differences is one of the most difficult and challenging problems. Nearly all teachers recognize the existence of these differences, yet in practice the teacher's main goal often seems to be to try to get all his pupils up to grade level—an impossible

[5] Arthur E. Traxler and Agatha Townsend, *Eight More Years of Research in Reading,* p. 65. Educational Record Bulletin, No. 64 (New York: Educational Records Bureau, 1955).

[6] Albert J. Harris, *How to Increase Reading Ability* (4th ed.; New York: David McKay Co., Inc., 1961), p. 123.

and frustrating goal for the genuinely slow, and an unstimulating one for the bright. Since teachers have such difficulty, considerable improvement can be expected when the teacher, receives help from a curriculum consultant, reading consultant, or remedial teacher.

Perceptual Development

Perception and reading. Perception is meaningful experience brought about by sensory stimulation. What one perceives is determined not only by the stimulation received from the external object situation but also by one's background experience which provides possible meanings and by the immediate mind set or anticipatory attitude. Teachers should strive to help pupils acquire a wide experiential background and to provide guidance in the anticipation of meanings.

Basic to success in reading are the following: (*a*) sufficiently clear visual perception to be able to distinguish the printed form of a word from other word forms; (*b*) sufficiently clear auditory perception to be able to distinguish a spoken word from similar sounding words; (*c*) simultaneous attention to the printed and spoken word, allowing the formation of a learned association; (*d*) increasingly clear perception of letters and letter groups within the total word configuration; (*e*) increasingly clear perception of the sound elements within the spoken word; (*f*) association of the sound elements with their printed equivalents; and (*g*) functional use of the perceived parts as aids in the perception of the words, either in im-

mediate recognition, or, failing that, through a combination of analysis and synthesis.

Visual perception. Current methodology in the teaching of reading assumes that it is easier and faster for a child to learn to respond correctly to the appearance of a word as a whole than to perceive it part by part and put the parts together. This viewpoint originated from pioneer work of Cattell, who demonstrated that, on the average, words could be recognized in a shorter time than single alphabet letters. This was reinforced by eye-movement photography, which showed that, in good reading, words are perceived as units or in groups, and was given a theoretical base by Gestalt psychology, which emphasizes the primacy of the whole over the parts. The development of perceptual skill starts in infancy with perception of a rather vague whole against a dim background and progresses toward increasingly sharp and clear apprehension both of the quality of the whole and of its details.

According to Vernon, young children tend to see things as a whole, but this is dependent upon the "goodness" of the shape; whether it is a coherent whole with a clear outline and fairly obvious structure or consists of a complicated mass of details without obvious interrelations. Some children have great difficulty with reading because they are less likely to see words as wholes than as meaningless jumbles of details. Other children have trouble because they react to the word as an undifferentiated whole with insufficient attention to the features which distinguish one word from another.[7] To be successful in word recognition, the child must be able to perceive both the whole and the distinctive parts.[8]

Research studies have shown that certain tests of visual perception skills are significantly related to success in beginning reading. Every reading readiness test has at least one subtest which purports to measure visual perception. Published readiness materials contain many exercises designed to improve visual perception. Using these with all beginners is questionable because many children are already well advanced in perceptual skill when they enter school and do not need them, while others find these materials too difficult. It is probable that direct practice in the discrimination and comparison of letter shapes and words is more useful than practice with pictures of objects or geometrical designs.

The problem of reversals in the perception of words and letters has been recognized as a fascinating one for many years. Inability to distinguish between shapes which are mirror images of each other is quite common among five-year-olds but decreases rapidly with the training in perception and in the left-right direction that is ordinarily given in kindergarten and first grade. In a small minority of children, directional confusion persists for several years and is a serious impediment to progress in reading. This problem of reversed orientation in reading

perception has become confused with left- and right-sidedness, but it is becoming clear that the major question for reading is the presence or absence of directional confusion rather than which hand or eye is preferred. Directional confusion, in some cases, seems to be a symptom of a special kind of immaturity and, in others, seems related to changed-handedness. Children with directional confusion can usually respond to instruction which stresses left-right sequence.[9]

Auditory perception. Although auditory perception requires adequate acuity of hearing, it may develop slowly in children whose acuity for sounds is normal. Much development takes place during the preschool years. Since children tend to pronounce words as they hear them, the gradual disappearance of immature pronunciations (*muvver* for mother, *wothe* for rose) indicates a corresponding sharpening of auditory perception. A school child's indistinct enunciation is often the first clue to poorly developed auditory perception.

Research indicates that initial consonants are easiest to perceive, followed by final consonants, long vowels, short vowels, and consonant combinations. Training in auditory perception —in listening to words and comparing their beginning sounds, middle sounds, and final sounds—is likely to be valuable to children whose initial scores in auditory perception tests are low.[10] Practice in hearing sounds within words, sometimes called "ear train-

[7] M. D. Vernon, *Backwardness in Reading: A Study of Its Nature and Origin* (Cambridge: Cambridge University Press, 1957), chap. ii.

[8] Jean T. Goins, "Visual and Auditory Perception in Reading," *Reading Teacher,* XIII (October, 1959), 9–13.

[9] Vernon, *op. cit.,* pp. 27–30, 81–110; Harris, *op. cit.,* pp. 249–60.

[10] Joseph Wepman, "Auditory Discrimination, Speech, and Reading," *Elementary School Journal,* LX (March, 1960), 325–33.

ing," improves readiness for phonic instruction, and the first step in introducing a new phonic element should be practice in hearing the sound. For children whose auditory perception remains poor in spite of training, instruction in phonics is likely to be ineffectual.

11. EYE MOVEMENTS IN READING*

Miles A. Tinker

WHAT role do eye movements play in reading? It is obvious that the eyes move when one reads. But just how these movements take place and how they are organized into certain patterns as reading improves is not self-evident. Parents and teachers undoubtedly would like to know more about the basic characteristics of eye movements in reading and how the patterns of these movements reflect degrees of proficiency in reading.

Nature of Eye Movements in Reading

It is a popular belief that during reading the eyes move steadily and uninterruptedly along the line of print. Observation of a reader's eyes will demonstrate that they move in "jumps" rather than in continuous sweeps.

* From Miles A. Tinker, "Eye Movements in Reading," *Education*, LXXIX, No. 9 (May, 1959), 575–79. Reprinted by permission of the author and The Bobbs-Merrill Co., Inc., Indianapolis, Ind.

Actually, the eyes make several stops, each a fixation pause, along a line of print. The eyes move from one fixation pause to the next with a quick jerk known as a saccadic movement. These movements are so rapid that nothing is seen during the moves. This is easily demonstrated. Look steadily at the image of your right eye in a mirror. Now look over to the left and then back to the right. Although you can feel your eyes move and other people can see them move, you will be unable to detect any movement in the mirror. The image always "looks" motionless. Your eyes have been "blind" during the quick jump from one fixation to the other.

The fixation pauses are the only periods of clear vision. When the eyes are motionless during the fixations, word perception occurs. These pauses total on the average about 90 per cent of the reading time while the interfixation moves total 6 per cent of the reading time. During reading, therefore, the eyes are motionless during the fixation pauses, i.e., a large portion of the time. Thus reading involves a series of peeps along the line of print.

In reading, the first fixation pause is located near the left end of the line of print. The eyes then move in a series of fixations along the line from left to right. If the eyes have made too long a "jump" for adequate perception of the successive words, or if some of the material needs reexamination to achieve better understanding, the eyes make a backward move toward the left to get another view of the words or for a more detailed examination of the printed material. This backward move to refixate words is called a regression. When the eyes reach the right end of a line, they make a long "jump" back to the beginning of the next line. This is called a return sweep. If the return sweep is too short so that the first fixation in the new line does not furnish an adequate view of the first words at the left end, there is a regression to remedy this. We shall now see that the reader who make the fewest and briefest fixation pauses is the more efficient reader.

Eye-movement behavior is of significance to the teacher for it provides external signs of the internal working of the mind during reading. Thus consistent progress from left to right with few fixation pauses along the line of print is ordinarily an indication of a clear understanding and a rapid grasping of the material read. On the other hand, many fixation pauses with frequent regressions tend to reveal poor comprehension with slow, laborious, and inadequate grasping of the meanings and ideas represented by the printed material. Repeated fixation pauses and regressions clustered about a word or phrase ordinarily indicate mental confusion of the reader with an ability to grasp the meaning of that word in relation to the rest of the sentence. The nature of the eye-movement patterns (number and spacing of fixation pauses and regressions), therefore, reveal quite well how the mind operates in trying to understand and grasp meanings during reading. It is important that the teacher understand these relationships between eye movements and the reading process.

Observing Eye Movements

Direct observation of eye movements by means of the "peep-hole" method is probably the most practical of several techniques available to the teacher. Proceed as follows: Upon a 9 x 12 inch cardboard attach two paragraphs of 6 to 10 lines of reading material of appropriate difficulty, one paragraph just above the center of the card and the other just below the center. In the middle of the cardboard cut a small hole, ¼ to ⅜ inch in diameter. Hold the cardboard at the proper reading distance directly in front of a pupil and place your eye immediately behind the opening. You now have the most advantageous viewpoint from which to see the successive movements and fixation pauses of one of the pupil's eyes as he reads the material on the cardboard. The movements are seen most easily when you fixate your attention upon the dividing line between the colored zone and the white of the pupil's eye. The fact that the pupil sees only the reading material before him reduces the distraction that would occur if you were to attempt direct observation (as looking over the top of a book) without concealing your face behind the card.

This method may be used to determine the number of fixation pauses per line of print, to detect the presence of regressions, and confusions shown by detailed examination of a word or phrase. Even after practice, this method is not entirely accurate since some eye movements will be missed. Nevertheless, the technique is quite satisfactory in the classroom where the teacher wishes to detect signs of very good and very poor reading in comparison with the average, or wishes to find out what the eye movements of a particular pupil are like.

To insure a fair degree of accuracy, practice in counting the eye movements of another teacher for a few paragraphs should be undertaken before working with the children. Since there is a fixation pause at the end of each move, the number of pauses per line is easily obtained. Count the number of eye movements for the whole paragraph and divide by the number of lines. Do not attempt to note regressions and words that cause confusion while counting the interfixation movements. Look for these other things when a second or a third selection is read.

Where precision in measurement is desired, as in research investigations or in a reading clinic, a photographic technique is ordinarily used (or an elaborate electrical method). For surveys of the field and description of apparatus for recording eye movements in reading, see reports by

Tinker.[3, 4, 5] Research studies, employing these techniques, have provided a wealth of information about eye movements in reading and consequently about how children learn to read and information concerning their difficulties in trying to read.

Eye Movements of the Beginning Reader

In the beginning, the proper direction of eye movements in reading must be learned. Obviously the eyes should begin at the left end of a line of print and move in a series of fixation pauses consistently to the right. It is erroneous to assume that this orientation comes naturally. The child on entering school has been accustomed to use his eyes only for examining pictures or other objects of various kinds. This means that his eyes move to the left just as readily as to the right and that neither the direction nor the order of the movements is consistent and predictable. At first the child naturally tends to observe words as he has viewed objects. This attack is, of course, inappropriate and if not remedied, difficulties will soon appear. The child should be taught from the outset to make the left-to-right sequence of progression (eye movements) along a line of print.

On first contact with the reading situation, therefore, the eye movements of the child may be described as merely a looking at or an examining of the words. No consistent tendency in the direction of sequences is present. After some experience in reading, although still near the beginning of the first grade, the child's eye movements are characterized by many fixation pauses per line of print, by fixation pauses of relatively long duration, and by frequent regressions. There is marked irregularity in both fixation pause duration and orderliness of eye-movement sequences. There is emerging, however, a tendency for the fixation pauses to move from the left end of a line toward the right. Improvement comes with reading experience. Toward the end of the first year the average child is making fewer fixation pauses per line. The progression from left to right is more consistent and the fixation pauses are shorter and less variable in duration.

Development of Proficiency with Age

Growth in proficiency of eye-movement habits is revealed in three ways: (1) By increase in the span of recognition, that is, by the number of words perceived in a single fixation pause. If a line of ten words is read with 8 fixation pauses, the child has a span of 1.25 words per fixation on the average. A decrease in fixation pause frequency would indicate an increase in span of recognition. (2) By an increase in the rate of recognition, i.e., the time devoted to each fixation pause. Long pauses reveal a slow rate of recognition; short pauses reveal a fast one. (3) By regularity of the sequences of fixation pauses along the line of print, i.e., freedom from regressions in the material read. Frequent regressions indicate marked irregularity while few or no regressions reveal a decided regularity from left to right along the line of print.

Recent studies of eye-movement changes with age are reported by Gilbert [2] and by Ballantine.[1] In silent reading there was a rapid decrease in the number of fixation pauses and regressions per line of print from grade 1 through grade 4. Although there were further decreases up through the higher grades and high school, the major changes had taken place by the fifth grade. Poorer readers continued to show more improvement than good readers for grades above the fifth. Fixation pause duration decreased rapidly from the first grade to the fifth and only slowly, or not at all, at higher grades. It is apparent that the average child achieves fairly stable eye-movement habits by the end of the fourth or sometimes during the fifth grade. There is, however, a slower rate of improvement from the fifth grade to the adult level although relatively very small changes do occur from the ninth grade up to the adult level.

It would seem that progress in the development of efficient eye movements reflects in some degree practice in reading instruction in the grades. Rapid progress is made as long as marked emphasis is placed upon the teaching of reading and slower progress when the emphasis is shifted to other subject matter. Probably a faster rate of progress in the upper grades would be maintained if more emphasis were given to reading instruction at those levels.

Eye Movements in the Reading Clinic

Inefficient reading is accompanied by characteristic eye-movement behavior. In marked contrast to efficient reading, the diagnostic signs of poor reading are many and long fixation pauses, and irregular sequences of fixation pauses along the line of print. With some very poor readers these movements approximate an aimless wandering of the eyes to and fro. These faulty eye movements are seldom the cause of poor reading. For the most part they are merely symptoms which reflect inefficient reading habits. The experimental evidence indicates that the processes of perceiving and comprehending in reading determine to a large degree the eye-movement patterns employed in that reading. That is, eye movements readily adapt themselves to mental processes. Complex eye-movement patterns (many fixation pauses and regressions), therefore, ordinarily denote confused mental processes while few fixation pauses per line of print with few or no regressions for the most part reflect clear and rapid comprehension.

It has been repeatedly demonstrated that the increased proficiency in reading achieved by special training is accompanied by more efficient eye-movement patterns. Fewer fixation pauses and regressions occur, and the sequences of movements become more regular. This occurs without any special training or pacing of the eye movements.

Analysis of photographic records or direct observation of eye movements may be employed as an aid in diagnosing reading difficulties. Nevertheless the eyes themselves seldom need to be trained to make more effective movements. One exception is that inaccuracy of the return sweep from the end of one line to the beginning of the next may be largely and quickly overcome by specific practice.

What Can the Classroom Teacher Do About Eye Movements?

The outstanding principle concerning eye movements in reading is that they reflect quite accurately the clarity of perception and comprehension taking place in the mind of the reader. Knowing this, the classroom teacher can make good use of her knowledge about reading movements of the eyes: (1) She can emphasize the development of the essential left-to-right movements along a line of print when the child is beginning to read. (2) She will be able to use direct observation of the reader's eyes as an aid in diagnosing reading difficulties. (3) She will appreciate the fact that although eye-movement patterns are good diagnostic signs of reading disability, specific training of eye movements is ordinarily not necessary to bring about improvement in reading. More efficient eye movements automatically appear as the reading is improved by other approved methods.

Eye-movement behavior is an essential part of the reading process. The efficient teacher should understand the nature of eye movements in reading and how she can use this information to advantage.

The study of eye movements in reading is for the most part a research technique. The information gained through experimentation helps us to understand better the reading process. Contrary to the views of some writers, nothing in the research findings suggest that eye movements as such should be paced or trained to improve reading proficiency.

REFERENCES

1. BALLANTINE, FRANCIS A. "Age Changes in Measures of Eye-Movements in Silent Reading," *Studies in the Psychology of Reading,* University of Michigan Monographs in Education, No. 4. Ann Arbor: University of Michigan Press (1951), 65–111.

2. GILBERT, LUTHER C. "Functional Motor Efficiency of the Eyes and its Relation to Reading," *University of California Publications in Education,* XI, No. 3 (September, 1953), 159–232.

3. TINKER, MILES A. "Eye Movements in Reading," *Journal of Education Research,* XXX, No. 4 (December, 1936), 241–77.

4. ———. "The Study of Eye Movements in Reading," *Psychological Bulletin,* XLIII, No. 2 (March, 1946), 93–120.

5. ———. "Recent Studies of Eye Movements in Reading," *Psychological Bulletin,* LIV, No. 4 (July, 1958), 215–31.

R E A D I N G   R E A D I N E S S

12. A PROGRAM FOR SIX-YEAR-OLDS*

Helen Garrett

A GOOD program for the first grade, designed to permit every child to work at his own maturity level, must perforce retain many of the informal features of a good kindergarten. For children of six do not put away their spontaneous growth patterns of the year before. It continues to be true for the first graders, as it was for children in the kindergarten, that only by providing opportunity for children to move about, find their own way of participating satisfactorily, and talk together can the teacher watch and guide them.

Children Need to Talk

In a first grade where the children are not allowed to talk, the teacher

* From Helen Garrett, "A Program for Six-Year-Olds," in *When Shall We Begin To Teach Reading?*, prepared by Helen Garrett, Division of Elementary Education, New York State Education Department (Albany, N.Y.: The University of the State of New York, 1949), pp. 36–40. Reprinted by permission of the author and the University of the State of New York.

does not know her children, their stage of maturity, their ideas, their hopes, their interests. She does not even know how they use the English language and does not give them practice to note mistakes for later correction, or opportunities consciously or unconsciously to correct their own mistakes. Such a teacher teaches as if from a ruled line outward. Everything behind the line is a blank.

A stranger comes into the room of such a teacher, a stranger who likes children and wishes to know them. She looks at all the eager little faces with their odd, stifled expressions. She asks a question of them. "Have any of you a little dog?" Many hands go up. "Tell me about your little dogs," she suggests.

The answers and comments flow swiftly. "My little dog ran away." . . . "I have a kitty." . . . "Dogs are bad. They bite." . . . "My puppy wath wun over by a twuck yethterday." . . . "I ain't got no dog." . . . "I hate dogs. They're mean." . . .

58

"My ittie dog ith bwown." . . . "I love doggies but my mummy says they is dirty." . . . "I can't has a dog 'cuz they makes me has asthma." . . . "My grandma won't let me have no dog but my daddy an' me wants one." . . . "Dogs is wicked. They kill sheep." . . . "No, they don't kill sheep. I got a black and white spaniel. He don't kill no sheep." . . . "A dog's better'n sheep anyway. Sheep ain't no good to no one." So it goes on until everyone has spoken. Has the stranger learned something about these children? Is she in a better position to work with these children where their interests lie or not? Does she find many concepts to discuss with them? Does she discover language problems related to reading? Of course, she does.

Children Need Activity

In a classroom where there are many activities, many "jobs" to do, and individual as well as group participation in the curriculum, the teacher will discover innumerable places where she can guide and help her children. She will recognize the socially gifted child but may discover he needs more time and assistance in reading than his best friend who is his devoted slave. She helps a very dependent child to learn to take care of himself. She appreciates that the child who always plays at the sandbox because he has never had this opportunity before and is exploring its possibilities, is different from one child who plays there all the time because his family has never given him any experience with books or crayons, and

not knowing their possibilities and being afraid of trying, he therefore hesitates to branch out beyond his familiar medium. And she knows that the first boy is likewise different from the boy who is always at the sandbox because he likes to "boss" everybody else playing there and has not discovered any of the satisfactions inherent in playing or working by himself.

She will find a shy child who is unusually musical and an overactive one who also is musical. Together they can enjoy more music than the others and help each other overcome some of their social handicaps. A child who gives every evidence that he will have difficulty with reading loves to paint at the easel. She gives him extra time there so that when he begins to realize that others can easily surpass him in reading he will have already gained self-confidence from his ability in painting. Indeed, she will always know how her first graders are growing and what their "emotional tone" is that day. Their needs are in her blood stream. She does not know how to ignore them.

Activities in a first grade classroom will include, to this end, blocks and block building, paints and large painting paper, toys for house play and for farm and animal play. There will be a live pet to take care of and to handle gently. There will be clay, a workbench, tools and wood. There will be a library table with books. There will be a science corner or shelf where young experimenters can study the uses of magnets, magnifying glasses, pulleys, tops, water and sand, and many other objects. There will be plants to water. A first-grade room will be a very busy place indeed all of the time, a veritable hive of bees.

Social Experience in the Group Is Necessary

In addition, however, to the long periods in the room when the individuals or groups select their own activities, there will be short periods when the group as a whole works together. Singing, rhythms, or the use of percussion instruments may bring all of the group together. Discussion periods, the making of plans, and talking over the care of materials will be a total group experience also. Story-telling and reading aloud is another reason for sitting down together and, of course, everyone goes on group trips.

Every day and many times a day in this classroom social learnings figure. Games are learned, sides are chosen, children learn to take turns and to wait for others. They find it necessary to be considerate and helpful. They make choices and play fair. They take part in play and plans initiated by others. They learn to contribute and be responsible for elements in the class program. This is part of the class *curriculum,* these social experiences. They are not extraneous experiences to no end.

The Importance of Reading

Reading is a part of the curriculum, too, for reading is a matter of importance in our culture. It is one of the chief working tools of the times. But it should be recognized as a means to an end, not as an end in itself. This end may be the acquiring of specific knowl-

edge, enlargement of our horizons, or immediate enjoyment and pleasure. It may be a surcease from sorrow or offer relaxation from strain. It may lift our minds to the infinite. For those who can read well and with pleasure, it is an unending joy. But learning to read can and should be an interest that continues as long as we live, and grows with our knowledge of the world. The concept that learning to read takes place in the first grade, or in the first and second, or in the first three grades is an oversimplification of fact. In the first grade, children can only consciously begin upon a long process that we hope will give increasing pleasure thereafter. Consequently, the real purpose of the first grade is to help children grow and enjoy enough satisfaction in reading so that they will be encouraged to continue to learn more about it. Also during the year they must experience a sufficient sense of achievement and success to be willing to work hard and conscientiously throughout the first two, three, or four years in the grades, when the rudiments, and the rudiments only, are generally learned.

The wise teacher of the first grade will not start the year with reading. She will start the school year with getting to know her children and with giving them time to know her and one another. When the first excitement of coming together in the fall is past and the children are moving about the classroom at their normal tempos and have learned to take good care of themselves; when the children show through their language that they can express their thoughts in intelligible form and can understand the thoughts of the teacher; when they are accustomed to many of the routines of the day, have some interesting understandings in common, and are ready to put their minds upon the new business of reading; then will the teacher direct the attention of the children to reading. For then she will know she is building on a firm foundation so that what is learned in this direction will be understood, remembered, and used.

13. A STUDY OF THE COMPARATIVE READING ACHIEVEMENTS OF EARLY AND LATE SCHOOL STARTERS*

Richard S. Hampleman

Introduction

FOR approximately thirty years school people have been speculating about the problem of the best age at which to start teaching children to read. As a result of some early study of the problem, it was concluded that children were having difficulty with reading because they were being started too young. Some schools moved back the dates by which pupils had to be six years of age before they could start school in September, from February 15 or January 15 to January 1 or December 15, or even earlier. Other schools approached the problem from

* From Richard S. Hampleman, "A Study of the Comparative Reading Achievements of Early and Late School Starters," *Elementary English*, XXXVI, No. 5 (May, 1959), 331–34. Reprinted by permission of the author and the National Council of Teachers of English.

another angle—kept the same rule for entrance age, but saw to it that no pupils were put in beginning reading groups until they were six years of age or over.

Later studies began to indicate that perhaps other factors, more important than chronological age, also operate to affect the problem of the proper time to begin reading instruction. Mental age, teaching techniques, and certain reading readiness factors which might be strengthened by kindergarten and first grade pre-reading experiences, were now considered to be of more value in predicting readiness for reading than was chronological age.

It is the opinion of the author, however, that school people can get changes made in the chronological age requirement far more easily than they can get the public to accept school entrance on the basis of mental age or reading readiness test scores. Therefore, to be practical, more study should be concentrated on that chronological age at which beginning reading can be taught most successfully.

The question this study will attempt to answer is, "Are pupils who start school at the age of six years four months or over better readers in the sixth grade than those who start school below the age of six years four months?"

It is the opinion of the author that there should be some important difference between the two groups. Those who are approximately one-half year older should be more successful in reading than the younger ones for three main reasons. Since they are older chronologically they will (1) be somewhat more advanced in mental age, (2) have more experiences to assist with readiness, and (3) have better eye coordination. Thus, even though chronological age by itself may not be an excellent prognosis for reading success, other factors which may be more important are advanced, to some extent, as chronological age advances.

Related Research

A review of related studies shows that the bulk of them were done in the 1920's and 1930's. All but one of them has studied the relationship of various factors to reading achievement in grades one or two. One study uses fourth grade subjects.

One group of studies indicates that chronological age should be six years to give a child a satisfactory start in reading. Most of them say that age seven may be better if the child is immature physically, mentally, or emotionally. Correlations found between chronological age and reading achievement are .09 and .12.

Studies of the relationship between mental age and reading achievement show that a mental age of six to seven years is necessary for beginning reading. Correlations between these two factors range from .50 to .69.

The best predictors of reading success discovered in the literature were mental age, teacher rating in November, and various combinations of such factors as mental age, reading readiness tests, and teacher rating plans.

A number of studies point to other factors more important to success in beginning reading than any fixed chronological or mental age. These factors are individual attention to the needs of slow learners, rich experience background, reading programs centered around experiences, and quality of techniques and materials used. A conclusion running through these studies is that mere postponement in the time of beginning to teach reading will not in itself insure that all children will learn to read.

The present study is different in that it is the first to compare the relationship between school entrance age and eventual reading success as far along as the sixth grade.

Methods of Research

Data used in the study were obtained from the school office of the Bloomington, Indiana, Metropolitan School District. These facts were collected:

date of birth, reading achievement score (age-equivalent) on the *Stanford Achievement Test, Intermediate Complete, Forms F* and *J,* date this test was administered, and all available intelligence quotient scores.

Data were collected only for those children who entered the first grade in September, 1947, finished the sixth grade in June, 1953, and had all of their schooling in the Bloomington schools. Working with these criteria, 58 pupils out of 181 in the class were selected for study.

All of those who were six years, three months of age or younger at entrance were put in Group 1, and those who were six years, four months of age or over were placed in Group 2. Mean and median reading achievement scores were then figured for each group.

In order to be able to compare the mean and median achievement of the first and fourth quarters of the whole group of subjects, Group 1 was divided into two equal parts, Group 1A and Group 1B. Group 2 was divided into two nearly equal parts, Group 2A and 2B.

Intelligence test scores were not used in this study to equate the two groups. They were used only to assist in the analysis and interpretation of results. In that connection, the score used was the median I.Q. score of the three to six scores found for each child.

Analysis and Results

Table 1 will help clarify relationships in the analysis of the data which answers the main question of this study, "Are late school starters more suc-cessful in reading by the time they finish the sixth-grade than are early starters?" Group 2, the older children, have a mean reading achievement score slightly more than four months higher than Group 1. The median score for Group 2 shows them to be seven months superior. Intelligence quotients for the two groups are essentially the same, means both being 106, and medians being 108 for Group 1 and 103 for Group 2. In the mean chronological age, Group 2 is five months older. As a result of this data it is clear that those children who started to school at age six years, four months or more, as a group are superior in reading achievement at the sixth-grade level to their younger classmates.

The results shown by a comparison of data for Groups 1A and 2B (youngest and oldest quarters) are even more impressive. Table 2 shows the means and medians of these two groups along with the corresponding chronological ages. The mean of the oldest quarter, Group 2B, shows a superiority of almost seven months over the youngest quarter, Group 1A. Comparing these groups by medians shows an even greater superiority—eleven months. Intelligence quotients for the two groups are essentially the same in both mean and median scores. The older group has a mean difference in age from the younger group of almost eight months and a median difference of seven months.

Since the older group in this study, Group 2B, showed more superiority to Group 1A in reading achievement than might have been expected, the data was analyzed in one other way in an attempt to shed further light on the

TABLE 1

Mean and Median Chronological Age, Intelligence Quotient, and Reading Achievement Score of Two Groups

Group Number	Mean Chron. Age *	Median Chron. Age *	Mean I.Q. Score	Median I.Q. Score	Mean Read. Ach. Score *	Median Read. Ach. Score *
2	146.51	146.00	106.25	103.00	148.86	146.00
1	141.53	141.50	106.13	108.00	144.70	139.00
Difference	4.98	4.50	0.12	−5.00†	4.16	7.00

* Expressed in months.

† This difference is marked minus (−) to indicate that it is the reverse of all the other differences shown.

TABLE 2

Mean and Median Chronological Age, Intelligence Quotient, and Reading Score for Upper and Lower Quartiles

Group Number	Mean Age *	Median Age *	Mean I.Q.	Median I.Q.	Mean Reading Score *	Median Reading Score *
2B	152.19	151.00	103.63	100.50	146.56	146.00
1A	144.27	144.00	103.27	100.00	139.73	135.00
Difference	7.92	7.00	0.36	0.50	6.83	11.00

* Expressed in months.

matter. Of the fifteen in Group 1A, there were only five up to grade level (143 months) in reading. Four of these five had an intelligence quotient of 110 or better. The fifth one had an I.Q. of 99, yet was up to grade level. One who was not up to grade level (eight months below) had an intelligence quotient of 115.

Of the sixteen in Group 2B, there were nine up to grade level and five of that nine achieved this with intelligence quotients below 110. One of these five had an intelligence quotient of 87. Six of the seven in Group 2B who did not achieve grade level had intelligence quotients below 100. The seventh one had a score of 102.

Conclusions

A comparison of the two groups, Group 1 and Group 2, indicates that there is an interesting difference between them in reading achievement. Although it has been well established by earlier research that many factors may influence reading readiness, it seems fairly certain, as a result of this study, that school administrators can advise parents that their children have a considerably better chance for success in reading by starting to school a few months later, rather than a few months earlier. This would be especially important in those cases where birth-date causes doubt as to the best time to send a child to school. The administrator can be more confident of a good prognosis if an intelligence test is given. Those children who have a considerably higher intelligence quotient than 100 would have an excellent chance for success in reading even if they were only six years, three months of age or below. Those children with intelligence quotients below 100 would have very little chance for success in reading if they were this young.

The differences in reading achievement between the older and younger groups observed in this study, although not statistically significant, are nevertheless interesting enough to merit further attention. It is possible that such differences would be significant if the number of cases studied were larger. Such a study is now in progress.*

REFERENCES

1. ARTHUR, GRACE. "A Quantitative Study of the Results of Grouping First-Grade Classes According to Mental Age," *Journal of Educational Research* 12:173–85, October, 1925.
2. BIGELOW, ELIZABETH B. "School Progress of Under-Age Children," *Elementary School Journal* 35:186–92, November, 1934.
3. BONEY, C. DEWITT, and AGNEW, KATE. "Periods of Awakening or Reading Readiness," *Elementary English Review* 14:183–87, May, 1937.
4. DAVIDSON, HELEN P. *An Experimental Study of Bright, Average, and Dull Children at the Four-Year Mental Level,* Genetic Psychology Monographs, Vol. 9, Nos. 3–4, Clark University, Worcester, Massachusetts, 1931, pp. 119–289.
5. DEAN, CHARLES D. "Predicting First-Grade Reading Achievement," *Elementary School Journal* 39:609–16, April, 1939.
6. DEPUTY, E. B. *Predicting First-Grade Reading Achievement, A Study in Reading Readiness.* Teachers College, Columbia University, Contributions to Education, No. 426, New York, 1930, 61 pp.
7. EAMES, THOMAS. "Comparison of Children of Premature and Full Term Birth Who Fail in Reading," *Journal of Educational Research* 38:506–8, March, 1945.
8. GATES, ARTHUR I. "The Necessary Mental Age for Beginning Reading,"

* The author reports that a replica of the above study was made with 323 sixth-grade pupils in Macomb, Illinois. A difference of 6.3 months was observed between the mean reading achievement scores of the older pupils (group 2) and the younger pupils (group 1). The difference favored the older pupils and was significant at better than the one per cent level. A difference of 7.7 months was observed between the mean reading achievement scores of the oldest one-fourth (group 2b) and the youngest one-fourth (group 1a). The difference favored the older one-fourth of the pupils and was statistically significant at better than the 1 per cent level. The mean I.Q. scores for these groups slightly favored the younger pupils (groups 1 and 1a).

The correlation between intelligence and reading achievement in this study was .71. Among the older pupils (group 2), 30 per cent of those who had I.Q.'s below 100 were up to grade level, and 98 per cent of those who had I.Q.'s of 110 or better were up to grade level. Among the younger pupils (group 1), 10 per cent of those who had I.Q.'s below 100 were up to grade level, and 84 per cent of those who had I.Q.'s of 110 or better were up to grade level.

Elementary School Journal 37:497–508, March, 1937.

9. GATES, ARTHUR, and BOND, GUY L. "Reading Readiness: A Study of Factors Determining Success and Failure in Beginning Reading," *Teachers College Record* 37:679–85, May, 1936.

10. HILLIARD, GEORGE H., and TROXELL, ELEANORE. "Informational Background as a Factor in Reading Readiness and Reading Progress," *Elementary School Journal* 38:255–63, December, 1937.

11. MONROE, MARION. *Children Who Cannot Read, The Analysis of Reading Disabilities and the Use of Diagnostic Tests in the Instruction of Retarded Readers,* Chicago: The University of Chicago Press, 1932, 205 pp.

12. MORPHETT, MABEL V., and WASHBURNE, CARLETON. "When Should Children Begin to Read?" *Elementary School Journal* 31:496–503, March, 1931.

13. PETERSON, INEZ B. "The Reading-Readiness Program of the Ironwood Public Schools," *Elementary School Journal* 37:438–46, February, 1937.

14. REED, MARY M. *An Investigation of Practices in First Grade Admission and Promotion,* Teachers College, Columbia University, Contributions to Education, No. 290, New York, 1927, 136 pp.

15. SAMUELS, FRA. "Sex Differences in Reading Achievement," *Journal of Educational Research* 36:594–603, April, 1943.

16. THOMPSON, J. L. "Big Gains from Postponed Reading," *Journal of Education* 117:445–46, October 15, 1934.

17. WILSON, FRANK T., and BURKE, AGNES. "Reading Readiness in a Progressive School," *Teachers College Record,* 38:565–80, April, 1937.

18. WILSON, FRANK T., and FLEMMING, CECILE W. "Correlations of Reading Progress with Other Abilities and Traits in Grade I," *Journal of Genetic Psychology* 53:33–52, 1938.

19. WRIGHT, WENDELL W. *Reading Readiness—A Prognostic Study,* Bulletin of the School of Education, Indiana University, Vol. 12, No. 3, Bureau of Cooperative Research, Indiana University, June 1936, 46 pp.

14. READINESS IS THE BEST PREVENTION*

J. Kendall Hoggard

TEACHER, teacher, I can count to a hundred!" six-year-old Kaye announced the first time she could get her teacher's attention. It was Kaye's first day in school and she was eager to get started.

She not only could count to a hundred, but in the days to follow her teacher noted that Kaye knew what numbers meant and that she had an excellent speaking vocabulary on a variety of subjects. Kaye recognized many words such as her name, mother, school, car, boy, girl, children, and book when she saw them. She had traveled, and she had a rich background of information drawn from books her parents had read to her. The teacher knew that, without a doubt, Kaye and the four or five other children in her room with the same type of background would have little trouble learning to read.

In this same room, however, was a small group which represented the other extreme. Gale was one of these. Gale was full of life, was well adjusted, talked at length concerning her home, and showed every indication of being alert and intelligent. Yet, Gale had no concept of numbers, her experience with books and stories was very limited, and she did not know her address or telephone number.

On the third day of school Gale was observed at noon buying candy. She had selected six cents worth and had offered the clerk one cent for full payment. Obviously, Gale—for the first time—was up against the stark reality of the value of money.

An investigation of the home background of these two children revealed no marked differences from an economic standpoint. The children were approximately the same age, both healthy, neither had any physical defects, and vision and hearing were normal. From all that could be observed both were very intelligent, and yet, Kaye and her group were ready to read while Gale and her group were not.

The above situation is repeated over and over in almost every first grade room in America each year. In studying this illustration three problems immediately present themselves: First, is there anything the home can do to help the pre-school child get ready for school? Second, what can the school do for children like Gale in order to prevent them from developing into reading problems? Third, how can the school and home more effectively work together at the pre-school and first grade level in order to insure better adjustment of all first grade children?

* From J. Kendall Hoggard, "Readiness Is the Best Prevention," *Education*, LXXVII (May, 1957), 523–27. Reprinted by permission of the author and The Bobbs-Merrill Co., Inc., Indianapolis, Ind.

Is There Anything the Home Can Do to Help the Pre-School Child Get Ready for School?

There certainly are many things that parents can do in order to get their children ready for school. The school needs to help the parent realize this fact. Furthermore, the school needs to recommend specific activities to the parents of pre-school children. Vague generalities are not enough.

In the first place, every person interested in children should know that reading is only one phase of the language development process. Contrary to popular opinion, learning to read does not begin at the age of six or seven, it begins with birth and continues throughout the life of the individual. Before a person can read he needs a wealth of experience so that words have meaning and association with persons, objects, and events. These experiences are the first stage in language development and they are the foundation upon which the other stages depend.

As the child grows and develops, he enters the second stage, which is called hearing comprehension. At this point, he learns that certain words which he hears others speak represent certain things. As his hearing vocabulary is increased, the child attempts to speak, and, as time goes on and his experience with sounds increases, he is able to enter the third stage, which is speech production. Now he can talk and make others understand him.

For most children the age of six to seven is the time at which initial experiences with the fourth stage, formal reading, take place. In this stage the child must learn to associate sound and meaning with the words he sees. A large part of his first years in school will be devoted to teaching him to make these associations. Simultaneously, he will enter the fifth stage, writing. Learning to write should be delayed, in the opinion of most authorities, until the child has a reading vocabulary of from three to four hundred words.

This brief description of the stages in language development is intended to show that a large part of that development takes place before the child enters school. The parents who know and understand these stages will give attention to the experience, hearing comprehension, and speech production aspects of language development in their pre-school children.

Almost without exception, every home in America can see to it that its children have the rich experiences that pre-school children should have before entering school. Family excursions to the park, to the zoo, to the open country for city children and to the city for rural children, will contribute greatly to the knowledge of the child. Family picnics, fishing trips, Sunday drives in the family car, trips on the train and bus, visits to museums, the airport, the beach, the mountains and rivers are experiences which will enable the child to grow into reading.

Books should be introduced into the life of the child between the age of one and two. Many homes make a practice of reading together at bedtime which is an excellent way of sharing experiences and extending horizons. Parents can draw heavily on the great store of books that are now available in every supermarket, drugstore, and newsstand in America. Literally hundreds of different titles are available for as little as 25 cents to as much as one wishes to pay.

There should be a balance between the modern and new stories of the times and the golden ones which have delighted children in the past.

Public libraries are full of books that tell the story of the American heritage, and the librarian will be delighted to help the parent select books that are appropriate to be read to the three-, four-, or five-year-old.

Television also offers an excellent opportunity to children if it is properly used. Parents should make every effort to watch television with their children so that they may know what concepts and ideas they are being exposed to. Programs should be well-selected and those that may be harmful should be avoided. When necessary, parents should give the child help in understanding and assimilating material so as to avoid confusion.

Broadened experiences, a wise introduction to the world of books, and constant selectivity and supervision in materials are valuable contributions that any home may make in helping the pre-school child get ready for that eventful first year in school.

What Can the School Do for Children Like Gale in Order to Prevent Them from Developing into Reading Problems?

The first grade, without a doubt, is one of the most critical periods in the life of the child. Here for the first time the six-year-old leaves the shelter and close associations of the home and steps out into a strange new world. This world will make many new demands, and the child will be confronted with an array of new experiences to which he must try to adjust. For some this adjustment will be accomplished with little difficulty. For others it will be the beginning of years of frustration and anxiety for they are destined to become known as reading problems. Yet, with the exception of 5 per cent of all children who go to school, most reading disability can be prevented. Prevention starts at home, but it must be continued and extended by the school if it is to be effective.

One of the chief causes of reading failure is rushing children into the initial reading program before they are ready. Gale is not ready. In far too many instances, however, children with Gale's language deficiency will enroll in schools where the teacher's chief concern is to get them started on reading without giving any attention to readiness.

Recently, the writer made a survey of 72 schools for the purpose of finding out practices in regard to reading readiness. It was alarming to find that 27 schools started all first graders in the pre-primer during the first or second week in school. It was more alarming to learn that four school systems started all first graders in the primer. The explanation was made that since the primer contains all the vocabulary to be found in the pre-primer, the program simply starts with the primer in order to save time.

Such a policy illustrates well the fact that far too many teachers and parents still expect beginners to read soon after school starts in September. In these situations some children are under so much pressure that learning to read becomes an unbearable task. The classroom is filled with fear and tension which serves to aggravate the language deficiency of children like Gale.

Reading authorities are in agreement that reading readiness is the very foundation of prevention. More, not less, attention needs to be given to reading readiness at all levels of learning, but especially at the first grade level.

Under proper leadership, first grade teachers should be anxious to take care of the readiness needs of all the children in their room. The question they most often ask is, "Where can I get help?"

It cannot be emphasized too strongly that all acceptable reading programs now available to schools have marvelous readiness programs. With these programs, teachers' manuals are offered in which the author sets forth his philosophy and outlines his plan for carrying out the program.

In addition to offering specific suggestions, the manual outlines the plan of organization the author recommends. The example of Kaye and Gale illustrates the fact that children vary widely in their readiness for reading. This means that in the early part of the year most teachers will need two groups—those who are ready for reading and those who are not. The children in the latter group may require weeks or months of help in language development before they are ready to read. Some of this group, however, will develop faster than others, so as the year progresses other reading groups are formed by the teacher as needs arise. These groups must always be flexible. In addition, many activities such as music, art, science, and playtime require different groupings.

The author's plan for organizing these activities deserves the most careful study by the teacher. There are no short cuts, and the school that gives little or no attention to the readiness program is creating reading problems in children like Gale.

Can the School and the Home More Effectively Work Together at the Pre-School and First Grade Level in Order to Insure Better Adjustment of All First Grade Children?

Yes, indeed, and the school must lead the way. One community has found a very effective way to outline to parents the pre-school and first grade needs of the child.

This school system is in a town of 25,000 people and has twelve elementary schools. Through the use of a continuous census, the school has the name and address of the parents of most pre-school children.

In February and March a series of conferences are planned in each elementary school for parents who will have children entering the first grade the following September. Written invitations are sent to every known parent in the district while others are reached through the press, radio, and T.V. The announcements carry an outline of the program and a list of specific questions to be discussed. Questions like the following are included: What can I, as a parent, do now in order to get my child ready for school in September? Does failure to learn to read during the first few months of school mean that my child has a low I.Q.? Will my child be taught phonics? What is included in the process of learning to read? Should I teach my child to count? My child is trying to write; what should I do? What is reading readiness?

As a rule, these conferences are well attended. In one school with an anticipated first grade enrollment of 100, 81 parents attended.

The principal of each school is in charge of the program. The meeting usually starts with a thirty minute talk by the Director of Instruction in which the school's philosophy is outlined. Many of the questions mentioned above are covered in this talk. At the end of the speech, the principal of the school acts as moderator and the parents are encouraged to ask questions. The first grade teachers with the Director of Instruction act as a panel to whom questions are directed.

For years this school system has produced a parents' handbook, "Ready for First Grade." These are distributed and explained. Included in the 24-page handbook is information on reading readiness. The handbook also contains specific suggestions as to what the pre-school child should be taught, recommended summertime activities and a list of 100 appropriate books from which the parent may choose the ones he wishes to read to the child. Books written by reading specialists for parents' use are also suggested.

After the handbooks are distributed, plans for two additional conferences, which occur after school starts in September, are announced. The first meeting comes at the end of the fifth week of school—usually the first week in October. During this week, all first grade children are dismissed at noon. Starting at 1 p.m. on Monday and continuing through Friday, individual parent-teacher conferences take place. Each conference is scheduled with the parent ahead of time and lasts approximately thirty minutes.

The second conference, which is held between Thanksgiving and the Christmas holidays, is another one to which all first grade parents are invited. At this final conference, explanation is given as to why one group is reading while another is still in reading readiness. Time is allowed at the meeting for parents to ask further questions concerning their child's progress.

It would be hard, indeed, to overemphasize the excellent accomplishments of these conferences. Complaints from first grade parents to school authorities have almost ceased. Parents and teachers alike have nothing but praise for the plan, and home and school have gone a long way toward understanding each other.

The number of parents who are trying to teach their own children formal reading have almost disappeared. Few parents need ask, "What can I do to help my child?" They know, and they are ready to follow suggestions that are given.

Parents and teachers in this system are proud of their Kayes, Gales, Jims, and Johns. They are all different and their individuality must be accepted and cherished. Any school program which is worth its salt will provide for these needs through a program centered around a philosophy of preven-tion. The home can help and it wants to help, but the school must lead the way.

15. CHILDREN WHO LEARNED TO READ AT HOME*

Dolores Durkin

FIRST grade and first steps in reading usually go together. In fact, teachers take it for granted that their new first-graders have not learned to read. The discovery of a six-year-old who is reading comfortably at fourth-grade level naturally excites admiration. But it causes embarrassment, too, when the child is also completing the sixth week of a reading readiness program.

For us the discovery of a six-year-old who was reading at an advanced level provoked curiosity because so little is known about precocious readers. The desire to know more led to the research study reported here, a longitudinal study of children who learned to read at home before entering first grade.[1] The study was designed to consider two basic questions: What accounts for preschool ability in reading? What is the value of learning to read early?

* From Dolores Durkin, "Children Who Learned To Read at Home," *Elementary School Journal,* LXII, No. 1 (October, 1961), 15–18. Reprinted by permission of the author and The University of Chicago Press.

The ability to identify at least eighteen words from a list of thirty-seven was used as the criterion for selecting children for the study. In the fall of 1958 this list of words was used with 5,103 beginning first-graders in a California community.[2] The children were asked to read, individually and orally, as many of the words as possible. In this way, twenty-nine girls and twenty boys became the subjects for the study.

Once identified, these forty-nine children were given the Gates Primary Word Recognition Test and the Gates Primary Paragraph Reading Test. The two tests were administered within the first two weeks of first grade, before instruction in reading began. Because the purpose of the testing was to establish the upper limits of the subjects' reading ability before first-grade instruction, other tests were also used under certain circumstances. Whenever a child got a perfect score on the Gates Primary Paragraph Reading Test, he was given the Gates Advanced Word Recognition Test and the Gates Advanced Paragraph Reading Test. If he got a perfect score on the latter, he was given the Gates Reading Survey.

The same testing procedure was followed in February and in June of the first year of study, and in September, February, and June of the second year.

When first identified, in the fall of 1958, each subject was also given the Revised Stanford-Binet Scale. Later, the parents, teachers, and finally the children themselves were interviewed to isolate the factors, other than intelligence, that might account for preschool reading ability.

After two years of study, what do we know about the forty-nine early readers? Results of the reading tests are summarized in Table 1. The reading-grade level of each subject at each testing period is represented by the median of the grade equivalent derived from the scores of the various tests.

Results of the Revised Stanford-Binet Scale showed intelligence quotients that ranged from 91 to 161. The

TABLE 1

Reading Progress of Forty-nine Early Readers over a Two-Year Period

Date of Testing	Reading-Grade Level	
	RANGE	MEDIAN
September, 1958	1.5–4.5	1.9
February, 1959	1.7–5.7	2.8
June, 1959	2.3–5.6	3.7
September, 1959	2.3–6.5	4.0
February, 1960	3.1–7.6	4.6
June, 1960	3.3–8.9	4.9

median for the total group of subjects was 121.

When the children entered first grade, the coefficient of correlation between their intelligence as measured by the Revised Stanford-Binet Scale and their achievement in reading as measured by the various tests was .40. Subsequently, the coefficient of correlation between intelligence and gain in reading achievement for each school year was calculated. For the 1958–59 school year the coefficient of correlation was found to be .44; for 1959–60, it was .25.

What did we learn about the families of these forty-nine early readers? How did the children learn to read at home?

Socioeconomic data gathered in parent interviews showed that seven of the families were of professional or upper middle-class status.[3] Fifteen were of the lower-middle class, while twenty-six could be classified as upper-lower, and one as lower-lower class.

The professional literature had not prepared us for these findings. Success in reading has so often been associated with membership in the higher socioeconomic classes that it was surprising to find that more than half of the early readers came from families of the blue-collar class.

Other interview findings, however, suggested a possible reason. Interviews with parents in the lower socioeconomic classes consistently revealed a ready and even an enthusiastic acceptance of preschool reading ability. In contrast, parents in the higher socioeconomic classes showed concern and even guilt feelings about their children's ability to read before entering school. Certainly this difference in attitude might account at least in part for the social-class distribution of the subjects in this study.

Through the interviews we also learned that each of the forty-nine families had from one to eight children, the average number being three. Forty of the subjects had at least one older brother or sister. As it turned out, help from these older siblings often accounted in part for early reading ability.

Sixteen of the children explained in interviews that an older brother or sister had first taught them to read. Later, interviews with parents indicated that in only four instances the help in reading came exclusively from a sibling; in twenty-four instances the help came from both a sibling and a parent.

In any case, having a sibling—especially a sister who is about two years older and likes to play school—appears to have something to do with early reading ability. That the younger child had a keen desire to keep up with the older one is also relevant, for when the older one entered school the younger was prompted to learn to read and to print.

Five of the sixteen children who told us they had learned to read with the help of a brother or sister described the lessons in these words:

She [sister] was the best reader in the class.
She got books for me. She told me what the words said.

When my sister's not too busy, she tells me words.

She brought home papers with lots of words.
She studied, and she kept telling me words.

My sister taught me how to sound out words.
Now she doesn't play school so much because I know lots of things.

He [brother] told me every word in each book.
He said, "Write these and you'll remember them."

Perhaps the moral of this part of the story is that teachers instruct not only the children in their classrooms, but younger brothers and sisters as well.

Parents sometimes say of their preschool child: "He learned to read all by himself." Data on these forty-nine early readers indicate that none of them learned without having had some kind of help. Usually help took the form of answering persistent questions about words the children saw in books and newspapers, on signs, labels, and TV programs. For eleven of the children, however, the help came from parents who wanted to teach their child to read.

Various factors prompted these eleven parents. Five mothers in the group said their children were so persistently interested in learning to read that they decided to teach them. One father in a bilingual family explained that his oldest daughter had difficulty in learning to read and had to repeat first grade. Consequently, when each of his other three children reached the age of five, he started giving them help in reading to avoid future problems in school.

One mother—and she was the only mother in the study who was a teacher—said her daughter was ready to learn to read when she was about five, so she started giving the child help at home. The other four mothers in this group of eleven parents said they taught their children to read early because they felt it was their responsibility as parents to get them ready to do well in first grade. For them, this meant giving the child a head start in reading.

What is the value of a head start? One way of approaching this question is to compare the achievement of the thirteen subjects who first got help at home when they were three years old with the achievement of the subjects who first got help at a later age. Data on this kind of comparison are summarized in Table 2.

Since the group that first got help at three years of age and the group that first got help at five years of age are comparable in number and in intelligence, their reading achievement over a period of two school years can be compared, though the comparison yields no clear-cut answers.

As Table 2 shows, the average achievement of the group that got help at three years of age was 2.6 at the beginning of first grade. For the group that first got help at five years of age, the average achievement was 1.7. At the end of the second year of school, the group that first got help at the age of three still showed greater achievement than the group that first got help at the age of five, but the lead was reduced by four months. Similar comparisons in later years should prove interesting and helpful in de-

TABLE 2

*Reading Progress of Forty-nine Early Readers as Related to
Various Factors in Pre-school Instruction*

			Reading-Grade Level		
Instruction	*Number of Pupils*	*Intelligence Quotient* MEDIAN	SEPTEMBER, 1958 MEDIAN	JUNE, 1959 MEDIAN	JUNE, 1960 MEDIAN
AGE STARTED					
3 years	13	128.0	2.6	4.3	5.3
4 years	22	111.5	1.8	3.5	4.9
5 years	14	127.0	1.7	3.1	4.8
FREQUENCY					
Very often	21	119.0	2.5	3.8	4.9
Rather often	21	112.3	1.8	3.5	4.7
Intermittent	7	132.0	1.6	3.7	5.4
INTENT					
Deliberate	11	114.3	2.4	3.5	4.5
Not deliberate	38	123.5	1.9	3.7	4.9
INSTRUCTOR					
Parent only	21	112.0	2.6	3.9	5.1
Sibling only	4	123.5	2.4	3.8	5.8
Combination	24	124.5	1.7	3.3	4.8

termining the ultimate value of an early start in reading.

Another and more significant attempt will be made to consider this question. A control group is to be established. It will be made up of children who started school with the children in this study but who could not read when they entered first grade. Their intelligence will be comparable to the intelligence of these subjects, and they will have had the same classroom teachers. The question now is: What will this second group be like as readers?

REFERENCES

1. This report is based on a paper read at a meeting of the American Educational Research Association in Chicago, February, 1961.
2. DOLORES DURKIN. "The Precocious Reader," *California Journal for Instructional Improvement*, II (December, 1959), 24–28.
3. W. L. WARNER, M. MEEKER, and K. EELLS. *Social Class in America* (Chicago: Science Research Associates, 1949).

16. AN EXPERIMENTAL STUDY OF THE READINESS APPROACH TO READING*

Beatrice E. Bradley

TEACHERS are increasingly aware that, in order to progress satisfactorily, children must make good adjustments to school, and teachers realize that a readiness program should be constantly keyed to promote such an adjustment. However, they are troubled by a number of problems. If children participate in a readiness pro-

gram, will they lose by not receiving instruction in reading upon entrance to Grade 1? If a readiness program is provided, when should the teacher begin formal instruction in reading? What types of activities and learning situations are inherent in a readiness program? The initiation of this study grew out of a sincere attempt to find some answers to these problems.

The problem. Will a child lose or gain if formal systematic instruction in reading is not provided until the child is ready? Clarification of this problem

* From Beatrice E. Bradley, "An Experimental Study of the Readiness Approach to Reading," *Elementary School Journal*, LVI (February, 1956), 262–67. Reprinted by permission of the author and The University of Chicago Press.

was sought through a study of two groups of children who had different programs during their first two years in an elementary school. The experimental group participated in a program which was built on the concept of readiness and was designed to stimulate growth in all areas of development. Formal systematic instruction in reading was not given any child until he was considered ready. In the control group, formal systematic instruction in all academic subjects was provided immediately upon entrance to Grade 1.

The number of children who participated in this study was small. Results of the study, however, point to procedures of instructional practice which might profitably be used with larger and with heterogeneous groups.

Procedures of the Study

Two groups of first-grade children, each consisting of thirty-one children, were matched as closely as possible on the basis of sex, chronological age, intelligence quotient, and the father's socioeconomic status. Each group was studied for a two-year period as it progressed through Grades 1 and 2. A comprehensive test at the end of the third year was administered for additional study.

The teacher of the experimental group remained with the group for the two-year period. The teachers of the control group each had the group for one year. All the teachers selected were matched as closely as possible as to amount of training, years of experience in the particular grade, and ratings of teaching efficiency.

Through a group meeting in which the program for the experimental group was explained, the co-operation of the parents of these children was sought.

Program with the Experimental Group

The experimental group worked in a classroom which was arranged to stimulate the children and to provide them with materials for many types of activities. Work centers around the room provided for the many interests and levels of development of the children. Materials were within easy reach of all and offered challenging opportunity for adventure.

Determination of the readiness of the group. A complete picture of the readiness of the experimental group was necessary before a program of work could be planned. The developmental history of each child was reviewed. A check was made on the state of his health. The analysis included an appraisal of his social, emotional, and experiential background. His language development also became an object of study. The Van Wagenen Reading-Readiness Test revealed pertinent information on the child's ability to perceive relationships, his ability to make visual and auditory discriminations, his memory span of ideas, and his general background of information. Scores on the Philadelphia Verbal Ability Test provided the child's intelligence quotient and mental age.

The teacher then attempted to adjust her program to the child, accepting him at the level of development he had reached upon entering Grade 1 from kindergarten. She also continued, by means of informal appraisals and objective tests, to continue her study of the child and to measure his growth. In late December of the first year, Marion Monroe's Reading Aptitude Tests were administered to determine the child's reading aptitude at that time. To appraise the growth of the children in the entire group, the Pintner General Ability Test, Verbal Series, was given in March. The mental age of each child was again reviewed.

Guidance in group living. Throughout her work with the experimental group the teacher attempted to do the following:

1. Provide experiences which would enrich and widen the child's understandings of the world around him through excursions outside of school and work within school.
2. Furnish opportunity for the child to relate language to experience, to build his vocabulary, and to improve his auditory and visual discrimination.
3. Present every type of creative expression and experience, and develop manipulative power.
4. Build emotional stability.
5. Initiate group experiences, with many opportunities for planning, setting standards, and living happily and cooperatively with others.
6. Help the child become self-reliant and mature.

Instruction in reading. Groups in reading were formed when the teacher's judgment and the results of objective tests indicated that the child was ready for the complicated task of reading. Considerable weight was given to the child's language develop-ment; to his background of information as revealed in his ability to interpret ideas read or told to him; and to his sustained interest in trying to read words, signs, and labels.

The first group received instruction in reading after five months in the readiness program; the second group, after eight months; and the third, after ten months. The first group received two formal lessons a week; the second group, three lessons; and the third group had a reading lesson every day. Each lesson was forty minutes in length.

Program with the Control Group

The children in the control group worked in a classroom whose decoration in the main consisted of children's work in art, handwriting, spelling, and arithmetic. This work was always attractively displayed on bulletin boards. An attempt was made to stimulate the group's interest through books placed on a low table and through storybook characters mounted on colored paper.

Appraisal of the group. An appraisal of this group followed traditional school procedure. The individual's intelligence quotient was obtained by means of the Philadelphia Verbal Ability Test. The general physical condition of the child was determined by the school physician. The speech teacher examined the group for speech difficulties. The results of this appraisal in no way affected the teaching procedures. The teacher made no attempt to study individuals by means of objective tests or informal appraisals. Instruction in every subject was begun immediately.

The subject areas. In each of the areas the group was instructed in the subject matter indicated in the guides of the school district. Planning, motivation, presentation, and review of the work were responsibilities of the teacher. From the total amount of subject matter to be covered, the teacher determined in advance each day's requirements. Lessons in the skills were balanced with lessons in other subject areas.

Instruction in reading. Instruction in reading was given from the same basic reading series as was used by the experimental group. In the first month of Grade 1 every child was given instruction from the easiest preprimer. Those children who made the most progress and were able to assimilate the vocabulary and to read fairly fluently were placed in the first reading group. The children who had great difficulty were placed in the third group. All others were in the second group. Each group advanced as rapidly as it could. A daily forty-minute reading lesson was given to each group.

TABLE 1

Results on Reading-Achievement Tests Given to Experimental and Control Groups during Second Year, at End of Second Year, and at End of Third Year

Name of Test and Date of Administration	Number of Pairs	Mean Score		DIFFERENCE (IN FAVOR OF EXPERIMENTAL GROUP)	t.	PROBABILITY
		EXPERIMENTAL GROUP	CONTROL GROUP			
Philadelphia Reading Test, Grade 2 A (November 1 of second year):						
Word recognition.....	31	24.10	27.58	−3.48	3.70	<.001
Phrase recognition....	31	10.29	17.87	−7.58	5.57	<.001
Paragraph comprehension	31	3.97	8.97	−5.00	4.90	<.001
Chicago Reading Tests, Grades 2, 3, 4 (June of second year):						
Comprehension of words	31	15.93	15.77	.16	.16	>.8
Comprehension of phrases and words..	31	13.45	13.64	− .19	.22	>.8
Comprehension of story, directions, and paragraphs	31	21.83	22.41	− .58	.35	>.7
Iowa Every-Pupil Tests of Basic Skills, Grades 3, 4, 5 (June of third year):						
Silent-reading comprehension	24	27.67	24.17	3.50	1.05	>.3
Vocabulary	24	23.79	20.58	3.21	1.83	>.05

At the end of the first year the teacher listed the names of the children in each group and the work that they had covered. The second-grade teacher started to teach the groups at the book level indicated by the first-grade teacher.

Interpretation of Test Results

The children in both groups were given standardized reading tests in November, December, and June of their second year, and in November and June of their third year. The data were treated statistically by means of the *t* technique. The means of the raw scores were obtained for interpretation.

Testing in the second year. In November of the second year each group was given the Philadelphia Reading Test for Grade 2 A, which consists of three parts: word recognition, phrase recognition, and paragraph comprehension. The results (Table 1) show that the control group was significantly superior in reading achievement at that time, the level of significance being better than .001. (It is fairly common practice to interpret a difference as significant when it would arise due to chance not more than 5 times in 100, that is, when the probability (*P*) associated with the difference is .05 or less. That practice is followed here.)

By the end of June of their second year the children in the control group had received systematic instruction in reading for twenty months. Group I of the experimental pupils had had such instruction for fifteen months; Group II, for twelve months; and Group III, for ten months. In mid-June of that year Test B of the Chicago Reading Tests, Form I for Grades 2, 3, and 4, was administered. The results shown in Table 1 indicate in comprehension of words a mean difference of .16, in comprehension of phrases and words a mean difference of .19, and in comprehension of story, directions, and paragraphs a mean difference of .58. These differences are not statistically significant.

Testing in the third year. In November of the third year the Philadelphia Reading Test for Grade 3 was given. The mean difference of the raw scores was 2.42 in favor of the experimental group. The difference, although not statistically significant ($.20 > P > .10$), suggests that the experimental group was achieving somewhat better than the control group.

In June the Iowa Every-Pupil Tests of Basic Skills, Form L, Grades 3, 4, 5, were administered to the experimental and the control groups. The results in Table 1 indicate that there are no significant differences in the achievement of the groups.

On the test in punctuation the mean scores of the experimental group (not presented here) showed marked superiority over the control group, the difference being significant at the .001 level. In the capitalization test the experimental group showed a superiority over the control group at the .01 level. In the tests in alphabetization and in fundamental operations in arithmetic, the experimental group showed a superiority over the control group at the .02 level. In sentence sense and in vocabulary and fundamental knowledge in arithmetic, the experimental group's superiority was significant at the .05 level.

Even though the experimental group had not been given systematic instruction in reading until the children were considered ready, the results on the standardized tests reveal that this group had caught up with the control group in reading achievement by the end of the second year. The experimental group continued to equal or better the progress of the control group during the third year. In the review of the data obtained from the scores made in the tests on basic skills at the end of the third year, it is apparent

TABLE 2

Grade Equivalents of Scores on Iowa Every-Pupil Tests of Basic Skills Made in June of Third Year by 24 Pairs of Pupils in Experimental and Control Groups

	Range of Grade Equivalents		Median Grade Equivalent		Number of Pupils Whose Scores Fell Below Grade 4.0	
	EXPERI-MENTAL GROUP	CON-TROL GROUP	EXPERI-MENTAL GROUP	CON-TROL GROUP	EXPERI-MENTAL GROUP	CON-TROL GROUP
A. Silent reading comprehension:						
Reading comprehension ...	2.2–6.5	1.8–7.2	3.8	3.7	14	16
Vocabulary	3.2–5.7	2.2–6.3	4.1	3.8	11	13
Total test	2.8–5.8	1.9–6.5	4.0	3.7	13	16
B. Work-study skills:						
Map-reading	2.7–4.7	2.2–4.7	3.3	3.3	19	18
Use of references	2.2–6.8	1.7–6.2	4.7	4.2	10	12
Use of index	1.8–7.6	2.4–5.5	4.8	3.8	7	13
Use of dictionary	2.0–6.6	2.0–9.1	3.8	3.8	15	14
Alphabetization	2.5–7.2	2.9–7.2	4.5	4.2	7	12
Total test	2.7–6.2	2.1–5.1	4.1	3.7	8	16
C. Basic language skills:						
Punctuation	2.9–7.4	2.2–4.8	4.4	3.6	4	17
Capitalization	3.3–6.4	2.2–5.8	4.8	3.8	7	18
Usage	2.3–9.0	2.3–9.6	5.5	5.5	2	8
Spelling	1.6–5.2	1.8–7.5	4.1	3.8	9	14
Sentence sense	1.0–7.7	1.0–7.0	5.0	3.3	8	16
Total test	3.1–5.6	2.6–6.0	4.6	4.0	5	12
D. Basic arithmetic skills:						
Vocabulary and fundamental knowledge	3.3–6.1	2.1–5.2	4.3	4.3	5	8
Fundamental operations ..	3.0–4.8	2.0–4.5	4.0	3.6	11	20
Problems	2.7–5.2	2.7–5.0	4.1	3.8	9	16
Total test	3.3–4.9	2.0–4.6	4.2	3.8	8	18

that the experimental group showed slight gains, some statistically significant, over the control group in a majority of the areas tested.

For a consideration of the grade equivalents of the scores obtained on the Iowa Every-Pupil Tests of Basic Skills, see Table 2. The spread of achievement in the two groups is indicated, as well as the number of pupils obtaining scores with grade equivalents below 4.0.

Major Conclusions

The soundness of the readiness approach to all school learnings is reaffirmed in a review of the findings of this study. The following major conclusions may be drawn.

1. Test results clearly indicate that the children who participated in the readiness program attained a degree of achievement in reading equal to that of the control group by the end of the second year. By the end of the third year the experimental group was up to grade standard in reading and continued to equal the progress of the control group.

2. By the end of the third year in other skills, such as work-study skills, basic language skills, and basic arithmetic skills, the experimental group was above grade standard and showed slight gains, some statistically significant, over the control group.

3. The early intensive start in reading and other academic subjects did not result in greater gains for the control group. Obviously the time spent in the early months of the first year on academic learnings could have been used with profit to develop the

social and emotional growth and the experiential background of the children in the control group.

4. The pupils in the experimental group had many more experiences than those in the control group. Included in these were activities involving oral language (planning, questioning, building standards, reporting, and evaluating), the creative and manual arts, firsthand experiences, and participation in the democratic processes. Any gains that this group may have made in these areas were in addition to the achievement they made in the academic subjects.

Implications for the Educational Program

The amount of time spent in a readiness program is an individual matter. It depends on the child's readiness for reading and other academic subjects. The amount of time now devoted to developing readiness is certainly insufficient and in some instances nonexistent. This situation might be the result, on the part of the teacher, of an unwillingness to accept the philosophy inherent in such a program. This attitude may derive from timidity, a lack of training in techniques, a lack of understanding, pressure on the part of fellow-teachers who are loath to receive children in Grade 2 who are "unprepared in the skills," and administrative and parental pressure. All these drawbacks could readily be dispelled by a fearless acceptance of the proved premise that the child, who should be the first consideration, benefits in meaningful ways by the delay of a formal program and that mastery of the so-called "three R's,' while important, takes its logical place in the total child picture only when he is ready for such mastery and not before.

Primarily the readiness program and all its implications become the responsibility of the teacher. He can meet this responsibility much better when parents, fellow-teachers, administrators, and leaders in education are persuaded that here is a program predicated on a sound philosophy of pupil growth. Not only the skills but other much-needed avenues of instruction lead to the development of an individual worthy of his place in an ever-growing, challenging society. Only wholehearted acceptance of the philosophy of readiness can dissolve what is often blind resistance to any departure from so-called "traditional practices," the best of which may be retained in a program of more progressive thinking.

It becomes incumbent upon administrators and teachers to lend their leadership and support to activities which have for their purpose such a development of the child as outlined here. This leadership involves on their part an unequivocal indorsement of the principles of child development. Further it involves unremitting effort to alert communities to the need for adherence to those proved principles of child growth.

17. BUILDING READINESS FOR READING IN FIRST-GRADE CHILDREN THROUGH SPECIAL INSTRUCTION*

Lillian Orme

ELEMENTARY–SCHOOL educators know that much of pupil nonpromotion occurs in the first grade,

* From Lillian Orme, "Building Readiness for Reading in First-Grade Children through Special Instruction," Thirty-Fourth Yearbook, *National Elementary Principal,* XXXV (September, 1955), 43–46. Reprinted by permission of the author and *National Elementary Principal.*

that inability to read is a leading reason for nonpromotion, and that many nonpromotions represent a failure of the school rather than of the pupil. Placing responsibility on the schools is justified after viewing the success of later remedial instruction which is adjusted to the abilities and interests of children. This outcome suggests that many children might have succeeded from the beginning had their initial instruction been as well adjusted to their needs as the remedial teaching.

With this knowledge in mind we experimented with a special program of initial instruction at the W. W. Yates School in Kansas City, Missouri. Our specific purposes were: (a) to develop a special readiness program with emphasis on the reading needs of first-grade pupils, (b) to test the value of readiness materials, and (c) to determine the degree of success of this program.

Experimental Procedure

The matched group technic was used. Entering first-grade pupils were divided into two groups, one control group and one experimental, each group having the same distribution of intelligence test scores as determined by the *Revised Stanford-Binet Scale*.[1] Two rooms of first-graders taught by two regular teachers made up the control group. One room, taught by the writer, made up the experimental group.

During the first month in school, all the first-graders were given the *Metropolitan Readiness Tests*.[2] The scores showed that slightly more than 78 percent of all the children were not ready for formal instruction in reading: 77 percent of the experimental group, 82 percent of one control group, and 76 percent of the second control group.

[1] Louis M. Terman and Maud A. Merrill, *Revised Stanford-Binet Scale* (Boston: Houghton Mifflin Co., 1937).

[2] Gertrude H. Hildreth and Nellie L. Griffiths, *Metropolitan Readiness Tests* (New York: World Book Co., 1950).

MATERIALS AND METHODS

The materials and methods used with the experimental group differed appreciably from those used with the control groups. The experimental group used reading readiness and preparatory books, pupil workbooks accompanying the basic readers, suplementary materials such as picture cards, phonetic cards, charts, tests, and other books and related content.

Materials for reading in the control groups were not designated by the experimenter. They were allowed to proceed with their reading instruction in nearly complete freedom of choice of materials and technics. Principal materials used in the control groups were the basal reading series, supplementary texts, preprimers, flash cards, charts, and similar ones. The absence of direction of procedures and technics for the control groups was to establish or to maintain as nearly as possible the conventional or normal practice of reading instruction. The only restriction was that reading readiness books were to be used only by the experimental group.

For the experimental group a longer time was allowed for the readiness period before beginning teaching the reading skills. The length of the readiness period depended upon the developmental level of the individual child, his adjustment, and progress. The program of special instruction was designed to include: (a) the city-adopted course of study, (b) activities to meet specific needs, and (c) provisions for the varying rates of progress of pupils.

The room of the experimental

Center of Interest	Purpose
Reading Center Reading table, chairs, bookcase, bulletin board, reading easel, readiness books, charts, *Our Big Book,* basic readers, workbooks, pictures, word phrases and sentence cards, phonetic cards, chalkboards, pocket card holder	Children worked directly with the teacher for development of reading readiness and of reading.
Library Corner Reading table and chairs, picture and story books, preprimers and primers, mounted pictures and picture cards, scrapbooks, picture dictionary	Free reading by the children
Play Corner Playhouse equipment, dolls, toys	Dramatic play and social experiences
Science Center Tables, shelves of specimens and exhibits, magnet, aquarium	Interest and observation
Arithmetic Center Abacus, beads, bottles (half pint, pint, and quart), buttons, clock dial, play money, ruler, yardstick, splints, calendar, geometric forms	To help develop number readiness and build number concepts
Painting Center Easel, newspapers, cloths, tempera paints, large brushes, jars	Medium for self-expression and development of physical dexterity
Sharing Center Games, puzzles, toys, things children bring from home, class projects	Child interest in and sharing with others

group was arranged in seven centers of interest with appropriate materials.

RESULTS AT END OF THE FIRST YEAR

At the end of the first year, all the children were given the *Gates Primary Reading Tests.*[3] The scores of the children of the experimental group were above those of the children in both control groups. A gain of two months on the average was made by the experimental group over the first control group and three months over the second control group.

RESULTS AT END OF THE SECOND YEAR

The pupils entered the second grade in the normal enrollment process.

[3] Arthur I. Gates, *Gates Primary Reading Tests* (New York: Teachers College, Columbia University, 1939).

Since each class remained fairly intact, there was opportunity for further study of the effects of the readiness program. The writer did not teach the pupils in the second grade. Although no special instruction was provided during the second year, the probability of permanence of the earlier instruction was indicated by the results of the *Gates Advanced Primary Reading Tests* [4] which were given to the pupils at the end of that year. The children who had been in the experimental group maintained superiority in all areas of the tests. The predictive value of the reading readiness tests used before beginning reading was shown by the fact that those pupils who reached or exceeded the norm on the readiness tests invariably succeeded with reading, and conversely, the poor risks remained poor risks except for the few who received the adjusted program

[4] Arthur I. Gates, *Gates Advanced Primary Reading Tests* (New York: Teachers College, Columbia University, 1943).

of instruction in the experimental group.

Implications for School Programs

Children of the first grade who are found to have deficiencies in readiness should neither be excluded from the first grade and put with younger children in the kindergarten nor forced into a beginning reading program for which they are not ready. They should be given a definite program of readiness training which offers them a chance to succeed, with methods and materials adjusted especially to meet their needs and abilities.

At all times the first-grade program must be planned for the continual development of the skills necessary for reading progress. By presenting a varied and rich reading readiness program the first-grade teacher is assured of guiding a maximum number of pupils to success in reading.

18. JUNIOR PRIMARY IN THE VAN DYKE LEVEL PLAN*

Helen Roche

THE problem of keeping children out of formal reading until they had reached the necessary state of readiness was chosen to meet a community need. On an individual psychological examination administered to all kindergarten children in October, 1953, the average IQ was found to be 99. This pointed up the fact that we had a high proportion of children whose mental ages were lower than their chronological ages. Also, the majority of the children seemed not to bring an adequate experiential background to the reading situation.

In September, 1953, a pilot study conducted in our schools researched the possibility of replacing the rigid grade system by a flexible plan of pacing the child to his own rate of speed in the reading situation. The plan was called The Level System.

Assumptions and Hypothesis

1. Maturation is an individual characteristic of each child and his progress must be individually tailored to his needs.

2. According to the normal curve of distribution, one third of the children entering first grade have not reached the mental age of six years and six months.

3. A mental, social, and emotional maturity equivalent to that of an average six-year-six-month-old child is a prerequisite for reading.

4. Lack of adequate functional visual and/or auditory acuity greatly limits the chance of success in the reading situation.

The hypothesis entertained was that a period of reading readiness between kindergarten and formal reading was essential for some children.

Subjects

The experimental group consisted of all children in the district who left kindergarten in February, 1953. The control group was composed of those who had left kindergarten in February, 1952. Only children of these original groups who were in the Van Dyke Schools four years after leaving kindergarten were used.

Setting up the Study

Personnel involved were Director of Elementary Education, principals of elementary schools, psychologist, reading diagnostician, and teachers of the experimental group.

* From Helen Roche, "Junior Primary in the Van Dyke Level Plan," *Journal of Educational Research*, LV (February, 1962), 232–33. Reprinted by permission of the author and *Journal of Educational Research*.

Groups	No. in Group at Start of Research	No. in Group at End of Research
Experimental	179	103
Control	103	83

All children of the experimental group, on leaving kindergarten, were given the Pintner-Cunningham group psychologist test. If it was considered necessary, an individual psychologist augmented this information.

Each child's vision was screened on the Keystone Telebinocular and referral to an ophthalmologist was made when indicated. All children were checked for emotional and social maturity against check lists constructed by the personnel involved. Any child whose mental, social, or emotional age was less than six years and six months was placed in the readiness situation. The other children were placed in Level 1 (Beginning Reading).

To insure a complete set of records for both the experimental and control groups, numerous forms and individual record charts were constructed. Meetings on released time were held for teachers of the experimental group in order to involve them in planning procedures and evaluation processes. Teachers of the control group were instructed only on methods of keeping records.

Procedures and Techniques

When the experimental group left kindergarten, placement was made in terms of the results of the tests that had been administered. Children ready for formal reading were placed in Level 1, those needing more readiness than the basic series provided were placed in Junior Primary A. The very immature and slow learning children were placed in Junior Primary B. Whenever possible, the Junior Primary children were placed in a room where no formal reading was taught. Groups were to be flexible and mobile. When the control children left kindergarten, they had all been placed in Level 1 and followed the Level System Plan.

There were five Reading Readiness books available plus all the material constructed by the teachers for use in the Junior Primary. The number used by each child depended on his individual need. The reading readiness slides of the Keystone Tachistoscope were also used as a basic tool. Emphasis was placed on teaching the necessary skills of functional visual and functional auditory acuity. To move from Junior Primary to Level 1, a child had to have the mental, social, and emotional maturity of the average six-year and six-month-old child. He also had to score average or above on the Metropolitan Reading Readiness Test.

At the end of two years, one of the most important findings of the research became apparent, namely, that a child might score average on a total Reading Readiness Test, but be in a very low percentile in areas measuring functional visual and/or functional auditory acuity. Such a child was doomed to failure on Level 6 (1A) or Level 8 (2B), although he might have succeeded on Level 2 (Preprimer) and Level 4 (Primer). All children in the experimental group who had failed a test on any level had a diagnostic study made of all their previous reading tests. Generally, such a study uncovered the fact that the child had previously failed in specific areas at least two books before his total score showed failure.

Previously, the child was offered some reinforcement of all skills and techniques at the level where he had failed. With this new insight, efforts were made to pick out those areas where inadequacy was evident and to give specific help there. Discussion of this problem at teachers' meetings resulted in the cooperative construction of consonant cards and geometric figure cards which were to be used in reinforcing functional visual and functional auditory acuity.

As the experimental group moved into formal reading, teachers became adept in the use of diagnostic techniques. They were able to identify causative factors of failure. Discussion of this new insight resulted in construction of materials and workbooks for reinforcing techniques introduced, but not permanently fixed, in the developmental program.

Findings

Because of the disparity in the numbers in the experimental and in the control groups, results were figured on a percentage basis. Only children of the control group who were in our schools in February, 1956, and those of the experimental group who were present in February, 1957, were used in computing the statistics. Findings are:

1. Children in the experimental group showed superior achievement.

A smaller percentage of them scored below average and a higher percentage of them scored above average than did the control group.

2. Results of the Iowa Basic Reading Tests administered to the control group in February, 1956, and to the experimental group in February, 1957, showed that 52.8 percent of the experimental group scored at or above 4A as compared to 34.3 percent of the control group. This in spite of the fact that over one-third of the experimental group were delayed in Junior Primary before they started formal reading.

3. The greatest benefit to the Van Dyke Plan resulted from the fact that teachers of the experimental group who were participating in the Action Research taught in rooms close to rooms used by teachers of the control group. Their enthusiasm, newly developed philosophy, and knowledge of new skills and techniques spread from teachers of the experimental to teachers of the control group. These in turn subconsciously resorted to the use of the same teaching methods.

4. A hopeful finding was that educators are willing to study any new plan that will promote child growth. To lend credence to this idea, seventy-two interested administrators and teachers visited the Van Dyke Schools last year. They observed the plan in action. These visitors came from Metropolitan Detroit, outstate Michigan, Canada, and Ohio.

5. A retarding factor in the progress of the program was the teacher who was unwilling to cooperate. There were also a few teachers who were still unable to recognize the opportune

time to accelerate or slow down a child's program. A rather prevalent disadvantage was that primary teachers desire to "even up" reading groups.

6. A finding that was both a surprise and a disappointment was the necessity for central leadership to achieve continuing success on a high level. This might be due to the fact that teachers are retiring and new teachers are taking their places.

Conclusions

The findings of this research led to the following conclusions:

1. Children not ready for reading profit more by being kept in a readiness situation until prepared for formal reading than by being placed in Level 1 (1st grade), failing, and having to repeat the work.

2. Moving children ahead into the formal reading program only after they succeed on the Junior Primary Level does not delay their school progress. Their rate in moving ahead depends on their speed of maturation in mental, social, and emotional areas. This cannot be accelerated.

3. Programs in which teachers cooperate in the planning and execution produce enthusiastic participation on the part of teachers and are reflected in the attitude of the children.

4. Material constructed to meet specific district needs is more readily accepted and more frequently used if it is a result of group action.

BEGINNING
READING   INSTRUCTION

19. IT HAPPENED ONE SEPTEMBER*

Odille Ousley

THE road machines arrived before the children that September morning. The school bus had to detour slightly to reach the entrance to the school yard. And the excited children leaned all over each other to see what was puffing and clanging along on what had yesterday been "the bumpy road that goes by our school."

This was news! It was the wonderful noisy news that the children brought into the first grade that morning. Jane squeezed her bunch of marigolds tighter around their already droopy necks. John dragged behind him the brown sweater that Mother made him bring. Sara shifted her lunch money from her right hand to her left, then back again to the right, and in the excitement it fell noisily to the

floor before she succeeded in placing it in the proper receptacle. Then she hurried to the nearest window where she edged herself in between Tom and Sue, who had been fortunate enough to arrive earlier. Eagerly they watched the workmen and the big machines.

Before long all the children had the best grandstand seats available. Miss Clarke had taken them out to sit on the dry grass on the edge of the school yard where the three black machines were doing their noisy best to resurface the bumpy old road.

The children looked and they listened. They watched the black composition as it was spread smoothly over the old road, and they heard the puffing and chugging of the machines at work. They liked it all!

And as the children sat under the tree near the road, in the flicking shadows that the September sun made on the grass, Grace had even seen the

* From Odille Ousley, "It Happened One September," in *Contributions in Reading, No. 5* (Boston: Ginn & Co.). Reprinted by permission of the author and Ginn and Company.

startled robin overhead as he sharply questioned the right of a noisy chugging machine to disturb his peace and quiet.

Making a Co-operative Chart

Later when the children went back into their room, they had plenty to talk about. They had seen the blue-coated policeman who was there and the man with "the long pusher that looked like a wooden rake." Billy wanted to imitate the chug, chug, chug of one machine, and Linda said, "There were three of them. I counted one, two, three machines."

So the spontaneous discussion proceeded and Miss Clarke chose sentences and phrases here and there, which she wrote on the board. "Yes, Linda," she said, "there were

> One, two, three machines."

Soon a co-operative story had grown out of the discussion and was on the board before the group. Billy proudly pointed to his "chug, chug, chug." And Linda could tell just where it said "One, two, three machines."

This is the story:

> The Road Machines
> We went to see the machines.
> Big, black machines.
> Chug, chug, chug!
> One, two, three machines.
> Chug, chug, chug!

A few days later, when the road was dry and hard, the group took another walk and sat by the side of the road and watched the cars go by. When they returned to their classroom, this story was recorded by Miss Clarke:

> Cars on the Road
> We saw many cars.
> We saw red cars.
> We saw blue cars.
> Mary saw a bright green car.
> The cars went fast.
> Honk, honk, honk!

After the stories were printed on large pieces of tagboard, the children drew pictures of machines and cars to decorate the charts.

It was evident from the spontaneous interest in the preparation of the charts and pictures that machines have a definite fascination for children—and perhaps the bigger and noisier they are, the better children like them. Anyway, Miss Clarke decided that the visit of the road machines at just this time had been a fortunate, if not a premeditated, incident.

Some of the children were encouraged to read the charts and did so with as much pleasure as they had experienced in the preparation of them. The charts were not used for drill and not read for the purpose of word mastery. Perhaps their chief value was that they helped the children to see their own, simple, oral sentences appear in a new written form. "That is what I said," exclaimed Sue. "There it is on the chart. *The cars went fast.*"

Watching the cars, discussing and recording the experience, and finally reading the finished story were so closely associated in the children's minds that they were not three separate experiences but *one* unified meaningful experience. As Grace said, "It happened on Tuesday. There it is on our chart. I'll read it for you." Through such experiences a child develops an awareness of reading. And this awareness of the relationship between oral and written form is fundamental in building the concept of reading for meaning. The child, in such an activity as described here, reads something that he helped to write and consequently brings understanding to the printed form. Reading can be a very real experience, even at the beginning —an experience as real as cars, airplanes, tricycles, and bright red apples. As real as the chug, chug, chug of a big black machine on a Georgia road on a hot autumn day.

First Reading Books

Books can be real, too. Book characters can be as real as the child who lives next door. An early introduction to simple attractive books is important in developing an eagerness for reading. These lively and colorful first books offer to beginning readers a welcome invitation to open the pages and join in the fun of the friendly children in "our new story book."

Miss Clarke did not rely altogether on experience charts and incidental reading to introduce her children to reading. It soon became evident that most of the children were ready for books—readiness books and simple pre-primers.

Being an experienced teacher, Miss Clarke knew that a well-built readiness book in a basal series is more than a delightful picture book. It *is* that and more, too. It is a picture book with a purpose. The purpose may be at times artfully and attractively concealed, but it is there all the time. Here are found lively stories presented in a carefully planned picture-sequence. Here are

activities that help to orient a child to his new environment.

Well-built readiness material is not a substitute for actual experiences of children or for teacher guidance. It may, however, be of great assistance in helping the teacher develop some of the essential skills and abilities of this period, such as left-to-right progression across the page and the ability to note likenesses and differences— first in forms of objects and later in simple words. Visual and auditory acuity are important factors in learning to read, and the exercises which foster these important abilities are usually as interesting and fascinating as any of the games the child enjoys during the day.

Readiness books also provide many opportunities for picture interpretation, informal storytelling and discussion, and choral reading. In providing these opportunities for speech improvement and growth in other linguistic abilities, the child's general language ability is greatly strengthened as he approaches the problem of learning to read.

At no time does the skillful teacher bring pressure on the child not ready to read. In many instances her own judgment will lead her to recognize the children who are ready for reading instruction. She also finds that a readiness book which has diagnostic features can help her in studying the needs and abilities of the group and that it re-enforces her judgment.

There are decided advantages, too, for many children in the early introduction of an easy pre-primer. Even with its limited vocabulary this can be exciting and dramatic. With only twenty-one different words it is as good in its own way as a book with one hundred and twenty-one words. This simple book must consist of stories with real plot and concrete text. All first-grade teachers know that the day a child gets his first pre-primer is a wonderful day for him. Here in a small easy-to-handle volume are stories with real plots and bright and satisfying pictures. These are read-on stories that are both simple and exciting. *"Ride fast,"* and a shiny tricycle wins the race with an old wagon. And he can read the book himself!

Another happy day for the first grader is the day he finishes his first pre-primer and is allowed to take it home for the first time to read to his parents who are eager to share in this "freshly minted miracle" that is taking place. Susie has learned to read!

20. EXPERIENCE CHARTS*

New York State Education Department

RECORDS of the children's activities make the best type of reading material for the beginning stage. These records are developed jointly by the children and teacher through conversation about an experience, after or before the actual happening which is to be recorded. Usually the records are worked out first on the blackboard and later transcribed to a homemade paper chart and reread by the children, under the teacher's guidance. All such records are loosely described as "experience charts."

* From *That All May Learn to Read*, Elementary School Aids to Teaching Language Arts, Leaflet No. 3 (Albany, N.Y.: Bur. of Curriculum Development, Div. of Elementary Education, 1949), pp. 18–20. Reprinted by permission of the New York State Education Department.

Experience charts are of immense value in developing readiness for learning to read. In the first place, they have vividness and personal interest because they are based upon the children's own experiences. Sometimes they even contain a child's own name or the name of a friend. Second, they provide one of the group experiences through which the children learn to function together. Third, the discussions involved naturally lead to language development. The making of experience charts gives great opportunity for all the children to think and speak more coherently, more fluently, and in a more mature style. They gradually set a procedure which individual children will use later in writing their own stories.

The use of charts also develops continued attention and interest in reading, perception of likeness and differences in word symbols, and left-to-right eye movements. The content of each chart is charged with meaning for the children; as a result reading itself becomes a meaningful process, and the child's speaking vocabulary is enriched by meaningful concepts.

Finally, experience charts furnish opportunity for providing a sight vocabulary basic to preprimers by the repetition of key words in different charts. This sight vocabulary will help the child when the time for book reading arrives.

The following incident shows how one teacher developed such a chart with two children in her group who were ready for experience chart reading. The incident recorded on the chart had been told by Margaret as soon as she reached school. Margaret said: "We have kittens at our house!" Much excited talk among the children followed, as the little girl told how Tabby had brought one of her new babies from the barn and laid it at Margaret's feet!

At an appropriate time, the teacher gathered Margaret and Bob near the blackboard and said:

"This morning Tabby came from the barn with something in her mouth. What do you think it was?"
"A kitten!" chorused both children.
"We can write *Tabby has a kitten,* on the blackboard," said Miss A. "Watch!" ———— She wrote the sentence in clear manuscript, reading it as she wrote. "Can you read this, Margaret?" They read it together. Bob read it.

"What did Tabby do with her kitten, Bob?" asked Miss A.
"She gave it to Margaret."
"We can write *Tabby gave the kitten to Margaret* on the board." Miss A again read as she wrote the sentence. The children read the sentence in unison.
"What did Tabby say?" asked Miss A. The children grinned, "Meow! Meow!"
"Meow," said Tabby wrote Miss A.
"Now, let's read all of this again." They read in unison, teacher and children together:

Tabby has a kitten.
Tabby gave the kitten to Margaret.
"Meow!" said Tabby.

The following day the children found the story they had helped to make transferred to a reading chart with a colored illustration of a charming kitten pasted at the top of it. Several children clustered around the chart, exclaiming over the picture, while Bob and Margaret tried to read the story.

The experience chart, then, serves as an excellent approach to reading; but it also has an important function of its own. Children continue to have activities and experiences, particularly in connection with their social studies and science programs, things they have actually done, which are important for well-rounded child development. The experiences form one of the bases for discussions and are a constant center for language development. Charts summarizing these experiences and discussions provide reading of a different quality from reading stories in a book. They continue to have a place of their own, even though books are also freely read. The good teacher continues their use throughout the primary grades, or until the children have developed the ability to record their own experiences.

It should be kept in mind, however, that experience charts have certain limitations.

1. The vocabulary is not controlled, with the result that the beginning reader may be confronted by a confusing number of new words at one time.
2. They may foster memory reading rather than actual reading.
3. Their construction demands a great deal of the teacher's time.
4. If the charts are used too much for developing word recognition, they may become boring and dull, thus defeating their main purpose.
5. Unless the teacher is skillful, the charts may be lacking in literary quality.

The following suggestions will help teachers to improve the development of this type of reading material.

SUGGESTIONS FOR THE CONSTRUCTION OF EXPERIENCE CHARTS

1. The charts should record significant experiences that the children themselves have had.
2. The sentences should be short, simple, and well-constructed.
3. There should be repetition of words and phrases that are basic to the next stage of learning.
4. Care should be taken to avoid the division of phrases at the end of lines.
5. Letters should be printed in clear and consistent manuscript writing.
6. Letters should be placed close together with ample space between words, so each word can be seen as a unit.
7. Letters should be large enough to be seen by all pupils in the group.
8. The bottom of each line should be about three inches below the bottom of the line above it.
9. The charts should be placed at the eye level of the children.

21. MORE WAYS THAN ONE*

R. Van Allen

Nature Speaks †

I went to the hills a few days ago
And I heard nature speaking soft and low,
Some folks say you can't hear her speak
But I heard it all right 'cause I took a
    peek.
Her language is beautiful indeed
Because she made something grow from
    every seed.
The humming of bees, the singing birds,
The pounding of buffalo running in herds,
The rustle of trees, the spatter of rain,
The moaning of wind when I walk down
    the lane.
Nature speaks in *more than one way*
And you can hear her every day.

SO many teachers and administrators in the San Diego area were interested in knowing a variety of well-balanced, basic approaches to teaching reading that the curriculum staff of San Diego County was asked to develop a research framework to involve hundreds of children in a program which used more than one way of teaching reading. The three-year study, "Three Approaches to the Teaching of Reading," is reported in a series of five monographs on improving reading instruction. This study probed into

* From R. Van Allen, "More Ways Than One," *Childhood Education,* XXXVIII, No. 3 (November, 1961), 108–11. Reprinted by permission of the author and the Association for Childhood Education International, 3615 Wisconsin Ave., N.W., Washington 16, D.C.

† Poem composed by a ten-year-old boy, National City, California.

method, materials, and the learning process. Its basic point of view was that no single approach to the teaching of reading can be *the best* or *only* solution. Its research framework attempted to include reading problems related to the diversity of our school population and our increased information concerning human growth and development.

Three Ways Studied

As the research team investigated many so-called "approaches to teaching reading," it selected three for detailed study: the *basic reading* approach, the *individualized,* and the *language-experience* approach. These selections were made because a teacher could:

1. define a valid purpose
2. describe a basic plan
3. secure materials for instruction
4. organize for teaching in a classroom situation
5. plan a direct reading instruction program, including skill development and vocabulary development
6. include an extended enrichment program
7. provide for individual differences
8. evaluate in terms of reading skills, reading attitude, and personal-social interaction of teacher with pupils.

The three approaches were tested in many classrooms. Teachers were asked to take part in a program of inservice education which would prepare them to teach one selected approach for a period of time, ruling out all other approaches. It was during this period that observations and test results confirmed the hypothesis: *There are numerous effective ways of teaching reading in our schools.*

When a teacher selected an approach that he understood, had the necessary materials to carry out the program as well as a supportive inservice education program, the results of any of the three well-defined approaches were more than satisfactory.

Of the three approaches used, two are well-described in the professional literature on reading instruction. Either the basic reading approach or the individualized reading approach had been used by most of the teachers in the study. However, the language-experience approach had not been described well enough before this study to give teachers guidelines to use it as an approach. Prior to this study, most of the teachers using elements of the language-experience approach did so as supplementary activities. *The language-experience teachers who ruled out all other approaches found that their children made as much or more progress on the skills (measured on standardized reading tests) as did the children who had direct teaching of skills.* With these results we had to ask ourselves some soul-searching questions about reading instruction:

1. Is the use of a predetermined controlled vocabulary as significant in reading instruction as we once thought? Is there enough control in the daily natural language of the individual to guide early word recognition without systematic control from outside sources?

2. Are choppy, unnatural sentences of present day preprimers and primers easier to read than more natural sentences? Could it be that the concept difficulty is enough greater in unnatural sentences than in sentences of real language that vocabulary control is outweighed as a factor in making reading simple and easy?

3. Are children's reactions to reading as important as their word-calling skills? Can an overemphasis on reading as a skill apart from listening, speaking, and writing develop negative attitudes?

4. Does a highly structured, predetermined sequence of reading materials and activities produce an attitude of language and thought conformity? Is it just as important to develop in children a feeling that their own ideas are worthy of expression and that their own language is a vehicle of communication?

5. Do all important reading resources exist outside of the child and in books, or should we develop the idea that a child's own thoughts may be used as a basis for the development of instructional reading materials?

6. Does the level of social interaction between teacher and pupils have as much to do with achievement as the method used? If a child really understands what he is doing, is there a greater possibility of development?

7. Does a child profit more from reading something *he* has selected than from reading pre-selected materials at all instructional periods?

8. Can we afford to continue evaluating reading programs on the basis of achievement scores of standardized reading tests? What about attitudes toward reading? Personality development? Self-expression abilities of pupils who are expected to be thinking, contributing citizens in a democratic society?

These and many other questions are confronting teachers and administrators who are willing to take a serious, penetrating look at reading instruction. As they search for answers to these questions they become more and more aware of the *need to look at reading as a means of arousing meaningful responses on the basis of individual experiences of the learner.* They realize that some of the concepts which have been developed concerning important areas of instruction, such as basic sight vocabulary, phonics instruction, reading materials, motivation for reading, classroom organization, and evaluation of pupil progress must be updated and expanded.

Many teachers are now dealing with basic sight vocabulary on an individual basis—from oral language to written language to recall of written language. This usually results in recognition of high frequency words as a result of repetition. *Each child gradually gains a personally tailored sight vocabulary which is functional and which is in excess of words introduced in the controlled programs. Control becomes an individual matter.* Ceilings are lifted for all children at all grade levels.

"See It" Rather Than "Say It"

Phonetic understandings are being developed more and more from a "say it" to a "see it" sequence. This insures that understandings are applied to the real language experiences of each individual, including skills in listening, speaking, word recognition, and spelling. This emphasis is merely applying what we have known for a long time: *There is a closer relationship between phonics and writing than between phonics and reading.* The natural desire of young children to create stories provides a powerful motivation to acquire skill in selecting the correct symbols to represent the sounds of oral language.

Pupil authorship is developed more and more as teachers take their clues from children and record their thoughts or encourage the children to record their own. Many materials for reading are developed by the children. In addition, children select their own reading material for pleasure and for enrichment reading. Those who author the most materials tend to be the ones who read the most from other authors. Assigned reading is used only for purposes which are understandable and useful in solving problems.

When teachers bring reading and other communication skills together in the instructional program, there is no way, nor any need, to distinguish between the reading program and other language activities. The development of all language skills makes possible the continuing use of each child's own experience background and thinking as he grows toward reading maturity.

Simply stated, teachers who are "taking a peek" at the many children in their classrooms can hear them saying—

What I can think about, I can talk about.
What I can say, I can write.
(Or: You can write it for me.)
What I can write, I can read.

I can read what I can write and what other people can write for me to read.*

REFERENCES

ALLEN, R. VAN. "Concept Development of Young Children in Reading Instruction," *Claremont College Reading Conference.* Twenty-fourth Yearbook, 1959. Pp. 12–21.

ALLEN, R. VAN and HALVORSEN, GLADYS C. "The Language-Experience Approach to Reading Instruction," *Ginn and Company Contributions in Reading No. 27.* Boston: Ginn & Co., 1961.

ARTLEY, A. STERL. *Your Child Learns To Read.* Chicago: Scott, Foresman & Co., 1953.

ASSOCIATION FOR CHILDHOOD EDUCATION INTERNATIONAL. *More About Reading.* Washington, D.C.: The Association, 1959.

BOYER, ALTA. "Reading and Creative Writing in a First-Grade Classroom," *Claremont College Reading Conference.* Twenty-fourth Yearbook, 1959. Pp. 22–28.

BURTON, WILLIAM H. *Reading in Child Development.* Indianapolis: Bobbs-Merrill Co., 1956.

DARROW, HELEN FISHER and ALLEN, R. VAN. *Independent Activities for Creative Learning.* New York: Bureau of Publications, Teachers College, Columbia University, 1961.

DARROW, HELEN FISHER and HOWES, VIRGIL M. *Approaches to Individualized Reading.* New York: Appleton-Century-Crofts, 1960.

HYMES, JAMES L., JR. *Before the Child*

* R. Van Allen and Gladys C. Halvorsen, "The Language-Experience Approach to Reading Instruction," *Ginn and Company Contributions in Reading No. 27* (Boston: Ginn & Co., 1961).

Reads. Evanston, Ill.: Row, Peterson & Co., 1958.

NATIONAL SOCIETY FOR THE STUDY OF EDUCATION. *Development in and Through Reading.* Sixtieth Yearbook, Part I. Chicago: University of Chicago Press, 1961.

RUSSELL, DAVID H. *Children's Thinking.* Boston: Ginn & Co., 1956.

SAN DIEGO COUNTY DEPARTMENT OF EDUCATION. *A Handbook of Independent Activities to Promote Creativity in Children.* San Diego, Calif.: The Department, 1959.

————. "Report of the Reading Study Project," *Improving Reading Instruction Monograph No. 1.* San Diego, Calif.: The Department, 1961.

————. "A Description of Three Approaches to the Teaching of Reading," *Improving Reading Instruction Monograph No. 2.* San Diego, Calif.: The Department, 1961.

————. "A Teacher Inventory of Approaches to the Teaching of Reading," *Improving Reading Instruction Monograph No. 3.* San Diego, Calif.: The Department, 1961.

————. "An Inventory of Reading Attitude," *Improving Reading Instruction Monograph No. 4.* San Diego, Calif.: The Department, 1961.

————. "Analysis of Pupil Data: San Diego County Reading Study Project," *Improving Reading Instruction Monograph No. 5.* San Diego, Calif.: The Department, 1961.

STRANG, RUTH M. and LINDQUIST, D. M. *The Administrator and the Improvement of Reading.* New York: Appleton-Century-Crofts, 1960.

VEATCH, JEANNETTE. *Individualizing Your Reading Program.* New York: G. P. Putnam's Sons, 1959.

ZIRBES, LAURA. *Spurs to Creative Teaching.* New York: G. P. Putnam's Sons, 1959.

22. MISS KING'S FIRST GRADE*

New York State Education Department

IT'S the first day of school and here come David, Anne, and Joe, washed, combed, and polished for their introduction to first grade.

David is six and a half years old. He lives on a large farm and has never been to school before. He's a sturdy, handsome little boy, his cheeks tanned and his hair bleached by a summer in the sun. David's farm life has given him opportunities for outdoor play, for the observation of nature, of animals and of the machinery on a modern farm.

He is independent and self-reliant, and has been quite accustomed to chores and duties at home. But he holds back a bit this morning, for he has had little opportunity to play with other children, almost no contact with books, and school life is new and strange to him.

Little Anne is a shy figure this first day of the new school term. She is not yet six years old and is very different from the self-reliant David. Immature and younger than most of the other children, she sits quietly, taking almost no part in the children's activities. She seems unable to cope with

* From "Miss King's First Grade," in *That All May Learn To Read,* Elementary School Aids to Teaching Language Arts, Leaflet No. 3 (Albany, N.Y.: Bur. of Curriculum Development, Div. of Elementary Education, 1949), pp. 7–11. Reprinted by permission of the New York State Education Department.

the task of modeling a clay bunny, or even of buttoning up her sweater.

Anne had a hard time adjusting to kindergarten last year, too. She was frequently ill and missed many of the kindergarten experiences. Her mother accompanied her to and from school each day, and it is still evident that Anne has never been allowed to learn to do things for herself.

Joe, on the other hand, is confident and alert as he steps into the room, at home with his friends from kindergarten days. He is six years and four months old and has had a background of experiences both at home and at school which has made him ready and eager for first grade. For Joe, and for some of the other children who have reached a similar stage of development, a program of activities will soon begin to unfold the joys of reading, and after a few weeks these boys and girls will begin to find out for themselves "what it says."

As the days go by, our three little friends are absorbed into the busy routine of their grade. At first, Miss King provides a great many whole group activities for the children, and also continues many features of the kindergarten program. She patiently teaches the children "things we do in the first grade," while they are becoming adjusted to her, to the classroom, and to one another. As the early weeks pass, she carefully observes each child and provides group and individual activities that gradually lead to reading readiness. On a basis of this continuing observation, and on the results of informal tests which she gives about the middle of October, she begins to group the children according to their "readiness" for reading instruction.

The children in Joe's group, the most mature of those who have had a year of kindergarten and who were already using picture books, are beginning to look at easy story books and to show definite interest in what printed words say. They love to tell about their experiences, to retell stories that have been told to them, and to make up stories of their own. They enjoy listening when stories are read or told. Soon these children will be reading *sentence-stories* from the blackboard and from experience charts. In a few more weeks they will be using reading readiness workbooks in addition to experience charts. Then, gradually will come the pre-primers and, after the children have a sight word vocabulary of 80 to 100 words, the primers.

Dave is having experiences in contributing to discussions, looking at picture books, playing games with the other children and happily splashing great amounts of red paint on easel paper to make "our barn." He and two other children who have not had a kindergarten year, but who are well over six and rather mature in their development, will soon be reading from experience charts, too.

Anne is getting better acquainted now. She is beginning to play happily in the "doll corner" with three of the other little girls. Because the teacher and the other children have been kind and helpful, she can button her sweater and take care of herself in other ways now. She loves to draw and paint pictures, and is beginning to enjoy listening to much longer stories at "storytelling time." She joins the other children in singing, and takes part in *choosing* games like "Sally Saucer" in which the children choose one another.

It is difficult for her to learn that there are times when the teacher cannot stop to listen to what she has to say, or to come to look at what she is doing. But she, along with all the other children, is off to a happy year's start.

Miss King's Classroom

Miss King's classroom itself contributes to the year's good beginning with its interesting work centers of available tools and materials, toys which help children learn, its large playhouse, and its collections of bright story books and picture books. Today the children's new pet, a turtle, has the charming picture book, Toddle, The Little Turtle, enticingly placed beside its bowl. A toy train stands in front of the opened pages of The Little Engine. The bulletin board has one or two gay pictures with a short sentence under each, and these are changed frequently.

Miss King's Class in December

Let's look in at Miss King's class on the morning of December 16th, some three and a half months after the opening of school in September. The children have just finished talking over their plans for the day, and have scattered into small groups to work on various activities. School will soon close for the Christmas holidays, and the children are busy getting ready to entertain their mothers later in the week at a Christmas party. Three children are hanging the colorful paper balls and garlands, which they had made the previous afternoon, upon a partly decorated Christmas tree.

There's Anne busily at work with another little girl cleaning and rearranging the playhouse so that it will look nice when the mothers come. And there is Dave, a member of a group drawing a snow scene on the blackboard. Other children are making pictures for a large class book about Santa Claus. One small girl is weaving a bright rag rug for the playhouse floor. She says it is her Christmas gift to the other children. Still others are working at their desks making decorations for a tiny Christmas tree that stands in the playhouse.

Six of the children have brought their chairs and are forming a reading group. Here we find our friend Joe opening his reader in workmanlike fashion and locating the story he is going to read. We are surprised to see that David is also in this group, and is coming now to join them with a picture book under his arm.

All the children in the room are working busily, and with close attention to their particular tasks.

The teacher turns to the reading group, in a circle around her in small chairs. They talk quietly so that we cannot distinguish their words from across the room. It is evident, however, that she asks the children questions about their stories, that they answer with interest, that they ask her questions, and that they also read aloud to the group.

"Joe read that so well today," says Miss King. "Perhaps he would like to read it to your parents on Friday. What do the rest of you think?" They all agree that Joe would be a good person to read to the parents. Mary volunteers that she could read part of that story. She shows the page she could read. It is agreed to divide the reading. "Good," says Miss King. "Now we have two readers to add to our program."

Then the teacher explains what the children are to do next. She points to their "Plans for the Day." The children pick up their chairs and carry them back to their desks.

"Let's have William's reading group now," says Miss King. Four children gather near the blackboard. After a brief discussion, the teacher prints on the board "Tony is a farmer." (One boy's name is Tony.) "Who can read it?" asks the teacher.

The children in the reading group are having trouble with the word *"Tony."* They keep calling it *this.* Now they have it! It is their own *Tony* they are reading about!

A second story-sentence is printed, and followed by another.

"William is a farmer, too."

"Tony and William gave us a Christmas tree."

As each sentence is placed on the board in manuscript writing, the children read it. William's smile unites with Tony's in a duet of pride as he, too, recognizes and reads his own name in the story.

Now the teacher says, "Find the

words that tell what Tony and William gave us."

The children read, and the teacher praises freely. "My, that's fine! Can you read it again as well as that?"

"Could we read all three of these stories for your mothers on Friday? I will make them into a reading chart for you. Then we can read them again tomorrow."

These children return to their desks, and nine other children bring their chairs, and primers in hand, seat themselves around the teacher. She introduces a new word by means of a story-sentence on the board; then the group settles down to absorbed reading and discussion. They are all working on the same story this time. We discover that it is a Christmas story that they are planning to divide into parts and use at their Friday's celebration.

There is only one child in the next reading group. Miss King explains to us later that this little girl is seven years old, had been making good progress in reading, but has been absent for six weeks because of illness. Working with her alone for a while will help her regain the confidence she lost during her absence.

Anne is one of five children who are not yet actually reading. We notice that at "story-telling" time, the teacher pays particular attention to these five children, and makes sure they look at, discuss, and enjoy the pictures in the book she is reading to the children.

No special premium seems to be placed by Miss King upon learning to read. It is treated rather as a natural and normal process that everyone gradually acquires. "First reader" children do not feel superior to "primer" readers; nor do "primer" readers seem to notice particularly the nonreaders, or those who thus far are reading only from blackboard and charts. In fact, the use of experience charts will continue all through the year for every group. Moreover, there are many other interesting activities in progress in this room in which all the children are sharing. Therefore, these differences do not stand out. Four months of school are about over, and we find children in various stages of the early beginning-to-read period.

We expected to find this variation, since the children in any group, as in this one, are at different stages of readiness for reading on the day they enter first grade. They must and should progress at varying rates as readiness gradually develops.

23. INDIVIDUALIZED PLAN OF INSTRUCTION IN WINNETKA*

Carleton Washburne

HAVING satisfied ourselves in a previous experiment [1] that it is safer not to try to teach beginning reading to most children until they are mentally six and a half, we raised the question whether there is any harm in longer postponement. We set up a controlled experiment, which was carried out over a period of eight years. This experiment (full data concerning which have not yet been published, since we are following the children into high school) consisted in postponing all formal instruction in reading, writing, and arithmetic until the middle of the children's second year in school and substituting a very complete program of activities and informal exposures to reading and number situations.

For each child in the experimental group there were three control children who had the same mental age, chronological age, and intelligence quotient and who came from homes of approximately the same socio-economic status, as far as could be judged by the teachers through personal knowledge. The children in the control groups did not begin systematic reading until they were mentally six and a half years old, but many of them had reached this mental age when they entered Grade I. All the control pupils began to read during their first year, and from that time on they were given regular periods each day for systematic instruction in reading and writing and arithmetic, although they spent approximately two-thirds of each day in a wide range of activities, excursions, etc. The children in the experimental group, as indicated, had a similar but richer and more extensive program of activities occupying the whole school day and had no drill, reading classes, or other systematic academic work.

In the middle of the second year, all children were tested, and it was found, as was to be expected, that the control children were much more advanced than those in the experimental group. From that time on, the control children and the experimental children were given practically identical programs and later were often mixed in the same classes. For both groups, work in reading (and arithmetic and writing) was largely individual but partly in small groups. Both groups

* From Carleton Washburne, "Individualized Plan of Instruction in Winnetka," in *Adjusting Reading Programs to Individuals,* William S. Gray (ed.), Supplementary Education Monographs, No. 52 (October, 1941), pp. 90–95. Reprinted by permission of the author and The University of Chicago Press.
[1] Mabel Vogel Morphett and Carleton Washburne, "When Should Children Begin To Read?" *Elementary School Journal,* XXXI (March, 1931), 496–503.

continued to have a varied and extensive program of activities during those parts of the morning and afternoon when they were not engaged in academic work.

At the end of the second year the experimental group was still markedly behind the control children, although it had gained on the latter. By the end of the third year the two groups were approximately equal. By the end of the fourth year the experimental group was a half-year ahead of the control pupils. Those who had postponed all systematic learning until they were approximately eight years of age mentally, on the average, had, in two and a half years, done a half-year more of work than the other children had done in four years. All were measured with the Stanford Achievement Test.

The superiority of the experimental group continued right through the grades, each child being measured against his own controls, with only three exceptions: one, a boy who was in an emotional tangle and under the care of a psychiatrist; one, a girl whose eyesight was seriously impaired; and one, a child who was absent from school a total of about one year out of eight. At the end of Grade 8 the children in the experimental group were, on the average, a year and a half ahead of the control children on the Stanford Achievement Test.

While this experiment involves a small number of children, nearly half of the pupils in the original experimental group having transferred from the Winnetka schools before the end of Grade 8, the consistency of the results, child by child, subject by subject, and year by year, was striking

and gave clear indication that, instead of harm, the postponement of formal work resulted in positive benefits to the academic program. These were more than matched by positive benefits from the standpoint of social activity and zest for learning, separately measured.

As far as I am aware, no experiment has ever shown any harm from postponing systematic academic work in reading. One early report by me for the Committee of Seven indicated that pupils in schools which merely postponed formal arithmetic without, as far as we know, substituting educative activities did not make as good progress in arithmetic as those in schools which began academic instruction earlier.[2] This report was based on a testing program and not on controlled research and probably has little or no bearing on the present problem in reading.

In general it seems to be a much safer hypothesis to assume that children will profit by postponing formal instruction until they are fully ready than to assume that it is preferable to attempt to force reading on children as soon as they enter school. This hypothesis is borne out by our knowledge of psychology. We know that nothing succeeds like success and nothing fails like failure. The child who attempts to read before he can attain success proportionate to his ability becomes discouraged, dislikes reading, reads as little as possible, falls farther behind, becomes more discour-

[2] Carleton Washburne, "When Should We Teach Arithmetic?—A Committee of Seven Investigation," *Elementary School Journal,* XXVIII (May, 1928), 659–65.

aged, dislikes it more, and so on in a vicious circle. The child who, when he attacks reading, is highly successful with it is delighted by his success, likes reading, reads more, achieves more skill, likes it better, and so on in an upward spiral.

Similarly, our knowledge of mental hygiene bears out our hypothesis. We know the great importance of security to the child. We recognize that to expect a child to do a task and then attach the moral stigma of low marks or failure when he is unable to do it, is well calculated to undermine security. On the other hand, to wait until the child has the experience and the maturity necessary for success in his work and then give him the happiness and the encouragement accompanying such success helps to build up security.

In accordance with this research and this line of reasoning, the Winnetka public schools have, for several years, completely removed from teachers any pressure for academic achievement in the first two grades and particularly during the first year and the first half of the second year in school. There are no fixed standards of sight words or phonics to be learned, no set of reading skills to be achieved during this period. Each teacher is given the utmost freedom to gauge by every means available when a child is ready and to follow her own judgment as to when to begin systematic instruction.

In order to free teachers from the pressure of parents, who traditionally expect children to begin to learn how to read the first day they come to school, the superintendent has a conference with all parents of first-grade children in each school building during the first few weeks of school each year. At this conference he outlines in popular form the point of view stated above. He points out the wide individual differences among children, as shown by the date of the appearance of the first tooth, the beginning of speech, the beginning of walking. He reminds them that the child whose dentition comes late eventually chews just as well as the child whose dentition is early, that the child who does not begin to talk until he is nearly two years old may be just as articulate later as the child who begins to talk at one. He calls the attention of the parents to the fact that children, when they graduate from the Winnetka public schools, have, on the average, a reading ability three years higher than the national norms. With this reasoning and the reassurance of ultimate success, most parents cease to bring pressure to bear on the teachers to teach their children to read. The few unreasonable parents would be nagging the teachers anyway and simply have to be accepted as a necessary evil. The teacher's loyalty is to the children, and she must have the stamina, backed by the administration, to stand up for what is right for the youngsters.

In addition to removing pressure from the teachers, the administration makes possible a broad program of activities and experiences in the primary grades, by allowing the teacher freedom of action and supplying the teacher with the necessary equipment and facilities.

Furthermore, the administration furnishes the teacher with as adequate knowledge of her children as possible.

Each child is given an individual Binet intelligence test either by the psychologist or by kindergarten teachers who have been trained by the psychologist. Each child is given a thorough physical examination, and any defects in hearing or vision or general health are reported to the teacher. For each child there is a cumulative record, and, if the child has been in the nursery school and kindergarten in Winnetka, a full report from the preceding teachers is available to the first-grade teacher. To this she adds her quota of information for the benefit of the second-grade teacher.

Finally, from the administrative standpoint, teachers are given definite information concerning the relative difficulty of the books they are going to use. The Winnetka Research Department, under grants from the Carnegie Corporation and with the cooperation of the American Library Association, has made elaborate studies of what constitutes the difference in difficulty between various books. A formula has been devised whereby one can predict, with reasonable accuracy, the degree of reading ability that is necessary to read any given book. The teachers therefore know, not from the publisher's guess, but from a careful statistical analysis, for just what level of ability the various available books are most suitable.

With this backing, the teachers follow their own best judgment, the knowledge they have attained through various courses and extensive reading, and their observation of each child under their care. In general they attempt to see that the children have a great variety of experience and much

opportunity for oral expression before they begin any systematic work in reading. The teacher exposes the children to reading situations through writing assignments on the blackboard, writing out stories that the children dictate and putting them on the blackboard or on a chart, and providing many picture-books, in which the children can browse. The pupils often ask questions about the words appearing in these books.

The teacher encourages parents to give children similar experiences, without attempting to teach them to read. At the present time the primary-grade teachers are preparing a manual for parents, describing concrete ways in which to broaden children's basic experience and use of language without attempting to give any systematic instruction in reading but to provide a basis for what will later be done in the school.

The teacher watches the response of each child to this sort of environment. When, in terms of his response and in terms of the data that the teacher has, she believes the child to be ready for reading, she takes him and a small group of others who are likewise ready and begins reading according to the more or less standard, present-day procedures—having the children dictate stories which she writes on a chart; having the children read what they have dictated; helping them to become familiar with words that are repeatedly used; gradually moving into very simple pre-primers; and ultimately working from the recognition of sentences, through the recognition of phrases, and the recognition of words, to the recognition of phonetic elements. Meanwhile, the children are reading books of gradually increasing difficulty.

From time to time the teacher checks the children's knowledge of the common sight words and gives any drill needed. Later, usually some time during the second year, she checks the pupils' recognition of phonics, and, for those children who have not acquired sufficient phonetic ability to work out new words made up of the commonest phonetic elements, definite group work and practice are given in these elements.

After one small group in the class has begun this systematic work in reading, the teacher, watching other children's reactions, forms a second small group. This process continues through the first two years of school until all children are in one group or another. Transfer from one group to another is frequent and exceedingly flexible.

Emphasis throughout the lower grades is on extensive reading of easy material. Our aim is to give children a delight in reading and fluency in it. We do not attempt any breakdown of the general reading skill into such parts as "reading to follow directions," "reading to remember details," "reading for gist," etc., until the children have reached fifth-grade reading ability. In the meantime they are, of course, doing some reading for detail and for following directions in connection with their various types of school work and their activities outside school. By the time they reach fifth-grade reading ability, most of them are pretty well up to standard in each of the various phases of reading. A Gates test is, however, given when they reach fifth-grade reading ability, and any deficiencies noted receive appropriate practice.

This program of freedom from pressure, allowance of plenty of time for maturity and experience before systematic work begins, individual progress, and extensive reading of material that is well within the child's range of ability has resulted in our having very few cases of remedial reading and in an exceptionally high average in reading ability. For almost all of the pupils, reading remains a pleasure throughout their school lives.

24. READING INSTRUCTION FOR THE SPACE AGE*

Glenn McCracken

THROUGH the ingenious imagination and inventiveness of a few Americans, this great nation of ours pushes on to newer and more phenomenal peaks of achievement each decade. In science and medicine, in industry and transportation, in architecture, and even in recreation, this country astonishes itself anew every few years.

Regardless of these achievements, it is rather generally agreed that the American people have not found an effective way to teach their children to read! Such incongruity in the otherwise prodigious development of our twentieth-century culture is beginning to assume an aura of almost incredible aberration.

The elementary schools of this country are not being asked to help land some of our citizens safely on the moon, or to design missiles capable of striking and obliterating selected targets ten thousand miles distant. They have much more modest assignments, the most important of which is to teach our children how to read the English language well. While a generous six-year period has been allotted for the accomplishment of this latter goal, nobody claims that the job

* From Glenn McCracken, "Reading Instruction for the Space Age," *Education,* LXXX, No. 9 (May, 1960), 545–48. Reprinted by permission of the author and The Bobbs-Merrill Co., Inc., Indianapolis, Ind.

is being fulfilled with distinction. Surprisingly enough, few people seem genuinely worried over the dilemma.

A great surge of activity presently is being directed toward producing scientists who will be capable of saving the United States from extinction, but nearly all of that interest concerns the secondary levels of the educative process.

Some day we must become aware that it is not easy to make great scientists out of young men and women who can't read their course books. Quality instruction must start at the beginning of the child's formal training. Thus, the onus descends now upon education to make startling new appraisals of its reading instructional methods.

The New Castle Experiment

Here at New Castle, Pennsylvania, we have been making such evaluations at the primary-grade level for more than a decade. Early in 1947 we began to prepare the equipment, materials, and teaching techniques for the testing of an entirely new approach to the teaching of reading, namely, the correlated-visual-image approach. This program now is rather widely known as the New Castle Reading Experiment. It has proved that children can be taught to read with far greater facility than heretofore had been anticipated.[1]

By September, 1949, the program was ready for use at the first-grade level. The New Castle Reading Experiment materials include filmstrips (textfilms) which were designed to accompany, page by page, the entire content of a particular primary basic-reading program. There is at least one film frame for every reading lesson in the books.

There also is a textfilm manual which suggests daily teaching procedures to the teacher. The textfilm frames include condensed versions of the reading stories appearing in the books and, of course, all of the new vocabulary and reading-skills exercises. All of the initial reading instruction takes place at a projection screen where every lesson appears as a large (36 by 48 inches) lifelike color image. The books are used for extended practice only.

In a typical teaching situation at any of the primary-grade levels, the film version of the lesson will be flashed on the screen after the room lighting has been dimmed. Teacher and pupils (the entire class works together) then will engage in vigorous discussion of everything appearing on the screen. They will talk about the story title, exchanging ideas as to why some words have capital letters and other words do not. They will discuss the picture at length, debating the various elements being portrayed, and then will proceed to the story itself.

In talking about the story content, the children will examine carefully

[1] Glenn McCracken, *The Right to Learn* (Chicago: Henry Regnery Co., 1959).

each paragraph, finally arriving at class agreement upon why first sentences are indented, why some words have capital letters, why each kind of punctuation is used, etc.

In examining the various words, certain children will go to the screen and mark off with chalk (while the image appears on a chalkboard) the many beginning, medial, and ending sounds they find in the words. They will pronounce these letter-combination sounds as they work with them, and, finally, they will show how the sounds go together to form words.

When all of the children understand the pronunciation of each word, they will have practice in reading the various sentences fluently, with proper enunciation and with comprehension. Next the pupils will transfer their attention to the textbooks where they will experience additional practice and where the teacher will test their ability to read their new words as they appear in different circumstances.

The projection screen affords such an excellent medium for teaching phonics that the New Castle teachers have added more and more phonics to their program each year. While we started out to feature a visual-teaching medium, our program now is described more accurately as a visual-phonics approach to the teaching of reading. Pupils in our primary grades are fascinated by the reading films. They call them "movies." Beginning classes often work vigorously and excitedly on one lesson, for nearly an hour at a time, with scarcely a glance away from the screen. For this reason, we consider "interest" to be the principal value of the film reading method.

Other values include: clarity of presentation; communication of thought among the children as they all discuss the same image together; opportunities for reticent pupils to grow in social confidence as they go to the screen to lead class discussions; and the almost total elimination of discipline distractions.

During the past ten years, we have accumulated at New Castle forty-three pages of tabular evidence proving the superiority of the visual-phonics reading method. Furthermore, in the more than twenty other American public school districts and in two Canadian schools, where the same teaching method has been employed, almost identically superior reading results have occurred. We have estimated that in the thirty-eight beginning classes at New Castle and elsewhere, which have been taught by the visual-phonics method, reading achievement, as measured by a well-known primary reading test, has been improved about 40 per cent.

Reading Improvement

In order to substantiate this rather startling claim of 40 per cent reading improvement at the first-grade level, we offer herewith a summary of our Table 14. It describes the reading progress of a first-grade class at the Arthur McGill School in New Castle during the 1952–1953 school year.

There were thirty-five children in the group, nine of whom had attended kindergarten. The median IQ was 108. Three of these IQ's were above 125, while eight were below 100. At the end of the eighth month of school

experience, twenty-four of the children scored above 3.0 on the primary reading test. The next ten pupils scored between 2.48 and 2.91. The other child produced a reading grade-equivalent of 2.08. Thirty-two of these pupils achieved above the seventh month of grade two and, therefore, realized two or more years' progress in eight months.

The poorest reading score (2.08) was produced by a boy whose IQ was only 82. Although his mental age was 5-0, he was reading with above-average ability. The pupil with the next lowest ability had an IQ of 85 and a mental age of 5-0. His reading score was 2.91, almost third-grade level.

The greatest improvement in our experimental classes, where the teaching has emphasized "visual" and "phonics" features, has occurred among slower-learning pupils. Our first-grade tables show that below-norm reading achievement scores have been practically eliminated. Children whose IQ's range between 70 and 90 have learned to read. Nearly every one of them has produced reading grade-equivalents above the national average.

Every child whose parents have been advised (at the onset of his entrance into the first grade) that he lacked mental readiness for the reading experience has come to school anyway. Each one has learned to read at a better-than-average rate for his grade level. And all of these supposedly unready pupils now are successful students in intermediate grades and in high school; some of them rank in the upper-third of their classes.

Our first-grade tabular evidence further indicates that pupils with average abilities have produced superior reading scores, and that children with gifted abilities read better than comparable students who are taught by traditional methods. This latter evidence is somewhat confounding to some reading specialists who assumed that, because we did not group our pupils into ability sections for initial instruction, our gains with slower learners would be accomplished at the expense of the brighter children.

As might be expected, our pupils do not maintain quite the same extraordinary reading progress in the second grade. Nevertheless they continue to read far above average. For example, the aforementioned beginning class produced a median grade-equivalent of 3.9 in the second grade. Only the child with an 82 IQ scored below the norm, and he was just one month below (2.7).

In the third grade, this typical class produced a reading grade-equivalent of 5.1, and, again, only the one child scored below the norm. The boy with an 82 IQ fell to three months below average (3.5).

In the sixth grade, this same class scored a median of 8.4 on the battery average of a well-known achievement test, which was administered to them in February. Once again, the pupil with the IQ of 82 produced the only score that was below average. At this grade level, he was, however, within three months of the national average.

The children in this class can read. Their junior-high teachers tell us this year that they can read well in all of their course books. They will enter senior high school fully prepared for success. And this class is typical of those who have been taught by the visual-phonics method.

An entirely new approach to the teaching of reading in this country is imperative. The New Castle Reading Experiment has proved that nearly every child can be a good reader if his reading program is interesting, imaginative, and modernized in other ways.

CHAPTER V

MEASURING READING
OUTCOMES
AND DETERMINING NEEDS

25. USING TEST RESULTS TO IMPROVE READING
INSTRUCTION*

John Martin

WITHIN any given classroom, there is certain to be a wide range of ability and achievement, regardless of grouping practices. Yet some teachers work with a class as though all pupils were able to read from the same sources, at the same rate, and with the same degree of understanding. This is hardly a realistic approach to teaching reading—or any subject.

In the same vein, a child may be called a disabled reader solely upon the basis of his performance. In some instances, in spite of a performance

level which measures up to his expected capacity, he may be considered a disabled or retarded reader. Performance would indeed be a valid criterion if all children were alike physically, mentally, and emotionally. But this, we know, is not true. Children, like everyone else, have varying degrees of ability.

Should he be so misclassified, it is extremely likely that instruction will present a hardship to the pupil. If the teacher believes a child is not functioning up to his capability, he is likely to assign tasks that are too difficult. Parents, too, may exert undue pressures if they feel their child is not working at the level they expect. And conversely, a pupil can be thought to be achieving at his maximum when actually he is not being challenged

* From John Martin, "Using Test Results To Improve Reading Instruction," *National Elementary Principal*, XL, No. 7 (May, 1961), 43–44. Reprinted by permission of the author and *National Elementary Principal*.

sufficiently for his level of capability.

Proper classification of children's abilities, then, is essential. The teacher must determine the individual pupil's capabilities and the degree to which he is utilizing them, and then apply this information as a basis for improving instruction. Tests, carefully interpreted, offer an excellent starting point for obtaining this information, which the teacher must have to provide more individualized instruction.

Proper Use of Tests

Teacher opinion is invaluable in diagnosis, but one must go beyond this point in identifying and classifying reading problems. Measurement of intelligence and measurement of reading skill are necessary. As an analogy: A child is injured on the playground and the teacher observes the symptoms of obvious pain, discoloration, and swelling of the affected area which indicate that a bone may be broken. He can not be sure of his diagnosis, however, until the school nurse or physician examines the patient and an X-ray is taken. Only then can it be determined whether or not the bone is broken.

The same principle applies to diagnosing reading difficulties. The teacher may believe a pupil is retarded in reading because of his stumbling efforts in oral reading. But how can he be certain? One guide is through testing. Comparison between reading ability and intelligence helps to determine if the pupil is actually retarded. If the mental age is considerably higher (one

and a half years or more) than performance (achievement age), then we can say with some conviction that the pupil is disabled.

Some achievement tests yield grade level and conversion may be necessary to compute achievement age. The procedure is: 1) Add the average entrance age, usually given as 6.2, to the grade level obtained on the test; and 2) Subtract one. Note that 1 is subtracted since the pupil is placed in grade one rather than grade zero at his initial enrollment. As an example, a grade level score of 3.5 would result in an achievement age of 8.7 ($3.5 + 6.2 - 1$), which is the approximate mean age of a child in the fifth month of the third grade.

Another method would be to employ the expectancy formula found in *Reading Difficulties: Their Diagnosis and Correction,* by Bond and Tinker. The expectancy formula gives the grade level of achievement expected. The expected level is then compared with the level found in the achievement test.

Retardation in reading does not correlate highly with low mental ability, nor should it be construed to be synonymous with mental retardation. In many cases, the pupil of superior intelligence is not performing up to his capability. Should such be the case, he may be a retarded reader. He *is* retarded in light of his own ability. For example, an eleven-year-old pupil who has an achievement age of eleven but a mental age of thirteen is properly classed as a retarded reader. Conversely, a nine-year-old child with an achievement age of eight and a mental age of eight is not a retarded reader, since it would be correct to assume that he is performing to the best of his ability.

Both the intelligence tests and the achievement tests which a teacher uses in identifying reading problems must be interpreted with care. Certainly, intelligence tests are not infallible. The mechanics of administering, scoring, and interpreting may produce questionable results. The type of test is also important. Group administered tests, while the most feasible in school situations, are not as thorough as individually administered tests. Careful examination of the instrument is essential to be sure that it is not heavily weighted with items necessitating verbal skills. When reading ability is overstressed, the child who cannot read well is penalized. If a child scores considerably lower than the teacher estimated, an individual test should be given whenever facilities and personnel are available. Should facilities be lacking, a different group administered test may be used to check the results of the first test.

Careful use of the achievement test is equally important. Standardized tests are probably more convenient, but teacher-made tests are also helpful indicators of ability and achievement. Since group administered reading tests are inevitably silent reading tests, they should be supplemented by individual oral reading so the examiner may "hear" the child read. Oral reading is helpful in determining why the pupil scored as he did. Additional information can be obtained from the results of a silent reading test by analyzing specific items to see if there is a pattern of learning difficulties.

Diagnosis the Basis for Instruction

All of these procedures are of little value unless instruction is improved as a result of following them. Diagnosis should always be the keystone for the improvement of any form of instruction.

Once a child's reading skill and potential have been determined, it is essental that he be given materials and instruction on his own level, regardless of what that level may be. A fourth-grade teacher, for example, may have to teach reading from the second- to sixth-grade levels; a fifth-grade teacher, from the second- through eighth-grade levels. Much of this diversity can be handled by the way the class is organized; but some cases require more individual attention than the classroom teacher is able to provide. It is perfectly legitimate in these situations to suggest that parents solicit tutoring from some qualified person in the community. It should not be implied that the teacher has no responsibility in such cases; he should work with the child as much as time permits. In the usual classroom situation, the teacher should provide individualized reading instruction during which he works for short periods with each child sometime during the week.

Test results—properly interpreted—can be an invaluable aid in diagnosing learning difficulties in reading. Mistakes can be made in subjective teacher evaluation unless appropriate measuring devices are employed and careful individual analysis is made of the results. Once reading problems have been identified, the teacher is obligated to work with the child on his own level—supplying him with appropriate materials, working with him individually, and, if necessary, encouraging his parents to seek qualified help for him outside the school.

When used in the ways described here, tests serve their true function as tools for instructional improvement.

26. WHAT DOES A TEST BATTERY TELL A TEACHER?*

Albert J. Mazurkiewicz

GENERALLY speaking a test battery that a teacher administers tells him much or nothing. If we judge the value of tests by the emphasis on testing which the NDEA program has made, we might assume that standardized tests have tremendous values. If, however, we examine the use to which standardized test results are usually put by the average faculty or school system, we must assume that such tests have very little value. That this is so, is reflected in the comments of principals and superintendents who are agreeably surprised when one asks to use their school records for reference purposes, and state "This is the

* From Albert J. Mazurkiewicz, "What Does a Test Battery Tell a Teacher?" Proceedings of the 41st and 42nd Annual Education Conferences Held at the University of Delaware, IX (1959–60), 91–94. Reprinted by permission of the author and Russell G. Stauffer, Director of The Reading Study Center at the University of Delaware.

first time anybody ever looked at or wanted to use our test data." The implication, borne out by further questioning, is that most school systems administer tests which are duly marked, scored, and filed, rather than used to determine some useful things about the children whose time was used in taking these tests.

Standardized tests, as commonly thought of, have several distinct values in terms of appraising pupil growth in reading as well as in evaluating the various mental abilities of pupils. Since tests of reading are constructed to measure the wide range of the reading ability found in typical classes, they can serve to screen out slow or fast pupils, as well as those who require special attention. In general, achievement tests provide the teacher with data concerning the specific skill attainment level of each pupil and the range of the group's achievement. Since standardized tests imply standard procedures in administration and scoring, the use of such tests permits comparison of pupils within classes, as well as one class with another.

The test battery used provides the information for the teacher to classify pupils for individualizing instruction; plan for small group work; select reading materials appropriate to the child's or group's needs; plan for remedial or corrective work; obtain information about children in the quickest fashion so as to permit instruction to get under way rapidly, as well as to formulate reports for conferring with parents. The test battery also provides data for use in formulating hypotheses concerning specific children's learning difficulties. The test battery, therefore, is useful only in terms of the elements included in it and, as such, the battery must be related to the specific things the teacher wants to know.

If a test battery is minimal and comprises an intelligence test and a reading test at any given grade level, much useful information can be acquired by the teachers if that teacher is wise. Such information reinforces or modifies his classroom observation, anecdotal records, cumulative records, and previous teachers' experience. Of course, the wise teacher uses his professional skills to examine the test used before examining the results of such testing so as to determine the reliability and validity of the results obtained, as well as the standard error of measurement to determine how much the obtained results might vary from the child's or group's true scores.

An intelligence test, be it verbal,

non-verbal, or a combination of the two, can be used as an estimate of the potential capacity level of a given student and the score achieved treated as a functional capacity level. By obtaining an intelligence quotient the teacher immediately has information concerning the rate of growth he can normally expect of a given child. If a score is 100, we assume that the child has the functional ability to learn at a normal rate. (All things being equal, he should, for instance, achieve 10 months' reading growth in ten months.) If his IQ is 120, the teacher would recognize that the child can learn at a 20 per cent faster rate than the average child. If the score is 80, he recognizes that the child should be expected to learn at 20 per cent less rapid rate. In the latter case, the teacher would recognize that this child will need concrete materials for manipulation in most learning activities, with various activities scheduled to reinforce learnings. In the first case, the IQ of 120, the teacher would plan to provide enrichment activities, independent research and work activities, special projects, and so forth.

But, before going further, the teacher's analysis of the test itself would modify his thinking and planning for work with children. She would recognize that in Jimmy's case, where the results are so low that they don't agree with her classroom observation, perhaps some extraneous factor was interfering with his performance. Perhaps, because he has a reading problem, the verbal type test used penalized him unfairly, or the test was not geared to his abilities but rather geared to a mythical average. She would treat such test results with caution and plan for retesting with non-verbal materials or ask for elimination of a purely verbal intelligence measure from future testing.

Assuming that a test composed of verbal and non-verbal parts was used, he might examine sub-test scores of a same or different item variety to determine whether concept development was being interfered with or he might examine the difference, if any, between verbal and non-verbal scores to determine whether a lack of reading ability might have influenced a lower verbal score, or examine this same difference to note that since the non-verbal score is considerably lower than the verbal that further investigation of the "why" might be necessary. It might be a reflection of a lack of aptitude, of anxiety under timed or pressure conditions, of neurological problems, of poor physical state at the time of the testing, and so on. Suggestions, hints, or clues to a child's behavior are the elements a teacher should get from such tests in addition to the gross scores achieved.

In the case of the reading test given, the wise teacher notes that Jimmy's grade equivalent score of 7.2 is at the mean of his class and this theoretically indicates that Jim is achieving as well as the average member of his class. The teacher might apply formulas using this score and his IQ score and achieve a Reading Quotient which might suggest that Jim is a developmental reader. If the teacher did do so, he would expect to find that Jim would have one word recognition error in every twenty words of seventh grade material read

and achieve 75 per cent comprehension on ten questions drawn from that material. Unfortunately, if the teacher tried the many Jimmy's out on such material, he would find that this is rarely the case.

The grade placement score is misleading and open to misinterpretation. Rather than being treated as an achievement score (and, therefore, to most people synonymous with instructional level) the score is best thought of and generally found to be, a frustration level score—the level at which no useful reading is taking place, the level at which the child can be found to have many word recognition errors and/or comprehension difficulties. Grade scores on standardized tests do not necessarily indicate the grade level of the basal readers to be assigned because grade designations of readers and grade equivalent scores on tests have been established by different means.

Such scores need interpretation, and modification, based on the teacher's experience with the child. The score, whether grade placement or percentile, tells the teacher how a given student compares with his group or the normative group and tells the teacher whether and how much the student has progressed when this test score is compared with his previous year's test scores. The norms provided by test publishers are *not* to be thought of as scores children in a given grade should reach.

No test score is diagnostic, nor are so-called diagnostic tests usually diagnostic. Diagnosis is the job of the teacher when results of tests are available. Based on his knowledge of what these test results are the teacher compares them with observed facts and works out tentative hypotheses concerning the learning difficulties of his children. By examining past scores, clues to such difficulties are discovered. Vocabulary difficulties, for instance, would naturally suggest reasons why a student's comprehension or rate of reading is low. But a vocabulary grade or percent score tells nothing about the kinds of difficulties the child is having. An examination of the item responses will lead the teacher to a recognition of these difficulties. A child's response to a multiple-choice item might reflect an over-dependence on configuration clues or on initial, medial, or final portion of words. Such response might reflect guessing, gaps in experience, an inability to apply word recognition principles, or an unwillingness to try test items.

Where tests exist, which identify the kinds of comprehension skills being sampled, more information is readily available to the teacher to aid in establishing corrective instruction proced-

ures. Unfortunately such information is misused by some teachers in that they devise class procedures to teach these particular skills so as to aid the student to do better on similar items. In effect they teach the child to pass the test and eliminate the value of such tests.

A test battery, whether it is an achievement battery, or a battery of tests chosen by the teacher for specific diagnostic purposes, produces information in direct proportion to that which was fed into it. Test users need to know exactly what the tests were designed to measure and recognize that norms provided turn measurement into evaluation. Given a simple measurement, the norms permit comparison with a standardization sample which may or may not be similar to one's own and which, therefore, must modify the teacher's interpretation of the achieved scores. The teacher obtains data from these simple measurements and test responses which provide clues for further action on the part of both the teacher and the learner.

27. INFORMAL INVENTORIES*

Emmett Albert Betts

SYSTEMATIC guidance in reading is, first of all, differentiated guidance. One of the first steps in systematic guidance is to estimate levels of the individual learners in the class. Until this is done, discussions of word analysis, semantic analysis, critical reading, concept development, group dynamics, and bibliotherapy deteriorate to the patter of faddists.

BASIC INFORMATION

To put reading instruction on a systematic basis, two questions must be answered. First, what is the highest level at which the child can read "on his own"? This is usually called the *independent* reading level. Second, what is the highest level at which the child can read under teacher supervision? This is usually called the *instructional* reading level.

MERITS

An informal reading inventory has several merits. First, the teacher is given direct evidence on achievement and needs in terms of available instructional material. Second, the teacher is

* From Emmett Albert Betts, "Informal Inventories," in *Handbook on Corrective Reading for the American Adventure Series* (New York: Harper & Row, 1952), pp. 3–8. Reprinted by permission of the author and Harper & Row, Publishers, Inc.

provided with a technique for detecting everyday needs in the classroom. Third, the child is convinced of his needs and sees how to improve his skill. The procedure is sound, understandable, and practicable.

To promote general language competence, the teacher guides her pupils in terms of their reading levels. Wholesome attitudes toward reading are fostered.

Achievement Levels

BASAL LEVEL

With the exception of non-readers, a learner usually can read material at some level of readability without *symptoms* of frustration, such as lip movement, finger pointing, word-by-word reading, tension movements, high-pitched voice, reversal errors, lack of attention to punctuation, and low comprehension. At this level he can pronounce all of the words without hesitation.

The highest readability level at which the individual can read without symptoms of frustration is the basal level. Often this is also the independent reading level. As succeeding levels of reading ability are attempted, two things happen. First, the number of symptoms increases. Second, each symptom becomes intensified.

INDEPENDENT LEVEL

The independent reading level is the highest level at which the learner can read with full understanding and freedom from frustration. The reading is done without tension movements, lip movement, finger pointing, and other evidences of difficulty. Silent reading is characterized by a relatively fast rate of comprehension and absence of vocalization. Oral re-reading is characterized by rhythm, accurate interpretation of punctuation, accurate pronunciation of more than 99 per cent of the words, and a conversational tone. At the independent level, the reading is fluent. The learner practices good reading habits.

INSTRUCTIONAL LEVEL

The instructional level is the highest level at which the learner can read satisfactorily under teacher supervision in a group situation. For normal progress, this reading has the same characteristics as independent reading, with one exception. The child may require help on the recognition of words, but never more than 5 per cent. If he must have help on more than one word in twenty, his comprehension bogs down. He becomes frustrated.

At a level just above the independent reading level, word recognition and/or comprehension needs may appear. If this is the only problem, the instructional level may be at this point.

FRUSTRATION LEVEL

Above the instructional level, symptoms of frustration usually increase rapidly. For example, at the next higher level, the rhythm of oral reading may tend to break and silent lip movement may be evidenced. At succeeding levels, there may be finger pointing, tension movements, a high-pitched voice, and other symptoms of frustration. This tendency to lip movement deteriorates to whispering and then to mumbling over unknown words.

Materials for Inventory

The materials used for an informal inventory are those found in a classroom equipped to meet the wide range of reading levels therein. They may be graded textbooks, graded current events materials, or other instructional materials graded in reading difficulty.

In order to guide reading development systematically, the teacher needs to have two types of information: (1) the reading achievement levels of each individual in the class, (2) the relative reading difficulty (readability) of each book used. THE AMERICAN ADVENTURE SERIES is graded in readability. Hence, the teacher who uses this series needs only to determine the starting level book for her group.

For an individual inventory, a series of graded materials is used. Short selections are read, beginning at a low level of readability and continuing until the individual's independent reading level is identified. Symptoms of difficulty are used as indicators of lack of achievement.

. . . .

Procedure for Inventory

The informal inventory is one of the most direct and effective means of appraising reading levels and needs.) By using a graded series of reading materials, the teacher or clinician may observe responses in a reading situation. It is possible to estimate reading achievement levels in a well-motivated situation. In addition, specific needs may be evaluated in terms of related needs and background skills. An informal inventory is easily ad-

... is simply the observa-
... idual as he reads at
... levels of readability.
... evel, which causes
... ntinues until the
... reading achieve-

... inventory situation may embrace an individual or a group. In a class of twenty to thirty-five pupils, there may be two or three who should be studied individually. However, the chief advantage of this no-cost inventory is that the teacher is provided with a technique for estimating reading levels and needs in *all* reading activities everyday. It is as valuable in a group situation as in an individual situation.

GROUP INVENTORIES

Reading achievement may be assessed in two types of group situations. First, during each directed reading activity, the teacher notes both reading levels and needs. For some of the pupils, the material may be too difficult; for others, the material may be too easy. Since the teacher's obligation is to challenge all learners in a class, she uses some system of grouping.

Second, a group inventory may be administered in the same way as an individual inventory. The teacher explains to the group the purpose of the inventory and interests the pupils in finding out about themselves. She also encourages the group to note the differences in reading difficulty of the materials used for the inventory. Then each individual is given an opportunity to read in a motivated situation. This is continued with increasingly higher level materials until some members show signs of frustration.

In general, the first procedure is more satisfactory. Since modern schools use a cumulative guidance folder for each learner, the teacher usually has the benefit of the previous teacher's observations. The data is used to form tentative groups. Reassignment to groups is based on observations during directed reading activities, supplemented by an occasional individual inventory.

INDIVIDUAL INVENTORIES

In some instances there is a need for learning more about the reading level and needs of an individual than can be learned from a group inventory. About 10 per cent of the learners in a regular classroom may profit from an individual inventory. In a corrective group, even more of the learners need to be studied in this manner. Since only five to fifteen minutes are required for each inventory, the time is well-spent.

ESTABLISHING RAPPORT

One of the chief values of an informal inventory is the understanding

it gives the learner regarding his own needs. He proves to himself that he *can read* at some level. He develops self-confidence and interest.

A few minutes used for explaining the purpose and procedure of an informal inventory are well spent. How well one reads depends considerably upon the emotional climate of the situation. An understanding of what is expected is essential to rapport between the teacher and the learner.

GENERAL PROCEDURE

At each readability level, three steps are taken:

1. Oral reading at sight of a page or less
2. Silent reading of a succeeding section of the material
3. Oral re-reading of the material read silently

EVALUATING COMPREHENSION

Following each of the first two steps, the examiner tests the reader's comprehension. For step 3, the examiner requests the individual to read orally the parts that answer specific questions.

Different types of questions are asked in order to evaluate the reader's ability to:

1. Recall facts.
2. Associate an appropriate meaning with a term.
3. Identify a sequence of events.
4. Draw conclusions.
5. Apply information.

ESTIMATING STARTING LEVEL

In order to give the learner a running start, begin with a very easy book,

e.g., FRIDAY—THE ARAPAHO INDIAN. Usually, this starting level can be estimated from a word recognition test and general observation.

ORAL READING AT SIGHT

This procedure is never used in a directed reading activity. However, it has many merits in a testing situation.

The learner is told that he is to begin reading aloud and that he will be asked questions about what he has read. He is then given a quick preview of the selection and some general questions to answer.

During the oral reading, the examiner notes hesitations, speed, rhythm, word pronunciation errors, interpretation of punctuation, and tension movements. Oral reading at sight induces difficulties. It brings to light pronunciation and comprehension needs.

SILENT READING

This is standard procedure in a directed reading activity. Generally speaking, the first reading of a selection is always done silently.

After the findings on the oral reading at sight are recorded, the examiner asks the learner to continue with silent reading. One selection is read orally at sight; a succeeding selection is read silently. This silent reading is guided by sequential questions about the short selection. The learner reads silently until he finds the correct answer. He either gives the answer in his own words or re-reads orally the correct answer, depending upon what the examiner wishes to observe.

During the silent reading, the examiner notes speed, lip movement, tension movements, head movement, and other evidences of confusion or frustration. A record is kept of unknown words, comprehension scores, and other relevant information.

ORAL RE-READING

At and below the instructional level, the oral re-reading usually is much more fluent than oral reading at sight. At the independent reading level, the oral re-reading is done without hesita-tion and without symptoms for additional help.

There are at least two ways proach oral re-reading. First, it be done as a check on answers silent reading questions. The learn merely reads answers to questions h locates by reading silently.

Second, the oral reading may be done following the completion of the silent reading activites. The learner may read orally the answers to different types of questions. Or he may re-read orally the whole selection for some specific purpose.

28. A MODIFICATION OF THE INFORMAL

READING INVENTORY*

Lester R. Wheeler and Edwin H. Smith

IT HAS long been known by those who work closely with children that grade placement scores on reading tests for primary grades often have little relationship to the child's actual instructional reading level. In the Reading Clinic we have found that pupils who cannot read a primer will often score above the second grade reading

*From Lester R. Wheeler and Edwin H. Smith, "A Modification of the Informal Reading Inventory," *Elementary English*, XXXIV, No. 4 (April, 1957), 224–26. Reprinted by permission of the authors and the National Council of Teachers of English.

level on some standardized reading tests. Naturally, we expect some variation, but it should be much less. We have found that certain primary grade reading tests tend to estimate a child's reading level approximately one grade level or more above the book level he can read for instructional purposes (4), substantiating the findings of Killgallon (1) a decade and a half ago. These findings are very important to the primary teacher in her classwork.

It has been suggested that, in order

to offset the over-estimations of standardized primary reading tests, we teach the child about one year below the standardized test level. Undercutting the test level about one grade seems to work satisfactorily on most tests. The errors tend to balance out and we have the reading instructional level of the average or statistical child; but it does not work with those who deviate widely from the normal.

Betts (1) and others have suggested practical methods for determining a child's instructional level through the use of basal readers to supplement the results of other tests. It is not our purpose in this article to enter a controversy over the readability of basal readers or the construction of group standardized primary reading tests. Our problem is more fundamental. The basic graded readers are our principal source material for the teaching of the primary child. If we are going to use the graded reader we must know the grade level book the child can read.

Basic readers and other materials differ in readability from series to series (1, 2, 3). They differ in the number of new words introduced per page, in sentence length, in percentage of new words per page, and in other readability factors. Readers differ in methodology, some readers being designed for use with a preparatory book and others with a supplementary book. Readers differ in interest level, with some readers high and others low in interest level. These and other differences have been noted by primary teachers and clinicians.

As the philosophy of individual differences reaches the action or practical stage, we may expect more and more emphasis placed upon a closer relation of the reading level of the child and the readability of materials. It is apparent that standardized reading tests for the primary grades often give a misleading idea of individual children's instructional level and the readers also differ in readability from series to series. Since both tests and graded readers present problems in practical teaching situations it would seem that another method of estimating a child's reading level is needed.

At the University of Miami Reading Clinic we use a combination of informal reading inventories such as selecting several paragraphs at random in several graded readers of a series and estimating the reading levels from these paragraph samplings. This method supplements other tests and is a practical test of reading in an actual schoolroom situation. It is important to select a set of readers of controlled readability and interest levels and the samplings should be based on a fair sampling of the book used. In order to reduce this risk we have added another step to the reading inventories.

Suggestions on How to Find a Child's Reading Level

1. Select a series of good basic readers which will, in your opinion, best suit the child.
2. Estimate roughly, from a standardized reading test, the child's instructional reading level and select a reader about one grade under the standardized test level or grade placement.

3. Have the child read the first complete sentence at the beginning of the pages sampled and keep a record of his errors. A suggested form for recording errors is given on the following page.

4. As the child reads, count as errors mispronunciations, omissions, substitutions, hesitancies over three seconds, distortions and word assists by the teacher. Do not count as errors mistakes on proper names.

5. If the percentage of errors per hundred words is more than 3 to 5 per cent, drop down to the next grade level in the series. If the percentage of errors is less than 2 per cent, move up to the next grade level in the series.

6. When you have found the level at which the child's errors constitute approximately 3 to 5 per cent of the running words, test his paragraph reading. Select four or five paragraphs and have the child read these, both silently and orally, noting the difficulties.

7. Remember that series differ in difficulty; therefore, teach the child in the series used to evaluate him, or retest him in the series to be used for instruction.

8. If the child passes the sentence test but not the paragraph test, teach him on the level indicated by the sentence test. This holds true ONLY on the primary level because at this level few children have difficulty with the concepts offered, and the vocabulary problem is not so much one of meaning as of recognition.

9. Children who show difficulties of organization, retention, and understanding can be taught in material where they know at least 95 per cent of the running words.

10. We might summarize the following practical underlying assumptions from clinical and teaching experience:

   (a) A child can read materials without any assistance when he knows and understands 98–99 per cent of vocabulary and comprehends 75–90 per cent of main ideas. This is his independent, library, or free reading level.

   (b) The child's instructional or teaching level is where he knows and understands the meaning of 95–98 per cent of vocabulary and comprehends about 75–90 per cent of main ideas. "Instructional level" implies the child needs word analysis of unknown words and comprehension direction.

   (c) The child's frustration level is when he recognizes or knows less than 95 per cent of vocabulary and comprehends less than 75 per cent of the main ideas. Frustration in reading generally increases with a decrease in recognition, meaning vocabulary, and general comprehension of materials he is reading.

11. One of the main purposes of the diagnosis is to determine the free reading and instructional levels for teaching purposes, and also to learn the frustration level where

Informal Reading Inventory Check Sheet
Used at University of Miami Reading Clinic

Name ————————— Date ——————————— Age ———— Grade ————

Vocabulary Difficulties   Series Used ————————————————
Phonics poor ———————————   Instructional level ——————————
Syllabication poor ————————   Independent level ——————————
Use of configuration poor ————   Frustration level ——————————
Use of picture clue poor ————   Probable Mental level ——————
Sight vocabulary poor ————————   *Comprehension Difficulties*
Use of context poor ————————   Sentence reading poor ——————
                                              Paragraph reading poor ——————
Perception difficulties   Memory poor ——————————————
Reverses words ——————————   Organization poor ——————————
Reverses letters ——————————   Detail reading poor ————————
Omits beginnings ——————————   *Rate Difficulties*
Omits endings ————————————   Directional problem ——————————
Omits words ——————————————   Word by word reader ——————
Sounds confused ——————————   Regression movements ——————
Sounds added ——————————————   Points at words ——————————————
Omits sounds ——————————————   Loses place easily ——————————
Other factors ——

---

the material is too difficult for the child to read.

REFERENCES

1. BETTS, EMMETT A. *Foundations of Reading Instruction.* New York: American Book Co., 1946.
2. ————. "Readability: Its Application to the Elementary School," *Journal of Educational Research,* XLII (March, 1949), 438–59.
3. KEARNEY, NOLAN C. "Sentence Length in One-hundred and twenty-one Representative First Grade Readers," *Journal of Educational Research,* XXXVIII (February, 1945) 447–61.
4. SMITH, EDWIN H. "Comparison of Standard and Informal Test Levels," *Unpublished Study,* Reading Clinic, University of Miami, 1956.
5. SMITH, EDWIN H. and WHEELER, LESTER R. *Unpublished Data for a Readability Formula,* Miami, Florida, University of Miami Reading Clinic, 1954.
6. SWEET, MARIE E. "A Comparative Study of the Relationship Between Recognition Vocabulary and Comprehension," *Unpublished Study,* University of Miami Reading Clinic, 1956.
7. WHEELER, LESTER R. and SMITH, EDWIN H. "A Practical Readability Formula," *Elementary English,* XXXI (November, 1954), 397–99.

29. THE DIAGNOSIS OF READING DISABILITIES*

Albert J. Harris

SOMETIMES names that we use to label certain things or objects or events are very impressive, but when we look more carefully into the meaning we find that the label does not really tell us any more than a much simpler term would convey. Medical specialists, for example, have devised quite a number of special terms to describe difficulties in learning to read. For example, the term *alexia* simply means inability to read. This can be subdivided into *acquired alexia* (loss of ability to read as a result of damage to the brain), *congenital alexia* (the person has never been able to read), or *developmental alexia* (the person has not developed any reading ability). Another favorite medical term is *dyslexia,* which simply means *that there is something wrong with the person's reading.* The term *strephosymbolia* simply means twisted symbols, or in other words, the individual has a reversal tendency.

The term *diagnosis* also seems formidable to some teachers. It is derived from Greek roots which mean "to know through" or "to know thoroughly." Taking this word out of the

* From Albert J. Harris, "The Diagnosis of Reading Disabilities," in *Corrective and Remedial Reading,* A Report of the Sixteenth Annual Conference and Course on Reading (Pittsburgh: Univ. of Pittsburgh Press, 1960), pp. 31–37. Reprinted by permission of Donald L. Cleland, Director of the Reading Laboratory at the University of Pittsburgh.

medical setting and applying it educationally, it refers to what is really a straightforward process. When we are diagnosing a difficulty, what we want to do is to find out what is wrong, what caused it, and what can be done for it. That is what diagnosis means as applied to reading disability.

Continuing the effort to explain diagnosis in plain and simple English, we may regard the diagnostic process as one that consists of asking five kinds of questions. These questions are summarized by the well-known little words: who, what, where, how, and why.

The first of these, *who,* means: who are the children who need special help? All children whose reading seems to be significantly below grade level need some special attention. Within this large group, usually consisting of one-quarter to one-third of all the children, we have to make some differentiations. We need to distinguish, first of all, between those whose reading problem is just one aspect of generally slow mental development and those who have the potentiality of making considerable improvement. The generally slow child, who is usually reading close to his mental ability level and sometimes manages to read somewhat above it, does not need a remedial program, but rather a total curriculum which is adapted to his limited learning abilities. He needs to be recognized and appreciated for doing the best that he can, and relieved of the pressure of trying desperately and vainly to come up to the normal group. The other children, who are below both the standards for age and grade and their general level of intellectual functioning, are children with reading disabilities, ranging from slight to severe.

Children who have slight to moderate reading disabilities are generally able to be helped considerably by the classroom teacher, working with them either in groups and helping them in the areas of their greatest difficulty, or providing them with some highly individualized help in the general classroom setting. The remainder, the severely disabled readers, need a much more careful diagnostic study and need to be given remedial help individually or in quite small groups, and usually outside of the classroom setting.

The task of estimating the mental ability of a retarded reader is not an easy one to solve. In the primary grades, the group intelligence tests in common use do not require any reading, and therefore are less likely to underestimate seriously the intelligence of a poor reader than the tests used above the third grade. The majority of the group intelligence tests now in use in schools at the fourth grade level and above present most of their questions in printed form, so that the child who cannot read the question is automatically low. For this reason, group intelligence test results must be interpreted with caution when trying to establish the mental ability of a poor reader. Individual testing by a trained psychologist is generally much more accurate in indicating what the child is able to do.

Assuming that one has a dependable measure of the child's mental age or level of mental development, it is simple to determine his average level of reading performance, express it in terms of an age score, and compare it with his mental age. If the mental age is significantly higher, there is a disability, and the greater the discrepancy, the more serious the disability.

The second question, *what*, asks: at what level can the child read? In answering this question, we find that teachers and school administrators tend to place too much reliance on the scores obtained from standardized reading tests. While average and good readers tend to get most of their scores on such tests by actually reading and answering the questions, the scores of poor readers are often based largely on guess-work and so they frequently over-estimate the level at which the child can really read. Standardized reading tests are very good instruments for comparing groups and for measuring rate of progress of groups. They are somewhat less satisfactory as measures of the status or progress of an individual child.

Increasing emphasis has been given in the past few years to the actual tryout of a child in a book to see if the book fits him. Usually we try to distinguish between the instructional level, at which the child can read fairly well when given instructional assistance of the usual sort, and the independent level, at which he can read for pleasure and without any assistance. Determining these levels for the disabled reader is extremely important, since we find over and over again that one of the reasons that certain children do not improve is that the materials with which they are being taught are just too hard for them.

With disabled readers, it is unsafe to rely on silent reading alone. It is necessary to listen to the child's unrehearsed oral reading in material of varying levels of difficulty, and to test his sight vocabulary and word analysis skills.

The next question, *where,* is an inquiry into the specific reading skill or skills that are central to the child's difficulties with reading. For example, let us assume that a sixth-grade child scores at fourth-grade level in a standardized silent reading test. Presumably his reading comprehension is quite inferior. But if we test his word recognition skills, we find that they are even more limited, since he has a small sight vocabulary and cannot read many words of greater than second-grade difficulty. Under these conditions, it seems evident that the word recognition problem is more central than the comprehension problem, or, in other words, he cannot understand the material primarily because there are too many words that he cannot recognize. The special help that he would need would have to concentrate more on word recognition skills than on comprehension. Similarly, many children who are very slow readers are slow readers because they have to hesitate and pause to puzzle out words, and again the central difficulty would not be the rate problem but rather a word recognition problem.

The next question, *how,* signifies: how does the child proceed in reading? What is he trying to do? What goes on in his mind? Here we can ask a number of questions, all of which are highly significant.

First, how does he attack words? Does he read only the words that he knows and wait to be told the others, or does he make some effort to figure them out? If so, does he try to sound words letter by letter, or by phonograms, or does he try spelling the word, or some other technique? In order to be able to answer these questions it is helpful to try the child on words presented individually rather than in continuous material, because some children have become such expert guessers that many of their shortcomings in word recognition pass unnoticed when they are allowed to guess from context. Furthermore, it is very helpful, when the child does not recognize the word immediately, to ask him to do his thinking out loud so that you can find out what he is trying to do and why it works or doesn't work. This is perhaps the most helpful single technique in reading diagnosis that I know. Sometimes more can be learned by listening to a child as he tries to figure out two or three words that can be gained from hours of other kinds of testing, in terms of providing insight and understanding about the child's difficulties.

A second question is, how does the child approach the reading material? With what intentions, expectations, or mental set? Is he reading to try to find out something, or is he just trying to say the words? In oral reading is he reading to himself out loud, or is he trying to read with expression so as to communicate to others? ⌐

A third area of inquiry is, how does the child feel about reading? Many children who have difficulties in reading approach printed material with fear and trepidation. They may anticipate that they will make many mistakes and that somebody will laugh at them. They assume it is going to be difficult and frustrating. If this is true about a child, then obviously helping him to change these feelings to more constructive ones would have to become a major objective in trying to help him. Answers to this kind of question are sometimes not easy to obtain, but once the child trusts you he will very frequently be able to tell you frankly just how he does feel about reading.

A fourth area of inquiry is, how does the child respond to instructional help? Does he seem indifferent, resistive, passively accepting, or gratefully enthusiastic? If he is already enthusiastic, perhaps one can concentrate on *what* to teach him; but if he displays very little responsiveness, perhaps major attention will have to be given to motivation for a considerable length of time, and skills development may have to be kept at a minor level of importance. It is desirable to inquire not only into his response to instruction in general, but whether he responds differently to different kinds of activities or different kinds of material. Sometimes finding a book that appeals greatly to a child's special interest may provide a magic key to getting him started. Sometimes a child who is a slow learner with one method of instruction may respond ever so much

faster to a different method. Experimental tryout of a variety of materials and a variety of teaching approaches may play a very important and practical part in the total diagnostic program.

The final question, *why*, is an attempt to get to the heart of causation. The causation of reading difficulties is very complex and frequently there are more causal handicaps for a particular child than we need in order to account for the difficulties that he is experiencing. Sometimes even in an intensive study by a group of specialists in a clinic it is difficult to do more than conjecture as to what the causes really were when the difficulty started several years ago. Nevertheless, the effort to find out what causal handicaps have interfered with the child's learning is very worthwhile, and even if we do not find full and complete answers, we often discover contributing factors or handicaps about which something can be done.

It would be a mistake to assume that it is always necessary to understand the causes in order to help the condition. From a practical standpoint, it is useful to make a diagnostic distinction only when there is a difference in treatment involved. For example, if there are half a dozen kinds of organisms that can cause a sore throat and they can all be treated with the same antibiotic, a sensible physician does not bother to make laboratory tests to decide which particular organism is the cause this time. Instead, he prescribes the antibiotic and the sore throat gets cured. On the other hand, if there is an abdominal pain and he does not know whether it is a digestive disturbance or an inflamed appendix, it is very important for him to make a diagnostic differentiation because the treatment of these conditions has to be so different.

In reading diagnosis, the first differentiation that has to be made is between those children whose problems are specific to reading and those who are generally slow. In this way we narrow our range of special inquiry to those children who can really profit from special attention. We look through the accumulated school records for any information that they can throw on how long he has had trouble in reading, what previous teachers have recorded about him, recorded intelligence and achievement test results, attendance, physical factors, conduct and personality ratings, and so on. A talk with his mother is desirable. This search may or may not cast light upon the causation. We should then proceed to a straightforward analysis of his reading problems, leading to the formulation of a teaching plan. If the parents are cooperative and interested, it may be helpful to suggest that the possibility of a significant visual or other physical defect be checked by comprehensive private examinations.

At this point it is proper to proceed with a remedial program, even though several areas of causation have not been explored at all deeply. If the child responds well to remedial help, it is an academic question whether or not we ever get answers to those questions. If after a reasonable period of tryout the child is making very disappointing progress, it is wise to try to get additional diagnosis in those areas that have not previously been covered. For example, it may be desirable to find out, through referral to a psychologist, psychiatrist, or mental hygiene clinic, whether the child's emotional problems are such that he cannot at present profit from remedial instruction. Proceeding one step at a time, in this way, we are able to avoid wasting our precious resources of psychological and psychiatric examinations, which are usually limited in availability, and use them for those cases that really need them, rather than giving every child a thorough diagnostic study.

In summary, diagnosis is nothing more than the application of a straightforward, common sense, problem-solving approach to the study of children who have difficulties in reading. We try to find out what is wrong, what caused the difficulty, and what can be done for it. We do it by intelligent use of our common question words— who, what, where, how, and why? We first single out those children who require special attention to their reading, and then we try to find out the level at which they can profitably be taught, specific reading skills that need to be tackled first, the incorrect procedures that the child is using so that we can correct them, and, finally, we try within the limitations of the study procedures available to us to find the causes of the child's poor reading and what handicaps may still be preventing him from effective learning.

CHAPTER VI

GROUPING FOR EFFECTIVE READING INSTRUCTION

30. THE STRUCTURED READING PROGRAM*

Theodore Clymer

IN PRINCIPLE no informed person can be opposed to a reading program which adjusts to individual differences, just as no one who understands children and how they learn can object to a program which is organized or structured. However, when we speak of *the* individualized method and *the* structured method, we pass beyond general principles and go on to spell out specific procedures on which there can be a clear and careful evaluation based on research, classroom practice, expert opinion, and logical analysis. In other words, when we progress from principle to prac-

* From Theodore Clymer, "The Structured Reading Program," in *Controversial Issues in Reading and Promising Solutions,* Supplementary Education Monographs, No. 91, compiled and edited by Helen M. Robinson (December, 1961), 75–80. Reprinted by permission of the author and The University of Chicago Press.

tice, we can see, compare, and perhaps resolve differences.

In the space available four questions will be treated in turn. They are: What are the characteristics of an effective, structured reading program? What are the major dangers in a structured program? What are the problems in an individualized program? And finally, what does research reveal about these two approaches?

What Are the Characteristics of an Effective, Structured Program?

Three carefully developed teaching tools form the foundation of an effective program. These tools are the end product of a careful application of research in child development, reading methods, learning theory, and children's interests.

The basic reader. The basic or basal

reader is designed with a careful control and gradual introduction of vocabulary, concepts, and mechanical features which research has demonstrated create learning problems for the pupil as he develops reading skill. In addition, the content of the basal reader is carefully selected to meet the standards of both child interest and literary quality. Except for some obvious problems at the pre-primer level where vocabulary is limited, the stories of well-designed basal series fulfill the criteria of good literature.

The value systems and social customs portrayed in primary basal readers have been criticized as "middle class" and therefore not in harmony with the background many children bring to school. To these critics we may ask, "What is wrong with middle class values?" Is working diligently, helping with a family project, caring for pets, treating neighbors, friend, and family with kindness and respect a poor set of values to develop? We may also ask these critics, "What value systems shall we substitute?"

The teacher's manual. The teacher's manual or guide is a second essential tool in a structured reading program. If full use is to be made of the basal reader, the teacher's manual must play an important role. It is only by consulting the manual that we learn the word-recognition skills, concepts, and comprehension abilities the author intended a particular selection to develop. The sequence of skills and abilities the program is designed to develop is revealed through the teacher's manual. The manual is not a recipe book—and it should not be used as one. You cannot add thirty-five children, fold in

one teacher, slowly blend eight units from a basal reader, and get good reading by the end of the year. A manual is a rich source of ideas and suggestions. In no way does it circumscribe teaching; in no way can a manual replace an intelligent, alert teacher who is professionally prepared to teach reading. The manual suggests; it does not bind; it enriches, not limits. Any teacher who uses a modern teacher's guide knows that a selective adaptation of the ideas presented must be made because there is just too much in the manual for time to permit the use of all the suggestions presented.

A crisp, new-looking manual with a sparklingly clean cover leaves me depressed. Unless such a manual has just been requisitioned, it is serving little purpose other than to decorate the teacher's desk. My preference is a dog-eared, well-worn manual with clippings inserted, notes for additional questions and activities liberally sprinkled in the margins, with underlining and comments throughout. Such a manual is serving the purpose the authors intended.

One additional suggestion for effective use of manuals: One copy for the classroom and one for home is ideal if the budget will permit it. Such a plan effectively solves the problem of your being where the manual isn't. More than once I carried the manuals home for careful study, made my selections and additions of questions and activities, then arrived at school the next day and discovered that I'd left my homework at home. Two manuals help to solve this problem.

From these comments you can see

that my view is that a manual serves as a guideline, not a navigation chart. Intelligent selection, adaptation, and additions by a professionally trained teacher are prerequisites for effective use of the manual. Use of a manual is not the mark of a poorly prepared instructor—rather, its use indicates a teacher who understands the reading process and the importance of sequence in developing reading skills.

The workbook. First of all, we are not discussing workbooks in general but the workbook that *accompanies the basal reader* the children are using. In this workbook we have the third of our essential tools, but perhaps the tool which must be used with the most discretion. The workbook usually provides a follow-up on the skills taught through the basic reader lesson. In certain series the workbook serves as a preparatory activity to reading selections from the reader. In either case, construction of the workbook is such that it provides additional practice on vocabulary, word-recognition skills, and comprehension abilities which are congruent with the sequence and scope of the reading program.

Selection and adaptation are keynotes to use of the workbook. Certain children, or groups of children, may not need further practice in the skill presented on certain pages of the workbook. A lesson on initial consonants, for example, may be omitted when a group is already proficient in this skill. Conversely, additional exercises must be provided on certain abilities for some children when they fail to achieve proficiency upon completion of the exercises provided by the workbook. No author can even hope to prepare a program which will be a "perfect fit" for every child. Here again, the teacher's professional judgment to supplement, to adapt, and to reject is required. Workbooks can and have been misused. Such misuses are not inherent in this third tool of the program. Our problem is not to eliminate the workbook but to be intelligent in its use.

Correction of workbook exercises is essential for good teaching. These exercises cannot be completed and then forgotten. Both the pupil and the teacher must be aware of problems and strengths which are revealed by performance on these exercises. Children often should have the opportunity to locate and correct their own errors. Research in learning reveals that immediate knowledge of success or lack of success is closely related to growth. Applying this psychological principle requires that the pupil be informed— the sooner the better—of the results of his efforts.

To summarize our discussion on the use of the basal reader, teacher's manual, and workbook of the basal reader, we can say that these tools, when used intelligently, critically, and professionally, offer a program for instruction with sequence and scope which is unparalleled by other approaches.

Time provisions. The program described to this point is not accomplished in a few minutes stolen from a crowded curriculum. At all grade levels —including the high school—we must take a firm stand and provide time for teaching reading. Schools with successful programs provide generous time allotments for reading instruction. Primary teachers somehow find the time. Intermediate grade teachers put up a valiant battle to find time for reading instruction. Unfortunately they don't always win the struggle. In the junior and senior high organization, reading is often lost in a welter of scheduling problems and activities. The answer to the time problem is to list in order of importance the objectives of the curriculum. If such an approach is taken, reading can easily claim its rightful proportion of the time available in the school day. Fifty to sixty minutes daily is certainly not excessive in the intermediate grades. One period a day for at least one semester per year is not an unrealistic demand in the junior and senior high school. There *is* time in the school day. Our job is simply to take what is needed for reading.

Grouping within the class. Two years ago this Conference considered the problems of grouping practices in adjusting to individual differences. The proceedings of the conference suggest that the final solution for individual differences must be found in the instructional practices of the teacher. Grouping plans, no matter how intricate, cannot produce groups of pupils who can be given uniform instruction. Since differences in reading ability within classes are here to stay, we must adjust our instructional program to these differences through grouping within the classroom.

Providing appropriate organizational routine, worthwhile independent work, and instruction for three or perhaps more groups is a topic of great concern to all of us, but this topic is unfortunately beyond the scope of our presentation in this session. Two comments are pertinent here. First, accomplishing this task is not easy. Careful planning, skill, and hard work are blended together in generous proportions to achieve the goal of good group instruction. The second comment is one of simple mechanics of instruction: as the number of instructional groups increases, the amount of the teacher's time available for any one group decreases. Sixty minutes of instruction with three groups allows the teacher to spend twenty minutes with each group. The same instruction time would allow ten minutes per group if six groups are used. Thirty groups (an individualized approach) would permit two minutes per group in a sixty minute period. A little speculation reveals that the advantage of greater homogeneity of instructional groups is soon offset by the smaller amount of time available for teaching a group.

Provisions for organization. A major contribution of a structured program is the organization provided in reading instruction. This organization is apparent in a number of ways. Consider first the provision for introduction of vocabulary, background, and concepts when a small group uses the same material. In this setting it is possible for the teacher to prepare the pupils to read the selection with understanding and without undue problems because of unanticipated vocabulary. If each member of the class is reading a different selection or book, such preparation is obviously impossible.

A second way in which the structured program provides organization is through a thorough comprehension program. Purposes for reading should be varied and carefully selected so that all the major comprehension skills are given a balanced emphasis. Such balance and organization is not likely to result from a happenstance selection of purposes. The manual, by providing a full range of purposes for reading, insures that effective comprehension abilities are developed.

A third way in which a basic program provides organization is in a carefully developed and sequential program of word recognition. In actual practice an effective and broad word-recognition program may be one of the most difficult aspects of reading to manage without aid from a basic system. How can we insure that our students have been (1) exposed to all appropriate aspects of word-recognition and word-analysis skills, (2) introduced to these in the most effective sequence, and (3) developed in a balanced manner so that neither over- nor under-dependence upon any one technique occurs?

Use of a basic program is no guarantee of perfect performance in word-recognition skills. Yet it seems clear that the probability of a broad, effective program is greatly enhanced when carefully prepared materials are used. *Topical and personal reading.* With all its aids, organization, and careful development of skills, the basic program will fail dismally if it does not do one more thing. It must stimulate reading beyond the basic text. The basic program is only the "how to read" aspect of a total reading curriculum. Simply "knowing how" is not enough to develop effective reading ability. Once the skills are taught they must be practiced in a variety of situations in which students read on topics of concern to class enterprises— whether related to the content of the reader, the social studies, or science curriculum. In addition to reading related to class projects, problems, and other assignments, personal reading must form an important part of the total reading curriculum. By re-emphasizing the importance of personal reading, the "individualized reading program" has performed a real service for it has made us sensitive to the contribution which the child's free-time reading can make to reading growth.

A reading curriculum which neglects topically organized reading and fails to provide a well selected collection of good books for personal reading—and time for reading them—will not achieve the goals we hold for a modern reading program.

What Are the Major Dangers in a Structured Reading Program?

There are certain dangers in the use of basal reading programs. The recognition of these dangers and proper planning can do much to avoid these problems. Three major dangers are discussed below.

Uniform application. Because the basic program is so well organized and so much aid is given the teacher in providing exercises, activities, and directions, it may be tempting for a teacher to administer a uniform program of instruction to all children, regardless of need. This problem may be one of in-service education for the school systems. It may also mean that the teacher-training institutions have failed to show the teacher how to organize his class for differentiated instruction. Whatever its origin, the problem is real and should be acknowledged.

The text as the total program. As was pointed out earlier, the basic text cannot be considered the entire reading curriculum. Programs which stop with the basal reader have failed to provide sufficient experiences with other worthwhile materials and cannot fully develop reading skills. An effective program will extend throughout the day, touching on all content areas and will stimulate reading of a wide range of materials.

Failure to apply insight. Because they respect the research and scholarship of the authors of basic reading series, teachers may be hesitant to deviate from the suggestions in the manual or to alter directions for workbook pages, or in other ways apply professional insight in the use of basal materials. But no author claims to have designed a program to meet all needs and to be suitable for every situation. The effective use of basal readers involves professional insight to meet special needs of children. Professional judgments are still the province of the teacher and must remain so, if our programs are to be truly effective.

31. GROUPING IN THE TEACHING OF READING*

Albert J. Harris

TWENTY years ago, most teachers of reading were pretending that they could teach reading effectively with all the children in the class doing the same thing at the same time. Instruction was planned for the average; the quick learners suffered from boredom, and the slow learners, from frustration and failure. Today we are all impressed with the fact that individual differences are large and important,

* From Albert J. Harris, "Grouping in the Teaching of Reading," *The Reading Teacher,* V (September, 1951), 1–3. Reprinted by permission of *The Reading Teacher.*

and in theory there is complete agreement that instruction must be adapted to individual differences. But how is this to be done?

The first approach tried was "homogeneous" grouping. This meant separating the children in a particular grade into classes by putting the brighter ones into one class, the slower ones into another class, etc. This was possible in large schools but not in small ones. Although teachers in general liked this system, and research showed that achievement was neither better nor worse on the average than in non-homogeneous classes, it has declined in popularity in recent years.

There are three main reasons for this decline: (1) Wide differences within a class still remained even in "homogeneous" classes. (2) It was difficult to avoid the development of a caste system, with the members of the slower classes the victims. As one boy in such a class put it: "We're not *supposed* to learn; we're the dummies." (3) Teaching methods were developed which could deal successfully with a fairly wide range of ability within a class.

In teaching reading, the most prevalent way of adjusting to individual differences is to divide the class into smaller groups with the teacher working directly with one group at a time. Such a procedure can be very effective. But in practice many difficulties have arisen, and teachers in many communities are raising questions. Let us take a look at some of these questions and see how they can be answered.

Is Teaching by Groups Worthwhile?

During the past twenty years, many reports have been published of programs which involve grouping for reading instruction. Most of them show substantially better results than those obtained with undifferentiated instruction. Research has not yet determined the best way of adapting classroom instruction to individual differences. Indeed, it is probable that there is no one best way and that different conditions require different solutions.

But grouping in itself does not automatically produce better learning. It simply is a means to the end of giving

children, whose learning is at different levels, work that is suited to their different needs. If the same materials and methods are used in each group, the main value of grouping is wasted. If the poor readers are given reading material which is too hard for them, it does not matter much if they try it in a small group or as part of the whole class. And poorly managed group instruction can result in a chaotic classroom.

Should All Reading Be Done by Groups?

Reading activities in modern schools are of three main types: developmental, recreational, and functional. Group reading lessons are primarily for developmental reading. Recreational reading is often best managed by periods of "free reading," with each child reading silently in a library book he has chosen. Functional reading includes those reading situations in which reading is used primarily as a way of finding out things. For some functional reading situations the whole class may be able to work together, as in a current events period. In others, the class can be divided into small groups or committees, each with a special assignment. In such committees, it is often desirable to have a wide range of reading skill, so that the members of a committee can supplement one another instead of each duplicating the others' work. On such a committee, a good reader can do wide research reading about the topic, while the poor reader can take major responsibility for illustrations, handwork, or other related activity. It is desirable for committees of this sort to have a different kind of composition from the grouping used for developmental reading lessons.

Some reading activities can be done by the whole class. These include appreciation activities such as audience reading, choral reading, oral book reports and discussions of individual reading, and informal dramatizations based on reading. Other whole-class activities can include certain kinds of developmental lessons, such as practice in alphabetizing and other special skills.

There should also be periods of completely individualized reading, of which there are two main types. The free reading period, which is primarily for recreational reading, has already been mentioned. In the intermediate and upper grades it may be desirable to have a period for individual practice to overcome particular weaknesses; for these, specific types of practice exercises, such as can be found in published workbooks, are needed. During individualized reading periods the teacher can find an opportunity to give individual help to those who need it, to give informal tests, and so on.

With some whole-class reading activities, some completely individualized reading, and some reading done by committees, it is obvious that a well-balanced reading program is not confined to developmental reading taught by groups.

How Should Reading Groups Be Set Up?

A teacher with a new class is often able to set up a preliminary grouping on the basis of reports from the previous teacher, or standardized test scores. If such information is not available, the first two or three weeks should provide opportunity for careful observation of each child's reading performance, and provide a basis for setting up groups.

In most classes, there is quite a wide range of reading ability and the main basis for grouping should be in terms of reading grade level as estimated by the teacher. If the class is fairly homogeneous, it may be advantageous to set up groupings in terms of specific skills on which help is needed; this is usually possible only in the higher grades.

For teachers who are inexperienced in group teaching, it is often desirable to start with two groups: a large group including the average and superior readers, and a smaller group which requires easier reading material.

As the teacher becomes more accustomed to working with groups and more sensitive to individual needs, additional groups may be set up. The best readers may be separated from the average group; or they may be taken care of by numerous supplementary assignments, by acting as helpers, by engaging in activities designed to develop special skills, and so forth. There may be a few children who need special help with a particular skill, such as phrase reading or vowel sounds; a special group can be set up for them, to be disbanded when its purpose has been accomplished. Some teachers are able to work effectively with as many as five or six groups. For most teachers, however, three groups represent a practical maximum. For many, a two-group program, supplemented by whole-class reading activities, individualized reading activities, and varied functional reading, will provide effectively for reading needs.

After children have been assigned to groups, the teacher must be alert to signs of wrong placement. Perhaps Mary can keep up with the high group only at the cost of great effort, and Jimmie's improvement has been such that moving him up to the high group may be worthwhile. While children should not be shifted back and forth just for the sake of variety, changes in group placement should be made whenever the need becomes evident.

How Can Good Social Attitudes Be Fostered?

Most important is the teacher's own attitude, which the children tend to imitate. If the teacher can praise a good try by the worst reader in the class with real enthusiasm, the class will follow suit. Children are usually very good judges of one another's performances. Whether they will be kind or cruel to one another depends to a very great extent on the example which the teacher sets. The teacher who accepts and expects individual differences in learning usually succeeds in establishing a healthy social climate in the group.

The combination of group activities with whole-class reading activities, individualized reading, and committee assignments diminishes the danger that children will label each other according to their group placement, which is somewhat more likely to occur if all reading is done in the same groups.

While the fact that one group reads better than another cannot be hidden, the names assigned to the groups should not emphasize that fact. The children will often like to choose their own group names, which may be taken from Indian tribes, athletic teams, animals, and so on.

How Can Efficiency in Group Work Be Achieved?

(1) Very important is the need to provide each group with reading material that is easy enough to insure success, and capable of attracting attention and maintaining interest. The slowest group usually requires material one or more grades below the official grade; and it should, of course be new to them and not a repetition of something read in a previous grade.

(2) Careful planning is required. A weekly schedule should be drawn up, showing what each group is to do during each reading period. The time required for planning decreases with experience, but even expert teachers should avoid relying on the inspiration of the moment. The manuals which accompany modern sets of readers are rich sources of inspiration for specific lesson plans in reading.

(3) Each group must be given clear, specific directions. These should include directions to follow if the main assignment is finished before the end of the period. It is desirable for the directions to be visible, so that a child who forgets what to do next does not have to interrupt the teacher.

(4) Movable furniture which can

be rearranged to suit the group activity is highly desirable. However, effective group instruction can be carried on in old-fashioned classrooms with desks bolted to the floor in rows.

(5) The length of periods should be adjusted to the attention span of the children. If a period is prolonged beyond the fatigue limit, the result is restlessness, noise, and misbehavior. If reading seems to need more time, it is often better to add an extra period than to lengthen the periods.

(6) In the primary grades, it is often necessary to assign the children who are not in the reading group with which the teacher is working to some activity that can be done without much help from the teacher, such as drawing, painting, clay work, and so forth. If all groups in a class are capable of doing fairly independent reading, it is feasible for all groups to be reading at the same time.

(7) Many teachers find it helpful to have a chairman for each group. Although the temptation is to use the best readers as chairmen of lower groups, morale is usually better if the chairman is a member of the group, either elected or appointed on a rotating basis. The assignment of good readers as "helpers" to poor readers may also be helpful.

(8) Group instruction does not eliminate the need for individual attention; it just makes it a little easier. Within each group there is always considerable variation not only in general reading level, but also in the pattern of specific reading skills. A slow child may need very simple thought questions; a shy child may profit from extra praise and encouragement; one may need to slow down for greater accuracy, while another needs to speed up. Much individualization can be done during the group sessions with the teacher. However, sometimes one finds a child who just cannot function in a group and needs much individual help, which may have to be given outside of class hours.

32. HOW TO TEACH A CLASS GROUPED FOR DIFFERENTIATION IN BASAL READING*

Willa T. Wynn

IN *Teaching Elementary Reading,* Tinker says, "Grouping is a device which facilitates the adjustment of instruction to individual differences."[1] This device has long been accepted as standard practice in the primary grades; however, there are those who use the technique without a clear understanding of the what and the why of the procedure. Consequently many misunderstandings and inconsistencies occur which tend to defeat the real purpose. Although the difficulties are many, grouping *is* an attempt to meet the problem of the wide range of reading abilities in the classroom. In a third-grade class the range of reading abilities may vary from primer level to a few children who can use a fifth-grade book with ease. In the usual sixth grade we normally find a spread of six or seven grades in reading ability. Children who vary so widely cannot be taught efficiently as one group using the same methods and materials. Some sort of grouping is essential.

Let us say that "Once upon a time" there were three teachers. After attend-

ing a university class each decides to try out Grouping for Basal Reading. Teacher X divides her class into three groups of twelve children each. That day Miss X teaches the same reading lesson three times. The next day Miss X goes back to her former classroom organization. For her the procedure was time-consuming, boring (to the children too), and entailed much more seatwork to be prepared. Our Miss Y is very enthusiastic; she divides her thirty-six into six small groups. With little readiness or preparedness for a new situation, her children become confused and bewildered. Naturally they become noisy; time runs out and little is accomplished. Result, Miss Y is discouraged and drops her experiment. But, as in all fairy tales, we still have Miss Z. She, too, is looking for some way to provide for the difference in reading ability among the thirty-six children in her classroom. Miss Z plans with her children, and together they set up two groups. After both teacher and pupils become more experienced with the device, another group is formed. Result, Miss Z is able to organize her room and class in one way to meet some of their varied problems.

There is no detailed recipe or paper pattern to put down and cut around. Each one of us must adapt the basic procedures to fit the varying needs of

* From Willa T. Wynn, "How To Teach a Class Grouped for Differentiation in Basal Reading," *Report of the Ninth Annual Conference on Reading* (Pittsburgh: Univ. of Pittsburgh Press, 1953), pp. 128–37. Reprinted by permission of the author and Donald L. Cleland, Director of the Reading Laboratory at the University of Pittsburgh.

our class from time to time. There is no *best* method that will work for everyone and everyplace. The success of our device, according to Tinker, depends largely upon the following six points:

"1. the professional competence of the teacher
2. the availability of materials
3. the range of ability and age of the group
4. the experience and interest of the children
5. the specific needs
6. the amount of experience the children have had in working together." [1]

The *Cincinnati Primary Manual* [2] recommends that a class have three groups of from twelve to fifteen each. The slowest group should be the smallest, if possible. Each group should have about forty minutes of systematic instruction daily—in two periods, one in the morning and one in the afternoon. Besides this basal instruction, there is time for functional reading, recreatory reading, and also special corrective work.

A very important factor is the physical arrangement of the room itself. Hildreth, in *Readiness for School Beginners,* [3] says, "In modern classrooms for beginners the atmosphere is that of a workshop or playcenter." There should be attractive pictures, picture books, blocks, materials for drawing, painting, and construction work, woodworking tools, a work bench, easels, bulletin boards, dolls, and a seemingly endless list of toys, clay, nails, and so forth. If possible a primer-type typewriter, a phonograph and records, a radio, a piano, and low tables and chairs

are desirable. In arranging the various centers of interest the teacher should keep the following questions in mind:

"1. Are the arrangements best for the activities in mind?
2. Is friction created by lack of space?
3. Are there sufficient passageways? Is the fire exit free?
4. Is the lighting good—especially where the reading circle and reading table or library are located?
5. Are needed materials accessible?
6. Are storage spaces suitable?
7. Are noisy activities away from quiet activities?
8. Is display space adequate?" [3]

All in all we strive to create an informal social atmosphere. The materials which the children use should be within their reach. If shelves are not available, the old reliable orange crate may be used to advantage. The reading circle should be located away from traffic lines, but near board space with an easel and a table easily reached, for there are times when the smaller children need the support of the table for the large-size workbook pages. It is considered an unwise practice to seat children in groups according to ability. Such segregation tends to emphasize and make groups inflexible. Mixed seating arrangements make for better social relations.

But beyond the furnishings and the physical equipment, the children's progress is greatly influenced by the atmosphere created by the teacher's attitude. If the teacher feels at ease and is encouraging, the children are more friendly and responsive.

Naturally, the first weeks are spent in learning to know the children. The first-grade teacher will want to discover which children are ready to read and which are not. After the children have become acquainted with the school, the teacher, and their classmates, some one of the Readiness tests should be given. Those children who have never been to school before should be given an Intelligence test also. Meanwhile, physical factors should be checked—in most schools this is taken care of by the School Doctor, Dentist, and Nurse. The home background—the language or languages spoken by the family, the family status—books and toys in the home, experiences the child has had, the trips taken, places visited noted for each child—not in questionnaire form but by listening to the children talk and observing how they work and play together in the classroom and on the playground. It has been suggested that this accumulated information be placed in a notebook using one page for each child. I have tried several ways of keeping the findings so they are handy and usable. I find that the 5 by 8 filing cards prove the most usable for me. They are durable, not too big, and can be shuffled and re-sorted more conveniently. Above the first grade the teacher may find much information on records of each child. Some schools are now using a Reading record card, also. This shows the books or parts of books read by each child and also the Achievement test scores. But it will also prove valuable to make an informal survey of her own to find each child's reading level. (Things do happen over the summer vacation period that may change the child's attitudes.) Those whose performances show that they are below the grade level should have more thorough testing to diagnose their difficulties.

The groups within a first grade might include some children ready for initial instruction in reading a group which needs help in visual and auditory discrimination before being introduced to the reading process; and a third group of immature, slower-learning children who will probably need a longer, intensive readiness period. Classes vary greatly, as you well know. For instance, last year I started out with a class of forty-one children. Their I.Q.'s ranged from 56 to 138; M.A.'s from 3-9 to 7-10; three spoke little or no English; eleven had serious speech problems which needed the attention of the Speech Correctionist; two had poor hearing; four were definitely left-handed while two others still showed no definite hand-preference; and one showed symptoms of a visual problem. The results of the Metropolitan Readiness Tests and observation of the children showed that eight were ready for reading, seventeen scored low normal, and sixteen rated poor risk for reading instruction. At first, this class grouped itself into four sections—one reading group and three readiness groups—with emphasis on language, visual and auditory discrimination. These groups were very flexible. There were some children who belonged to all three of the readiness groups for a time at least. Later a second group proved ready to start reading. About Christmas time a third group started on their first pre-primer. The fourth group did not start the pre-primers until late in January.

One of the most perplexing problems confronting primary teachers is the matter of the children who must work alone while one group works under the teacher's supervision. The best advice I have been able to get was given by Miss Agnes Burke of Columbia University. Miss Burke told us how she introduced and developed what we have grown accustomed to calling "Quiet Time." Since then, the Association for Childhood Education has published a very helpful *Portfolio for Primary Teachers* containing twelve leaflets. Number Eight is called *When Children Work Alone.*[4]

"The day comes when the teacher feels that she can introduce a quiet time successfully. Having in mind three or four rather definite things which the children can do with a minimum of leaving of seats and without asking help from anyone, she tells the children, 'This afternoon I need to do a little writing, so I shall not be able to help you with your work. Will you please plan to do something that you can do without asking for help?' Then she discusses possibilities with the children and helps them make their choices. She has already planned for and made accessible most of the needed materials. When all are at work, she sits down with pencil and paper and takes notes, indicating which children are having difficulty following quiet time plans and what she can do to help the situation. After a few moments, before any child has had an opportunity to become disorderly, she puts away pencil and paper, thanks the children, commends them for working well, takes them out of doors for a good rollicking game.

"In planning the next day's quiet time she takes advantage of the notes she had taken the day before and forestalls some of the difficulties. Always she takes plenty of time to see that the children have good, stimulating ideas to carry out, that they can carry them out without assistance, that the children have the material they need and that the period is short enough to be successful, for these are the means by which she teaches the children to use a quiet time. Gradually she lengthens the time and builds up, with the children, standards of behavior.

"At first the teacher spends all of her quiet time studying to make it a satisfying and successful one for the children. When habits are pretty well established and the children are learning to take care of themselves, she may say, 'Today I would like to talk with Bobby while you are working. We will talk very softly so we will not disturb your work,' and she spends the time giving lisping Bobby extra help. She works with individuals or with a few children until she feels she needs to pay little attention to the children at their seats, then she gradually forms her reading groups. Often time is taken after each reading class to give all the children in the room the recreation of a jolly game and before each class the teacher looks at the children's work to enjoy it with them and to re-stimulate efforts with questions and comments."

It is very important that this quiet time result in helpful attitudes toward work and in habits that improve schoolroom living. A quiet time in which children work alone gives the children a chance to use their time wisely, to finish what they undertake, and to rely on themselves. The need for comparative quiet is talked over with the children. They suggest, discuss, and decide upon any rules or standards to be made. Last fall, after several building block *crashes* had interrupted our small group game of Listen, the class finally made the rule—Building blocks are for Work Time, not Quiet Time. Likewise, for several reasons which they discussed, regular clay was also limited to Work Time and plastic or green Clay placed on the Quiet Time list. One of the characteristics of the Six-Year-Old is that he has difficulty in making decisions, so many teachers arrange to assign work to be completed to the best of the child's ability before any other work may be taken. Before the day is over the assigned work is shown, enjoyed, discussed, evaluated, and used for whatever purpose it was made. Sometimes, practice exercises are given as quiet time work. Great care must be taken to see that the children understand what they are to do, and are able to do it. Otherwise, they will practice and learn incorrect habits and skills and perhaps learn to dislike reading. There are many ways to insure correct responses. Several sets of self-correcting materials have been published. *Puzzle Plans* is one example. Teacher made materials for quiet time practice should be made self-correcting, for practice makes perfect that which is practiced.

The task of providing for independent activities is one of the major problems confronting primary, and especially first-grade, teachers. Non-readers must take their turns working alone also. A few of the activities they may carry out successfully are:

1. Draw a picture about something that was discussed by the group.
2. Make a picture book. Look for pictures of dogs in the magazines on the shelf. Cut them out and paste in the scrap book being made by their group.
3. Copy or trace child's own name. Use carbon paper.
4. Classify pictures. Two kinds placed in a manila envelope.
5. Simple puzzles.
6. Sort objects as to size and color.
7. Sort pictures by initial sounds.
8. Draw pictures to verbal directions.

The work assigned should be interesting, challenging, and suited to the individual needs and abilities. It should reinforce the work of the classroom. After reading is begun, a larger variety of activities may be used. Exercises and games pairing pictures and words; classifying pictures; puzzles somewhat more complicated; directions given to make something; answering yes and no questions about a story read. Numerous writing experiences—copying a short story — illustrating it; writing notes to sick classmates, invitations, making labels or signs, and so on. Workbook exercises may be used by some of the children as independent work after the first item on the page is done under the teacher's supervision and the children clearly understand what is required. Usually, the slower learning children need supervision on the entire page to make the activity worthwhile.

Our Pittsburgh System provides us with a number of printed exercises called Reading Readiness exercises. These were worked out by a committee of teachers and are of great assistance. Our Section on Elementary Education under Dr. Elizabeth Graf and her assisting supervisors held a series of Workshops for Teachers-in-Service. One of these was devoted to Seatwork. For about five meetings teachers discussed, exchanged, or pooled their ideas and problems. Although attendance was purely voluntary, the workshops were well attended and proved very valuable.

At the second and third grade level, we find still more variety in the independent activities. The children may be asked to:

1. Arrange a group of sentences in sequences to tell a story.
2. Find all the root or base words in the story they are reading.
3. Arrange the new words of the story in alphabetical order.
4. Match words of opposite meanings.
5. Match words of similar meanings.
6. Pick out the sentence that best tells what the paragraph is about.
7. Match words with meanings.
8. Divide words (from the story) into syllables.
9. Solve crossword puzzles from the story.
10. Write the compound words in the story.

No matter which of the basal series your school uses, you will find the Teacher's Guide or manual of great assistance. In all fairness to the series and to yourself, the manual should be consulted. Many students and beginning teachers have the attitude that any use of the manual shows a lack of initiative and creativeness. The suggestive helps have been the work of experts in the field and the ideas have been proved by use. Much spade work has already been done for you. With so many individuals for whom to provide, any additional ideas are welcome. However, on the other hand, I do not subscribe to any slavish following of the manual. No system of reading can possibly take the place of the creative teacher who knows how to capitalize on her own situation. We should tailor the good thinking of the experts to fit our own group of children. Many helpful ideas are to be found in the manuals. One particular guide gives three different sets of suggestions for presenting the basic material to slow, average, and superior groups.

In a basal series each step is vital to sequential learning. All too often children in the superior group skip steps in the skills program and spend more time on the enrichment activities. The ability to maintain their superior rate of progress at later levels will depend in part upon the development of a step-by-step sequence of skills that can be used to unlock new and more difficult work. Dull drill is not necessary but the ideas and process should be made clear. In like manner, the slower group may need more time for vocabulary building, re-teaching, and checking and any or all steps may take longer to develop; but these children should not be deprived of the poetry and other creative activities if they are to achieve social-emotional maturity. We must expect some children to take longer than others, but all should have their chance to succeed. Slow children may need more than one period or presentation to master an item. With flexible grouping, a child may join another group temporarily. A child who has missed out on a skill through absence may work with another group until he has caught up or bridged the gap in the sequence of his learning.

To individualize instruction and provide the environment in which every child will find what he needs, it is necessary to provide meaningful learning experiences: films, filmstrips, demonstrations, excursions, picture books, books, and many opportunities for dictating and then reading stories of the experiences they are having. The child's progress in reading can be no faster than his ability to talk intelligently and to think with words. At one of our previous conferences it was brought out that language develops first and that reading ability depends upon linguistic ability.

No commercially prepared material can do as much for the beginning or the slower-learning reader as the class developed chart which influences more than just the reading-side of the child. The chart, based upon experience, is close to everyday living and therefore is personally important; it is prepared co-operatively and helps develop responsible members of the group. For the slower reading groups the reading experience charts provide excellent opportunity to assist in acquiring ad-ditional and difficult vocabulary. Chart reading is not a complicated form of reading, but children are eager to read their own stories. Charts help the child catch on to the fact that reading is talk written down.

Chart making is not unduly time consuming, if the necessary equipment is at hand.

Flexibility is the key to success in using the device known as grouping. Large blocks of time are needed. A tentative time schedule should be set up as a guide. Time devoted to each group may vary, for a point should be clinched at the proper moment. Tomorrow the group that was cut short today may have extra time. The growth and development of the children should be always in mind. Sixes and Sevens need physical variety in their activities; it is essential that frequent changes are possible. I find it a good plan to discuss with the class in the morning planning time what is to be done and with them plan the schedule for the group turns. No group has priority and no one group should always be last. Sixes like to know what they are going to do; sudden changes upset them. The teacher should have a tentative schedule worked out so that group lessons may be balanced. For satisfactory development, each child must find something at which he can succeed, so because the low average and slow learner may not be able to achieve much success in the complex area known as reading, we must help him find success in perhaps music, art, or recreational activities.

Just as the first-grade teacher found her children at various stages of readiness, so the second-grade teacher must expect variations in reading ability, necessitating divisions in her class. And so on, all along the line, differences seem to multiply. The *Cincinnati Primary Manual* [2] recommends that a third-grade class have a daily period of systematic instruction in addition to as much as two hours of activities closely related to reading. For pupils reading below grade expectancy, two periods of systematic instruction should be provided. As stated previously, grouping has long been standard practice at the primary level with the number varying from three to five. At the intermediate level, the general tendency is toward two groups. Logically, it seems to me, if education tends to increase individual differences, more groups would be necessary. But I shall leave that question to be discussed by more experienced "intermediates."

According to Dr. Albert J. Harris, in the *Reading Teacher* for September 1951,[5] "the published reports of programs involving grouping for reading instruction show substantially better results than those with undifferentiated instruction." With classes averaging from thirty-five to forty-five in number, individual instruction is impossible to attempt. So far, grouping has been the next best answer. Of course to many observers or teachers who have not given it a fair trial, the procedure

bears close resemblance to a three-ring circus. There are times, too, when the teacher wishes she were twins or triplets. Somewhere I remember reading this little commentary:

"Is this type of teaching easy for the teacher? No. But it is gratifying because of the real growth shown by the boys and girls. She knows, too, that any teaching or experiences *short* of a well-balanced program is synonymous with the story told of an old man sitting on his back doorstep fishing in a mud puddle. When asked what he was doing, he replied, 'Fishing.' 'But, don't you know there are no fish in that puddle?' he was asked. 'Yep,' replied the old man, 'but it's so convenient.'"

REFERENCES

1. TINKER, MILES A. *Teaching Elementary Reading,* Appleton, Century, Crofts, 1952.
2. CINCINNATI PRIMARY MANUAL. *Bulletin No. 95,* Cincinnati Public Schools.
3. HILDRETH, GERTRUDE. *Readiness for School Beginners,* World Book Co., 1950.
4. ASSOCIATION FOR CHILDHOOD EDUCATION. *Portfolio for Primary Teachers, No. 8 When Children Work Alone.*
5. HARRIS, ALBERT J. *The Reading Teacher,* September, 1951.

33. GROUPING HELPS CHILDREN SUCCEED IN THE INTERMEDIATE GRADES*

Marie B. Clark

SHOW me a child who is happy in school and I'll show you one who feels that he is an important member of a group, one who is conscious of personal achievement.

Teachers of grades four, five, and six know that in every classroom there is a wide range in the abilities, interests, and experience backgrounds of the many Johns, Marys, Sues, and Pauls who trip hopefully back to school in September. The "new" teacher holds the key to another year of adventure for these children and she will be held largely responsible for the growth and achievement, the happiness and security which they attain. Because teachers differ as widely as children in amount and kind of training, in energy, in resourcefulness, and in temperament, the effectiveness of any program—and of the reading program in particular—depends largely upon the teacher herself. The plan which works well for one may be quite difficult for another.

A plan which does not work at all is to have all children in the grade, be it fourth, fifth, or sixth, reading the same material. We are agreed that these children have widely different interests,

* From Marie B. Clark, "Grouping Helps Children Succeed in the Intermediate Grades," *Teachers Service Bulletin in Reading*, Vol. XIV, No. 1 (October, 1952). Reprinted by permission of the author and The Macmillan Co., New York, N.Y.

abilities, and backgrounds. It follows necessarily that different materials and different approaches must be used to teach them all to read successfully.

Each day, as I face the children in my classroom, I am deeply moved by the conviction that every child has a right to his share of my help; that he not only expects to succeed, but also needs to do so; that he wants to read and read well; and that I am the one who must open the doors of learning to him in such a way that his hopes are realized.

Who is he?

I. He is the average child in the classroom. By average, I mean that his ability, his interest, and his past experience make it possible for him to carry the normal load for his grade level.

II. He is the below-average child. His reading ability may be two or more levels below his grade placement. Because of emotional insecurity, defective eyesight or hearing, prolonged illness, or delayed readiness for the school program, he is not quite able to carry the regular work. He will need much extra help.

III. He is the gifted child—one might call him the neglected child. It has been said that about one percent of the school population have Intelligent Quotients of 130 or above. Approximately half of these gifted children do not go to college. Many of them do not even go successfully through the grades. Too often the gifted child becomes bored or creates a discipline problem because he can read material two to six grades above his average classmate; his ability is not challenged, his interest is not stimulated, and so he develops undesirable study habits. As a result his work begins to lag behind that of his classmates who may actually have less ability. It is time that we did something constructive to develop and use the abilities of this group.

If reading instruction is to be effective for all these children of different abilities, grouping within the classroom is a *MUST*. How it is done depends upon the teacher and her training, the size of the classroom, the size of the enrollment, the materials available, and so forth. There should never be more groups than a teacher can handle at one time. Generally speaking, three is a workable number.

If possible, the furniture in the classroom should be so arranged that it is conducive to groupings. Tables and chairs or movable desks can be easily arranged. Screwed-down desks can be mounted on strips and arranged in a hollow square, double circles, or small groups. Or, the desks can be screwed to the floor after they have been arranged in group situations.

Grouping at the intermediate level may be according to the skills to be developed. These include: reading for information, recalling facts, noting details, predicting outcomes, finding the central idea, proving statements, outlining, summarizing, skimming, drawing conclusions, using the dictionary, developing word analysis (root word, prefixes, suffixes), and using various attacks in word recognition.

The most effective grouping takes into account children's interests. Boys and girls in grades four, five, and six are interested in everything—animals, science, mystery, adventure, biography, fancy, myths, current events, history, home, school, humorous stories—so there is ample choice for groupings. Whatever method is used, the grouping must be flexible so that no child will feel embarrassment because of his placement and so that every child may be an active participant in several groups. A classroom atmosphere which encourages children to ask questions and find out for themselves is conducive to such flexible grouping. Interesting pictures, a library corner, bulletin boards changed often, science tables, display and storage shelves, plants, aquarium, terrarium, a workshop corner all help stimulate interest in various fields.

The teacher should use the results of standardized tests, intelligence tests, diagnostic tests, individual cumulative records passed along by the previous teacher, as well as her own observation of each child's reading behavior in determining the level of instruction for the groups. Systematic reading instruction, based upon a careful analysis of reading habits and using materials within the reading level of the various groups, is necessary for the achievement of good results. Let us assume that we mean good results for every child, not for just a few. Within every group there is need for attention to individual differences which can not be overlooked. Until the child is provided with material he can read, both his time and the teacher's are wasted. Durrell says, "A selection is considered too difficult if the child has difficulty with more than one word in twenty, or if he reads in a slow, labored manner." [1] Therefore, the material on which the group is to start work should be less difficult than this.

The manuals accompanying basal texts have a wealth of research and good teaching techniques behind them, and each particular reading series has a consistent plan of vocabulary and skill development. These make it possible for teachers to shift a child from one group to another as his needs and achievement vary. The manuals list books and selections for extended reading.

Let us presume that for a particular class a basal text is used and that there are three groups. Three short reading periods are not satisfactory, but every teacher can have at least two groups a day for special instruction. The children in the below-average group are a part of the entire class and need to be recognized as such. Those children want the regular text whether they can read it or not. They will be happy, reading in a different book, if they can still take part in the discussion with those of higher reading levels. This can easily be managed if the teacher will use the "each one teach one" method. An above-average child in the sixth grade will enjoy taking one child or a small group over to the reading table and reading the story

to them. Then, during the discussion or sharing period, each child will be able to make his contribution.

The superior group does not need as much supervised help from the teacher, but will have more time for extended reading activities: reference work, extensive reading in relation to the story, perhaps reading the entire book from which a selection is taken, doing recreatory reading, creating dramatizations, illustrating parts of the story, working in clay, developing marionette or puppet shows, making the marionettes and puppets themselves, and helping slower-learning children to get the story. This group, however, does need specific instruction in order to develop further their skills in reading. This is especially necessary in those school systems where systematic reading instruction ends with the sixth grade. In these schools the sixth-grade teacher must be certain that all the children in her class master the essential reading skills before they leave the grade. The average group will need more help from the teacher. The slower group will need intensive daily help.

While the average and above-average groups are given instruction, the slower group will have a study time for work-type lessons or extended reading. While the average group is being aided by the teacher, the upper group may help the lower one. While the average and below-average groups are being guided by the teacher, the superior group extends its reading in various ways, reads widely in areas related to the story, or does free or recreatory reading. Every third day or so, the three groups meet together,

[1] Durrell, Donald D., *Improvement of Basic Reading Abilities* (Yonkers-on-Hudson, New York: World Book Co., 1940).

after they have had sufficient preparation for participation. Different groups may present various interpretations of the story; or they may re-create it for school assembly, the sharing period, or another group.

For the enjoyment of poetry, which all children love if it is presented well, all three groups may be taught together. This is particularly good for the listening period. Then grouping may be effected on the basis of collecting poems the children like, creating original ones, or just hearing more read by the teacher or a good reader. All creating of poetry should be absolutely voluntary without any fear of threat or failure. The time has passed when children *had* to learn a certain selection or *had* to "make up" a poem. Every effort should be made to help children feel relaxed and comfortable during the poetry sessions. As they begin to feel the rhythm and the musical quality of what is being read, they will begin to enjoy poetry.

To enrich the basic reading program, it is wise to have not only sets of supplementary readers for group reading, but also one or two copies of many different books varying widely in interest range and level of reading difficulty. It is more fun to share a story or to listen to one if it is different from all the others. Teachers have seen children literally wilt because some child gave the exact story, report, or news that another one had planned to give.

Science and social studies offer excellent opportunities for re-grouping or for committee work. Herein lies the advantage of grouping *within* the classroom rather than *by* classrooms. It's fun to work with John and Harry in reading because they read about as well as George does, but George likes working science experiments with Howard and Guy, and in social studies it's fun to have some girls on the committee, too. These arrangements are possible because there are a dozen books with science experiments, about animals, the new plastics, television, magazine articles about the stars, airplanes, radar, space ships, and so on. Within the group, each child can find material which he can read and interpret and which is different from all the others. One committee from each group goes to the school or public library to get more materials on the area under discussion. With so much available, browsing really is fun.

A class in social studies, for another example, is studying China. Committees are chosen for various sections. "How chosen?" one asks. Therein lies a method many teachers neglect to use. Let the children choose the part on which they want to work; then help them find material they can use. There will be homes, ways of travel, schools, religion, government, the war, ways of making a living, natural resources, games and entertainment, customs, and many other phases. Material may be gathered from social studies books and readers from third-grade level up, through reference books, stories of Chinese life, newspaper articles, magazine stories, movies, filmstrips, and so forth. Globes, maps, pictures are invaluable aids also. The material available is unlimited to the wide-awake teacher who groups children according to interests and finds materials within their abilities. This cannot be done if every child is expected to do what everyone else does; if the slow learner is frustrated because the material is too difficult; if the gifted child is held back to the level of the average because the teacher "can't find enough hours in a day."

Reading is a systematic development of skills, an extension of interests, hobbies, and so on, based upon the needs, abilities, interests, and experience of children, and no one ever "gets through." Reading is not a race nor is it a mold through which all must pass. Reading does make for individual progress and consistent growth.

How to group children depends upon the teacher's training and understanding. Grouping children is just as necessary in grades four, five, and six as it is in the primary grades; it is possible to do whether classes are large or small; it contributes to emotional security better if done within the classroom rather than by classrooms; groups must be flexible to be most effective. Teachers find such grouping a sure way to help every child succeed.

34. EVERY CHILD READS SUCCESSFULLY IN A MULTIPLE-LEVEL PROGRAM*

Kathleen B. Hester

EFFECTIVE grouping of children for instructional purposes is one of the most powerful keys to succesful reading. When differences in reading achievement of children within a classroom began to be recognized in the 1920's, teachers started to assemble children into "fast," "average," and "slow" groups. After a short time, parents began to resent having their

* From Kathleen B. Hester, "Every Child Reads Successfully in a Multiple-Level Program," *Elementary School Journal*, LIII (October, 1952), 86–89. Reprinted by permission of the author and The University of Chicago Press.

children labeled as "slow" learners. To overcome this difficulty, teachers attempted to camouflage the groups by allowing the children to select their own group names, as "Birds," "Butterflies," and "Bees." The pupils themselves were not misled by such names. To give an example, one child said to a special teacher, "Are you going to work with me?" When the teacher replied that she was, the child continued, "You don't need to bother because I am in the 'dumb' group."

This type of grouping takes care of differences by means of acceleration only. It implies that every child has the same needs and that the difference is merely in how slowly or how rapidly the material is covered. Yet research studies tell us that various children have different needs.

Providing for Individual Differences

Numerous studies on child growth and development have been conducted in recent years. The findings indicate that the growth pattern of each child varies from time to time and is different from that of other children. If reading is to be one of the means used to help the child achieve his maximum growth, the teacher must recognize the varying needs of children and must pace each pattern of growth by supplying instructional materials in accordance with the needs and interests of each child. The reading program must be set up to help every child feel secure in his school life and develop gradually and successfully into a competent, self-confident person.

If teachers accept this philosophy, it becomes necessary for them to do more than give lip service to the idea of providing for individual needs. They can no longer set up three or four reading groups among which the only differentiation is that of speed in covering the material. Providing for individual need means that the teacher must adapt the instructional program to fit each child in the classroom. This is not so difficult as it appears at first. It does not mean that each child must be taught separately. It *does* mean that the teacher must provide a flexible plan of grouping, since the needs of a child may vary from day to day.

The teacher of the elementary-school classroom says, "That is good theory, but how can it be done with thirty-five or forty children?" To find out, let us examine a few of the classrooms where the reading program is flexible enough to give each child the specific help he needs for maximum growth and development. These teachers, in both urban and rural schools, are enthusiastic about the excellent results obtained, not only in producing better readers, but in producing happy, well-adjusted children.

Classroom Experiments

Application in an urban school. Mrs. P., a first-grade teacher in a large city in southern Michigan, met the needs and interests of her children through "invitational reading classes." A glance at Mrs. P.'s diary shows the typical problems of a first-grade teacher.

It was late in the afternoon of September 6 when I entered the last child's name in my class book, and I stopped to reflect for an instant as to why! oh, why! had my mother ever consented to let me become a teacher.

As I glanced over the names, bits of information came back to me, given the first day of school by well-meaning parents, such as: "Billy is allergic to most everything; here is his medicine; it must be given every day at 10:30, and oh, yes, he will need a shot once a day. I will bring the hypodermic needle tomorrow. Please do not give it to him in front of the other children; he is very sensitive."

Another, "Be sure and let Jimmy go to

the toilet whenever he wants to go. We have never insisted on habits at home. He still wets his bed at night and is very nervous."

Then, "Here is my son. I hope you can do something with him. He is spoiled, we know, but he is our baby."

And finally came big, smiling Ted, all alone. He had been a failure according to all reports, and this was to be his second year in the first grade. There was a question about his mental ability.

There were others with problems but only these seemed to stand out very clearly. What was I going to do?

Mrs. P. observed the children carefully and noted on check sheets bits of information about mental, social, emotional, physical, and educational factors concerned with readiness. Standardized reading-readiness tests were given later. The following information was recorded:

I found there were eighteen children with scores between 50 and 64, which meant they were ready for reading and were rated high; one with a score of 38, which is average; and eleven below 35, in the low grouping bracket. Eight of these eleven would not be six years old until November. The scores ranged from a perfect score of 64 to a double zero, which means twenty-eight points below the lowest possible score marked on the test.

Mrs. P. set up three groups, as she had done in previous years. The results were unsatisfactory. She summed up the situation in the following way:

My poor little average pupils did not have a chance with the "ready to read." My below-average pupils didn't care if they ever learned to read. And I was slowly losing my mind.

It was at this time Mrs. P. sought help. Plans were made to experiment with the multiple-level instructional plan, or, as the children call it, "reading by invitation." Consent was readily given by the elementary supervisor and by the principal. The parents were very much pleased with the plan.

To inaugurate the program, several interest centers were set up in the room. Peg boards, colored pegs, colored beads and strings, puzzles, clay, and drawing paper were provided. A library corner was set apart, with two portable screens, two tables, four chairs, two davenports, two bookcases (all constructed from orange crates and painted royal blue and cherry red), and a floor lamp. Attractive books were placed on the table and in the bookcases. A doll, a doll buggy, and play dishes were put in a playhouse in this corner, also. A painting easel afforded even the spoiled baby a chance to express himself.

Three reading classes were started: one which provided readiness work preparatory to beginning reading; a second in which more advanced readiness work was done; and a third in which formal reading instruction was given. During a pupil-teacher planning period, the children were told they might come to any or all of the reading groups, stay as long as they wanted, and leave when they were ready, provided that they found a useful occupation elsewhere in the room.

Once a week, on a day chosen at random, each child was given an opportunity to tell a story he had read or to read the story written on the blackboard during the course of a "sweep-check" vocabulary test. The story on the blackboard contained all the new words introduced during the week. The checkup was not compulsory, but, after fourteen weeks of school, the pupils who had not wanted to look at a book in September were asking their turns to read or to tell about what they had read. The results were gratifying. By January every child in the room was reading successfully at his level. The child who had received a double zero on the standardized reading-readiness test was attending every reading class. Every afternoon at dismissal time he would ask, "Do we have to go home now?" The child whose mental ability had been questioned was a well-adjusted boy who was reading successfully at primer level. Needless to say, the parents were strongly in favor of continuing the program.

Application in rural schools. Rural teachers who teach nine grades—beginners through the Grade 8—have used the multiple-level instructional program to meet the needs of each child in the school. Mr. Mac, who teaches a one-room school in rural Michigan, says of his work:

One year ago I was not as pleasant a teacher as I could be. I would not greet the children enthusiastically in the morning. I dreaded their coming to school. It meant seven trying hours and a good headache. My program was stiff and uninteresting. Today I am enjoying teaching, and, more important, my happiness has been reflecting in the children.

This change in attitude was brought about by the improved reading program. The usual number of reading classes were set up. At a meeting with the parents, the present-day philosophy of reading instruction was ex-plained. Parents were helped to understand that reading-growth patterns of children vary, just as do their physical-growth patterns. The parents were asked to co-operate in the work, and the program was discussed with the children, also. Mr. Mac describes the working of the program in this way:

Our reading classes have changed from what they used to be. A fourth-grader may be found with a third-grade reading class, but this is his own choice. I do not force children to attend reading classes composed mainly of younger pupils; I invite them. Sometimes they refuse; sometimes they accept. Those that accept come with no inferior feeling, and we enjoy our reading classes to the utmost. Those who refuse at first soon join in because of the fun we have.

Many times a child who has been absent chooses to attend several reading groups until he has "found himself" again.

Mrs. B. has met similar success in her one-room rural school. She says:

The value of grouping children according to their reading needs has been brought more forcibly to my attention. I have found that my children enjoy reading more, read with less nervous tension, and are more interested in learning to read when they are reading at their own levels. They do not feel they are being forced to do something that is too hard for them to do.

How the Children Are Grouped

The multiple-level instructional program allows the pupils to join any group or groups that meet their needs. It is explained to the pupils that everyone has specific reading needs. If pupils find the work too difficult in the group which they normally attend, they are invited to work with a group of pupils who are reading at a lower level. If one group is working on a specific reading skill, such as vocabulary development or some aspect of comprehension, any child who feels he can profit by the work is free to join them. In this manner the groups are flexible. The children soon become able to select the group or groups which best meet their needs. Many times a child chooses to work in two or more groups to satisfy his needs. There is no feeling of inferiority.

Many teachers question the ability of the children to select wisely. After trying the plan, however, they are soon convinced that often children sense their own weaknesses more accurately than do teachers. The basic psychological principle of success functions. A child, just as an adult, will participate in, profit by, and enjoy, work in which he is successful. Just as teachers welcome an opportunity to join a group working on a problem that is troubling them, so are children happy for the chance to gain the help they need for greater success.

35. "READING LEVELS" REPLACE GRADES IN THE NON-GRADED PLAN*

John I. Goodlad, Fred E. Brooks, Irene M. Larson, and Neal Neff

ALTHOUGH grade classifications have been removed from only a scattered few elementary schools in America, several ungraded plans have been in operation long enough to provide us with some guidelines for

* From John I. Goodlad, Fred E. Brooks, Irene M. Larson, and Neal Neff, " 'Reading Levels' Replace Grades in the Non-Graded Plan," *Elementary School Journal,* LVII (February, 1957), 253–56. Reprinted by permission of the author and The University of Chicago Press.

further development of what might become a trend. Three of these plans were selected for study with a view to seeing their development in some time perspective.

The original plans studied revealed a good many dissimilarities. Common to a number of them, however, was some attempt to relate children's progress to reading levels, which were determined largely from the basal reading series used. The Nathaniel

Hawthorne School in University City, Missouri, the Cabool Elementary School, also in Missouri, and most of the schools in Green Bay, Wisconsin, were found not only to be organized without grade levels but also to be cognizant of reading ability in classifying pupils.

It must be emphasized that organization of the elementary school around reading levels is not the only approach to the removal of grades. In fact, some exponents of non-grading maintain that rigorous attention to reading levels actually defeats the original intent of ungraded structure. In the discussion that follows, reading levels serve merely as a device for clarifying some of the problems and procedures that accompany the change to non-grading. They are not intended to prescribe the basis for establishing non-graded plans.

Getting Started

Non-grading apparently grows out of dissatisfaction with some other related aspect of schooling. At Green Bay, for example, first-grade teachers were dissatisfied with making promotion decisions regarding slow starters who were moving along nicely toward the end of the year but who still were not up to "grade" standard. At Cabool the present plan grew out of the demand of parents after a report-card committee of parents and teachers had labored together for months. Teachers and parents at Nathaniel Hawthorne School had difficulty in relating old methods of reporting to a developing concept of individualized, continuous pupil progress.

Apparently teachers want a model when they seek to replace long established practice with something new and, in the eyes of many, radical. Merely intellectualizing the desirability of change, no matter how specifically that change is conceived in the mind's eye, is not enough. Green Bay teachers studied reports of the Milwaukee plan, well established at that time, and also visited schools there and conferred with teachers and supervisors.

Significant change is not a unitary thing, conceived as a whole and transplanted in its totality from conception to implementation. Rather, an idea takes root, grows a little, and perhaps lies dormant for a time. But then, as soon as some outgrowth of the idea becomes operative, new ideas spring forth, and many kinds of changes follow. At Cabool the initial idea of a primary department grew almost immediately into an organization embracing three departments: primary, intermediate, and upper. At Green Bay two schools began with the organization of primary units. Others followed, one after another, until by September, 1955, the plan was in operation in eight of twelve schools. The Nathaniel Hawthorne teachers found the removal of grades to be just an early step in formulating a whole new concept of pupil progress and in effecting accompanying readjustment. The search for a way to trace and report the actual progress of children led to the identification of reading levels.

Reading Levels in Operation

The teachers of the Nathaniel Hawthorne School, in moving to an ungraded primary unit, wanted to maintain some concrete way of determining the actual progress of a given child. It was agreed from the beginning that (1) there should be flexible classification levels; (2) these levels should relate to the length of time a child had been in school; (3) these levels should in some way be related to the basic reading program being used; and (4) the classification system should be related to a standardized testing program.

The teachers soon found that they really had two classification problems: first, grouping to determine the classroom unit to which a child was to be assigned; second, grouping within a given classroom. In seeking answers to the first problem, the teachers developed the following general principles:

1. Pupils should stay with a teacher for a period of at least one year.
2. There should be a normal range of ability in each group.
3. Pupils should be grouped as closely as possible by chronological age.

A classification-index system based on semesters in school was established. Normally a child moves through Semester 6 in completing the primary unit at the end of the third year in school. Slower children, who took as long as four years to complete the classification unit normally completed in three, might be classified as "Semester 7" or "Semester 8."

In answering the second problem, that of grouping within a single classroom, a flexible system of reading levels was adopted. Standardized tests are given frequently to determine present reading performance, but these results are related to other indexes of maturity determined by the teacher. It is conceivable that a child will move through several reading levels in a given year.

At Nathaniel Hawthorne there are nine classification levels through which a child may proceed in completing the three-year primary unit:

Level R.—Pupil not able to read; readiness developed.

Level 1.—Preprimers and primers (testing at a grade level of approximately 1.6).

Level 2.—First readers and many supplementary readers of primer level (testing at a grade level of approximately 2.0).

Level 3.—Second reader with four or five first readers that can be read with fluency and comprehension (testing at approximately 2.6).

Level 4.—Second readers with several easier second readers read with fluency and comprehension (testing at approximately 3.2).

Level 5.—Third readers with many easy high-level second readers read with fluency and good comprehension; child displays good word attack and some independent reading (testing at approximately 3.8).

Level 6.—High-level third-reader material with ability to read with fluency and good comprehension; child does independent reading (testing at approximately 4.2).

Levels 7 and 8.—These levels provide for pupils in the primary school who read well in library books and who read other textbooks, in areas such as social studies and science, with fluency and understanding.

We see, then, that a child classified as 5-7 is in the first semester of his third year at school, reading at the seventh level described above. Such a pupil obviously would go on into an intermediate unit or the fourth grade, whichever existed, at the end of the year. Another child, classified as 5-3, also is in the first semester of his third year at school, but he probably would continue in the primary school for a seventh or even eighth semester.

Children entering school at Cabool are tested during their second week to determine mental age and reading level. Then, after several weeks of observation, teachers in the primary department determine assignment of pupils to rooms and reading groups. Instructional materials and equipment are centralized and classified in order that teachers may locate quickly what they need in providing for the several levels to be found in a given room at any time.

Teachers in Green Bay schools date the time each reading level is reached. Parents are able to see progress as it occurs, instead of waiting a year and then perhaps being disappointed because actual progress is lost sight of in the face of retarded over-all attainment. Changes from group to group, either within classrooms or between classrooms, occur at any time on the basis of social adjustment to a group or of academic progress (mainly reading).

Change Brings Its Own Burdens

Some school practices have been with us a long time and are firmly intrenched. This is certainly true of the grade structure. During the past century, not only have pupils come to be classified by grades, but, in addition, courses of studies and textbooks have been so classified. Teachers have come to think of themselves as second- or fourth- or sixth-grade teachers and to conduct their professional affairs accordingly. *Unfortunately, many proponents of change do not appreciate fully and early enough just how firmly the graded concept is established in the minds of teachers and parents!*

Green Bay brought in the parents just as soon as the teachers were generally agreed on the professional soundness of the suggested plan. Mothers and fathers discussed all aspects of the proposal at evening meetings. But some parents and teachers still have difficulty in seeing that non-grading permits the use of realistic standards for children of widely varying abilities. Non-grading, properly conceived, most certainly is not a first step in the abandonment of standards.

The chief burden shouldered by educators in moving to non-grading is that of continuously educating parents and teachers to the plan. There are always new parents and, too frequently in schools today, new teachers. Few of them come from schools using ungraded schemes. As a result it is constantly necessary to interpret policies to the newcomers.

Initiating Non-Grading: a Word to the Wise

Are you contemplating moving from graded to non-graded structure? If so, those who have walked the road before you have a few words of advice.

1. Develop understanding first. A year or more of study by parents and teachers before any specific change is

made will pay rich dividends. Both groups need to understand the wide range of abilities and attainments represented in a first-grade class. Normally, under good teaching the spread increases instead of decreases as children advance. Teachers and parents must come to understand the barriers placed in the way of normal, continuous progress by the grade concept and its concomitants. They need to understand, too, what the removal of grades will and will not do.

2. Move toward non-grading a step at a time. Teachers may first be helped to divorce themselves from their grade stereotypes by moving along with their pupils into the next grade before ungraded units actually are established. In this way the teachers come to understand more readily the tremendous grade-to-grade overlap of abilities and attainments. There seems to be some advantage, also, in removing the grade barriers a year at a time as a first-year entering group begins to advance through the school. In a relatively short time—six to eight years—only transfer pupils will know what it is to deal with grades and the accompanying externally imposed pressures.

3. Try to see an actual model early in the planning. Some persons must see really to believe and understand. If the model is common to the experience of all, it provides a discussion base from which local plans may evolve more readily.

4. Once the step has been taken, go all the way. Removing grades in name only is not enough. Grade signs must be removed from doors and replaced with "Primary—Miss Smith,"

"Intermediate—Miss Brown." Progress must never be thought of in terms of "promotion and non-promotion" or "skipping and repeating." The considerations implied by these terms simply do not exist; they have no part in nongrading. This is difficult for some parents and teachers to understand— *very difficult!* Concepts of individuality, heterogeneity, continuous progress with each child moving at the rate that is best for him, must be hammered away at continuously!

5. Rigorous record-keeping and careful, periodic testing are essential. *Continuous* progress does not mean *haphazard* progress. Those persons in charge have a tremendous responsibility for assuring that each child is placed where he can profit most, where his progress in all aspects of development is optimum. Without careful observation, without periodic tests, without occasional shifting—group to group and class to class—children will be misplaced.

6. Stick to the instructional methods previously assumed to be sound. If the removal of grades suggests new and more appropriate methods, so much the better. But non-grading is an organizational, not an instructional, device.

7. Experiment. Determine what happens when children are moved through a four-year primary unit beginning with kindergarten in three rather than four years. Determine the effects of remaining in such a unit for five rather than four years. Seek to isolate the most significant factors determining satisfactory pupil placement. Find out what areas of instruction can be taken care of best through com-

pletely individualized methods, through small groups, and through total group techniques. Non-grading in itself is little more than door-opening. With the door open, look beyond to see what comes next in finding what we need to know and doing what we know to do.

36. MEETING CHILDREN'S READING NEEDS IN THE MIDDLE GRADES: A PRELIMINARY REPORT*

Cecil Floyd

I HAVE forty pupils in my fifth-grade room and forty-five minutes a day for basal reading instruction. Some of my pupils read on a second-grade level, and some on an eighth-grade level, and others on all levels in between. How am I going to provide for all these ranges or levels in my room in the time I have for reading instruction?"

Such statements are frequently made by teachers searching for the solution to the problem of caring for the wide range of reading abilities in Grades 4, 5, and 6. These teachers have been told by college instructors, by school supervisors, and by school administrators to provide reading instruction of such nature as to care for the individual differences of pupils. Teachers

* From Cecil Floyd, "Meeting Children's Reading Needs in the Middle Grades: A Preliminary Report," *Elementary School Journal,* LV (October, 1954), 99–103. Reprinted by permission of the author and The University of Chicago Press.

have been made to realize that in any grade they must expect to find children at various stages of development. These two factors have been recognized by all those who are concerned with teaching reading to children, but it has been difficult to put the ideas into practical programs.

Many attempts have been made to produce workable solutions to the problems arising in the classroom in which there is a disparity of reading levels. In some of these, two or three reading groups are found within a room. In others, remedial classes of one type or another have been used. In most cases the attempts have achieved rather mediocre results.

In any fourth-, fifth-, or sixth-grade class, pupils will be found who are able to read only second-grade material, while others are able to read eighth- or ninth-grade material. Children on or near the proper reading-grade level have usually received fairly adequate instruction, but this has not been true in the case of those who have deviated at either end of the scale. Obviously it is impossible for any teacher to teach thirty-five to forty-five children effectively in a short period of forty or fifty minutes a day when such great ranges of achievement exist.

During the past four years we in the Joplin public school system have been diligently at work on the reading curriculum. Modern materials and methods of instruction, well-trained teachers, and an in-service training program of many facets have been part of the reading curriculum. We felt that we had done much to improve the type of instruction that was being offered. In spite of all this, we realized that all children were not being given the opportunity to progress according to their potential rates and abilities. Some were not being sufficiently challenged, while others were still reading, or attempting to read, on the frustration level.

A Method of Procedure

In light of these conditions, a plan was conceived for an experiment to be conducted during the second semester of the 1952–53 school year in Grades 4, 5, and 6 of the Irving Elementary School. Several planning sessions were held with the principal and the teachers who were to conduct the experiment. At these sessions, decisions were reached as to methods, materials to be used, the part of parents in the program, and the explanation to be given to the pupils.

It was decided that the first step necessary was the determination of the reading levels of the pupils of Grades 4, 5, and 6. The Iowa Every-Pupil Tests of Basic Skills, Test A, Silent Reading Comprehension, Form L, Grades 3–5 and Grades 5–9, were chosen as the tests to be administered. Some of the fifth- and sixth-grade pupils with known ability took the fifth- to ninth-grade test. Previous school records, teachers' knowledge of children, results from previous tests, plus cumulative-record data, in addition to the test results, were considered in establishing the reading level for each child.

The average reading-grade level on the test for all fourth-grade pupils was 4.25; for the fifth grade it was 5.3; and for the sixth grade, 6.3. Since the tests were administered before the end of the fourth month of the 1952–53 school year, it was evident that all three grades were practically at the norm as shown by the reading tests. It was also evident that a wide range of abilities existed in each grade, making the task of adequately providing for all these levels a most difficult one for each teacher if the traditional organization were followed.

The teachers decided to use the period from 11:15 to noon each day for the basal instructional program. If the pupils were to be taught in groups, with all pupils in each group falling into a narrow reading-level range, it was found that provision must be made for at least nine groups. Since five teachers were to be included in the experiment, four of these teachers must of necessity teach two groups each. Table 1 shows the homogeneous grouping which was used as the method for forming classes for the basal instructional period. It was found that all these groups contained children from each of Grades 4, 5, and 6.

In addition to this forty-five-minute period, each teacher placed on her daily afternoon program a twenty-five minute period, during which a recreational-reading program was conducted. For this period, pupils remained with their regular classroom teacher, and the homogeneous grouping plan was not used. Materials on all levels of readability were furnished. Thus each child was still reading material on his reading level. Activities included not only guidance by the teacher in the selection of books to be read but also discussion periods, art periods pertaining to illustration of books and characters, and visits to the public library.

It was felt that, if the program were to be successful, it would be necessary to purchase new reading materials—materials which these children had not previously used. It is a well-known precept that a remedial-reading program, which this program would be for some children, is usually predestined to failure if materials are used with which the pupil has had previous frustration. Accordingly, it was decided to purchase a new series of basal materials on all grade levels from Grade 1 through Grade 7. In addition to this basal material, many other types of materials were also purchased for use by all groups.

An announcement was sent to the parents of all the pupils in Grades 4, 5, and 6, inviting them to attend a meeting at which the reading experiment was explained and discussed. A large percent of the parents attended this meeting. Parents were not told anything concerning the reading level of their children or how the groups were to be divided. They were told that we felt we could do a better job of caring for the needs of pupils by this type of organization, and they were asked to give their co-operation and to help evaluate the results of the

TABLE 1

Groups Established According to Reading-Grade Levels

Teacher and Group	Grade Range
Teacher 1	7.0–9.2
Teacher 2:	
Group 1	5.6–6.4
Group 2	6.5–6.9
Teacher 3:	
Group 1	4.4–5.2
Group 2	5.3–5.5
Teacher 4:	
Group 1	3.0–3.9
Group 2	4.0–4.3
Teacher 5:	
Group 1	1.1–1.7
Group 2	1.8–2.9

program. Questions were asked by the parents, and they unanimously expressed a willingness to do everything in their power to assist in the program. They were invited to visit the reading classes at any time.

Before putting the program into operation, an assembly was called at which a brief explanation of the procedure to be followed in the new reading program was made to the pupils. They were informed that a new and interesting plan was to be tried, and they were told to which teacher's room they were to go for their reading class.

It was decided to discontinue giving a mark in reading during the experiment, and a new type of report to parents was devised for this subject. The report included comments by the teacher concerning the pupil's progress in the following areas: word skills, oral reading, silent reading, number

TABLE 2

Average Gain in Reading-Grade Level for Each Grade after Four Months of Instruction

Grade	Reading-Grade Level		Gain in Months
	AT BEGIN-NING OF EXPERI-MENT	AT END OF EXPER-IMENT	
4	4.25	4.9	6.5
5	5.3	6.17	8.7
6	6.3	7.65	13.5

of recreational and supplementary books read, and suggestions and remarks. Another section of the report provided a space for comments by parents.

Evaluation of the Experiment

An attempt was made throughout the experiment to evaluate it objectively and subjectively.

Two weeks before the end of the semester, the Iowa Every-Pupil Test of Basic Skills, Test A, Silent Reading Comprehension, Form M, was administered. The experiment had then

been in progress for four months. Reading-grade levels ranged from 2.2 to 10.5. The average gain in reading-grade levels was computed for Grades 4, 5, and 6. Table 2 shows the gain in months of achievement for each grade.

Individual gains in reading achievement varied from a few months to more than two years. According to test results, one sixth-grader gained in reading-grade level from 1.9 to 4.2. A fourth-grader gained from 1.8 to 3.7. Practically all pupils made substantial gains.

The following were typical comments from parents:

This is a splendid program you have started. Every remark you made on Jim is true. Can you make any further suggestions for me to help him?

I believe this reading program is very successful. Joyce has enjoyed it so much, even anticipating it from day to day.

I am very proud of Sarah's work. I feel that she has taken more interest in reading. She reads a lot more at home now.

We think Irving School is fortunate in being the school to initiate this reading program.

I think the new reading program is a very fine thing, and accomplishes so much more.

Comments such as the following were heard from pupils:

This is a good book—I can really read it.

This is the first time I ever read a book all by myself.

I thought it was hard to learn to read very well, but it really isn't.

Teachers' reactions can be noted from such statements as:

I have never worked so hard, but I feel as if I am really achieving results.

It isn't difficult to remedy the troubles in reading for most children if you really know how.

So much more can be accomplished in the time allowed if you don't have so many levels to teach.

It was noticeable during the experiment that pupils were interested and enthusiastic. More reading and much wider reading were evident. Many pupils who had done little reading of recreational material in the past read several books each. As the reading ability of pupils improved, their work in various content subjects also improved. The progress and enthusiasm of those who possessed superior reading ability were marked. Often these pupils are the most retarded in terms of ability, and their acceptance of the challenge was gratifying.

Further experimentation will be made, using more pupils and teachers, a greater variety of materials, and careful evaluation in terms not only of achievement, but of personality traits, social behavior, emotional security, and the like. Following further experimentation a more accurate evaluation of the plan can be presented.

CHAPTER VII

INDIVIDUALIZED READING

37. WHAT IS INDIVIDUALIZED READING?*

Albert J. Harris

THE continuing popularity of the annual reading conferences here at the University of Delaware is a tribute to Dr. Stauffer's genius at selecting topics which are at the growing point in reading. For example, the 1950 conference on "Parents and Reading" was one which attracted nation-wide attention and has stimulated a great deal of thinking on this problem. Individualized reading is now one of the central issues in the whole area of reading instruction for those who are looking ahead. For this reason, it is highly appropriate that Delaware should once more take the lead in giving thoughtful consideration to an important new development.

Individualized reading can be de-

* From Albert J. Harris, "What Is Individualized Reading?" in *Individualizing Reading Instruction,* Proceedings of the 39th Annual Education Conference, Univ. of Delaware, VI (March, 1957), 12–17. Reprinted by permission of Russell G. Stauffer, Director of the Reading Study Center at the University of Delaware.

fined in a number of ways. To me it can be most adequately defined as follows: "A completely individualized reading situation is one in which no two children in the class are reading the same thing at the same time." (2) It is obvious that there can be many kinds of individualized reading plans and programs, some of which will be described briefly below.

Historical Development of Individualized Reading

The roots of individualized reading can probably be found in the tradition of European universities in which students "read" for a degree rather than accumulate courses. Attendance at lectures is in such universities an optional matter with the student, and he obtains his degree by passing a searching set of examinations rather than by spending a given amount of time at the university or taking a specified number of courses.

In the United States, there are several factors which seemed to have paved the way for a trend toward individualization in instruction. Perhaps the first and most important of these is our democratic emphasis upon the value and worth of the individual, in contrast to those societies of a totalitarian nature in which the individual as such has little or no value.

Certainly one of the major contributing factors has been the growing awareness of individual differences as studied systematically by psychologists. Starting with the pioneering work of Cattell in this country and Binet in France, marked individual differences were found in practically every human trait which could be measured. Immediately after the end of the first World War, group intelligence and achievement tests were developed which began to be used in the schools in the early 1920's. The pioneer test surveys of that era showed tremendous ranges in both ability and achievement, and a correspondingly high degree of overlapping in the abilities of children at different grade levels.

A third contributing factor was the growing interest in dynamic psychology. As psychologists became interested in problems of motivation and began to study the interests of children, one fact that showed up most impressively was the very wide range of individual likes and dislikes found among children of any age. Those who attempted to utilize this information in school practice actually moved in the direction of trying to find a variety of learning activities to suit the interests of individual children.

It would be a mistake to assume that all of the work on individual reading is very recent. As early as the middle 1920's, Lou La Brant was exploring the values of a free reading program in the high school associated with Ohio State University. (3) At about the same time, Carleton Washburne was beginning to introduce individualized teaching methods into the public schools of Winnetka, Illinois. (8) By the end of the 1930's there were several important contributions to this topic. In 1938 the annual yearbook of the *National Elementary Principal* (4) contained brief descriptions of several programs which were essentially individualized reading programs. During the same year Luella Cole published a book (1) which advocated essentially an individualized study skills method of teaching reading. The following year, Witty and Kopel (9) wrote eloquently on the values of an individualized reading program, particularly at the secondary school level. In 1940 Olson (5) put forth the ideas about individualized reading which have since become the basis for much work in this area. During the 1940's relatively little was written about individualized reading but a great deal of work continued to go on quietly in a number of places. During the last three years a marked increase in new publications and accounts has appeared.

Many Phases of the Reading Program Can Be Individualized

Probably the first approach to individualization in reading took place in the revolt against the uniform intensive study of a limited number of "masterpieces." Starting at the secondary school level, teachers began to explore the values of an extensive reading list from which the child could select a book on which to report, as compared to requiring that every student read exactly the same material as every other student. Emphasis in the free reading program was placed on the possibility of developing individual tastes and interests, and of making literature more vital and important in the lives of the students.

A second area in which individualization was introduced early was in the area of research and study. The development of the project method, with activity units, subdivision of responsibility among several pupils, individualized reading upon specific questions, and individual and group reports, tended to break the lock-step reliance upon the uniform textbook in content areas.

A third area in which individualization began to creep in was in the area of oral reading. Here the development of the "audience reading" procedure, in which one child reads an interesting selection while the rest of the class listens attentively as an audience, served both as an incentive to encourage wide individual reading and as a method of individualizing the oral reading program.

A fourth major type of individualized reading has been the use of at least part of the time allotted for reading instruction for individualized practice in the specific skills in which boys and girls needed special practice. A carefully detailed description of how this could be done was presented by Cole (1) back in 1938. This approach

required, however, a wealth of practice materials which were not available to most teachers, and that is probably a major reason why more has not been done with this particular kind of individualized reading. Only within the past three months have we had the announcement of the publication of a set of materials designed to be used in the way that Cole advocated almost twenty years ago.

The fifth type of individualized reading, and the one which is the center of current interest, involves the replacement of class or group developmental reading instruction by individualized reading procedures. This is sometimes done with an entire class, and sometimes it is done with only one group of children within a class.

Individualized Developmental Reading

Developmental reading, as described in books on teaching reading and in the manuals prepared by authors of basal readers, generally involves a fairly common series of steps. The first step is preparing the children for advance reading, which involves motivation, the development of new concepts and ideas, and the teaching of the recognition of new words. The second step is usually guided reading, done silently, and followed by discussion of meanings. The third step is usually re-reading for a specific purpose, and may be done orally or silently. The fourth step generally consists of related activities which may involve specific pages in a workbook, word recognition and word attack skills, or other specific reading skills.

The final step is usually some form of enrichment activity such as reading additional material on the same theme, related poetry, music, art activities, and so forth.

In contrast to the typical developmental reading procedure, individualized developmental reading eliminates most of these steps. Each child is helped to select a book that is appropriate for him. When reading time comes, he reads ahead in the book silently, getting help from the teacher or another pupil as he needs it, and reading orally to the teacher or discussing his reading with the teacher as often as the teacher can get to him. Preparation for reading is almost completely eliminated, except in so far as help in selecting a book is concerned. Reading is not guided by any specifically stated purposes except that of getting ahead in the book. Comprehension is checked occasionally. Rereading is usually eliminated in favor of doing a large amount of varied reading. Workbooks usually have no place in such a program, and training in word recognition and word analysis skills, if given, is usually outside of the pattern of individualized reading and given on a group basis at some other time. Enrichment activities may take any of a number of forms.

With regard to the materials to be used in such an individualized reading program there are two main points of view. There are, on the one hand, those who stress the importance of a very gradual introduction of vocabulary with ample repetition. These people favor the use of basal readers arranged in a sequence so as to have a maximum overlapping of vocabulary between one book and the next, particularly for children whose reading skills are at primary grade levels. On the other hand there are those who follow Olson (6) in believing that the child is the best judge of what he is ready for in reading material, and they believe in giving the child access to a wide variety of reading material and letting him choose for himself. The slogan of this group is "Seeking, Self-Selection, and Pacing."

With regard to the details of how individualized instruction can be carried on, there are many differences of opinion. On these details there are some quite positive opinions but little or no evidence resulting from experimentation. The whole field of individualized developmental reading is at the stage where experimentation is something for the future. At present we have descriptions of specific efforts and programs rather than comparative evaluations.

There are a number of questions which need to be considered by anyone who is contemplating the introduction of individualized reading as a substitute for developmental reading of a more systematic sort on a group or class basis.

1. *With how large a class is this method practical?* Most of the descriptions thus far printed are about classroom situations in which the teacher has fewer than 25 children. The difficulty of conducting individualized reading would seem to become greater as class size increases, and the point at which any possible advantage of individualization might disappear has yet to be determined.

2. *What are the minimum materials*

necessary for introducing an individualized developmental program? One recent writer has stated rather positively that a minimum classroom collection of 80 to 100 varied books is necessary in order to do individualized reading. Other writers are more modest in their requirements.

3. *Is individualized reading best suited to children who are bright, or can it be used with all children, the average and the slow as well?* Most of the reports to date have been based upon individualization with relatively bright groups of children.

4. *How is the teacher to diagnose individual needs* and so be able to determine what to teach children and how to teach it to them in the individualized program?

5. *How much help does a classroom teacher need to introduce such a program and to keep it going smoothly?* Is it necessary for the teacher to be able to call upon a consultant or supervisor for a good deal of help in order to make such a program operate?

6. *Are all phases of the reading program equally amenable to individualization?* It seems probable that some phases of the reading program are more easily done on an individualized basis than others. In a symphony orchestra some parts of the total selection are best carried by the piccolo, some by the violins, some by the trumpets, and some by the bass viols. It may be that we will find that different forms of class organization are most appropriate for different parts of the total reading program, in the same way that different instruments help to harmonize and to give enrichment in a symphonic selection. To organize the class in the same way for all reading activities may be equivalent to trying to play all orchestra parts on one instrument.

Conclusions

1. In this consideration of individualized reading, it is evident that the trend toward the introduction of individualized procedures in reading instruction has been based on solid general psychological principles and has been proceeding gradually over a period of about thirty years.

2. Individualization has been carried out for many specific parts of the reading program. Some of them, such as individualized recreational reading and individualized research reading, are widely used.

3. There is great interest at present in the attempt to replace systematic developmental reading instruction by an individualized reading procedure.

4. Many questions about the practicality of such a procedure are in need of careful study. Individualized reading is still a very new development in education. We are just beginning to learn some of the answers concerning it.

REFERENCES

1. COLE, LUELLA. *The Improvement of Reading.* New York: Farrar & Rinehart, 1938.
2. HARRIS, ALBERT J. *How to Increase Reading Ability,* Third Edition. New York: Longmans, Green and Co., 1956, p. 115.
3. LA BRANT, LOU L. *An Evaluation of the Free Reading in Grades Ten, Eleven, and Twelve, for the Class of 1925, The Ohio State University*

School. Columbus, Ohio: Ohio State University Press, 1936.

4. *Newer Practices in Reading in the Elementary School,* 17th Yearbook of the National Elementary Principal, Vol. 17, No. 7, July, 1938.

5. OLSON, WILLARD C., and DAVIS, SARITA. "The Adaptation of Instruction in Reading to the Growth of Children," *Educational Method,* Vol. 20, 1940, pp. 71–79.

6. OLSON, WILLARD C. "Seeking, Selfselection and Pacing in the Use of Books by Children," *The Packet,* Boston: D. C. Heath and Co., 1952.

7. VEATCH, JEANNETTE. "Children's Interests and Individual Reading," *The Reading Teacher,* Vol. 10, No. 3, February, 1957, pp. 160–165.

8. WASHBURNE, CARLETON C. "Individualized Plan of Instruction in Winnetka," in *Adjusting Reading Programs to Individuals,* Supplementary Education Monographs, No. 52. Chicago: University of Chicago Press, 1941, pp. 90–95.

9. WITTY, PAUL A., and KOPEL, DAVID. *Reading and the Educative Process.* Boston: Ginn and Co., 1939.

38. WHEN SHOULD I INDIVIDUALIZE INSTRUCTION?*

Don H. Parker

HOW can I individualize instruction? A better question would be *"When* should I individualize instruction?"

To answer this, let us first examine the total schooling process—the twelve years between the ages of six and seventeen or eighteen, during which we attempt to offer schooling for all the children of all the people.

* From Don H. Parker, "When Should I Individualize Instruction?" *Grade Teacher,* LXXIX, No. 8 (April, 1962), 66–67, 136–37. Reprinted by permission of the author and Teachers Publishing Corporation, Darien, Conn.

Schooling includes two separate and distinct elements: *training* and *education. Training* is skill-getting. *Education* is skill-using. In the *education* part of schooling, the child uses basic skills gained in a systematic training situation to generate and use knowledge in a "project" or "unit of study" situation meaningful to him.

Traditional schooling consisted mainly of skill-getting and packing in knowledge. This was called "education," although it was really only training. This overattention to skill-getting and fact-packing led to a kind of schooling not appropriate for all of the children of all of the people. Many children were unable to relate what they learned to life. As learning became less and less meaningful, the child dropped out of school.

Then came the "progressive" movement, in which emphasis was on *use* of skills and knowledge in a lifelike situation. Around 1915, with the impact of Dewey's philosophy, schools began emphasizing education as an active, rather than passive, process; learning was experimentation instead of imitation. Kilpatrick was to say that learning should involve purposeful activity and should begin with a problem that created interest and developed initiative.

Unfortunately, the progressive movement tended to throw the baby out with the bath. Skills and knowledge received less and less attention in favor of project work. "Skills," said the progressive, "would come as the child discovered a need for them." This was all very well, but progressive education failed to provide such skill-getting and knowledge-learning situations for the child when he was ready.

Nor was there any systematic track of reading, writing, and arithmetic skills except that laid out by the textbook. Teachers who did a good job on projects often did a poor job on skills and vice versa. Too often, the result was that neither was done very well. Sometimes the teacher simply focused on either skills or projects, to the neglect of the other, thus producing unbalanced schooling.

Do we have to settle for either/or? Can't we have both? We can if we have a basic track of skill-getting on the one hand, *and,* on the other, projects in which the child discovers the usefulness of his skills for successfully cooperating and competing in a group project. Equally important, the education part of schooling furnishes the situation in which he will discover the need for more knowledge.

We can now answer the question, "When should I individualize?" Answer: for the *training* part of the schooling process, individualization of instruction should be the rule when we want to help the child learn such basic skills as reading, writing, spelling, and arithmetic.

When should I "group"? Answer: for the *education* part of the schooling process. Here the goal is to give the pupil an opportunity to *use* the skills he has learned in a lifelike situation from which he can pull out his own meanings.

While it is possible to learn a skill —and much knowledge—in a relative vacuum, the *profitable use* of our skills comes only as a member of society. Somebody has to buy them.

Why not grouping for the learning of basic skills in the first place? Because in the group of six or eight or ten children, the group norm is so obvious that children will feel the need for an attempt to conform to it, whether they conform upward or downward. The best reader and the worst reader in a group so "stick out" that both are uncomfortable. From this standpoint, there is possibly more sense in trying to teach reading in a group of 35 than in a group of eight, since the "false norm" is spread thinner and therefore is less obvious. Grouping for instruction in skills, then, probably actually does more to inhibit learning than it does to help it.

Even more important, however, is the fact that in "grouped" instruction relatively little learning takes place because there is so little opportunity for *learning behavior* on the part of each child in the group. Few teachers can take the time to make sure that each of six, eight, or ten children learn each skill introduced during a twenty-minute reading session, for example.

As the year moves on, feelings that kill rather than build a learning situation soon develop. "What's the use?" says the slower learner. "They just run off and leave me." Equally tragic and wasteful is the case of the faster learner. "Why don't they hurry up? I finished a long time ago!"

A major fallacy in the "grouping-for-instruction" theory seems to be that it is somehow believed that *all* children in a group of six, eight, or ten are getting practice, while *one* child is doing the learning behavior. The fallacy here is that *watching* behavior and *doing* behavior are not the same.

Skill-getting is an internal, active, and a completely individual thing. It is not a matter of simply listening. It is a matter of doing something—of behaving. It requires not only taking in, but giving back.

The behavior required in learning one of the skills of reading, for example, is quite precise. The learner first meets the skill; learns what it is, what it does. Next, he engages in practice, or the attempt to perform the skill himself. During this practice he needs a feedback after each attempt. He needs to know whether he has "hit the mark" or whether, in his next at-

tempt, he should "correct his aim" by different behavior. Gradually, he eliminates the wrong behavior and retains the right.

It takes no scientific training to understand that the behavior just described can only take place in the mind of the learner, that no one can do it for him.

This brings us to another important fact of life and reason why basic skill-getting must be a completely individualized learning opportunity: *Where two or more pupils participate in a learning situation, significant individual differences exist in both learning rate and capacity.* If maximum learning is to take place, it is necessary to provide a situation in which each child may start where *he* is and move ahead as *fast* and as *far* as his learning *rate* and *capacity* will let him.

By individualizing instruction in the basic skills, two important things are accomplished: (1) Pupils learn better and faster than they do in grouped instruction and (2) the teacher's time is saved for the more important work of being a learning consultant and/or a curriculum planner for each pupil.

"But," you say, "if I have trouble finding time to teach three groups in reading, for example, how can I possibly find time to teach all 29 of my pupils individually?" Answer: Shift your emphasis from teaching to *learning.* "Laboratory-ize" your instruction so that, after a major learning sequence is introduced, instruction is individualized and largely self-operating.

Individualizing instruction in this manner is not as difficult as it sounds. At present many teachers are using various kinds of workbooks, but they are often being used on a one-level basis or, at best, in two or three groupings. Why not use workbooks at several levels, giving the right workbook to the right child, according to his learning ability? Even better, and less expensive, break such materials down into even smaller "learning units" so the child gets the satisfaction of completing a job.

Further, many teachers spend long hours correcting the workbook responses. When they do this, they are actually robbing the child of a good half of his learning opportunity. Why not give the child responsibility for correcting his own work from a key, which can be prepared by the teacher and which children can soon become expert in using?

Still further, since children like to know (as do we all) "how am I doing?" why not devise a way so that the results can be recorded on some form of running record or progress chart? In this way, both pupil and teacher can get the "feel" of progress and some idea of where to look for the trouble, if progress is not being made.

With several instructional levels available, how will you know at what level each child should be working? The results of any good standardized test will be found helpful. Simply take the child's score and reduce it by *at least* one grade level (often two) to arrive at his functional level—the level at which he is able to work comfortably at that time. For example, if a pupil in the fifth grade shows a reading comprehension score of 4.5, he should be given material to work on at a beginning third grade level. The same would hold true for pupils testing above the level of the grade in which they are sitting. In the case of reading, an informal reading inventory can be a helpful supplement in questionable cases.

Self-programming, laboratory-type, individualized instruction, as described above, has been worked out by teachers in reading at both primary and elementary levels. Similar work has also been done in spelling, some phases of writing, and in arithmetic. Materials used have been workbooks and textbooks disassembled and reassembled by hand into kits stationed about the room.

Regular laboratory periods are scheduled in each skill area, usually in the morning when minds are fresh. This is followed by unit or project work in late morning or afternoon, involving planning, generation of knowledge through reading, films, TV, and so forth, and application of skills and knowledge in forwarding the group's project and the individual's part in it.

When children work in groups, should they be homogeneously or "ability" grouped—slower ones together, average in another group, superior in another, gifted in another, and so forth? There is much to recommend heterogeneous project groups— and the more heterogeneous the better.

For one thing, homogeneous grouping tends to set up a "caste system" which is not the best training for working toward the democracy we idealize. For another thing, there are enough varied activities in a well-planned project or unit to meet a wide range of ability levels.

This description corresponds much to the lifelike situation of a large research group in which there are the head scientists, the apprentice scientists, the technicians, the clerical workers, the tool makers and finally the maintenance people who simply keep things clean and in order. As work gets under way, functional groups and subgroups will develop, ranging from two pupils to, at times, the entire class, with assigned "project groups" running around six, eight, or ten. Relating the roles of individuals from project to project can further broaden the learning experience of each pupil.

Thus, a group project, in itself, can afford a great amount of individualization or individualized learning opportunity, if the teacher will simply let it happen. The teacher's role in the education part of schooling is that of planning coordinator, resource person on locating needed knowledge, and consultant in evaluating learnings growing out of the project for each project group and for each individual. It is these all-important *education* activities for which the teacher's time should be saved—and can be saved when *training* activities are individualized.

What will be the end product for children in such a project situation? The product of each child, while different from that of his classmates, should represent *his* best work. Naturally, there will need to be a somewhat "standardized" type of product each pupil will be responsible for producing to demonstrate his grasp of the central theme of the topic, and to give meaningful practice in *using* the tool skills

he is learning systematically in the training part of his school day. There should also be a unique product from each pupil—a drawing, a model, a "book," a role in a play, and so forth, that will stimulate creativity and deepen part-whole comprehension of the central theme.

In overview, we have considered the questions: *How* can I individualize and *when* should I individualize? We have seen that both individual and group instruction are desirable in the total schooling process. In the training part (skill-getting), individualized instruction is essential if learning is to take place as effectively as it can. In the education (skill-using and knowledge-generating) part of the schooling process, a combination of group planning, individual study, and group participation is usually most desirable.

Possibly one-half of a pupil's time would be spent in basic skill training. The other half of his time would be spent in project work in science and social studies. In the primary grades, a larger proportion of time would be devoted to training in skills; in upper elementary grades, more time would be devoted to the education part of schooling, as children become more ready and adept at planning and responsibility-taking. By recognizing the two separate elements of schooling, providing for both individualized and group learning situations, and concentrating on *learning* rather than on *teaching,* you can provide a balance in the two kinds of growth each of your pupils must experience: growth *as an individual* and *as a member of society.*

39. INDIVIDUALIZED READING: AN APPROACH TO INDEPENDENT READING*

May Lazar

DURING the past few years, there has been throughout the country a great deal of concern about reading, especially children's reading. Numerous articles have appeared in newspapers and magazines. There have been discussions and debates over television and radio. These activities point to a widespread interest in how well our children read and what they read. They also reveal that there is apprehension and much controversy as to whether children are reading as well as formerly and as to whether present-day methods used in our schools are adequate.

Educators who have worked closely with children and who have conducted numerous research studies know that (1) our children today are reading as well as, if not better than, children of the past; (2) our children today are reading more than ever before. Librarians report that many more books are being taken out by children than in the past; in fact, the shelves are frequently depleted. Book dealers, too, report greater sales than ever before. As a result, publishers of children's books have been making available more books as well as more attractive

* From May Lazar, *Individualized Reading: An Approach to Independent Reading* (New York: Franklin Watts, Inc.), pp. i–vi. Reprinted by permission of the author and Franklin Watts, Inc.

books than formerly. The Individualized Reading approach gives further indication of the wide reading done by today's children.

In the face of such positive evidence, do we need to ask whether our children are really reading? They are!

This bulletin, through its discussion of reading in general and of Individualized Reading in particular, will point the way as to how our children are becoming effective readers.

What Is Reading?

There are many points of view and confusions concerning this important activity. Reading is a complex process which involves seeing the symbols on a printed page, recognizing these symbols, synthesizing them, and comprehending the meanings of the symbols and the ideas of the writer. It has been recognized for some time that reading is not a subject or a specific area to be studied at a certain time every day through preconstructed lessons in a textbook. Reading is not a simple activity that can be defined in a few words. It is not just *looking* at words and *saying* them, not just *looking* at words and *sounding* them. Reading is a technique which opens to the reader the whole world of literature. Reading is actually communication. Reading involves meanings—word meanings; idea meanings. To get at meaning involves interpretation. The past experiences of the reader help him greatly in assimilating the new ideas he finds before him. Interpretation, then, is carried over into broad realms.

The mechanics are necessary at all times in order to read, but reading goes far beyond the mere mechanics of seeing and saying the words. Unfortunately there has been too much emphasis on the mechanics of reading and not enough on the thinking aspects of reading. In the last analysis, reading is a thought process, involving "reading between the lines" or making inferences, making judgments, and critically evaluating the content of the matter read.

The details of how one arrives at the stage of "thinking in reading" will not be discussed in this bulletin. In other words, the specifics of methodology is too large an area to present here. There are many teacher reference books and educational articles which offer excellent suggestions to help teachers with the basal reading instruction necessary for children's independent reading.

What Is Basal Reading Instruction?

The term Basal Reading Instruction is often somewhat confusing because it is construed to mean the development of reading through basal reader systems. Basal Reading Instruction implies the need for getting the tools associated with reading in order to learn to read independently. It is not exclusively related to a specific text or set of texts. There is no one set of rules, or materials, or procedures for Basal Reading Instruction.

Instructional methods are developed through effective procedures which stem from the teacher's knowledge of the needed skills; e.g., how to develop word recognition; how to pronounce and understand the words; how to synthesize meaning from combinations of words, phrases, sentences, and paragraphs. A teacher must be familiar with these basic techniques and fundamental skills regardless of any special "system." She cannot expect the so-called basic texts to "relieve" her of her role as a teacher. These texts are not the sole source of Basal Reading Instruction. The interrelationship between Basal Reading Instruction and Individualized Reading will be discussed later.

What Is Individualized Reading?

There have been many attempts through the years to develop a reading program which would reach each individual child with his own unique needs. For a long time the "three-group approach" has been featured in most classrooms as a possible solution for handling individual differences. It was found, however, that this three-group approach was not reaching the individual child and was not compatible with the newer ideas on child development and learning. Today it is recognized that achievement in reading depends not only upon the child's personal capacities and upon his school and home experiences but also upon his own personal drives and interests. Suitable experiences must be constantly provided in order that his reading potentialities be developed to the fullest.

This objective seems to be attained best through Individualized Reading—a dynamic approach to reading which has been tried in many schools throughout the country. Intensive study and repeated observation indicate that Individualized Reading meets individual needs through its effective classroom instructional organization, its provision for wide reading of a variety of materials, and its flexible arrangement of reading activities and experiences.

Individualized Reading is not a new method of teaching reading. It is a way of thinking about reading—a new attitude toward the place of reading in the curriculum, toward methods and materials, toward class organization, and toward the relationship of the teacher and the child. It provides experiences and opportunities for satisfying the child's basic drives—exploring the materials available, choosing those that appeal to him, and reading them at his own pace. Thus the child has an active role in the learning process.

How Is Individualized Reading Carried on in the Regular Classroom?

GETTING STARTED

The teacher must—

1. Provide an adequate supply of materials with a wide range in readability, interest, and theme. This is essential if "self-selection" is to be successful.

2. Prepare the child for the new approach. Through careful guidance the children are led to see that reading can serve their purposes and that a good mastery of the skills is needed to make them independent readers.

3. Teach the children the routines necessary for smooth class management. This will encourage independence. Children will need help in keeping records and reports.

4. Help the children in choosing their books. They may need time and guidance in order to make adequate choices.

5. Provide many interesting reading experiences in order that the reading activities function in normal situations.

CARRYING THE PROGRAM FORWARD

The daily reading "period" may include individual, group, or class experiences or it may be a combination of several depending on the specific and immediate needs of the children and their degree of independence in reading. The teacher will arrange individual sessions with the children as often as she can, but there is no set rule as to how frequent or how long these sessions will be. The teacher hears the child read from his "self-selected" book and keeps records of his abilities, interests, and difficulties. She helps him then and there with his specific problems and makes provision for further practice assignments.

There are frequent class and group discussions in which the children share their reading experiences. These are usually very lively sessions in which enthusiasm for and interest in further reading are developed. Other group work will involve definite instruction in needed skills, introduction of new skills, and checking of skills previously learned. These group sessions may involve a few children, a larger group, or the whole class. "Individualized" does not mean that the child performs alone in every instance. It can readily be seen that there is no stereotyped program, no set pattern of procedures. The reading experiences and activities may differ from day to day. There is considerable variation from class to class and from school to school.

The teaching of the skills or Basal Reading Instruction is an important part of Individualized Reading. No child can possibly be expected to read books, either readers or trade books, unless he has some of the necessary basal techniques. Inadequate techniques may bring on frustration. Thus in Individualized Reading, as in any approach, there must be careful provision for the development of the reading skills—that is, providing Basal Reading Instruction.

The problem is not so much how Basal Reading Instruction should or should not be achieved. The problem is—how best can we train children for wide, enjoyable, independent reading? The individualized approach seems to be the answer since it provides for both the development of skills and enjoyment of the material used. When a child reads independently and reads widely, he has the opportunity to fuse and practice all the skills he knows at his own pace. Moreover, when a child chooses books independently, he has the opportunity to enjoy his reading more fully.

In Individualized Reading where the teacher has *no definitely prescribed patterns* to follow, she has the opportunity to use her resourcefulness and flexibility in methods as well as in the use of materials. She learns more about children, their needs, and how they learn. She gains more knowledge about children's literature and the many sources of information that will broaden and deepen children's thinking and understanding. She becomes a truly *creative* teacher.

How Are Children's Reading Interests Stimulated?

The ultimate aim in all reading programs is to help children become interested, independent readers. Through the years, library books have always been available. The public libraries have for many years featured children's books and children's story hours which have stimulated interest in reading. In the schools, too, there have been class libraries and central school libraries. Why then were the library books not read more widely? Free-choice reading was generally restricted to a special "library period." This had a limiting effect on children's wide reading and thus restricted their choices and interests. Moreover, the arbitrary categorization of materials into "basic" instructional texts, supplementary readers, and recreational or library books (with the major emphasis on the use of instructional texts) also retarded the free development of wide interests.

In Individualized Reading there is

no such categorization of materials. As was pointed out before, all reading materials are basic and may be used for reinforcement of needed skills. In addition, they give enjoyment to the reader. It cannot be emphasized too often that if individual differences are to be recognized, an adequate supply of materials must be on hand in each classroom. This includes books, magazines, pamphlets, dictionaries, and other reference material. These must be selected with full knowledge of the range of abilities of the children in the class. For example, in a fourth-grade class, the children may range from first-grade ability in reading to seventh- and eighth-grade levels or higher. Thus the books provided would cover a range to meet these various needs. Close adherence to grade level designations is fast becoming obsolete. Recognition of individual differences is of utmost importance.

In selection of books, a wide range of interests must also be considered. The selection should include fiction, science, social studies, specific biographies and history episodes, art and recreation, sports, and the like in order to take care of as many preferences as possible. Even an individual child may have different interests at different times. At one time he may chose fiction, at another time science facts; at still another time he may work on a specific research assignment. For example, one day Johnny may be absorbed in the First Book of Airplanes; the next day his interests may lie in the direction of football. For special holidays, he may choose a biographical story or an historic episode.

Even at the primary level, there are many attractive and interesting books written for very young people. Every day more and more are being published. They are so attractive that if they are available in primary classrooms they will lead to wider reading and thus pave the way for Individualized Reading.

It has been said at times that children cannot make proper selections such as is needed in Individualized Reading. They may flounder a bit at first, and many books may be handled in the process of selection. Individualized Reading with its provision for self-selection is not a "laissez-faire" matter. The teacher must guide the children in making selections appropriate to readability and interest; she must inculcate adequate concepts in their minds as to the purposes of reading and the need for having adequate techniques. Through such guidance, they come to know the great enjoyment experienced through reading.

Each teacher develops her own ways of stimulating interest. She might talk to the children about books and often read to them. She acquaints them with the new acquisitions, displays the book jackets, talks about the authors, and reads short excerpts from the story. She encourages some children to read aloud to the class. The "sharing" or discussion period in the Individualized Reading approach does wonders for stimulating curiosity and interest. Allowing books to be taken home is also an incentive for wide reading. If, while reading in school, a child has to stop at a very absorbing part of the story and if he can take the book home and finish it, this satisfies his immediate interest and leads to further reading.

An adequate supply of appropriate materials, self-selection by children, and well-planned guidance on the part of the teacher are the most important factors for developing ongoing and permanent reading interests.

What Are the Important Values in Individualized Reading?

Children have learned to read in the past through various approaches. Children have learned and will learn to read with basal readers. But what have they lost in the process? Individualized Reading offers many advantages over and beyond the more obvious results of other reading programs, such as are indicated by test scores, grades, and other objective indexes. What then, are the special advantages inherent in Individualized Reading that make it superior to other approaches? The following summary highlights the most important values which distinguish Individualized Reading from other approaches:

1. Individual differences are truly considered and provided for to a greater extent.

2. Undesirable group competition is eliminated—the gifted child and the slow learner work independently on their own levels.

3. Children read more, read faster, and comprehend better, and at the same time experience more enjoyment. They read more varied materials.

4. Reading and the other language arts become more closely integrated, and greater growth is evidenced especially in oral and written expression and in critical thinking.

5. The child experiences greater self-worth—he takes more initiative, demonstrates greater self-management, and gains more independence.

6. Parents and librarians report increased interest in reading on the part of the children and more actual reading outside the school.

7. There is more creative teaching —the classroom becomes a more lively, interesting place. The environment and activities take on greater resemblance to real-life situations.

8. Reading as a major part of the curriculum has at last found its true place.

40. INDIVIDUAL READING INSTRUCTION IN A THIRD GRADE CLASSROOM*

Vivian L. Loveless

LET'S come into the room with these eight and nine year olds and watch them as they work. A few arrive at a time by bus or walking, and before long each child has taken a book from the open shelves or reading table and is busily reading at his own desk. A few will be working at other reading activities which I will describe later. This first period usually lasts until 9:30 or 10:00 o'clock or even later (of course with short breaks for lunch orders, Bible reading, and so on). Children read at many other times during the day, also. During the morning reading period the teacher checks more closely with the child on book selection. Each child is reading at his own rate, seeking information and enjoyment, and working out his own new words as best he can. One at a time they come to me for help if they cannot make out a word or if the meaning is not clear. "Is this 'conductor'?" A nod or a word of praise for getting the word alone assures the child. Perhaps no more is needed this time. Or, if context only was used, I may help the

child analyze the word into syllables, and perhaps note the short "u," particularly if we have just been studying short vowel sounds.

Most of the children's growth in word recognition and comprehension skills comes in these work periods, while I help them individually with context clues and phonetic and structural analysis. I emphasize that each child must come TO ME whenever he needs help because, although his little friend "knows the word just as well as I do," he "does not know how to be as good a teacher," and that I will teach them how "to read for themselves."

Each child has been given the *Gates Primary Reading Test* or the *Gates Advanced Primary Reading Test* near the end of the second grade. The previous teacher also left a record of the books each child had read under her instruction, and included comments on library reading, phonetic skills, and so forth. This provided a basis for planning the books to provide so that the children could begin.

For fluency, and emphasis on thought content, I wanted some easy reading. I also wanted some common reading to lead into group discussion. So we began with the Macmillan Co. Reader, *Today We Go* (2-1) this year with two-thirds of the children. They

* From Vivian L. Loveless, "Individual Reading Instruction in a Third Grade Classroom," in *Individualizing Reading Instruction,* Proceedings of the 39th Annual Education Conference, University of Delaware, VI (March, 1957), 24–26. Reprinted by permission of the author and Russell G. Stauffer, Director of the Reading Study Center at the University of Delaware.

were told to read no farther than the first chapter, a trip across America, very interesting to these much traveled children at the end of their vacation, and leading right into transportation, their social studies topic. After study the children who had tested at around grade three, met as a group, read the stories orally and discussed them. Those children for whom the book was too hard for fluent reading, and who had an easier study book, joined this *Today We Go* circle for enjoyment if they wished. The more advanced readers only discussed the stories and ideas growing from them along with the occasional oral reading of some passage.

As the year has progressed we have used the district adopted basic texts in the same way. Assignments have largely been "You must not read farther than chapter two this week" or again "Please read chapter three in *Streets and Roads* and chapter three in *More Streets and Roads* by the end of next week while we are interested in animals." Those who need close check up, extra skill help, or oral reading practice meet in groups for preparation in the common room study time. In third grade I expect each child to have met certain difficulties before coming to a reading group. There is not time for groups to meet every day, nor is it needed. However, all slow readers do some oral reading with the teacher each day. For most of the children the above mentioned reading takes only a small part of their school time. Their reading is largely self-selected with teacher approval.

There are many other texts in the classroom, or brought in from our textbook depository. The classroom library has books on science and social studies. Our school has a good library from which teachers check out trade books for use in their rooms. The children go to the library for a class period each week, and individually at other times for reference needs. We also use *My Weekly Reader,* Editions 2, 3, and 4.

When our schools were new, and had no libraries, I kept my room supplied with adequate reading material by checking out books from the County and Wilmington libraries, exchanging for new ones every month. While teaching in an Oklahoma school I found it necessary to get the books from the state library.

Most of our learning comes from our wide reading. Sometimes the reading is for pure enjoyment. More often the children are following up some field of interest opened by the class, a small group, or an individual. Practically all the instruction in reading for those children above third grade level is given individually as they read trade (or library) books.

As a third-grade teacher, I do very little oral reading to the class. The superior children do it. Three or four (or ten) prepare and take turns reading. Some books so read are *Dr. Dolittle, Arne and the Christmas Star, The Wizard of Oz* (in the unabridged original text). I only take my turn as one of the group.

Each child records his completed reading in a booklet. These reports show the date the book was finished, the title, the author, and at least two or three sentences reviewing each book read at school. However, in order not to discourage reading, only the title and author are required for books checked out for home reading. I discuss many books with the children individually. Often a child reads a page or two to me.

When we find a common need in word structure or phonetics, it is worked on by the class. Each child has a "sound" folder in which he has examples of short vowel sounds, lists of *"er, ir, or, ur"* words, and so on. He may be referred to this when he comes to me to ask about a difficult word, and so learn how to solve it himself. We make much use of dictionaries. A few children who need the practice use the workbooks that accompany the basic texts. I feel that most of the children with whom I am working this year make better use of their school time by other wide reading, and only a rare use of workbooks. They do use the *Weekly Reader* exercises.

In summary, we read widely for enjoyment and information because there is so much we want to know. Help is given as needed. Any grouping used is flexible. So there is no ceiling on the learning. Sometimes two children work on an interesting library book together, helping each other. Last week one boy began reading *Streets and Roads* (3-1) at chapter three because he could and the others were reading it. In the meantime he is finishing the last half of *More Friends and Neighbors* (2-2). He also has time for library books.

41. YOU CAN INDIVIDUALIZE YOUR READING PROGRAM TOO*

Mary Ann Daniel

RECENTLY many articles have been written stressing the effectiveness of individualized reading programs. I became as enthusiastic as

* From Mary Ann Daniel, "You Can Individualize Your Reading Program Too," *Elementary English*, XXXIII, No. 7 (November, 1956), 444–46. Reprinted by permission of the author and the National Council of Teachers of English.

anyone else who has read these articles —here at last was a method which could cope with the wide range of reading abilities within a classroom. The best way to meet individual differences is to deal with them individually. Now, my classroom was going to be different! Reading was going to be fun! All of my pupils were going to read and like it, I hoped.

As I gazed at the 36 faces—some eager, some apprehensive—on the first day of school in September, I wondered if my plan would succeed. It sounded perfect in every article I had read. But 36 fifth grade youngsters! My school district, in a rather well-to-do suburb of Philadelphia, believes in grouping for reading. Almost every classroom in our eleven elementary schools has three reading groups. This year, a new reading series was purchased which encouraged the ability grouping. The size of my class and the policy of the school district would certainly encourage the "old-fashioned" ability grouping!

I was determined to make an attempt to work out a plan for a combination — group and individualized reading program. The first thing I did was to check the reading ability level of all of the children. This was done for grouping and for my beginning records for the individualized reading. Each child read a paragraph from a story, we talked about it briefly, and we also talked of how they felt about reading in general. It was both amazing and discouraging to discover the number of children who responded, "I hate it; I can't read."

We had our regular reading groups. I gradually worked out the policy, for the top group first, that one day a week they could read any book they selected during a reading period. I checked what they read individually that day. The other two groups responded, just as I hoped they would, by demanding to know why they couldn't read a book of their own choice also. Soon everyone was making his own selection from our room library of approximately 150–200 books.

From there it was easy to guide the children into forming a Book Club. The first undertaking of the club was a book exchange. Books were brought from home—sometimes six or eight at a time by one youngster. The books were all excellent ones! Only one child brought in a comic book, and the youngsters themselves decided they didn't want any more! The first president of the club, who was an extremely capable little girl, planned programs for the care and handling of books, book quizzes, rearranging and classifying the library shelves (the fifth grade star football player took charge of this task), and getting others interested in reading. From this last topic they decided to present book reviews at least once a week. At first our book reviews were merely short résumés. The more imaginative youngsters later presented drawings, puppet shows, and short plays. These activities took place during a regular reading period or in the afternoon. Much of the time formerly spent on workbooks was being devoted to these creative activities. Our workbook exercises still got done, however!

Reading periods, when we had the individualized program, always ran 40 to 60 minutes. This was never too much time; in fact, the majority of the children requested more time. During that time I called individuals, volunteers first, over to a corner where we talked about what had happened in the book thus far, discussed the characters and their actions, made predictions of what was to come, read a paragraph orally, and discussed how the book had helped them as individuals. Any difficulties the child had were noted, and later they were worked on. If there was a common problem for five or six youngsters, we went over it together. Individual problems were naturally taken care of individually without wasting the time of the entire group. I found that with my weakest students, who had a great deal of difficulty, it was easier to give them individual assistance either before or after school.

The children kept a diary of the books they read. They made a very short comment about each book, told whether they liked it or not, and discussed what they gained from having read the book. I might say the last two items were the most difficult for them. They could not understand, at first, that it was permissible to say they did not like a book. All of the children thought they *had* to say they liked every book they read. Many of them did not understand what was meant by, "How did the book help you become a better individual?" We had several discussions on this, and more and more of them gradually included that item in their diaries. I found that short book reviews of this type were a help in finding books they would like to receive for Christmas. Brief résumés were written about the most appealing books; these were typed and mimeographed and sent home for Christmas suggestions. After reading several books, the children were encouraged to write their own stories. These were put into book form— bound and illustrated—instead of just written on "good penmanship paper." These books were kept in a conspicu-

ous place so that they were available for reading at all times. What could thrill a child more than to see someone pick up his "bound book" to read?

Of course the time for telling about a book read is most valuable. It is amazing to watch the methods of presentation change and improve as the children do more and more of this reporting. At first all of the reports seemed to follow the same pattern: "This book was about. . . . If you want to know what happened read it." I thought to myself, "Where is all the creativity that is supposed to develop in this reading program?" An original presentation by just one youngster was all that was needed to inspire the others. Soon we had radio reporters, plays, pictures, drawings on the blackboard, papier-mâché puppets, string puppets, and book reviews written in our classroom newspaper. The more creative the presentation, the more irresistible the book became to the other youngsters.

As this program was going on, I still had my regular groups about three days a week. The creativeness from the individual program carried over to the groups. We did more dramatization and felt freer to skip around in the book and select stories that had a particular interest at that time instead of reading from the first story to the last in the correct sequence. I have found that all of the children, in the group reading and individually, felt much freer to come to me for assistance. While working in groups, instead of waiting for everyone to finish, those who finished first worked on their book diaries or methods of presenting books read.

As I have watched this reading program develop since September, I have been most pleased with its results. It has enabled me to know more about the level and ability of each child. Thus I have been able to give more worthwhile individual and group assistance. Naturally, as the children read more books, they become more skilled in self selection of books. They are very capable of selecting books that they understand and that are well-written. The weaker pupils are not embarrassed by their selection of easier books, and the superior readers are not held back. Everyone exhibits more enthusiasm and interest in reading. Because the slower readers select books they are able to read, they soon develop confidence in their reading ability, and their whole attitude towards reading is changed. In the individual program the children want to read; the more they read, the greater degree of success they feel in all of their school work.

42. RECORD KEEPING FOR INDIVIDUALIZED READING*

Muriel Fisch

INDIVIDUALIZED reading may be used more and more widely as we see that our children profit more from this type of free choice instruction in the elementary schools than from basal reading teaching. The transition from the reader series program to individualized reading, however, requires careful planning on the part of the teacher and the keeping of even more careful records of the progress of each child. Following is a system of record keeping which worked quite satisfactorily in the sixth-grade class with which I used the individualized approach. The child and the teacher each kept records, and we shall consider them separately.

Teacher's Records

Any notebook will do for the teacher's records. Allotting a double page for each child, I arrange the entire class (boys and girls together) alphabetically. Each page is organized as in Diagram I.

* From Muriel Fisch, "Record Keeping for Individualized Reading," Grade Teacher, LXXVI, No. 2 (November, 1958), 90–91, 93. Reprinted by permission of the author and Teachers Publishing Corporation, Darien, Conn.

Page 1		Page 2		
Tony B.				Tony B.
		Conference Dates		
BOOKS READ	INTERESTS COMMENTS	SKILLS NEEDED		
		Idea	Word	Other

In the "Books Read" column I put the date, title, and author of book taken. I have found it worthwhile to date each entry even when the book was soon discarded by the child. In looking over accumulated notations, a pattern of behavior often begins to show, which guides me in helping a particular child.

The "Interests and Comments" column is a sort of catchall for notations. For example, if the child is a stamp collector I note it here; if he said sometime that he hated school, I put that down.

At the top left-hand corner of the first page I write the Reading Grade Level and the Vocabulary Grade Level, based on standardized tests.

In this individualized approach to teaching reading, "Skills Needed" is the most difficult part to decide. Which are important and which should wait for later? I make a list at the end of my notebook of those skills which my school system wishes emphasized at each grade level represented by the children in my class. I classify them under "Ideas," "Words," and "Other." Then I further subdivide "Idea Skills" into "Understanding Ideas," "Interpreting Ideas," and "Organizing Ideas." The "Word Skills" column is for recording "Word Meaning," "Word Analysis," and "Dictionary Skills." As I work with each child in individual

conferences, I glance at the list and decide which of his needs for his grade level seems most urgent. That need I jot down in the appropriate column.

Under the "Other Skills" column I note such items as "Choppy phrasing in oral reading," "Silent reading: moves lips." Here, too, I write down what the child shared with the class during the "Sharing Period."

When a child has made his book selection, either from the public library or from the school library, I test his ability to read the book without frustration, using the standard of fewer than five errors in a hundred running words. If the book is too hard, then I help him find a simpler book on the same subject or on an interest I have noted in the "Interests" column.

Library Records

Both children and teacher bring in books for the classroom library from which children may select in the course of the term. The ideal is ten books per child, although I have gotten along with far fewer.

A card is kept inside each on the shelves. Author and title are written across the top, and columns for "Borrower's Name," "Date Borrowed," and "Date Returned" below. A duplicate set on smaller cards, with just author and title, is kept in my files as a record of total number of books in the library. It is convenient to use different colored cards for books belonging in the separate library sections.

The Reading Period

My reading period is forty minutes a day, allocated as follows: thirty minutes for everyone to read silently, except for the child who has an individual conference with me. I see six children for five minutes each in such a period. Then five minutes is used for writing summaries and five minutes for sharing.

During the individual conference I hear the child read, or test some of the other skills at his level. I concentrate on one skill per conference. After a period of two or three weeks there are usually from six to seven children needing help on some particular skill. I take these during the silent reading period and work with them as a group. At the back of my book I note the date, the skill taught, and the children participating.

About once a month I take the reading period to teach to the whole class a skill that is needed by the majority of the children. For this purpose I use a reader because each child needs a copy of a common text.

Child's Notebook

The child's notebook may be arranged in the following way:

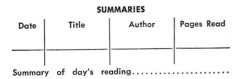

SUMMARIES

Date	Title	Author	Pages Read

Summary of day's reading.....................

The last column contains notation only of pages read during class periods. Gaps therefore indicate home reading. The summary is a sentence or two telling the most important action which took place within the pages read. To assist the child in writing summaries I ask him to answer two or three of

the "W's": Who, What, Why, When, Where.

The back of the child's notebook is set up as in Diagram 3:

VOCABULARY

Date	Book	Page #	Word in phrase

Word, dictionary meaning, and new phrase with word.....................

During the individual reading period the child tries to make out any new word from the context. Only if he finds it impossible to continue and make sense of what he is reading does he stop to look up the word in the dictionary, noting the page on which the word occurred. During the summary period he makes the entry on his Vocabulary page, using the phrase from the story and then one of his own.

In the center of the notebook the child keeps suggestions for making summaries, vocabulary notations, and sharing. For example:

Sharing an excerpt:

Introduction: Just enough (one or two sentences) so that the class can understand the part being read.

Excerpt: One or two sentences or a short paragraph which is exciting or mysterious, to share with classmates.

After the sharing of an excerpt, there is a show of hands of all children who, having heard the excerpt, wish to read the book. They can reserve the book by signing on the card for the book, leaving, of course, the "Date Borrowed" column blank.

Sharing vocabulary:

(Choose a word which you think the

majority of the children may wish to add to their day-to-day vocabulary.)

Write the word in a phrase on the board.

Underline the word.

Give the meaning and a new sentence orally.

It is necessary for the teacher to go over with the child the item he expects to share with the class. This is done during the individual conference. Shy children need considerable encouragement at first, but the teacher's

enthusiasm for a new word or for an especially exciting passage may give the necessary boost. Sharing his contribution alone first with the teacher helps. No comments are made during the brief, five-minute sharing periods.

At the completion of a book, a child may write a review, a character study, a poem about an event or person in the story. He may draw a scene or a portrait of a character. He might make a book jacket—any individually satisfying culmination at his own level.

43. THE PLACE OF INDIVIDUALIZED READING IN A WELL-PLANNED PROGRAM *

Harry W. Sartain

Some Experimental Evidence on Individualized Reading

INDIVIDUALIZED reading has a unique and worthy quality. The personal nature of the conferences between the pupil and the teacher has a highly salutary effect on the child's attitude. He feels that the teacher is interested in him as an individual as well as in what he is reading. He responds to the

* From Harry W. Sartain, "The Place of Individualized Reading in a Well-Planned Program," in *Contributions in Reading*, No. 28 (Boston: Ginn & Co., 1961), pp. 3–6. Reprinted by permission of the author and Ginn and Company.

teacher's encouragement, and, according to most reports, he reads considerably more.

Unfortunately this great strength is offset by a serious weakness in individualized reading—inefficiency. The most conscientious teachers find themselves frustrated in their efforts to schedule as many conferences as the children really need; often they feel that they can take time to teach only a part of the needed skills. They have doubts about the permanence of learnings which are not systematically reviewed. They spend an inordinate amount of time in preparing ten to fifteen individual reading skills lessons each day, and then feel that they are forced to present them somewhat superficially because of time limitations.[15]

Some capable teachers who have experimented successfully with a totally individualized program, have preferred to return to basal reading in small groups or to a combination of procedures. They usually find that their classes can be divided into three to six groups of children, who are able to learn and utilize new skills at approximately the same pace. The planning for six groups can be far more thorough and systematic than that needed for thirty individuals. More important, it permits the teacher to introduce the new words and concepts which the children need in order to read with maximum comprehension and pleasure. The discussion of stories read by *a group* deepens the children's insights, critical reading abilities, appreciation of literary qualities, and ability to express reactions acceptably to others. All these attributes of basal instruction in small groups attest to the greater efficiency of this type of organization over the totally individualized approach.

In brief, it can be said that the individualized system has one outstanding strength—the personal pupil-teacher conference, and one tremendous weakness—inefficiency. Most statistically controlled experiments have revealed that capable pupils, with the aid of well-educated, experienced, and dedicated teachers, can learn to read approximately as well in the individualized way as through basic grouping.[1,15,19] Since not all children are of good capability and not all teachers

organize well the work of thirty children, it would seem unwise to recommend that all classes utilize the individualized plan. It will be much more fruitful to combine the best features of individualized reading with the proven practices in basal work. Some teachers have been doing this in various ways for years.

Adding Individualized Reading to the Basic Program

When incorporating individual work into standard programs, teachers usually follow these procedures with some variations.[16]

1. Divide the class into several small groups for instruction in the basic skills. A minimum of three groups will always be required for adequately differentiated pacing. Five groups will usually accommodate all but the very unusual pupil.

2. If possible, use a "new" basal series for each group. Fresh material for every group greatly improves the children's reading interests, makes basic reading a real thought-getting process, and reduces the stigma associated with grouping. If three basic sets are available, differences in the progress rates of groups will probably be large enough so that books used by the first groups will seem new when read later by the fourth and fifth groups. As each group of children moves into a different classroom for the next school term, *they should continue to work in their own basal series.* Of course, each group should progress through the series at the rate of its capability, regardless of the grade designation.

3. With most groups use only the

one set of basic materials during the year. This will make it possible to teach a skills program *completely* instead of piecemeal, as is sometimes done when classes race through several series.

4. Utilize the teacher's manual consistently to teach thoroughly the complete skills program for each group. Do not dwell on a specific skill longer than is needed for a group to learn it. However, if the lessons in one manual are not adequate for the group concerned, supplement them from the manuals for other series.

5. Use the basic reader workbooks in the same way to reinforce the skills program and to enrich the study backgrounds. Most children may need most of the pages in their workbooks, but do not hesitate to let a child skip exercises that he does not need. Freely supplement those exercises that are not adequate for some individuals. Do not flood the class with additional workbooks and worksheets which simply keep them busy repeating exercises which they have learned earlier.

6. Collect in the classroom all the additional "basic" readers, supplementary readers, and good trade books that can be obtained. The bibliographies in teachers' manuals can be of invaluable aid in selecting books. One to three copies each of more than a hundred different titles are necessary for an adequate program. They should range in difficulty from approximately four years in the first grade to eight years in the sixth grade. They can be placed on shelves in three or four very general difficulty classifications to simplify selection by pupils. Colored paper slips in each book can direct children in returning them to shelves that are similarly labeled.

7. During all the time when they are not engaged in basic study, the children should enjoy the reading of books and stories of their own choosing from this room library and from other sources. Thus they are introduced to the skills through the basic materials, and they gain proficiency through extensive independent reading. The basic readers may create interests which children will want to follow, or pupils may wish to read along other paths. Now they have something to challenge them in every spare moment during the day, plus homework for those who want it! The teacher is relieved of the preparation and correction of endless seatwork exercises, and can spend more time with groups and individuals.

8. Arrange to have the children share their independent reading with others in several ways. A few of these are:

a. Individual conferences with the teacher as often as possible. These can take place while others are reading silently or during specially scheduled periods. Since skills are taught systematically through the basic program, these conferences need be only long enough to show real interest in the child's work, to motivate further reading, and to provide occasional assistance with individual problems

b. Conferences between two pupils about favorite stories

c. Storytelling, sometimes to the whole class, but more often to small groups of personal friends

d. Oral reading of favorite parts in groups of about four students

e. Dramatization of a story enjoyed by several pupils

f. Making and displaying dioramas or peep shows that illustrate books

g. Designing book jackets that will attract others to read the books

h. Making mobiles to stimulate the imagination in respect to certain stories

i. "Auctioning" books by telling successively more tantalizing events in the plot, but not reaching the climax

j. Having characters in different books meet, either in writing or "in person"

k. Making paper doll illustrations

l. Giving the story action on the flannelboard

The number of ways in which books can be shared is as unlimited as the imagination of the teacher and the class.

9. Have the children keep records of independent reading. The satisfaction gained from their accomplishments will spur them on to further reading. The forms of the records should be changed frequently. Some are:

a. Scrapbooks of illustrations and summaries of stories

b. Charts showing different types of literary materials read

c. "Collection boxes" of "souvenirs" from good stories

d. Charts on which stories are evaluated according to criteria set by the class

e. Devices to which segments are added for each book read—the "bookworm," the giraffe that "stretches upward" with books, the flowering "garden" of books, the "tower" of books, etc.

10. Keep card records of special learning difficulties of individual pupils. Occasionally bring together several children from various groups for help with a common problem. Schedule at least a couple of fifteen-minute periods a week for this type of corrective teaching in flexible groups.

Organizing Combined Programs

The procedure for dividing instructional time between basal and independent reading will depend upon the wishes of each teacher and the needs of the pupils. A few possibilities follow.

INDIVIDUALIZED SUPPLEMENTARY READING

This is the procedure that has been referred to in most of the preceding paragraphs. It is easily managed in both primary and later grades. The basic lessons are taught in small groups. The individualized reading proceeds continuously whenever children are not working on basic assignments. While the teacher is engaged with one group, the others will complete workbook requirements and then spend all remaining time on independent reading. The teacher can relate the sharing activities to language instruction in order to schedule more time. Frequently the "telling time" periods that begin the day can be devoted to telling about books in the interesting ways mentioned earlier. A few brief individual conferences should be scheduled daily in place of the time the teacher would otherwise spend in explaining and correcting needless seat work. Supplementary individualized reading can be added to all of the additional plans that are suggested.

ALTERNATING BASIC AND INDIVIDUAL READING PERIODS

In primary grades most teachers have long periods for reading instruction twice during the day. In some classrooms, the books used in the morning are different from those used in the afternoon. Basic and individualized work can be combined easily by scheduling the sequential skills work in the morning and the self-selected reading during the afternoon period. This is probably the simplest way for the teacher to make a first attempt at individualized reading.

PERIODIC REINFORCEMENT OF BASIC SKILLS WITH INDIVIDUALIZED READING

At any grade level a group may alternate a few weeks of study in the basic materials with extended periods of individualized reading. In this situation the teacher will keep a group in basic books and workbooks while a new phase of skill building is being introduced. Before the next skill or set of skills is presented, the children may put aside the basic materials and spend a few days or weeks practicing the new skill through individualized reading. Such an organization insures sequential learning and gives specific direction to the instructional emphasis in each phase of the individualized program. In each room some of the groups will be engaged in basal reading while others are reading self-selected materials. Because the skills have already been introduced, the individual conferences can be quite brief, allowing the teacher time to work effectively with the other children in basal groups.

The less capable children should spend a smaller proportion of time on independent than on basic work. One experiment with ten second-grade classes [15] revealed that slower pupils make appreciably less progress when they do not receive direct instruction daily. The plan of alternating extended basic reading with individualized work can be especially well adapted to the needs of slow pupils. Since the reading program of each group is different, the teacher can give slow groups fewer weeks of individualized work without calling this to the attention of other children. Thus the less capable pupils can spend most of their time on sound skills development, which will help them to feel more comfortable in all classroom study situations.

The periodic reinforcement plan is probably the easiest for a teacher who has never scheduled *independent* reading before. Individualized reading can be undertaken with only the ablest group while the teacher tries out varied techniques of conferring and record keeping. As one feels secure with the procedures, he can apply them to other groups.

COMPLETION OF A BASIC PROGRAM BEFORE BEGINNING INDIVIDUALIZED READING

Here each group completes the basic program in its assigned series before the end of the year. The reading periods for the remainder of the year are spent in self-selected reading and individual conferences. Again the brightest children, who complete a basic program fastest, will spend the most time in individual work. This is commendable because they are capable of profiting from self-directed study. Some schools encourage the most able groups to move beyond their grade levels in the basic books. In this case the teacher must judge the point at which the introduction of new skills should cease in favor of more individual practice. Slower children should still have the privilege of independent supplementary reading as a part of their seat work.

BASIC AND INDIVIDUALIZED STUDY COMBINED IN THE TOPICAL READING UNIT

This is the most complex way to produce this combination, but teachers who have practiced it for several years find the plan to be particularly rewarding. Progress through the basic readers is paced in such a way that two or more groups, preferably the whole class, are reading on approximately the same theme. Examples of such topics are "Imaginative Tales," "Children of Other Lands," or "Stories of Heroes."

Together the pupils and the teacher plan a project which will require extensive independent reading on the topic. The project may be a set of puppet shows, a museum, a radio broadcast, or a program for parents. The children search through all of the room and building library materials to obtain every bit of available information. To aid each other, they evaluate materials; they build a class bibliography; they keep records; and they organize material for sharing. In the process they practice many of the work-study skills that have been introduced.

This instructional organization is especially recommended for the intermediate and upper grades because of the content of their readers. Also there is more possibility of children being sensitive about grouping as they get older. Under the topical unit plan they work in groups only two or three times a week. The other periods are spent in planning, sharing, and activity work which cuts across group membership.

Summary

The "Miss Tracy's" throughout the country have found that there need be no conflict between sequential basic reading in groups and individualized reading. Emphasis on the latter has reawakened teachers to the value of the one-to-one relationship between teacher and pupil. However, there is a heritage of other valuable techniques that has grown through many years of research and practice. By incorporating extensive independent reading and personal conferences into a sound basic program, teachers can take another stride forward in the fruitful teaching of reading.

REFERENCES

1. ACINAPURO, PHILIP. "A Comparative Study of the Results of Two Instructional Reading Programs— An Individualized and a Three Ability Group Pattern," Unpublished Doctoral Dissertation. New York: Teachers College, Columbia University, 1959.

2. BETTS, E. A. "Approaches to Differentiated Guidance in Reading," *Education*, 70:582–99, May, 1950.

3. BUREAU OF EDUCATIONAL RESEARCH, BOARD OF EDUCATION, CITY OF NEW YORK. "Books for Individualized Reading" (mimeographed), Revised 1960.

4. ————. *Individualized Reading Interim Report*, 1957. 29 pages.

5. CARR, CONSTANCE. "Individualizing Development of Abilities and Skills in Reading: A Description and Critique of Emerging Practices," Unpublished Doctoral Dissertation. New York: Teachers College, Columbia University, 1959.

6. CAVANAUGH, CECELIA L. "Every Child's Reading Needs are Unique," *Instructor*, March, 1959.

7. DARROW, HELEN M., and VIRGIL M. Howes. *Approaches to Individualized Reading*. New York: Appleton-Century-Crofts, 1960. 102 pages.

8. EVANS, N. DEAN. "An Individualized Reading Program for the Elementary Teacher," *Elementary English*, 30: 275–80, May, 1953.

9. GRAY, WILLIAM S. "Role of Group and Individualized Teaching in a Sound Reading Program," *The Reading Teacher*, 11:99–104, December, 1957.

10. KARLIN, ROBERT. "Some Reactions to Individualized Reading," *The Reading Teacher*, 11:95–98, December, 1957. (See additional articles in this issue.)

11. MIEL, ALICE (Editor). *Individualizing Reading Practices,* Practical Suggestions for Teaching, No. 14. New York: Teachers College, Columbia University, 1958.

12. ROBINSON, HELEN M. "News and Comment," *Elementary School Journal*, 60:411–20, May, 1960.

13. SAFFORD, ALTON L. "Evaluation of an Individualized Reading Program," *The Reading Teacher*, 13:266–70, April, 1960.

14. SARTAIN, HARRY W. "A Bibliography on Individualized Reading," *The Reading Teacher*, 13:262–65, 270, April, 1960.

15. ————. "The Roseville Experiment with Individualized Reading," *The Reading Teacher*, 13:277–81, April, 1960.

16. ————. "In Combining Sequential and Individualized Reading," *Sequential Development of Reading Abilities* (Helen M. Robinson, Editor), Supplementary Educational Monograph No. 90, Chicago: University of Chicago Press, 1960, pp. 187–90.

17. STAUFFER, RUSSELL G. "Individual and Group Type Directed Reading Instruction," *Elementary English*, 37:375–82, October, 1960.

18. VEATCH, JEANNETTE. *Individualizing Your Reading Program*. New York: G. P. Putnam's Sons, 1959. 242 pages.

19. WITTY, PAUL, with ANN COOMER and ROBERT SIZEMORE. "Individualized Reading—A Summary and Evaluation," *Elementary English*, 36:401–12, 450, October, 1959.

20. YOUNG, MARION. "A Report on Self-selection in Reading," *Elementary English*, 35:176–81, March, 1958.

C H A P T E R   V I I I

W O R D   P E R C E P T I O N
A N D   P H O N I C S

44. A REPORT OF A CONFERENCE OF READING EXPERTS*

"Sight-Words" vs. Phonics

LARGELY, the public confusion about the teaching of reading is the result of constant repetition by some critics of the charge that our schools employ mainly a so-called "Sight-Word" (Look-Say) method of reading instruction, to the neglect of phonics. It has been alleged that as a consequence large numbers of our children are failing to learn to read acceptably. This assertion is based on the false premise that reading instruction can be done by one single method —either by "sight-words" (look-say) or by phonics. Reading and the teaching and learning of reading are not as simple as that.

* From "A Report of a Conference of Reading Experts," in *Learning to Read*, a 31 page pamphlet with a foreword by James B. Conant (Princeton, N.J.: Educational Testing Service, 1962), pp. 3–10. Reprinted by permission of the Educational Testing Service.

Let us answer the "sight-word" charge first.

It is not true that our schools, in general, use primarily a "sight-word" method. It is not true that our schools, in general, do not teach phonics.

We hold that reading cannot be taught through "sight-words" (look-say) alone. Such teaching would require our children to memorize, word by word, the mass of printed words. No reading authority advocates so impossible a procedure.

We consider phonics one of the essential skills that help children identify printed words that they have not seen before and then understand the meaning that those words represent. Without phonics most children cannot become self-reliant, discriminating, efficient readers.

In our reply to the false "sight-words" charge, we are not endorsing all reading instruction as good. Some

201

of it is excellent, much of it is good, and some of it is poor. However, we are certain that little of it is as poor as it sometimes is caricatured by critics who present exceptions as typical examples.

There are understandable reasons why some reading instruction is not good. The main reason is the shortage of good teachers, which is a plague that affects the teaching in all educational institutions, be they schools, colleges, or universities. Many teachers are inexperienced, as evidenced by school systems in which as many as one-third of the teachers are in the first three years of their teaching careers; and many teachers have become masters neither of the components (constituent parts) of reading instruction nor of the teaching of those components. Other reasons are large classes, meager libraries, inadequate equipment, insufficient books and supplies, poor public support—both moral and financial.

What Reading Is

Briefly stated, experts in reading instruction everywhere agree upon the common sense proposition that there are two major acts to be performed in the process of reading: (1) recognizing the printed word on the page; and (2) understanding and dealing with the meaning intended in the passage.

Adults have forgotten how complex this reading process really is. They recognize instantly almost all the words they read and only occasionally hesitate over an unfamiliar word. When they meet one of the many words that have several meanings, they automati-

cally wait to assign the exact meaning until context makes it clear. They read words in groups—not one-by-one— since it is grouped words that express ideas. They even find that the precise meaning of a particular sentence may be determined by other sentences with which it is combined. And they have no trouble with the mechanics of reading down the page and from left to right along the lines and through the words.

All this, and much more, adults think of as the single act of reading. They read with an ease made possible by the accomplished total habit of years of reading. Few of them remember exactly how they learned to read, and they are unaware of how simply children must start to learn to read and how carefully constructed must be the learning activities that lead to reading skill.

Reading is indeed a complex process; and because reading has so many facets, the teaching of reading also is complex. No single device, such as phonics or sight-words, can reach across the range of skills that an efficient reader uses. We are agreed that there is no single best way of learning to read, and therefore no single best way of teaching children to read. Wise reading teachers make appropriate use of all the tools and techniques available at the time most suitable for using them. They do not speak of *the* method of teaching reading because they understand that teaching reading is a composite procedure that assembles and uses the best methods that professional theory, research, and the practical common sense of competent teachers have been able to devise. . . .

Word Recognition Skills

It should always be remembered that when children come to school they want to learn to read. It is good sense to capitalize on this desire at once. Therefore, as the children begin to learn the reading skills, it is rather standard practice for good teachers to see to it that they simultaneously learn a few printed words that are common in children's speaking vocabularies and that they will thereafter recognize when they see them. With these few words as a base, the children can begin utterly simple reading almost immediately—for instance, a sentence of only two or three words.

For many reasons, these beginning words are readily learned. They are common, simple words. They are few in number, learned one by one and not as a list of words. They are learned in meaningful situations, and as a rule come from the children's own conversation in the class. The oral context in which they are used leads to their meaning. They illustrate the reading skills being learned and provide further practice of those skills.

The learning of these few initial words is not a mere feat of memory but is the result of the composite procedure by which in the very early stages of reading instruction children begin to learn how to identify printed words. Because of their use in the very beginning reading, these words are usually called "sight-words"—that is, they are words that once learned will thereafter be recognized whenever they are seen. They are the beginning of the "reading vocabulary" that all persons must possess who are going to read well.

Thus, with the learning of these few initial words, the children at the same time are beginning to use the skills with which they soon will be able to figure out other words that they will meet in their reading each day. We call these skills the "Word Recognition Skills." An essential among them is the "phonics" that some critics say the schools omit in their instruction of reading.

When children first come to school they can recognize a vast number of words when they hear them spoken. They know both the sound and the meaning of these words. Sound (pronunciation) and meaning are tied together. The number of such words is well into the thousands and is greater than has sometimes been thought.

However, many children at that age do not know what *sounds* are represented by the *letters* in the printed word. Therefore, they have to learn to relate the letters in the printed word to the sounds in the spoken word. With the variety of sounds that most letters have, this is not a small task. It is here that phonics enters in, for phonics is the study of the relationship of the letters and letter combinations in words on the printed page and the sounds in the spoken words.

When children acquire mastery of phonics, they can produce a pronunciation for most of the words they meet. How will they know whether this pronunciation is correct? If the word is one that they already know by sound, they can check the pronunciation by their own knowledge. For the familiar words, then, phonic skills help the children tie the printed symbols (letters and words) to both pronunciation and meaning.)

On the other hand, for totally new words phonic skills lead usually only to unverified pronunciation and do not lead to meaning at all. In short, like the rest of us, children can pronounce words with no idea whatever as to their meanings. But the whole purpose of reading is to get meaning. That is why good teachers insist upon uniting phonics instruction with instruction in the word recognition skills through which meaning is ascertained.)

The mastery of the skills that lead to recognition and meaning of words may not be left to chance or haphazard practice. If this seems obvious, then it should be equally obvious that learning the word recognition skills should be carefully planned and expertly guided if it is to be effective. This means that the heart of the reading instruction program really is a competent, dedicated teacher who knows both the theory of reading instruction and the ways different children learn.

The number of word recognition skills varies from one reading authority to another, but basically they can be grouped under two types:

1. *Learning to respond to the phonic (sound) clues provided by the letters standing in the word, including the recognition of such parts of words as syllables, prefixes, and suffixes.*

This skill is usually spoken of as two separate skills: (a) *phonics* and (b) *structural analysis.* Teaching phonics and structural analysis calls for teachers who have mastered the fundamentals of these skills and who know how to teach them to children. For teachers who do not meet these criteria, schools should provide in-service training. So far as their students are concerned, teacher education institutions should make certain that their prospective reading teachers do master those fundamentals.

2. *Learning to recognize words by the meaning clues provided by the other words standing in the material being read, and to confirm these recognitions through use of the other word recognition skills.*

Training and practice in using meaning clues in identifying new words also requires the help of a skillful teacher. It is *not* mere random guessing, but a skill that can be highly developed. It requires thinking through the context so that meanings are chosen systematically and logically.

These skills must be practiced until they become automatic. Furthermore, children should be encouraged to use them simultaneously rather than separately. In actual reading they are probably more often used simultaneously than independently.

As children identify words through facility in the use of the word recognition skills, they learn to recognize those words instantly as wholes through their unique patterns of letters. For instance, once a word and its meaning are firmly determined (for example, the word "teacher"), that word should thereafter be recognized instantly as a whole because of the unique pattern of the letters in it. That is how the "reading vocabulary" that all good readers must possess is built. We do not go through life figuring out what a word means every time we meet it. In fact, we have not really learned a word until we do recognize it instantly as a whole. Expert readers are those who have acquired huge reading vocabularies and who have to stop only occa-sionally to unlock a new word.

In summary, if a program of reading instruction is to be effective, it is essential for it to provide a carefully planned word recognition program, based in the beginning stages upon words common in children's speaking vocabularies. This program should be taught regularly and systematically; and its sequence and terminology should be consistent within a school system from year to year. . . .

45. WHAT RESEARCH TELLS US ABOUT WORD RECOGNITION*

Nila Banton Smith

WORD recognition, or "word perception" as we often call this phase of reading, is the most fundamental of the reading skills. Without ability to recognize words, the reading process cannot proceed. Important as word-recognition skills are, experimental research did not concern itself with this aspect of reading until rather late in our history.

* From Nila Banton Smith, "What Research Tells Us about Word Recognition," *Elementary School Journal,* LV (April, 1955), 440–46. Reprinted by permission of the author and The University of Chicago Press.

Delving into historical research, we find that during the beginning centuries of reading instruction children were taught to read by the alphabet method, and the only technique which they were expected to use in attacking an unrecognized word was simply to spell it. By some mythical process, spelling the word was supposed to tell an individual how to pronounce it.

The writer [19] found that the use of phonics did not enter American reading instruction until after the Revolutionary War, and then it came in as a patriotic, rather than a pedagogic, measure. Noah Webster, who wrote the first series of American readers and who was highly activated in terms of patriotic motives, sought some means of unifying the diversity of dialects which existed in the United States following the Revolutionary War. Unity was an essential aim at that time because on it depended the future existence of the young nation. The idea of teaching all children in the country to give the same sound to each letter and to each of the important groups of letters occurred to Webster as a means of teaching all young Americans to pronounce words in the same way. And so phonics was introduced vigorously in his *Blue Back Speller* and taught for many years for the purpose of unifying spoken language in America.

Eventually, however, the patriotic emphasis on teaching phonics subsided, and teachers discovered that learning the sounds of letters aided children in recognizing words in reading. Patriotism and phonics parted ways, and pedagogy took over where patriotism left off. Pedagogy gave phonics a new function, that of helping children to attain independence in attacking new words while reading, and in this role, phonics has been continued in classrooms down to the present time.

The years between 1840 and 1860 constituted a period of vigorous protest against the A-B-C method by educational leaders, and in some quarters against the method of teaching the sounds of letters. During these years, Bumstead [4] and Webb [26] began publishing readers based on the word method. Many school people were intrigued by the startling discovery that children could recognize whole words without knowing the letters and began using this method. The majority of schools, however, continued to use the phonic method in teaching children to read.

So much for the historical research in regard to word recognition. Although it is only in comparatively recent years that experimental research has begun to invade this area of reading, there are several studies which can be reported. These studies seem to fall mainly under four headings: "How do we recognize words?" "Is phonics effective?" "When should phonics be taught?" "What elements should be emphasized?"

How Do We Recognize Words?

The earliest experimental studies in word recognition had to do with perception. They were conducted for the purpose of ascertaining the general nature of the word-recognition process. While not directly concerned with phonics, these studies certainly pointed toward word analysis.

Huey,[14] a pioneer in investigating this problem, concluded some four decades ago that, in the case of the fluent reader, the general form or outline of the word is a sufficient visual cue to its recognition:

The aid supplied by the context tips the balance in favor of the unitary recognition of the word. . . . With very familiar words, the letter recognition is checked in its incipiency. . . . With new words, the recognition of certain letters may quite complete itself before the whole word is known [14:103].

Hamilton [11] and other early investigators agree with Huey. Several years later, Vernon [24] also concluded that both the total word form and its distinguishing characteristics are important aids to recognition. She further concluded that children in the process of learning to read are influenced more by significant parts of words than are adults with mature reading habits.

These and several others who have investigated perception seem to agree that, in the majority of cases, the general characteristics of a word are the clues by which it is recognized but that, when some unfavorable condition arises or when the words are strange or difficult, additional distinctions within the word are required. As early as 1925, the following aids to word recognition were identified: the context, the total configuration of a word, significant details of words, phonetic analysis, and use of the dictionary.[10] At the present time we teach children the use of all these methods of attack plus another one just recently added, the study of word structure. Phonics, however, is the only one of these which has been the target for much research. The effectiveness of teaching phonics has been challenged by many investigators.

Is Phonics Effective?

Among the earliest studies reported in regard to the effectiveness of phonics were those conducted by Currier and Duguid from 1918 to 1923. After five years of experimentation with different primary-grade groups, Currier reported:

1. Phonetic drills have a very real value but are not essential to every child as a part of the daily program in primary grades.

2. Phonetic drills should at all times be employed with discretion and adapted to the needs of the individual child or special group.

3. Word-pronunciation drills have proved to be of much value [6: 452].

Another early study was the Newark phonics experiment conducted by Sexton and Herron.[18] The experiment involved nearly a thousand pupils in Grades 1A and 1B, who were also followed through Grade 2. Some of the groups were taught phonics; others were not. The results favored the teaching of phonics strongly. Nevertheless, they showed that there was less difference between phonic and non-phonic groups than between groups having different teachers. Good teachers obtained unusually good results whether or not they taught phonics, and vice versa.

Garrison and Heard,[8] working with four classes of children during their three primary years, concluded that children having phonics learned greater independence in pronunciation than did the no-phonics group.

Agnew [1] carried on some rather extensive studies with primary-grade children in Raleigh, North Carolina. His conclusions indicate that, while comprehension in silent reading was not affected by isolated phonics, longer periods of phonetic study did increase word recognition and pronunciation as checked in oral reading. Tate [20] also concluded that isolated phonics instruction increased ability to recognize words but that it did not affect comprehension.

Other investigators have found positive correlations between phonics and comprehension. In the study of Tiffin and McKinnis,[23] the correlations between scores on a phonic test and three silent-reading tests varied from .55 to .70. Russell [17] also found that phonics contributed to comprehension.

Templin,[22] who investigated phonic knowledge as related to reading and spelling in Grade 4, concluded that a substantial amount of phonic knowledge had been acquired by fourth-grade pupils. She also found that, in unfamiliar test situations, the poor spellers and poor readers applied their phonic knowledge less well than did good spellers and good readers, while the difference was not significant when phonic knowledge was measured in familiar words. This may indicate a real difference in the ability of children of similar intellectual level to transfer what they know from one situation to another. On the other hand, it may be related to the various methods of teaching. One wouldn't expect that isolated methods of teaching phonics would transfer as much as related methods.

Gates and Russell [9] conducted a study with three groups of pupils. Group D received the smallest amount of phonics or word analysis; Group E was given moderate amounts of informal, newer-type word analysis, comparisons, and the like; and Group F was provided with large amounts of conventional, phonetic drill. Pupils in Group E, who were given moderate amounts of informal, newer-type word analysis work, exceeded those in the

other two groups in all tests of word recognition and comprehension.

Tate, Herbert, and Zeman [21] also found that incidental teaching of phonics, in connection with children's needs in working out words encountered in their reading, was superior either to the teaching of isolated phonics or no phonics instruction.

House [13] studied the effect of a program of instruction on pronunciation skills in the middle grades. The results of his experiment showed a distinct superiority of pupils who were given specific training with carefully prepared instructional materials over those who received no such training. This investigator pointed out that word-analysis skills can be taught more effectively not only when systematic instruction is given but also when the functional use of what is taught can be integrated with such instruction.

To sum up these conclusions, it appears that we have a considerable body of evidence to the effect that phonics instruction is valuable but that its greatest value is realized only when it is closely related to children's needs and is given direct application to words which cause them trouble in their daily reading.

When Is Phonics Instruction Most Valuable?

In years gone by, phonics instruction was begun on the children's first day in Grade 1, and intensive instruction in learning the sounds of letters and combinations of letters was continued all through the early and later first-grade period. At present the trend seems to be to provide some kind of phonics readiness program in Grade 1 but to delay more intensive phonics instruction until Grades 2 and 3.

The research done on phonics would seem to justify this delay. Sexton and Herron,[18] in the Newark phonics experiment previously cited, drew the conclusion that the teaching of phonics functions very little or not at all during the first five months in Grade 1 but begins to be of some value during the second five months and is of great value in Grade 2.

Dolch and Bloomster [7] found many individual differences in regard to the mental age at which children were able to work profitably with phonics. Their general conclusion, however, was that a mental age of seven years was necessary for a child to make the best use of phonics. Garrison and Heard,[8] mentioned previously, also concluded that much of phonics instruction should be deferred until Grade 2 or Grade 3.

All these studies point toward a delay of phonics instruction for the average child until Grade 2. I find nothing in research, however, which indicates that we should not provide for the development of phonics readiness in Grade 1 so that those children who need phonics will be prepared to work with it when a more intensive phonics program is offered at the second-grade maturity level. *BBEaw*

What Should Be Taught in a Phonics Program?

A summary of research on phonics would not be complete without a mention, at least, of studies which have

been made to determine phonic content. A pioneer study to determine the relative importance of phonics elements was conducted by Vogel, Jaycox, and Washburne,[25] who analyzed the vocabularies of readers and standard vocabulary lists to find out which letter groupings occur more commonly. An early study of Cordts [5] also analyzed primary reader vocabularies for phonetic elements. Two more recent studies have been reported by Black [3] and by Oaks [16] in regard to frequency of consonant and vowel sounds, respectively, in primary reading vocabularies. The length of the lists from these studies prevents their presentation in this article.

Miscellaneous Studies

A few studies, broader in scope than the phonics studies, have been made. Bennett,[2] for example, conducted an analysis of word-recognition errors made by children. The analysis was concerned with 37,274 errors made by retarded readers at about the third- or fourth-grade level in school placement. The errors which she found had to do with the final letters, the initial letters, median vowels, reversals of initial consonants, reading of a whole word or part in right-to-left sequence, final -s errors, and substitutions.

Hester [12] checked the word-recognition ability of 130 pupils referred to a reading clinic, all of whom were below third-grade level. She found that 18 of the pupils had no difficulty with the letter names, sounds, or blends. One hundred and twelve of the pupils lacked partially or entirely the knowledge of phonics essential for independent word attack. She concluded that, whereas configuration clues and context clues are essential in good reading, failure to teach the child the sounds of letters will leave him unable to attack new words independently when the other methods fail.

In recent years we have been hearing a great deal about auditory perception and visual perception, both of which are fundamental factors in word recognition. One study in this area, that of Murphy and Junkins,[15] is well worth noting. It involved three groups of children: an experimental group of pupils which was given thirty auditory discrimination lessons as a part of the regular reading instruction, a second experimental group which was given visual-discrimination lessons, and a control group that continued its regular program of instruction. Auditory and visual discrimination tests were given to all groups at the end of six weeks. As would be expected, the group with auditory training excelled in this type of perception, while the group with visual training excelled in visual perception. The most important result was the gain in the number of words retained of those taught. The experimental groups doubled their capacity, while the control group made little progress. Later experiments indicated that reading failures in the first grade were greatly reduced when a combination of training in both auditory and visual perception was provided.

Summary

In conclusion, we might say briefly that research tells us:

1. It cannot be assumed that *all* children need phonics.

2. Phonics is effective with children who need word-recognition help, but its greatest effectiveness is attained when it is taught functionally and is related to children's reading needs.

3. It is advisable to delay intensive phonics instruction until a child has attained a mental age of seven years.

4. Phonics instruction is most valuable at the second- and third-grade levels.

5. The use of configuration clues and context clues should be supplemented with phonics.

6. It would be well to give more attention to both visual and auditory discrimination in teaching all types of word recognition.

REFERENCES

1. AGNEW, DONALD C. *The Effects of Varied Amounts of Phonetic Training on Primary Reading*, pp. 8–50. Duke University Research Studies in Education, No. 5. Durham, North Carolina: Duke University Press, 1939.

2. BENNETT, ANNETTE. "An Analysis of Errors in Word Recognition Made by Retarded Readers," *Journal of Educational Psychology*, XXXIII (January, 1942), 25–38.

3. BLACK, ELSIE BENSON. "A Study of the Consonant Situations in a Primary Reading Vocabulary," *Education*, LXXII (May, 1952), 618–23.

4. BUMSTEAD, JOSIAH F. *My Little Primer*. Boston: Perkins & Marwin, 1840.

5. CORDTS, ANNA D., and McBROOM, MAUDE MARY. "Phonics," *Classroom Teacher*, II, 427–29. Chicago: Classroom Teacher, Inc., 1927.

6. CURRIER, LILLIAN BEATRICE. "Phon-

ics and No Phonics," *Elementary School Journal,* XXIII (February, 1923), 448–52.

7. DOLCH, E. W., and BLOOMSTER, MAURINE. "Phonic Readiness," *Elementary School Journal,* XXXVIII (November, 1937), 201–5.

8. GARRISON, S. C., and HEARD, M. T. "An Experimental Study of the Value of Phonics," *Peabody Journal of Education,* IX (July, 1931), 9–14.

9. GATES, ARTHUR I., and RUSSELL, DAVID H. "Types of Materials, Vocabulary Burden, Word Analysis, and Other Factors in Beginning Reading," *Elementary School Journal,* XXXIX (September and October, 1938), 27–35, 119–28.

10. GRAY, WILLIAM SCOTT. *Summary of Investigations Relating to Reading.* Supplementary Educational Monographs, No. 28. Chicago: University of Chicago Press, 1925.

11. HAMILTON, FRANCIS. *The Perceptual Factors in Reading.* Columbia University Contributions to Philosophy, Psychology, and Education, Vol. XVII, No. 1, pp. 52–53. Lancaster, Pennsylvania: Science Press, 1907.

12. HESTER, KATHLEEN B. "A Study of Phonetic Difficulties in Reading," *Elementary School Journal,* XLIII (November, 1942), 171–73.

13. HOUSE, RALPH W. "The Effect of a Program of Initial Instruction on the Pronunciation Skills at the Fourth-Grade Level as Evidenced in Skills Growth," *Journal of Experimental Education,* X (September, 1941), 54–56.

14. HUEY, E. B. *The Psychology and Pedagogy of Reading,* pp. 102–16. New York: Macmillan Co., 1912.

15. MURPHY, HELEN A., and JUNKINS, KATHRYN M. "Increasing the Rate of Learning in First Grade Reading," *Education,* LXII (September, 1941), 37–39.

16. OAKS, RUTH E. "A Study of the Vowel Situation in a Primary Vocabulary," *Education,* LXXII (May, 1952), 604–17.

17. RUSSELL, DAVID H. "A Diagnostic Study of Spelling Readiness," *Journal of Educational Research,* XXXVII (December, 1943), 276–83.

18. SEXTON, ELMER K., and HERRON, JOHN S. "The Newark Phonics Experiment," *Elementary School Journal,* XXVIII (May, 1928), 690–701.

19. SMITH, NILA BANTON. *American Reading Instruction,* pp. 69–70. Newark, New Jersey: Silver, Burdett & Co., 1934.

20. TATE, HARRY L. "The Influence of Phonics in Silent Reading in Grade I," *Elementary School Journal,* XXXVII (June, 1937), 752–63.

21. TATE, HARRY L., HERBERT, THERESA M., and ZEMAN, JOSEPHINE K. "Nonphonic Primary Reading," *Elementary School Journal,* XL (March, 1940), 529–37.

22. TEMPLIN, MILDRED C. "Phonic Knowledge and Its Relation to the Spelling and Reading Achievement of Fourth Grade Pupils," *Journal of Educational Research,* XLVII (February, 1954), 441–54.

23. TIFFIN, JOSEPH, and McKINNIS, MARY. "Phonic Ability: Its Measurement and Relation to Reading Ability," *School and Society,* LI (February 10, 1940), 190–92.

24. VERNON, M. D. *The Experimental Study of Reading.* Cambridge, England: Cambridge University Press, 1931.

25. VOGEL, MABEL; JAYCOX, EMMA; and WASHBURNE, CARLETON W. "A Basic List of Phonics for Grades I and II," *Elementary School Journal,* XXIII (February, 1923), 436–43.

26. WEBB, RUSSELL. *Webb's Normal Readers.* New York: Sheldon, Lamport & Blakerman, 1856.

46. TEACHING A BASIC READING VOCABULARY*

Edward Fry

RECENTLY the popular press and some professional journals have placed great emphasis on the phonics approach to the teaching of beginning reading. Educators might well look again at their reading instruction programs with a view to assessing the efficiencies of teaching words as "whole words."

The fact that a high percentage of all beginning reading material is composed of relatively few words has been well proven and is easily demonstrable. In a recent study done in the Loyola Reading Clinic, for example, samples of reading material used in the first three grades were taken from the reading texts issued by three major publishers. The three hundred commonest words in the English language, referred to as the "Instant Words" because they must be recognized instantly before the child can gain real reading facility, were found to make up an average of 63 per cent of the sample. The range varied from 58 to 77 per cent, depending upon the publisher. This means that more than half of all the words a child encounters in reading texts during the first three years of his reading experience come from a list of only three hundred words. What

* From Edward Fry, "Teaching a Basic Reading Vocabulary," *Elementary English,* XXXIX, No. 1 (January, 1960), 38–42. Reprinted by permission of the author and the National Council of Teachers of English.

is more, the same three hundred common words also comprise nearly one half of most adult reading material—the front page of our daily newspaper, the magazines and popular books we read. It seldom dips below 40 per cent, even in technical articles.

On the surface, then, learning to read would appear to be a task which is ridiculously easy: If 300 words will do such a large percentage of the job, why not begin with just these words, teach them quickly, and get it over with at once? There must be an easy way to do it.

Exponents of the phonics approach would insist that learning the sounds of words is the key to the integration of words-and-meanings. But many of the first three hundred Instant Words do not yield to the commonly taught phonics rules. Even if the rules could be made to work out well in all cases, we should still not expect a student to achieve any degree of reading fluency if he has to sound out most of the words he learns. Try, as an example, to sound out the words "of" or "was" using the phonetic rules of nearly any system taught to primary children or to students in remedial reading classes. It is most inappropriate.

What is needed is some means of making these relatively easy and oft-repeated words instantly recognizable on sight. It is by no means a simple task. In the first place, the Instant Words are largely devoid of subject-matter meanings or object reference (such subject-matter words as "sleeping" or "horseback" can be taught with comparative ease). In the second place, it takes time for the child to assimilate what he has learned.

Experience had shown that, normally, mastery of the first three hundred Instant Words (or of any basic vocabulary list, for that matter) could be expected to take nearly three years for primary children. An average child in an average school situation learns most of the first one hundred words toward the end of the first year. The second hundred words are added during the second year. It is not until some time in the third year that all three hundred words are really mastered and used as a part of the child's own vocabulary. This is not to deny that second and third graders can "read" many more words than the 300 Instant Words.

One can expect to decrease the learning time required in the case of older students—illiterate adults and students in upper elementary and secondary remedial reading classes. Still, their learning of the first three hundred Instant Words is found to parallel closely their attained reading ability level. For example, a person who can just manage to read upper second-grade material barely knows most of the first two hundred Instant Words. This is in line with the findings of Dolch and others.

Methods of Instruction

Methods for teaching the Instant Words vary with the teacher, the pupil, and the educational situation. We at the Reading Clinic say that any way that is successful is fair—that any method that works is a good method.

We use card games, easy reading, tachistoscopes, flash cards, and spelling lessons augmented by lavish praise, stern talks, competition, or a play-therapy climate. The pupil learns to read words in books, on flash cards, in his own compositions, or off the screen when words are flashed at 1/25th of a second. We teach him alone and in large groups, in the classroom and out under the trees. But all the while we are constantly telling him three things by word and deed: (1) We care about him. (2) We want him to read. (3) These Instant Words are important.

Easy Reading is one of the best ways of teaching the Instant Words. By "easy reading" is meant, simply, that if a child *can* read on the second-grade level of material (whether with help or hesitatingly), for him "easy reading" is reading first-grade materials. Betts gives an excellent definition of easy reading—when a child can pronounce 99 per cent of the words. Another Betts rule-of-thumb is that when the child averages fewer than one mistake for every twenty words, the material is "easy" for him. Easy reading is especially beneficial because it is certain to contain the Instant Words, and a child who barely knows these words gets practice in recognizing them. Easy reading makes it easier to apply context cues. Each reading gives the child a feeling of success, and encourages him to try to learn more.

Some primary children become discouraged at the sight of a whole page of printing. And children in remedial reading classes have sometimes learned to hate a page of printing. For these pupils it is often well to teach them reading in a completely different setting. We have had success with reputedly "hopeless cases" by having them do a fair amount of reading from filmstrips projected on the screen. There is something about a partly darkened room with its illuminated image that attracts attention, much as the television screen does for us all. We try to induce a sort of game atmosphere by flashing the word on the screen as quickly as an eye blink (tachistoscopically) and daring the child to see it. If he does catch the word, he can write it down, paying attention to proper spelling. When called upon, he can tell the teacher the word and earn the reward of proving how good he is. (Perhaps the child is virtually being trapped into reading, but the process is painless.) In case he does not know how to read the word, the teacher or another student reads it aloud, so that he can hear it and associate the visual-written image with the sound. In any event, right or wrong, the student sees the word on the screen again, and corrects his written response or writes it for the first time if he missed it altogether.

Repeating the showing of each word, and pronouncing the word immediately after the student has attempted to write and say it (we can assume that most students will try to say the word to themselves, even if not called on) gives what the psychologist calls the "knowledge of results," a very effective tool in learning and motivation. In addition to knowledge of results, some of the learning principles involved in the process are (1) "learning set," *i.e.* paying attention to the right thing; (2) multi-sensory approach, *i.e.*, the use of eyes, ears, speech, fingers, with their corresponding areas of the brain, (3) learning small units which increase the frequency of the rewarding effect of knowledge of results; and (4) the sheer novelty of the use of the screen which is unlike other reading experiences.

It is not necessary to have a tachistoscope to take advantage of many of these learning principles. Flash cards do many of the same things. Both flash cards and the tachistoscopic presentation of words can be done in large groups or individually. In fact, either can be self-administered by the student, although self-administration often makes correction a problem. We frequently use flash cards with small groups. The teacher flashes the word as quickly as possible. The student who says the word first gets to hold the card. The point of the game is to see who gets the most cards. Inequities in reacting time or ability can be partially offset by giving each student a turn at recognizing the word; when he misses, the next student gets the turn. Students sometimes work alone with a small pack of flash cards, separating them into two piles, (1) the card he knows, and (2) those he does not know. When he is finished, the teacher or a superior student checks up on the "know" pile and then helps him with the "don't know" pile.

Bingo is an excellent game for teaching Instant Words to large groups, but it is equally useful for small groups.

Twenty-five words can be placed on a card (five rows and five columns) in random order, with a card each for as many students as are playing. The teacher calls off the words in random order, or may take the precaution of drawing the word cards out of a hat. Markers can be small squares of cardboard. The first student to get complete row or column or diagonal line wins. Oftentimes, even though there has been a winner, the class likes to play on until the board is filled, so that every word is covered. If played until the board is filled, the teacher can sometimes spot poor readers by the number of uncovered words. In a teaching situation where some of the students do not know all the words, excellent instruction can ensue by having the teacher show the card or write the word on the board after saying it; this gives poor readers an equal chance at winning, which is always desirable.

Another game played with great success is called Pairs. This is a rummy-type of card game for from two to five players. First a deck of fifty cards is made by the teacher or by an able child. The fifty-card deck contains twenty-five pairs of identical cards, thus using exactly one group of 25 Instant Words (see appendix). Each player is dealt five cards. The first player asks one other player if he has a specific card (the asking player must hold the mate in his hand). If the asking player gets the card, he has a "pair" and may lay it down. If not, he draws a card from the deck. The object is to get as many pairs as possible. For most efficient reading instruction, the players should know some but not all of the words used in a given deck. If the asking player does not know how to read a card, he may show it and any player or the teacher may read it for him. Likewise, the player being asked may request to see the card asked for, so that he may compare it with the cards in his hand.

Once in a while it is good to review easy words already mastered, just for fun; but, generally, instructional games should follow the same rules as the selection of instructional reading material, *i.e.,* not too easy, and not too hard.

We have suggested only a few of many possible specific methods for teaching the Instant Words. Experienced reading teachers know and use many more. In remedial reading, especially, a variety of methods is desirable.

Summary

The fact that 63 per cent of all words used in the first three years of reading consists of just 300 basic words points to the desirability of stressing the teaching of this fundamental vocabulary so that these words may be recognized instantly.

Teachers are cautioned not to expect it to be too easy a task to teach the first 300 Instant Words, for mastery of them frequently corresponds to approximately the third grade level of reading.

A number of methods used successfully in teaching these words were explained: (1) encouraging easy reading, (2) tachistoscopic drill with writing, (3) use of flash cards, (4) a bingo game, and (5) a card game called Pairs.

Some of the psychological principles of learning were mentioned with particular reference to the method of using filmstrips, but many of them are common to the other methods as well. The learning principles include knowledge of results, learning set, multisensory approach, frequent rewarding, and novelty.

REFERENCES

BETTS, EMMETT. *Foundations of Reading Instruction.* American Book Company, New York, 1950.

DOLCH, EDWARD. *A Manual for Remedial Reading.* The Garrard Press, Champaign, Illinois, 1945.

FRY, EDWARD. "Developing a Word List for Remedial Reading," *Elementary English,* November 1957.

————. "Instant Words" (Filmstrips), *Learning Through Seeing,* Sunland, California, 1957.

APPENDIX

THE INSTANT WORDS *

First Hundred Words
(*approximately first grade*)

Group   1   the a is you to and we that in not for at with it on can will are of this your as but be have

Group   2   he I they one good me about had if some up her do when so my very all would any been out there from day

Group   3   go see then us no him by was come get or two man little has them how like our what know make which much his

Group   4   who an their she new said did boy three down work put were

* Copyright by Edward Fry, Director, Reading Clinic, Loyola University of Los Angeles.

before just long here other old take cat again give after

Second Hundred Words
(*approximately second grade*)

Group   5   saw home soon stand box upon first came girl house find because made could book look mother run school people night into say think back

Group   6   big where am ball morning live four last color away red friend pretty eat want year white got play found left men bring wish black

Group   7   may let use these right present tall next please leave hand more why better under while should never each best another seem tree name dear

Group   8   ran five read over such way too shall own most sure thing only near than open kind must high far both and also until call

Third Hundred Words
(*approximately third grade*)

Group   9   ask small yellow show goes clean buy thank sleep letter jump self fly don't fast cold today does face green every brown coat six gave

Group 10   hat ear write try myself longer those hold full carry eight sing warm sit dog ride hot grow cut seven woman funny yes ate stop

Group 11   off sister happy once didn't set round dress fail wash start always anything around close walk money turn might hard along bed fine sat hop

Group 12   fire ten order part only fat third same love hear yesterday eyes door clothes though o'clock second water town took pair now keep head food

47. BASAL TECHNIQUES IN TEACHING PHONETICS*

Arthur I. Gates

THE modern reading method provides a carefully organized program for developing a wide reading vocabulary. This program is concerned with the development of word meanings, word recognition, and word analysis. Word meanings should become richer and more exact. Word recognition should become quicker and more accurate. Word analysis—that is, insight into the visual and auditory characteristics of words—should become easier and surer. Although these three phases of reading vocabulary should be developed together in a mutually helpful program, this article will discuss chiefly the teaching of phonics or phonetics.

Unfortunately for clarity of discussion, phonics and phonetics mean many different things to teachers. In this article, teaching phonetics or phonics will mean merely instruction in the use of the auditory or sound characteristics of words in improving word perception and independence in word recognition. A number of types of phonetic ability are of great value in learning to read. They are useful primarily as tools to use in achieving familiarity with "new words" as they are introduced and in working out the recognition and pronunciation of unfamiliar words either in isolation or in the course of reading. What the most valuable skills are can best be indicated by pointing out the various devices which children can profitably use in learning to recognize words.

In the first place, it should be noted that ability to recognize words "at sight" at a single glance without detailed study, and the ability to work out the recognition of unfamiliar words by visual analysis without any type of phonetic analysis, are possible. As a matter of fact, children can learn to read very well without any phonetic training or any phonetic ability whatsoever. This was clearly demonstrated in an experiment in teaching deaf-mute children to read.[1] These children, who could not hear at all, learned to read and spell by means of visual analysis alone.

The fact that deaf-mute children and others do learn to read without utilizing phonetic clues is no argument for neglecting training in phonetics. The normal child learns more effectively and is more versatile when he can utilize both phonetic and visual

* From Arthur I. Gates, "Basal Techniques in Teaching Phonetics," in *Teachers' Service Bulletin in Reading*, Vol. VII, No. 9 (May, 1946). Reprinted by permission of the author and The Macmillan Company, New York, N.Y.

[1] A. I. Gates: Methods and Theories of Teaching the Deaf to Read. *Journal of Educational Research.* June 1925; and Helen Thompson: *An Experimental Study of the Beginning Reading of Deaf-Mutes.* Teachers College Contributions to Education No. 254, Teachers College, Columbia University, 1924.

clues. On a visual basis alone, a word can be recognized by noting its total shape or configuration and by singling out various tell-tale visual features within the word just as faces can be distinguished on the basis of visual clues. The modern program endeavors to help pupils become very expert in recognizing words by visual clues and it undertakes to teach them to use sound clues also. In most words, phonetic units form very effective visual clues, often the best ones. For example, the component word "day" in *daytime* or *Wednesday* is very useful in the visual recognition of these words and it is also a simple and useful phonetic element. Syllables, such as *an, ing, et,* and so on, are by definition phonetic units and have proved to be very useful clues in word recognition. Such combinations of letters as *br* in *bring,* or *th* in *thing* (typically called phonograms) are good visual as well as phonetic clues. Single letters can with value be made the basis of the phonetic approach in the case of short words, such as *hat, cat, boy,* and often a letter is the essential basis of distinguishing the words by sight.

Investigations have shown that the most useful clues for the recognition of words vary from word to word, and that to deal with a representative group of English words all the types mentioned above are desirable. In the early stages, where a large portion of the words are monosyllables, ability to translate the individual letters into sounds often comprises the best device for working out the recognition of an unfamiliar word. In the latter part of the second grade and later, where polysyllabic words comprise the larger

proportion of the new words, ability to detect component words and syllables of all kinds from short ones, such as *in,* to longer ones, such as *ight,* is indispensable. For example, it would be very difficult to work out the recognition and pronunciation of a long word, such as *automobile,* by sounding each of the ten single letters one after another. In many words several different kinds of units should be used. For example, if the child in the third grade is unable to recognize the word *vagabond* as a whole, a convenient way of working it out would be to detect the first syllable *vag,* the following letter *a,* and the final word *bond.* The program should therefore provide training for recognizing words by all the clues which have proved to be useful.

The newer program differs from older practice not only in attempting to teach the pupil how to take advantage of a wider variety of phonetic and visual clues but also in endeavoring to develop these skills by a better procedure. The first and most distinctive feature of newer practice is that instead of beginning with practice in sounding isolated letters or phonograms and then later in building up words by combining them, it begins by teaching the pupil how to locate useful elements in the whole word and to follow this by translating the elements into sounds and combining the sounds. This practice is based on the discovery that the first and, in general, the most difficult and important task in working out the recognition and pronunciation of an unfamiliar word is that of locating in the word those parts which can be either recognized by sight or, this failing, readily translated into sound. For example, if the pupil is confronted with the word *vagabond,* the first task is that of examining the word in such a way as to discover parts which he can translate into sounds. He may be familiar with the different divisions *vag-a-bond* but be unable to find them readily. The first attempt may result in *v-a-gab-ond,* or some other series of units which the pupil does not readily recognize. It is one thing to take the separate units *vag-a-bond* and combine or blend them into a word, but quite a different and a much more difficult task to take the word, find within it familiar elements, and then work out the total word sound. The modern method is to give the pupil in the word-analysis lessons the experience of doing precisely what he will be called upon to do when he encounters an unfamiliar total word. What he will encounter is a total word which must be analyzed and not a series of already separated word parts to be put together.

In the newer practice, two basal teaching techniques are employed. The first consists of providing the pupil with experience in making a direct attack upon the word immediately or shortly after it has been introduced, and later when it is encountered again for the purpose of locating the most useful (visual and auditory) clues. In some instances the teacher assists the pupils in locating these features. For example, after the word has been introduced in meaningful context, the teacher may present it for deliberate study. She may ask the pupils first to point out what seem to them to be the most useful parts or characteristics. If they do not themselves make what seems to the teacher to be the best analysis she may help them locate the best clues or deliberately point them out. In brief, she arranges for the pupils to study and analyze words both with and without her assistance.

The second basic technique is the comparison of each word with others that have been previously introduced. The teacher may select from the previously introduced words one or more of those with which the new one is likely to be confused or which contains similar parts or features. The basal problem for the learner is: How are these (two or more words) alike and different? By noting the parts that are alike the pupils are assisted to "generalize out" of the total word pattern particular word parts—letters, phonograms like *br,* syllables like *ing,* and component words like *day.* By doing this repeatedly, they come to recognize these elements quickly and accurately and to recall their sound. This helps them to recognize these same parts in words encountered later. This procedure also aids the pupils in detecting features of words which must be noted to avoid confusing one word with others. For example, when *ring* is compared with *sing,* the pupils, by noting the common element *ing,* learn to recognize it in these words and they also learn that the initial letters are essential means of distinguishing them. Thus they learn to perceive each word in the most fool-proof manner and to analyze out of it the characteristics which will be useful in unlocking many other words.

As a means of helping pupils learn to make these analyses by themselves, a variety of devices is utilized. A good one consists in incorporating in comprehension questions or exercises words likely to be confused or words containing common factors. One of these words must be chosen to answer the question or solve the problem, and in order to choose it the pupil must successfully distinguish it from the other similar words. For example, if the pupil has read a story, he may be given a comprehension exercise which includes the following:

                    brick.
The monkey did a funny lick.
                    trick.

In solving this exercise the pupil must have clearly in mind the proper meaning, then search for the word which conveys that meaning and distinguish it from others which closely resemble it. Here the pupil is given practice in utilizing context clues and word-form clues at the same time. Since the exercise presents the most similar words of those previously studied, the pupil's perception of words is sharpened to the degree necessary to enable him to read without error at this stage. Later, of course, words even more similar, and therefore more likely to be confused, may be introduced in an exercise of this type. In this way the pupil is not only assisted in analyzing out the common elements of words but is also given experiences which enable him to perceive words precisely enough to keep pace with the demands of his growing reading vocabulary.

The basic techniques underlying the newer method may be briefly summarized as follows:

1. Teaching the pupil to use all the clues, both visual and phonetic, which highly proficient readers find useful.

2. Teaching the pupil to do what he will be called upon to do in actual life, namely, to find the most helpful clues or features in a whole word encountered alone or in a phrase or sentence. The teaching procedure should include:

a. Demonstrating to the pupils the best methods of analyzing typical words.

b. Guiding the pupils in their own efforts to analyze and "study over" words.

c. Inducing pupils to study words regularly by themselves to discover the familiar and distinctive features.

d. Setting-up exercises which force the pupil to analyze and compare words carefully in order to solve the problem.

These are the basic features of the newer program. Needless to say, the details of material and teaching procedure vary considerably with the grade and with the abilities of the child. It should be noted, however, that the method outlined can and should be put into operation, practically speaking, on the first day the pupil is introduced to reading. As soon as the pupil has been introduced to three or four words, the teacher can begin to show him what features of these words to note and she can put them side by side or one above the other and guide him in comparing them. When the next words are introduced, the pupil can himself try to find their tell-tale features and see the similarities and differences among them. At the early stage, of course, the teacher should provide a maximum of guidance and demonstration but even at this early stage it is reasonable and desirable to expect the pupils to do something for themselves in the way of "studying over" words, noting similarities and differences, and trying to find ways to distinguish the words from each other.

There is, in other words, no problem of "when" to introduce phonics or word analyses. The teaching of phonics becomes an intrinsic part of this broader program of word study and word analysis. It begins on the first day of school and continues throughout all the grades.

In this program much depends upon the teacher's skill in helping the pupils find the features of words most useful for visual recognition and phonetic translation and in "analyzing out" the most useful common factors—letters, phonograms, syllables, and "little words in big words." Among other things she needs to know, when she introduces a "new word," is what words previously introduced in her basal program are most likely to be confused with it. As anyone realizes who has tried to compare, say, in the second grade, a particular word with all those previously introduced in the basal program, finding the most significant words for comparison is a large task. The authors of basal programs can help the teacher enormously by publishing, in the teachers' manuals, suggestions for analyzing and comparing words based upon a careful study of each of the words in comparison with all the words previously introduced. Such material would afford an excellent basis for a word-study program in each lesson.

48. PHONICS: CONSONANTS*

Emmett Albert Betts

THE story is often told of Amanda and Rebecca, who often spent their afternoons in the parlor knitting and commenting on life in general. One

* From Emmett Albert Betts, "Phonics: Consonants," *Education,* LXXXII, No. 9 (May, 1962), 533–36. Reprinted by permission of the author and The Bobbs-Merrill Co., Inc., Indianapolis, Ind.

afternoon Rebecca looked up from her knitting and said, "Mandy, do you know that *sugar* is the only word in which the *s* has the *sh* sound?"

Amanda kept to her knitting, lost in serious thought. After a while, she looked up and asked, "Becky, are you sure?"

No, Mandy had not thought of the *sh* sound in *sure!*

Our badly spelled English has many letters for the same sound. The *sh* sound, for example, is spelled *sh* in *shore,* s in *sure,* c in *ocean,* ch in *Chicago,* t before *i* in *nation,* ss in *passion.*

Then again the sound of *b* is represented by *b* in *bat* and *bb* in *rabbit.* But in *climb* it has no sound!

The letter *c* has no sound of its own, representing *k* in *cat,* s in *city,* sh in *vicious,* and so forth. Neither does *x* have a sound of its own, representing *ks* in *box,* g-z in *examine,* and so on. The letter *q,* of course, has no sound of its own, usually representing the first part of the blend *kw,* as in *queen* and *square.*

In the words *hot* and *hat,* the vowel sound is the cue to the meaning of each spoken word. On the other hand, in the words *race* and *raise,* the consonant sound is the cue to the meaning, the hissing *s* sound of *c* in *race* and the buzzing sound *z* of *s* in *raise* offering the only clues to the differences in meaning.

Consonant Settings of Vowels

While the key to the syllable is the vowel, its setting usually is a consonant before and/or after it. This consonant setting may be fairly simple, as in *at* or *cat.* Or, it may be made more complex by consonant blends, as in *(gl)ad* or *(spl)ash.* Then, too, the vowel setting may include a number of consonant letters representing no sound at all, as in *(w)rite* and *ni(gh)t.*

Whole-word Approach

One of the first steps in teaching consonant sounds is to help the child tune

his hearing to them. He is taught, for example, to hear the simple sound of *m* in *my* and the blend of *st* in *stop.* Then he is taught to hear, for example, the simple sound of *l* in *tail* and the blend of *lt* in *felt.* In teaching both first and last consonants, the child first learns to hear the undistorted consonant sounds in spoken words before he identifies the letters which stand for those sounds.

It is easy for the child to say the sound of long *a,* the sound of *er,* and other vowel sounds in isolation without distorting them. On the other hand, he needs more sophistication in order to say the isolated sounds of *b, v, d,* and other consonants without distorting them. Therefore, it is necessary for him to hear and say consonant sounds in combination with vowel sounds; that is, in syllables and words.

Confusion results when the child is taught that *buh-erd,* for example, is *bird.* *Bird* is a one-syllable word, but the distortion of the consonant sound produces a two-syllable word. This confusion is compounded when an attempt is made to teach him to hear the syllables in *singing, kindly,* and *happen.*

Sounds of Consonant Phonograms

Pupils are taught how to draw their own conclusions—to make their own rules—regarding the sounds of consonants. As stated before, this approach puts emphasis where it belongs: on understanding rather than the rote memorization of rules.

In learning the sounds represented by the letter *c,* for example, the pupils need (1) to hear the consonant-vowel blend (e.g., *ca* of *cat*) of the spoken word and (2) to examine the written form of the word. In this instance, they might use these words from their reading vocabulary: *cake, call, came, can, cat.* After the study of these words, the pupils may conclude that *c* before *a* usually has the sound of *k.*

Later they may add to the rule the *k* sound of *c* before *o*, as in *coat, color, come, cookies.* Then they may add the *k* sound of *c* before *u*, as in *cut, cup, cub, cute,* and so forth.

Consonant Blends

When consonants are thoroughly learned, the pupils are well on their way to phonic independence. Before learning the consonant blend *st,* for example, they need to be well grounded in the sounds of *s* and *t*. In short, each element of a consonant blend is learned before blending the sounds.

A consonant blend is a grouping, or a cluster, of sounds. The goal of instruction is to teach the pupils to group letters, as the *st* of *stop*, automatically —to prevent an inefficient letter-by-letter word attack in reading and letter-by-letter spelling. The grouping of the first two consonants of *stop*, for example, cuts the word down to the two parts *st* and *op* or *sto* and *p*, bringing the word under control for the pupils.

This learning to *group* letters into phonograms pays big dividends when they meet in their reading *brook, chair, friend, through,* and other long one-syllable words. But still bigger dividends are paid when they are confronted with *broken, chimney, station,* and other words of more than one syllable.

At this point a word of caution is necessary. The *wh* of *who, whole,* and so on represents the single sound of *h*. However, in *which* it represents the *hw* blend. The phonogram *sh* in *she* represents a single sound and, therefore, is not a blend. Likewise, the *th* and *ng* of *thing* represent single sounds, hence are not blends.

Steps in Teaching Blends

These steps are taken to teach consonant blends:

1. *Listening and saying.* To teach the pupils to hear the *st* blend, for example, have them say *stop* and *story* as they listen to the first sound.

Then, read, in a conversational tone, a list of three or four words and have the pupils raise their hands when they hear a word beginning with the same first sound as *stop*. For example, use *toy, stay, took, stand.* Avoid other consonant blends beginning with the *s* sound, as in *(str)eet*.

After the pupils have become fairly sharp in hearing the *st* blend, introduce words beginning with *s* and *sh*. For example, use *soon, star, she, step.* Then have the pupils say each word, listening to the first consonant sounds.

2. *Seeing the consonant phonogram.* For this purpose words from the pupils' reading vocabulary are used. First, the pupils listen to the initial consonant blend and say the *whole* word; for example, *stop* and *story.* Second, the teacher writes the words on the board and has the pupils say the words and identify the *st* letters representing the first sound.

Finally, they may study other words beginning with *s, t,* and *st.* For example, use *see, time, stop.* First, they listen to the initial consonant sound or blend as the teacher says them. Then, they say the words to get the feel of the first consonant. Finally, they identify the letters in whole words that represent the single sounds and the blend.

3. *Blending consonant and vowel.* Additional help may be given by having the pupils study vowel-consonant blends, as the *sto* of *stop* and the *stor* of *story.* By blending the consonant cluster with its vowel, the pupils can say the *sto* of *stop* or the *stor* of *story* without distorting the sound of *st.* After the pupils hear and say the vowel-consonant blend, then they identify the letters representing it in written words.

4. *Blending first consonants.* Some pupils need more help to get the "feel" of consonant blends. For them, these steps to teach the *st* blend, for example, are taken:

a. *Hearing the separate sounds of the blend.* Either using a picture or spoken words, have the pupils tell which words begin with the same sound as *sun: Sue, hen, seven.*

Use the same procedure for reviewing the initial *t* sound. For example, which words begin with the same sound as *toy: red, to, take.*

b. *Hearing the blend.* Then ask, "Which of these words begins with the first sounds of *sun* and *to: soon, story, to?*"

Or, ask, "In which of these words do you hear the sounds of *s* and *t* together at the beginning of the word: *soon, story, to?*"

c. *Seeing the letters of the blend.* Write on the chalkboard: *soon, story, to.*

Have the pupils say each word and

listen to the *s* of *soon, t* of *to,* and *st* of *story.* In each example, have them identify the letters representing the consonants sounds.

5. *Applying the learning.* These steps are taken to help the pupils apply their skills to first consonant blends:

a. Use the skill to identify new words with the same first consonant blend; for example, apply *st* skill to new words to be introduced in a succeeding reading activity, as *stay, step, still, stood, storm,* and so forth.

b. Blend the first consonant sound with other rhyming parts to make new words; for example, the *st* of *stop* with the *ep* of *step, ill* of *still,* etc.

c. Help the pupils to apply their skill to unknown words in their silent reading. For example, if the pupil needs help on *step,* ask, "What word do you know that begins like *step?*" (*stop*) Or, ask, "What are the first consonant letters?" (*st*) Then, "What word do you know that begins with *st?*" (*stop*) Finally, "What is the word?"

6. *Meaning.* At all points in the development of phonic skills, the meaning of the word is kept uppermost in the minds of the pupils. For example, in silent reading situation, they always check the meaning of the word in its sentence or paragraph setting.

In Summary

Phonic skills are usually taught by beginning with the spoken word and ending with the written word. That is, the pupil is first taught to hear the *kw* sound of *qu* in the spoken word *quick,* for example, before attending to the letters *qu* in the written word *quick* which represent that blend.

On the other hand, when anyone reads he is confronted with the written word and, therefore, must reverse the process. For example, when he sees the *qu* of *quick* he recalls the *kw* blend—if he has been taught this skill. Therefore, the pupil is taught how and when to apply his phonic skills to unknown words. If he has not learned his phonic skills, his situation is as hopeless as trying to beat water uphill with a stick. If he has learned them, his success with the systematic examination of written words is always clearly in sight.

49. RECOGNITION OF LONG WORDS*

E. W. Dolch

A PRACTICAL schoolman of long experience said some time ago that he did not see why there was so much fuss about reading. "It is all very simple," he said. "You just know the little words, you sound out the big ones, and you know what it says. No one can stop you."

We now know which are the little words that are most useful, and how to teach them, but the problem of the "long words" is still with us. A recent research points out that this is no small problem. Some time ago a list was published combining eleven big studies in vocabulary. This list contains 19,000 words. (It includes the Thorndike 20,000 but leaves out the proper names on that list.) These are probably the 19,000 most common words in reading matter in English. As a check, this list was gone through in order to count the number of one-syllable words, that is, the "little words." In the whole 19,000, there were only 3,000 one-syllable words. That leaves just 16,000 words of more than one syllable. These 16,000 are the most common "long words." But from them on, most of the rest of the words in the 600,-000 word dictionary are "long words," that is, words of more than one syllable.

If we think of the three primary grades as the time to learn the common words, that is, the "little words," we can then think of all the rest of schooling as the time for the "big words." This fact is pointed up by a study of the spelling lists used in

* From E. W. Dolch, "Recognition of Long Words," *Education,* LXXV, No. 9 (May, 1955), 604–8. Reprinted by permission of Mrs. E. W. Dolch and The Bobbs-Merrill Co., Inc., Indianapolis, Ind.

schools. These lists are obviously common words. But look at the lists for the various school years. It will be found that during the primary years, the great majority of the words are monosyllables, or little words. But these words are "used up" in a few years. Beginning with the fifth year list (words met with during the fourth year in reading) the lists are about half polysyllables, that is, words of more than one syllable. (We know that the dictionary says a "polysyllable is a word of several syllables, especially of more than three," but let us, for purposes of simplicity call a one-syllable word a monosyllable, and a word of more than one syllable a polysyllable. This is a usage that would help discussion and thinking very much.)

The real point is that, beginning with the new subjects of the fourth grade and for the rest of school and of after life, the problem of every school subject and of every kind of reading is the "long word" or the polysyllable. Monosyllables do still come up at times, but they are few. It is true that we continue to meet *inflections* of monosyllables, such as those with the ending *-ing,* and so on. But these are still monosyllables if we teach the children how to take off the inflectional ending. Inflected or "changed monosyllables" are not what we can properly call "long words."

Attacking the Long Words

A very common method of attack on a long word is to take off prefixes and suffixes. This is a good method, especially when we are emphasizing word meaning. Prefixes and suffixes do alter the meaning of a root or stem, and the way they alter it should be known. Therefore, emphasis should be put on prefixes and suffixes just as soon as the children can discover this alteration of meaning. Obviously, it should not go faster than they can discover it. For instance, the prefix "un-" in "undo," "untie," "uncommon" and the like will easily be discovered, and the effect of the prefix can be understood. But that does not mean that the children should at once take up the meaning of "pre-" and other prefixes. We always tend to try to go too fast with this matter of prefixes and suffixes. If we let the children call them to our attention, then we will have a guide as to when to study them. The study of prefixes and suffixes would naturally begin with the third grade perhaps, and continue on through all the other grades and into high school. But we will not follow the common practice of trying to crowd the subject into a short time, thus doing violence to the children's language by trying to get them to think of unfamiliar roots or unfamiliar changes in those roots.

However, the greatest defect of the approach through prefixes and suffixes is that these concern relatively few words and do not give a general method of attack on all long words. Stauffer found that 24 per cent of Thorndike's 20,000 words have prefixes, but this also says that 76 per cent of those common words do not. That is, roughly three words out of four in the elementary school do not have prefixes. So let us teach prefixes and suffixes at the proper time, but let us also ask how one should attack other words which do not have prefixes or suffixes.

A second common attack on long words is "finding small words in big words." Here we do not mean the finding of stems in words that have regular endings, such as finding "look" in "looking." That really should be called "identifying the original word." Instead, we mean working out a long word by the aid of groups of letters in them that happen to be little words. An instance is seeing the word "tent" in "contentment," or the word "public" in "publication." We all know that children do use this method of working out big words. We all use it. However, should this method be recommended? One study with this method was made on words in fourth-grade readers. The results showed that, about 40 per cent of the time, the correct word resulted, and about 60 per cent of the time, the wrong result was found. We all know instances of error, as when one pronounces the word as "*can*-ine" instead of "*ca*-nine" just because the small word is seen at the beginning. Even though the chances of real help are many, we must conclude that this method cannot be fully recommended.

Third, the most common method of teaching attack on long words is just showing children how particular words are actually divided. A child may be sent to the dictionary and asked to write a long list of words divided as done in the dictionary. Or when a child comes to a long word, he may be told what its usual division is. So all we do is just to say, "Well, these words are divided this way." This telling how particular words are divided does not give a method. It does not give rules. It actually leaves it to the child, consciously or unconsciously, to form his own rules or method. Most teachers and most textbooks know only this method. They can say how any particular word is divided, but they cannot say what the rules for division are. The child has to find them for himself if he is to do so at all.

Rules for Recognition of Long Words

There is, however, a definite help that can be given children for the recognition of long words. There are rules that help in *recognition of what word is meant*.

First, however, we must emphasize that these are *not rules for the pronunciation of English*. Rules for that purpose are given at the beginning of the large dictionary in twenty pages of fine print. The pronunciation of English is a very complicated thing. The sounding of different letters, of different syllables, and of different words depends on language origins, on word relationships, on letter relationships, and so on. No school child, not even a school teacher, can know all of these things. The only safe way to find out just how any word is pronounced in English is to get out the dictionary and study the respelling that is given after the word. No simple rules can take the place of such a study.

Second, we are dealing only with the *recognition of words that a child has already heard*. He may or may not know the meaning, but he does know the sound of the word if he could only recognize it. We are definitely not dealing with words which the child has never heard. If he tries to work out a word and does not recognize a familiar sound, he must ask someone what the word is or go to the dictionary and find out just what the sound is. As we have said, no rules can give the correct sounding for English. An attempt to sound out words that have never been heard gives such mistakes as "for-*mu*-la," "hypo-*thesis*," and so on. Instead, we are dealing only with the recognition of long words that the child has heard before. Reading can give him meaning, but it cannot give him the correct sound if he has never heard it.

Third, recognition of long words requires intelligence. Very often, the context suggests what the word might be, and the rules for recognition tell quickly if that is the right word or not. Rules for recognition can never do more than get the reader *near* to the right sound. They can never, as we have said, give the exact sound. Then if the reader gets close to the correct sound, his intelligence, together with the context, will tell him what the word is.

The Three Rules for Recognition of Long Words

1. *Every vowel or vowel combination means a syllable.*

Children are interested to listen to someone and to hear that every syllable means a vowel or vowel combination. They can count the syllables in words heard. They can say words they look at and see that "every vowel or vowel combination means a syllable." Of course "vowel combination" means

vowels that go together, such as *oa, ou, oi,* and so on.

In class, the teacher can write long words on the board and ask a child to take the chalk and put a check mark over every vowel or vowel combination. The check marks show the number of syllables.

2. *Divide syllables between two consonants that are between vowels or in front of one consonant that is between vowels.*

Children can understand the reason for this division. If the vowels make the noises or sounds, the consonants show how the vowel sounds are begun and how they are ended, as in *seen, rich,* and so on. So if we find two consonants between vowels in a long word, the first usually ends the syllable before them, and the second usually begins the syllable after them. But children should look out for the digraphs, such as *th, ch,* and so on. They are never divided.

3. *Usually a syllable that ends in a vowel has the long vowel sound, and a syllable that ends in a consonant has the short sound of the vowel.*

This rule for recognition begins with the word "usually" just because there are many exceptions. For recognition, we recommend that the child try the sound that the rule would give; and if the word is not recognized, try the other sound. It is recognition we are after, and not the exact sounding shown in the dictionary. We must also look out for the vowel with *r,* as the *r* is practically never divided from the vowel, and it has a special sound (*far, her, sir, for, fur*). Of course there are more vowel sounds than the short, the long, and the sound with *r* but again we are only trying to *get close* enough to recognize the word. Only the dictionary gives the fully accurate sound.

Method of Presentation

In teaching these rules for recognition of long words, one should emphasize, as we have, that it is only recognition we are after, not the accurate pronunciation, which can be found only from the respelling in the dictionary.

Then it is advisable to give the children sample words that illustrate the three rules and that can be used to remember them. Proper names are good for this purpose, especially local geographic and other names. In the West, the word *Kansas* illustrates division and the short sound of vowels; the word *Dakota* shows division and the long sound. In the Midwest, *Wisconsin* shows the short sound, and *Ohio* the long sound. In the East, *Pennsylvania* illustrates all the rules, but shows more than two consonants between vowels, and an exception to the long sound in the letter *i*. In our rule 3, the word *usually* must be emphasized.

But the best practice with the three rules comes in all the school subjects. In spelling, the children can try the rules to see if they work. "Do the sounds of the letters give the sound of the word?" If they do, they can be used to remember the right spelling; if they do not, the exception can be used to remember the right spelling. In arithmetic, new words can be tried out to see if they follow the rules. In history, science, health, all new words can be checked by the whole class. Classes like to do this. It will help them to give attention to the spelling problem in every word, and will develop skill in use of the Rules for Recognition.

With small children, exceptions to rules discourage. But older children are interested in exceptions. Here the teacher can give added information that will be most interesting. For instance, the word "Philadelphia" does not divide before the single consonant *l*, but there is a reason. We have a rule that in pronunciation we usually do not divide a root. The root here is "phil" which we see in "philanthropy" and elsewhere. That is why this word does not follow the rules at that point. In the word "helper," the rules would divide into *hel-per,* whereas the rule for not dividing the root would give us *help-er.* Which do we really say? The children will be much interested to try this out. If the class finds a violation of one of the rules and goes to the dictionary, they will often find very interesting information about the meaning or origin or structure of words.

To summarize, beginning with the fourth or fifth grade, long words in reading are the big problem. We can use no rules to tell us the right sound for words we have never heard, but for words we have heard, there are rules for recognition. We will find that the children have much fun in the use of these rules, and they will have a big part of their reading problem solved. To repeat what the schoolman said, "You just know the little words, you sound out the big ones, and you know what it says. No one can stop you."

50. POEMS MADE UP TO TAKE OUT*

Margaret Fishback

Spellbound

It's true, I do not like to spell,
Nor do I do it very well.
If "handle's" "l e," why not "travle"?
Such mysteries I can't unravle.
There's also "pare" and "pear" and
    "pair,"
Though which is which, I've ceased to
    cair.
I master demons such as "guide"
And "guard" with pardonable pruide,
But when it comes to "hear" and "here,"
I can't decide which way to stere.
And then I'm faced with "hair" and
    "hare"

* From Margaret Fishback, *Poems Made
Up to Take Out* (New York: David McKay
Co., Inc., 1963), pp. 13, 50, 52. Reprinted
by permission of the author and David
McKay Co., Inc.

To plunge me further in despare.
Indeed it seems to me absurd
To grapple with the written wurd—
I'd better throw away my pen
And never, *never* write agen.

Not Hard to Swallow

I wonder what would help my cough . . .
    A cup of coughey *should*.
At least it wouldn't bump me ough,
    And it *might* do me gould.

Homb, Sweet Homb

I'll comb
My domb
Then romb
To Nomb.

51. NOT BACK TO PHONICS—FORWARD TO PHONETICS!*

Helen Bowyer

WHY make a problem out of reading—at least so far as word recognition goes? Why not undercut the whole time-waste of "isle, style, mile, guile"—the memory burden of "meter, liter, heater, teeter"—the reason-flouting of "since, rinse—sense, scent—cent, sent"? It could be done with a system of sound-sign relationships at least as teachable as that through which Russia expedites the education of her young.

One such system is World English, which America's Simpler Spelling Association and its British ally have so long been offering.

You can try it out in the demonstration (slightly modified) which follows. Pronounce *ae, ee, ie, oe, oo* as in *maelstrom, fee, fie, foe, fool—aa* and *au* as in *bazaar* and *bauble—uu* and *ou* as in *put* and *pout*—italicized *th* as in *thin* and *both—zh* as in *pleasure* or *Persian*. Give all other letters and digraphs their most common present values, but notice that short *i* supplants *y* in such words as *perfectly* and that *t* and *z* supplant *d* and *s* wherever they more truly represent the sound.

"Yoo aar oeld, Faathur Wilym," the yung man sed,
"And yoor haer haz bekum veri hwiet,
And yet yoo insesntli stand on yoor hed,
Doo yoo *th*ink at yoor aej it iz riet?"
"In mie yoo*th*," Faathur Wilym replied too hiz sun,
"Ie feerd it miet injur the braen,
But now that Ei'm purfektli shoor Ei hav nun,
Hwie Ei doo it agen and agen."

"Buuli for him," chortld oeld Paul Hoil, kiking wun Purzhn slipur tordz the seeling, the uther *th*roo the dor.

Here in eighty-three words we have forty basic spelling units matched one-to-one with the forty basic sounds of our American speech. Together they constitute an alphabet as consistent and predictable as that through which the Soviet Union manages to have its children *reading* by Christmas of their first school year.[1] That it holds a similar promise for us is demonstrated daily through those missionary fields of Asia, Africa, and the islands of the

* From Helen Bowyer, "Not Back to Phonics—Forward to Phonetics!" *Phi Delta Kappan*, XLII, No. 5 (February, 1961), 207–10. Reprinted by permission of the author and *Phi Delta Kappan*.

[1] Soviet first graders start, of course, at age 7. Many are already reading well. Some learn in kindergarten, but more pick it up for themselves, according to Deana Leven, an English authority who taught for five years in a Moscow school. She says, "Russian is so nearly phonemic that children can and do learn to read in two or three months with very little adult help, once they know the alphabet."

seas where the Committee for World Literacy actively pursues its work. It uses this system, or a close approximation, in the beginning teaching of English. The committee's showing puts to shame our traditional system with its traditional spelling.

World English is not the only system actively engaged in providing one character and *one only* for each separate sound of our mother tongue. We have only to open our desk dictionary to find another literally staring us in the face. What do I do when I need to know whether the *ch* of *Eustachian* is that of *ache* or *aitch* (h)? Or whether *sophist* starts off with the vowel sound of *soap* or *sop?* Just what you do when you are not too certain about the beginning *X* of *Xanthippe,* her midriff *th,* or her final *e.* You look at the parenthesis after her entry and find that, at least among us barbarians, she is to be called Zantipē. And I hope that on this or some other such occasion you felt something of the exasperation of that sound-headed tenth-grader of mine who exploded into: "Why ain't they wrote that way in the first place? Why does a feller have to fool around with two spellings for one word?"

Why, indeed? Especially as he would only have to cross a bridge at El Paso or Brownsville to find himself in a world where a feller has to learn but one spelling. And that so simple and consistent he can all but automatically pronounce the whole vast vocabulary of his native *idioma,* just by application of the alphabet he learned way back in the early weeks of his first school year. It is a world where, in consequence, a seventeen-year-old graduates from his *Preparatoria* a good two years beyond his U. S. age-mates in almost every study which demands an easy and accurate command of the printed word. And a world, be it added, of twenty hemispheral allies whose respect for our culture we can ill afford to lose.

Our various dictionaries differ somewhat as to the symbols of their second spelling system, but as to its necessity they are as one. Says the *Funk & Wagnalls* unabridged (p. xxiii), "That we should be compelled to respell words in order to show how they are pronounced is a pity and an absurdity, since the original and proper function of spelling is to do that very thing. The maker of a German or Italian or Spanish dictionary has rarely any need to respell a word in order to tell his own countrymen how the word is pronounced. But in English the necessity exists and must continue to exist as long as our so-called orthography continues on its present footing. Hence arises the problem of a scientific alphabet."

There was a time when the National Education Association was acutely conscious of this problem. Way back in 1903 its Department of Superintendence called a conference to seek a solution. Together with the American Philological Association and the Foreign Language Society, it organized a committee which eventually produced the alphabet which, with some modifications, still appears in the *Funk & Wagnalls* unabridged dictionary as Key I to its respellings. But any hope the NEA may then have entertained that this alphabet would come into general use was doomed from the start by the diacritics used to indicate the value of its vowels. These diacritics, to a greater or lesser extent, still cripple today's dictionaries, even those compiled for the fourth and fifth grader. When a nine-year-old turns to his Thorndike for the pronunciation of *falcon, urge, ruthless,* why should he be faced with the strangeness of *fôkən, èrj, rüthlis,* when the familiar *faukn, urj, roothles* not only portray their sounds as well, but give him a sense of at-homeness in his dictionary which would lead to a more frequent and pleasurable use thereof?

Perhaps the greatest single service the NEA could now render in the reading area would be to authorize a series of school dictionaries making this simple change. It would be almost the only change needed to bring most dictionaries to an all-Roman letter key of maximum simplicity and trustworthiness. Their consonants are already close to that ideal. Like World English, they discard *c, q, x,* turning their redundant functions over to the perfectly able letters herewith indicated: sistern, *k*up—brus*k, k*wit—a*k*sis, e*g*zit, Zeno. Like W. E. too, they keep unchanged the diagraph *sh* but deprive *ch* of its prerogatives in *ch*imera and *ch*auffeur. Again, they add a second *th* to differentiate between *th*in and *th*en, and *zh* to represent the soft sibilant of plea*s*ure, rou*g*e, Per*s*ian. And all join World English in eschewing the double consonant, as such, and dropping all those silent letters which falsify pronunciation in such words as "lim*b*, e*d*ge, si*g*n, *gh*ost, *h*onor, ca*l*f, *m*nemonic, solem*n, p*seudo, deme*s*ne, li*s*ten, *w*rite." Moreover, all confine *y* to its purely consonantal function, as in *yet* and *banyan,* and respell *lyric, ugly, pity* as *lirik, ugli, piti.*

In short, with little more than a Romanizing of their parenthetic vowels, our dictionaries could not only facilitate a greater and more pleasurable resort to their pages but could provide young America with advance preparation for that inevitable day when our spelling will no longer be "a pity and absurdity" —when, as in that Latin world just across a bridge from Brownsville or El Paso, the entry will take care of its own pronunciation and mere application of one's first-grade alphabet will ensure correct spelling of every native word one writes, from *aardvark* to *Zyzzogeton.* And when in consequence, our Johnny will finish his eleventh grade neck and neck with Juanito in every subject which demands effortless command of the mechanics of reading.

Do we really have to go through a "back to phonics" era before we permit that day to dawn? We tried phonics for over three centuries. When, in all that time, were the bulk of our school children reading before Christmas of their first school year? Or even by June? Not in 1768, certainly—else why would Benjamin Franklin write: "Whatever the difficulties and inconveniences of changing our spelling are, they will be more easily surmounted now than hereafter. Sometime or other it must be done or our language will become the same with Chinese as to difficulty of learning and writing it."

Nor, certainly, in 1878, when a meeting of ten thousand teachers, led by professors from fifty leading colleges and universities, sponsored a memorandum to Congress which read, in part: "It is currently stated by leading educators that the irregular spelling of the English language causes a loss of two years of the school life of each child, and is a main cause of the alarming illiteracy of our people."

Nor when Andrew D. White was president of Cornell. Else why would he have lashed out at "the fearful waste of time on the part of millions of our children in learning the most illogical mode of spelling, probably, that this world has ever seen; the only result being to weary them of books and blunt their reasoning faculties."

Nor in 1906, when Theodore Roosevelt made his gallant attempt to bring the beginning of rational spelling into the Government Printing Office.

And even less in the late 1920's, else why the nationwide junking of the phonic method and the nationwide substitution of the whole word tactic?

If that has proved a jump from the frying pan into the fire, it doesn't alter the fact that the frying pan was a bad place to be and not one to jump back into. And it's no use saying the pan has been so improved it is practically a new utensil. I've glanced through most of the recent "how to" books which make this claim, and not even with a powerful glass can I see any essential difference between their handling of "does, dozen, cousin—us, bus, fuss—has, gas, pass" and the method on which I grew up and taught in my teacher-training days. Which one of them reduces by a single item the 250 spelling units in which our forty basic speech sounds are awash? Which deals more effectively with the scatterbrained transcripts of our simple *f* sound now cavorting through "if, staff,

giraffe, graph, laugh, calf?" Or with *f* and *gh,* which compound the disorder by ousting *v* and *p* from *of* and *hiccough?* Or with *gh,* which muscles in on *through, naught, et al.* without performing the shadow of a service today?

Is there a back-to-phonics proponent from Maine to California who could look a second-grader in the face and tell him these words are as easy to read, write, and spell as would be their simplifications into "staf, jiraf, graf, laf, kaf, ov, hikup, throo, naut?" Or assure a worried parent that after four years of phonic training his offspring will be getting more out of his future history texts if they are strewn with "monarch, foreign, usurp, allegiance, villeinage, demesne, ecclesiastic" rather than "monark, foren, yoozurp, alleejens, vilenaj, demeen, ekleeziastik" —and if all words between were spelt in conformity with these last?

At least Rudolf Flesch, whose *Why Johnny Can't Read* started the jump back into the frying pan, couldn't do it. He makes no bones about the fact that while the pan is preferable to the fire, there's an incomparably better place to be than either. Speaking of the world-famous Dr. Frank Laubach of the missionary Committee for World Literacy, Flesch tells us: "He always starts by working out a phonetic alphabet for the language with which he is dealing and then teaches the natives in very short order how to read and write it. Yes, if you have a language with a perfectly phonetic alphabet, you are in a sort of dream world where teaching to read and write is no problem at all. This is [all but] true, for instance, in Spanish, Finnish, Czech. . . . But let's get back from this dream world to the harsh reality of English." [2]

The pertinent question is, Why should there be a harsh reality to get back to? Who or what imposes it upon us? What is there in our Bible or our Constitution which obligates us to retard our children's education with 250 chameleon spellings for their forty speech sounds? What hypnosis makes us waste the time and blunt the reason of our first-graders on "who, do, you, two, blue, flew, shoe, through," when the rhyme word *too* points an obvious way out? And why must we hold sacrosanct the classic elements of *philosophy, pseudo,* and *zephyr* when Spanish, chief heiress of the Latin tongue, spells them *filosofia, seudo, cefiro?*

[2] As quoted in "How To Be a Perfect Speller," Rudolf Flesch, *Saturday Review,* January 14, 1961.

CHAPTER IX

DEVELOPMENT OF VOCABULARY

52. LANGUAGE DEVELOPMENT*

Albert J. Harris

THE ability to communicate with others by means of verbal symbols is the most distinctively human characteristic. Speaking and writing are active phases of communication; listening and reading are receptive phases. All phases depend upon a common structure of language, which in turn depends upon a base of common experiences. In the development of civilizations, the attainment of a complex spoken language has been necessary before reading and writing could be developed to a substantial degree and before the individual needed to learn reading and writing.[1]

Vocabulary. One of the most significant aspects of language development is the growth of vocabulary. Starting off slowly in the first half of his second year, the child tends to increase his vocabulary rapidly during the second half of that year and from then on. Early estimates of vocabulary size have been greatly increased in more recent studies; M. E. Smith estimated an average vocabulary at age six of about 2,500 words,[2] while M. K. Smith's corresponding estimate is

* From Albert J. Harris, "Reading and Human Development," in *Development in and through Reading,* Sixtieth Yearbook, Part I, of the National Society for the Study of Education (Chicago: Univ. of Chicago Press, 1961), pp. 25–27. Reprinted by permission of the National Society for the Study of Education.

[1] Dorothea McCarthy, "Language Development in Children," in Leonard Carmichael (ed.), *Manual of Child Psychology* (2nd ed.; New York: John Wiley & Sons, Inc., 1954), pp. 492–630; and "Research in Language Development: Retrospect and Prospect," in *Proceedings of the Fortieth Anniversary of the Iowa Child Welfare Research Station,* pp. 3–24 (Child Development Monographs, Vol. XXIV, Serial No. 74, 1959).

[2] Madorah E. Smith, *An Investigation of the Development of the Sentence and the Extent of Vocabulary in Young Children.* University of Iowa Studies in Child Welfare, III, No. 5, 1926.

23,7000.[3] All research has relied on small samples drawn from the entire vocabulary of the language, and the sampling techniques used and types of questions asked have had marked influence on the results obtained. Vocabulary grows not only with respect to words whose meaning is understood but also in the precision of meanings, the number of alternative meanings known for a word, the ability to apply the word correctly, and the ability to think of the word when needed. Listening and speaking vocabularies develop during the preschool period and provide a base for the development of reading vocabulary, which becomes about equal in size to the listening and speaking vocabularies when word recognition skills have been mastered; writing vocabulary lags somewhat behind.[4]

Sentence structure. By the first grade, the very short and grammatically incomplete sentences of the preschool period have developed into complete sentences of several words. Templin's data suggest that sentence length has increased in recent years; the mean sentence length which she found for six-year-olds in the 1950's (6.6 words) was higher than that for nine-year-olds in the 1930's.[5] Both sentence length and sentence structure show progressive development throughout the school period. Compound and complex sentences make up less than one-tenth of first-grade sentences, while more than half of the sentences in college compositions are complex.[6]

Concept development. The words children can use and understand give us a good insight into the development of their concepts and ideas. Usually the first words a baby learns deal with the concrete objects and activities in his environment. The common adjectives, such as "big" and "good," are used by children at an early age, but their meanings are highly specific at the beginning. The understanding of class names, such as "animal," and of words like "because," which cannot be concretely pictured, develops slowly and is frequently overestimated by parents and teachers. Children often use such words with only a very incomplete and limited understanding of their meanings.

Clarity of speech. The ability to pronounce sounds correctly increases steadily during the preschool period, and approximately 90 percent of all sounds are given correctly by most children at the age of six years. Consonant sounds are mastered somewhat later than vowel sounds, and consonant blends and final consonants tend to be perfected last. The degree to which articulation defects are due to poor auditory perception on the one hand or to muscular incoordination on the other is still an open question. Accuracy of articulation is strongly related to most other aspects of proficiency in speech, such as word usage, sentence length, sentence completeness,

[3] Mary K. Smith, *Measurement of the Size of General English Vocabulary through the Elementary Grades and High School.* Genetic Psychology Monographs, XXIV (November, 1941), 311–45.

[4] *Ibid.,* pp. 343–44.

[5] Mildred Templin, *Certain Language Skills in Children, Their Development and Interrelationship.* University of Minnesota Institute of Child Welfare Monograph Series, No. XXVI, 1957.

[6] McCarthy, *op. cit.,* pp. 551–62.

and complexity of sentence structure.[7]

Interrelations among communication skills. Since listening, speaking, reading, and writing all deal with recognition, comprehension, and organization of language patterns, it would be surprising if there were not a substantial relationship among them. Although some children who have trouble with reading do not show other language problems, a great many of them are also poor in spelling, and problems of penmanship and speech defects are significantly prevalent. For some of these children, it would be more proper to speak of a generalized language disability than to indicate one area of linguistic functioning as the focus of the problem. For the child who has such a general language disability, it is desirable to provide a modified reading program paced according to his linguistic development; this may be considerably below his general intellectual level. Help should be given in listening and in oral self-expression as well as in reading and writing.

53. THE CONCEPT BURDEN OF INSTRUCTIONAL MATERIALS*

Mary C. Serra

RESEARCH establishes the fact that the concept burden of instructional materials is too heavy. It points to a growing tendency to lighten the load in content-subject textbooks, particularly in series of books designed for basal reading instruction. It emphasizes the need to consider the concept burden as well as the vocabulary burden of instructional materials and suggests a growing concern with the distinction between mere verbalism and well-established concepts based on experiences. Some of the studies in this area have little or no individual statistical significance, and their specific findings are open to question. The agreement among them, however, cannot be ignored.

Social Studies

Bedwell [1] studied children's comprehension of concepts of quantity in third-grade reading materials in the

[7] *Ibid.,* p. 575.
* From Mary C. Serra, "The Concept Burden of Instructional Materials," *Elementary School Journal,* LIII (May, 1953), 508–12. Reprinted by permission of the author and The University of Chicago Press.

social studies. Both definite and indefinite terms were found to be of differing degrees of difficulty. Children demonstrated that it was possible to have a factual knowledge of a term without having a functional concept of the same term. Even in the restricted field of concepts of quantity at the third-reader level, the load was too heavy for the children, and verbalism resulted. Definite and indefinite terms for quantity were misinterpreted because children lacked concepts based on experience. This makes it clear that concept burden is relative, to be evaluated only in terms of the established concepts possessed by the intended readers.

Ritter [11] carefully studied the words and meanings (and, by inference, the concepts) used in two popular fourth-grade textbooks in geography. Her finding were glaring when contrasted with the usual vocabulary burden of basal reading series. In the basal reading books for Grade 4 that had been published near the date of her study, the authors, who can be presumed to have given careful consideration to children's capacity to acquire new vocabulary effectively, introduced roughly 1,000 new words. Ritter found that 2,195 technical, difficult, or unusual terms were introduced in one fourth-grade geography. In basal reading instruction, nothing is more important than the building of reading vocabulary in the basis of well-established concepts. In geography textbooks, vocabulary control is relatively incidental. One author of a geography textbook doubles the burden that the authors of readers feel children can carry.

The second geography textbook analyzed by Ritter was somewhat shorter in terms of the total number of running words. The number of new words in the second geography was 1,093. The authors of basal readers add all the new words that they believe children can acquire. Authors of textbooks in history, science, and geography seem to pay little attention to vocabulary load.

In one of the geography books that Ritter analyzed, one technical, difficult, or unusual word was added for every 34.5 running words. In the second book, one new term was added for every 49 running words. In either, the load would be just about right for instruction in reading, but it is certainly excessive in geography, where instruction in reading should be incidental. It is also doubtful that the "difficult" and "unusual" words in geography textbooks are symbols of concepts that children ordinarily have already established. With basal readers, the problem is intentionally kept at the level of associating verbal symbols and established concepts. Readers deliberately attempt to convey and develop concepts. Thus the significance of the contrast, between these books and textbooks in social studies increases.

Springman,[14] in a study of sixth-grade pupils' understanding of statements in social-studies textbooks, found that only about half of the children fully comprehended the statements. For statistical reasons, his findings cannot be interpreted to mean that children do not understand half of what they read. He does, however, demonstrate that the concept load was much too heavy for the children he tested. Springman's findings imply that the number of concepts in textbooks would constitute an excessive burden for many children. In his study he used fifty sixth-grade pupils. The children were requested to read passages from two geography textbooks. They were then asked to relate in their own words what the selections meant to them. Out of a total of 594 responses, 52.18 per cent showed either partially correct or vague meanings. Not one child demonstrated correct comprehension of the selections read.

Basal Reading Materials

Marcum [8] made a direct attack upon the concept burden of primary-grade basal reading materials. She analyzed the concepts expressed in fifteen series of preprimers, primers, and first- and second-grade readers and found the following numbers of concepts:

110 different concepts in 15 preprimers
406 different concepts in 15 primers
719 different concepts in 15 first-grade readers
1,487 different concepts in 15 second-grade readers

The range in the concept load at the different levels was as follows:

10– 55 different concepts per preprimer
48–101 different concepts per primer
73–182 different concepts per first-grade reader
188–389 different concepts per second-grade reader

At any one level, not more than 17 concepts were common to all series, and only one concept was common to all preprimers.

Marcum listed the concepts, classified by level and series, to aid teachers in determining the experiences that children need to prepare them for reading in a basal series. Vocabulary lists are commonly printed in the back of each book in basal readers. Marcum's work suggests that an analogous listing of concepts used in each book would be available.

It is the intention of lower-level basal readers to cause children to associate printed symbols with spoken symbols that are already associated with well-established concepts. The early stages of learning to read should not be complicated by the need for concept development. With a "concept vocabulary" or "concept list" at hand, the teacher could determine the appropriateness of a given book in terms of the concepts already possessed by children or could provide appropriate experiences to build the needed concepts before using the book.

Sims [13] concluded that the concepts which a child will need for handling materials adequately through reading can be determined by analysis. She recommended the compilation and use of "concept vocabularies" or "concept lists."

Ogle [9] found that the concept burden varied from one series of basal readers to another at the primary-grade level. He classified the concepts and found twice as many relating to house and home as in any other classification, with concepts of metals occurring least often.

Investigating the language of relativity as related to readiness, Osburn, Huntington, and Meeks [10] found no systematic attempt to include concepts of comparison relationships in readers. Such of these concepts as were used seemed to have been included by accident. The authors of this study believe that children should receive systematic training in dealing with relationships and that textbook writers should provide the occasion for it in their primary-grade materials.

Hildreth [4] advocates a lighter vocabulary load in primary-grade reading materials. She notes that easy vocabulary seems to require less teaching expertness. The inexperienced teacher succeeds with easier books, whereas even the experienced teacher has a difficult time with a heavy vocabulary. Probably an easier concept load would also lighten the teaching burden.

As of 1938, Hockett [5] reported that the basic vocabulary of "recent" primers and first readers was not so extensive as that in older books. There was more repetition of words in "recent" readers than in earlier editions. There is no evidence that this trend has been reversed. Fewer words and more experience with them are the major promises of the authors of basal readers. The same approach could well be assigned to the treatment of concepts.

As late as 1939, Herbers,[3] in dealing with third-grade basal readers, found that children revealed inadequate and incorrect concepts of words, phrases, and sentences. Some materials which were used by pupils with facility showed hazy and erroneous concepts. It is not clear from Herbers' report whether she was actually measuring concepts or language facility. Either way, she established the point

that, at the time of her study, the problems connected with the vocabulary burden and probably with the concept burden of third-grade readers had not been solved.

Gunderson [2] found some hopeful signs in 1942. She concluded, in substance:

1. Basal readers for the first three grades make provision for the development of meaning vocabularies in verbs.
2. The large number of synonyms introduced at progressive levels enabled children to become aware of the common, as well as the more specific, meanings of words.
3. The vocabulary load increases from the preprimer to the third reader for growth in accuracy of comprehension and depth of interpretation.
4. More colorful and precise words are introduced in the second and third readers for finer interpretation, developing shades of feeling, and a sensitivity for meaning.

Gunderson's study dealt with words and their meanings rather than with concepts, but her study shows the serious attention given by authors of basal readers to the nature of learning in children.

The real harm in overloading instructional materials with concepts is that overloading produces verbalism (or no learning at all). Looby,[6,7] investigating the understandings that sixth-grade children derive from their reading of literature, found that verbalism is rampant. Children's understanding of "the stern of his ship" placed the stern from one end of the boat to the other. "Breathing space" meant a space in the mouth. A statement that a man was "slain" meant that he had servants. Yet children read and used these words.

Simpson [12] found wide variance in the specific meanings that children attach to terms indicating differing degrees of frequency. For example, one-fourth of his subjects believed that "frequently" meant less than 40 per cent of the time; while another fourth of them thought it meant more than 80 per cent of the time. A similar treatment for the term "seldom" produced quartile scores at 6 per cent and 18 per cent of the time. The probable confusion in interpretation of instructional materials containing such indefinite terms is obvious. Resulting verbalisms are easily predicted.

In books overloaded with difficult terms, a large portion of these terms are not associated in any usable manner with established concepts. In some cases, children can ascribe no meanings to the terms. In other cases they ascribe wrong meanings, vague meanings, or partially correct meanings. In any case, where correct meaning is not ascribed, the best that can result from reading a term is verbalism.

Summary

There is a scarcity of research dealing directly with the concept burden of instructional materials. From the investigations that have been made, the following conclusions can be inferred.

1. The concept burden of social-studies materials is excessive.

2. Difficult or unusual concepts are not repeated sufficiently often in social-studies textbooks. That is, con-

cepts are expressed in the books but are not developed for the children who read them.

3. The problem of concept development is complicated by the vocabulary burden through the too frequent use of indefinite terms.

4. Verbalism can be avoided only by associating words with concepts that have their roots in experience.

5. There is a tendency today to reduce the concept load of instructional materials, particularly of basal reading series.

REFERENCES

1. BEDWELL, MARGARET. "Comprehension of Concepts of Quantity in Third Grade Social Studies Reading Material." Unpublished Master's thesis, University of Iowa, 1932.

2. GUNDERSON, AGNES G. "Provision in Readers for Developing Meaning Vocabularies in Grades I, II, and III," *Elementary School Journal,* XLIII (September, 1942), 41–46.

3. HERBERS, SISTER M. B. "Comprehension Difficulties in a Third Grade Reader," *Elementary English Review,* XVI (February, 1939), 53–57.

4. HILDRETH, GERTRUDE. "Word Frequency as a Factor in Learning To Read and Spell," *Journal of Educational Research,* XLI (February, 1948), 467–71.

5. HOCKETT, JOHN A. "Vocabularies of Recent Primers and First Readers," *Elementary School Journal,* XXXIX (October, 1938), 112–15.

6. LOOBY, RUTH. "The Meaning Derived by Children from Words and Phrases in Literature." Unpublished Doctor's dissertation, University of Iowa, 1937.

7. LOOBY, RUTH. "Understandings Children Derive from Their Reading,"

Elementary English Review, XVI (February, 1939), 58–62.

8. MARCUM, DIXIE M. "Fundamental Experience Concepts and Primary Basal Reading Materials." Unpublished Doctor's dissertation, George Peabody College for Teachers, 1943.

9. OGLE, F. A. "Concepts of Primary Reading." Unpublished Doctor's dissertation, Colorado State College of Education, 1934.

10. OSBURN, W. J.; HUNTINGTON, MIRRIEL; and MEEKS, VIOLA. "The Language of Relativity as Related to Reading Readiness," *Journal of Educational Research,* XXXIX (April, 1946), 583–601.

11. RITTER, OLIVE PEARL. "Repetition, Spread, and Meanings of Unusual, Difficult, and Technical Terms in Fourth Grade Geography Texts." Unpublished Doctor's dissertation, University of Iowa, 1941.

12. SIMPSON, R. N. "The Specific Meanings of Certain Terms Indicating Differing Degrees of Frequency," *Quarterly Journal of Speech,* XXI (October, 1944), 328–30.

13. SIMS, RUTH LYTLE. "Concept Analysis of Primers and Preprimers," *Elementary English Review,* XV (December, 1938), 302–5.

14. SPRINGMAN, JOHN H. "A Study of Sixth Grade Pupils' Understanding of Statements in Social Studies Textbooks." Unpublished Doctor's dissertation, Colorado State College of Education, 1941.

54. THE BILINGUAL CHILD AND HIS READING VOCABULARY*

L. S. Tireman

Introduction

THERE is no magic formula to solve all the reading problems of non-English-speaking children. They must master the same reading skills as the English-speaking children master. The difference is that they must do so while learning a new language. Almost anything that can be said about the reading habits of one group applies also to the other. The principles of learning seem to be the same, but they vary in the degree of application. Success for the teacher of these pupils is compounded of an appreciation of their difficulties, a knowledge of the

* From L. S. Tireman, "The Bilingual Child and His Reading Vocabulary," *Elementary English,* XXXII, No. 1 (January, 1955), 33–35. Reprinted by permission of Mrs. L. S. Tireman and the National Council of Teachers of English.

language and reading skills to be mastered, a vast amount of patience, and a real liking for children.

The reading problems of most bilingual children arise, generally, from the home situation. The economic status, the education of the parents, the general cultural level, the emotional pattern, the health standards, mobility, rural or urban residence, and the attitude toward the English language are interlocking factors. The product of all these factors is the child with whom you work.

A foreign culture background does not mean inferiority; it means difference: difference in attitude of the parents toward the significance and value of education; difference in the belief in general education; in the extent of personal sacrifices needed to send children to school; in willingness to deprive oneself of the income he might receive if the child left school and went to work. These items bear directly on the matter of regularity of attendance and the age of dropping out of school and consequently on the child's reading ability. Another difference is in the language of the home. The mother tongue—the language of the hearth—is a dear possession. It carries with it intimate and cherished memories and is the vehicle of customary communication. Consequently parents make a real sacrifice when they give it up for another language in which they are less comfortable and less secure. Indeed they will not relinguish the mother tongue unless they are convinced that their children will profit from the increased opportunity to think and speak in the new language.

The economic status of the parents affects the reading situation of their child, English-speaking or non-English-speaking. It so happens that a large proportion of the non-English-speaking parents will fall in the low-income bracket with a resulting meager environment. This situation affects directly the number and kind of experiences the children have, the amount and kind of available reading material, and the number of years the children can remain in school.

Because of the considerations mentioned, the average non-English-speaking child will not perfect reading skills as quickly as the English-speaking child. His difficulties will persist for many years both in easily recognized forms as well as the more subtle ones. One of the most fundamental problems relates to the matter of vocabulary. In its most readily recognized aspect this appears as a lack of English words. In its more subtle aspect, it refers to the inability to distinguish between shades of meaning as expressed by words. As is well known, we do not get meaning from the printed word, we put meaning *into* the printed symbols. These odd little characters, d-o-g, mean nothing at first. But through many and varied experiences, both joyous and sad, the word becomes meaningful.

In any case, vocabulary growth is dependent upon experiences, real and synthetic. If the home environment of the bilingual child provides only meager experiences, the school must compensate by a rich and satisfying program. The collecting and care of a science corner will make some words meaningful that otherwise are empty.

Anyone can learn the word *fish,* but meaning comes through observing and studying them. The word *Korea* does not mean the same to me as it does to a man who fought in Korea.

The non-English-speaking child lives in a strange world where many words are vague, indistinct, foggy, cloudy, and obscure. Is it any wonder that he is frustrated and emotionally disturbed? Here are samples:

blot—"Where blood comes" (clot)
spool—"A place where there is water" (pool)
habit—"We habit be quiet" (had better)
rack—"When they go fast they rack (wreck) the car"
won—"The Indians have a wig*won*"
task—"They cut the *tasks* of the elephant"
bushel—"The name of a big bush"
climate—"The natives climate (climbed up) the trees to get coconuts."
oyster—"A kind of bird in the zoo" (ostrich)
run on the bank, run in a stocking, a home run, run a race, a run for your money.
the cross-eyed bear (the cross I'd bear)
the car stopped at the fork in the road

If one examines these misconceptions, he finds many that are logical. You and I make the same type of error when we try to speak in a foreign language. Example: That famous salutation of one of our leading American politicians when he addressed an audience south of the border "Señoras y caballos." [1]

These are only the overt signs. The tragedy of the situation is that for every misconception we note there are

dozens, and probably hundreds, that occur to confuse the reader and *we are unaware of them.* We only know that the child fails to comprehend and are irritated or sympathetic depending upon our own understanding of the problem.

A teacher of bilingual-speaking children will find much meat in an experimental study by Gray and Holmes.[2] Miss Holmes presents experimental evidence which shows conclusively that "specific guidance is of relatively more value to pupils of limited initial achievement" than an indirect method. By specific vocabulary instruction, Miss Holmes means (1) to form clear, vivid associations between word meanings and their oral and written symbols; (2) to promote the meanings of words and phrases; and (3) to provide opportunity for pupils to use the new words appropriately in either oral or written form.[3]

Experienced teachers find some of the following techniques to be especially helpful:

1. tape recording
2. vocabulary notebooks in which all new words are listed, with synonyms or definitions and sentences
3. exercises in selecting accurate words to express meaning
4. listing words often confused
5. listing words with similar words to show differences in meaning
6. listing words with antonyms
7. listing descriptive words
8. dramatization with specific attention to choice of words

[1] The salutation is "Señoras y caballeros" (Ladies and gentlemen). The speaker confused the second word which means *horses.*

[2] William S. Gray and Eleanor Holmes, *The Development of Meaning Vocabularies in Reading* (University of Chicago, 1938), p. 140.
[3] *Ibid.,* p. 45.

9. oral exercises with the specific intention of using the new words to be studied

10. habitual use of the dictionary

This program takes much time. The teacher must decide which is more important for the child—to learn to pronounce mechanically a large number of meaningless words or to use a smaller number with understanding. Many a social science lesson in the upper grades is sterile because the teacher has followed the former practice. In the schools of Europe where bilingualism exists, it is a common custom to use the content subjects for language instruction. For example: a history lesson may provide something to talk about in the language that is being learned. They feel that it is rather purposeless to try to talk unless one has something to say.

The writer finds phonetic and structural analysis useful for the English-speaking child who has an adequate oral vocabulary. For, as he analyzes the word, he has the possibility of recognizing it through the ear. However, for the non-English-speaking child who has a limited oral vocabulary, these tools are less helpful.

Accordingly, we recommend for the bilingual child the introduction of many experiences to increase his meaningful vocabulary and, in addition, a direct attack on these words to fix them in his vocabulary.

In summary:

1. Meaning is attached to words by numerous and varied experiences.

2. If the home environment is meager, the school must compensate.

3. Experimental evidence supports the direct attack on vocabulary.

4. Such a program should receive major attention in all subjects and in all grades throughout the elementary school and probably in the secondary school.

55. VOCABULARY DEVELOPMENT IN THE CLASSROOM*

Lee C. Deighton

How Context Operates

THERE are four general principles of context operation which can be stated with some exactness. They are stated at this point to permit their being checked against the instances of context which will be quoted later. The *first* general principle has already been stated—context reveals the meaning of unfamiliar words only infrequently. The *second* is that context generally reveals only one of the meanings of an unfamiliar word. Most words in common English usage have more than one meaning recorded in the dictionary. These dictionary entries are only an interpretation by the dictionary editors of the common denominator in a great many instances in which a particular word is used. The dictionary entries are indispensable to us as a point of departure in understanding a word. However, dictionary entries do not limit the use of words. Dictionary entries are shaped, changed, and altered by individual contexts, each of which is different. This in brief is why a single context can illuminate only one phase of a particular word. Which phase

is developed will be determined by the demands of the particular context. In presenting this matter to children it is worth repeating over and over again that no word has one fixed and inalterable meaning, that no one context revelation will suffice for all the later uses of the word which may be met.

The *third* principle of context operation is that context seldom clarifies the whole of any meaning. Occasionally, context will provide a synonym, but it must be remembered that synonyms are never exact equivalents. Words are not like coins of even value, to be substituted at random in the exchange of communication. Context more often provides only clues from which the reader may infer the meaning of an unfamiliar word. It is important to make clear to developing readers that the whole meaning of an unfamiliar word can never be gathered in the first encounter with it. Meaning comes from experience, and the wider the experience with a word, the richer will its meaning be for the reader.

From this follows the *fourth* general principle—that vocabulary growth through context revelation is a gradual matter. It is a matter of finding one clue here and another there, of fitting them together, of making tentative judgments and revising them as later experience requires. It is a matter of

* From Lee C. Deighton, *Vocabulary Development in the Classroom,* Bureau of Publications, Teachers College, Columbia Univ., 1959, pp. 2–6, 15–16. Reprinted by permission of the author and the Bureau of Publications, Teachers College, Columbia University, New York, N.Y.

building meaning into a word over a period of years.

Limiting Factors in Context Operation

In addition to these four general principles, there are certain limitations on the effective use of contexts in classroom study. The first of these follows from what has just been said. *What a context may reveal to a particular reader will depend upon his previous experience.* It is unfortunately true that some words exist for most of us *merely as words*—as spoken sounds or printed symbols having only the vaguest of meanings for us. We have not tied these words into our personal experience. We have not objectified them. We have not applied them as labels to physical objects or to the observable qualities of physical objects or to the behavior of persons and things. We recognize these words and we can restate them, perhaps, in other words with more or less success, but we have not attached them to the living experience of our physical world. The degree to which we have objectified the words which compose a context will determine the success with which we use that context to uncover the meaning of an unfamiliar word.

The key words in the context may themselves be unfamiliar to the reader. Although the construction of a context may indicate to the experienced reader that an example or restatement is being given, the inexperienced reader may completely miss the restatement and assume that new material is being added. Inexperienced readers must not be expected to derive as much help

from context as experienced readers get. This factor of experience is really a limitation on the effective use of contexts in classroom study.

There are two other limitations worth noting. The first of these is that the portion of context which illuminates an unfamiliar word must be reasonably close to the word if it is to act effectively. It may appear in the same sentence. It may appear in the same paragraph. It may precede or it may follow. If it follows within reasonably close space, it can be used effectively by the average reader in his average haste to cover the material in hand. If it precedes the unfamiliar word by so much as a paragraph, its effectiveness is limited. If it precedes by several pages, it has even less value except to those careful readers who take the time to re-read for understanding. In ordinary adult circumstances, there are few of us who take the time for re-reading. In classroom practice there is always time to re-read; and there could be no more salutary exercise in vocabulary development than to assist and then, as pupils experience grows, to require the pupil to dig out the preceding passages which reveal the meaning of an unfamiliar word.

There is another limiting condition in the effectiveness of context which exists irrespective of experience or reading patience. *There must be some clear-cut connection between the unfamiliar word and the context which clarifies it.* This connection may be made by repeating identical sentence structure; by repeating the construction in which the unfamiliar word occurs and substituting a synonym; by use of pointing words or phrases such as *such as, like, for example, this, that, those,* and many others.

The importance of these constructions and these connecting words is apparent when we examine a context which lacks them. For example,

We were flying at 22,000 feet. M. called for echelon starboard. Our Hurricanes moved into single-file, each plane to the right of the plane in front.

The unfamiliar words are *echelon starboard.* The next sentence describes an echelon starboard, but there is nothing to indicate definitely that it does. How is the reader with no previous knowledge of *starboard* or of *echelon* to know that the next sentence is not a completly new idea?

By contrast note how the parallel construction in the following example reveals what is meant specifically by *moisture.*

The letters they carried were wrapped in oiled silk to protect them *from* moisture, either *from* water in fording streams, or perspiration of the horse.

It is not meant here that the word *moisture* is an unfamiliar word for the average reader. The example is cited simply to show the operation of context. Similar examples may be found with the same pattern involving words of real difficulty for the most widely read adult. The importance of the example is its illustration of how parallel construction ties context closely to a key word.

To restate: Context reveals the meaning of unfamiliar words only infrequently. A single context reveals only a part of a meaning of a particular word. The building of meaning from context is a gradual process. The effectiveness of context in revealing meaning is limited; it depends on the previous experience of the reader, on the proximity of the enlightening context to the unfamiliar word, and on the clearness of the connection between the context and the word upon which it bears. . . .

Context reveals meaning most simply by outright definition. It reveals meaning by citing examples, and these contexts frequently employ signal words: *such as, such, like, especially, for example, other, this* or *these* (followed by a synonym), *the way* or *in the way that.* Occasionally, when these signal words are not employed, the linking verb is used to show the connection. A third method of explaining an unfamiliar word is the use of modifiers. A fourth method by which context reveals meaning is through restatement in which certain signal words can always be counted upon as introducing a restatement: *in other words, that is, to put it another way, what this means, which is to say,* and all the possible modifications of these. In addition restatement employs two mechanical devices as signals: the dash and the parenthesis.

The classroom study of these four methods of context revelation may reasonably be expected to yield good results for perhaps half of the context situations which will arise in classroom reading. For the other half, there are no key words and no mechanical devices. The reader must rely on inference. Sometimes these inference contexts show the connection between the unfamiliar word and the explanatory matter by employing repetition of sentence pattern, by repetition of key words, by use of familiar connecting words like *however, yet, therefore, similarly.* Frequently the connection is established only through repetition of thought or statement of its opposite.

There are many instances of infer-ence context which contain none of these connecting devices. They may be dealt with profitably as they arise, in the hope that teacher guidance will encourage the pupil to use his own resources in reading for meaning rather than to pass by all unfamiliar words.

56. BUILDING VOCABULARY WITH A FOURTH-GRADE CLASS*

Marguerite P. Archer

ONE Friday morning during their library period, I asked Mrs. Curran's fourth grade, "When you write stories, what word do you have to use so much that you get tired of using it?"

The children guessed *and, the,* and *a,* but I commented that we usually just accepted these words. Then I gave an example of dialogue and they triumphantly exclaimed, "Said!"

I quickly replied, "That's it! Said! *Said* is a word we don't *have* to use so often that we get tired of it. What words could we use instead of *said?*"

The answers came so fast that I could hardly write them down. Occasionally there would be a lull and Mrs.

* From Marguerite P. Archer, "Building Vocabulary with a Fourth-Grade Class," *Elementary English,* XXXVII (November, 1960), 447–48. Reprinted by permission of the author and the National Council of Teachers of English.

Curran or I would start a new trend of thought. "Suppose these people are angry with each other." "Maybe they're not angry. Suppose something funny is said." Within twenty minutes' time the class had discovered forty-four words to use instead of *said.*

At that point we stopped listing so that the children could withdraw books. Two volunteers sat down to copy the words neatly for the bulletin boards in their classroom and in the library. I pointed to two lists made by other classes and Martha inquired, "How many did the other class get?"

"Forty-eight," I admitted, knowing quite well that she meant the other fourth-grade class.

"That's only four more than we got! Somebody think of some more!" urged Katie.

Before they left the library the class

had fifty-one words. They also had a challenging piece of information: Mr. Gillespie's sixth grade had compiled a list of seventy-eight words for *said*.

At noontime Peter T. walked in. "Could you use blasted?" he inquired hopefully. *Blasted* was accepted and so was *boasted*. Jeff contributed *taunted* and *retorted* after school.

On Monday Sally triumphantly declared, "We didn't say *told*. There are times when you could say *told* instead of *said*." Jeff came next with *exaggerated*. Marilyn reread the list and wrote down *joked*.

Tuesday noon Peter returned. "Is *jabbered* all right? It doesn't have to be slang."

"You're right," I acknowledged. "It doesn't. You've added another word."

"*Added!*" grinned Peter.

When the children had their next library period Tuesday afternoon my first remark was "I suppose you all know that some of the class has continued your list."

"*Continued!*" Ralph echoed gleefully.

On Tuesday Mrs. Curran was absent. So the youngsters took down their list and read it to the substitute teacher. As they read it more words were added.

"Do we have *stuttered?*" queried Barbara.

"I thought you said *muttered*," Tommy interjected.

As I moved my head up and down in agreement Jimmy said *nodded*. By this time the list was back on the board with eight children clustered around it. Diane, Sally, and Linda were leafing through the unabridged dictionary. Anthony and Tommy L. be-

gan to open books and hastily scan the contents. More youngsters dashed to get books. Peter L. took a magazine and others hurried to the rack. When they found new words they would burst out with a joyful exclamation, and someone would run over to the board for a hasty check.

Luckily I had a clerical period during the next half hour. "They're supposed to have English now," the substitute commented hesitantly.

"This *is* English!" I laughed. "Let them stay."

"Yes, of course," Mrs. Zisson smiled. "The plan book has the same thing—vocabulary development."

I reassured her. "That's fine! Mrs. Curran will be pleased."

Then I asked the children to sit down in the circle so that we could read the additions to the list. "Mrs. Zisson has consented to your staying," I announced.

"*Consented!*" cried the chorus with Vic in the lead.

"I didn't mean to tell you any words myself," I ruefully retorted.

"Do we have *told?*" Frank asked.

"Yes, we do; but we don't have *shuttered*," was someone's answer.

"*Shuttered* isn't the word you mean. That means having shutters like a house," I explained. "The word is *shuddered*. How would you spell it? Sound it out."

When that detail had been corrected I called for volunteers to copy the additions which had been squeezed onto a small piece of paper.

"Why don't we mimeograph it?" inquired Lester. "Then everyone could have a copy."

By the time the project was "finished" on Wednesday afternoon the children had listed one hundred and four words. The principal, Mrs. Dyring, had given her happy approval to the mimeographing; and the secretary, Miss Flynn, had left space so that more words could be added.

Reports on the duplicating kept coming back to the library. "Miss Flynn says we can make enough for the other classes, too!" "Miss Flynn made up a story with the first twenty words in it!"

Linda, from Mr. Gillespie's sixth grade, came in after school. "Those fourth-graders had a hundred and four words for *said*. Isn't that wonderful?"

"Yes," I agreed. "It is wonderful." She was absolutely right.

Words to Use instead of "Said" by Mrs. Curran's Grade 4

1. sobbed	27. screeched	53. boasted	79. named
2. declared	28. protested	54. taunted	80. murmured
3. replied	29. stated	55. retorted	81. reasoned
4. suggested	30. laughed	56. told	82. consented
5. exclaimed	31. chuckled	57. exaggerated	83. shuddered
6. dictated	32. giggled	58. joked	84. mouthed
7. questioned	33. snickered	59. jabbered	85. sighed
8. complimented	34. smiled	60. added	86. remarked
9. complained	35. frowned	61. continued	87. considered
10. answered	36. grinned	62. stuttered	88. claimed
11. proclaimed	37. snarled	63. muttered	89. discouraged
12. congratulated	38. glared	64. nodded	90. informed
13. asked	39. requested	65. began	91. encouraged
14. advised	40. stammered	66. warned	92. corrected
15. argued	41. informed	67. called	93. begged
16. quarreled	42. recited	68. fretted	94. whined
17. inquired	43. demanded	69. confessed	95. observed
18. yelled	44. commanded	70. crowed	96. cursed
19. screamed	45. cited	71. bragged	97. wept
20. shouted	46. conversed	72. chattered	98. sorrowed
21. cried	47. claimed	73. read	99. comforted
22. whispered	48. thundered	74. admitted	100. conceded
23. commented	49. roared	75. ordered	101. continued
24. pouted	50. growled	76. mentioned	102. mumbled
25. blurted	51. grunted	77. consoled	103. snapped
26. bellowed	52. blasted	78. reminded	104. gulped

57. CEILING UNLIMITED*

Mildred Z. Wiersema

RECENT publicity on the importance of reading in this expanding world has given both young people and adults an urgent desire to read. Both groups realize that without the benefits gained from reading, their world is very limited. Research shows that a definite correlation exists between success in life and a good vocabulary. Since most adolescents and adults stop learning to read in the sixth grade, it becomes necessary in the secondary schools to continue the study of reading, and particularly the development of vocabulary, which is the basis for increasing rate and comprehension in reading.

Words must be read, not "read around," if meaning is to become precise and intelligible. Hundreds of devices are being used effectively, but some presentations have an added usability by being able to challenge both slow and rapid learners to perform with success at their levels. Perhaps in an assignment with an unlimited ceiling a teacher can provide some help for those students who are on their way to building a more effective vocabulary by:

1. Directing the Take-off
2. Guiding the Upward Lift

3. Sustaining the Air-borne
4. Encouraging the Solo Flight

This is just another way of stating that the basic principles of learning—purposing, motivating, perceiving, associating, evaluating, and applying—can still be followed, even in the use of small techniques. On top of it all, it should be remembered that the old childhood rhyme offered some valuable advice:

Learned with pleasure,
Learned full measure.

There are many vocabulary-building devices that may be used to challenge students to maximal accomplishment.

Word Autobiographies

Why not shake hands with a word and get to know it better? Here is an effective way to let a word introduce itself.

Words can be classified as *anyday, everyday,* and *someday* varieties. In a conspicuous place list unusual words from any of these three varieties that spring from reading or discussion. A follow-up study on structure, history, adaptations, and usage of these words can be made for better word perception. From such a list students can choose words for a genetic study, presenting findings as autobiographical accounts. A format can be agreed upon by the class, setting up this pertinent

* From Mildred Z. Wiersema, "Ceiling Unlimited!" *Education,* LXXX (October, 1959), 76–79. Reprinted by permission of the author and The Bobbs-Merrill Co., Inc., Indianapolis, Ind.

material: origin, meaning, changes, pictorial material, and sentence illustrations. Individual, group, and class work can be employed in the project.

Students respond to this type of no-ceiling assignment. Some students will do superior artistic illustrations with mediocre work in word research which might be maximal for them. Others will resourcefully use cutouts from magazines for illustrations and do optimum work in a genetic study. Some students will struggle to finish a one-word study, while others will enjoy completing several words which have become entangled in their spiraling interest.

Variations of this project include making personal dictionaries, a miniature collection of alphabetized words which the student wishes to study and to include in his speaking and writing vocabulary; booklets of word origins; and board displays of words in many categories, such as name words, technical words, three-letter words, and others. Making students word-conscious is a great step forward in vocabulary building.

"What's My Line?"

A vocabulary study without upper limits for quality or quantity of research by students of varying abilities could be called "What's My Line?"

This device was used while working in a unit on "Choosing Careers" in a non-college sophomore English class. Each student made a list of technical words that he could use in the discussion of his chosen career. Under the title were placed ten words that might be the most difficult to reveal clues for the line of work involved. On the sec-

ond page were listed the next ten most unrevealing words. Other pages were added with ten words each until the list was exhausted or the words became too easy to guess the category. The last page contained the name of the occupation. When mounted on the bulletin board, the list was a challenge to the viewer to guess the line of work from the first ten words, or the next ten, or the last ten, which were followed by the name of the occupation.

The project has merit in several aspects. It draws on skills and hobbies of the students who may have had little success in formal classroom work in English. These students receive recognition for their contributions to the learning that takes place in the classroom. Pride in special knowledge leads to pride in the completed project: its format, its execution, and its acceptance. The exceptional students will find quite a challenge to their resourcefulness in seeking information in school, home, and community. Variations can be made to include phrases or sentences which identify various sports, animals, or characters in literature. This project gives an opportunity to use several communicative skills while the students are widening their vocabularies.

"Nyms" for Vocabulary Growth

Any study of the relationships of words as designated by the "nyms"—antonyms, homonyms, and synonyms—will be rewarding in vocabulary development. Most of the words have created some associations for the students, so new aspects seem to be learned rather quickly.

Devices for this study are numerous, but some adaptations of these practices may be helpful. One class made a book of homonyms, alphabetized and complete with definitions and sentence illustrations of each. Individual students made few or many contributions, according to their abilities. Alphabet tabs attached to the appropriate pages made the book usable for other classes.

Each member of another class made a card file for himself. Still another class made a hall display of a study in antonyms using separate cards for each set, which included meanings, use in sentences, and pictorial examples. The alphabetized arrangement was usable later as a class study and reference when the cards were replaced in a file box.

Good students made up their own tests for synonyms and antonyms by selecting ten words for Set A and ten matching words for Set B. After rearranging Set B, the class members tested themselves in speed and accuracy by matching the sets properly.

Lists of names of the male and female of various species were matched in an antonym study: lord—lady, gander—goose. Short paragraphs were constructed by the students in which underlined adjectives or adverbs were to be replaced with synonyms. The word choices were discussed from the standpoint of effectiveness. These devices could be used by individuals or groups.

As a culminating project, the students brought copies or clippings from texts or home materials to illustrate the "nyms." With these samples underlined in red pencil, the students were able to apply the newly gained knowledge in word relationships and were encouraged to use these words in speaking and writing, as well as in reading.

Board displays and, later, filed collections were shared with other classes. One class made tests of these words on one side of a paper with answers on the reverse side. The paper was slipped inside a plastic book cover upon which pencil checks could be made to answer the tests. After the answers had been checked, the pencil marks could be erased and the test could be used over and over. These tests were arranged in sets and used for do-it-yourself study.

The idea of making learning materials for themselves and then passing them on to other classes seemed to heighten the students' interest in a completed project.

Assembling Words

A helpful device for comprehending word structure is through the development of word clusters. A root of a word was selected from a word under scrutiny in reading or discussion and placed with its meaning on the board. Affixes with their meanings were added as resourceful students ferreted out words from their dictionaries, glossaries, and personal knowledge. Each root, affix, and finished word was carefully checked in an unabridged dictionary, as spelling similarities and variances could be misleading.

On another panel of the board were listed the words formed, their meanings, and illustrative sentences. All students contributed to the project in developing word-building skills.

When the study was fully worked out, the words were transferred to tagboard and mounted on the bulletin board where examples of these word usages from newspapers and magazines could be clipped to them. The studies were finally collected in a class booklet.

Many students duplicated the studies in folders for personal use; some were displayed and shared with other classes. Many variations of this graphic presentation are possible.

This type of vocabulary-developer adapts itself to the slow learner, who can select simple roots and common affixes, and also to the rapid learner, who can be challenged to make

Word Assembly Line

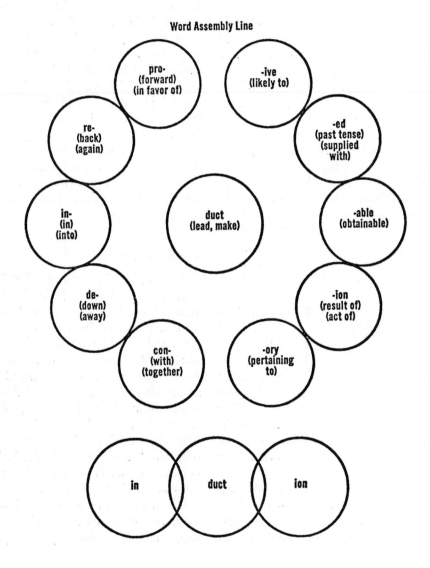

extensive surveys to complete his study.

Achieving Goals

Little or no learning takes place if the student's interest is not involved. However, the teacher can whet the mental appetite and satisfy the intellectual hunger by providing proper materials, a stimulating environment for learning, and an enthusiastic manner.

When a student's interest is involved, he is ready for the Take-off on a project. Use of the major aids to word perception—structural clues, contextual clues, similarity word-form clues, and the final court of appeals, the dictionary and other reference works—constitutes the know-how necessary for the Flight.

The culmination of these studies is the mastery of the "Big Idea" behind the word. With the newly acquired word-concept added to the vocabulary, and the many others which join it, the student gains the confidence needed for the Solo Flight on his own.

58. STIMULATE READING . . . WITH A DICTIONARY*

Edith F. Miller

MAKING a dictionary as a class project provides a valuable addition to the reading program and can be adapted to any grade level.

As a first step, in the first grade, I prepare a set of large cards, each with a word on one side and the same word

* From Edith F. Miller, "Stimulate Reading with a Dictionary," *Grade Teacher*, LXXIX (February, 1962), 51–52, 106–7. Reprinted by permission of the author and Teachers Publishing Corporation, Darien, Conn.

below a picture on the other side. In the lower right-hand corner of the side with the word only, I put the beginning letter of that word. This gives an added means of identifying a word —"dog" will not be called "puppy," "Mother" will not be called "lady" or "woman," "ship" will not be called "boat."

The words on the cards are those with which the children are already familiar from their basic readers, from class activities, from the special weeks and holidays already passed, from writing exercise books or number study—in short, from any source the children have used.

Making the Cards

Except for the colors and a few verbs, all of the words are nouns. If the children are familiar with only the singular form or the plural form of a word, it is wise to include the other form, also, as the words are put on cards.

As soon as I start making the cards, I ask the children to help me find the needed pictures. We keep a pile of magazines on hand and the children look for the pictures, colored if possible. These are cut out and mounted. In many cases there will be duplicate pictures which are saved for later use. A good drill in reading is furnished by tacking on the bulletin board the cards which need pictures. As pictures are found, the children tack them under the cards. Later the class helps to decide which pictures shall be used on the cards.

The pack of cards may be used in a variety of ways. The teacher may show the cards, word side only, to the entire class, allowing the children to take turns reading them. The children love to see who can get the most cards. The cards may be used in the same way in a small pupil-led group. Other games may be made up by the class and played by the children in small groups. The cards also provide a good means of developing self-help when a child uses the pack or part of it by himself. Individual children may be tested on the entire pack by teacher or a pupil-partner and the words missed isolated for further drill.

Next Step

After intensive use of the pack of cards, I make a large booklet titled "Our Very Own Picture Dictionary." Each letter of the alphabet appears at the top of a page in the book with several blank pages following each lettered page. When I show the blank booklet to the children, I also show them some published picture dictionaries and picture dictionaries made by previous classes.

The children are most enthusiastic about making their own dictionaries. First their cards are sorted out according to the first letter. We play games with the sorted cards. This proves a good way for them to see, for example, that all "b" words start with the same sound, while the "a" words may have different sounds.

After this activity, we look for the pictures needed for our class picture dictionary. Many of the duplicate pictures which we did not discard are now used. The children do all the cutting and they arrange the pictures in the book in the order of the alphabetically listed words. I check this arrangement before they do any pasting. Then I print the words under the pictures.

As new words are learned, pictures are found and pasted in following the original words; thus the new words cannot be in alphabetical order. New cards are made and, if desired, these are kept in a separate pack so that drill on cards may be centered on the newly introduced words.

Personal Dictionaries

Several months after the beginning of the project, I arrange all the words alphabetically and make duplicate sheets so that each child may make his own copy of "Our Very Own Picture Dictionary." Space is left for illustrations which may be pupil-made but usually are procured from catalogues, old text books, gummed seals, conservation stamps, used greeting cards, informals, and magazines.

At the close of the school year, the finished picture dictionaries are taken home. Parents are always impressed with the many words that have been mastered, especially if they realize that only comparatively few words of the children's reading vocabulary can be illustrated. A copy of the dictionary is also sent to each second grade where the pupils go in the fall.

Second Grade and Up

Second-grade pupils who have not made picture dictionaries in the first grade would enjoy the project, following practically the same procedure. Whether they have had the experience in the first grade or not, any second-grade or third-grade group would enjoy adapting the idea by making "A Picture Dictionary of Science Throughout the Year," "A Picture Dictionary of the Seasons," "The Circus," or any topic they study. "A Picture Dictionary of Christmas" is always popular and the number of words added by that one theme alone is amazing.

Third-grade children may use the pack of cards or omit that part of the plan if preferred. If third-grade pupils make dictionaries toward the end of the year, they are mature enough to make up simple definitions for some of the words after studying picture dictionaries carefully. They are happy to make their dictionaries a little more like dictionaries for grownups. Of course, the teacher will have to write many of the definitions with them and for them. Pupils in the third grade and above usually prefer to draw their own pictures rather than to cut them out and paste them.

Fourth-grade pupils can write more of the definitions themselves and should also show how to pronounce each word. Since the fourth grade is the one where dictionary work is usually stressed, making a class dictionary is a natural activity for this grade and provides the needed practice in the use of the pronunciation symbols. Studying glossaries found in their own texts and in sample books helps in all phases of dictionary writing. Thus the transition from a picture dictionary to one with definitions and very few pictures is gradually made.

Pupils in grades above the fourth proceed in the same way. The topic chosen for the dictionary should always be one of real interest to the children. These upper-grade dictionaries will include many words other than nouns.

The dictionary made by a class may be used as a reference or as reading material by other classes, and often inspires creation of their own dictionaries by the other classes.

Transitional Step

As an intermediate step between the picture and name on a card and the "real" dictionary on a given topic, you might like to try this idea, applicable to any grade:

Choose any area where the children need some help in understanding terms —it might be art, music, science, geography, arithmetic, and so forth. Make up a list of terms which you want your children to understand. Give each child one term which can be illustrated. Have each child print his term neatly in red crayon at the top of a sheet of drawing paper. He will then draw an illustration, putting the part which illustrates the specific word in red crayon.

In arithmetic, for example, the term SUM would be lettered in red at the top of the paper and an addition example would be put on the paper in black crayon, with the answer in red. Children can see at a glance that a SUM is the answer to an addition example. However, the definition—"SUM is the answer to an addition example"—will be put on in small letters.

In geography, physical features lend themselves well to this idea; in art, it is possible to illustrate "angles," "vanishing points," "planes," and similar terms; in science, words such as "antenna," "insect," and "larva" may be clearly shown.

Every child may make as many of these sheets as desired. A border of these terms, arranged alphabetically, is a help in spelling when the children are writing on the topic. Understanding of a topic is an outgrowth of such an activity. The pupils sometimes like to make their own booklets of the words in the border, illustrating when possible. This activity could lead very naturally into making a dictionary including terms that cannot be illustrated.

Outcomes

The most important outcome of making dictionaries is that pupils will come to love words and *want* to know more and more of them and their meanings. They will become more articulate in their oral and written reports, in the expression of their thoughts and feelings. Knowledge of words increases the enjoyment of reading and greatly stimulates the desire to read.

Other outcomes include:

1. Picture dictionaries made in the primary grades provide a good foundation for the formal dictionary work of the fourth and later grades.

2. Alphabetizing is introduced sequentially beginning in the first grade and continuing until any list of words can be easily alphabetized by the children. This helps them to find words in a real dictionary easily.

3. The children experience satisfaction through the self-help their systematic study of dictionaries has made possible.

4. The number of words learned thoroughly by this one means is astounding—both words from standard lists and words from special content fields.

5. The finished dictionaries are popular with both children and their parents. The parents can see the progress the children are making in learning.

6. The practice in writing definitions is a real contribution to exact and precise English.

59. VOCABULARY—KEY TO COMMUNICATION*

James I. Brown

THE process of communication may be likened to the flow of traffic on a four-lane highway. Two lanes —the reading and listening lanes— carry a stream of facts, ideas, feelings, and impressions in our direction. The other two lanes—writing and speaking —carry our ideas, feelings, and impressions out to others. But highways, of themselves, do not take anything anywhere. We need cars, trucks, buses, and other vehicles to move people and goods from place to place. In our communication analogy, words are the all-important vehicles. And if our word supply is inadequate, our communication is of necessity inadequate also.

The Key Role of Vocabulary

In essence, word power is reading power. For example, if the word *impeded* is not known, it is impossible to read with understanding the sentence, "His progress was impeded." Even the most common words present similar difficulties. An analysis of the 500 words most used in the English language reveals 14,070 separate meanings—an average of 28 per word. The sentence, "He reached for the fast," actually contains no uncommon words, yet it is meaningless unless we know one of the less common meanings of

* From James I. Brown, "Vocabulary— Key to Communication," *Education*, LXXX (October, 1959), 80–84. Reprinted by permission of the author and The Bobbs-Merrill Co., Inc., Indianapolis, Ind.

the common word fast—"a mooring rope or hawser." Obviously, any improvement of vocabulary is an improvement of reading ability.

The same thing is true in listening. A boy was returning a well-worn dirty book to the public library. The librarian looked at the title, at the smallness of the boy, and said, "This book is rather technical, isn't it?" Planting his feet firmly on the floor, the boy said defiantly, "Well, it was that way when I took it out."

Word power is indeed listening power. Research done in connection with the construction of the *Brown-Carlsen Listening Comprehension Test* pointed up that fact. The subtest measuring the ability to recognize meanings of words from contextual clues correlated more closely with the total score on the test than any of the other four subtests.

And in the expressive skills of writing and speaking, we must have a ready, large supply of words if we are to express ideas with a minimum of loss. If our vocabulary is limited, our written and spoken communication is to that degree limited. In short, the pen is mightier than the sword only when the writer has the word power to make it so.

A Multi-Purpose Approach

The teacher who emphasizes word study at the elementary level, secondary level, or college level, is, by that one move, making students better in four different areas—reading, listening, writing, and speaking. When we spend class time teaching punctuation, we expect students to write better. When we teach basic speech skills, we expect students to speak better. When we use the tachistoscope to develop improved word-grouping habits or greater perceptual speed and accuracy, we expect them to read better. And when we help them discriminate more accurately between speech sounds, we expect them to listen more effectively. On the other hand, by attention to vocabulary, we can help the student improve, not in one, but in all four areas of communication.

If we stop here in our analysis, however, we may be overlooking the most important of all reasons for emphasizing word study. Psychologists, linguists, and anthropologists are quick to remind us that we think with words. Sapir puts it this way: "Thought is hardly possible without the symbolic organization brought by language." In a sense, then, a new word is more than just a word; it is a new thought, a new idea, a new concept, a new picture. In this sense, word power is thought power and, as such, deserves even more attention throughout the whole range of formal and informal education.

A Master-Word Approach

With this as background, suppose we examine a somewhat new approach to word study, suitable for use from the elementary level right into college.

A study of word origins has from time immemorial been an accepted approach to vocabulary development. Lists of prefixes, roots, or suffixes appear somewhere in most textbooks for English. With an estimated 60 per cent of our language coming from Latin and Greek sources, that would seem a highly desirable move. But in the usual alphabetical listing, *deca-* may appear side by side with *de-*, which has well over a hundred times the number of derivatives, and *echino-* may be side by side with *ex-*, with its over two hundred times the number of derivatives.

A fresh look at the old approach would seem in order, one which would bring the most important of these Latin and Greek elements into much sharper and clearer focus. One measure of the importance of a prefix would certainly be in the frequency of its appearance in English. With this in mind, a research project was undertaken fifteen years ago which involved working through the entire collegiate dictionary, listing all prefixes and counting the number of words in the dictionary containing a form of each one.

Out of that research, fourteen master-words were put together.[1,8] They contained twenty prefix and fourteen root elements, elements found in over 14,000 words of desk dictionary size, or an estimated 100,000 of unabridged dictionary size. Just as a master-key will unlock many different doors, so these master-word elements help unlock the meanings of thousands of derived English words. For example, a student may come across the word *prescience* in a vocabulary test. Does it mean *poise, discernment, helpful-*

ness, foresight, or *knowledge?* Although he may never have seen that word before, if he knows that *pre-* usually means "before," he should arrive at *foresight* as the most reasonable choice.

This research into the frequency of prefix and root elements in English provided an answer to the question: Which prefix and root elements deserve most attention?

How Should They Be Taught?

The related question, "How should they be taught?" seemed even more interesting to explore.

Six years ago, in checking the effectiveness of our instruction in reading here at Minnesota, we used forms of the *Diagnostic Reading Test* as pre- and post-test measures. As a control, we administered the same test to students in other sections of our freshman program. The analysis of results showed that instruction in reading was most helpful in increasing reading rate. Here the below-average readers taking training made an average percentile rank gain of 60, as compared with a 20.6 gain for those in the other group, about three times as much improvement. Gains in comprehension were also good, the reading students making a 51.8 percentile rank increase, as compared with 23.9 for the others. In vocabulary, however, the reading group and the other group made almost identical progress—15.2 as compared with 14.9, a difference of only .3 in favor of those taking training in reading. This was the only area of the three checked where the below-average students had not passed those in the other group. These findings [2] suggested the need for additional research and for moves to strengthen that part of the reading program.

A study by Tyler [6] of the relative permanency of different kinds of learning from the field of zoology seemed to have important implications for word study in general. In this study, students were rechecked fifteen months after completing a zoology course and taking the final examination. There was an 80 per cent loss in recall of facts, a 72 per cent loss in recognition of technical terms, a 22 per cent loss in names of organs identified from pictures, and no loss in application of basic principles. Ability to interpret new experiments was the only area where there was a gain in performance over the fifteen-month period. From this study, Tyler concluded that rote memory is the greatest waste in education.

Apparently the most important question is not, "Did you learn it?" but, "How did you learn it?" Learning involving rote memory of unrelated facts seems relatively temporary. Learning involving problem-solving processes and associative reasoning seems relatively permanent.

There are those who teach reading as thinking, thus involving these higher mental processes. What about teaching vocabulary as thinking, for the same reason? More specifically, can the fourteen master-words be taught so as to shed light on the behavior of prefixes and roots in general, so as to establish habits of reliance on the higher mental processes, and so as to capitalize more fully on visual cues which reduced forgetting so effectively in the area of zoology?

As a step in that direction a 40-item test was devised [4] to aid in diagnosing depth of performance at four different levels—memorization, identification, application, and generalization. Three of the levels are beyond the level of rote memory, each involving a somewhat different kind of thinking, designed to add permanency of learning.

The first ten questions in the test can be answered correctly by any student with a rote knowledge of the prefix and root elements being studied. In a sense he may say he knows the material, but not in depth, as the remaining three parts of the test will reveal.

The next ten questions are intended to measure his ability to spot these key elements accurately as they appear in words. Obviously, it is possible to know that the prefix *com-* means "together" and still not recognize its presence in such words as *collaborate, incomplete,* or *correlate.* Yet until the student can deal with these elements well enough to take that second step—recognizing them in a word—his rote knowledge is of little real value.

The move from theory to practice is always a difficult one in any learning process. We know so many things in theory, about learning or child psychology, yet it is the rare individual who applies that knowledge to full advantage in learning or dealing with children. The third part of the test attempts to measure the student's ability to apply this theoretical knowledge to the practical problems of understanding, defining, and using words more effectively. In this section, relatively uncommon words are used. Each, however, has a familiar prefix or root which should bring the student to the right answer—if he can apply his knowledge effectively. Many students who make a perfect score on the first two parts will still have trouble with part three, application.

Even this is no place to stop, if we are to make full use of this approach. The last part of the test is designed to measure how effectively the student is able to generalize about the behavior of other such elements on the basis of the few prefix and root elements studied. A statistical analysis of the results of this approach with 162 of our students was quite encouraging.[9]

Visualization

To enlist the aid of some visualizing techniques and materials was the final step in rounding out the picture.[5, 7] The visual material permitting maximum flexibility for the teacher in a normal classroom situation is a set of 48 specially designed cards, 2½ by 7½ inches in size.[7] While designed for use with a flannel board, they lend themselves equally well to use in front of a class as flash cards.

The fourteen master-words are printed in bold type on one side, one per card, the back side providing an accurate and immediately available visual image to reinforce and accelerate the learning of these key elements. In addition there are 34 prefix and root cards with the prefix and root on one side, their other spellings and common meanings on the back. Suggestions for using these cards at the elementary and secondary level are also provided.

While results with this new approach

have been quite encouraging, further research is even now in progress, for our rapidly expanding problem demands ever improved methods and approaches. It has been estimated that we need a vocabulary one-third larger than that needed a hundred years ago. Radio alone has put five thousand new words into our dictionary. Fortunately many of the new words that come into our language every year are built around old familiar prefix, root, and suffix elements. Once the student has accustomed himself to dealing with these fundamental elements of word construction, he is properly prepared for the new words as well as for the old.

To be sure, this is just one of many different ways of approaching the problem of vocabulary development. Other teachers no doubt will have even more useful suggestions to report, or modifications to make. More research in this vital area is badly needed, to bring additional insights, to blaze new trails, and to further our over-all educational efforts which are so dependent upon effective communication and underlying word power for results.

REFERENCES

1. BROWN, JAMES I. "A Master-Word Approach to Vocabulary," *Efficient Reading* (Boston: D. C. Heath & Co., 1952).
2. ———. "Report of the Committee on Reading Comprehension," *Journal of Communication,* VII (Winter, 1957), 184–85.
3. ———. "1958 Supplementary Report of the NSSC Reading Committee," *Journal of Communication,* IX (March, 1959), 32–34.
4. BROWN, J. I. and SALISBURY, R. *Building a Better Vocabulary* (New York: The Ronald Press Co., 1959).
5. LEX-O-GRAM (Chicago: The King Co., 1954).
6. LINDQUIST, E. F. (ed.). *Educational Measurement* (Washington, D. C.: American Council on Education, 1951).
7. MASTER WORD SET (Minneapolis: The Judy Co., 1958).
8. STEVENS, L. A. "The Fourteen Words That Make All the Difference," *Coronet,* XL (August, 1956), 80–82.
9. THOMPSON, ERNEST. "The 'Master-Word' Approach to Vocabulary Training," *Journal of Developmental Reading,* II (Autumn, 1958), 62–66.

CHAPTER X

READING FOR MEANING

60. CONTRIBUTIONS OF READING TO PERSONAL DEVELOPMENT*

David H. Russell

IN HIS autobiography, *Safe Conduct,* Boris Pasternak says that the biography of a poet is found in what happens to those who read him. What *does* happen to a reader?

We read at four levels. At the first level we are largely concerned with the association of printed words with their sounds. In some school situations children are drilled in word-calling— "barking at words" without much attention to meaning. At the second level we read for literal meanings. We get the facts or we follow explicit directions. Such reading may have many functional values for the child finding out about India or for the suburbanite engaged in a week-end do-it-yourself project.

The other two levels of reading are

* From David H. Russell, "Contributions of Reading to Personal Development," *Teachers College Record,* LXI, No. 8 (May, 1960), 435–42. Reprinted by permission of the author and *Teachers College Record.*

more complex. At the third level we interpret what we read. That is, we go beyond the literal comprehension of the fact or the main idea to read between the lines. We draw some conclusion of our own from the passage— we envisage or predict or infer. Sometimes we reflect on the author's point of view or the relation of the material to other things we know—we evaluate or analyze critically. But we also read at a fourth level or depth. Sometimes the passage takes us beyond thoughtful analysis or critical review to a more stirring experience. We feel "the shock of recognition." We recognize a new or an important idea in the actions, characters, or values described. The impact of the material is such that we receive fresh insight into our own or others' lives. In our reading we are changed, a little, as persons.

Most reading is done at the second, literal level, and most of the writing and research in the field of reading have had to do with the first two levels. We know a lot about word perception, the teaching of phonics, and ways of developing comprehension of the printed page. Such activities make many contributions to the individual. The young child enjoys his new-found skill of working out new words, and the world's work and its weekend hobbies involve the use of much factual reading matter contributing to knowledge and skill. Reading has always been one of the individual's most important resources for gaining knowledge. Granted a modicum of reading skill in the individual, books and libraries are storehouses of information for him. Thus, reading at the second level may have many influences on personal development, as in increasing skill in making model airplanes or in preparing a traveler in Spain to get the most out of direct experiences in a foreign country. The main branch of the Berkeley Public Library has approximately 375 books whose titles begin with the words "How to———," starting with *How to Abandon Ship* and including *How to Live with Children.* Reading at the second level can be a big help to us!

At the third level, we are not so sure of our ground as we are when concerned with word recognition or literal comprehension. A feature of recent research, however, has been considerable work on critical and creative reading abilities. In a recent study at the University of California, for example, Clark [4] developed twenty-three lessons in reading to predict beyond the given facts and tested some ways of teaching these in the classroom. He found that

tests of reading to predict were relatively independent of vocabulary and comprehension. In going from literal comprehension to personal interpretation as in prediction a reader puts more of himself into his reading. He thinks beyond the line of print. The perceptual process is the stimulus to many kinds of thinking—to drawing analogies, to checking a writer's point of view, or to beginning an attack on a personal problem. As suggested below, more work needs to be done in exploring this process of thoughtful reaction to an author's ideas.

It is at the fourth level, however, that our knowledge is slight and our needs are great, and so it is with effects of reading on individuals that this discussion is chiefly concerned. Can Pasternak or other poets influence us deeply? Do we really have *Books That Changed the World,* as the optimistic title of one publication suggests? Can a book, story, or poem change one person, much less the world? Can reading have the effect Lincoln believed it could have when he first met Harriet Beecher Stowe? On that occasion he said, "Is this the little woman whose book made such a great war?" In a world of television, radio, comic books, parents, and teachers, can a book be an experience which changes the nature of reality for the young reader? In the words of Ciardi, can it make him "quietly passionate" about an idea or a cause? Or can a book help a person to the self-insight attributed to a man who, seeing his neighbor going by in a new pink Cadillac, said, "There, but for me, go I!" Can a book fill a boy with courage or help him find himself? Or is this too much to ask, even of great literature? Reading may be useful at all four levels, but somehow this fourth level seems the most tantalizing and important of all.

Some Possible Effects of Reading

The kind of reading that we do affects the contribution of the reading matter to our development. In the primary school grades so much of the effort goes into the first level—into the mechanics of reading, into getting the words right, toward following the sequence of the writer's thought—that the chance of added dividends is unlikely. Similarly, in the later grades, the poor reader, or the child deciphering material much too difficult for him, has little opportunity or stimulus to interpret a story or to find materials meaningful to his larger concerns or problems. Piekarz [11] has shown that when children are unable to read a passage with reasonable ease they have fewer reactions to it, with many more responses at the literal-meaning level than at the implied-meaning or evaluation level.

Accordingly, the time and effort given to the making of fluent, skillful readers at the elementary and secondary school levels may be worthwhile, not only in terms of specific aspects of reading skill but also because such reading is a basis for operation at the two higher levels of reading. Children need word-attack skills and ability to follow directions, not because they are merely going to read words or to follow directions blindly, but so that, having clearly recognized words or accurately interpreted directions, they can then go to the meanings behind the words and, if necessary, to questions about the validity of the directions.

Such an interpretation of reading is not a derogation of reading skills. Many children and adolescents work very hard to attain word recognition skills and the ability to grasp the literal meaning of a paragraph, passage, or chapter. Indeed, success in these matters may make a contribution to personal development beyond that of the facts read because of the "nothing succeeds like success" formula. The child who learns to read skillfully not only pleases his parents but contributes positively to his self-concept. The converse is even clearer. The child who has reading difficulties at the first two levels may have emotional and personality problems associated with his reading. The primary causation may not be so important as the *fact* that reading difficulties are affecting his total development adversely.

When poor readers have not achieved fluency in reading, they must have help. For these pupils various types of remedial programs have been developed in schools.

For young children, one aid to fluency is to have their parents and teachers read stories to them, more complex stories than they can read for themselves. For their own first reading practice there seems no reason why children should not begin on easy, graded materials developed in light of many of the things we know about the psychology of learning. In the preschool and early primary years, children can be challenged and helped to reach higher levels of reading by the ideas in the stories read to them.

An example of such reading–listening situations affecting total development is given in a recent master's thesis by Webster.[21] She found in a group of eighty first-graders that thirty-five expressed fear of the dark and five indicated fear of dogs. Accordingly, in groups of seven children, she read to and discussed with the children five stories dealing positively with the dark and with dogs—stories such as Margaret Wise Brown's *A Child's Good Night Book* and Ruth Dixon's *Three Little Puppies*. Three months later, an impartial judge agreed with Webster's analysis of interviews: twenty-nine out of the thirty-five children had, it seemed, reduced their fear of the dark and all five of the children had lost most of their fear of dogs. Such a study needs verification with more careful controls, but it suggests that, for young children, the "read-to" situation may affect a child's emotional development.

As a child develops the ability to read for himself some books and stories of merit, the second level of reading flourishes. He finds out not only the secret of the lost treasure but something of the lives of early Americans or something about woolgrowing in Patagonia or in Queensland. The purpose of many books, newspapers, and magazines is to inform. We live in a difficult period of man's history, and the problems which beset us demand our best knowledge and efforts. Therefore, we read for main ideas, for facts, for following a sequence of events, for seeing relationships, and for arriving at conclusions.

Teachers of English at the secondary school and college level have not always considered such reading part of their domain. Of course they must also be concerned with the third and fourth reading levels of interpretation and with the impact of great literature. The value of the information contained in a book has little or nothing to do with its value as literature. One level is concerned with getting a fact right and clear, the other is concerned with some basic human expression or need. One makes for grasp of the immediate, the other, as Bernard Berenson remarked of great pictures, makes for the enhancement of life. Most of our school texts are written and should be used at the level of accurate comprehension. I believe the problem is not "either-or" and that the teacher of English must be concerned with both kinds of reading. Skill at the first two levels seems to be basic to achievement at the third and fourth levels. But it is in the realm of imaginative literature that we usually get to the third and fourth levels of reading. It is here that writing is intrepid in its approach to problems, ingenious in its solution of difficulties, in a way that the child or adolescent cannot achieve by himself. It is at these levels that reading can operate in depth and make its greatest contribution to individual development.

Fortunately, some research evidence is beginning to be accumulated about reading at the third level of interpretation of printed materials. May I quickly suggest a variety of findings. (*a*) Most children do not seem to respond to some of the commoner literary devices such as metaphor or personification before they are in their teens.[23] (*b*) Children's interpretations are influenced by their attitudes and expectancies toward what they are reading, by their previous "set" in the reading situation.[5] (c) When asked to respond to short stories, adolescents give interpretational reactions as a dominant type of response; other categories of response, in order of frequency, are narrational, associational, self-involvement, literary judgment, and prescriptive judgment.[19] (d) Responses to a piece of literature are largely an individual matter. Children and youth with different experiences, personalities, and needs see different things in the same character, story, or poem—and one interpretation may be just as "true" or "honest" as the other. Consequently, teachers of reading and literature should beware of looking for the one "correct" interpretation.[14] (e) With adolescents, literary judgments and emotional involvements vary inversely. In other words, children and adolescents tend to suspend objectivity when emotionally involved.[19] (f) The most common emotional involvements of adolescents in fiction seem to be "happiness binding" (the desire for a happy ending) and insistence upon certainty in interpretation.[19] These half-dozen statements can be extended in a consideration of the process of interpretation. Perhaps the samples are enough to show that we are beginning to accumulate some research evidence about some of the psychological factors which are involved in interpretation, whether of a good story in a third reader, a chapter or poem in a high school anthology, or an individual example of an author's work.

Unfortunately, the evidence about effects at the fourth level of reading is sparse. Perhaps it will always be shaky in the scientific sense and we shall always have to rely in part on individual testimony regarding the effects of books or literature. Down through the generations, great and good men have testified to the influence of a book or books in their lives. The Greeks believed in the effect of literature on the growing boy, and Plato wrote in *The Republic,* ". . . we should do our utmost that the first stories that they hear should be so composed as to bring the fairest lessons of virtue to their ears." Much later, Stephen Vincent Benét wrote, "Books are not men and yet they are alive." Luther Burbank, the great horticulturist, testified that his whole life was changed by reading one book, *The Origin of the Species.* But the testimony of these and other men and women, interesting in itself, does not constitute evidence in the scientific sense. What about the individual's readiness for change? What about other supporting or conflicting influences in classroom, home, or community? Can a biography of sacrifice and social service influence a twelve-year-old girl for whose parents the good life consists of cocktail parties and Las Vegas weekends? If we as teachers are trying to influence the ideas and lives of young people through literature, we need to know much more about the role of the individual himself, the content of the materials, the total situation in which the reading takes place, and the overt reactions to be expected in speaking, writing, and action.[14]

To some teachers such analysis of the four factors influencing the impact of reading on the individual makes the whole process needlessly complex. Not every teacher of reading in the fourth grade or of literature in the tenth grade can take time to know individual children and materials in such intimate fashion, nor can they easily arrange maximum environmental conditions for reading to affect individual development. Perhaps the problem is still one for research rather than classroom practice, and yet somehow the two must be combined. All elementary and secondary teachers of literature know that some pieces are more effective than others with a group but may not have tried to discover the reason. Why does one story "hit" a group of ten-year-olds or another, a group of fifteen-year-olds "just right"? What kind of matching of material and reader can a teacher accomplish? How can this be individualized at the secondary as well as the elementary school level? What are maximal conditions when "boy meets book"?

The evidence that reading affects lives is largely confined to the subjective, individual testimony illustrated above and to some reports of bibliotherapy in individual case studies.[8, 15, 7, 24] Studies by Russell,[12] Smith,[18] and Weingarten[22] have attempted to get at the effects of reading by requesting direct reports of them from teachers and from elementary and secondary school students. Such reports may all be too optimistic because of the desire of students to give congenial answers but they do suggest that the effects of reading may be widespread and sometimes profound. The present scattered findings can be substantiated or refuted by further research. Perhaps at the moment the teacher can only adopt the optimistic view that there are certain things that are true even if not experimentally verified. Perhaps such a faith is needed if one is to teach literature well. The possibilities are so vast that this article concludes with a few more examples of research explorations in unmapped territory.

Research on Interpretation

In addition to the investigation by Squire cited above and the studies supporting the six conclusions stated earlier, some careful investigations have been made of the interpretive process in reading. These date back at least to 1917, when Thorndike[20] published his classical study of ways children misinterpret paragraphs. One reason for flagrant errors in interpreting a factual passage he attributed to the overpotency of certain words. He said, "The mind is assailed as it were by every word in the paragraph. It must select, repress, soften, emphasize, correlate, and organize, all under the influence of the right mental set or purpose or demand." This statement was explored further by Hinze[9] in a recent doctoral study at the University of California. She was interested in the cluster of associations the reader may have with certain words as explored by Jenkins, by Osgood and others. She first selected two passages, one factual (about scientific discoveries) and one emotionally charged (part of a Kafka story). Before the students saw these passages they were asked, in interview, to associate all the words they could with certain individual words from the two selections and to rate the words as positive or negative associations. Later, the students read each passage and interpreted its meaning. Hinze found clear evidence that when students had consistent emotional responses to the words in the passage, that is, all positive or all negative reactions, they tended to interpret the paragraphs objectively or "correctly," but when some of their emotional responses to the individual words were opposed to the dominant association, that is, when they had "conflict words," they had trouble giving a clear interpretation of the passage. Conflict words, in contrast to unidirectional words, caused significantly greater misinterpretation of the affective materials.

Some other investigations have given clues to the kinds of interpretation a teacher can expect. In a study [23] in England, the subject of the work was found to be most important for young children. Before they were twelve they made judgments about the ethical intention of the writer, and after twelve there emerged some feeling for "literary quality" as shown in structure and the aptness of simile or metaphor. In an American study, Harris [6] analyzed students' responses to literature into four types: translating; summarizing; inferring tone, mood, and intent; and relating technique and meaning. He devised tests of seven specific recognition skills but found on factor analysis of results that one general factor was adequate to account for the intercorrelations of the test results. This suggested that comprehension of literary materials may be a general function.

A study by Groff, [5] however, emphasized the factors of individuality and attitude in interpreting paragraphs. He found that as a child reads critically, his interpretations are influenced by his attitude toward the content type of material read and his attitude toward reading as a school activity. In a factor analysis of scores on twenty-seven variables Bauer [2] found that achievement in reading was positively related to two variables, "self-expressiveness" and "drive for achievement," but negatively related to social adjustment and absence of excessive fears. Personality factors may influence reading behavior.

Another unpublished study of interpretation is that of Scribner,[16] who found wide differences in the interpretation of poems by students, teachers of English, and literary critics. These differences are not great in the interpretation of relatively clear-cut poems such as Robert Frost's "The Road Not Taken." Even here, however, in a group of eighteen-year-olds, Scribner got such divergent interpretations of the main theme as—

The necessity of making decisions in life.
The idea that one road may be better than the other.
The idea that it is important to think for yourself and make your own decisions.
He took the less traveled road.

These may seem varied responses from a group of eighteen-year-olds to a relatively simple poem, but Scribner found that variety in interpretation becomes much greater for the more "difficult" or ambiguous poem such as Blake's "Tiger," both in the student group itself and in terms of differences among students, teachers, and critics.

Why do students interpret a poem, story, or novel differently? We have already suggested one group of causes in the student or reader—his reading ability, his background of experience, his attitude and expectancies, his needs perhaps. The second group of causes lies in the piece of literature itself. As Hinze found, an overlap in these two occurs in the reader's associations with the individual words. It also occurs in the pupil's sensory perception of a poem or other piece of imaginative writing—his response to images in seeing, hearing, feeling, or even smelling. The piece of literature itself may affect the reader's interpretation through the arrangement or pattern; for example, the rhyme scheme or the use of onomatopoeia.

Finally, there is the symbolization in the story or poem. At the elementary level the lion is the symbol of courage, a flag of nationality, and Loki of trouble and mischief among the gods. With older children, we begin to get values attached to symbols. Some things are true and good, as motherhood, and some wrong or unworthy, as cowardice. Studies of school reading texts by Anderson [1] and by Child,[3] of children's biographies by McConnell,[10] and of best-selling fiction by Harvey [7] are examples of analyses of content of reading materials which *may* influence a reader. Thus the reader himself and the content of the material, particularly the symbolic content, may influence interpretation.

This research report is sketchy, and necessarily so. Most of it consists of spot checks instead of long-term studies of the effects of reading. We need to know much more about both cross-sectional and longitudinal aspects of each of the four factors influencing interpretation and personal development through reading. Since the days of the *New England Primer* we have had the feeling that, somehow, reading can help create a virtuous life. Almost three hundred years after the *Primer* perhaps the goal is still a good one.

REFERENCES

1. ANDERSON, PAUL S. "McGuffey *vs.* the Moderns in Character Training." *Phi Delta Kappan,* 38:53–58, November, 1956.
2. BAUER, EDITH B. "The Interrelatedness of Personality and Achievement in Reading." Doctoral dissertation, University of California, Berkeley, 1956.
3. CHILD, IRWIN L., and OTHERS. "Children's Textbooks and Personality Development: An Exploration in the Social Psychology of Education." *Psychological Monographs,* 60, No. 3, 1946, 54 pp.
4. CLARK, CHARLES M. "Teaching Sixth-Grade Students to Make Predictions from Reading Materials." Doctoral dissertation, University of California, Berkeley, 1958.
5. GROFF, PATRICK J. "Children's Attitudes Toward Reading and Their Critical Reading Abilities in Four Content-Type Materials." Doctoral dissertation, University of California, Berkeley, 1955.
6. HARRIS, CHESTER W. "Measurement of Comprehension of Literature." *School Review,* 56:280–89, 332–43, May, June, 1948.
7. HARVEY, JOHN. "The Content Characteristics of Best-Selling Novels."

Public Opinion Quarterly, 17:91–114, 1953.

8. HERMINGHAUS, EARL G. "The Effect of Bibliotherapy on the Attitudes and Personal and Social Adjustment of a Group of Elementary School Children." Doctoral dissertation, Washington University, 1954.

9. HINZE, HELEN A. "The Individual's Word Associations and His Interpretation of Prose Paragraphs." Doctoral dissertation, University of California, Berkeley, 1959.

10. MCCONNELL, GAITHER A. "An Analysis of Biographical Literature for Children." Doctoral dissertation, University of California, Berkeley, 1952.

11. PIEKARZ, JOSEPHINE A. "Getting Meaning from Reading." *Elementary School Journal,* 56:303–9, March, 1956.

12. RUSSELL, DAVID H. "Teachers' Memories and Opinions of Children's Literature." *Elementary English,* 26:475–82, December, 1949.

13. ————. "Personal Values in Reading." *The Reading Teacher,* 12:3–9, October, 1958.

14. ————. "Some Research on the Impact of Reading." *English Journal,* 47:398–413, October, 1958.

15. RUSSELL, DAVID H., and SHRODES, CAROLINE. "Contributions of Research in Bibliotherapy to the Language Arts Program." *School Review,* 58:335–42, 411–20, September, October, 1950.

16. SCRIBNER, MARION. "Responses of Students, Teachers and Critics to Selected Poems." In manuscript, University of California, Berkeley.

17. SHRODES, CAROLINE. "Bibliotherapy: A Theoretical and Clinical-Experimental Study." Doctoral dissertation, University of California, Berkeley, 1949.

18. SMITH, NILA B. "Some Effects of Reading on Children." *Elementary English,* 25:271–78, May, 1948.

19. SQUIRE, JAMES R. "The Responses of Adolescents to Literature Involving Selected Experiences in Personal Development." Doctoral dissertation, University of California, Berkeley, 1956.

20. THORNDIKE, EDWARD L. "Reading as Reasoning: A Study of Mistakes in Paragraph Reading." *Journal of Educational Psychology,* 8:323–32, June, 1917.

21. WEBSTER, W. JANE. "Some Effects of Stories on the Reduction of Fears of First Grade Children." M.A. Seminar Study, University of California, Berkeley, 1960.

22. WEINGARTEN, SAMUEL. "Developmental Values in Voluntary Reading." *School Review,* 62:222–30, April, 1954.

23. WILLIAMS, E. D., WINTER, L., and WOODS, J. K. "Tests of Literary Appreciation." *British Journal of Educational Psychology,* 8:265–84, November, 1938.

24. WITTY, PAUL A. "Promoting Growth and Development Through Reading." *Elementary English,* 27:493–500, December, 1950.

61. NEW APPROACHES TO THE STUDY OF INTERPRETATION IN READING*

William S. Gray

INTEREST in improved techniques in the study of interpretation in reading stems from three facts: the increasing demand which current life makes on readers for breadth and depth of interpretation; failure to increase ability to interpret in many recent reading improvement programs in colleges and at the adult level; and slow progress during the last two decades in securing a more penetrating understanding of the nature of the interpretative process. Before describing recent approaches to the problem it may be helpful to view the problem briefly in historical perspective.

One of the earlist efforts to identify objectively the processes involved in understanding what is read was reported by Thorndike [1] in 1917 as a result of detailed studies of children's errors in sentence and paragraph reading. On the basis of the evidence secured, he concluded, first, that the understanding of a paragraph involves the same sort of "organization and analytic action of ideas as occurs in thinking of supposedly higher sorts"; second, that in effective reading the mind selects, represses, softens, empha-

* From William S. Gray, "New Approaches to the Study of Interpretation in Reading," *Journal of Educational Research,* LII, No. 2 (October, 1958), 65–67. Reprinted by permission of Mrs. William S. Gray and *Journal of Educational Research.*

sizes, correlates, and organizes "all under the influence of the right mental set or purpose or demand"; and third, that "the fishing around in the text" for something to use in answering a question "and its use without reorganization is one of the most debased forms of reasoning—selective thinking —which school work shows."

A second milestone was established by Judd and Buswell [2] in a study of different types of silent reading. On the basis of eye movement records they concluded that the mental processes in reading vary with the kind of material read, its difficulty, and the purpose for which it is read. They also distinguished between silent reading for "understanding and appreciation" and "analytical study." They pointed out that as long as instruction fails to distinguish between different types of reading "pupils will adopt a purely incidental method." Since most of them are uncritical of their methods, improvement will be slow and more or less accidental unless guidance is provided.

Stimulated by such findings, teachers made vigorous efforts during the twenties and thirties to improve comprehension. At least four procedures were used widely: first, the use of questions, both fact and judgment; second, detailed studies of the form, organization, and structure of the passages read, which led ultimately to questions concerning the value of a knowledge of grammar and syntax; third, the procedures recommended by semanticists who pointed out that meanings of words are influenced by the context in which they are used, by the author's purpose and mood, and by the kind of material read—historical, scientific, emotive. They also differentiated sharply between literal and implied meanings and emphasized the importance of interpreting passages in the light of their broader context. A fourth procedure consisted of vigorous training in reading for various purposes.

Paralleling these developments, research specialists sought to identify through the use of various correlation techniques the factors which exert most influence on comprehension. As early as 1924, Hilliard [3] reported the results of a detailed study which showed that intelligence and meaning vocabulary are more closely related to comprehension than any other factors studied. The third factor in order of importance was ability to organize, which implied capacity to grasp relationships and to reconstruct ideas. During the next two decades many similar studies were reported. Various summaries of findings led to the conclusion that many factors are involved in comprehension which are related but not identical. As a result, pointed questions arose concerning the nature of the techniques that would discriminate more sharply among factors.

The technique which seemed most promising at the time was factorial analysis. Since 1930 more than a score of studies using this technique have been reported. A striking example was Davis' study [4] in 1944 in which the following factors were identified: "knowledge of word meaning"; "ability to reason," that is "to infer meanings and to weave together several statements"; "ability to identify the writer's intent, purpose, or point of view"; "ability to grasp the detailed statements in a passage"; and "knowledge of literary devices and techniques." Such findings appeared to be very promising until Thurstone used a different procedure on Davis' data and found only one common factor. More recent investigators also report that they found only one common factor in addition to meaning vocabulary.

On the basis of findings to date, the use of factorial analysis has not greatly advanced our knowledge of the basic factors in interpretation or methods of improving competence in thoughtful reading. Whereas the basic methods used may be mathematically unique and valid they do not provide methods of interpreting the data on which all can agree. Furthermore, the analyses made have not gone beyond the answers to the questions in the tests used. As a result, it has become necessary to search for other techniques which are more productive. Some investigators have adopted the procedures used by Thorndike, to which reference was made earlier, and are studying the errors and difficulties of children and adults in reading assigned passages. A recent study by Black [5] of the difficulties which students who are preparing to teach in England face in understanding what they read illustrates both the technique used and the nature of the findings.

Other investigators are now making use of retrospective and introspective techniques which were first used by Huey [6] in studies of the interpretive process in reading more than a half century ago. In 1953, Swain [7] reported the results of a study among college students in which introspection was used in identifying the conscious thought processes involved in answering questions based on the passages read. She sought to find out among other things whether attention was focused primarily on the analysis of language or on the reconstruction of meaning. Her findings when compared with the results of other studies indicated that a reader, varying with his level of competence, may focus most of his attention on word perception, on the analysis of language in identifying the author's meaning, or on the restructuring of meanings in the light of his experiences, interest, or specific purposes. A second study which used both introspection and retrospection was made by Piekarz. [8] She secured recordings of interviews with high level and low level readers in the sixth grade following the silent and oral reading of selected passages. During the interviews, each pupil verbalized his thoughts and feelings concerning what he had read and answered thirty questions, the answers to which involved nine aspects of interpretation.

An analysis of the responses showed that the higher level readers made a greater variety and number of responses, implying greater penetration. Their responses were more evenly divided over three broad areas, namely, literal meanings, implied meanings, and evaluations. They tended to remain objective and impersonal in their interpretations, to use their general background in enriching the author's meaning, to restrict their responses to the text, and to refer to their personal experiences only in proving a point. Finally, they seemed to be able to view the selection impersonally and to see both sides of an issue objectively. Even though they possessed strong feelings toward the ideas presented, they were able to control their reactions and to distinguish clearly between their own opinion and those of the author.

The lower level readers, on the other hand, limited their responses to literal meanings and gave only passing attention to implied meanings and critical reactions. They had difficulty in maintaining an objective attitude and in distinguishing between their own and the author's ideas. For example, many of the words read stimulated the recall of experiences that led them far beyond the author's intended meanings. The evaluations expressed stemmed from an emotional rather than an intellectual base and were highly personal in nature.

Using an interview and retrospective techniques with adults, Gray and Rogers [9] secured evidence which clearly supported the conclusions of Piekarz. Of special significance was the fact that the mature readers had mastered the skills of word recognition and those involved in a clear grasp of meaning and concentrated on the evaluation of the ideas read and their reconstruction into patterns that served their purpose. In this connection each reader exhibited compelling interests, or indeed, a central point or radix which influenced directly the nature of the interpretations made. To a surprising extent, the evaluation and reconstruction of ideas were directed by their concern for efficient living and a better society.

In an effort to gain added insight concerning the processes involved in problem solving while reading, Bloom and Broder [10] made use of introspections with college students. They found, at first, that success in problem solving is usually accompanied by tension followed by relaxation when a solution is found. The tension usually varies with the complexity of the problem. They found, second, that as individuals give attention to a problem, certain aspects and details appeared to stand out and to occupy the foreground of attention while other details remained in the background. Four characteristics of this foreground-background relationship were identified: the speed with which they were recognized, the strength with which they could be held, the amount of detail which could be brought to the foreground, and their degree of relevance. Finally, three major steps leading to the attack on a problem were identified. First, the reader attempts to dispose of unfamiliar items; second, he selects a point that stands out as a possible starting point; and finally he attempts to limit the problem. This last step was found to be more characteristic of superior than of poor students.

The studies to which references have been made provide clear evidence of the value of the use of retrospective and introspective techniques in studying interpretation in reading. They reveal as clearly as any technique used thus far the nature of the thinking involved. By securing recordings of the reader's responses, it is possible to analyze them in as much detail as often as may be desirable. The subject can also be re-examined at points in order to verify or extend conclusions.

The use of introspection and retrospection can be adapted to the study of various kinds of reading situations. For example, Jenkinson [11] has just completed a study in which blanks were left in the passages read, the demands made on the reader being similar to those in an expanded completion test. However, the blanks occurred at strategic points which made it possible to study the influence of selected aspects of a passage on its interpretation. Letton is now completing an illuminating Ph.D. study of the interpretative process when reading poetry. Rogers is well launched on a study at the high-school level which aims to compare the interpretative processes in a typical structured assignment situation and in free reading, using equivalent passages with respect to difficulty and human interest appeal.

The foregoing discussion should not be interpreted as critical of techniques that have been used widely in the past in the study of interpretation. As indicated earlier, the study of difficulties and failures of readers, using the Thorndike or Black techniques, can be very illuminating. The chief aim has been to call attention to another approach which merits careful considerations in planning studies of the interpretative process in reading.

REFERENCES

1. THORNDIKE, EDWARD L. "Reading as Reasoning: A Study of Mistakes in Paragraph Reading," *Journal of Educational Research,* VIII (June, 1917), 323–32.

2. JUDD, CHARLES H., and BUSWELL, GUY T. *Silent Reading: A Study of Its Various Types,* Supplementary Education Monographs, University of Chicago, 1922.

3. HILLIARD, GEORGE H. *Probable Types of Difficulties Underlying Low Scores in Comprehension Tests.* University of Iowa Studies in Education, Vol. II, No. 6, 1924.

4. DAVIS, FREDERICK B. "Fundamental Factors of Comprehension in Reading," *Psychometrika,* IX (September, 1944), 185–97.

5. BLACK, E. L. "The Difficulties of Training College Students in Understanding What They Read," *British Journal of Educational Psychology,* XXIV (February, 1954), 17–31.

6. HUEY, EDMUND B. *The Psychology and Pedagogy of Reading* (New York: The Macmillan Company, 1912), Chapter VIII.

7. SWAIN, EMELIZA. *Conscious Thought Processes Used in the Interpretation of Reading Materials,* Unpublished Ph.D. dissertation, University of Chicago, 1953.

8. PIEKARZ, JOSEPHINE A. "Getting Meaning From Reading," *Elementary School Journal,* LVI (March, 1956), 303–9.

9. GRAY, WILLAM S., and ROGERS, BERNICE. *Maturity in Reading: Its Nature and Appraisal* (Chicago: University of Chicago Press, 1956).

10. BLOOM, BENJAMIN S., and BRODER, LOIS J. *Problem-Solving Processes of College Students* (Chicago: University of Chicago Press, 1950).

11. JENKINSON, MARION. *Selected Processes and Difficulties of Reading Comprehension,* Unpublished Ph.D dissertation, University of Chicago, 1957.

62. LET'S READ AND HEED!*

Ann Ess Morrow

Cause for Lament

"IF boys and girls would only think as they read!" Mrs. Jones remarked, and her tone was truly mournful. Maybe that was why she wore black that day.

"Think as they read!" exclaimed Mr. Loring. "I'd be grateful if they'd just think." He was somewhat impetuous himself and was inclined by his example to impart the trait to youngsters in his charge. "I always seem to have children who somersault into activities. Emotional acrobats I call them. They often suffer afterwards from consequences of their rash enthusiasm. Like the time Jane suggested free reading, and everyone thought that was wonderful. Why, several brought magazines that day with cover girls that needed covering!"

"And I'd be grateful if they'd just read," put in Miss Donahue. "My pills lack skills—no wonder they misbehave! And believe me, building background that should have been built grades ago is no fun when the book that's to be covered is dedicated to one grade level with people under and above it. For I do have one or two superior students who crave a speedy

* From Ann Ess Morrow, "Let's Read and Heed!" *Education*, LXXVIII, No. 3 (November, 1957), 131–35. Reprinted by permission of the author and The Bobbs-Merrill Co., Inc., Indianapolis, Ind.

pace," she added. "That makes them restless, too."

"Now mine think without reading," volunteered Mr. Thomas. "They're always quoting what someone told them, instead of ferreting it out from print. And everything is colored by emotion. There's just no reason to it, but plenty of reason for it, because it's so much easier that way."

"Mine think all right," observed Mrs. Anderson, known for her sense of humor. "They always think as they read—but the two don't go together quite like apple pie and cheese. They read about the Pilgrims and dream of the new little blonde across the room. Sometimes, though, they keep their thinking and their reading together, then veer off. Take a story about Pocohantas, for instance. They concentrate on Indians so hard first thing you know they're deep in powwow plans for Saturday night. Or else they're wondering how I'd look if I were scalped. They ought to know," she laughed. "I blew my top the other day."

Flippant and exaggerated though these remarks may be, there are elements of truth in them recognized by all of us.

Knowledge of Mechanics Essential

Truly thoughtful reading can best be done when boys and girls have freed themselves from a consciousness of the mechanics—when the reading process becomes a fluid activity, well lubricated, instead of halting or rusty. This brings about more glow than woe, for facility of reading will always be a source of pleasure. One is free to look beyond the words then and to come upon intended meaning. But when one's biggest goal in life sometimes is the verbalizing of a word that bothers with its bulk or startles with its strangeness or confuses with its connotation, meaning fades like a photographer's negative forgotten in the sun.

Meeting of Needs Vital

Yet it is not so simple as all that. For varying degrees of mastery of such reading skills as perception and recognition and attack will always exist in any heterogeneous classroom. And for these the worthwhile teacher must provide. Just helping boys and girls to read correctly, then, will advance them on the way to thought. And the way loses bumpiness and becomes highway smooth if there is a two-way variety within the group—variety of levels recognized and provided for, and variety of types of material to increase the possibilities of print appeal. Thus the aim of a teacher with a read-to-heed goal is to develop fluent readers, first of all—by development of basic skills and by meeting individual needs, a process worthy of thought as deep as that engaged in by that famous statue of Rodin. This will leave the children freedom to concentrate on meaning. For how can John think critically if he has not yet found the means of reading what he is to think about?

Thought Involved in Act of Reading

The very act of reading involves thought. Youngsters mend faulty pronunciation sometimes by learning how to blend; they arrive at meaning by obtaining clues from context. They identify words by recognition of parts, by associations, by careful observations of visual details. And once they do all this, they're not too far from starting on their way to locate information.

They like to make inferences, too. Even small children understand this art. "I'll tell Daddy if you don't behave," they're told at times.

"But if I do, she won't," the lad concludes. And weighs the fun involved against displeasure to be registered, and regulates his way of acting according to his decision. Surely if they understand a process, it is easier to apply it when they read.

Also, in order to think effectively while reading, boys and girls must realize that different rates are both permissible and necessary—that speed is just as right at times as are care and slowness. And once Sue realizes that differences in people lead to differences in reading, she likewise comes to see that differences in purpose lead to differences in rate.

Emotional Problems as Deterrents

Mary Alice couldn't read well at all the other day—and couldn't answer questions afterwards about the story because she was obviously upset as she read. Something looming large upon her personal horizon had happened before she reached this room and kept putting itself between her and the printed pages. So that day she didn't think at all. She just pronounced words, and didn't even do that too well. But her teacher, Mr. Henry, had much of Solomon in him. He did not chide or seek to pry before the group. He quietly asked if she'd care to stop in a few minutes after school, and called on someone who was not perturbed.

Later that day he listened to a story that unfolded in an atmosphere of sympathy and rapport, and just by listening helped to ease the emotional problem which Mary Alice was more easily able to solve. Next day she was her cheerful self. She read and thought well then.

Capturing of Interest Vital

Tom doesn't think much as he reads, either, unless he's reading of his dominating interest. It isn't just girls who are eager to meet that man in the moon, it seems. Tom hopes to make the trip himself some day, and searches out in print all he can about it. But he doesn't seem to like anything else. And because he doesn't like to read the assigned selections from Franklin's *Autobiography,* he doesn't even try to think. Miss Gleason recognizes this, fortunately, and tries to lure him into finding traits that Franklin had, like practicality and reasoning ability, that travelers in space would need. Before, he'd merely done a print-squint. But now he sees that they're connected, he, too, thinks.

Bewilderment a Negative Factor

Timothy is too bewildered by it all to think. To find suddenly that in a strange book he is to cover ten pages in a minimum of time in a class where he feels lost is just too much for him, who seems the counterpart of Alice in Wonderland. At least, he wonders what it's all about and how he'll manage to go on living, and when he thinks, he uses question marks lavishly, but most of them remain inside. If only he were in a class not quite so big, the teacher would realize his problem and clear away the fog. But as in so many schools today, the class is far too big for one, yet not enough for two. And Timothy suffers for it.

Problem of Prejudice

Beverly discovers she is reading a spirited defense of the Republican party, when her entire family has long been steeped in donkey symbolism. And because she's sure she'll disagree with it the way her folks will do when she confides at home, she turns off her thoughts faucet-fashion, and lets not one opposing thought drop down. The challenge to the teacher now is clear—to show the need for tolerance and for ideas arrived at through one's reason, rather than through emotions or through ideas that come all packaged for posterity. It's so easy that way when opinions come all ready-made. Then no one has to think. When Beverly sheds her prejudice, she, too, will read with thoughts unhampered. No, it isn't just the dentists who have patients. Teachers do, too—a never-ending supply.

Establishment of Purpose Sought

John's problem is different. He can't read and think at all if he's not sure about the aim. If Mrs. Jones gives him an outline of questions to be answered in the reading, he is reassured. He knows what is expected, and he becomes secure. But like a country liberated suddenly from authoritarianism, he feels an overwhelming need to be told exactly what to do. But guidance like this can also be overdone and quell initiative. For boys and girls eventually must come to set their goals themselves. They never must rely on guidance so strongly that without it they are lost. And right there lies a danger.

Adjustment Needed to Techniques

Alice is the kind of reader who recognizes the technique that's needed, but somehow can't apply it. She knows that she should skim to find exactly how long ago it was that dinosaurs inhabited the earth, when she has only two minutes to find a needle answer tucked within a verbal haystack of perhaps some seven pages. But she hasn't yet learned to sweep along and light on partial phrases, to scoop up topic sentences and breeze through waiting pages. Her conscientiousness she applies to every word. Each one she says within herself as fast as possible, which really isn't fast at all, for other folks have left her pages back. Thus she concentrates on individual symbols with a multiplicity of jerky eye-fixations, when what she needs is rhythm of movement, with point of focus in the middle of a span grown large.

Jim's just the opposite. He knows that thoughtful reading is required here to find exactly why a certain person reacts the way he does—and he is so addicted to the printed drag-strip that when he does slow down, the squealing of his reading brakes counteracts the sound the meaning makes.

Again, the alert teacher notes all this and offers exercises that provide opportunities to practice skills. She uses reading exercises that are timed by way of stimulating rate, and tests the comprehension of the children by determining the accuracy with which they answer questions that relate to subject-matter.

She uses reading as a means of strengthening vocabulary and of studying words in parts and whole, facilitating better understanding of the way that words are spelled and said. She gives the students paragraphs designed to bolster word attack and to show them further how to blend. She also checks on use of context as an aid to meaning.

The children find it challenging to keep a record of their growth of skill. They closely watch the charts they sometimes make and feel an academic glow when real improvement shows. They come to see the techniques personally needed and eventually are able to apply them.

Dr. Byron Van Roeckel of Michigan State University has a plan for encouraging this skill. He advocates for this a three-minute reading exercise each day as class begins, an exercise the purpose of which changes with the date. One day they read to find a fact designated by the teacher; another, to find a passage and interpret; and then again, to summarize. And as the purpose changes, the children see that rate and technique also change.

Figurative Language Difficult

Figurative language, too, is cause for thought. On conversational level, this creates no problem, for similes and metaphors are raisins in the dough of common speech. Ellen knows that Tom's a square although he's more rotund than angular; and Sally Lou will always be a doll, despite vivacity and pace that keeps her breathing fast. But when *Poor Richard* states that hunger's like a pickle, or Shakespeare claims that all the world's a stage, she looks a bit incredulous and shifts to literal thought. Like others, she's perturbed by the imaginative quality of figurative speech. Yet through the skillful guidance of the teacher, she must come to see the beauty of figurative expressions that give life and color to ideas that otherwise might wear an ordinary look.

Teacher's Role Significant

The teacher, then, must develop judgment, both in herself and others. She must know how to cater to the individual needs of boys and girls and then act upon the knowledge. She must have the children come to see that some statements are emotional and colored by one's viewpoint—like "Rainy days are awful." Perhaps they are to picnic planners or to those who launder with no dryer inside or who walk from beauty shops unprotected from the deluge. But ducks and gardeners and raincoat salesmen find the day delightful. Some statements, however, are based on logic and cannot be changed—the proverb kind—like practice that makes perfect. The children know that statement well and so accept it with a gesture. Yet Gerry is a child who really thinks. He quickly adds that it should be the kind of practice that is right for that particular skill, or practice of the wrong technique will only hinder.

Critical Thinking Fostered

As they read, too, they must come to recognize that some folks are much more qualified to give opinion than others who may even shout in print. Thus elderly folks who have no children sometimes think from tales they read all teenagers are wild. A teacher who deals with them knows how wrong this is. Besides, if anyone is wild, *she is!* She guides them into seeing they should test authority, to see if experience and background warrant belief in what is said. Or if the statement's one of prejudice, then what has caused all this, and what is being overlooked, and how can this be fairly put?

Under skillful guidance, they come to identify such factors as they read, and then they list the errors in thinking. Perhaps the facts are insufficient for generalization; or maybe they're not even related, like voting for a student representative because she's cute. They must evaluate and challenge opinions that they find untrustworthy and veer from jackrabbit thinking, with its emotional hippety-hop from bases insecure. And they must come to realize, too, that sometimes statements are for general acceptance, that there are times we do not challenge.

Thus they must learn to weigh, to evaluate with wisdom, rather than with emotion. And teachers must recognize and act upon these facts if they're to guide the wise way. For in the words of Josiah Royce, "Thinking is like loving and dying. Each of us must do it for himself." Only when this process accompanies interpretation of the printed symbol has one really learned to read and heed.

63. LEVELS OF DISCUSSION IN READING*

Nila Banton Smith

READING content is one of the most productive mediums to use in developing thinking abilities through discussion. Are we making the fullest use of this medium for this purpose? Are we conducting discussions at a level which is too low, in many instances, to stimulate real thinking on the part of boys and girls? Are we, too often, simply asking them to repeat, parrot-like, what is said in the book rather than guiding discussion in ways which will encourage them to probe for deeper meanings and to evaluate critically?

We shall present a few examples to illustrate the possibilities of different

* From Nila Banton Smith, "Levels of Discussion in Reading," *Education*, LXXX, No. 9 (May, 1960), 518–21. Reprinted by permission of the author and The Bobbs-Merrill Co., Inc., Indianapolis, Ind.

levels of discussion, as applied to reading content.

Literal Comprehension

Guidance directed toward literal comprehension is the lowest rung on the ladder of discussion possibilities insofar as stimulation of thinking is concerned.

For example: The children are reading a story about two children and their toys. "With what was Ann playing?" asks the teacher. "Ann was playing with her doll," comes the answer. And this statement is given in so many words in the text. "What was Jack doing?" and the text says quite definitely that "Jack was playing with his rocket."

Questions of this type require only slight mental activity on the part of the teacher and little or no thinking on the part of the pupils. Such questions undoubtedly give children practice in recalling and reproducing statements or facts and have a place in detailed factual reading. It is doubtful, on the other hand, whether this form of questioning helps children to develop the ability to glean the types of meaning from reading that they need to enrich their lives to the fullest extent.

Through continued practice, however, children often become so glib in answering this reproduction type of question that they convey the impression of having achieved a high degree of excellency in "comprehension."

A thirteen-year-old boy named Larry recently was sent to the writer for diagnosis. He had above-average intelligence and was considered a "very good reader," but he was failing in other studies. As a part of the diagnosis, the boy was asked to read the story of Johnny Appleseed. A class of graduate students observed and read the story also. When Larry had finished, he was asked several questions which could be answered by restating what had been said directly in the text:

"How long ago did Johnny Appleseed live?"

"More than a hundred years ago."

"What was his real name?"

"Jonathan Chapman."

"How did he spend his time?"

"He planted apple trees."

These and additional questions of the reproduction type were asked, and Larry answered all of them unerringly in the words of the book.

"Do you think Larry needs help in comprehension?" the graduate class was asked.

"No," came the unanimous response, "his comprehension is perfect!"

Interpretation

Larry had been checked on his literal comprehension, but the discussion had been extremely limited. What happened when he was asked some questions at a higher level of comprehension—in other words, questions which called for interpretation of meanings not stated directly in the text?

"Why did Johnny choose to plant his trees deep in the wilderness where the settlers had not yet come?"

"He wanted to be alone while he was working," Larry replied.

Larry had missed an important implication in drawing this conclusion. Johnny's real reason for planting the trees before the settlers arrived was, of course, so that the trees would grow and bear fruit by the time the settlers moved in. Larry's reason made Johnny an unsocial person who didn't want anyone around him while he was working.

Several other questions of the thinking type were asked. Larry's replies to all of them were equally faulty, and all of them failed to evoke any give-and-take discussion.

Larry is only one out of hundreds of intelligent pupils who learn the superficial knack of giving back what the text says, but who never tap the significance of meanings which can be gleaned only through the use of mental processes of a higher type.

One of the most productive ways of developing ability to derive meanings in reading is through discussion in which the teacher makes a special contribution by throwing in questions here and there, which stimulate cause-and-effect reasoning and which point up the necessity for making comparisons, drawing inferences, arriving at conclusions, and gathering generalizations.

In a third-grade classroom recently, such a discussion took place. The children had read a story about Fred, a boy who visited his Uncle Bill, a sheepherder who lived in a covered wagon in the foothills. During the first few days of his visit, Fred was concerned with his uncle's shepherd dogs, who stayed out with the sheep at night, even in bad weather. One night, Uncle Bill took Fred out to the herd while a storm was raging. He called the dogs. They appeared from the midst of the herd of sheep, but they "did not want to leave their wooly hiding place." Fred said, "All right. I won't worry about them anymore."

The children and the teacher discussed the story as they went along, and also, after they had finished. Everyone entered into the plot with interest and enthusiasm and relived the experiences of the characters. As all of this was taking place, however, the teacher kept uppermost in her mind the importance of stimulating children's thinking in working with meanings derived from their reading. Now and then, at appropriate times, she asked questions to which there were no answers directly in the text—questions which called for inferences, generalizations, comparisons, and reasoning.

"In what part of the country do you think this story took place?"

The children referred to details in the text and pictures and soon concluded that the setting of the story was in the Rocky Mountain region.

"Why do you suppose one of the dogs was called Taffy?"

None of these children ever had seen warm taffy pulled and noted its golden-brown color when it is in this elastic state. The colors they associated with taffy were greens, blues, pinks, and yellows, which they found in the salt-water-taffy boxes that their parents had brought from Atlantic City. The children lacked the experience necessary for this concept; therefore, the teacher told them about taffy in its natural state and compared its color with Tom's sweater and Jan's hair. The children then easily reasoned why one of the dogs was called Taffy.

"Compare the way that Fred felt at the beginning with the way he felt at the end of the story. Why did he change?"

At no point in the story does the author tell how Fred felt, nor is there any statement in regard to why he changed. The children, however, were able to find telltale words and phrases that indicated how worried Fred was all through the early part of the story, and other words and phrases which revealed his satisfaction and peace of mind toward the end of the story. It simply required one major generalization on their part to uncover the cause of this change in the boy.

Thus a wise teacher can guide discussion fruitfully in connection with children's reading dozens of times every day. And, thus, deeper meanings emerge from the printed page, and the real significance of the printed symbols becomes fully apparent.

Critical Reading

Critical reading is another aspect of the reading-for-meanings area of development—an aspect which requires carefully guided discussion. Critical reading makes use of both literal comprehension and interpretation. It involves both getting the facts and interpreting deeper meanings. In addition, it calls for the personal judgment of the reader in deciding upon the validity of the material. In critical reading, the reader evaluates and passes judgment upon the purpose, the fairmindedness, the bias, and the truthfulness of statements made in the text.

Jean was reading a story in a pre-primer about children who made a playhouse by spreading newspapers across the backs of two chairs. Among other things the story said that Furry, the cat, played with them, too, and ran about on top of the playhouse.

Jean stopped in her reading and remarked, "Furry couldn't have run on top of this playhouse, because it was made of newspapers." Jean was doing critical reading.

Tommy, a second-grader, read these statements in some arithmetic material that he was given: "Nancy went to the store to get some milk. Milk was 12 cents a quart. She got two quarts. How much did she pay for it?"

"There's something wrong here," said Tommy. "Milk costs more than 12 cents. I paid 21 cents for a quart at our store yesterday." Tommy also was doing critical reading.

In this age of multitudinous attempts to influence our thinking through the use of printed material, much more emphasis should be placed on critical reading. Youth should be taught to look for slants and biases and tricks of propagandists so that they will be in a position to judge the validity of statements which they read in all printed material.

In the primary grades, we need to rely largely upon guided discussion of books children use in the classroom to develop critical reading. However, more direct work can be done in the upper grades, not only with books used in the classroom but also with materials brought in from the outside.

Ask the children to bring to class newspapers from different publishers; then have them compare several reports of the same event and note the variations. Much worthwhile discussion will ensue. Guide them in passing on the newspaper's reputation for containing "uncolored reports," and on the writer's reputation for presenting facts accurately. Encourage spirited discussion as the children pick out statements which they think are opinions and statements which they think are facts.

Ask the pupils to bring in articles from the various columnists and discuss each one in terms of personal opinion versus facts, biases, radical ideas, and attempts at sensationalism. The same procedure can be used with magazine articles, pamphlets, and books.

In addition to the aforementioned experiences in evaluating, students should become acquainted with methods and tricks used by the propagandists. Each member of the group may bring in a clipping of an advertisement, an excerpt from a speech made during a political campaign, or an article on any topic, in which the writer tries to influence readers in their thinking or actions. Let each child read his selection aloud. Following the reading, encourage free discussion concerning the writer's motive and techniques that he uses to accomplish his purpose.

These are only a few suggestions for developing critical reading through discussion. The teacher who is acutely aware of the significance of critical-reading skills in our current life will find many opportunities each day to help her pupils to grow in this important area of reading achievement.

Summary

We have intended, in this article, to emphasize the urgency of developing children's ability to enter into mental action and reaction with meanings embedded in printed symbols, both those that are immediately apparent and those that lurk between the lines of type. Furthermore, we have tried to point out that on-the-spot discussion, guided by a skillful teacher, is probably one of the best mediums which can be used for this purpose.

The teacher, however, must prepare carefully for any discussion. She must be ready with sagacious questions and remarks; ready to follow and guide discussions into worthwhile channels; ready to "step out" when children are taking over in ways that are truly conducive to growth in their thinking processes; and ready to "step in" when a question will stimulate further mental activity or when a remark will afford subtle guidance in arriving at a sound judgment.

Discussion of reading content under such conditions well may result in the fullest realization of Edward Thorndike's terse but significant definition of some years back: "Reading is thinking."

64. CREATIVE READING*

Constance M. McCullough

I HAVE seldom seen Mabel so excited. Mabel is a first-grade teacher now on our faculty, but she has taught all the grades. When she gets steamed up, she boils all over. Most of us on the staff are busy enough thinking about what we are doing today and what we'll do tomorrow. But not

* From Constance M. McCullough, "Creative Reading," in *Contributions in Reading,* No. 15, pp. 1–4. Reprinted by permission of the author and Ginn and Co., Boston, Mass.

Mabel. She's always worrying on a higher level about bigger things, never just the thing itself but its implications for the next two centuries. Today was no exception.

"You know what people make me mad?" Mabel asked.

"Well, no," I said. "I know what people made you mad last week and the week before, but I'm not sure about today."

"These people *always* make me mad," she replied. "No special week for them."

"All right," I said, "who are the villains?"

"They are the people who go around saying that children can't think about what they read. What a menace! They act as if children aren't a part of the human race, as if they were the offspring of parrots instead of *homo sapiens*."

"Mabel," I cautioned, "do you think these people are worth your high blood pressure?"

"Is the future of this country worth it?" she countered. "If all of us taught the way they do, the bunch of rubber stamps we'd produce would be ready for a dictator to harvest in another twenty years."

"You don't harvest rubber stamps, Mabel," I objected. "Now, tell me, what's all this about?"

In a nutshell, this was her complaint. These "people"—she is always tactfully vague about their identity—believe that young children can't do creative thinking. They believe also that some children of low mentality never do think creatively, that probably only a few of the top pupils in their classes are capable of it. They are always indefinite about when the ability to think for oneself asserts itself, and are likely to believe it happens in the grade *above* the one they happen to be teaching. In fact, they sometimes go back to that early idea that you taught children how to read in the elementary school, and then, about the sophomore year in high school, had them think about what they read.

When these "people" claim that children or people of low mentality can't do creative thinking, they mean that the only kind of question these children can answer about their reading is the kind that can be answered by quoting verbatim from the book. "What color was little Red Riding Hood's hood?" Answer: red. "How long did the Hundred Years War last?" Answer: one hundred years. "What did Jack say to Suzie on this page?" Answer: "No, no, Suzie. Oh, oh, no!" This burned Mabel to a crisp.

That "Non-Thinking" Child May Surprise You

Mabel pointed out that these same young children who supposedly cannot think about what they read are very capable of thinking about everything else in their lives. They ask good questions and make worthwhile observations.

"For instance," said she, "look at my nephew. He's no Einstein, but he came home the first day of kindergarten and said, 'My teacher's okay.' How do you suppose he decided that? With somebody's blueprint? No. He drew on his catalogue of people in his experience. He added up all the nice things she'd done and said that morning, and he sized her up as being a good egg."

"Well, now," I said, "why wouldn't such a child show a teacher that he can think about things he reads as well as about things he observes in other ways?"

"That's easy," Mabel answered. "What if the teacher never gives him a chance to think about his reading? He'd get used to *not* thinking when he reads. Reminds me of my dog during the rabies quarantine. You know, I had to keep her on a seventy-five foot run of wire. Well, one day the wire broke, but when I came home, there she was, running up and down, straining to meet me, as though she were still tied. And she wasn't a dumb dog, either. If you're kept in prison long enough, you don't realize freedom when you have it. That's what happens to children's minds. Think what that means for the next generation of adults—reading newspapers and magazines and books. They'll be swallowing every piece of bait that's offered. A fine mess for a democracy!"

I began to see why Mabel was so upset.

"But if high-school teachers get the students to use their heads when they read, won't that fix up the future adults?" I asked.

Give the Child a Chance to Think —and Early!

"Hmph!" sniffed Mabel. "How well do you think the intellectual processes can be developed after six or eight or ten years without stimulation? Haven't we learned from the research in the teaching of reading that every skill needs to be exercised at every educational level if the child's development in reading is to be well balanced and sound? If you asked me which I'd rather employ as a thinker, someone who had just started to think or someone who had been thinking all his life, which do you think I'd take?"

"I'm not asking, Mabel," I said. "I know."

"And the worst of it is," she continued, "that some children are never given a chance to think about their reading, even in high school."

"Why so?" I knew she expected me to rise to this bait.

"It's as simple as simple," she replied. "When all the youngsters in a class are given the same book, and that book is aimed at the reading ability of the average person in the class and at the mental ability of the average person in the class, what do you suppose happens to the below-average reader or the below-average mind? The same thing that can happen to any of us, even to the best readers in our classes. It can happen to us teachers, if we're given something too difficult in reading level or too remote from our experience or too complex for our mental capacity."

"You mean you could make the same geese out of all of us by picking the right book to baffle us?"

"Exactly," she said. "Given the right conditions, any one of us can look stupid."

"The worst of it is," she continued, "that some children get accustomed to reading without understanding. We are teaching them to accept fragments of understanding—factual crumbs off the table—as a satisfactory diet. We are giving them the idea that the educated man is a parrot of little-understood facts, unrelated and apropos of nothing."

"Mabel, you devastate me," I protested. "What can the elementary teacher do about this?"

Every Child Has Creative Possibilities

"I'm glad you asked me." Mabel liked her audiences to worry with her. "First," she proclaimed, "every elementary teacher should take a mighty oath that she believes in the creativeness of every child in her class. Not just the bright-eyed front-seater with the golden curls, but everybody.

"Secondly, she should accept the responsibility for finding out the level on which each child is comfortable as a thinker."

"Wait a minute," I interrupted. "What do you mean by that?"

"Well, there are two ways of doing this," Mabel responded, "the incidental and the deliberate. I'll give you an example of the incidental way first. As the teacher discusses stories with children, as she reads aloud to them and asks questions, as she listens to them retell and comment on stories they've liked, she will notice that a particular child tells a simple story well, but gets mixed up or forgets parts about harder stories. She begins to sense his level of thinking ability.

"The question, you see, is how far up the child can go in complexity of plot and breadth of experience and difficulty of vocabulary just in stories

he *hears,* how far up he can understand. Certainly we should have him reading only on levels of his understanding if we expect him to answer thought-provoking questions about his reading.

"One direct method of finding this out is to give a standardized test in which the teacher reads successively harder stories to the class and each child responds to questions about them. Or, the teacher can make up her own test, using selections from the different books of her reader series, and asking questions about them."

"You mean, then, that we shouldn't have children reading *above* their thinking level," I ventured.

"Can you think of anything sillier," she retorted, "than to sit down for an evening with a book you can't understand? Why should children think it's sensible if it is so obviously silly to us adults? What is gained by hours of mouthing words without knowing the score? Let's be sensible."

"All right," I said, "but what about your reading groups? The children aren't all alike. In any group, somebody understands better and somebody else understands worse, somebody finishes first and somebody else draws up the rear. How are you going to meet those differences?"

Keep a Sharp Eye on Grouping

"There is no need," Mabel said firmly, "of putting a child above his intellectual level in a reading group. Few children can read so well that the teacher will be fooled into putting them above their level as thinkers. Probably some are placed *below* their mental levels. The crucial point is in the initial grouping and in the teacher's willingness to make changes if she sees a child doesn't fit into his group. If she made an error in judging his ability, she should be willing to admit it. Or if the child's ability to read seems to take a spurt, or if it seems to lag or falter, she should recognize the change and make an adjustment. Children should be placed at the level where they can read with understanding. That won't be above their intellectual level. In fact, a lot of children don't even approach their intellectual level in reading, any more than adults do as well as they could in the things they attempt."

"What you're saying, then," I summarized, "is that the teacher's test of whether a child should be with a group reading a certain book is whether he can answer thought-provoking questions about that material, not just whether he can mouth the vocabulary or parrot the words of the author."

"It takes you a while, but you do get a point," said Mabel.

I thought that one over for a moment.

"Suppose," I said, "you've grouped your children, everything is perfect, and now you are going to teach the group a story. How will you get at this thought-question business? How will you achieve a creative approach to reading?"

I shouldn't have asked that question, for Mabel had me pinned there until the custodian came around with a threatening mop and ran us out of the building. But she did say some things worth mulling over.

Mabel's Creative Approach to Reading

She has children speculate about the pictures that illustrate a story. She doesn't stop with asking, "What is happening in this picture?" That is just the factual level. She probes, "How did these people get into this fix? What do you think will happen next? How do you think John feels from the way he looks and from what's happening to him? How would YOU feel?"

Sometimes the picture is fanciful. "Is this picture about something that really happened? Why don't you think so?" (Hens don't wear hats. Lollipops don't grow on trees.) Sometimes the picture is of an unfamiliar animal. "Does he look like any animal we know?" (He has a head like a squirrel, fur like my cat, and a tail like a Fuller brush. His paws are funny. More like a duck's feet.)

If she uses the picture as a stimulus for adding purpose to the silent reading of the story, she may ask, "Does this picture make you wonder something about the story?" (Yes, I'd like to know how they got into that fix. I'd like to know how they got out of it. I'd like to know what it's like to live in a house like that and dress like that and do that kind of work. Maybe this story would make another good puppet show for us; I'm going to read to see whether it would and what scenes I'd have.)

Sometimes the title of the story sets Mabel and her group off into speculation. "Why do you suppose this story is called, 'The Black Sheep'? Have you ever heard of anyone called a black sheep? Why was he called that? What do you think may happen in this story? Let's read to see how the person in this story got that name."

"I give the children something to look for in the story," said Mabel. "That makes their reading more efficient. For each story I try to think of a different kind of thing for them to look for."

I protested, "But Mabel, don't you consider the purpose of the author, don't you think of the chief value of the story, in deciding on that purpose?"

"Of course," she replied. "I always read the story first myself to see what I think he's driving at, and I check with the teacher's manual to see whether the lesson plan there gives me a clue to the author's purpose, if I'm not sure. And I often use the unit theme such as courage or understanding children of other lands, or whatever the unit is about, to determine my question." . . .

65. CHILDREN CAN READ AND THINK CRITICALLY*

Russell G. Stauffer

CHILDREN can read and think critically about matters relating to their experiences. This is as true of six-year-olds, or pupils usually in a first grade, as it is of ten-year-olds or sixteen-year-olds. A six-year-old may not be motivated, or intellectually able, to comment on the validity of historical doctrines, such as the Marshall Plan, but he may think critically about ideas in a story, as one boy did when he questioned the fact that three ducks in a line were "a *long* parade of ducks."

* From Russell G. Stauffer, "Children Can Read and Think Critically," *Education*, LXXX, No. 9 (May, 1960), 522–25. Reprinted by permission of the author and The Bobbs-Merrill Co., Inc., Indianapolis, Ind.

This six-year-old boy exhibited use of the integrants needed for critical reading-thinking. He not only had had experience with ducks, but also he apparently had examined his experiences, indexed certain facts, noted relationships, and reached certain generalizations. Hence, he took advantage of post learning so as to deal with a new problem—in this instance, information gained through reading. As a result, he obtained maximum return on what he had learned from his experiences and from his reading skill.

Unexamined experiences result in vague notions that represent gross, sweeping, wholesale generalizations. Therefore, the notions usually are largely ineffective in nature or based on emotional overtones, and permit only muddled, bungled thinking. By contrast, examined experiences can result in orderly, effective thinking. The person doing the examining makes his own associations and comparisons and reaches generalizations that usually are workable and acceptable to other authorities.

Undoubtedly, the aforementioned boy had experience with ducks, and, most likely, he had more than one experience. He was the son of a farmer and lived on a farm. Not only did he have experience with ducks, but also he had seen them walking one behind the other in single file. In addition he probably had seen files of different length. Somewhere, at sometime, he must have compared lines of ducks and noted that some are longer than others. This kind of comparing and indexing he may have done completely on his own, or in the presence of, or with the aid of, a more experienced person— an older brother or sister, or an adult.

Another interesting feature about this boy's conclusion is the fact that, at sometime or other, he had gained generic knowledge about the word "long." Apparently he had reached acceptable or relevant conclusions about what is long and what is short, insofar as a line of ducks in single file is concerned. This means that he demonstrated considerable sensitivity to linear dimension as well as to estimating. Certainly, at this stage, he could not discuss these two processes with a mathematician, but certainly he is developing readiness that can be capitalized on to prepare him to do so later.[1]

Undoubtedly, too, the boy had a generic meaning for the word "parade," since he understood its use as applied to the ducks in a line. It may be that this was the first time he had dealt with the word "parade" as used in this context. If this was the case, he had done what good readers do when they read: he had extended his concept of the word "parade" by regrouping previous experiences with parades and adapting them to this new situation. Reading can extend and refine experiences.[3]

What has been said so far is probably almost minor in comparison with the point about to be made. This boy not only had examined the material in the perspective of related objective evidence, but also he had compared the evidence with some norm or standard.[5] In this case, the norm he had obtained for "a long parade of ducks" was a personalized estimate—a judgment that was, nevertheless, pertinent and discriminate. Other people, experienced with ducks, would agree with this boy's estimated norm, and this is the measure of validity.

While it is evident that this boy's personalized judgment was a "considered" judgment and not a "casual" one, it also is evident that his conclusion was neither thoroughly objective nor completely definitive. To establish an accurate norm on the length of unselected duck parades would require research and analysis of data. This boy is not ready to do such research work, but he exhibited the attitudes and presence of mind that, at a later date, may qualify him for research work. Even so, in his own way, he demonstrated the fundamentals of critical reading and thinking which result in reader "yardsticks" that, at some mature stage, may be converted into more definitive reader norms.

Another Example

In another situation, a group of six-year-olds was reading a story about a pony. During the course of the discussion, the group, with the aid of the teacher, generalized by saying that all ponies are little. As a matter of fact, ponies were compared with midgets.

One boy challenged the concept that all ponies are little. When the teacher asked him why he doubted, he replied, "Indian ponies aren't little." The teacher was taken aback by the boy's comment, and the group seemed unconvinced. So the teacher asked, "How do you know this is true?" To which the boy replied, "I know! I see them on television."

Almost at once two other boys joined the first in support of the idea. The three of them persuaded others in the group to accept the idea that Indian ponies are not little and to reject the idea that all ponies are little.

In this situation, the boys used concepts gained through secondhand experience, by means of television. As every good teacher and parent knows, many ideas are gained through pictures, both "stills" and "movies."[7] The ideas gained through secondhand experience are useful—though only if they, too, are examined and evaluated.

Many other instances similar to the "duck parade" and the "pony size" could be reported to support the points being advanced. It is felt, however, that additional examples are unnecessary. Further examination of the aforementioned illustrations, though, reveals another point of considerable value.

In both episodes, it is quite clear that the boys had examined and evaluated their experiences and that their judgments were based, most likely, on many experiences. It is seldom that one experience is sufficient to allow a person to generalize. It is necessary for adults to have many experiences if they are to make sound judgments, and, certainly, it is even more necessary for children to have varied experiences if they are to do formative situational thinking.[2]

Consequently, "field trips" need to be planned carefully and repeated if they are to yield the concrete "stuff" that permits a learner to acquire imagery resources, to test ideas in action, and to evaluate conclusions.

For example, one first-grade teacher took her class to a city post office, where the postmaster took the children on a guided tour. Later, the teacher expected the pupils to talk about the money-order window and how people use money orders, but they wanted to talk about a boy who had fallen off the bus at the post office. Surely, this semicreative teaching showed considerable lack in the ability of the teacher to evaluate the suitability of materials and resources in terms of their contribution to the learnings and aspirations of children.

If it is agreed that field trips should be projected creatively and wisely, then it must be agreed that directions to teachers, as provided by teachers' manuals, should be equally mature and productive. Yet, commonly, these manuals instruct teachers to motivate the reading of a story by telling part of the story; by explaining that the story to be read is a surprise story; by asking the pupils to read to see what Tom said; by saying that the first sentence on the next page will tell what happened and when it happened; by telling children that today's story is about a merry-go-round, showing pictures of a merry-go-round, and telling about how people get off and on and ride horses that go up and down.

This is the kind of pabulum which results in teaching and reading that become "uncreative by responding to requirements, following directions, and waiting to be told what to do." [8]

Reading Is a Thinking Process

Children bring with them to school many concepts and opinions that can be used while reading. What is required is that the teacher direct reading as a thinking process in order that children may put to work their experiences, making comparisons and judgments. This means that children must be taught to reflect on relevant antecedent events from their own experiences, so that they may set their own purposes for reading; may reason while reading; and, subsequently, may accept or reject what they find as proof for their speculations. This way of directing reading teaches children to take full advantage of past learning when reading to accomplish new purposes.

Training of this kind can be accomplished in two ways—in a group-directed reading activity and in an individualized reading situation. In a group situation, the children benefit from shared experiences, estimates, and predictions, since each one reads the same selection or story. This method permits each member of a group to compare his predictions with the predictions of others to see how different members manipulated story information in order to predict; to compare his conclusions with those reached by others; to evaluate the skills he has used; to note whether or not others used the same skills and why; and to scrutinize the way others extended and refined concepts and generalizations gained through reading.

Furthermore, in a group where all members deal with the same material, authority for the acceptance of proof rests with the group as well as with the teacher. Each member serves as an auditor, examining and weighing proofs and conclusions presented—frequently by oral rereading.

This kind of reading-thinking can be done in a group situation only if the materials used are well constructed.[6] If a basic reader contains stories that are well conceived in terms of plot; language structure; illustrations that supplement a story rather than betray it; episodes that are realistic; interest areas that not only capitalize on a variety of experiences common to children but also extend their experiences—then thinking-reading skills can be acquired, sharpened, and refined.

If a well-conceived plot has been read in such a way as to enable the readers to think, then pupils can grasp the deeper, underlying principles of thinking and learning in a generic way. This, in turn, gives pupils the power to use the generic understandings about thinking when reading other kinds of materials.

Individualized training in reading helps the pupil learn how to make decisions about what he likes and dislikes; how to select material on his own; how to be diligent about seeking answers;

how to keep records; how to prepare reports—in short, how to be a self-reliant reader when on his own.

These are skills essential to a well-rounded reader-thinker's education. If they are to be acquired, training in self-selection on an individualized basis must be provided along with a wide range of materials.[4]

In summary, it is quite clear, I believe, that children can read and think critically about matters relating to their experiences. It also is clear that, to prepare pupils to be effective readers, teachers must teach reading as a thinking process. If they do so, then basic readers with structured content may be used appropriately to direct group-type reading-thinking activities. And, when this is done effectively—along with a sound program of self-selection through individualized instruction—skilled, well-rounded, efficient readers will develop.

REFERENCES

1. BRUNER, JEROME S. "Learning and Thinking," *Harvard Educational Review,* XXIX (1959), 184–92.
2. DEWEY, JOHN. *Democracy and Education* (New York: The Macmillan Co., 1916).
3. GRAY, WILLIAM S., and ROGERS, BERNICE. *Maturity in Reading: Its Nature and Appraisal* (Chicago: University of Chicago Press, 1956), p. 273.
4. LAZAR, MAY. "Individualized Reading: A Dynamic Approach," *The Reading Teacher,* XI (December, 1957), 75–83.
5. RUSSELL, DAVID H. "Higher Mental Processes," *Encyclopedia of Educational Research,* ed. Chester W. Harris (3d ed.; New York: The Macmillan Co., 1960), pp. 645–61.
6. STAUFFER, RUSSELL G. "Productive Reading-Thinking at the First-Grade Level," *The Reading Teacher,* XIII (February, 1960), 183–87.
7. WITTY, PAUL A. "Some Results of Eight Yearly Studies of T.V.," *School and Society,* LXXXVI (Summer, 1958), 287–89.
8. ZIRBES, LAURA. *Spurs to Creative Teaching* (New York: G. P. Putnam's Sons, 1959), p. xxii.

66. CRITICAL EVALUATION*

Martha Dallmann

THE problems in teaching reading that confront the intermediate-grade teacher can be divided into two categories. One deals with difficulties due to the fact that some pupils, after they have reached the fourth grade, do not possess the skills ordinarily acquired in the primary grades. To help such boys and girls the teacher must follow many of the suggestions usually given to primary-grade teachers.

In addition to this problem, the intermediate-grade teacher has a second type of responsibility. Her task is not only remedial but also developmental in nature. She must help the child make steady progress, commensurate with his capacity, toward becoming an effective reader. One of the most crucial of these phases of teaching reading in the intermediate grades—critical evaluation—is discussed in this article.

What Is Critical Evaluation?

Maybe what is meant by critical evaluation can best be explained if the reader first has clearly in mind what is *not* meant by that term. When we say that we want boys and girls to learn to evaluate critically what they read, we do not want them to become unduly

* From Martha Dallmann, "Critical Evaluation," *Grade Teacher,* LXXV, No. 1 (September, 1957), 46–47. Reprinted by permission of the author and Teachers Publishing Corporation, Darien, Conn.

skeptical of everything they read. If, as a result of training in critical evaluation, the child becomes suspicious of everything in print and out of it, the time spent in helping him read critically has been worse than wasted. An individual who has become a "doubting Thomas" is not the one who is likely to have the maximum opportunity to lead a full and rich life, satisfying to himself and helpful to others.

As the term *critical evaluation* is used in this article, it refers first of all to skill in knowing when to take time to question the authenticity of a selection. Second, it involves knowledge as to how to determine the way in which data can be checked, if necessary. Third, it requires that the reader should be able to read with enjoyment and profit without being handicapped by an overly critical attitude.

How to Make Evaluations

Guidance in critical evaluation should not be postponed till the intermediate grades. The theory that a young child cannot think has been refuted by psychology as well as common observation. Equally outmoded is the claim that before a child learns to read with comprehension, including critical evaluation, he should be excellent in recognizing words in print. It is now believed, upon good evidence, that it is far more effective to have the child develop almost simultaneously skill in word recognition and comprehension. Consequently, the intermediate-grade teacher does not need to assume that her pupils have had no experience in evaluating what they read. The effective primary-grade teacher will have encouraged growth in such appraisal by asking the child questions like, "What do you think will happen next in the story?" or "What makes you think that the author is right?"

Guidance in critical evaluation should not be limited to reading situations. Every day there are many excellent opportunities to help the child grow in power to evaluate. Making use of such opportunities will result, not only in increased ability to read intelligently, but also in more discrimination in situations other than reading.

Here are some of the ways in which the teacher can help the child evaluate:

1. After a pupil has given a talk, the rest of the class can indicate what points mentioned by him brought out the theme the speaker wished to establish. If irrelevant facts were mentioned, the classmates could designate which ones they were.

2. If boys and girls hear two conflicting points of view, they can be given an opportunity to tell which, if either, is the correct one. Thereupon, they can be asked to give evidence to support their answer or to collect data that will help establish which point of view is correct.

Guidance in critical evaluation of what is read can be accomplished both through practice-type situations and

through more informal procedures. A few practice exercises that can be used are illustrated on the page opposite this. Two ways in which the teacher can make use of nonpractice-type situations to help boys and girls learn to evaluate critically are:

1. Ask the boys and girls to read a story, that they are also reading for other purposes, to find out what arguments given in it best support the point that the author wishes to prove.

2. Have the pupils compare two stories as to suitability for a given purpose, like dramatization, reading to another group, or inclusion in a bibliography.

If practice exercises are used in order to develop power in critical evaluation, adaptation to individual differences should be made. Not all boys and girls need such exercises. Some can acquire this skill through other types of opportunities that arise. Other boys and girls, however, can profit greatly if these other chances to become better able to evaluate critically are supplemented by practice exercises. The exercises to be done by any pupil should serve a helpful purpose.

Boys and girls need to recognize the purpose of doing a practice exercise. It is not enough for the teacher to know specifically why she is asking an individual to do an exercise. If the pupil himself is not able to recognize the activity as worthwhile, she should make clear to him its value. It is only then that the pupil is likely to do his best, both at the time when he takes the exercise and later on when he is in a position to make application of his learning. . . .

HOW TO RECOGNIZE "LOADED" WORDS

Some words are referred to as "loaded" words because they are "loaded" with emotion, and are used to arouse the emotions of the reader. Pupils may be asked to indicate which of the following words is a "loaded" word or group of words. Write *yes* to the left of each "loaded" expression and *no* on the other lines.

....a. dwelling   ....e. my native
....b. loved   land
     ones   ....f. home
....c. native   ....g. house
     land   ....h. liberty
....d. nation

HOW TO DISTINGUISH BETWEEN FACT AND OPINION

1. In order to acquire skill in differentiating between fact and opinion, the boys and girls can indicate which of a series of statements like the following are, in part at least, a matter of opinion. They can give their answer by writing *yes* to the left of each sentence that is a statement only of fact and writing *no* if the sentence is, at least in part, an expression of opinion.

....a. Fifty years ago today the Delaware Ice Company announced the purchase of the Krause property on 21 North Sandusky Street.

....b. The most enjoyable vacation anyone can have is to spend a week in a summer home on the banks of the St. Lawrence River.

....c. The public library in Moscow is one of the largest in the world.

....d. Thomas Jefferson wrote the Declaration of Independence.

....e. The German people are the most industrious people in the world.

2. To provide the pupils with still more practice in distinguishing between fact and opinion they can be asked to rewrite each statement in an exercise like the one above that expresses, at least in part, an opinion. Rewrite it so that it is a statement of fact only. For example, the statements in the preceding paragraph marked *b* and *e* can be rewritten in this manner.

b. The most enjoyable vacation I have ever had was a week that I spent in a summer home of friends on the bank of the St. Lawrence River.

e. Many Germans are very industrious people.

HOW TO ARRIVE AT CONCLUSIONS

Besides checking the validity of conclusions at which an author arrives, the boys and girls can get help in deciding upon data sufficient to warrant a given conclusion. For example, the pupils could be asked to write paragraphs to show that generalizations like the following could be accepted as reliable. It is important that the conclusions stated are some on which pupils have, or can fairly easily acquire, information adequate for establishing the generalization.

a. Schools of China and Japan are somewhat alike.

b. Air exerts great pressure.

c. Oxygen is necessary for burning to take place.

d. In the book, *Rabbit Hill,* the

animals act, in many respects, like human beings.

HOW TO COMPARE INFORMATION FROM DIFFERENT SOURCES

To help pupils realize that reports on the same topic may be unlike, each pupil may be asked to read two references on any one of the list of topics. In evaluating the information they received from the references, questions like the following may be discussed:

Possible Topics

a. Early life of Jane Addams
b. Causes of the Revolutionary War
c. The conquest of Poland
d. Why Andrew Johnson was impeached

Questions for Discussion

a. What information was given in one of the references that was not given in the other(s)?

b. If there were any disagreements in the reports, what were they?

c. How do you account for any disagreements that you may have found?

d. Which reference, do you think, gave the right statements (in case you found disagreements)?

e. How could you set about to try to find out which is correct (if there were disagreements)?

HOW TO READ NEWSPAPERS CRITICALLY

1. Boys and girls can be asked to write *yes* to the left of each of a group of sample headlines of newspapers if the headline is sensational. To the left of each of the other headlines, they can be asked to write *no*.

....a. Six-year-old Has Harrowing Experience

....b. Fire Destroys Block in Business Section

....c. University Safe Loses Five Hundred Dollars

....d. Route 23 Is Turned into Graveyard

2. After the pupils have studied the difference between news items and editorials, they could evaluate some news items and editorials, or excerpts from them, by answering questions or following directions like these:

a. Is it a news item or an editorial?

b. Give reasons for your answer to *a* above.

c. If the material is in the form of a news item, write an editorial on the topic. If it is an editorial, write the news items that could have been written on that topic.

d. Compare your rewritten article with the original, by giving reasons for considering one a news item and the other an editorial.

HOW TO USE THE COPYRIGHT DATE FOR CRITICAL EVALUATION

To give the pupils practice that will make them realize the value of copyright dates of books, the teacher may make available a list of books, some with old and some with recent copyright dates. The pupils may be asked to examine each of the books on the list in order to be able to answer questions like the following. It will, of course, be necessary to have in the group of available books all those to which reference is made in the questions that are asked.

a. Is your history book written recently enough so that it can report on events during the last five years?

b. For what purpose could you use the copy of the McGuffey *Readers?*

c. What is the copyright date of Virgil Hillyer's *A Child's Geography of the World?* Find two items of information in the book that are now out-of-date. Find two items of information that still hold true even though the book was written long ago.

C H A P T E R   X I

READING IN CONTENT AREAS

67. THE DEVELOPMENT OF LOCATIONAL SKILLS*

Martha Dallmann

IN this article, suggestions for teaching three types of locational skills are given: (1) developing efficiency in locating information in a nonreference book (2) acquiring skill in using encyclopedias and (3) learning to find materials in a library.

Basic Considerations

The teacher should take inventory of what skills her pupils already possess. Even in the beginning of the fourth grade, the teacher will find that many of the pupils have some ability to locate information in print. It is upon this foundation of *what the children already know* that the teacher needs to build, rather than upon some

* From Martha Dallmann, "The Development of Locational Skills," *Grade Teacher,* LXXV, No. 5 (January, 1958), 56–57. Reprinted by permission of the author and Teachers Publishing Corporation, Darien, Conn.

theoretical conceptions of what skills boys and girls should have when they enter her grade.

Develop skills in terms of the resources available. When you are teaching boys and girls to use the index of a book, use the indexes of books that the children already have. Similarly, when teaching encyclopedia usage, use those encyclopedias that are provided in the school or that the boys and girls have in their homes. And again, when teaching how to find materials in the library, let the children learn in terms of the library facilities which are available, either in the room, or the school or the public library.

The boys and girls should be given a thorough foundation in the techniques and skills needed in locating information. These skills include finding words arranged in alphabetical order, using entry words, locating a page rapidly, and knowing for what type of information to look in a given kind of book. Unless, for example, a pupil is efficient in finding words in alphabetical order, he will have trouble when using the dictionary, an index, an encyclopedia, and the card catalogue of a library.

Locating Information in a Nonreference Book

Essential knowledge and skills. Some time before the pupil leaves the elementary school he should have learned the purpose and location of the parts of a book that serve as aids to finding information in the book: the introduction or preface, the table of contents, the appendix and the index. He should know how to use these divisions of a book to locate information in the book. Furthermore, he should be able to use chapter headings, center heads, and side heads as aids in locating information. He should also know that not all books have these various means for facilitating the location of information, and he should realize in what types of books each is likely to be found—for example, he should not look for an index in a book of fiction.

Since the introduction to a book often gives some clue as to what to expect in it, boys and girls should learn what type of aid they may be able to find in the introduction and how to make use of the information there. They also need to realize that the sole purpose of most introductions is not, however, to help the reader learn to locate information within the book.

The pupils should realize that the table of contents can be very valuable in finding information. They need to know that it contains chapter headings, at times divided into subheadings; that the chapters are listed in the contents in order of appearance in the book; and that the page on which each chapter begins is given. They should acquire efficiency in using the contents to decide, in the case of some books, where to look for information on a given topic.

Important points for children to learn about the index are:

1. If there is an index, it is almost invariably located in the back part of the book.

2. The topics are given in alphabetical order.

3. The main entries in an index are usually subdivided.

4. References indicate on what pages information on main entries and subdivisions can be found.

The following skills in using the index are some of the most significant ones: (1) ability to decide under what key words to look for information on a specified topic or question (2) speed in finding an entry in an index (3) skill in interpreting the various types of information given in an index and (4) ability to make effective use of a reference in an index after it has been located.

The boys and girls should also learn what type of information is likely to be given in appendices to books and how to make use of this information. At times this involves learning how to interpret tables. They should also learn how to use chapter headings, center headings, and side headings in such a way that they do not spend time looking for information in parts of the book where it is not likely to be given.

Methods. In teaching this topic of how to find information in a book, the teacher should utilize meaningful classroom situations as much as seems profitable. Most of the work should not be in the form of exercises; a large part of the needed practice should be obtained as the boys and girls need to find information on some problem or question of significance that confronts them. Frequently, however, some of the pupils will need supplementary practice exercises.

The following are a few of the ways to develop skill in finding information in a nonreference book:

1. Ask the boys and girls to find as quickly as they can, but without haste or tension, the title of a story in one of their basal reading books.

2. Provide incentive for making a table of contents or an index for a notebook that is being made either as a class, a committee, or an individual project.

3. Have some of the children report on the type of information given in the introductions to various books they are using. Ask them to note in particular that which serves as an aid to finding information within the books.

4. Have the boys and girls decide which one of several specified words would probably be the entry word to use when trying to locate information on a specified question.

Using Encyclopedias

Essential knowledge and skills. The boys and girls should learn what types of information can be found in an encyclopedia, how the information is arranged, what aids to the speedy finding of material are given in each set of encyclopedias, and what method each has for giving references to material in addition to that included in the encyclopedia. The pupil should also be helped to develop skill in finding and utilizing material found in the encyclopedia.

Methods. The following are some procedures to help boys and girls use encyclopedias effectively:

1. When introducing the use of the encyclopedia, ask each child to browse through some volume until he can report one fact that he finds particularly interesting or significant.

2. After you have written on the chalkboard a diagram showing the volume guides of an encyclopedia, have the pupils tell the number of the volume in which they would look for information on a topic that you mention, such as George Washington Carver, the Battle of New Orleans, or state flowers.

3. Show the pupils the filmstrip, "How to Use an Encyclopedia," published by the Popular Science Publishing Company (distributed by McGraw-Hill Book Co., 330 W. 42nd St., New York 36, N.Y.).

4. Help the boys and girls make arrangements for a "quiz program" in which questions will be asked that are answered in one or more related articles in the encyclopedia. Let a committee of boys and girls, under your guidance, prepare the list of questions. They should inform the rest of the class of the articles on which they will base the questions, but they should not

tell their classmates beforehand what the questions will be.

Finding Materials in the Library

Pupils should learn the meaning and use of the following: the card catalogue, its arrangement and value; the three most common types of library cards—the title card, the author card, and the subject card; the arrangement of the books on the shelves; the placement of magazines in the library.

The teacher can do the following to help the boys and girls learn more about the library and how to use it.

1. Help the boys and girls make a card catalogue of books in their room library. Have them include title cards, author cards, subject cards, guide cards, and *See also* cards.

2. Suggest that a committee make a large diagram showing the placement of books in their room or school library.

3. Take the boys and girls to the public library so that the librarian can explain to them the arrangement of books and magazines in their local library.

4. Have the pupils put on a skit showing how to behave when in a library.

Skill in Locating Materials in a Nonreference Book

1. To provide practice in using the table of contents, the boys and girls could be asked to answer questions based on the table of contents in one of their textbooks.

Directions. Study the table of contents in your science book. Then write the answers on the lines.

_____ a. Into how many main parts is the book divided?

_____ b. On what page does the chapter begin that tells about the sun and other heavenly bodies?

_____ c. In which chapter would you find the answer to the question, "How fast does sound travel?"

2. In order to acquire skill in using the index to a book the pupils could do an exercise like the following.

Directions. Draw a line under the word in parentheses that you would use as entry word in an index under which the answer to each of these questions would be found. When you have finished, use your index in your social studies book to find out whether your answers are correct.

a. What were the provisions of the Missouri Compromise? (provisions, Missouri, Compromise)

b. Why was the transcontinental railroad one of the greatest events in the history of communications in America? (transcontinental, railroad, America)

c. What were the fears of the seamen who were with Christopher Columbus on his first voyage to America? (seamen, Christopher, Columbus)

3. After the boys and girls have learned how to use other than main entries in indexes, they could be given an exercise like the following.

Directions. Find the answers to the following questions by consulting the index in your social studies textbook.

a. Under what main entry and

under what subentry in the index do you expect to find information about cranberries in New England?

Main entry _____

Subentry _____

b. On what page is a map given showing the territory included in the Northwest Territory? _____

c. On how many consecutives pages is information given about the Gold Rush of 1849? _____

Skill in Using Encyclopedias

1. In order to develop skill in deciding for what type of information they should turn to an encyclopedia, they could be asked to do an exercise like the following. After they had answered the questions, they could tell orally in what type of book they would look for the answers to questions that are not likely to be answered in an encyclopedia.

Directions. If you think a question will be answered in your encyclopedias, write *yes* on the line. Otherwise write *no.*

_____ a. How many bushels of potatoes were produced last year in the United States?

_____ b. What was the chief contribution of George W. Goethals to the building of the Panama Canal?

_____ c. What was the first message that was sent by telegram, by Samuel Morse?

_____ d. What does the word *compromise* mean?

2. If some of the boys and girls have difficulty in finding the exact sentences in an encyclopedia that give answers to their questions, give them questions like the following. If only one set of encyclopedias is available, only one pupil at a time can answer any one group of questions. In order to encourage the pupils to work as rapidly as possible, yet without haste or tension, tell them to keep a record of when they began the work on the exercise and when they completed it.

Directions. In an article on Niagara Falls in *Compton's Pictured Encyclopedia* (1955 copyright) answers are given to the following questions. When you have found the sentence that answers a question, write the first two words of that sentence. Time yourself as you do this exercise.

_____ a. How many cubic feet of water pours over the falls every minute?

_____ b. Who was the first white man to view the Niagara Falls?

_____ c. How are the falls and rapids illuminated at night?

Skill in Finding Materials in a Library

1. If the boys and girls have visited a local library and had the arrangement of books and magazines in the children's division explained to them, draw a diagram showing the location of the various bookshelves and exhibit tables and exhibit stands. Number in the diagram the places for books and magazines. Then ask the pupils to answer questions like the following, as they indicate the answer by means of the appropriate number listed on the diagram. Tell the pupils that for some

of the answers more than one letter is needed.

_____ a. Where are the books for the youngest readers kept?

_____ b. Where are the books on biography shelved?

_____ c. On what shelf (or shelves) would you look for the book *Abraham Lincoln* by Ingri and Edgar Parin d'Aulaire?

2. After considerable work on the card catalogue has been done, help the pupils, by means of an exercise like the following, to review some of the important facts learned. In many cases it will be advisable to take time for discussion of the answers after the pupils have completed the written work.

Directions. Write the answers to these questions.

a. In what order are cards in a card catalogue arranged?

_____

b. What kind of card in the card catalogue should be consulted if neither the author nor the exact title of a book is known?

_____

c. If there are books by an author and about an author in a library, which kind of card is filed first in the card catalogue, the books by him or those about him?

_____

d. What is the purpose of a call number?

_____

3. Ask the pupils to write the answers to the following questions concerning periodicals in the public library to which they have access.

a. What are the exact titles of two or three magazines for boys and girls that are ordered by your library which are interesting to you? What is one thing you like in particular about each?

b. What is the name of the reference book that gives information about magazine articles? Where is this reference book kept in your public library?

68. STIMULATE READING WITH INDIVIDUAL RESEARCH PROJECTS*

Edith F. Miller

IN my group there were always some children who finished before the others, who I felt would profit by directed reading activities, which at the same time would allow some opportunity for creativeness. A research project aimed at making booklets proved both popular and profitable to the three groups in my class.

Pick a Topic

First of all, each child was asked to choose a topic about which he really wanted to find out more. In our experiment, any topic was accepted, but some teachers may prefer to make a list from which the children may choose.

After the children handed me their choices, I had an individual conference with each child. If a child had chosen a topic which was too broad, such as *Animals,* we narrowed it down to *Woodland Animals* or *Water Animals.* If the topic was too narrow, such as *The Frog,* we changed it to a broader topic such as *Amphibians.* The list of topics was posted so that children could help each other find informa-

* From Edith F. Miller, "Stimulate Reading with Individual Research Projects," *Grade Teacher,* LXXIX, No. 4 (December, 1961), 28, 29, 84, 85. Reprinted by permission of the author and Teachers Publishing Corporation, Darien, Conn.

tion and pictures.

When the upper group held its first meeting, I presented each child with a typed slip which had key words and phrases which had to appear somewhere in his finished work. For example, the girl studying *Insects* had to include:

1. Definition of an Insect
2. Some Harmful Insects
3. Some Helpful Insects
4. Insect Communities
5. How Nature Protects Insects
6. Metamorphosis

The boy studying *Aviation* had on his list:

1. Lighter-than-air
2. Heavier-than-air
3. How the Airplane Helps Us (Besides transporting people and things)
4. Famous Flights

I tried not to make the list too long for I did not want to discourage anyone. Another year I shall have each child make his own list and add to it if necessary.

The middle group's first meeting was used to make an outline of the subtopics needed in the study of their common topic—*Dogs.* They decided on:

1. The History of Dogs
2. The Care of Dogs
3. The Training of Dogs

4. Working Dogs

5. Dogs as Pets

At their meeting, the children in the slow group helped each other compile about five questions which would be answered in their booklets. The child who had *Pets* as a topic had the following questions on her list:

1. What are the most popular pets in America?

2. Which pets can you train to do tricks?

3. How do you keep your pets well?

4. What are some unusual pets?

5. What pets did early people have?

Sources of Materials

To the first meeting of each group, I brought a number of things which interested the children. They especially liked a large box which had been decorated with pictures of gaily wrapped presents. In this "Present Box" I had put many small pictures, conservation stamps, canceled stamps, some typed poems—in fact any surplus material I had which would later help in illustrating their booklets. As time went on, pupils added "presents," too.

Each child was given a large tension envelope in which all his collected material could be kept safely, and a place was reserved for storing these.

We discussed sources of information. The children realized this was to be primarily a reading project but that other sources would also be used, including firsthand observation, TV, movies, slides, trips, our museum collection, the radio, and talking with people. In our own classroom we had a good set of encyclopedias, many books, and a picture file. We discussed the use that could be made of poems, stories, newspapers, magazines, our own textbooks, pamphlets, and the Public Library.

Organizing Notes

Some children looked up many references and inserted bookmarks with their names on them before doing any reading. Others digested one source at a time. As they read, they took notes. Here, too, they needed help, and we found that stapled sheets of paper with a question or topic at the head of each page seemed the best way to keep the material organized. For example:

What animals are in the woods of New Jersey?

1. Deer

2. Fox

3. Rabbit

How do insects protect themselves?

1. Some look very fierce.

2. Some have a bad smell.

3. Some are born by the thousands.

The notes were reorganized into the children's own stories. When a child had all the information he needed, he would write up the topic. I would then check it and after all revisions and corrections were made, it was ready to go into his booklet.

Children worked on their topics during the reading period whenever their assignments in reading were completed. Occasionally, we spent our entire reading or language period working on the topics so that I could supervise and give help. In addition to the work done in school, many children were so interested in their topics that they voluntarily worked on them at home.

Deadline

Eventually, I set a deadline for the research material to be in, all key words included and all questions answered. Each child worked to complete his work by "Due Date" and I kept a close check on the progress.

As this project was primarily one on reading, all pasting and drawing was postponed till the bulk of the reading was done. This prevented the children from using the reading time to draw pictures.

We used an art period to begin this phase of the project. First we talked about careful selection and arrangement of the pictures to be mounted. We discussed the use of judgment in placing the right pictures with pertinent stories.

For the next two weeks, "Work on your topics" meant drawing, sorting, arranging, cutting, pasting, or copying rather than reading, but books were constantly referred to even in this stage of the project.

Mounting some pictures on colored paper, making decorative borders or end sheets, making pictures in silhouette or all in one color, or using water color illustrations were among the many original ideas which made the finished booklets so attractive.

When all the pages were arranged in order, holes were punched and the booklets were bound with wool or with soft cord that would not tear the holes.

Reading Party

After the booklets were thoroughly checked, they were used as directed reading material for about a week. The children knew that we were to have a "Reading Party" to which guests were to be invited. Each child was to be prepared to read or show anything in his booklet. The children wanted to read the booklets the other children had made, too, so they were placed on a table for easy access and a list of things to look for was put on the board. The list included:

1. A good introduction
2. An index
3. Original poems
4. Some surprising information
5. A good poem
6. A well-copied song
7. An attractive border
8. A well-arranged page
9. Something funny
10. A clearly written article

Each child kept a list of outstanding things he thought should be shown at our Reading Party. For example:

1. Elizabeth's cover
2. Elizabeth's information on How A Jet Flies
3. Cindy's introduction
4. Bill's last page
5. John's cartoons

On the day of the Reading Party, the children showed their covers, most of them gay with cut paper letters. Two children read their Introductions and one read his index. I asked for specific things by saying, "You must see the graph John made"; "Now everyone who made a map will show it"; "Grace made up an original poem." After that, each child showed his favorite pages. Then each child brought out his list and made his request for the display of something unusual in the other children's work.

The Values

After the Reading Party guests left, each child was given a questionnaire. No names were to be put on the papers and it was understood that the class secretary would tally the results and that they were to be perfectly frank in their answers. The results, given below, showed how worthwhile the children felt the project had been.

A QUESTIONNAIRE ON OUR
READING RESEARCH PROJECT

	Yes	No
1. Did you enjoy the research project?	23	4
2. Did it help you to read more widely?	23	4
3. Would you recommend it for next year's fifth grade?	26	1
4. Are you still interested in your topic?	23	4
5. Did it help you to organize the facts you found?	27	0
6. Did you use many kinds of sources of information?	23	4
7. Will the next research project be easier for you?	24	3
8. Did you add many new words to your vocabulary?	18	9
9. Do you remember much of the information you learned?	25	2
10. Did you enjoy our Reading Party?	27	0

There were many values throughout the project such as sharing, judging, planning, and participating, which are hard to measure but which were natural outgrowths of this experience in research.

One development I had not anticipated as an outgrowth of our study was an interest in new hobbies. For example, I attribute the wave of insect collections largely to the two splendid booklets on that subject which were made as part of our project. And, when one girl phoned me during the summer to ask me to recommend a good book to help her identify insects and another phoned to say, "I'm working more on my topic this vacation just for fun," I knew that the effects of our reading-research project had gone deeper than I had ever dreamed possible.

69. THE DEMON OF ARITHMETIC—READING WORD PROBLEMS*

Martha Gesling Weber

RECENTLY a group of teachers was asked to list some of the troublesome areas in the teaching of arithmetic. "Getting children to read story problems with sufficient understanding to be able to solve them seems to be the *demon* of arithmetic," answered one of the teachers immediately.

"It isn't that we don't teach arithmetic," said another teacher. "We just don't teach reading. My children do all right as long as we work with numbers."

"It must be something more than reading, though," replied a third teacher thoughtfully. "I have children who read very well; yet they have trouble with their word problems in arithmetic."

Perhaps no field of study in arithmetic is more complex than that which deals with the factors involved in solving word problems; so it is not surprising that "getting children to read story problems with sufficient understanding to solve them" was classified by the first teacher as being the demon of arithmetic. What is the relationship that exists between the reading of

* From Martha Gesling Weber, "The Demon of Arithmetic—Reading Word Problems," *Monograph for Elementary Teachers,* No. 71, pp. 1–3. Reprinted by permission of Martha Gesling Weber and Harper & Row, Publishers, Inc., New York, N.Y.

word problems and the solving of them?

What Is a Word Problem?

In arithmetic the pupil is asked to work two kinds of problems: word problems and number problems. Interestingly enough, neither word problems nor number problems may present a matter of doubt or difficulty from a psychological point of view; that is, there may be no doubt in the child's mind as to what is to be done. Problems in arithmetic are "problems" because the pupil must translate the meanings of the symbols into the terms of one of the four fundamental processes: addition, subtraction, multiplication, or division.

Word problems are called word problems because words are used in the writing of them. Number problems are called number problems because they are written with mathematical symbols (number figures and number signs) and according to a prescribed form; for example,

$\frac{115}{-78}$ is a number problem.

Word problems are seldom made up just of words, for number figures are found in almost all word problems. However, since all number figures have number names, it is possible to write a word problem using nothing but words. When the number name is used instead of the number figure, the problem is said to contain a "hidden number."

To understand more fully what a word problem is, let us see several ways in which it is like a number problem and an important way in which it differs.

Number Problem	Word Problem
72 −31	Tom had 72 chickens. He sold 31 of them. How many chickens did Tom have left?

In both problems the number concepts to be recognized and understood are the same (72 and 31). In both problems the mathematical operation to be performed is the same (subtraction). The difference between the two kinds of problems does not necessarily lie in the number concepts used or in the mathematical operation to be performed. The basic difference lies in the way in which the operation to be performed is indicated.

In the number problem the operation is indicated directly by the number sign minus (−) and by the form in which the number figures are written. In the word problem the operation to be performed is not indicated directly, but must be supplied by the pupil through his understanding of the ideas expressed by the words and number figures. The pupil can be conditioned to respond with the correct computation to the sign minus (−) without understanding the idea which the sign represents, but he cannot solve the verbal problem unless he understands one of the ideas involved in the concept of subtraction. Not even the recognition and understanding of each word and mathematical symbol in a word problem will guarantee that the pupil will understand the idea involved in the fundamental operation to be performed. He must understand the idea or ideas underlying the fundamental operations, and he must be able to recognize those ideas operating in specific quantitative situations when those situations are described in terms of the words and number figures. Lack of understanding of the ideas underlying the fundamental processes is one of the principal reasons why students have trouble with word problems.

For this discussion it can be seen that number problems and word problems are alike in that they both contain (1) number concepts and (2) a mathematical operation to be performed. They differ in the way in which the operation to be performed is indicated. This difference forms the basis for our definition of a word problem. A word problem is an arithmetical situation described symbolically in which the operation to be performed is not indicated directly, but must be supplied by the student from his understanding of the ideas expressed by the words and number figures.

What Is Reading?

Reading is the process by which meaning is put into written symbols. Written symbols may be of different kinds. The following are all symbols which must be read, and they must be reacted to meaningfully if they are to be understood.

Symbol	Kind of Symbol
table	word
95	number figure
XXV	Roman numeral
—	number sign

In teaching the reading of any kind of symbol, the teacher has three major responsibilities:

1. *The development of skill in recognizing the symbols.* Some skills we use in recognizing words are general configuration clues, context clues, phonetic analysis, and structural analysis. What skills do you use in developing recognition of number figures?

2. *The development of a rich background of experiences that will make the symbols meaningful to the child.* Since meanings are not inherent in symbols, the child must first attach meaning to the symbol if he is later to put meaning into it. He will be able to do this only if he has had many experiences with that which the symbol represents.

3. *The development of a positive attitude toward reading.* This is the teacher's most important responsibility. The learning situation in which the understandings and skills are developed must be purposeful to the child and so structured that he will see that symbols, either oral or written, are used to express ideas.

In our schools emphasis is placed on teaching the reading of two kinds of symbols: word and mathematical symbols (number figures and number signs). Because the activity in the classroom centering around the development of the meaning and recognition of words is called the reading period, many teachers do not realize that they are teaching reading when they work with the activities which lead to the recognition and understanding of mathematical symbols.

This column must be read	even as	*This column must be read*
	1	A number figure representing a number concept. The word symbol representing the concept is *one*. All number figures have number names. Although number figures and number names are written differently, they are pronounced the same and mean the same.
	3	Another number figure representing a different number concept. All number figures are a part of a number system and represent concepts that have definite relationships to one another in that system. The child grows in his understanding of arithmetic through his growth in understanding the number system.
		A mathematical symbol representing one kind of mathematical operation. Word symbols representing the same process are

+

and, add, and *plus.* The four fundamental processes may all be represented by simple signs: +, −, ×, and) ‾‾‾‾ or ÷.

$1 + 2 = 3$

A sentence (a statement of an idea) expressed in mathematical symbols. In word form, this sentence would read as follows: One and two are three, or one plus two equals three.

$$\begin{array}{r} 64 \\ -31 \\ \hline \end{array}$$

One of the forms (called algorisms) used in writing down mathematical symbols for computation. In this form, these particular symbols represent an incomplete thought which may be expressed verbally as follows: Sixty-four minus thirty-one is . . . .

Did you really read all of the second column? If you did, you will have begun to recognize that the simplicity of representing the number system hides the complexity of the relationships involved and makes the recognition of these symbols far easier than the understanding of them. At the root of much of the trouble which children have in reading word problems is a lack of understanding of the ideas and relationships that make up the number system.

The Relationship Between Reading and Word Problems

If the definitions given for word problems and reading are accepted, it follows that whenever a word problem is presented in written form, a reading situation confronts the child. Usually it is not until the introduction of word problems that teachers begin to consider the reading in arithmetic. Then the emphasis is placed on the recognition of the general and specialized vocabularies often to the exclusion of the mathematical figures appearing in the problem and the mathematical operation to be performed. Why is the language of words stressed in the reading of word problems?

1. Many teachers still think of reading only in terms of words, not in terms of mathematical symbols.
2. There are more words than number figures to be read.
3. Mathematical symbols present far less difficulty insofar as recognition is concerned.

Consider the following problem found in a third-grade text:

One day 29 children went for a hike. There were 3 teachers with them. How many people went for the hike?

There are sixteen different words in this problem and only two number figures. Many children in the third grade may still be having difficulty in recognizing such words as *with, were,* and *went;* and though they may meet for the first time such words as *people* and *hike* without recognizing them, they will be able to recognize the figures 29 and 3. Since there are more words than figures to be recognized and since children seem to recognize mathematical figures more easily, the emphasis in reading word problems is placed on word recognition.

The concern of many teachers with word recognition skills is a legitimate one. The first phase of any reading activity is apprehending or recognizing the symbols. It stands to reason that if the child cannot recognize the words, he is not going to be able to read a word problem. Further questioning of the teacher who said, "We just don't teach reading," brought out the fact that her pupils were having trouble with the mechanics of word recognition. The comments of the other teachers in this particular group and in other groups indicate that a careful control of the general vocabulary used in writing word problems is essential if the pupil is to center his attention on "thought-getting."

The wide differences in reading ability that are found at any grade level make it difficult to control vocabulary so that the teacher will be safe in assuming that the words will be recognized by every pupil. The teacher will find that difficulties in word recognition will be lessened if the general vocabulary used in word problems is simpler than that being developed in the reading instruction period. Word problems might well be written using a vocabulary *at least one grade level below* the grade placement of the arithmetic symbols and ideas being developed; problems for the fourth grade might be written using only the vocabulary developed through the third grade, problems for the third grade using only vocabulary developed through second grade, and so on.

Since it is generally accepted that all children are not "ready" for reading at the same time and since all children do not grow at the same rate, differences in reading skills become greater rather than smaller with each succeeding grade level. The higher the grade level, the wider should be the lag between the difficulty of the words being developed in the instructional reading program prepared for a given grade level and those included in the word problems.

70. FIVE STEPS TO READING SUCCESS IN SCIENCE*

Metropolitan School Study Council

Science

Many reading difficulties faced by pupils studying science arise from the introduction, all at one time, of numerous new concepts, the interpretation of mathematical formulae, and the solving of problems. To read science material successfully, pupils must master certain reading skills:

1. Locating pertinent details
2. Distinguishing between main ideas and supporting details
3. Visualizing
4. Following directions
5. Drawing inferences

To help pupils learn these reading skills, teachers will find the following sample procedures valuable as guides in developing similar lessons in their classes.

Reading skills often essential to science are included in the sample procedures in the Social Studies section of this manual. The teacher may wish especially to refer to the procedures for "Skimming" and "Reading Critically" in that section.

Five-Step Approach in Science

STEP ONE: READINESS

1. Relating the experiences and knowledge of the pupils to the new material

* From *Five Steps to Reading Success in Science, Social Studies, and Mathematics,* Revised, Metropolitan School Study Council

2. Arousing the pupils' interest in the section
   a. The challenge of solving a problem
   b. The desire to satisfy a problem
   c. The practical value of scientific knowledge

STEP TWO: CONCEPT DEVELOPMENT

1. Developing vocabulary
   a. Words and phrases new to the pupils
   b. Familiar words and phrases with new connotations
2. Clarifying ideas of measurement
   Space   *Energy*
   Time   *Mass*

STEP THREE: SILENT READING

1. Asking pupils to find answers to specific questions
2. Asking pupils to discover and follow the steps of the experiment or problem

STEP FOUR: DISCUSSION (ORAL OR WRITTEN)

1. Helping pupils to evaluate their answers to questions

(New York: Teachers College, Columbia Univ., 1960), pp. 1–7. Reprinted by permission of the Metropolitan School Study Council.

2. Helping pupils to discover or to understand principles or theories
3. Helping pupils to see the practical application of principles or theories

STEP FIVE: REREADING (SILENT OR ORAL)

1. Checking accuracy
2. Examining critically

Reading Skill: Locating Pertinent Details

STEP ONE: READINESS

Pupils are aware that green vegetables are a necessary part of a balanced diet. The teacher should stimulate the pupils' curiosity about the reasons for this.

STEP TWO: CONCEPT DEVELOPMENT

The meaning of the following words and concepts should be clarified before the pupils begin the reading. These words and phrases should always be presented in written context.

green plants	fats
carbohydrates	minerals
proteins	cellulose

STEP THREE: SILENT READING

The pupils then should be asked to read the selection, keeping in mind the questions, "What are green plants made of?" and "What do green plants make?"

"Green plants have been broken down, chemically, to find out what they are made of. They are made of certain carbohydrates, proteins, fats, minerals, and water. But chiefly they are made of a woody material called cellulose and contain large amounts of starch and sugar. . . . Sugar is made first. Green plants make starch, cellulose, and even fat and proteins, from the sugar." [1]

STEP FOUR: DISCUSSION

The discussion should stress that green plants, broken down chemically, provide substances for building body tissue and providing energy. Pupils should be able to name the substances.

STEP FIVE: REREADING

Rereading may be necessary to check the number and kind of substances found in green plants.

Reading Skill: Distinguishing between Main Ideas and Supporting Details

STEP ONE: READINESS

The reading selection that follows concerns the endocrine glands. Before being asked to read this selection, students should be made generally familiar with what the endocrine glands are. The teacher should make clear to students that the purpose of reading about the endocrine glands in this instance is to discover the results of over-secretion of growth hormones in the pituitary

[1] Raymond W. Burnett, Bernard Jaffe, and Herbert S. Zim, New World of Science (Morristown, N. J.: Silver Burdett Co., 1953), p. 136. Quoted by permission of the publisher.

gland. To stimulate interest, the readiness lesson might also include a discussion of the following:

1. Why individuals vary in height
2. What causes circus giants

STEP TWO: CONCEPT DEVELOPMENT

The meaning and pronunciation of the following words should be clarified before the pupils begin the reading. These words and phrases should always be presented in written context.

pituitary gland	*hormones*
lobes	*somotropic*
anterior	*giantism*
secretes	*acromegaly*

STEP THREE: SILENT READING

The pupils should locate details about the results of over-secretion of the growth hormone.

"The *pituitary gland* consists of two *lobes*. The *anterior* lobe *secretes* several different *hormones*. One of these, the *somotropic* (so-mo-TROP-ic) or growth hormone, regulates the growth of the skeleton. If an over-secretion of this hormone occurs during the growing years, tremendous height may be attained. This condition is called *giantism*. Circus giants over 7 feet tall, weighing 300 pounds, and wearing size 30 shoes, are examples of this disorder. If the over-secretion occurs during adult life, the bones merely thicken, as they cannot grow in length. However, the organs and soft tissues enlarge tremendously. This condition is known as *acromegaly* (ak-ro-MEG-a-lee). Victims of this disorder have greatly thickened jaw bones, enlarged noses, and greatly enlarged hands and fingers." [2]

STEP FOUR: PURPOSEFUL DISCUSSION

The following questions should be on the blackboard while the pupils are reading. Such questions aid in giving direction to the reading.

1. What condition is caused by an over-secretion of the pituitary hormone during *the growing years?* Give an example.
2. What condition is caused by an over-secretion of the pituitary gland during *adult life?* Describe the symptoms.

STEP FIVE: REREADING

The rereading may be oral or silent. Pupils may skim through text material seeking the proof of an answer they have given and then read orally to prove the point.

In this particular lesson, pupils may find it necessary to reread to correct errors in spelling or pronunciation of *somotropic* or *acromegaly*. They may want to read to check on the details concerning the circus giant or the symptoms of acromegaly.

Reading Skill: Visualizing Concepts

STEP ONE: READINESS

The teacher should arouse the interest of pupils in the atom by discussing the frequent use of *atom* or *atomic* on the radio, in the newspapers, in the

[2] Truman J. Moon, Paul O. Mann, and James H. Otto, *Modern Biology* (New York: Henry Holt, 1951), p. 502. Quoted by permission of the publisher.

movies, and on television. The pupils should be led to ask what an atom really looks like. The purpose of reading the selection will be to find the answer to that question.

STEP TWO: CONCEPT DEVELOPMENT

The pupils should become familiar with the pronunciations and definitions of the following words and phrases. These words and phrases should always be presented in written context.

atom	positively charged
electrons	protons
negatively charged	neutrons
particles	electrically neutral
nucleus	mass of the atom
planetary	
electrons	

STEP THREE: SILENT READING

The teacher should ask the pupils to try to picture the structure of the atom and to try to compare the size of the nucleus and its electrons.

"There is plenty of evidence to show that an *atom* consists of *electrons, negatively charged particles,* whirling about a *nucleus.* These outer electrons, usually called *planetary electrons,* are lightly scattered about the nucleus and at relatively remote distances from it. The nucleus, on the other hand, is *positively charged* and consists of a closely packed group of *protons* and *neutrons.* A proton has a positive electrical charge, whereas a neutron is *electrically* neutral and probably results from the union of a proton and an electron. A proton is almost 2,000 times heavier than an electron so

that more than 99.9 per cent of the *mass of the atom* is in the nucleus." [3]

STEP FOUR: DISCUSSION

To test visualization powers, students could:
1. Draw the structure of an atom
2. Compare the structure of an atom to our solar system
3. Make a model of an atom from clay and wire

STEP FIVE: REREADING

Some rereading may be necessary to check the accuracy of the proportions of the drawing or model.

Reading Skill: Following Directions

STEP ONE: REREADING

In preparation for an experiment, the pupils have already discussed the use of levers as simple machines. They have learned, by observation, about levers in daily use like the crowbar, scissors, and sugar tongs. They have also learned that levers are used to do work with less effort and with more speed. They are now ready to read the directions for an experiment that will actually demonstrate the scientific principle involved.

STEP TWO: CONCEPT DEVELOPMENT

The meaning of the following words and concepts should be clarified before

[3] John C. Hogg, Otis E. Alley, and Charles L. Bickel, *Chemistry, A Course for High Schools* (New York: D. Van Nostrand Co., copyright 1948), p. 274. Quoted by permission of the publisher.

the pupils begin to read the experiment. These words and phrases should always be presented in written context.

equilibrium   unlike weights
parallel forces   products
balance   vary
fulcrum   sum

STEP THREE: SILENT READING

Each pupil should be instructed to read each detail carefully and execute each step as stated.

"*Experiment* 33a. *Equilibrium* of *Parallel Forces.—Balance* a meter stick in a clamp or on a *fulcrum.* Hang or stand two *unlike weights* on the stick and move them until the stick balances. Then measure the distance from each weight to the balancing point, or fulcrum. Multiply each weight by its distance to the fulcrum and compare the *products. Vary* the set-up as much as you like, using different weights . . . or three weights, or many weights. In every case you will find that the product of weight times distance for the left weight equals the product for the right weight (times distance from the fulcrum). When several weights are used, add the products for those on the left and check against the *sum* of products for those on the right." [4]

STEP FOUR: DISCUSSION

After each pupil has performed the experiment, he should compare the re-

[4] Robert W. Fuller, Raymond B. Brownlee, and D. Lee Baker, *Elements of Physics* (Boston: Allyn and Bacon, 1953), p. 106. Quoted by permission of the publisher.

sults to determine whether or not the phenomenon is consistent.

STEP FIVE: REREADING

If results indicate that there are some pupils who have not accurately followed directions, the pupils should re-read to discover their errors and do the experiment again step by step.

After the lesson has been satisfactorily completed, the class is ready to discuss the scientific principles involved in the experiment.

Reading Skill: Drawing Inferences

STEP ONE: READINESS

The teacher can prepare the class for reading the selection by discussing why many distributors of food pre-package or wrap all foods they display. Pupils will probably mention the danger of contamination from handling by customers or from flies. It should be suggested that there may be another reason why local health suggestions usually require that most perishable foods be packaged or displayed in an enclosed display case.

STEP TWO: CONCEPT DEVELOPMENT

The meanings of the following words and concepts should be clarified before the pupils begin to read. These words and phrases should always be presented in written context.

microscopic   original formation
germs   carbon dioxide
decay   minerals
chemical   ptomaine poison
   compounds

STEP THREE: SILENT READING

The pupils should be asked to figure out from the facts in the selection the answer to the following question:

What is a third reason for packaging or covering food in stores? ". . . When the *microscopic germs* that float about in the air settle on foods, they start *decay*. The materials in the goods are broken up to form new *chemical compounds*. Some of them are the same as those which entered into the *original formation* of the foods; namely, *carbon dioxide, water*, and *minerals*. When decay takes place, new compounds with bad odors are also produced, and the food changes in taste. The food may even become poisonous. *Ptomaine poison* is an example of this." [5]

STEP FOUR: DISCUSSION

In the ensuing discussion some pupils will probably say that the answer is not stated. Others who have arrived at the correct answer should then explain how they reached the conclusion that food is wrapped as a protection against contact with the air as well as with persons, animals, and insects.

STEP FIVE: REREADING

Those pupils who did not make the correct inference will reread to find the facts from which the inference was drawn.

71. WE MUST CLEAR THE LANDSCAPE TO GET AT THE SOIL*

Mauree Applegate

EVERY elementary schoolteacher longs to teach artistically. In her mind's eye she sees herself stopping to take advantage of the extra teaching opportunities that arise in every class —the new vocabulary word that pops up unplanned, the question apropos to the moment, the path down which a pupil's quick mind darts that should be explored—now. But since the elementary teacher must, she tells herself,

* From Mauree Applegate, "We Must Clear the Landscape to Get at the Soil," *Grade Teacher,* LXXV (January, 1958), 38, 86. Reprinted by permission of the author and Teachers Publishing Corporation, Darien, Conn.

[5] Ira C. Davis, John Burnett, and E. Wayne Gross, *Science* (New York: Henry Holt and Co., 1952), p. 514. Quoted by permission of the publisher.

cover the curriculum as well as un-cover the children's ideas and thoughts, she is afraid of being led away from the narrow path of today's lesson plans.

This argument is as out-of-date as woolen petticoats and red flannel un-derwear. It is high time that teachers and superintendents recognized that teaching is a profession and that mem-bers of a profession must be allowed to use their own judgments in their daily planning. Too few teachers can plan their own days!

All we can do for a child during the day is to lead him to *think,* to *read,* to *write,* to *speak,* to *listen,* to *do* and *create* better than he has been doing. No matter if we taught him fifty sub-jects a day, those seven skills would embrace all we could teach him. So why teach him to do all seven in one day? We teachers need to cover less ground during one school day and do a better, slower job in leading and guiding a class to learn. The guidance of learning is one thing that cannot be hurried. Rote learning can be pushed and shoved and driven from behind, but guided learning is forever a slow process.

The language arts and the social studies are "naturals" to be taught to-gether. Nine-tenths of all that we teach in the social studies is a form of lan-guage arts. Therefore, why not inte-grate (not correlate) classes where we can and thus have time enough for better teaching?

Instead of the old question and an-swer method, the social studies class must embrace good discussion. Why? In a question and answer period, the responsibility lies wholly with the teacher; by contrast, a discussion de-velops responsibility where it belongs —in the student. Just consider the skills which a good discussion develops in children: together the teacher and chil-dren plan the outline that covers the material to be discussed; together they decide the criteria by which the discus-sion can be evaluated; and together they evaluate the discussion after it is over, deciding in what ways their next discussion can be improved. Together, too, the class decides the qualities and duties of a good discussion leader and evaluates carefully the good points of each one. *If a discussion did nothing else but teach children to plan and to evaluate, it would be eminently worth-while.*

But think of the *questioning* ability a good discussion strengthens. The abil-ity to question others so as to get a large answer to a little question is be-coming a lost art in the schoolroom. Tell me, Teacher, have you evaluated your own questions lately? How many questions do you have to ask before you get the information you want? Are your questions tweezer-like ones, pull-ing out one skinny answer at a time? Are your questions phrased so that they are inclusive, or are you able to ask only short-answer questions? *Ask your-self how you rate as a questioner.*

Together with your students make a chart of possible starters for inclusive questions:

Why
Trace the beginnings of
Compare
Contrast
Explain the reasons for
Evaluate
Prove that
Enumerate and explain

Name the

Trace the

and so on and on.

Think also of the opportunities that a discussion offers to disagree gracefully, and what skill is needed more in adult living?

"That's an interesting idea, but I wonder if it would hold in an argument. Black says that. . . ."

"That's true, James, but have you thought. . . ."

"I think that statement is only partially true, Mary. . . ."

"I'd be interested in seeing that statement in print, James. Every source I read said that. . . ."

"I disagree with you, Lillian. If that were true, then. . . ."

"I believe you misunderstood the author's meaning, Jerry. . . ."

"Could you possibly be mistaken, Ned, on your facts? According to Mearns. . . ."

To disagree gracefully is to be prepared for living together in peace.

Another social grace practiced is the chairman's bringing out each individual so that he contributes his best. It is wise to select a student of medium ability as the one to start a discussion, for the poorest student will "murder" the topic or question, while the best will give it so fully that the less loquacious gleaners who follow will find no straws of information left for them to gather and their attention will wander.

An intuitive chairman will get a quiet member of the class into the discussion by a well-worded, definite question—not the general, "Does anyone have anything more to contribute?" It is this being specific that gets the shy student into the discussion. Another technique which is often successful with the shy student is to ask him his opinion of something that wasn't in the book.

Obviously reading and organizing materials are the techniques of the language arts that play largely in a discussion: learning to locate materials in many books and magazines; having a committee make the bibliography of materials; learning how to read to a topic; learning to take notes for a discussion; assembling and organizing those notes. Talk about *reading* in the social studies—the social studies *is* reading! If your social studies class and your reading class could be combined at least three days each week, think of the time one could save in the process. There is reading in almost every class in the school day, and yet in grades 5 to 8, some teachers think they must have a reading class, just for reading. It's like the nurse's aid who awakened her patient to give him his sleeping powders!

And not only does reading for a discussion come into the social studies, but reading for enrichment—the folk tales of the land or area you're studying; the more adult viewpoint presented by the more advanced student who read the adult book; the historical fiction and the travel books read by those who enjoy reading. If one must have a reading class on the same day as reading in the social studies class, why may one not be an enrichment of the other? Those who teach the social studies out of one book only are cheating this generation of wings and wheels.

Almost every language arts lesson cropping up in a social studies discussion is present, too, in report-giving, and inter-group sharing of information. There's no doubt about it, the social studies and the language arts are Siamese twins.

The social studies very much needs writing, both work-type and creative writing, as its voice. Summary writing, outline making and writing organized tests are three skills college freshmen badly need, as well as do the heads of business departments. They can be taught in simple form to any normal fourth-grader.

Students who have never written essay-type examinations before they enter college are placed at a great disadvantage. Life is not a mere filling out of blanks; it is a thinking things through, a padding out of an outline which isn't there. It seems to me we teachers in elementary and secondary schools are forgetting that the qualities and habits of thought we want adults to have we must begin in simple form as soon as children start to school. I don't believe it is fair to a child to begin his mental discipline at fifteen; any discipline acquired at that point is apt to be shrugged off as soon as schooldays are over. No discipline is of much account to a student unless it is automatic and habitual—in fact, it isn't a discipline until it is just that. America needs leaders, and leadership is the result of training and experience as fast as a child is ready to assume leadership. In an age when children are the most ready for leadership, we let them do little but play, and our country is the loser.

Creative writing, as well as the disciplined, work-type writing, is a vital need of the social studies. It provides two things: reality and expression, both badly needed when the material being studied is considerably removed from children's environment. Studying history and geography from many books and from visual aids, as we do nowadays, makes the imaginative child feel as if he were really there; in history he walks in shoes of our forefathers, and in geography he wears the sandals of the man across the sea. As he reads and listens, he gets empathy for other men.

And empathy is exactly what we want him to get. But feeling must be expressed in some way or it results in frustration. A homemade series of television shows or radio plays could grow out of your social studies units: stories written about heroes of old as if the children were there will make history a real experience; pretend-interviews with men whose spirits will never die help ancient heroes to become living men and women to our children. If we would have our children embrace the best of the past, we must make the courageous men and women of that past live.

Notice how fifth-grade Jill has taken true incidents from a popular book on Lincoln and woven these into a story:

Abe Lincoln was studying his only book when I came to the door that day. I asked if he would play with me, but I really didn't expect him to. He never would play when he had started to read. I asked him if he wanted to go swimming.

He said, "I'd get this book wet."

Sometimes he was impossible! Finally, he came out to play. That's when we had fun. He loved a joke. Once he put mud on his little brother's feet, turned him upside down, put his feet on the ceiling, and walked him along, leaving muddy footprints on the ceiling. Was his mother surprised!

When we got to the stream, we jumped in. Abe loved swimming, so I was surprised when he got out ahead of me. When I got out, our clothes were gone. It seemed to me Abe had a twinkle in his eye. A few minutes later, I found them, high up in a tree! That Abe!

When we got to Lincoln's, I said goodby to Abe. It had been a wonderful day! Tomorrow I hoped Abe wouldn't be buried in a book all day.

Eighth-grade Judy has written with empathy about Valley Forge:

Bleeding feet . . .
Tied with rags . . .
Hungry men . . .
Unite their flags . . .
This is the spirit of Valley Forge.
Mournful hearts . . .
Filled with cries . . .
Suppressed souls . . .
That never die . . .
This is the spirit of Valley Forge.

Seventh-grade Carol could teach many of us things that our hearts should know:

I am the Statue of Liberty, a symbol of friendship, freedom and brotherhood. I am proud and honored to be a bronze statue standing on Bedloe's Island welcoming all. I have stood there seventy-one years and there I will remain. I have welcomed tired, hungry, poor, and homeless and I shall never fail to.

But creative writing is only one of the language arts that are the voice of the social studies.

Creative drama, another of the language arts, is the life and substance of the social studies. Street and village scenes enacted of the countries studied, the folklore dramatized and made real —such activities can enliven the social studies to the point where children really learn the feeling of re-creating the long ago or the far away. I have seen children so really catch the spirit of the characters of the townspeople in the "Pied Piper of Hamelin" that I know that, for them, German history had truly moved back. I have seen role playing of the conditions in the time of Napoleon that was so real that I, too, felt the hunger of the peasants and suffered their wrongs. I have stood with a mob of children outside a paper drawing of Liberty Hall and in spirit listened to the bell issue forth the great tidings of liberty to all Americans. And I have felt great pride that America was free.

Few hearts are changed from mere knowledge; hearts are changed through deep feelings. We must feel deeply about our country. We must feel deeply about all the peoples of the earth.

Surely, we can trust our future into such capable hands as those of eighth-grade Kathleen:

As I was walking on Bedloe's Island feeling depressed about one thing and another I heard a voice. I stopped suddenly, bewildered. I looked around expecting something to happen. I then heard the voice again.

By this time a little crowd had gathered around me because I was conspicuous, looking around and mumbling to no one. But then the voice implored.

"Help! Help! Won't somebody help me?"

I thought it was funny that some of the Americans didn't hear the voice. The voice continued:

"I am the Statue of Liberty. My torch is dimming. Why won't you help me?"

I replied, "Before I help you, I would like to ask a few questions. What does your torch stand for?"

"My torch stands for the liberty of America; the forefathers of America had made her free. Some of her leaders are George Washington, who is the 'Father of His Country'; Abe Lincoln who gave slaves their liberty; and Patrick Henry with his immortal words, 'Give me liberty or give me death,' " replied the Statue.

I questioned further, "But the Americans have liberty. They can do as they please, when they please, and as they please as long as it doesn't interfere with the rights of others. Why, then, is your torch dimming?"

"My torch is dimming because the liberty of America would be threatened if she went into war. But you and your associates must keep the torch of liberty forever burning brightly, not only in America, but in all nations of the world," she informed me.

"But how can I do this?" I inquired.

"You can help me by acting honestly and wisely in your work and by letting your conscience be your guide," she replied. "You can do this because you are a delegate to the United Nations."

If we so arrange our school day so that we really have time to teach the social studies and the language arts, meshing them when we can, we can grow nearer to the day when all men will be brothers. The future does not come by leaving things the way they have been or are. Education changes, and teachers can change education. That is what we are for. Are you changing, or have you ossified into easy ways?

CHAPTER XII

MOTIVATING READING

72. STUDIES OF CHILDREN'S INTEREST — A BRIEF
SUMMARY*

Paul Witty and Associates[1]

WHAT do we mean by the term interest? A first approach to an understanding of the term might be for the reader to look back on his own childhood. For most of us there will be a nostalgic glow as we think about interests that led us to collect birds' eggs or stamps, or marbles or dolls. We shall think about the model auto, the play house, or the boat we built. And we shall reflect with great pleasure on the butterflies we mounted, or the animals we hunted and photographed.

The activities cited above were undoubtedly learned, yet they were "freely" chosen—usually just because we wanted to take part in them. They were often unassociated with work and were not usually the result of home or school pressures. In a way, these interests were the result of need for expression although the need was rarely recognized. Elizabeth Hurlock makes the following statement about interests:

An interest is a learned motive which drives the individual to act in accordance with that interest. It is defined as preoccupation with an activity when the individual is free to choose. When the child finds an activity satisfying, it continues to be an interest.[2]

E. K. Strong discusses interest and interests in this way:

* From Paul Witty and Associates, "Studies of Children's Interest—A Brief Summary," *Elementary English*, XXXVII, No. 7 (November, 1960), 469–75. Reprinted by permission of the authors and the National Council of Teachers of English.
[1] Robert Sizemore, Ann Coomer, Paul Kinsella, and Stanley Krippner (associates in the Northwestern University—Office of Education Study of Interests.) See also "The Role of Interests" by Paul Witty, Chapter VIII in *Development In and Through Reading*, Sixtieth Yearbook, Part I, *National Society for the Study of Education*.

[2] Elizabeth B. Hurlock, *Child Development* (New York: McGraw-Hill Book Company, Inc., 1956), p. 440.

Interests possess the four qualitative criteria of interest, i.e., persistent attention, feeling, activity, and direction. Two additional quantitative criteria, namely, intensity and duration, could be attributed to interest but it seems more appropriate to attribute them to interests.[3]

Jacob W. Getzels gives a short but useful definition. "An interest is a characteristic disposition, organized through experience, which impels an individual to seek out particular objects, activities, understandings, skills, or goals for attention or acquisition.[4]

For purposes of this article we have described interest and interests similarly: Interest is a disposition or tendency which impels an individual to seek out particular goals for persistent attention. The goals may be objects, skills, knowledges, and art activities of various kinds. The behavior patterns in seeking these goals may be regarded as particular interests such as collecting objects or viewing TV. They should be looked upon as acquired, although they are based upon such factors as the constitutional nature of the individual and his personality structure as affected by his unique experiences and his particular environment.

Methods and Values of Studying Interests

Various methods have been used to study or identify children's interests:

the questionnaire, the interview, the "log" of activities, the interest inventory, the anecdotal record, and observation under various conditions.

A child-study technique widely used by teachers is illustrated by the Northwestern University Interest Inventory.[5] Guided by the inquiries on the inventory, the teacher and the pupil discuss informally topics such as favorite leisure activities, hobbies, play preferences, movie and reading habits, and familiarity with community places of interest. The inventory also contains questions related to the child's personal and social problems. Included too are lists of play activities and of books to be discussed.

The writer and his associates at Northwestern University recently devised a series of questionnaires to be employed in studying interests.[6] The items were assembled from diverse sources and listed in four questionnaires which deal with the following areas: play and recreational activities; TV, radio, and movie preferences;

[3] E. K. Strong, Jr., *Vocational Interests: 18 Years after College* (Minneapolis: University of Minnesota Press, 1955).

[4] Jacob W. Getzels, "The Nature of Reading Interests," in *Developing Permanent Interest in Reading,* Supplementary Educational Monographs, Number 83, compiled and edited by Helen M. Robinson (Chicago: The University of Chicago Press, December, 1956), Chapter I, page 7.

[5] Developed from the Witty-Kopel Interest Inventory described in Paul Witty and David Kopel, *Reading and the Educative Process* (Boston: Ginn and Co., 1939).

[6] *A Study of the Interests of Children and Youth.* A cooperative research project performed (1958–59) in accord with a contract between Northwestern University and the Office of Education, U. S. Department of Health, Education and Welfare. Paul A. Witty, Director of Project (Northwestern University); Robert A. Sizemore, Assistant Director (Toledo Public Schools); Paul Kinsella (Skokie Public Schools); Ann Coomer (Chicago Public Schools); Stanley Krippner (Northwestern University). Report was submitted to the Office of Education, U. S. Department of Health, Education and Welfare in February, 1960. Parts of this article are adapted from this report.

reading pursuits; and vocational and educational interests.

A first step in the study of interests perhaps involves an examination of the findings of studies in various interest areas. Another step implies consideration of the ways interests can be used to promote growth in and through reading for individuals and for groups. We shall, in this article, summarize studies of activities, interests, and preferences of pupils in play and recreation; TV, radio, and the movies; reading; and vocations and education.[7]

Play and Recreational Activities

There are many studies now available of play and recreation.[8] The results vary widely depending on the techniques used, the time the studies were made, and the type of groups employed. In a widely quoted study, published in 1927, H. C. Lehman and the writer [9] considered play to be primarily those activities in which children engaged "just because they wanted to." They employed a play quiz which was submitted to thousands of children and

[7] In Chapter VIII of the *Sixtieth Yearbook* of the *National Society for the Study of Education,* these interests are related to effective reading instruction with examples from case-studies and classroom practice.

[8] Summaries of studies of interests have been made by Elizabeth Hurlock, *Child Development, op. cit.,* and by Irving R. Melbo and John A. Hockett in *Children's Interests, 12th Yearbook,* California Elementary School Principals, 1940. See also Dale B. Harris "Interests and Attitudes as Motives," Chapter V in *Forty-ninth Yearbook,* National Society for the Study of Education, Part I, *Learning and Instruction* (Chicago: University of Chicago Press, 1950).

[9] H. C. Lehman and Paul Witty, *Psychology of Play Activities* (New York: A. S. Barnes and Company, 1927).

youth. Comparable results were reported by Witty and Coomer for boys and girls studied in 1946.[10] In the latter study one may note a persistence of many play activities previously cited. It was found that by the time boys and girls were six years old they began to show differences in their favored pursuits. The six-year-old girl liked to play with dolls and miniature furniture. She enjoyed "playing house" and making things to use in a playhouse. She participated in some group games such as "drop the handkerchief," but she always took part in individual activities such as "jumping rope" and "playing jacks." When boys were six years of age they liked best to participate in more active but relatively unorganized games such as "tag" and "hide-and-seek." Most boys eight or nine years of age found pleasure in spinning tops, flying kites, playing marbles, and building houses. They experienced satisfaction in "playing cowboy" and similar games in which they pretended to be aviators, soldiers, sailors, or marines. Other group activities such as playing catch or games the boys referred to as baseball or football, were also popular; but these pursuits were unlike the more formal competitive sports enjoyed by older boys.

By the time the boys were twelve years of age they turned to more highly organized games such as tennis and baseball. From twelve to fifteen there appeared to be a sharp decrease in the amount of active, spontaneous play, and a tendency developed on the part of both boys and girls to take part to a

[10] Reported by Paul Witty, *Reading in Modern Education* (Boston: D. C. Heath and Company, 1949).

greater extent in sedentary pursuits. Going to the movies, listening to the radio, riding in an automobile, and watching contests gained favor during this period.

In 1949, Arthur T. Jersild and Ruth J. Tasch cited the results of questionnaires submitted to pupils in grades one through twelve. Among children's interests, the authors stressed the prominence of experiences involving bodily activity:

It is apparent that experiences involving bodily activity, doing something, or going somewhere are much more prominent than activities of a more intellectual or aesthetic character. Many children do mention reading (and other related matters such as going to the library) in describing what they like best, but the youngsters who mention the delights of reading or other intellectual pursuits constitute a small minority. Moreover, it is mainly the girls who mention such intellectual enterprises.[11]

Prior to the advent of television another study revealed a decrease in participation in games with increase in age. Children in grades five through eight in a midwestern community were asked to rank six activities (sports, games, radio, reading, movies, and hobbies) according to the way "they used their spare time." In 1949 it was reported that:

Reading was clearly overshadowed by sports, radio-listening, games, and movie attendance. The pattern of other activities did not vary greatly from grade to grade.

[11] Arthur T. Jersild and Ruth J. Tasch, *Children's Interests and What They Suggest for Education* (New York: Bureau of Publications, Teachers College, Columbia University, 1949).

Sports were consistently first; hobbies consistently last. Radio-listening stayed near the top, in second or third place for all the grades. Movies seemed to go up somewhat among older children, as might be expected. Games showed the only consistent downward trend with increased age.[12]

Still another investigation emphasized differences between the sexes in favored activities as well as the changing pattern of interests with increase in age. Children ranging in age from four to thirteen were asked to name their favorite play interests and activities. It was reported in 1951 that:

. . . the boys enumerated 109, and the girls 70 games with an overlap of 42 items. The greatest number of games was obtained from the boys and girls between 7 and 9 years and the smallest number was mentioned by the children between 4 and 6 years of age. . . .[13]

In recent years, TV has been almost invariably assigned first rank among children's preferred activities. A study made in 1954 by Constance M. McCullough in nine Oakland, California, schools clearly revealed this tendency.[14] These schools were located in three distinctly different socio-economic localities. One district was composed "largely of racial minority

[12] Inez L. Mauck and Esther Swenson, "Study of Children's Recreational Reading." *Elementary School Journal,* L (November, 1949), 148–50.

[13] Jacob H. Conn, "Children's Awareness of Sex Differences (II), Play Activities and Game Preferences." *Journal of Child Psychiatry,* XI, 1951.

[14] Constance M. McCullough, "A Log of Children's Out-of-School Activities," *Elementary School Journal,* LVIII (December, 1957), 157–65.

groups living in low-cost housing and employed as unskilled labor. . . ." Another group included three schools located in a district of native-born skilled laborers of average income. And the third group consisted of schools situated in a district representing upper-middle-class prosperity. Fifth-grade pupils kept a "log" for one week of their out-of-school activities including before-school, after-school, and after-dinner pursuits. Twenty-six "recreational" activities were cited 6,217 times; fourteen "work" activities, 2,922 times. Televiewing was first in popularity among both boys and girls. Next for the boys was active sports, followed by caring for pets, games, doing homework, straightening own room, and visiting friends. The girls mentioned televiewing first; and these activities followed: preparing meals, straightening own room, washing dishes, active sports, doing homework, and games. Reading of books was low on all lists except for the third group in which nearly half the children reported reading books.[15]

Throughout the recent Northwestern University–Office of Education study, the influence of the mass media—with TV first—was evident.[16] There were, of course, other passive activities which were cited at all grade levels. Despite the time devoted to the mass media, boys and girls still found time to take part in outdoor activities. Boys played baseball and football, swam, and rode bicycles; and girls enjoyed skating, jumping rope, building snowmen, and

[15] Constance M. McCullough, *op. cit.*
[16] *A Study of the Interests of Children and Youth.* Northwestern University—Office of Education, U. S. Department of Health, Education, and Welfare. *Op. cit.*

riding on sleds. Certain activities such as playing marbles, fishing, hunting, hiking, flying kites, and picnicking, which formerly enjoyed greater popularity, were less frequently cited.

We may note in these studies a wide range of play activities enjoyed at every level. Of course, some play pursuits are characteristic of younger children while others are followed by older pupils. Moreover, differences in the popularity of play activities depend upon factors such as the location of a school or group studied and the time or season of the year. Marked individual differences, too, are apparent in play preferences. In order to utilize play interests effectively in motivating instruction, it is desirable for a teacher to investigate the interests of each new group or class he attempts to instruct. Similarly, it is necessary for the teacher to study each pupil individually to ascertain his particular pattern of interests and preferences.

TV—Children's Most Time Consuming Activity

Diverse opinions have been expressed about the effects of TV upon children. Some writers emphasize the potentialities of TV as a positive force. Others minimize its significance, while still others stress undesirable results. Parents have asserted that TV is affecting adversely children's interest in reading and in other academic pursuits. Some teachers, too, have pointed to certain unfortunate features of TV insofar as children's interest and effort in school are concerned. Some have stated that TV is a "time trap for children" and that "TV produces not only idlers, but also bad taste and bad manners." It is certainly true that TV consumes a great deal of our time. For example, *Time* magazine of October 13, 1958, cited a report showing that 43 million U. S. homes had TV turned on an average of five hours and 56 minutes each day.

In seeking to evaluate the charges made against TV, one may profitably examine the results of investigations made since TV appeared.

In 1949, TV came to the Chicago area. By May, 1950, 43 per cent of the school children reported that they had access to TV. The percentages increased to 68 in 1951, 88 in 1952, and in 1953, to 92. In 1955 and 1956, 97 per cent had TV sets at home. Studies made by teachers in Chicago, Skokie, and Evanston in 1958 also yielded a percentage of 97.[17] In 1959, 99 per cent of the Evanston children had sets; more than one–third had two sets or more, and 3 per cent had color TV.

In 1950, the elementary school pupils spent on the average 21 hours each week with TV; and in 1951, the average dropped to 19 hours. There was a small increase during the next two years— to 23 hours in 1953. In 1955, the average was 24 hours, while in 1957, it was 22 hours. In 1958, the average for elementary school pupils was 20 hours, and in 1959, it was 21 hours.

From the first, high school students were found to give less time to TV than did younger pupils. Their average

[17] Paul Witty and Paul Kinsella, "Children and TV—A Ninth Report." *Elementary English,* November, 1958. Other studies have been published in former years in *Elementary English.*

for 1951 was 14 hours per week. In 1958, it was 13 hours, and in 1959, 12 hours.

In 1950, the children's favorite programs were (in order): *Hopalong Cassidy, Howdy Doody, Lone Ranger, Milton Berle,* and *Arthur Godfrey.* In 1952, *I Love Lucy* became the best liked program of boys and girls. *I Love Lucy* continued in first place until 1955, when acclaim went to *Disneyland. Rin Tin Tin* and *Lassie* also became very popular. In 1956, *Disneyland* again held first rank with *I Love Lucy,* third. In 1957, the favorites were *Disneyland, Mickey Mouse Club, I Love Lucy,* and *Lassie.* Changes took place rapidly and in 1958 the following favorites appeared: *Zorro, Disneyland, Bugs Bunny, Shock Theatre,* and *Mickey Mouse Club.*

By far the most popular program for elementary school pupils (grades 1–6) in 1959 was a new presentation, *77 Sunset Strip.* Another new program, *Huckleberry Hound* was second on the list of favorites and *Maverick* appeared in third place. In the primary group (grades 1–3), *Huckleberry Hound* won first place in 1959 while *Zorro* fell from first place in 1958 to fifth place in 1959. In the intermediate group (grades 4–6) *Zorro,* which had ranked first among the favorite programs of 1958, was replaced in 1959 by *77 Sunset Strip. Shock Theatre,* however, retained second place in 1959.

Maverick and *American Bandstand* were the most popular programs of high school pupils. Although westerns were popular, they appeared as favorites less frequently than in the younger groups.

Writers have asserted that children today tend to spend less time in outdoor play, hobbies, sports, and creative activities than they did in former years. This condition is sometimes attributed to the influence of TV. The studies of 1950–1951 did suggest some reduction in hobbies and in outdoor activities. However, several more recent studies showed a persistence of old hobbies and the appearance of new ones since TV arrived. For example, T. C. Battin found that 57 per cent of the boys and 59 per cent of the girls followed the same hobbies as before TV.[18] Moreover, 38 per cent of the boys and 34 per cent of the girls reported the cultivation of new hobbies, while only 5 per cent of the boys and 7 per cent of the girls indicated less hobby interest. It is true, of course, that many pupils today cannot recall a time when they did not have TV.

A recent report of high school boys by Joseph K. Balogh shows results somewhat similar to those obtained in the Northwestern University studies.[19] However, in Balogh's study, a sharper decrease in televiewing took place among high school students; the average sophomore spent twice as much time with TV as did the average senior. It was reported also by Lazarus (quoted by Balogh) that with the advent of TV a serious reduction in "creative activities" has taken place; e.g., playing musical instruments, singing, acting, writing, photographing, and so on. We have indicated that this finding while holding in some studies is not corroborated by others, as is apparent in the Battin investigation cited above. Our recent studies have revealed that, since the advent of TV, there has been a marked reduction in movie attendance outside the home; in radio listening, and in the reading of comic magazines.[20]

A British study of TV, sponsored by the Nuffield Foundation, reports data for 4,500 English children of ages 10 to 14. According to *Time,* December 29, 1958, this study disclosed that "Even heavy viewing does not necessarily make children more aggressive or listless, or discourage them from reading or studying."

In the Northwestern University— Office of Education studies, both teachers and parents continued to report the following behavior and adjustment problems associated with TV: fatigue, impoverishment of play, lack of interest in school, increased nervousness, reduction in reading, eyestrain, and mealtime disturbance. In recent reports, however, problems are not so frequently cited as in the earlier studies. A relatively small per cent of the parents and the teachers mentioned such problems in 1959.[21]

A few studies have been designed to disclose the relationship between the amount of televiewing and attain-

[18] T. C. Battin, *Television and Youth.* Report published by TV Information Committee, National Association of Radio and TV Broadcasters (Washington, D. C., 1954).

[19] Joseph K. Balogh, "Television-viewing Habits of High School Boys," *Educational Research Bulletin,* XXXVIII, No. 3 (March 11, 1959), 66–71.

[20] Paul Witty, "What Children Watch on TV," *The Packet Series Bulletin* (Boston, Mass.: D. C. Heath and Co., Winter, 1959–60), Vol. XIV, No. 2.

[21] *A Study of the Interests of Children and Youth.* Northwestern University—Office of Education, U. S. Department of Health, Education, and Welfare.

ment in specific school subjects. For example, in San Leandro, California, sixth and seventh grade pupils who televiewed the most, 22¾ to 69½ hours a week, were compared with those who televiewed very little, 0 to 9¾ hours a week. Some differences favoring those who televiewed very little appeared in arithmetic and reading, while little difference was found in the language and spelling attainment of the two groups.[22]

In the Chicago area studies of TV, excessive televiewing seemed to be associated with somewhat lower academic attainment.[23] In one early investigation the average time devoted to TV by pupils in the upper fourth of their classes on standardized educational tests was 21 hours per week, while the average for the lower fourth was about 26 hours. Similar results were obtained again in 1957 and in 1959. We should point out, however, that some pupils were led to do better work in school because of interests awakened by TV. Moreover, in the case of an association of TV with poor academic attainment, other undesirable factors, in addition to excessive televiewing were found.

Several other investigators have reported little relationship between televiewing and the marks pupils receive in school. For example, Donald G. Tarbet concluded from a study of televiewing habits of 1,500 sixth graders within a twelve mile radius of Chapel Hill:

It appears that an average of 20 hours of viewing TV per week is not detrimental to pleasure reading or to academic grades. Of course, sectional differences may have affected these results. With proper training in the schools, harmful effects of TV can be diminished or overcome.[24]

Another study now being carried on in California provides relevant data. In May and June, 1958, fifth- and sixth-grade pupils were divided into heavy viewers (3 or more hours daily) and light viewers (one hour or less daily). Comparisons were made, too, of the pupils in the first four grades who, according to their parents, spent more time televiewing than playing. The following conclusions were drawn: "On the basis of data on hand, we cannot say that heavy television viewing, at any stage of elementary school, significantly lowers school grades. What slight difference there was in grades was overall in favor of the heavy viewers." [25]

[22] Lloyd F. Scott, "Television and School Attainment." *Phi Delta Kappan,* XXXVIII (October, 1956), 25–28.
[23] Paul Witty, "What Children Watch on TV," *op. cit.*
[24] Donald G. Tarbet, "The Televiewing Habits of Pupils." *The Clearing House* (April, 1956), pp. 486–87.
[25] Stanford Institute for Communication Research, Preliminary Report No. 2, "Television," The San Francisco Study of Children and Mass Communication. Palo Alto, California. (Mimeographed reports, 1959.)

73. CHILDREN'S READING INTERESTS*

Robert L. Thorndike

Conclusions From This Study

AN analysis of the responses of some 3,000 children to the reading interest questionnaire made up of annotated fictitious titles suggests the following general conclusions:

(1) *Within the same sex, the interest patterns of groups differing by several years in age and/ or as much as thirty points in average IQ show a substantial positive correlation.* Though some titles show marked differences in interest level for different age and ability groups, for many of the titles the differences are quite small. In other words, there is a consistent pattern of boy-interests (and aversions) and, to a somewhat lesser extent, a pattern of girl-interests cutting across all age and intelligence differences. Although progressive changes with age are marked in the case of some titles, the 10-year-old boy and the 15-year-old boy are more alike than different in their interests. Of the ten titles which have highest appeal for average 10-year-old boys, five are still found in the top ten titles for 15-year-olds. The resemblance of the youngest and oldest of our groups might have been

* From Robert L. Thorndike, *Children's Reading Interests:* A Study Based on a Fictitious Annotated Titles Questionnaire (New York: Bureau of Publications, Teachers College, Columbia University, 1941), pp. 35–40. Reprinted by permission of the author and the Bureau of Publications, Teachers College, Columbia University.

less marked if a wider selection of mature titles had been included, but there seems little doubt that it would still have been present. This community of interest has been found for children 9 years old and older. It seems altogether likely that differences would have been sharply increased if it had been possible to test younger children.

(2) *In their pattern of reported reading interests, bright children (median IQ about 123) are most like a group of mentally slower children (median IQ about 92) who are two or three years older than they are.* The patterns of interest for bright and slow children of the same age are much alike (correlations of from .80 to .90 in the case of boys and .60 to .80 in the case of girls), but the resemblance is increased when the bright children are two or three years younger than the slow group. "Brightness," as shown by IQ, operates to produce some differences in topics of interest, but these are not marked, and it is only when the brighter child is also older that large differences tend to appear between him and his fellows. If he is somewhat younger than his fellows, the differences are reduced to a minimum.

(3) *Sex is conspicuously more important than age or intelligence as a determiner of reported interest pattern, at least within the range of age*

MOTIVATING READING

and ability here studied. Most of the correlations computed between patterns of interest for a group of boys and a group of girls were zero or negative. We find a community of boy-interests or girl-interests which can be discerned running through all age and ability groups, but there is no comparable pattern of 10-year-old interests which appears for both boys and girls. The differences associated with sex obscure any common effect of level of maturity. We must repeat that this does not mean that no topics have appeal for both boys and girls; some do, but as many do not. Knowing only that 10-year-old boys like a title, we have a fair basis for predicting that 15-year-old boys will also like it; knowing only that boys like a title, we have no basis at all for predicting whether or not girls will also like it.

(4) *The acceleration of interest in bright children does not seem to be entirely, or even predominantly a scholarly or bookish precocity.* Though it has not been possible to determine in detail areas of greatest and least acceleration of interest for the bright group, an inspection of the results suggests strongly that the acceleration is not concentrated in titles of a more academic character. It appears as clearly in an early interest in mystery and violent adventure as in an early interest in science and invention.

Practical Implications

Relevant to all these conclusions is a caution concerning the adequacy of the method employed. One must always be somewhat tentative in interpreting measures of interest obtained through questionnaires. The mechanics of the questionnaire and the gap between words and action may distort obtained results. Bearing this caution in mind, we may draw from the results of the study a number of practical suggestions for administrators, teachers, librarians, and publishers.

For the administrator. This study bears on the question of the desirability of accelerating bright and retarding slow children. The results suggest that no maladjustment of interests, as they were sampled, is likely to occur if the child is accelerated or retarded in school by one-half to two-thirds of his intellectual acceleration or retardation. It appears that his interests will, in general, be most like those of his classmates under such circumstances of acceleration or retardation. The bright 10-year-old will have more community of interest with a group of average 11-year-olds or 12-year-olds than with his contemporaries, and the reverse will be true of the slow child. Of course, the interests here studied represent only one facet of development and should not be over-weighted in determining policies of acceleration and retardation, but within the segment of the individual's development which was studied, interest acceleration is found to accompany intellectual acceleration.

For the teacher. No generalization about the reading interests of groups will take the place, for the teacher, of a knowledge of the personal pattern of choices of each individual. Any group trends in interest development should serve merely as a framework of general probabilities into which to fit the picture of the individual child. This study may be of value to the teacher in part by providing some of that framework of group characteristics and in part by suggesting a method by which she may quickly survey the interests of each of the children in her class.

Within the range of ages studied (10 to 15), the most conspicuous differences are those between boys and girls. Though there is shown a common interest in mystery stories, animal stories, and milder adventure stories, the teacher must expect boys and girls at these ages to reveal sharp interest differences. The stories of home life, of romance, of feminine school adventures will be emphatically rejected by the boys, who will be interested to a much greater degree than the girls in science and invention, in sports, and in violent adventure. In her provision of attractive reading experiences for this age range, the teacher will need to pay primary attention to the factor of sex.

The changes of interest with age, between 10 and 15, are gradual and, for many titles, small. The interests of earlier childhood in stories of talking animals, magic, dolls, child life, and so forth, show a sharp decline as the child grows older. But many of the animal, adventure, mystery, sport, travel, science and invention, and other topics show quite small changes even over a span of four or five years. Combine with this finding the result that bright children are somewhat accelerated in their interests and slow children somewhat retarded, and one is led to the conclusion that the age differences in a given class will not be of great importance in determining interest pattern. If the teacher becomes acquainted with the reading interests of that age which is most frequently represented in her group, she need not fear that the interests of the older or younger children in the class will be particularly different. Differences will be a function of individual background rather than of age within her class.

As far as intelligence is concerned, the teacher will be able to give the bright children reading on topics which appeal most to the average child a year or two later, while the slow child will be interested in topics which appeal most to the average child a year or two earlier. This will often mean, where there has been some acceleration or retardation of intellectual deviates, that the brighter and slower children in the same classroom will be interested to read about many of the same topics.

Often, of course, the slow child will be conspicuously retarded in reading ability, and in that case he may be able to read easily only those materials which were prepared for very much younger children. It seems from our results that, if the older boy is not made to feel that these are "kid" stories (by labeling them "Third Reader," or by the injudicious remarks of the teacher), he will willingly read material about animals, adventure, mystery, sports, science, and invention which is written in simpler style for much younger children; similarly, the older girl will willingly read the simpler material about animals, mystery, romance, and domestic activities. Materials of this sort are what is required for remedial reading with the older child.

As a method of studying the class

interests, the fictitious annotated titles questionnaire, either including the present titles or made up of a different pattern to fit the particular age group concerned, would be quite useful. Children in the fourth grade and above seem to have little difficulty in handling the procedure of the questionnaire, and frequently react to it with marked enthusiasm. A tabulation of the responses of a class will give the teacher a general picture of the interests of her group and suggest desirable additions to the class library. The responses of a particular individual will serve as a basis for (1) suggesting reading materials for him or (2) conferring with him about his reading.

For the librarian. The children's librarian in school or public library will find the results for titles and categories of interest in confirming or revising her estimates of what children of different ages like to read. It may be that upon some topics of high interest (such as aviation for boys of all ages or stories of jobs for the young adolescent) she is unable to provide reading material, and this will indicate gaps on her shelves which she should try to fill. Furthermore, the questionnaire supplies an efficient technique of surveying the interests of the children who do or might use the library. If it were modified to include the titles and annotations of books which the librarian was considering adding to her collection, it would provide an advance guide of the probable appeal of the various titles. Those titles could then be selected which seemed to meet the widest demand.

For the publisher. These results should be helpful to the publisher in selecting topics and plots for children's books, and the technique should be helpful in selecting titles for manuscripts which are already completed. Although practical experience has necessarily given the successful publisher a good working knowledge of what will and what will not appeal to children, he may find certain extensions of his knowledge in our tables. Of more practical value may be the technique of this questionnaire as a procedure for testing the appeal of several topics which are under consideration or of several different titles for the same manuscript. In the last case in particular, the spontaneous choices of a sample of children should provide an exceptionally valid indication of the appeal and drawing power of a title.

74. THE INDIVIDUAL AND HIS WORLD OF BOOKS * †

Leland B. Jacobs

MANY years ago, when I was a child, the branch library near our home was a haven of delight in leisure hours for all the children of our neighborhood. There we borrowed books from an extensive collection of children's literature. There we browsed. There we sought help from the patient, friendly children's librarian, whom we trusted to make suggestions for further reading. There we went on Saturday mornings to be enthralled at the weekly story hour.

At the entrance to the children's room there was a map—an artist's creation of a land that both does and does not exist. It was a map of bookland which we often studied and discussed with considerable enjoyment. That map included many of the stories that we knew best, but it also led us to become acquainted with other fine tales which we had not previously known. It helped us to recall vivid memories of books which we had read with pleasure. It also served as a roadsign pointing to further journeys in reading.

Should one return to that library today and still find that painting in the very same spot, he would undoubtedly be surprised at how out-of-date the map has already become. To be sure some of the mountain peaks of children's literature would remain the same, but so much new territory has been explored that the map would need to be reconceived in new dimensions. To the well-plotted fields of the past would have to be added the great frontiers of children's literature of today. A modern child reader could not travel very far with that old map. There is a wonderful new world of children's books, the mappings of which would include territory not known in my childhood.

Guiding Children into the World of Books

Although the mappings of the realms of children's books are important, they are really not enough to provide a great adventure for boys and girls in their reading. The mappings can indicate general contours. They may chart specific destinations. They do help an individual reader to locate himself. But for a truly educative experience in literature, the young reader needs guide service to go along with the mappings. The teacher and parent should be able to provide expert guidance through the child's world of books.

What are the characteristics of a

* Presented at 1954 Annual Institute on Reading, Temple University, 1954.

† From Leland B. Jacobs, "The Individual and His World of Books," *Education,* LXXIV, No. 9 (May, 1954), 523–26. Reprinted by permission of the author and The Bobbs-Merrill Co., Inc., Indianapolis, Ind.

good guide in this adventuring in literature? In the first place, the guide has zeal for the undertaking—a devotion that is contagious. He is personally so enthusiastic about literature that he generates in others his sense of the values of reading. He never has to feign interest because it never occurs to him to be anything but genuine. He so enjoys experiences in reading that he is anxious to lead others to similar pleasures.

In the second place, a good guide in the world of children's books seeks out all significant possibilities for new explorations. While he thoroughly enjoys leading the young down the main-traveled roads of the literary heritage, he keeps his eyes open for exciting new developments. He is alert to fresh fields of literary endeavor. He is willing to follow a new author into unexplored territory. He glories in original accomplishments in pioneering ventures in writing for boys and girls. At the same time that the good guide is using the highways of literature for the main course of the journey, he is also alert to capitalize on sallies and short trips into byways that promise new views and vistas for those under his guidance.

The good guide, furthermore, provides his services with no obligation of acceptance on the part of those for whom he is the leader. He assumes his obligation to point up the potentialities of each landmark and interesting literary work but, at the same time, he does not attempt to foist his ideas of worth and merit on children. He believes, rather, that the individuals must take from the guidance given what is most desirable or beneficial to

them. He avoids forcing the attention of young readers on his preferences. He views his job as that of orientor and surveyor so that the young ones can make choices with critical comprehensions of the selections available to them.

The good guide shares his valuable knowledge of the world of children's books generously. While he does not flaunt his erudition arrogantly, for the sake of impressing his young charges with his learning, he does use what he knows about children's books to whet their interests in further reading. He knows other books to recommend when the child says that he has enjoyed a particular title. He knows sources to which to turn with a child who is seeking books on particular topics or subjects. He collects stories about authors and illustrators that help the makers of children's books come alive for young readers. In other words, the good guide puts his knowledge to work in such ways that the one being guided seeks to learn more from the guide, turns to the guide for sharing the knowledge which he possesses, and thus discovers the joy of being knowledgeable in the field of litterature for children.

Yet another distinguishing characteristic of the good guide is that he varies his services from individual to individual and group to group. He does not develop a series of cliches, patent responses, and mechanical techniques. Rather, he studies and sizes up his present associates and ministers to their purposes and concerns. He does not expect all individuals or groups to respond to the same materials. He knows that he must have at his finger-tips information for the unusual as well as the usual child. He further recognizes that because of differences in backgrounds and abilities and experiences he must be prepared for diversity in tastes and expectations rather than uniformity. So he gauges his guidance to what seems to be right for the present members of his group and glories in the opportunity to be creative in his approaches and appeals to them. He trusts his services most when he senses the uniqueness of the children with whom he is currently working.

Finally, the good guide in literature is the one who whets children's enthusiasm for further exploration and further guide service. He is the one who helps young readers to feel that they are capable of doing some exploring on their own. He encourages them to seek out experiences in literature in which they can guide themselves. But simultaneously he helps them to realize that other guides may at times be beneficial. By his own actions in the guidance role he teaches them how to recognize a reliable guide when they meet him and how to use his services most profitably.

The World of Books in Schools

Whatever the grade level or the content area, children and youth have a right to expect their teachers to guide them expertly into the world of books. From nursery school and kindergarten through senior-high-school science, mathematics, or industrial arts, the learner should be able to turn to his teachers for guidance in reading beyond the textbook materials in use.

The learner will want guide service to fiction—fiction that entertains him, that whiles away the hour, that deepens his sensitivity to persons, to cultures, to human values. In the best modern schools it is possible for children and youth to peruse the great wealth of historical fiction, regional fiction, intergroup fiction, fiction of life in other lands, love and family stories, animal tales, sports stories, and, now, science fiction. The literature is available, waiting for teachers who will discover its potentials for classroom use. Will the physical-education teacher develop a library of sports stories for his students to enjoy? Will the science teacher see opportunities that science fiction may afford him? Will the teacher of social studies encourage children to live intimately in other times and other places through identification with characters in appealing stories? Will the kindergarten teacher have a library corner where five-year-olds can browse and begin to read picture-story books? If school staffs believe that children's fiction can contribute constructively to the well-being and welfare of children and youth, then they will work to provide time and facilities for bringing books and pupils together. They will develop classroom libraries that lure young readers into adventuring with a great variety of fiction, both realistic and fanciful.

But the world of children's books today is more than fiction. Many reputable publishers are working to provide children with significant informational literature also. They know that the active minds of children and youth are questing for knowledge and information and ideas about the physical, the natural, the social world in which they live. So from the presses come, in encouraging quantities, biographies of the great and near-great, books about animals, trees, stones, and flowers, expositions concerning water, weather, volcanoes, atomic energy, electronics. There are well-written informational books about peoples—Indians, Eskimos, Polynesians; about countries—Norway, Israel, Japan; about careers —engineers, painters, inventors; about public services—water supply, transportation, communication. There is enticing informational material about hobbies—cooking, sewing, magic; about play-group games, sports, stunts; about creative activities—ballet, wood-working, ceramics, weaving. There are fine informational books about religion, about occupations, about physiology, about mathematics, about man and mankind.

Again, the informational literature is here, ready to be tapped by creative teachers who recognize its values in the education of children and youth. Sometimes this informational literature leads learners to new ventures; sometimes it deepens their interests in knowledge. Sometimes it relates specifically to on-going curriculum activities; sometimes it expands the horizons of the students beyond the immediate classroom environment. For every teacher this wealth of informational literature is an educational gold mine if he will but make it available to the children or youth with whom he works, if he will use it in ways that result in a memorable experience of reading.

Through informational literature young readers can experience the joy of learning on one's own. They can discover that literature helps them answer their questions, aids them in being interested persons, and broadens their insights into the meaning of being human. They can feel the satisfaction of being well-informed, truly literate. Through reading they have a touchstone for educating themselves if their teachers keep this touchstone in active use.

In the modern school, surely it is not too much to expect that first the child, then the pre-adolescent, and ultimately the youth has satisfying contacts with all kinds of literature: old and new, fanciful and realistic, fictional and informational, prose and poetry. When such is the case, the individual and the culture must benefit. For the well-read individual, whether he be five or seventy-five, possesses a rich personal resource and is an asset in a democracy. It is, indeed, fine recompense for teaching when one's students catch sight of the joys of exploring reading so that, as Alexander Pope has said, "Hills peep o'er hills and Alps on Alps arise" in the wonderful world of books.

75. MAKING BOOKS COME ALIVE FOR CHILDREN*

Nancy Larrick

WHEN a three-year-old brings you a book to read, don't be surprised if it is about a submarine rescue or a man-made satellite. These are hot subjects today, even with the very young; and adults had better take heed.

If you would make books come alive for a child, I know of no better way to begin than with the child. He *is* alive. His interests and concerns will make the book come to life for him. Oddly enough, many an adult tries to make books come alive for a child by beginning with his own childhood interests. Frequently they lead to a dismal let-down.

Know Today's Children

Today's children are different from the children we remember we were. They have different interests; they are using different words. Indeed, they are living in a different world. A second-grader made this dramatically clear to me when I used the term, "prehistoric times." "Do you mean prehistoric times before television?" he asked.

That stopped me in mid-sentence until I began to think of the shatter-

* From Nancy Larrick, "Making Books Come Alive for Children," *Childhood Education*, XXXVIII, No. 7 (March, 1962), 311–15. Reprinted by permission of the author and the Association for Childhood Education International, 3615 Wisconsin Ave., N.W., Washington 16, D.C.

ing changes in our society since television began a new era.

Mass media bombard the modern home with world news. Technical terms are brought from their old hideout in the laboratory to become the language of the general public, including children. Nowadays children's interests are often as adult as their vocabulary. If you have any doubts, check the toy counter of the nearest five-and-ten. You will see space ships and submarines but few teddy bears and baby dolls. The little red wagon has almost faded away.

Librarians report growing demand for children's books about outer space and underwater exploration. Some first-graders are rejecting cowboy stories as too babyish. Instead, they are asking for books about electricity and radiation. Fifth- and sixth-graders often turn to adult books as more appealing than those written for young readers. *The Diary of Anne Frank* and *Thirty Seconds over Tokyo* are favorites with this age level.

Television producers receive quantities of juvenile fan mail about programs created for adults. Apparently children and their parents have the same reading interests and are viewing the same TV programs. Many of these deal with the conflicts and confusions of what we have been calling the adult world. It is small wonder, then, that today's child turns to books with different expectations from the child of 1930 or even of 1950. Through television, in particular, a child is likely to establish certain habits which affect his approach to books. For one thing, he is used to making a choice. His TV set permits him to select the program he will view. If one channel does not please him he switches to another, much as he swaps one comic book for another. He is used to being part of the adult world, watching the same television programs with his parents and exchanging views on an equal basis.

By Way of Contrast

Imagine a child coming from this kind of world into the traditional classroom. He reads, "Oh! Oh! See. See. Come. Come," in a book selected for him. He meets with a group, also selected for him, to hear others read the same colorless words at a pace that is not his own. And, as one youngster put it, "We read and read, but nothing ever happens in the story."

But something may be happening in the mind and heart of the child himself. He may be deciding that reading is deadly dull and therefore not for him. He may be finding out that this kind of book talks down to him ("Come, children," says Mother. "Come."), while television makes a man out of him, giving him the same straight talk that it gives his parents.

Further, he may rebel against the slow pace of the three-group lock step that means *read, listen, and wait.* He may not register his protest verbally. But, TV-trained as he is, he may tune out that which is not appealing. Day-

dreaming is one way to do it. Wriggling and squirming and interrupting are other ways.

Let Him Choose the Books

When a child is given the opportunity to choose the book he will read, he begins to see things in a different light. This is what he has done all his life with television. It is the procedure approved by the big, exciting grown-up world outside of school.

If each child is to have a choice, there must be many books from which to select: easy books for the slow reader; more advanced books for the better reader; baseball books; fairy tales; biographies; books about jet planes and outer space, about the moon and deep-sea diving. There must be fiction and non-fiction, poetry and prose.

Unless a child has been used to selecting books for himself, he will need some guidance. He may resent guidance of the "see-see-read-read" variety. But he will welcome guidance that is as straightforward as a newscaster's report.

The third-grader who follows the world series is a natural for *How Baseball Began in Brooklyn,*[1] by LeGrand. His sister, a horse fan, will thank you for a steer to *Misty of Chincoteague,*[2] by Marguerite Henry or *Little Vic,*[3] by Doris Gates. Space enthusiasts of all ages will be eager to know about *You Will Go to the Moon,*[4] by Mae and Ira Freeman; *A Book of Satellites for You,*[5] by Franklyn Branley; and that delightful bit of spoofing, *Miss Pickerell Goes to Mars,*[6] by Ellen MacGregor.

A book comes alive when it is in the hands of an interested reader. When an interest is already astir in the child, all you have to do is help him find the book which will kindle that interest further. That is the easiest kind of guidance.

To make it even simpler, there are numerous book lists which group favorite children's books by subject and age level. By using the index in the book list and reading the annotations, you have some guidelines by which to aid children in selecting books. Soon fourth- and fifth-graders will be consulting the same book lists when they choose books. Today's children like self-service, even in books.

Make the Introduction Alive and Personal

Beyond this, it is important to introduce children to new interests and to open new vistas which will lead to books. This is where the fun begins—the challenge, if you will—for a child's adventures into new kinds of books and new kinds of subjects depend in large part on the introduction he gets from adults.

A printed list of recommended books won't do it. Certainly, required reading selected by adults won't do it—not today, when children are accustomed to the spoken word of radio and television, to hearing enthusiastic, firsthand reports of world affairs and commercial products.

Take a tip from TV and make your introduction of a new book just as vital, just as personal. First read the book yourself; reread it if there's been a time lapse, letting yourself bask in its humor or pathos or whimsy.

Then while you are still aglow with it, read a chapter or two to children. Your delight in the book will show in the way you read it, and children will sense your enthusiasm. Soon they will want to be a part of it and ask for more.

Some of the real gems of children's literature need this kind of read-aloud introduction. Tell a ten-year-old that *Charlotte's Web,*[7] by E. B. White, is about a talking spider, and he may shy away. But read aloud part of that remarkable book, and Charlotte will have another devotee. The interest and sympathy in your voice and the magic of Charlotte's personality will do the trick.

The Borrowers,[8] by Mary Norton, and *Half Magic,*[9] by Edward Eager, profit from the same kind of introduction. Indeed, any book does. Read aloud a few chapters of a book you have already read and are sold on, and a listener's indifference is likely to vanish.

This is true for poetry, too. But you will have to read and reread before you meet your audience. The misreading of poetry can be as discordant as a soloist off key, and a dull listless voice will deaden interest from the start.

If your children have not been reading poetry, begin with something light, even humorous. Fourth- and fifth-graders love "The Tale of Custard the Dragon," by Ogden Nash. *The Golden Treasury of Poetry,*[10] selected by Louis Untermeyer, and *Time for Poetry,*[11] edited by May Hill Arbuthnot, are excellent collections of poetry for all ages. *Poems To Read to the Very Young,*[12] selected by Josette Frank, is just right for preschoolers.

Remember, too, that children today are used to seeing as well as hearing, so share the pictures as you read. In *Charlotte's Web,* Garth Williams' pictures of Wilbur the pig are irresistible. Even the most hard-bitten fifth-grade missile expert will soften before Wilbur's contented smile as he stands under Charlotte's web.

When you read *I had a little . . .*[13], by Norma Levarie, hold the pages so children can see as you read. The drawings are as gay as the text with suspense at the turn of every page. First- and second-graders, by the way, will soon be guessing what the next rhyming surprise will be.

Young and Old Alike

Read *I had a little . . .* the next time you have guests to dinner, and I think you will find they are as charmed as the children. Or read a chapter from *Charlotte's Web* to some of your contemporaries, and watch the reaction. These books have a quality that appeals to young and old alike. They have a subtlety, a sophistication if you wish, that lifts them above any grade-level label.

Watch for this as you search for books to introduce to today's children. Before you bring a book to a class, give it the read-aloud test. If it flows rhythmically to your adult ears, the chances are it will appeal to readers attune to adult oral-language media. If it speaks in the straightforward manner accorded grownups, children will be pleased.

If you are intrigued by the information in a book of nonfiction or glowing with satisfaction over a book of fiction, you can be sure that most children will do likewise.

It's up to you!

REFERENCES

1. LeGrand. *How Baseball Began in Brooklyn* (Nashville, Tenn.: Abingdon Press, 1958).
2. Marguerite Henry. *Misty of Chincoteague* (Chicago: Rand McNally & Co., 1947).
3. Doris Gates. *Little Vic* (New York: Viking Press, Inc., 1951).
4. Mae and Ira Freeman. *You Will Go to the Moon* (New York: Random House, Inc., 1959).
5. Franklyn Branley. *A Book of Satellites for You* (New York: Thomas Y. Crowell Co., 1959).
6. Ellen MacGregor. *Miss Pickerell Goes to Mars* (New York: Whittlesey House, 1951).
7. E. B. White. *Charlotte's Web* (New York: Harper & Bros., 1952).
8. Mary Norton. *The Borrowers* (New York: Harcourt, Brace & Co., Inc., 1953).
9. Edward Eager. *Half Magic* (New York: Harcourt, Brace & Co., Inc., 1954).
10. Louis Untermeyer. *The Golden Treasury of Poetry* (New York: Golden Press, 1959).
11. May Hill Arbuthnot. *Time for Poetry* (Chicago: Scott, Foresman & Co., 1952).
12. Josette Frank. *Poems To Read to the Very Young* (New York: Random House, Inc., 1961).
13. Norma Levarie. *I had a little . . .* New York: Random House, Inc., 1961).

76. STIMULATE READING . . . WITH READING

"JUST FOR FUN"*

Edith F. Miller

MY pupils don't read unless they have to."

"Don't children read for enjoyment any more?"

"How can I get my sixth-graders to read more?"

Many teachers ask these and similar questions, for it is true that today numerous organized outside activities, television and a heavy reading-for-information load in the school curriculum all limit the time spent in reading "just for fun." But it is an important part of the teacher's job to give children a background of fine literature and to help make recreational reading a vital part of their lives.

You might begin by reading to the children for about ten minutes daily, "stealing" the time, if necessary, from the period allotted to reading or language. Choose short selections of varied kinds. Poems, nonsense jingles, descriptive passages, editorials, the opening chapter of a good book—the possibilities are endless. The habit of listening is a good habit to develop in itself.

At one time I compiled a children's anthology of the class's favorite poetry. I made a cover entitled "Poems We

* From Edith F. Miller, "Stimulate Reading with Reading 'Just for Fun,'" *Grade Teacher,* LXXIX, No. 8 (April, 1962), 70, 134–35. Reprinted by permission of the author and Teachers Publishing Corporation, Darien, Conn.

Love" and typed the poems and illustrated them with tiny pictures cut from greeting cards and magazines. When I read to my next year's class from that anthology, they asked to add their own favorites to the book.

Another class liked some of the poems, but instead of making anthologies they became interested in choral speaking. The duplicated copies of their favorites were used as reading material for choral speaking.

Still another class became interested in the poems I read and in some poetry broadsides which I had purchased and displayed. Their interest led me to make some poetry broadsides of my own, using magazine illustrations and large lettering. I copied lines of poetry appropriate to the season and poetry about stars in which we were interested at the time. The boys and girls became interested in making broadsides of their own; each selected a few lines to illustrate with his own drawings.

Perhaps book reports will be the thing that will capture interest. I usually begin by giving some oral reports myself —sometimes I read some exciting parts, sometimes I show and explain some pictures, sometimes I tell about the author or tell how the book came to be written. The children are encouraged to give interesting oral reports of the books they have read. We use a three-minute egg timer to limit the length of each report and the children love turning it!

Often we write book reports during class time. A date is set by which each child will have completely read a book. Books are brought to school so they will be on hand only in case of difficulty in spelling names of people or places. We agree together on the directions for writing that particular report. The directions might be:

"Describe the principal characters in the story."

"Tell about the funniest or the saddest part."

"Tell why you would recommend this book."

"Describe the places where most of the action takes place."

I read the children many book reviews from newspapers and magazines so that they may see the quality and scope of published reviews. The boys and girls will enjoy writing reviews to be considered for publication in a class or school newspaper or magazine. One sixth grade delighted in writing short book reviews when they knew that their work would be typed and stapled into a booklet to be placed in the children's room of the public library and would thus be available for all the children in town to read. Other classes have enjoyed writing their reviews on filing cards to be placed under different headings—Mystery, Adventure, Biography—for use in their own classroom. Short personal comments on filing cards ("I thought this was a little hard, but if you like to read about airplanes you will enjoy it.") gave other children some idea of the difficulty of the books.

A reading nook proved popular in one class. We secured a large screen which we covered with heavy unbleached muslin. We screened off a small corner of our classroom and used masking tape to fasten material relating to books on the screen. A rug and two small rockers were brought in. There was room on the windowsill for a few books to be placed between bookends. The children loved their reading nook!

The children may choose to dramatize a well-known book. Everyone will discuss the story, decide on scenes, and divide into groups to dramatize the scenes informally. One or two practice periods may be needed before the meeting day when the scenes are presented. The children may bring in simple costumes or properties if desired, or they may use things already on hand—one boy used our dust-brush when he was Tom Sawyer painting the fence; a yardstick has played the role of cane, sword, or wand.

First attempts at dramatization are often very discouraging if the pupils have had little lower-grade experience with it. They may use distorted voices to show that they are acting or they may stand stiffly and not act at all. Using an easy reader for class reading and interpretation may help. At first the children may read the conversation from the books and act out their parts with books in hand. Making up additional dialogue to fit in where needed will help in interpretation. Dramatizing informally the stories in each reading group will also be a help. Children often feel freer when they act out plays they have made up themselves, so original plays based on their social studies help to produce results. I save copies of any plays my previous classes have produced. These furnish good practice material.

Puppet shows are also valuable. The children will do a great deal of reading as they decide on the stories and the scenes to be used, read selections to the rest of the class to get their reaction, dramatize informally, write the script, and practice their parts.

There are also many "incidental" ways of stimulating interest in books. Small signs put up by the teacher saying, "This is a good book for animal lovers" or "No boy should miss this" help to arouse interest in books. Many stories are available on records and playing one now and then stimulates the desire to read the books. A book section on the bulletin board with a constantly changing display of book reviews, riddles about books, library rules, book illustrations, pictures of authors—in fact, anything and everything about books—will get some children sufficiently interested so that they begin to do some reading.

Displaying one or two books on the library table with appropriate models is a sure-fire attraction. For example, a book on Woodland Animals displayed with museum models of red and gray squirrels, or a book about Vikings with the model of a Viking ship is sure to attract the boys and girls.

The teacher's role in arousing interest in books is always an active one. She will be alert to anything new pertaining to children's books—new books in the public library, a just-published book that has made news, a TV adaptation coming up, a live play or movie that she can recommend. She will work with the public library staff, encouraging her pupils to participate in any reading program planned by the library, and taking her class to visit the library. She may see that Book Week is observed in her classroom and in the school. By these and many other means, she will interest many of her pupils in fine literature. But above all, to make her efforts most effective, she herself must really believe that Reading Can Be Fun.

77. A SUMMER'S GROWTH IN READING*

Helen B. Aasen

IT was the last day of school. Sixty-four children walked through the wide doorways into the June sunlight and began their vacation with a book-mark in their hands, a bookmark the teacher had given them as they left fourth grade. The markers were shaped like a key and bore a reminder for the long vacation days ahead: "This key fits any public library. Be sure to use it this summer."

The key was a tangible token of a project I had launched a week earlier.

Time to Read

As a classroom teacher, I have long believed that summer is an excellent time for children to become better readers. The leisurely vacation months give boys and girls a chance to use reading skills they have learned throughout the year in the classroom. Unfortunately, however, many children do not read at all during the summer.

Like other classroom teachers, I know full well what can happen to reading skills when children do not open a book from the time school closes in June till school bells ring again in September. The story of rust-

* From Helen B. Aasen, "A Summer's Growth in Reading," *Elementary School Journal,* LX (November, 1959), 70–74. Reprinted by permission of the author and The University of Chicago Press.

ing skills is told in reading-achievement scores that show a big drop each year in the fall.

And Encouragement to Read

Can this summertime loss be avoided? I have long thought that it might be. In fact, I have felt that, given proper encouragement, children might wind up the season with a gain. Not long ago, when the opportunity presented itself, I put into practice some of my ideas for a summer reading program.

Ninety-six fourth-graders in the Minneapolis public schools took part in the project. The children, most of them from middle-class families, showed wide differences in abilities, interests, and achievement.

The experimental group was made up of sixty-four children: the thirty-one children in Classroom A and the thirty-three children in Classroom B. The average intelligence quotient for pupils in Classroom A was 104.7; for pupils in Classroom B, 108.4. The pupils in these two classes were encouraged to read during their summer vacation.

The thirty-two children in Classroom C made up the control group. The average intelligence quotient for pupils in this classroom was 102. These children were given no stimulation or encouragement whatsoever to turn to books. Nor were they told of the plans for the summer program.

On June 3, the children in all three classrooms were given the Stanford Reading Achievement Test, Form K. My purpose was to determine the reading-achievement level of each child at the start of the experiment.

The special program to stimulate reading in the two experimental classes began on the next day, June 4, and ended on June 12. Throughout that time, every effort was made to encourage the children to read.

Planning with the Children

At our first session, the children were told of the plan. We talked about various kinds of books they might like to read and the importance of selecting books that were not too difficult.

No book reports were to be required. Each child was simply to keep a record of the title of each book, the name of the author, and the number of pages read. Each pupil was given a special form on which to keep his record from June 4 to September 4.

The children themselves suggested the tally of pages: some books are longer than others, they pointed out. They also decided that comic books should not count, since they have more pictures than text.

The children became so interested in the project that we decided to talk about it for a short time each day till school closed.

After the reading-achievement tests had been scored, I had a brief conference with each child in the experimental classes. I told each pupil his grade

level in reading and explained what it meant. This information alone created intense interest in the program and kindled a desire to make gains in reading during the summer.

Titles That Entice

I felt it would help if I suggested books for the children to read. Before recommending titles, I made a survey of reading preferences in the experimental groups. Each child was given a list of sixteen types of books and asked to check his favorites. The list included adventure and mystery stories; humorous stories; fairy tales; biography; poetry; and books about animals, home and school life, boys and girls from other lands, cowboys, science, sports, hobbies, history, religion, music, and art.

The results revealed that these children preferred to read books about adventure and mystery. Their second choice was books about animals, and their third choice was books of humor. Boys and girls were about equally divided in these preferences.

Guided by the responses, I prepared an annotated list of thirty-five books. In choosing titles, I considered the breadth of appeal as well as the literary value of each book. I included a few easy books for the reluctant readers, who may be found in any group. Each child was given a copy of the list, and one day I brought the books to class and reviewed each briefly as I held it up. If a book appealed to a child, he checked it on his list to remind him to read it during the summer.

The school librarian gave us valuable assistance. She helped the children become better acquainted with the library. Under her direction, they learned how to use the card catalogue and how to find books on the shelves. On browsing day, the children paid a special visit to the school library, an excursion they enjoyed thoroughly. Colorful posters had been mounted on the walls. Attractive book jackets brightened the bulletin board. Each table had a tempting display of books specially chosen to stimulate young minds and appeal to varied tastes.

One day a librarian from the closest branch library came to school to talk to the boys and girls, bringing with her many samples of the newest, most attractive, and most interesting children's books from the library shelves. These, she told her audience, were only a sample of the books they could borrow from the library.

A show of hands revealed that two-thirds of the children already had library cards. Application forms were distributed to the other pupils, who needed no urging to fill in the blanks.

A Roving Library

I wanted to overlook no source of good books to which the children could turn during vacation. Each Tuesday, a bookmobile pulled up and parked a short distance from the school. The two classes in the program visited the travelling library. The children were told that the bookmobile would continue its weekly visits throughout the summer. The young visitors were invited to come and borrow from the attractive collection.

Films—Pathway to Books

Our film festival turned out to be a memorable event. Months before, during Children's Book Week, the pupils in Classroom A built a theater to show "films" they had made, films based on their favorite library books. The young film-makers arranged to share their productions with the children in Classroom B. Each pupil showed his own film and told incidents from the book. The showing added to the fund of appealing titles the children were collecting for summer reading.

Parents Were Partners

On the last day of school, letters were sent to the parents, announcing the project. The parents were reminded of the great influence the home has on reading, a fact borne out by research.

What role could the parents play in the project? How could they help their child in the program? "He will need all the encouragement that you can give him," the letter read. "Your interest in your child's reading is valuable. . . . Reading is contagious. . . . Your enjoying of good books will serve as an inspiration to him. Surround him with suitable books for home reading. Go with him to the public library. Let him share his reading with you. Read to your child, and discuss books with him. . . . Your cooperation and interest will be greatly appreciated."

What the Records Showed

On September 4, the summer-reading records of the experimental group were collected. On the same day, forms were distributed to the children in the control group, who were given several days to list their summer reading. The forms could have been given to the children in the control group in June. Had this step been taken, their record of summer reading might have been more reliable. But the forms might have stimulated the children to read and thus curtailed their usefulness as members of the control group.

Actually, there can be no guarantee that the records of either the experimental or the control groups were accurate. It is difficult to obtain accurate records on the amount of free reading children do. Quite likely, some of the entries showed only the approximate number of pages read.

On September 5, the Stanford Reading Achievement Test, Form J, was given to all ninety-six children. Grade equivalents derived from the scores on this test and the test given earlier were compared to note any change in the reading growth of each child. Then the grade equivalents of the children from the experimental group were compared with the corresponding data for the children from the control group.

Gains in Growth

The study produced evidence that a program of voluntary summer reading can be helpful.

The children who took part in the program showed greater growth than the children who did not. The results of the test given on June 3 showed that the average grade equivalent for the experimental group was 5.4. By September 9, the average grade equivalent for this group had increased to 6.1, thus showing a gain of seven months. Had it been possible to stimulate and encourage the experimental group throughout the entire summer, an even greater group gain might have resulted.

The average grade equivalent for the control group was 5.2 on June 3, and this score remained the same as of September 9, thus indicating no group change in reading performance for this period.

A much higher percentage of children from the experimental group showed gains in reading growth, and these children also showed greater average gains. Of the sixty-four children from the stimulated groups, about 68.8 per cent showed gains in reading growth, as against only 37.5 per cent of the thirty-two children in the control group. The average gain of the children who showed gains in the experimental group was one year and one month, as against seven months in the control group.

Twice as many children from the control group showed losses in reading skill, and their average losses were greater. Only 28.1 per cent of the stimulated groups showed losses as against 56.3 per cent of the children in the control group. The average loss in the stimulated groups was three and a half months; the average loss in the other group, five months.

The greatest gain in reading growth was three years and five months. This record was made by a boy from one of the stimulated groups. A girl from the control group showed the greatest loss—one year and four months.

The stimulated groups read considerably more than the children from the control group, who were not stimulated. The control group read 61 per cent of the average number of pages read by the children from the experimental group.

The Pupils Report

The children's own comments on the project are revealing. Many in the experimental group reported that they were finding more pleasure in reading. Several said they had a wider selection of book friends; their leisure reading was more varied. One child reported that she was more word-conscious, that her vocabulary had grown. Another child felt that his understanding of what he read had improved. Most of the children were certain that their speed had increased considerably. And nearly all were finding a new interest and a new joy in reading.

Summertime need not be an interlude when children's reading skills suffer from disuse. Given a well-planned program—and encouragement, cooperation, and guidance by teachers, librarians, and parents—summer can be a season when children's reading skills show vigorous growth.

CHAPTER XIII

MATERIALS FOR THE READING PROGRAM

78. VALUES AND LIMITATIONS OF BASAL READERS*

David K. Stewart

EDUCATORS are beginning to look critically at the graded elementary school. Some doubt its ability to meet the individual differences which are being brought to light by research in child development and in psychology and which are currently exaggerated by increasing enrolments. McGuffey in the 1840's was dealing with a relatively narrow range of abilities, not so narrow as he thought, but still not so wide as that found in today's mass enrolments.

Third-graders are not so much alike as they once seemed to be. All eight-year-olds are not magically attracted to the same book, even if the vocabulary and interest levels are equal. Some highly respected schools have eliminated grade organization. The vast majority of the schools, however, are graded, and they use graded basic readers.

The task of a reading teacher is complex. He must have the ability to organize a class of twenty-five or more individuals into teachable groups. He must organize a school day in such a manner that a number of unrelated subjects can be partially correlated and taught to each of those individuals. He needs a finger-tip knowledge of the concepts and skills that must be carefully taught at each child's readiness level. He must know enough about each child to reach the pupil at the right time with the learning that he is ready to receive. To do these things, the teacher of reading must possess a knowledge of child development equal to that required of the school psychologist. His understanding of

* From David K. Stewart, "Values and Limitations of Basal Readers," in *Materials for Reading,* Supplementary Education Monographs, No. 86, compiled and edited by Helen M. Robinson (December, 1957), pp. 51–56. Reprinted by permission of the author and The University of Chicago Press.

the reading process must also be complete.

The ideal school in which he works will provide secretarial assistance in the preparation of pupil-progress charts, work sheets, tests, and instructional devices. The school principal will be competent to help the occasional "un-ideal" teacher who comes to his school without adequate professional training. The school library and classroom bookshelves will contain all the materials needed for the interests of all the children. The pupils who are in need of special help will be referred to the school psychiatrist. The gifted children will be provided for adequately. The reduction in class range, coupled with reductions in class sizes and improvements in teaching methods, will eliminate all reading problems. There will be no more criticism of the work of the schools, and Johnny will live happily forever after.

It isn't going to happen this way, because there isn't any "forever after." In lieu of a magic wand that will serve as a panacea for all our problems we have to find effective tools of reading instruction that we can afford and can approve.

Various teaching procedures, ranging from the "regimented basic" to the "all-out" experience method, have been attempted. Some have been highly successful; others, dismal failures. Between the extremes in methodology are found the schools that follow the practice of using one or more series of basic readers intelligently. To some extent, these materials, with their accompanying manuals, workbooks, and filmstrips, determine the direction of the program. The manner in which

basal readers are used varies considerably. Some schools use a single basic, some a co-basic, and some a tri-basic approach. Which is the most effective? What is the value of the basal reader? What are its limitations? Are these programs pallid, or are they valid?

A Survey of Current Practices and Problems

The writer conducted a questionnaire survey of instructional practices in reading. This survey, including school systems responsible for the reading instruction of 250,000 children in 107 cities of over 25,000 population in 40 states, gives us some indication of current practices and problems. All the schools are making use of one or more basic reading series.

Ninety per cent of the responding schools are employing a single basic, co-basic, or tri-basic series. More than half of the schools use a single basic reader. Schools using a single basal reader are less critical of the training and preparation of teachers and administrators than are the other schools. Responses indicate that 87 per cent of the schools consider that the skills program contained in the basal reader is adequate.

The survey seems to indicate that the basal reader is the mainstay of the reading program in the 1957 version of the elementary school. Capitalizing on the errors of the twenties and thirties, when all systematized reading instruction was scorned by some schools, the basic reader, a better one, is back. Readers again are bringing stability and continuity to programs once described as haphazard, unplanned, and catch-as-catch-can.

In some cases it is suspected that the stability provided by the basal reader has been carried to an extreme, with the "basic" serving as a limitation rather than as a guide. The resultant loss of freedom and the stifling of the initiative of teachers and of children must be considered with alarm. The desirable value of continuity is counteracted by the inability of pupils to conform to predetermined instructional patterns. Inadequately trained teachers, doing their planning by fits and starts, are pulled along by the basic program, but the skills program of the "basic" can receive so much attention that the purpose of learning is lost in the process.

Yet our most effective tool is the properly used basic reading series. Highly trained educators and research personnel in the employ of the nation's leading publishers have developed and recorded patterns of reading instruction that promise the most effective results. There are guides for teachers which provide logically organized teaching techniques. The sequence of presentation of the skills program is not precisely parallel in any two of the popular reading series, but all agree upon objectives and purposes. Each would prove effective if used competently.

Administrative Responsibility and the Basal Reader

Although we would like to think that *we* are making the decisions, curriculum trends and instructional practices often are determined by price rather than by principle. Rising tax rates require us to economize in the purchase of materials, but the needs of children demand that we make effective use of what we have. Unfortunately many excellent teachers are not well enough acquainted with the materials in their hands.

The viewpoint expressed in this paper is that of one administrator, working in the public schools and responsible to parents and to a board of education. That basal readers produce desirable outcomes is an established fact. That there are problems inherent in their use has also been pointed out by every "expert" in the field.

There are more self-styled "reading experts" per square mile than we can use. People who do not consider themselves competent to criticize the plumber or the electrician think that they know every facet of the reading process. Some of our critics deserve an audience, but the picture is not always clear even to those of us who are on the inside. Nila Smith's statement regarding basal readers is significant:

The great majority of our public schools undoubtedly are not yet ready to dispense with a basal reader. The techniques of teaching reading through functional activities must undergo further development and refinement; new materials must be prepared; administrative difficulties must be overcome; and teachers must be better trained.[1]

Smith predicted that when the difficulties mentioned have been dealt with (in fifteen or fifty years), the basal

[1] Nila Banton Smith, *American Reading Instruction* (Morristown, New Jersey: Silver Burdett Co., 1934), p. 266.

reader will no longer be necessary. Her prediction was made in 1934, twenty-three years ago. The children now in our classrooms must be taught to read. While we are waiting for Smith's prediction to come true, we shall continue to use basal readers. "Forever after" is not here yet; maybe it isn't coming.

Listing the limitations of the basal readers as they are used in most schools is a relatively simple task. Our greatest single problem is in the area of personnel qualification. With competent personnel working at the elementary, secondary, and university levels and with sufficient funds to allow them time, material, and incentive for their work, we shall continue to improve the instructional tools and methods used in reading. Teacher-preparation levels are improving, and certification requirements are moving toward the Master's degree. Even with this steady improvement in teacher training, our schools are having to provide periods of internship.

Experienced teachers may profit from in-service training to as great an extent as do beginners. The major share of such a program for elementary-school teachers will be concerned with the improvement of reading instruction. The most important function of the reading supervisor has become the establishment of a program of in-service training for administrators and classroom teachers. The implementation of such a program is the responsibility of each school administrator. The guidebook of the basal reading series adopted for use in each school should serve as the textbook for the in-service training program in reading. The basic series furnishes a program of systematic, sequential instruction in the skills of reading.

Beginning teachers usually have acquired a knowledge of theory; most are able to generalize about the teaching of reading. The task of in-service training is to provide an understanding of the specifics. Supervisors and administrators in the schools must teach teachers to use reading tools effectively. Each teacher must acquire a knowledge of the skills presented at the levels above and below his own indicated area of responsibility. Such a knowledge is possible when a basic reading program is employed. With such knowledge a teacher is better equipped to provide for children's individual problems; without it he may not even be aware of their presence. When a teacher understands the basic reader, when he uses and comprehends the material available in his "basic manual," when he has the help he deserves from the other professional staff members in his school, then, and only then, can he teach effectively. He can know where his children are only if he knows where they have been and where they are going. Herein is found the greatest value of the systematic basal reading program.

Single Basic or Multi-Basic?

The use of a single basic reader will serve the purpose of sequential presentation better than using two or several series. Thought-provoking criticisms of the use of a single basic reader have come from classroom teachers. The problem of "the other group" is frequently advanced. Teachers contend that the story is not new to Group B if it has been read by Group A and that interest is lost. It is difficult to develop interpretation skills with a group that has already heard the lesson. Perceiving relationships, anticipating outcomes, and drawing inferences are skills that are taught best with fresh materials.

A room organization is suggested that provides a "reading corner," where children in the reading circle are somewhat isolated. A bookcase, a low folding screen, or the teacher's desk can be utilized to provide such an arrangement. It may be that school designers will one day find time to consider this problem. It is also possible that children and teachers can profit from the practice of keeping their voices at low volume. The retelling of a story may not be so insurmountable a problem as we sometimes consider it to be. Most stories are improved by a second hearing. But the greatest value in repetition is for the teacher; he probably does a much better job with each successive use of the material.

To avoid the problem of children overhearing a lesson before they should, some schools employ a different basic series for each group within the classroom. Such a procedure complicates the task of the teacher by requiring him to become familiar with each of the programs. In addition, the use of more than one "basic" in a classroom tends to create inflexible grouping. Children moving from one series to another encounter different vocabularies and different skill levels. Changes from one group to another can create gaps in the skill sequence. These same problems occur when children change groups within a single

series, but teachers with a well-defined skills program in mind can concentrate on the children's needs. A teacher should be able to direct his attention to the next skill rather than merely to the next page or the next book.

That a single basic reading program is *the* way is undoubtedly open to question. There is doubt of its necessity in schools where all teachers are fully qualified to plan and present a complete program. Schools that have written their own reading guides and have tested and proved their methods can manage quite well without a basal series. Schools that use a paperback phonics workbook in conjunction with one of the basal series (and describe this organization as a "co-basic program") are sorely in need of a single "basic."

There are teachers in every school system who have no need of a reading series. They could teach effectively with any kind of reading matter. They know the skills program so well that they are aware of children's difficulties before they look at test results. Yet these are the teachers who consistently like the "basics," who use them and appreciate them the most.

Readers Need Real Books

A single basic program does not preclude the use of supplementary materials. The reading of stories and books of all kinds, including other basal readers, is an intrinsic part of every "basic." Such materials are recommended for enrichment activities, further practice, remedial work, and for sheer enjoyment. To suggest that basal readers limit the learner to the stories contained therein is to exhibit a lack of understanding of their content.

Another important limitation that must be considered along with a discussion of the basal reader is the lack of support given the reading teacher by planners of the library budget. Such lack of support may be due to insufficient funds, or it may be the result of limited understanding. Teachers of reading need books. Books of all types must be available as the need for them is indicated in the basic manual or in the opinion of the teacher. After reading skills have been taught, it follows that they should be applied. The teachers' manuals for the basic series provide an excellent buyer's guide for the school librarian.

The availability and use of an adequate book collection will offset another of the limitations charged against the basal reader: the tendency for teachers to consider "reading" as an end in itself, rather than as a means of acquiring further learning. It is a lack of understanding of this concept that causes us to rush to the defense of the content of our reading materials. There is no reason to defend little Mabel's moronic tendency to repeat herself as she chases her puppy around the table for six pages of the pre-primer. What she is doing is morally acceptable in any society. The children reading the story actually laugh when Mabel knocks over the goldfish bowl. This interest is usually motivated by the teacher to a greater extent than by the story, but the source of the motivation is not too important. We are teaching skills: auditory perception; visual scrutiny; recognition of short vowels, soft consonants, and similes; drawing inferences; and many more. We don't teach them all the same day or the same year. We are not haphazard about our planning, though; we have a pattern to follow, and we are able to follow it because we have the tools we need.

We must remember: the basal reader is merely a tool. The carpenter has a tool that he calls a hammer. He uses it when he builds a house. If he is skilled in its use, he will build a strong house. Hammers are used to build ordinary houses and extra-special houses. Strong, fast carpenters do their work with the same kinds of hammers used by smaller, slower carpenters; both kinds of carpenters build houses. Carpenters never live in hammers. Pupils cannot live in basic readers.

The basal reader approach to the teaching of reading is the surest thing we have. It is not the only way. It is not a method that is designed to exclude other methods. The worst that can be said about basal readers is that we have not sufficiently explored their possibilities. At best, they are only tools of instruction. Teachers, principals, reading specialists, and all who are concerned with the reading process will continue to determine their effectiveness.

Indications

The best series has not yet been published, but it is good business for the publishers to continue to try for our approval. They have given us better teachers' manuals and improved reading materials for pupils. Even the most acute cases of hyperanxiety, found usually among parents and among professors in liberal arts colleges, would be soothed if they knew how carefully our reading materials are prepared for publication. It is probable that every comma has been measured by at least six doctors of philosophy. The publishers are even providing specialists who go out into the schools to help teachers use their materials effectively. Some publishers hold conference-workshops designed to help supervisors and administrators. The publishers may have merely mercenary motives, or they may be combining a need for capital gain with a desire to serve our educational system. Whatever the motive, the result is obvious: children are learning to read. The schools have more materials available in the reading field than can be found in any other subject area. We may eventually accept the proposition that reading is a part of the larger area of communication skills. Such a concept is certain to change our perspective regarding the teaching of reading

and writing and even spelling. It is entirely possible that spelling is already included and adequately provided for by a well-organized reading program.

The values and limitations ascribed to the basal reader really constitute a commentary on schools and teachers. The way in which we use what we have will continue to determine our effectiveness as educators. As long as we are making only partial use of the tools that the taxpayers purchase for our use, we shall not reach capacity achievement levels. Many of our schools need to examine their materials of instruction more carefully.

Concluding Statement

The basal reader will be with us a long time. It could be that "forever after" will really come, that television will actually replace the teacher. But until and unless these things happen, teachers must continue to be supplied by better basal readers.

79. THE PURPOSES OF WORKBOOKS AND TEACHERS' GUIDES*

Martha Thompson

THEY didn't just happen. We realize this when we look at the open pages of a complete series of reading workbooks and teachers' guides which are used in our schools today. What refinement has taken place in these tools, which enable teachers to guide boys and girls to successful experiences in understanding the printed page!

How Workbooks Developed

The child of yesteryear used a slate on which to practice the learnings that his teacher thought basic to his reading program. Today's child moves from reading level to reading level with the aid of scientifically planned workbooks. Between the time of the slate and today's workbook, there came a period of worksheets that were planned by the teacher to accompany the reading stories of the textbook in use at the particular grade level. Planning and duplicating the worksheet took much of the teacher's time and energy. Often the children were unable to read that

which they saw before them. The inability to read the assignment might have been due to the teacher's lack of knowledge of worksheet preparation. The vocabulary in the lesson may have been unrelated to that of the reader. The print may have been too light, or the teacher's printing may not have even resembled the type on the printed page. Sometimes teachers used cursive writing instead of manuscript, and then the children were really lost. Beyond all of this, perhaps the teacher thought of only two or three basic skills that were being taught in reading and therefore prepared work sheets that were much the same day after day. Materials were wasted; the teacher's and the pupils' time was wasted; and learning moved at a slow pace compared with the potential rate of development.

Two teaching aids were developed to upgrade the program. Duplicating machines appeared and brought results—if the teacher was not in too big a hurry or too tired to produce master sheets which were definitely related to the reading text and to the child's and the group's needs and, most important of all, which provided for developmental growth in basic skills and abilities. Then too, workbooks appeared, but they were unrelated to the reading textbook and therefore failed to con-

* From Martha Thompson, "The Purposes of Workbooks and Teachers' Guides," in *Materials for Reading,* Supplementary Education Monographs, No. 86, compiled and edited by Helen M. Robinson (December, 1957), pp. 71–74. Reprinted by permission of the author and The University of Chicago Press.

tribute to the growth potential which was awaiting development.

Modern Workbooks

The modern teacher knows, just as the teacher of yesteryear knew, that children need an opportunity to extend their basic learnings through practice. Today's teacher knows that the workbook which the child uses with his basic textbook is planned by skilled educators who have the knowledge of how best to develop specific skills and abilities from level to level in a sequential and systematic pattern of growth. The teacher knows that this "doing book" parallels the reader, complements it, and adds a variety of extending and enriching experiences. He knows, too, that there are workbooks which are textbooks in themselves (such as pre-reading workbooks for developing readiness) and review workbooks (such as those for use between the elementary and the junior high school grades). As the teacher is a member of a staff of instructors in reading, he takes in the entire "doing" program in order to help the child at his own level of learning. The teacher knows best the grade levels below and above his own grade. He realizes that workbooks should be used at every level to build toward independence.

A step-by-step procedure for using workbooks might be as follows: (1) The teacher works with the group, from the reading of the directions to the doing of the exercises, checking for and correcting any misunderstandings. (2) Without pencils, the teacher and the group work through the workbook page. The teacher then releases the children to print or write and finally evaluates, with each pupil, his strengths and his weaknesses. (3) The teacher and group, without pencils, work halfway through a page together, and the pupils are then released to work the entire page to the point of completion and correction. (4) The teacher and group work one sample together, and then each pupil works alone. (5) The children interpret to the teacher what they are to do, and they go on from there independently until the results are checked by the teacher. This procedure calls for teacher-pupil planning, as well as the use of class time to develop the plans and to evaluate the outcomes.

The workbook can be used as a diagnostic tool. As the teacher works with the children in evaluating (finding their errors and correcting them), he can list, on that particular page in his own workbook, the names of the pupils who will need more guidance when the basic skill is reviewed. If the workbook carries an index of basic skills, the child's name can be recorded on the very page presenting the same skill. (This is an excellent way to account for absentees and to make sure that they receive the lessons for developing skills.) Because they mark their own workbook pages, the children, too, can see where they are in error and can correct the mistakes immediately. Won't they cheat? No child cheats when the atmosphere of the classroom is conducive to honesty and when he understands the purpose of the lesson.

The workbook is used for learning and not as a grading device. To grade workbook pages alerts the child to look for a grade instead of realizing the value of the lesson. Teachers who trudge home with shopping bags full of workbooks or stay long hours after school to grade or even to mark errors in workbooks are missing the real advantage of the use of a modern tool of education.

At teacher-parent conferences, workbooks may be used to indicate to the parents where the child's strengths and weaknesses are. The parents will be pleased to see successful pages, for, if the child is working at his ability level, such pages will be numerous. Parents will be pleased to see errors corrected because they will know the child has seen his mistakes and learned from them. Parents will find out that today's workbooks are planned not to keep the child quiet by merely keeping him busy but to increase his ability to read through purposeful activities.

The Teacher's Guide

The guide for today's workbook and today's reader is the teacher's guidebook. It, too, has been improved through a series of changes. The first teacher's guide was probably the teacher's own plan of how to teach the reading lesson of the day. Then the author of the reading book probably thought that some teachers were missing the point, and he decided to tell them a little bit about how he would like to have his book used. Today's guidebook (thank goodness, it is no longer called a "manual") really does what it says! It guides the teacher so that teacher and pupils have successful experiences when using the reading books and the workbooks. Good guidebooks develop master teachers, who, through creative and thorough teaching, develop pupils who read up to, and beyond, their mental abilities.

A good guidebook reviews for the teacher the psychological development of the child who will be using the reader at a particular level. It requires the instructor to think of the mental, physical, and emotional development of the child in relation to the stories which are to be read and enjoyed while basic skills and abilities are being taught. The philosophy of the author of the particular series of books is presented, along with the objectives or goals to be reached. A basic or fundamental plan for developing and enriching the skills which are to be achieved is found in the guide. It may be a three-step or a four-step plan, but it has been established upon scientific findings to produce results.

Bibliographies have been added, listing titles of (1) supplementary readers which present stories related to those in the particular reader being used, (2) library books which are also related, (3) reference books, and (4) books for the teacher's own development. Lists of films and records are suggested to add to the extension and enrichment of the child's outside-the-book experiences. An index of the basic skills and abilities has been mentioned previously in connection with the workbook. Such a list is found again in the guidebook, and indications of the appropriate pages of the reader and workbook save the time of the teacher in planning for individual and group needs.

Additional assistance for teachers of

the upper elementary grades may be found in an appendix, which lists exercises for constructive help. Suggestions for charts and record cards are made in the guidebook. Tests, to find out at what level a child is reading before beginning to work with him and then to find out how far he has come, are printed for duplication. A teacher who avoids the guidebook is like the cook who shuns the new, easy, efficient ways to arrive at a dish "fit to set before the king"; or the businessman who fails to read the bulletins which come in the mail to tell him how to produce better products with less waste of time, energy, and materials; or the doctor who stacks his medical journals on the side of his desk and misses the new and better ways to help his patients. Both the newcomer to the teaching profession and the teacher of experience need to know the contents of the guidebook peculiar to their respective grade levels and, to assure a stronger school-wide program, those of the complete series as well.

Guidebooks must be used properly and faithfully, in sequence, if the program is to be successful. The teacher should always use them in planning the unit and then in planning the daily lesson. Day-to-day planning, month-to-month building, and year-to-year achievement will help boys and girls to acquire security through successful experiences assured by their strength in skills which have been developed by teacher after teacher. The teacher who is found using the guide is to be praised.

The guidebook, since it includes questions which arouse the children to think constructively and which set their imaginations on fire, is helping future citizens to share and compare in discussions that will lay the foundations for tomorrow's thinking adults. The teacher should be careful to state the questions exactly as they appear in the guide to insure responses which go beyond the usual replies to factual questions. Also, enough time should be allowed to let the children really express their feelings. Too often we rush over this wonderful opportunity to share and compare because we or someone else thinks we are wasting time.

Teachers, especially those who are experienced, should feel that, even when using the guidebooks, they can add thir own ideas and use their own initiative in their work with individuals and groups. As long as the results of the teaching contribute to the growth of the child's ability to read, there can be no complaint. Child, classroom, and total school behavior can be improved by *how* reading is taught and *what* reading is done.

Concluding Statement

No, workbooks and guidebooks didn't just happen, and they shouldn't just happen to be chosen for use by the children whom we instruct in our classrooms of today. A good reading program should mean careful selection of guidebooks, readers, and workbooks to insure the development of basic skills and abilities so that our boys and girls may continue to thrill to the printed page.

80. MATERIALS FOR INDIVIDUALIZED READING*

Patrick J. Groff

THE plan for individualized reading has been described elsewhere in some detail. Very briefly, this method of teaching reading provides for the individual reading needs and interests of the child as is impossible under methods that teach the child as a member of a group. It allows the child to learn to read at the rate that is commensurate with his own native abilities, level of development, and interests rather than at a rate set by a graded series of reading textbooks and their accompanying teacher's manuals. Each child's progress in learning to read is judged in relation to his personal capacities rather than against some hypothetical average. No bright child is hampered by having to keep to the learning pace of less able classmates. No dull child is forced to learn at a speed which he finds uncomfortable at best and frustratingly impossible at worst. No invidious comparisons are drawn between the reading abilities of individual children. Each child is, therefore, to a great measure released from undue pressure, monotony, frustration, boredom, tension, emotional blocking, and most important of all, from situations that develop within him undesirable attitudes toward reading.

After the individual child is able to recognize the small number of sight words necessary to begin reading pre-primers and very simple trade books (library books), he, thereafter, is given the opportunity to select which books or other reading materials he would like to read. The teacher's role is to act as a combination counselor-librarian-reading instructor. He provides large numbers of books he knows the child can read, helps guide the child in his selection of these (the child progressively develops his own powers of self-selection to the point where such guidance becomes increasingly unnecessary), and gives the necessary instruction in word recognition and other reading skills. The teacher meets with the child in individual conferences, and upon occasion in small groups, to provide this help.

The atmosphere of an individualized reading classroom is one of mutual helpfulness. Almost every child at some time can become an informal teacher and help another find a good, readable book or to recognize an unfamiliar word. Reports of teachers using the method suggest that everyone involved enjoys it—that is, the children, the teachers, and the parents. The children like it especially for the freedom it affords and the other aspects mentioned above. The teachers are attracted by the possibility at last to provide for individual differences and by the fact

* From Patrick J. Groff, "Materials for Individualized Reading," *Elementary English*, XXXVIII, No. 1 (January, 1961), 1–7. Reprinted by permission of the author and the National Council of Teachers of English.

that children seem to progress in their reading skills as adequately here as in the use of a group plan. Especially appealing to parents are the changes in attitudes noted toward reading and books by older children, or the desirable attitudes they notice are developed in beginning readers. All agree that the child's urge to express his independence can be taken advantage of through this method of teaching reading. Freedom and reading no longer are associated in the child's mind as antonymous terms.

The prime material requisite for the success of such a reading plan is implied in the preceding statements. Large numbers of books and other reading materials on various topics and on widely divergent reading levels (increasingly so in the middle grades) are an absolute necessity. Because of the peculiar problems of the beginning reader in the first grade, there is a lack of confidence among some first grade teachers that individualized reading will work at this level. This is principally because of the disbelief that there are enough reading materials especially written for first–grade readers. To dispel this doubt, there is included in the bibliography of this article a substantial compilation of easy-to-read books with which the first grade child will be successful after he has established a small sight recognition vocabulary. Of course, slower-learning second- and third-grade children will find these books fit their needs, also.

For individualized reading to be successful, the teacher must acquaint himself with children's books, both as to their content and reading difficulty. The quickest and easiest way to accomplish this is to consult a good reference book. The most useful reference for children's literature is the *Children's Catalog*.[6] This volume can be found in all public and school libraries, and arranges books not only by title, author, and subject matter, but also very briefly describes the plot and gives an estimate of the reading difficulty of each title. The children's books listed in this reference volume and its yearly supplements are selected for their *literary qualities*. By consulting this volume when he compiles his reading lists for his class, the teacher will know he will provide the very best literary experience possible. *Children's Catalog* is unsurpassed for this purpose. Another excellent source of books that are graded as to difficulty are the lists published by the Wisconsin Reading Circle.[45] Here again, careful judgment is made of reading difficulty and quality. These little pamphlets list books from the first grade reading level on to the eighth grade.

In selecting books for bright children the teacher should keep in mind that while bright children generally can read materials of much greater difficulty than the normal child, their interests, by and large, are the same as the more average child. Generally speaking, the teacher should provide for the good readers books whose subject matter are of common interest to children of their age group, but whose reading difficulty provides a challenge for these more able children. It is as important to adjust the reading material provided for the bright child–advanced reader as it is for the dull child-retarded reader. The teacher must beware of putting complete reliance on the statistical averages of children's interests that are the result of surveys, however. Instead, he should maintain a continuous survey of the interests of the individual children in his particular class. Only by supplying books in line with such informal surveys will he be assured of providing for interests that may diverge widely from the norm of a formal, large-scale survey. Such tremendously exciting things are happening so fast in the world today that large-scale surveys sometimes quickly get out of date. The teacher also should keep in mind that there are substantial differences between the reading interests of boys and girls and that these tend to increase with age. He should know that for the dull child or the retarded reader there are good lists [38] he can consult to find books that are more mature in their interest level than their difficulty level.

Records of the books children read should be kept on materials such as *My Reading Design*.[37] This is a circle graph on which the child indicates how many books he has read under headings such as Pets, Poetry, Aviation, Indians, Adventure, Seasons, and seventeen other categories. The value of using such a record is that it stimulates the child to see how many of the sections of the circle (each of which represents a category such as the above) he can fill in. It also provides a ready reference for the teacher to check on the variety of books a child is reading, and, thereby, provide for guiding his interests into other fields. The reverse side of the circle graph of *My Reading Design* lists under its major categories other subtopics about

which the child may be interested in reading.

In individualized reading, teachers especially must be on guard not to overlook the development of word analysis and other reading skills. Obviously, this means that they must know all the word analysis techniques and in what order they properly may be introduced. (The rate of introduction of such skills will depend on the individual child, of course.) If the teacher confesses to any weakness in this respect, he should have a copy of Gray's *On Their Own in Reading* [14] on his desk for constant study and referral. This detailed, comprehensive, yet thoroughly readable book gives help not only in the above, but provides examples for independent self-study of word analysis skills by the child. The teacher can use such examples as models and extend them into work sheets for the children who show the need for such help. Because so much of the word study and other reading skill drill that children do in individualized reading is of an independent, self-study nature, the teacher should have on hand source material for developing reading games and devices. The most well-known and widely-used of such sources is Russell and Karp's *Reading Aids Through the Grades*.[33] This inexpensive paperback volume is full of descriptions of reading games and devices to develop many different kinds of reading skills at all the grade levels. Source books of this nature that have been recently published are those by Starr: *Selected Reading Games and Devices for the Primary Grades* [41]; *for the Intermediate Grades* [40]; and Kingsly.[17]

School districts often develop manuals for independent reading activities that are useful in individualized reading. The teacher may consult his own school district library and/or those districts nearby for such material. The collections of independent reading activities made by Omaha,[29] Madison,[25] Alameda,[1] Arcadia,[2] San Diego [35] are excellent examples of this kind of help. The Iowa State Education Association has gathered together a collection of instructional games including many in reading.[16] Dallas Schools have written resource materials on "Making Friends with Books" and on using with children myths that could serve as guides in individualized reading.[9]

Publishers often provide useful materials for teachers. Ginn and Co. will send free, *Let's Play a Game*.[21] This is a booklet of suggestions for games and independent activities for developing reading skills. The *Dolch Materials School Edition Catalog* [10] contains many excellent teaching aids for independent reading activities. These are offered for sale, of course, but they also give many ideas for materials that the teacher himself can construct. Other publishers that send free bulletins, pamphlets, and other materials on reading upon request are American Book; Heath; Houghton Mifflin; Lyons and Carnahan; Macmillan; Row, Peterson; Scott Foresman; Silver Burdett; and World Book. Teachers affluent enough to be able to purchase flash cards, picture-word cards, word wheels, crosswords, word bingo games, rhyming puzzles, consonant and vowel games, consonant substitution cards, and the like should know there are many reliable companies that offer

such materials.[47] The *Non-oral Teaching Method* materials originated by McDade [24] can be used effectively in individualized reading because they stress developing reading skills in an independent, non-oral way.

There are several sets of self-testing, graded reading materials that can be utilized in the individualized reading program. The newest and most elaborate as well as most expensive of these is the *SRA Reading Laboratory: Elementary Edition*.[30] This is a box of 150 short stories and factual articles and 150 reading rate building exercises printed on cards and written at ten different grade levels from grade two through grade nine. (There is a Secondary Edition which runs through grade twelve.) The child first reads a story or article and then self-tests himself, keeping a record of his degree of comprehension. When he is able to read one level of difficulty with the prescribed percentage of comprehension and speed, he moves on to the next more difficult level. The *SRA Reading Laboratory* fits into the individualized reading program well because the teacher does no bookkeeping and keeps no scores on the reading done by the child. It does not interfere with the time available for the individual conferences that the teacher holds with each child. During the conference, the teacher would want to discuss with the child his record graph of reading scores and give suggestions for future work. The materials as set up can be used to both test reading skills as well as develop reading. Reading skill development materials by Gates and Peardon,[13] McCall and Crabbs,[23] Stone, Grover, and

Bayle,[42] Zirbes,[46] and the *Reader's Digest Reading Skill Builders* [32] are other materials of this type.

One source for individualized reading materials the teacher should not overlook is *Textbooks in Print*.[44] This is a paperback book published yearly that lists all the reading textbooks in print. All the supplementary materials, independent reading activity materials, readiness materials and word games and charts that are part of a reading textbook series are also included. In addition, *Textbooks in Print* lists practically all the workbooks on reading that are published. In the 1959 edition there are eighty-one different workbooks on reading listed for sale. This volume can be found in the professional library of the teacher's school district. The best way to utilize money available for this kind of material is to buy as many different kinds of workbooks as possible rather than many of one kind. The same policy should be used in the purchase of reading textbooks. That is, a few copies of many series should be obtained instead of many copies of one or two series. If two copies of each workbook are purchased, the workbooks can be taken apart, each page mounted on stiff paperboard and covered with a clear plastic material. The child can mark on the plastic with a grease pencil which, in turn, easily rubs off leaving the sheet clear and ready for the next user. The advantage of disassembling the workbooks is that all the pages that develop a certain reading skill can be grouped together (along with pages from other workbooks on the same skill). When filed, they form a storehouse of practice material for work on certain needed reading skills. A numerical designation for each page can indicate its relative difficulty.

The teacher using individualized reading should give some thought to the use of audio-visual materials for teaching reading. Especially valuable are those collections of materials of this type by Leestma [20] and the materials listed in the Children's Reading Service *Audio-Visual Catalog*.[7] The latter is published yearly. Both of these sources list recordings and filmstrips which are particularly valuable as reading readiness experiences for children not mature enough for books, or for children whose attention span with books is short. Often the young child will read for a short time then quietly listen to a record or watch a filmstrip designed to develop reading readiness and then return to a book. The intervals spent with books typically will steadily lengthen as the child matures. For the middle–grade child, there are available records and filmstrips that help stimulate reading by providing a visual and/or aural background of the book while putting new vocabulary into context. Examples of these kinds of materials are the Landmark Enrichment records and filmstrips.[18] For both intermediate and primary grade children the Weston Woods Studios have prepared sixteen iconographic motion pictures, filmstrips and records based on outstanding children's books such as Gag's *Millions of Cats* and McCloskey's *Make Way for the Ducklings*.[31] These latter films have received generous critical approval by authorities in children's literature. The Society for Visual Education has in their *SVE Filmstrip*

Catalog [43] a complete selection of reading filmstrips, as does the *Filmstrip Guide.* [12]

Magazines and paperback books, which are relatively inexpensive, provide sources of materials for individualized reading. Cundiff [8] lists 101 magazines that are appropriate for school use. Spache [39] and Larrick [19] both describe the magazines that are appropriate for the elementary school. Children's magazines cost about $2.50 to $3.50 for a year's subscription, and make excellent birthday and Christmas presents. Parents can be encouraged to consider them for this purpose. Children will readily bring such magazines to school, where they can be read by many others. *Humpty Dumpty's Magazine* [15] is one which has many stories that first–grade children can read. *The Arrow Book Club* [3] provides paperbound editions of children's books for only twenty-five and thirty-five cents. The child after joining chooses one book five times a year from an offering of sixteen books. At these prices the child can build up his own personal library at home. It probably is unrealistic to hope children would exchange these paperback books with the same verve they do comic books, but the classroom can be used as the setting for such exchanges. The Library Club of America [22] will send free pins and other materials to help get reading clubs started in the classroom.

Because individualized reading depends to such a large extent for its success on the development of self-selection skills, instruction in the use of the library, including the card catalog, should be undertaken as soon as possible. Primary–grade children can be taught the location of the nearest library, how to make applications for library cards, and where in the library to find books at their reading levels and interests. The teacher should plan for the intermediate grade children a more systematic program of experiences to develop book selection skills. Often the school district will publish guides, courses of study or lessons that develop the child's ability to make fruitful choices among the many books in the library. The manuals prepared by Omaha,[28] Nashville,[27] and Sacramento [34] are excellent examples of this kind of help. Fargo's *Activity Books for School Libraries* [11] are well-known references of this nature, and can be found in most school libraries. Mott and Baisden [26] give many profitable activities for building library skills. A workbook of independent activities accompanies this book. There are other publications the teacher can consult that provide detailed ideas for teaching proficiency in library use through games and devices.[5, 36] Buchheimer [4] has written a factual and accurate account of how a library is arranged and how to use it. This is an especially good preparatory book to lead third- and fourth–grade children into many of the library activities described in the above books and manuals.

REFERENCES

1. ALAMEDA, CALIFORNIA, UNIFIED SCHOOL DISTRICT. *Reading Activities, Grades 1–4.* Alameda: The Board of Education, 1955–1956.
2. ARCADIA, CALIFORNIA, UNIFIED SCHOOL DISTRICT. *Developmental Reading through Reading Games.*

Arcadia: The Board of Education, 1956.

3. *Arrow Book Club.* 33 West 42 Street, New York 36, N.Y.

4. BUCHHEIMER, NAOMI. *Let's Go to the Library.* New York: Putnam, 1957.

5. CAVANAGH, GLADYS (Editor). *Handbook of Suggestions for School Library Activities.* Madison: Wisconsin State Department of Education.

6. *Children's Catalog.* New York: H. W. Wilson Co. Published yearly.

7. CHILDREN'S READING SERVICE. *CRS Audio-Visual Catalog.* Brooklyn: Children's Reading Service. Published yearly.

8. CUNDIFF, RUBY E. *101 Magazines for Schools, Grades 1–12.* Nashville: Tennessee Book Co.

9. DALLAS, TEXAS, INDEPENDENT SCHOOL DISTRICT. *Elementary Education, Grade Four, Five and Six.* (Three volumes.) Dallas: The Board of Education, 1953.

10. *Dolch Materials School Edition Catalog.* Champaign, Illinois: Garrard, 1959.

11. FARGO, LUCILE F. *Activity Book for School Libraries.* Chicago: American Library Association, 1938. *Activity Book No. 2,* 1945.

12. *Filmstrip Guide.* New York: H. W. Wilson Co. Published yearly.

13. GATES, ARTHUR I. and PEARDON, CELESTE C. *Practice Exercises in Reading.* New York: Bureau of Publications, Teachers College, Columbia University.

14. GRAY, WILLIAM S. *On Their Own in Reading.* Chicago: Scott, Foresman, 1948.

15. *Humpty Dumpty's Magazine.* Bergenfield, N.J.: Parent's Magazine Press, Inc.

16. IOWA STATE EDUCATION ASSOCIATION. *Instructional Games.* Des Moines: The Association, 1959.

17. KINGSLY, BERNARD. *Reading Skills, Games, Devices and Aids to Improve Reading.* San Francisco: Fearon, 1959.

18. *Landmark Enrichment Records and Filmstrips.* New York: Enrichment Teaching Materials.

19. LARRICK, NANCY. *A Parent's Guide to Children's Reading.* New York: Pocket Books, 1958.

20. LEESTMA, ROBERT. *Audio-Visual Materials for Teaching Reading.* Ann Arbor, Michigan: Slater's Book Store, 1954.

21. *Let's Play a Game. Suggestions for Games and Independent Activities for Developing Reading Skills.* Boston: Ginn and Co.

22. *Library Club of America, Inc.* 28 West 44 Street, New York, N.Y.

23. MCCALL, WILLIAM A. and CRABBS, LELAH M. *Standard Test Lessons in Reading.* New York: Columbia University Press, 1941.

24. *Non-oral Teaching Method Primary Seatwork.* Chicago: Primary Educational Service. (Approved by James McDade.)

25. MADISON, WISCONSIN, PUBLIC SCHOOLS. *Word Games.* Madison: The Board of Education, 1951.

26. MOTT, CAROLYN and BAISDEN, LEO B. *The Children's Book on How to Use Books and Libraries.* Chicago: Scribner's Sons, 1955.

27. NASHVILLE, TENNESSEE, PUBLIC SCHOOLS. *Library Lessons for Intermediate Grades.* Nashville: The Board of Education, 1956.

28. OMAHA, NEBRASKA, PUBLIC SCHOOLS. *A Library Program for Elementary Schools.* Omaha: The Board of Education, 1951.

29. ———. *Reading Activities for Non-Reciting Groups in the Elementary Grades.*

30. PARKER, DON H. *SRA Reading Laboratory. Elementary Edition.* Chi-

cago: Science Research Associates, 1958.

31. *Picture Book Parade Motion Pictures, Filmstrips and Records.* Weston, Conn.: Weston Woods Studios.

32. *Reader's Digest Reading Skill Builders.* Pleasantville, N.Y.: Reader's Digest Services, Inc.

33. RUSSELL, DAVID H. and KARP, ETTA E. *Reading Aids through the Grades.* New York: Columbia University Press, 1951.

34. SACRAMENTO, CALIFORNIA, UNIFIED SCHOOL DISTRICT. *Manual and Course of Study for Elementary School Libraries.* Sacramento: The Board of Education, 1953.

35. SAN DIEGO COUNTY, CALIFORNIA, SCHOOLS. *A Handbook of Independent Activities.* San Diego: San Diego County Board of Education, 1959.

36. SCHOOL LIBRARY ASSOCIATION OF CALIFORNIA. *Library Skills. Teaching Library Use through Games and Devices.* San Francisco: Fearon, 1958.

37. SIMPSON, G. O. *My Reading Design.* North Manchester, Indiana: Reading Circle, Inc.

38. SPACHE, GEORGE D. *Good Reading for Poor Readers.* Champaign, Ill.: Garrard, 1958.

39. ———. *Resources in Teaching Reading.* Gainesville: University of Florida Press, 1956.

40. STARR, JOHN W. *Selected Reading Games and Devices for the Intermediate Grades.* Eugene: University of Oregon, 1958.

41. ———. *Selected Reading Games and Devices for the Primary Grades.* Eugene: University of Oregon, 1958.

42. STONE, CLARENCE R.; GROVER, CHARLES C.; and BAYLE, EVALYN. *Practice Readers.* St. Louis: Webster, 1947–1949.

43. *SVE Filmstrip Catalog.* Chicago: Society for Visual Education. Published yearly.

44. *Textbooks in Print.* New York: R. R. Bowker. Published yearly.

45. WISCONSIN STATE READING CIRCLE BOARD. *Wisconsin Reading Circles.* Madison: Wisconsin State Department of Public Instruction. Published yearly.

46. ZIRBES, LAURA. *Practice Exercises and Checks on Silent Reading in the Primary Grades.* New York: Columbia University Press, 1925.

47. These companies will send free catalogs of materials for independent reading: Beckley-Cardy Co., Chicago, Ill.; F. A. Owen Publishing Co., Dansville, N.Y.; Gelles-Widmer Co., St. Louis, Mo.; Gel-Sten Supply Co., Brookfield, Ill.; Ideal School Supply Co., Chicago, Ill.; Kenworthy Educational Service, Buffalo, N.Y.; Milton Bradley Co., Springfield, Mass.; Palfrey's School Supply Co., San Gabriel, Calif.; Plymouth Press, Chicago, Ill.; Primary Educational Service, Chicago, Ill.; School Aids Products Co., St. Louis, Mo.; and School Service Co., Los Angeles, Calif.

81. ELEMENTARY SCHOOL LIBRARIES*

William S. Corliss

THE development and use of independent work-study skills has been a problem of the junior and senior high schools for many years. Oftentimes, the major problem has been one of taking time at this stage of education to teach and refine the work-study skills as related to library usage.

Learning skills in library usage has been the primary concern of the junior high school pupil. The general procedure has been for the skills to be taught jointly by the English teacher and the librarian. They cooperatively develop a program for the child to use the skills.

It has been the desire of the elementary school administration in the Wayzata (Minn.) Public Schools to introduce, teach, and develop independent use of the library before the children finish the sixth grade. The program is continuous from the kindergarten through the sixth grade and calls for cooperative action on the part of the elementary school librarian, the elementary school teacher, the elementary school administration, and the public librarian in the city.

Before embarking on the project of full-time librarians in each elementary school, a list of the services to children and to professional staff was de-

veloped to serve as a job analysis in employment. The services to children included training in use of library resources, books, pamphlets, and magazines; training in citizenship, social adjustment; interest in books fostered through circulation; enrichment of the curriculum; training in research; reading guidance; broadening of reading interests; book talks, displays, individual counseling; care of library materials and other responsibilities of users; book talks and presentation of new materials to help develop new interest and discrimination; an atmosphere conducive to child use; building and maintaining a resource center for teacher use. The services to the professional staff were to include consulting teachers in selection of materials; developing bibliographies for teachers; promoting cultural and functional growth of the staff; indexing and organizing teaching materials; resource in library skill development; developing library collections for room library use as resource units; attending grade level meetings as a resource person; establishing the library as a work center, reading room and a materials laboratory, a resource center for books, magazines, pictures, maps, and audio-visual materials; and creating an atmosphere conducive to teacher use.

Other services to school related activities were to include the provision of a resource and reference center for

* From William S. Corliss, "Elementary School Libraries," *Elementary English,* XXXVIII (November, 1961), 494–96, 505. Reprinted by permission of the author and the National Council of Teachers of English.

PTA, clubs, and administration; co-operation with public library; sponsoring field trips during Book Week; furnishing bibliographies of available materials; working with other librarians and community leaders in planning and developing an over-all library program for the community or the area; and providing an atmosphere conducive to lay persons' use.

The skill development program for children, aimed at independent use of the library, was to be a cooperative endeavor on the part of the classroom teacher and the elementary building librarian. It was determined that the library should be one of the important places where work-study skills are applied on an individual, small group, or class basis. The following outline indicates the scope and sequence of skill development for library skills.

KINDERGARTEN

1. Listening to stories
2. Reading stories from pictures
3. Access to many easy, well-illustrated books
4. Re-telling stories, observing sequence
5. Handling books properly
6. Awareness of pleasure in books
7. Acquaintance with old favorites
8. Visits to school and public library

FIRST GRADE

1. Reading stories within child's reading level, silently or orally
2. Appreciation of relationship of illustrations to study
3. Thinking of books in terms of possible ownership

4. Discovering public library facilities
5. Access to an attractive library corner
6. Regular library periods for enjoyment of books
7. Observation of library rules: quiet behavior, clean hands, returning books to proper place

SECOND GRADE

1. Awareness of books as a source of information
2. Acquaintance with stories of humor
3. Telling stories that have been read and enjoyed
4. Insight into the contributions of illustrations to knowledge
5. Access to room collections of interesting books
6. Continued use of library corner
7. Learning proper methods of handling books and the techniques of opening a new book
8. Visits to school and public libraries

THIRD GRADE

1. Increased range of reading interest
2. Access to fable and folk lore
3. Appreciation of the color and beauty of good illustration
4. Awareness of the function of libraries as sources of information and pleasure
5. Training in finding books grouped according to special interest
6. Use of titles and tables of contents as aids in finding materials
7. Observation of library rules

8. Extended use of public library facilities

FOURTH GRADE

1. Access to books dealing with children of other lands
2. Introduction of use of encyclopedia
3. Function of index and guide words in using reference material
4. Practice in locating books in school library
5. Observance of good library rules
6. Emphasis on year-round use of public library

FIFTH GRADE

1. Access to many books dealing with the American Heritage
2. Access to biographies on various reading levels
3. Effective use of encyclopedias
4. Acquaintance with the Newberry and Caldicott Award books
5. Facility in use of the table of contents, index, and card catalog
6. Learning library methods of grouping books under the terms FICTION AND NON FICTION
7. Observance of good library rules
8. Continued emphasis on year-round use of public library

SIXTH GRADE

1. Acquaintance with the Dewey Decimal system of book cataloging
2. Appreciation of the infinite resources which books offer

3. Continued use of table of contents and card catalog
4. Student assistants in maintenance of school library and circulation of books
5. Observance of rules of good library conduct
6. Locating materials in reference books
7. Continued use of public library facilities

Some practical outcomes of this program have been realized. When a particular unit of work makes it necessary for a class visit to the library, the teacher and librarian may plan a worthwhile visit; the librarians compile short bibliographies for pupils and teachers for units; and they circulate annotated bibliographies of new reference and professional books. The librarians arrange to circulate current professional magazines; they work in the classrooms as well as in their libraries to encourage attitude and usage; the librarians help develop usage of the public library facilities, and serve the buildings as resource persons for audio-visual aids and equipment. Many of the fine educational services not seen at the outset of this program have developed and aided the elementary schools to attain an excellent record in reading progress as well as development of the independent work-study skills.

Independent reading in the elementary schools has grown tremendously since the program of full-time qualified librarians for each elementary building has been inaugurated. The measurable (Iowa Tests—S.R.A. Tests —Specific Reading Tests) growth and improvement in the reading accomplishment of the students has increased tremendously. The provision of the full-time qualified librarian in each elementary school precludes the necessity of searching for a mechanical means to teach developmental reading. It allows a school system to adhere to proven methods of organizing classes and the program of learning without searching out some mechanical panacea. It is the answer to the teacher's prayer when it is properly used in individualizing instruction in reading.

Work-study skills (as measured by tests and observation) have improved. The sixth–grade student is almost an independent user of the library resources. The junior high school English teacher and librarian need only refine some of the specific skills and continue the trend toward full use of the library facilities.

The elementary school teachers, the elementary school administrators, the junior high school English teachers and librarians, are in total agreement that the employment of full-time qualified librarians in our public schools has had a tremendous effect in upgrading all subject matter achievement and has contributed toward the goal of education—a self–motivated individual with the skills to find knowledge and apply it.

82. THE IMPORTANCE AND USE OF READING GAMES *[1]

Guy Wagner and Max Hosier

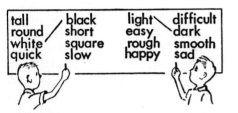

CHILDREN seem to learn more readily and with greater enjoyment when they have access to a variety of good teaching aids. This chapter is designed to emphasize the importance of reading games in the learning process and to make some practical suggestions for their use.

Good teachers have always lightened the day's work with games of some sort. Many of these games, however, had little relationship to the classroom routine. A good proportion of these games have been action ones, necessary to meet the physiological needs of children for action. As stated in a Dade County manual

Many classroom games provide

physical activity which is essential to desirable growth and development; others, though having little exercise value, help to relieve strain and tension. Social and recreational values are developed when the principles of good leadership and good followership, courteous sharing, and general group responsibility are stressed.[2]

Other games have been of the more quiet type, but were useful in giving functional practice in some important learning skill. The games in this publication are of this type; thus, they have learning as well as recreational value. They are designed chiefly to reinforce formal instruction in reading. Incidentally, many of these games also develop skills in subjects directly allied to reading: spelling, writing, speaking, listening, and dictionary work. These games also qualify as good "breather" or recreational activities, since they vary the routine of formal classroom work with the game element, adding freshness and zest to the curriculum.

Using the "Make-Believe" Element

As a rule, the games included do not rely on figurative speech or the element

* From Guy Wagner and Max Hosier, "The Importance and Use of Reading Games," in *Reading Games: Strengthening Reading Skills with Instructional Games* (Darien, Conn.: Teachers Publishing Corp., 1960), pp. 7–10. Reprinted by permission of the authors and Teachers Publishing Corporation.

[1] Some of the material in this part is based upon the article "Let's Put Instructional Games to Work," which was written by the authors of this chapter, appearing in the January, 1957, issue of *Education*.

[2] Dade County Board of Education, *Manual of Classroom Games for Elementary Schools* (Miami, Florida; January, 1954).

of "pretending." Children, however, like and *need* some opportunities to "make believe" and if a few games include this make-believe element it seems not only acceptable but advisable to use them. To illustrate, one of the games is entitled *Up the Ladder,* and in this game the children see how far they can get up the "make-believe" ladder that is drawn on a large piece of construction paper. The children "climb the ladder" by being able to give a word that begins like each key word that is placed on the respective rungs of the ladder. Of course, the children do not literally climb the ladder. They are, however, stimulated by the challenge of responding correctly so that they can, as rapidly as possible, reach the top rung.

In life, adults frequently enjoy and are motivated by this same type of make-believe activity. Frequently, community fund-raising campaigns are sparked and stimulated by a large thermometer placed in a prominent downtown location where workers and citizens can see and be motivated by the rate of the campaign's progress. We know, too, that many adults are very interested in and give complete attention to such games as charades, which call heavily on the elements of suspense and pretense. Life would be dull, indeed, if every experience in it had to be literal and realistic.

The moderate use of make-believe, as found in this book, must not be interpreted as approval of artificial or vicarious experiences when the "real" thing is available. But when children, in games, use make-believe ladders for real ones and apply the term "corral" to a circle-type game, they are not only

putting a little spice into their school life—they are also likely to be working harder and more enthusiastically in learning the basic skills.

Commercial Versus Teacher-Planned Games

When the term *instructional games* is used, there come to mind two rather distinct kinds. First, there are the commercially prepared games which are normally purchased for use in the home. These are sometimes purely of a recreational nature and would have little value in the classroom except perhaps at recess time or during the noon hour. The writers have found, however, that many commercial games do have instructional value especially in the so-called academic subjects. Schools might well make judicious use of such games as *Go Fish* (teaches consonant blends), *Match Games* (helps children rapidly recognize common words), *Puzzle-Plans* (helps children identify some commonly used nouns), *Spell It* (motivates interest in spelling), and *See and Hear* (gives practice in auditory discrimination).

The second and by far the more important classification of instructional games might be called "teacher-planned"—those which are designed or adapted by the classroom teacher for use with her particular pupils.[3] Often, children themselves come up with an

[3] It is not expected that the classroom teacher will spend an inordinate amount of time in preparing materials to be used in the teacher-planned games. Such work should be done by pupils, within reasonable limits. It is believed that games in this publication will serve as "time-savers" for the teacher as well as motivated learning experiences for pupils.

interesting adaptation of a familiar game and sometimes they create stimulating ones of their own. In classrooms throughout the country, teacher-planned games of this nature are used in varying degrees. Some teachers consider them to be of little value whereas others are convinced that teacher-planned games are an important learning aid. The authors are inclined to agree with the latter, although they recognize that the *game* way of learning is only one approach and should be used judiciously as a member of the instructional materials team. They also believe that the use of games is not an attempt to sugar-coat education; rather, it is an efficient device for helping make school life more purposeful and learning more meaningful.

In considering instructional games for classroom use we should ask one simple question, "Would this particular game make teaching more effective and pupil learning more efficient?" The first step, therefore, in using instructional games is to make selections only in terms of their obvious teaching values. When wise choices have been made, experience indicates that the question is HOW can these games best be used rather than SHOULD they be used.

Values of Instructional Games

No teacher would believe that all learning must be presented as a game. No teacher would suggest that all learning can be accomplished with games. Furthermore, no child expects all learning to be fun and no child wants to play games all day long. But both teachers and children want their classrooms to be happy places in which to work, and they certainly don't object to having working conditions enlivened by the planned diversion of an occasional game. Instructional games can facilitate learning for a pupil while giving him ample reward in terms of interest, and a variation in what is sometimes monotonous routine.

Children enjoy participating in games. They will give undivided attention and interest to a game while making a sincere effort to contribute to the best of their ability. Why will they do this? Close observation usually shows that children gain status or experience success through playing worthwhile games. Some basic psychological drives are satisfied through their participation in games.

Games afford many opportunities to present desired learnings or to give additional repetition or drill in a variety of ways. Because of the many settings in which the same learning or skill can be practiced, the pupil's interest is maintained. Instructional games can give, in an interesting way, the additional practice necessary to "fix" certain learnings. They can eliminate meaningless repetition and rote learning. The pupil will display that characteristic which is essential in any learning situation—INTEREST!

Sometimes a game may help pupils develop an insight that cannot be gained as well by any other method. Instructional games add a sense of visualization to the learning process and often give purpose to learning. *Many of these games are self-teaching and can be carried over into home activities.*

Perhaps the greatest value which can

be claimed for instructional games is that of motivation. Has any elementary teacher had to plan long hours and devise various ways to motivate a game? The answer is that good games are largely self-motivating. Because children inherently like games and can learn efficiently from them, their proper use in the classroom needs little other justification.

83. AUDIO-VISUAL READING TOOLS*

Amo De Bernardis

WE HEAR a great deal of criticism today about the unfortunate influence which the commercial motion picture, the radio, and now television may be exerting upon the development of the child—particularly in relation to his reading habits. There is a growing fear that the child listening to radio or watching the TV screen may have little time for books. But no such criticism can be made over the value which a school can derive from these audio-visual materials in promoting a better education for the child, and this includes more and better reading. When properly selected and used, the motion picture, the various types of recordings, the radio and television programs can become some of the best tools available to the classroom teacher, and can contribute a great deal to the school's reading program.

Too many people look upon reading merely as the ability to recognize words on a printed page and to repeat them aloud. They measure the child's skill in reading by his fluency, and are more concerned over the fact that some children find it difficult to recognize the printed symbol than the fact that many are unable to understand what they do recognize.

Consequently, unless the child has accumulated a background of experience, of contact with real objects or people, or their visual representation, he cannot hope to understand the printed word even if he can say it correctly. The audio-visual tools now available for the classroom teacher help the child acquire this essential background.

In the early grades the problem is simple. The symbols on the page refer to father, mother, baby, dog, house, or common action words—all of which are part of every child's environment, and therefore universally understood. However, even here audio-visual aids

* From Amo De Bernardis, "Audio-Visual Reading Tools," *Grade Teacher,* LXXII, No. 8 (April, 1955), 33, 79, 80. Reprinted by permission of the author and Teachers Publishing Corporation, Darien, Conn.

can be helpful, and the beautifully il-lustrated primers in the modern school are excellent examples of this merging of picture and word.

Once the child gets away from these simple elements in his home or his neighborhood, the problem is no longer as simple. He must find other means of acquiring the understanding of things not in his immediate environment. He must acquire new knowledge. For this purpose audio-visual tools, and to these we may add field trips, are important, even essential.

Field Trips

The field trip is rapidly becoming a standard audio-visual practice in almost all school systems. To conduct one involves a number of administrative problems: securing permission, arranging for transportation, and working out a proper time schedule. But the results of a successful field trip make the effort worthwhile. Each child who takes part has acquired a rich and vital experience which not only advances his education but can be made to develop a growing interest in oral and written communication, and eventually in the reading of print.

A trip to a factory, a farm, or a fire station has been a learning experience which then and thereafter seeks expression in language. After each field trip, children are eager to describe what they saw and reproduce the event in various forms. One is the reading chart which the teacher builds out of what the children relate. This helps to develop word recognition and, what is more important, to give real meaning to an abstract symbol. The class has

turned the field trip into a reading exercise which is both interesting and readable.

Motion and Still Pictures

One of the best substitutes for actual experience is the motion picture, and next to it, the filmstrip and the photograph. As in the case of the field trip, the full educational possibilities in them can be achieved only if the experience itself is followed by interpretation and criticism from the children. The pictures merely furnish facts and situations. The learning takes place when these presentations provoke discussion and debate. The film or filmstrip should really be regarded as motivation for further learning activity, not as mere enjoyment. Pictures stimulate the imagination, and the wise teacher encourages the full play of this imagination and its expression in a variety of ways —in speech, in writing, in art, and above all, in further reading.

Mounting and Arranging Flat Pictures

In addition to the motion picture, the filmstrip, and the slide set, there is the vast field of the flat printed picture. The professional photographer has covered the world with his camera—its people, its institutions, its occupations, its customs, its human relations. The result of his efforts may be found in every illustrated book, and especially in the numerous magazines devoted to science and travel—foreign places, foreign people, and all the scenes of American life and work.

Many of these pictures are available

to the classroom teacher, but to make the best use of them, they should be mounted and systematically filed.

One device used by many teachers for displaying pictures is the flannel board. Its simplicity, ease of construction, and flexibility makes this a valuable teaching tool. Words, phrases, sentences, and pictures can be displayed on it, and it is especially excellent in storytelling, since, with its aid, the story can be developed step by step and visualized.

Opaque Projectors

One of the most versatile tools in the reading program is the opaque projector. With its help, an infinite variety of materials from books, pictures, photographs, students' written or printed work, and even objects themselves may be projected on the screen for examination and discussion by the whole class.

Projection of a child's work so that all the class may see it at the same time and discuss it presents an excellent teaching and learning situation. The projected picture centers attention on material being discussed. Individual children may be called upon to read or interpret what is on the screen. Errors may be pointed out and corrections agreed upon, and the whole exercise made an opportunity for motivating further reading.

Audio Aids

A wise teacher has said that children should be grouped in their classrooms for instruction in reading not on their reading level, but on their *thinking* level. It is useless for a child to be able to recognize words he cannot understand or use in his own mental processes. Too much of this "parrot reading" has existed in the past and much of it is still to be found in many places in the present.

It is here that audio materials such as recording tapes and radio programs find their relationship to better reading. They motivate attentive listening; they provoke comment and discussion; they improve understanding. There are available for the classroom today recordings of almost infinite variety—speeches, narratives, descriptions, dramatizations, poetry, and almost anything that can be made through sound.

The tape recorder has made it possible for any classroom teacher to create his own audio aids. The mechanics of operation have been so simplified that even the pupils can operate the machine. The tape itself can be kept intact for repeated use in the future or erased and then re-used.

All these audio-visual devices and classroom methods must be used properly if they are to promote the cause of good reading. In themselves they are only tools, but in the hands of a good craftsman they can be made to create worthwhile education provided he doesn't forget the real purpose for which they are being used. If his objective is to increase the child's interest and ability in reading, then the teacher must keep this continuously in mind, and use every opportunity created by the field trip, the motion or still picture, the tape recorder, and every other device to advance the cause of reading. There is no such thing as an automatic tool for teaching. No matter how dramatic or exciting the visual, the auditory, or the actual experience may be, it takes the skilled teacher to turn it into an effective learning situation. In the last analysis, the teacher himself is the chief miracle worker. But the right tools will help him accomplish the miracle we call education.

REFERENCES

DALE, EDGAR. *Audio Visual Methods in Teaching* (Revised Edition), "English and Reading" Chapt. 26 (New York: The Dryden Press, 1959).

DAVIS, HUBERT J. *Teaching Reading the A–V Way,* Educational Screen, 31: 417–19 (December, 1952), 64 E. Lake St., Chicago 1, Illinois.

GORMAN, HARRIET. *Adventure with Film-Readers; How Motion Pictures plus Correlated Film-Storybooks Help Young Readers Read,* Educational Screen, 30:13–15 (January, 1951).

JACKSON, E. B. *More About the Flannel-graph in Teaching Reading Readiness,* The Grade Teacher, 65:26–27 (February, 1948).

LEESTMA, ROBERT. *Audio Visual Materials for Teaching Reading* (Ann Arbor, Michigan: University of Michigan Press, 1954).

RUSSELL, D. H., and KARP, E. E. *Reading Aids Through the Grades,* Teachers College, Bureau of Publications, Columbia University (New York, 1951).

SULLIVAN, L. H. *Using the Radio in Developing Reading,* The Elementary School Journal, 27:53–57 (June, 1946).

WILLEY, ROY DE VERL. *Using Audio-Visual Methods in Teaching Communications,* Elementary English, 276–83 (May, 1954).

Filmstrips that correlate with *Alice and Jerry* series of books, available through Society for Visual Education, 1345 Diversey Parkway, Chicago 14, Illinois.

Filmstrips, supplemented by study guides, for *Better Reading Series* (Pasadena, California: Stillfilms Inc.).

Wilmette, Illinois: Encyclopaedia Britannica Films, Inc. and Boston: D. C. Heath Co. have made available a series including such titles as *Three Little Kittens, Shep the Farm Dog, Farm Animals.*

A set of books to correlate with the Encyclopaedia Britannica Films series *Children of Many Lands* has been published by Row, Peterson and Company, 1911 Ridge Avenue, Evanston, Illinois.

ORAL READING

84. ORAL READING? CERTAINLY!*

Louise Willson Worthington

ORAL reading, once an almost lost art, is coming into its own again. Changes in mass communication have given it new importance and have opened new career opportunities for the skilled reader. Daily one hears news commentators, announcers, and entertainers use oral reading. On special days, such as Lincoln's Birthday, Independence Day, Thanksgiving, and Christmas, our hearts are moved by the voices of those who bring us *The Gettysburg Address, The Declaration of Independence, The First Thanksgiving, The Littlest Angel,* or *The Gift of the Magi.* The storyteller who entertains children or adults by television, radio, or recording is an accomplished oral reader.

Recently a well-known actor made a nationwide tour before theater audiences with a full evening's program of oral readings. Included in his repertoire were Mother Goose, fairy tales, historical documents, Shakespeare, and the Bible. His reception and acclaim bear witness to the effectiveness of the art of reading aloud and help to re-establish its appeal as an avenue of entertainment.

The message of the statesman, read to the listening world from a typed manuscript previously released to the news services, goes over the air waves in times of crisis, of rejoicing, and on other important occasions. If the speaker reads clearly and convincingly, his words are respected and heeded. If he reads haltingly, with wrong inflections and other evidences of inadequate comprehension, the faith of his listeners in what he is saying may be lessened. Thus the course of events can be influenced by the skill with which the speaker reads his message.

Not only statesmen and entertainers but men and women in all walks of life are finding new uses for oral read-

* From Louise Willson Worthington, "Oral Reading? Certainly!" in *Contributions in Reading,* No. 16, pp. 1–4. Reprinted by permission of the author and Ginn and Company, Boston, Mass.

ing. A fairly recent development is the amateur play-reading movement. In many communities small groups of adults meet informally in the homes of members just to read aloud. Sometimes they choose a current Broadway hit; at other times they prefer old favorites or one of the classics. No one is interested in developing the plays into little theater productions. The group merely enjoys a happy social experience, and each member adds to his appreciation of the drama.

The chairman of the local Red Cross Drive is allotted five minutes of radio and television time to launch the drive; to report progress; to spur the community to further effort. In order to cover his topic and to time it accurately, he prepares a statement of the proper length and reads it. The candidate who aspires to public office as city commissioner, sheriff, or judge is expected to state his case before camera and microphone. The president of the League of Women Voters must manage a fifteen-minute spot on the air in which she introduces the opposing candidates and questions them on campaign issues. The president of the PTA uses TV or radio channels to bring out the vote on school legislation. Whatever the occasion, the speaker who is able to present his case clearly and concisely is more likely to influence his listeners than the unskilled person who stumbles over his notes and reads them without force or conviction.

Oral Reading in Everyday Living

These are the new and more spectacular occasions for oral reading. A further look reveals that the average child or adult has frequent uses for oral reading in his daily living. An adult may—

1. Read a book aloud in the family circle or to friends.
2. Read to children.
3. Read a piece of information or something to prove a point to someone.
4. Read a report at a business meeting, or an announcement, or a set of resolutions.
5. Read an original paper or a book review to a group.
6. Read poetry aloud to himself to aid in appreciation or memorizing.
7. Participate in choral reading.
8. Read a message over the telephone.

Like their parents children read for a variety of reasons. Often they wish only to share a happy or memorable experience or to entertain friends or themselves. At other times their purpose is related to a problem that has arisen at home or school. The teacher who desires to take full advantage of the values of oral reading in her classroom will keep in mind several objectives. She will guide her pupils as they read aloud for such purposes as these:

1. To share scarce materials: a library book of which there is only one copy; a newspaper clipping; references in sources such as encyclopedias, a single copy of a text or supplementary book, a magazine article.
2. To broaden interests through sharing: different library books on a topic (these may cover a wide range of difficulty); several opinions from different authorities on the same topic; new interests introduced by children who have explored them and can present them

convincingly; original papers or stories.

3. To carry on classroom or school affairs; an announcement or a committee report; a plan for group action; the minutes of a meeting.

4. To settle an argument: excerpts from sources that prove a point, or clarify an idea, or present varying points of view.

5. To entertain: selections from books that others have not read; favorite poems; choral speaking.

6. To enhance appreciation of selections in which beauty is inherent in the language used; descriptive passages; selections rich in imagery and colorful words; musical and poetic passages.

7. To develop tastes for material of high literary quality and of many kinds.

8. To meet the needs of certain children for approval, worthy group membership, or sense of personal worth.

Reasons for oral reading occur naturally in every modern classroom. Throughout the day there are frequent occasions to read aloud in clearing up a point in a social-studies discussion, in reporting an experience in science, in re-examining a problem in arithmetic, in appraising a news story for the school paper, or in sharing a passage from a familiar story.

Differences between Oral and Silent Reading

As the teacher works to accomplish the purposes just mentioned, she must remember that oral reading, by its very nature, is different from silent reading.

First, oral reading is more complex than silent reading. When one reads silently, there is nothing between the mind of the author and the mind of the reader except the printed word. The reader follows the author's thinking, finds out what he has to say, interprets it in the light of what he already knows, and accepts or rejects it in the light of his experience and understanding. When one reads orally to others, however, one must not only *get* the author's meaning, but he must also *give* it to his listeners. His voice is the vehicle for conveying the ideas. The real measure of his success is not merely that *he* understands what the author has said, but that his *listeners* understand it, too. His success is measured by their reactions.

Second, oral reading requires accomplished listeners. The child receiving the ideas must have developed listening skills. These involve such mechanical abilities as hearing differences between *help* and *held* or *chair* and *share;* but they also include the power to grasp the main idea, to note sequence, or to follow directions. The child who has learned to do these things while reading silently does not necessarily do them while listening. Again, the oral reading situation may be more complex than silent reading.

Third, oral reading usually requires special preparation. The reader cannot effectively convey the author's ideas to an audience unless he already knows, before he reads aloud, what the author is trying to say. He cannot give his audience what he does not have himself. To permit him to attempt to do so makes failure a certainty. Not many adults like to be called upon to read orally, at sight, a selection of difficult material in the presence of their peers.

They need a moment or two to scan the material before attempting to read it aloud. Sometimes they offer an excuse to avoid having to read, such as, "I forgot my glasses." Children may have no such escape. Is it surprising, then, that in oral reading situations they may show evidences of strain and insecurity; read mechanically or in monotonous tone; read by "word-calling;" use high-pitched voices; and dread to be called upon?

Before reading orally, the child usually needs to read the material silently to make sure of his understanding of the ideas and his ability to recognize and comprehend all the words. Sometimes he may need to get help from his teacher so that he can be sure of a satisfactory presentation. This means that, for most school purposes, silent reading should precede oral. Exceptions are made when the material is very simple or the reader is unusually skillful.

Developing Oral Reading Skills

It seems clear, therefore, that if oral reading is to make its full contribution to the child and to the activities of the school, each teacher must help her pupils develop skill in using it. Oral reading is not something to be used occasionally; it is something to be learned as part of an organized, balanced reading program.

The teacher who wishes to help children learn to read aloud better should have these objectives:

1. To help children grow in oral reading skills, such as
   a. correct pronunciation
   b. articulation, so audience can hear
   c. phrasing in thought units
   d. speed suited to selection
   e. natural conversational pitch and tone, not too high or low
   f. emphasis and expression, as means of making meaning clear
   g. proper breathing
   h. posture, standing or sitting
   i. position of book
2. To develop wholesome attitudes about reading aloud and about listening to others read, such as believing that this is
   a. a good way to discover new ideas
   b. a good way to share what you like, and interest others in it
   c. a good way to help others
   d. a pleasurable experience
3. To help children set high standards for quality of performance
4. To help children develop discrimination in choosing what to read aloud
5. To help children grow in listening skills

Children are most successful in becoming good oral readers when they are aware of the uses of the skill and are eager to perfect it. Teachers, therefore, should be alert to recognize daily occasions for oral reading such as those mentioned earlier, and should take advantage of them. In these natural situations children will be given the specific help they need, and good learning experiences will follow.

For example, a fourth-grade group had been reading silently a selection about whales and in the lively discussion which followed a controversy arose about the eating habits of these huge animals. One child quickly located and read to the group a paragraph which explained and clarified the point in question. Often errors of interpretation are discovered in this way. One word misunderstood may change the meaning of a lengthy passage. Children using oral reading in a natural situation where a range of answers is possible lose their fear and tension because reading serves a useful purpose; they are interested and involved in the findings; they are eager to defend their opinions; they "know what it says."

Oral reading also takes place naturally when a child finds a library book or other reference which contains pertinent information that he desires to share with his group. Occasionally one or more pupils may read aloud the directions for doing some assignment in order to be sure that all in the group understand. Sometimes disagreements over factual details may develop in which oral reading has a function. The pupils then return to their sources to find and check their data and perhaps to verify their conclusions by reference to author or to copyright date, or by reassessing their comprehension and interpretation.

Often a class discussion about a story leads directly to oral reading. For example, after a group had finished reading "Tembo in the Moss-Draped Forest" in *Wings to Adventure,* the sixth reader of the Ginn Basic Reading Series, one boy located and read to the class a description of an African forest. Another obtained a copy of the book from which the selection in the reader is taken and read aloud other exciting excerpts. Thus, in a variety of natural purposeful settings, oral reading skills are developed and improved.

A Word about the Audience

Whenever the purpose of oral reading is to *entertain,* then it certainly follows that the material should entertain someone. This implies that there is an audience composed of listeners who do not know the material to be read, do not have copies of it before them, have real interest in what is to be read, and some good reason for hearing it. They expect to *listen.* They also expect, and rightly so, to hear something entertaining.

To hold the attention of his audience, the reader must be prepared. He has read the selection silently, has had help on the hard words and knows them, and perhaps has read the material aloud once to a listener who has helped him become proficient. He understands what the author has to say and wants others to understand, too. He knows that he will have an attentive audience which has not read what he will read. His listeners will not be looking for faults, but for enjoyment of his story. Narrative material is particularly suited to such situations. Poetry also has an important place. Library books provide a treasure house of suitable materials. Collections of reading texts contain splendid material.

Folklore and classic literature are particularly suitable for oral reading. Many of these old stories as well as modern ones which contain much conversation may be used for simple dramatization. Basal readers currently in use also contain stories in dialogue form, all ready for informal dramatizing. These dramatizations can be prepared rather quickly if kept simple with no costumes or stage settings. Children are chosen for the speaking parts, and one child takes the part of the "book," reading all the content that is not spoken by a character. Occasionally such a dramatization may be prepared more elaborately with simple costumes and staging for an invited audience of parents or children.

Some Specific Suggestions

A check list will enable the teacher to assess the extent and nature of her instructional problem in helping children become good oral readers. On a sheet of squared paper she may write along the left side the qualities which seem most important. At the top of each column she may write the name of a child. Beneath each name she may check what each child needs to work on. She may discuss his strengths and weaknesses with him and cross them out as they are overcome. Such qualities as posture, phrasing, place keeping, voice quality, enunciation, expression, speed, and pitch may in this way be checked. The check list may be used with necessary adaptations for the varying grade levels.

Such weaknesses as high-pitched voices, poor reading posture, many repetitions and regressions, sing-song voices, and facial grimaces may be habits or symptoms of tension, embarrassment, or fear of failure. They may also be signs of a physical deficiency. It is well to make sure of vision, hearing, and speech if the symptoms persist.

Patience, sympathetic understanding, and sustained effort may be necessary to break the "word caller" of a well-established habit. It probably originated when the youngster was asked repeatedly to read aloud material that he did not understand, containing words that he did not know. The material used for purposes of overcoming the difficulty should be very easy, with no strange words or ideas. If the child is asked to read the material silently first and then tell what it says, he is more likely to use a natural conversational voice. He can then be asked to read it as he would talk. It is well to remember that as he did not acquire the habit overnight, he will not overcome it in one practice session.

85. MORAL: GO ORAL—SOME OF THE TIME*

Ann Ess Morrow

EMPHASIS on silent reading—stressing of the oral—like players on a ball team, the two sides go to bat. First one is up, and then the other. Supporters cheer wildly, while opponents further crowd the world with noise. Truly, at times of tension, the wisdom of an umpire, like his clearsightedness, is indispensable.

Yet why go in for *either-or*-ing when the answer lies in *both-and?* Unless both teams were in there pitching, how could one get to first base; how could one ever score? When controversy wakes and players feel they have one strike against them, it seems as if the whole matter of reading becomes more strident than oral-or-silent. One thing is certain—teachers of reading must be on the ball. At any rate, there is a dual aspect. It is oral reading, entailing all the techniques of listening, which in itself is one of the four big communication skills, that we discuss here.

Hazards of Impromptu Reading

Among techniques to be avoided is a sudden request that someone read aloud expressively a selection he has never seen before. This happened to Linda once. The request came unexpectedly. She hurled herself into the

* From Ann Ess Morrow, "Moral: Go Oral—Some of the Time," LXXVIII, No. 2 (October, 1957), 72–77. Reprinted by permission of the author and The Bobbs-Merrill Co., Inc., Indianapolis, Ind.

strangeness of a context until then unexplored by her. Panicky, Linda stumbled over words she could have named correctly, had she not been confused in thinking.

When everyone laughed at the queerness of the emphasis she gave the lines, she did, too, but there was dampness in her laughter, for tears were close beneath. Suddenly she seemed to feel that insight was no longer hers, that she'd appeared ridiculous before the group.

She never forgot that afternoon. If only Mr. Jones had been ready to aid with difficult parts! Annoyance grew within her at having been forced to give an oral version of a completely strange viewpoint. Her irritation, thus, was aimed simultaneously at the teacher who occasioned it with thoughtless policy, and at the literature which caused it. So Linda lost the friendly feelings toward oral reading which she had had when circumstances differed. Next time, she resolved within, she'd have no part of it. Let others read aloud. She'd do hers silently.

Means to Appreciation

Jack Gibson, across the hall, is very fortunate. His reading teacher, Mrs. Lloyd, has real love for children and for literature, and her resonant voice and appropriate manner readily catch tone color, cadence, tempo. She uses them with such easy effectiveness that Jack can always see the loveliness of thoughts that come all wrapped in the cellophane of print.

Oral Reading Used Diagnostically

Mrs. Turner uses oral reading diagnostically. She watches Tommy hurdle words that seek to throw him, and makes a mental note to give more drill in word-attack; she notes Alice's plodding approach and methodical attempts to make strange words sound familiar and knows that here is a child who concentrates on letters, who does not see words as a whole. She knows when Henry reads aloud at his own level that he is building better concepts of himself, and she thrills to see his eyes glow as he proves to the others that he, too, can read, however halting the process may be. If it had been all silent reading, who would know? Not for a butter-broiled T-bone steak would Mrs. Turner let him attempt aloud material beyond his depth, for Henry, like everyone else, must attain success to some degree.

For Michael, oral reading serves another purpose. He reads glibly, well, and everybody loves to listen. Mike senses this, and reads to entertain. Because he does it well, he generates pleasurable feelings toward the act of reading orally. And his attitude of pleasure permeates the class.

Arousing Interest in Sounds of Words

Carol is romantic. She loves to read out loud. She knows that beauty sleeps in print, and with techniques and skills for wand, she wakens words to state of glow. When she thinks of reading that way, of the power of words to enchant, to carry her away to other worlds, in her imagination she becomes a little princess. Somehow she thinks of ballet, too, with rhythm in her toes and in the print, and beauty in both media.

If sometimes words become obdurate, reluctant to unfold their meaning, she makes them all conform by using skills which she has learned in school. Miss Robertson talked to them one day about the picture-power of words, about their individuality, and pointed out that ideas, like girls, are always looking for new clothes to wear. Now Carol thinks of colorless words that everybody uses—like *nice* and *went* and *said*—as all alike and sees them as automatons in uniforms of gray, and all of them together can not stir her like one word of vividness. And when she reads the words out loud, she reads them so that boys and girls come to see rapidity of movement in the short, crisp words, in leaping phraseology. They find it fun to realize that some words sound exactly like their meaning—that *buzz,* for instance, makes the same sound bees do, something she'd have missed if she'd read silently.

Miss Robertson is very wise. She knows when Mary goes to high school, she will learn a great big word that means that sound and meaning are sometimes related. She does not tell them now the word for it, but some day some one will.

Overcoming Fright at Symbol

One day John Greer learned it, but he was wearing longer arms and legs.

Yet he was frightened even then when he first heard *onomatopoeia*. He always was when man-sized words were purposefully tossed about. But since he'd learned its meaning first and then was given the symbol, he gained a feeling of amazement, of confidence, that what he had been doing easily, bore relationship to it.

Surely in employing this technique of interesting the child in sounds of words, one must remember its effectiveness is all but lost if the reading of the polished lines is to oneself alone. When Johnny actually hears these words and voices them himself, as well as hearing the teacher, his sensitivity tends to grow. The very act of vocalizing words of skill and artistry makes John aware of their potentialities and of effectiveness in speech.

Pleasure Often Attained by Listening

Laura, on the other hand, prefers to listen. She loves to have Miss Smith read stories aloud. It's best of all when all the boys and girls close books and do not try to follow trails of print. Miss Smith is really restful. She never crowds her reading into close parentheses of time, as if a waiting bus would leave in just two minutes. The teacher's voice is soft and warm and sunshine-filled, and words take on attractive forms because Miss Smith is saying them. The happy way she looks at boys and girls when she begins to read reveals to all that here will be adventure into pleasantness, a talking kind of music. And like the time when Johnny got the measles, everybody gets that way. *Euphony* the big folks call

the sounds that never plod in mud or splash one disagreeably. They glide along and soothe one like a lullaby, and yet one does not wish to sleep; he desires, instead, to listen to the teacher who is able to communicate her love for what she reads.

Unfavorable Attitudes Sometimes Built

Mr. Jackson isn't one bit that way. He seems to blow his voice right through his nose as if he didn't know the normal route that voices take. He never seems to use the alley of his throat. And somehow sounds get squeezed into unpleasant shapes, and pretty words grow bent and twisted, the way trees do sometimes. The children in his room think that oral reading isn't really nice at all. And Miss Arnett is not too helpful, either. Why, she has such a mild voice that when she reads of lions they seem like butterflies instead, and things get all mixed up again. And Mr. Timkins is so pompous he makes little fishes talk like whales.

Art of Oral Reading Slighted

Perhaps it is because teachers have been so trained in literary probing, dissection, and analysis that they have overlooked to a large extent the art of oral reading. Certainly one often sees the effects of an education which has paid too little attention to the area of oral interpretation so needed in our schools. How true it is that speech class rarely lures the needy, for who will willingly walk into a daily class of seeming torture when credits can be had an easier way? Thus the good at speech grow better, and the poor don't grow at all.

Need for Careful Selection

Miss Truett has a lovely voice that makes them feel the freshness ushered in by summer rain, but Susie cannot now enjoy her fully. One day the story that Miss Truett read was quite embarrassing, Susie felt, though it held nothing vulgar. Yet the teacher had somehow violated sensitivity by vocalizing thoughtlessly material too personal for listening by all. Susie could not put it into words, but she somehow felt Miss Truett lacking in that insight and sympathetic understanding so needed in one who helps to solve the problems of the children whom she guides. Truly boys and girls have sensitivities that are offended when they hear their inmost thoughts voiced boldly, thoughts and happenings exposed that almost seem like theirs, and which they would prefer to keep private.

Variety of Interpretation Needed

When Mr. Talbot reads a selection to the class, he insists that everyone see it his way, even though his vision is impaired by years of paper work. He won't admit that there's another way. Yet all the time he reads and as the children listen, they build word-pictures, too, and meaning takes on different forms for them. Sometimes, too, they ask among themselves, "Can't Mr. Talbot ever be wrong?" But no one dares to say the answer known by all. So they listen dully, their initiative cut off. When children have an eagerness to share their viewpoint, however, they tend to listen closely and appreciatively.

Oral Reading as a Complement to Silent Reading

Mary likes it best when oral reading is the climax to the silent reading, to the study she has made for purposes of gaining insight. By this time she has come to realize the significance of words, and so has been prepared for oral interpretation.

Most boys and girls, when in a sympathetic, permissive atmosphere, seem to find the act of reading aloud themselves brings to them an auditory and kinaesthetic pleasure—a pleasure so rewarding that it feeds their fondness for silent reading, too, and nourishes their understanding. This subsequently grows into ability to interpret with effectiveness when they are by themselves.

When children come to see that oral reading is a means to interpretation, they tend to realize to some degree its usefulness to them, and seriously attempt to better those reading skills so needed in both areas.

Good Judgment Needed in Assigning Poetry

Since true interpretation calls for the loss of neither thought nor feeling, it is difficult to attain. Teachers sometimes feel they make it all too easy for the children when they read aloud themselves; thus when the unit deals with poetry, they make assignments to be read at home. Yet, like Joe in reading class, this is not good. If there is silent reading to be done for homework, perhaps it should relate itself to problems arising from the poem, to furthering the understanding of the background of the poetry through study of the writer or of the period in which he lived or in which the piece of literature is placed.

Importance of Good Listening

The fact that listening is a fundamental tool can never be overlooked. As Mrs. Wilson reads expressively, adapting her tone and rate to the mood of what she reads, the children come to listen with a consciousness of sound. Although they are not ready yet, perhaps, to put it into words, they are developing awareness to the qualities of sound, like length and roundness. Marcia likes the long tones best because they seem so strong and positive to her; Tim is thrilled with roundness that makes him think of doughnuts. Similarly, others with awareness wakened can be stimulated to listen more keenly to the literature they read when they are by themselves. To most of them the printed page now takes on round and resonant proportions, instead of staying flat and silent.

Karen finds it difficult to handle symbols that are meaningless to her. She fumbles, mumbles, stumbles until she comes to Miss Green's room. Miss Green leads her to pastures verdant as the teacher's name, for she attaches meaning to the symbols causing trouble. Sometimes to exemplify the word, she shows the children pictures of concrete objects related to the meaning. She draws upon experience, and has everyone sharing eagerly.

Once Karen understands the meaning of a symbol, her reading rate is bettered, and she thinks reading's fun. If she knows words for what they mean, she's not afraid to speak them out before the class. Thus it is generally recognized that a close relationship exists between emotional response and sensory image. If the child is little stirred, the image is vague; if he is deeply moved, the image tends to be exact and clear.

Difficulties Caused by Over-Concern

Kenneth likes to know the meaning of expressions, too, but doesn't like the thoroughness with which Miss Fulbrook undertakes her explanations. It makes him think of how his mother cooked a turkey once. In her concern, she baked and baked it until it dried and fell apart. It's nice to have the teacher show by pause or emphasis or writing on the board what new words mean, but Kenneth gets involved in constant explanations to such degree that he forgets to put parts back into the story—and grows annoyed at interruptions breaking into thoughts he wants to follow.

Significance of Movement

Michele delights in finding how the movement in the lines contributes to the meaning. Miss Booth reads so expressively that almost anyone can see. Michele thinks of movement and the part it plays when reading to herself. She senses then the mournful tread of tragedy, the swiftness of a frightened bird. Once the words were all so whirling that she felt as if she'd just stepped off a merry-go-round, but it was fun to feel that way. And when Miss Booth was reading yesterday, her vivid words and breathless tones made Michele seem to sense the mad rush of a plane in flight, when actually she's never been in one. Truly, Miss Booth has a camera voice. It takes pictures, then shows them to the group.

Comprehension Difficulties Noted

Hilda reads out loud quite easily, yet when Mr. Williams asks her questions concerning what she's read, she grows quite puzzled and confused, and can't quite say what she's supposed to. Mr. Williams speaks of comprehension difficulties—and Hilda and Ruth and others, too, who do not find the meaning readily, agree to work together afterwards, with Mr. Williams' help, and they will have a special goal that's all their own—to understand material which they read. They want to do it because they know that this will help them greatly, both in and out of school.

Different Skills Required for Poetry and Prose

Mr. Henry makes them laugh sometimes because he looks so funny when he is surprised. He wears his eyebrows high when Glenda starts to read. He remembers that she reads prose well— then grows so startled when she trips on meter. Too often we believe falsely that because a child reads prose well, he necessarily reads poetry with similar skill. Yet this is not so, for his ability to deal with word-order, arrangement, figurative language is not so challenged in the field of prose.

Good Oral Reading Appreciated

Miss Greenhoe's room is filled with fervent little readers, yet she still sees values in reading aloud to them despite the freedom of their silent reading. She knows that they'll respond to oral language far more readily and at a higher level than if they were to read the full time independently. She uses this technique as if it were a ladder, and has the children climb to higher levels.

Possibilities of Choral Reading

Choral reading is another way of gaining interest in the oral, for boys and girls gain courage in their reading when they feel security in others reading, too. The fact that husky boys participate with willingness in many instances gives prestige to this form of reading. Experience indicates that if we can get the interest of the boys, the girls, also, show interest, for they tend to like those things that boys like, yet this is not the case when the situation is reversed.

Ralph especially likes choral reading. He feels that he participates in something bigger than himself, and in perfecting the interpretation, he tends to gain appreciation for it. Ralph likes to know the words and what they mean. In this way he gains mastery of thought and sees the thought in units. But choral reading is an area so broad it lends itself to pages rather than to paragraphs.

He also sees that there are values in recordings which allow selections to be listened to at will—excellent when one is studying enunciation and interpretation.

Order of Procedure Significant

In the matter of silent and oral reading, the order of procedure is of great importance, for, just as in our cultural heritage, marriage should precede the bearing of children, so in our educational practices, silent reading should precede the oral.

Both Approaches Necessary

Yet is it not easy to see that both approaches are needed? that each is supplementary to the other? For information or for pleasure, for speed or for reflection—silent reading; for appreciation of sound, for entertainment, for diagnosis, for identification of mood—the oral. Truly, when reading to ourselves, we learn to listen and to hear; when reading to others, we learn to show the close relationship between the mood and meaning. Each holds its own set of values; each, like the universe, calls for order in procedure. Therefore one without the other is incomplete—a philosophy upon which life itself is based.

86. TOWARD MORE PURPOSEFUL ORAL READING*

Emery P. Bliesmer

THE last few years have seen what is supposedly a recurrence of, or an increase in, emphasis on oral reading. There frequently seems to be implied the notion that our children are not having enough oral reading in school and that this is the reason some children are poor readers. This perhaps explains why we frequently still find, with some degree of prevalence, the

* From Emery P. Bliesmer, "Toward More Purposeful Oral Reading," *Education*, LXXIX, No. 9 (May, 1959), 547–50. Reprinted by permission of the author and The Bobbs-Merrill Co., Inc., Indianapolis, Ind.

practice of consistently having children read aloud, in a group, materials or selections which all have already read silently (some more than once) and have discussed and rehashed, both before and after the silent reading. If some children have prepared for the reading lesson by "studying" at home, chances are good that a number will already have read given selections orally a number of times also.

Under the above conditions, the purpose of giving information or pleasure to, or of sharing it with, others tends to be obviated. Further obviation ensues when all the "listeners" (??) in the group are following the selection silently (more or less) while someone is reading it orally. Consequently, oral reading in this type of situation is relatively purposeless. Where such practices or situations exist, there is little incentive for listening—except for children to see who can be the first to pounce upon the mistakes a reader might make. While there might possibly be some merit in helping children develop skill in quickly detecting errors made by someone while reading aloud, this can hardly be justified as a major purpose for oral reading; and certainly little security or self-confidence is promoted in the poor readers who are the consistent targets for such practice in pouncing.

Need for More Purposeful Oral Reading

"But," teachers might say, "my children want to read orally. If we don't let them take turns reading aloud in a group they complain." Or teachers might even have had the experience of having parents complain because their children were not having their daily stints at reading orally, in turn, during the reading class. Perhaps this might sometimes be a reflection of teaching method or practice. If reading a selection aloud, in turn, after the selection has already been read, studied, and discussed has been the regular reading lesson experience for children, they might well have "learned" that this is what "reading" is mainly.

Another seemingly strange observation frequently noted is that even the poorest readers will usually clamor or insist that they also be given their turns to read aloud. If a teacher tries to avoid embarrassing a child with his poor reading performance by skipping him (seemingly accidentally), she usually does not get by with it. The child will call attention to the omission and insist upon his turn. Perhaps he regards putting on a public display of his reading inadequacies as less humiliating or degrading, or being made to seem less different, than being singled out by omission or skipping.

Should we then omit oral reading entirely? Certainly not! While oral reading is not the major type of reading which is required and used most often (and we sometimes seem to forget this), oral reading skill is of importance. However, oral reading needs to be more than a means of showing that one can detect errors rapidly or that one is skillful in making all the right noises associated with given graphic symbols. It needs to be more purposeful than that. The oral reading practices or situations described previously, and often decried, are ones in which the oral reading is relatively purposeless. How, then, can provisions be made for more purposeful oral reading?

Modifying Reading Lesson Procedures

Frequently, slight adaptations or modifications of some typical reading lesson procedures can accomplish more purposeful oral reading. Must a reading selection always be read aloud in entirety, from beginning to end, and consecutively paragraph by paragraph? Why cannot parts of a selection be read aloud in other than a consecutive order? Why cannot some parts be skipped? The writer has had these suggestions be received in aghast fashion at times. "What about continuity of thought? What about omission of some important ideas or details? Won't the children miss a part of the story?" These have been some of the reactions. Certainly a selection or story needs to be read in entirety and in the order in which written if this is the only exposure to, or contact with, the material involved. However, in a reading class all the children will usually already have read the material silently (more or less) in (supposedly) a continuous, consecutive, and orderly fashion; so oral reading is not the major means by which such reading is, or should be, accomplished. Reading it again in this way, but orally rather than silently, would often make the reading somewhat purposeless.

Would it not be more purposeful for each of various children to read aloud, for example, a part he especially liked or a part which might be particularly effective in evoking imagery? The discussion which should usually follow the silent reading of a selection can also provide some very good purposes for oral reading. If two children should disagree on a certain point, each can read aloud the part which he used as a basis for his opinion. If the class seems to have missed some pertinent details relative to a given point, another good reason for having a part, or parts, be read aloud is afforded.

Children's responses on worksheets or workbook exercises also offer good opportunities for meaningful oral reading. Rather than merely marking responses as "right" or "wrong" and giving a score or "grade," it would be much better to have a child read the parts of a selection which he used as bases for his answers to some given items or exercises—and, thus, perhaps lead him to see or understand better why some of his answers might not be the best or the right ones. (Some right, as well as wrong, responses should be utilized in this way; otherwise a child may be apt to view any request to read a part of a selection aloud as an indication of a mistake or failure.)

If the teacher customarily reads the directions for worksheets or other activities to a class, some pupil might be given the opportunity to do this instead, at times. Attention might also be given to modifying or varying directions at times so that there is a real need to read directions before proceeding with given tasks; and such directions might be read to the class by a child before the other pupils have a chance to read the directions silently. After the silent reading of material, individual children might also be guided to the oral reading of parts not covered by specific guide questions for silent reading.

Situations outside the Reading Class

Thus far, mainly oral reading during the reading lesson or class has been dealt with. But we need to keep in mind that oral reading, as well as silent reading, is usually most functional and meaningful outside the reading class. We need to help our children become aware of, and direct their attention toward, this. There are many opportunities for purposeful oral reading outside the reading class. We need to look for such opportunities and, in some instances, modify or adapt our teaching procedures so that additional opportunities are afforded. Quite often certain materials the teacher is in the habit of reading to the class might just as well be read by some of the children, keeping in mind, however, that a child should be given a chance to prepare before he reads to a group. An announcement concerning a PTA meeting might be read to the class by a child before children are given these announcements to take home to their parents (and might be better insurance, in some cases, that the information will actually reach parents). A note of instructions or directives from the principal's office might be read by a pupil. A child who has received a letter from a former member of the class might be prevailed upon to read the letter aloud to the group. A reply to a class request to visit some local place can give one child some good oral reading experience. A particularly funny joke or a part of a story which has caused an individual to chuckle unusually might be shared with the class. If the teacher is reading a story aloud to a class (Why do we do so much less of this above the primary grades?), why could not several children, chosen from among the better readers, participate in this reading also?

Opportunities in Content Areas

Numerous opportunities for purposeful oral reading are to be found in the content areas also. If some point in arithmetic seems confusing or a particular arithmetic problem appears to be stumping some pupils, a class might listen and concentrate on understanding while one pupil reads the problem or other pertinent material aloud. An erroneous concept in science or social studies might be clarified better by having children listen while a child reads a relevant part of a chapter than by having the teacher tell or "explain." A whole class can benefit from listening to one of its members read material which is pertinent to a topic being studied but which has not been generally available to the whole class. Various modifications of procedures suggested for the regular reading class might also be readily used in content area classes.

Criteria for Purposeful Oral Reading Situations

The foregoing suggests some of the situations which might well be used in providing for purposeful oral reading. If they are consciously and consistently on the watch for such, teachers will be able to find many other meaningful opportunities. Relatively purposeless types of oral reading might be avoided more readily if the chief purpose or function of oral reading is kept in mind: to convey ideas to listeners, to tell them something. Obviously, if what is being read aloud is already general information for the supposed listeners, there is then no really good reason for listening—or no really good reason for oral reading in the first place. Another obvious, and frequently made, point to be kept in mind is that if what is being read orally can be read silently by supposed listeners at the same time, there, again, is no reason for listening. These points should perhaps be among the chief criteria used in the selection of situations which offer opportunities for purposeful oral reading; and constant and consistent application of these should aid in eliminating much of the oral-reading-for-its-own-sake practice—and make oral reading be more than a matter of making the right noises in response to given visual stimuli.

Increasing the opportunities for children to read aloud in functional and meaningful situations should aid in making the reading act or process more meaningful to children also. However, it may take a little time for some children (and some parents and teachers also) to accept and become acclimated to this more meaningful and functional approach, if they have become somewhat habituated to a more ritualistic and mechanistic type of oral reading practice. Some teachers may even find themselves in the situation experienced by a friend of the writer. One night early in the school year this teacher received a phone call from a rather disturbed mother who wanted to know why the teacher was discriminating against her Geraldine. The little girl had complained to her mother that the teacher was not letting her read very much in school. Actually, Geraldine had been given frequent daily opportunities to read, but in situations other than the "now-let's-read-around-the-circle-in-turn" one. On succeeding days after the phone call the teacher made it a point to comment favorably upon Geraldine's reading every time she read orally and to call her attention, indirectly, to the fact that she was reading. At the end of each day the teacher called the child aside, helped her recall all the various times she had read orally during the day and suggested (for further insurance, perhaps), "Don't you think your mother would be pleased to hear about all the times you read for us today?"

87. CHARACTERISTICS OF EFFECTIVE ORAL READING*

William S. Gray

A VIVID picture of the varied uses of oral reading in current life is presented in Dr. Shane's paper. The fact that the role of oral reading has expanded rapidly during recent years emphasizes the urgent need of training boys and girls to read well to others. To achieve effective results, we need a clear understanding of the attitudes and skills that characterize a competent oral reader.

Earlier Practice

As an approach to this problem, it will be illuminating to review briefly certain pages from the history of oral reading in this country. In early Colonial days, oral reading served a genuine social need. During evenings and on Sundays, those who could not read met in small groups to listen to the reading of the Scriptures. As far as I have been able to learn, however, little or no special training was given in the art of oral interpretation.

As revealed by a survey of the school practices that prevailed, initial instruction in reading was based on the use of the alphabetical method.

Further growth in ability to read was promoted through daily practice in reading aloud. The guidance provided aimed to correct errors in recognition and to develop ability to read independently and accurately. Obviously, oral reading was conceived as an instructional aid rather than as a mode of interpretation. A pattern of teaching was thus established which profoundly influenced much of the character of reading instruction for three hundred years.

At various times, however, following the Colonial period, vigorous effort was made to improve the quality of oral reading. During the Revolutionary period, for example, the chief purpose of much of the material printed was to promote loyalty to the new nation and to develop national unity and strength. These purposes were clearly reflected in the content of school readers and in significant changes in methods of teaching. The latter included: "(1) emphasis upon articulation and pronunciation as a means of correcting the numerous dialects that had sprung up in different sections, and of bringing about a greater unity in the American language"[1] (concern about these matters led to continued emphasis on the more formal aspects of oral read-

* From William S. Gray, "Characteristics of Effective Oral Reading," in *Oral Aspects of Reading,* Supplementary Education Monographs, No. 82 (December, 1955), pp. 5–10. Reprinted by permission of Mrs. William S. Gray and The University of Chicago Press.

[1] Nila Banton Smith, *American Reading Instruction* (New York: Silver, Burdett & Co., 1934), p. 69.

ing), with "(2) increasing attention to elocution." [2] This resulted in spectacular innovations. Note, for example, the following directions to teachers in Leavitt's *Early Lessons in Reading:*

Great pains should be taken to make reading appear like real life. The reader should place himself exactly in the circumstances supposed by the writer, and endeavor to possess the same feelings and passions. Children should never be allowed to pronounce a sentence or even a word, in that dull, monotonous humdrum style, which so often disgraces our common schools.

It is a very useful practice for the teacher to read over a sentence, before the scholar, giving it the proper pauses, inflection, and emphasis, and then to require the scholar to repeat it, until he can pronounce it with propriety. [3]

As a further aid some authors divided the line into metrical feet and marked them with a series of notations to help pupils read with ease and rhythm. In addition, great importance was attached to the learning and following of rules, such as to speak with a clear and distinct voice. As revealed by these and other suggestions, vigorous emphasis was given to one form of oral reading during the Revolutionary period. Although the ends sought were achieved largely through formal drill, imitation, and the memorization of rules, a foundation was laid for the personal interpretation of meaning by the reader.

By the middle of the nineteenth century, further progress had been made in the recognition of oral reading as a useful art. Furthermore, some of the basic requirements of effective oral reading were more clearly and explicitly defined. Note, for example, the following statement by McGuffey:

The great object to be accomplished in reading as a rhetorical exercise is, to convey to the hearer, fully and clearly, the ideas and feelings of the writer. In order to do this, it is necessary that the feelings of the author whose language is read, should be infused into the breast of the reader, and then alone can they be properly and fully expressed. . . . The best speakers and readers are those who follow the impulse of nature as felt in their own hearts, or most closely imitate it as observed in others. [4]

As aids in achieving the goals sought, McGuffey [5] provided training in harmony with the following suggestions: "Give to each letter (except silent letters), to each syllable, and to each word its full, distinct, and appropriate utterance"; make effective use of inflections according to the meaning to be conveyed; give proper accent in pronouncing words of more than one syllable; use emphasis effectively; modulate the voice to give variety and effectiveness to oral expression; and use poetic pauses skilfully "to make prominent the melody of the measure."

Although McGuffey recognized the great importance in oral reading of a clear grasp of meaning and of spontaneous, natural expression, his sug-

---

[2] *Ibid.*

[3] Quoted in Nila Banton Smith, *op. cit.,* p. 70.

[4] William H. McGuffey, *New Fifth Eclectic Reader* (Cincinnati: Wilson, Hinkle & Co., 1857) p. 9.

[5] *Ibid.,* pp. 10–32.

gestions to teachers gave little emphasis to such matters. Instead, he focused attention chiefly on the mechanics of oral reading and on the technical aspects of expression. He did this so thoroughly that the pattern of teaching he recommended was followed rigorously in many schools throughout the latter half of the nineteenth century.

By 1915 widespread protest developed against the formal practices in teaching reading that had prevailed. It took the form of a radical shift in emphasis from oral to silent reading, owing in part to the greater economy and efficiency of silent reading. Even specialists in oral interpretation, such as S. H. Clark,[6] one-time professor of public speaking at the University of Chicago, joined in the revolt. He pointed out that the very poor oral reading in the schools was due not to lack of technical exercises but rather to failure to understand fully the meaning of what was read.

Clark recognized the great importance of helping to clarify for the listener the meaning intended by the author, and he recommended that the reader employ such devices as appropriate grouping of words and subordination of ideas to achieve that end. His treatment of the problem of conveying feeling or emotion was brief, his chief advice being "to enter into the spirit of the text."[7] He believed that, if the reader experienced internally the emotional values of what he was reading, the bodily and facial expressions would "take care of them-

selves."[8] Neither did he attempt to give instructions concerning the use of the vocal mechanism, assuming that the voice, too, would respond intuitively once emotion was felt.

As revealed by the foregoing discussion, radical changes occurred in the teaching of oral reading during the century and a quarter following the Revolutionary War. From primary emphasis on oral reading as an instructional aid, much attention was given at different times to elocutionary aspects of oral interpretation, to technical aspects of expression, and to techniques of grasping the ideas and feelings inherent in what was read. During the twenties and thirties, so much attention was given to the development of efficient habits of silent reading that oral reading was sadly neglected in some schools.

We are emerging today into a highly significant period with respect to oral reading. Its importance as a useful art is clearly recognized. The large emphasis given to silent reading has provided new techniques for use in mastering basic reading skills and in grasping the ideas and feelings intended by the writer. Furthermore, oral reading has been freed from many of the formal practices which prevailed when it was taught chiefly as an instructional aid. We are now in a position to focus attention specifically upon the development of those attitudes and skills that characterize efficient oral reading.

The Current Scene

Today oral reading is considered to be (1) an instructional and diagnostic

[6] S. H. Clark, *Interpretation of the Printed Page* (Evanston, Illinois: Row, Peterson & Co., 1915).

[7] *Ibid.*, p. 257.

[8] *Ibid.*, p. 265.

instrument, (2) a useful art in communicating ideas to others, and (3) a fine art which conforms to certain aesthetic standards. In the discussion that follows, we shall be concerned primarily with oral reading as a useful art and to some extent with oral reading as a fine art.

In the effort to identify the characteristics of effective oral reading, an analysis was made of recent discussions by specialists in this field. The impressive fact revealed was that, in the judgment of all, and independent of the maturity level of the reader, four significant tasks are involved: grasping the author's intended meaning, sensing the mood and emotional reactions which the author intended to produce, conveying the author's meaning to the listener, and conveying mood and feeling. Although reading specialists discuss these tasks either separately or in varying combinations, all maintain that a high degree of skill should be developed in each of them.

Securing the ideas and feelings intended. Without exception, the fact was emphasized vigorously that a reader must secure a clear grasp of the thoughts and feelings intended by the author before he can convey them to others. The steps involved have been likened to the charging of a battery prior to its use for an important service. The ideas and feelings acquired supply the inner drive and condition both the mind and the body of the reader to the challenging task of reading well to others. Time and again the fact was pointed out that, without adequate impression, there can be only ineffective expression. As essential requisites in securing adequate im-

pressions, three characteristics of an efficient reader were discussed.

The first is ability to secure a clear grasp of the author's meaning. The attitudes and skills involved are similar to those required in any reading situation where full understanding is essential. As implied earlier, the reading specialists of previous generations directed attention largely to such items as the major point in a selection, coordinate and subordinate ideas, and the grouping of words and their sequence. Valuable as are these clues to meaning, they are based largely on an analysis of the structural elements of the passages read.

Current writers have adopted a far broader and more dynamic concept of the steps involved in securing the meaning of a passage. Of major importance is the need of a unified grasp of the story as a whole, of the message intended, or of the information presented. As a necessary background the reader should often know the kind of material he is reading, why the author wrote it, and, to some extent, the author's background.

As the reader gains a broad grasp of the author's meaning, he tries to identify its central theme, idea, or contribution. He studies the way in which the various ideas presented reinforce and expand the central idea. He examines the words and figures of speech used in their contextual setting and identifies the way in which they delimit, qualify, or enrich the meaning of the passage. As his search for meaning continues, he recalls parallel experiences in his own life, the geographic setting of the incidents related, their historical background, and everything he knows that makes clear the meaning of the passage. He also searches for meanings that are intended but not stated, for example, the kind of person a story character is as revealed by what he does or says. At every step in reading, vivid memory images are recalled or the reader reconstructs in imagination mental pictures of the things, scenes, and activities described.

A second requisite is ability to sense the mood and emotional tone which the author intended to create. Oral reading which fails to develop appropriate feeling responses falls far short of its goal. In order to produce desired effects, a good writer selects and organizes with great care the ideas to be presented. He also uses words and forms of expression purposefully and creatively in presenting specific ideas, in describing scenes and events, and in depicting character. Furthermore, he tries to build up vivid mental pictures that elicit emotional responses, and he uses such devices as repetition, rhyme, and sound to produce appropriate effects. His aim may be to convince his readers; to modify their attitudes; or to develop certain moods or feelings, such as joy, sorrow, hatred, fear. No matter what they may be, a good oral reader is able to identify and interpret all clues to the mood and emotional responses which the author intends to develop.

A third requisite is ability to react thoughtfully to both the ideas presented and the effects that the author is seeking to develop. A favorable reaction by the reader influences in a positive manner the vigor and effectiveness of his oral interpretation. If his reactions are unfavorable, they are more or less unconsciously reflected in his attitude, facial expression, or tone of voice while reading to others.

Conveying ideas and feelings to others. The task of conveying ideas and arousing feelings through oral reading is no less challenging than that of grasping the meanings and sensing the feelings to be conveyed. As preconditions for this step, three personal qualifications are discussed repeatedly in the literature.

In the first place, a good reader is eager to share with his listeners something to which he attaches real importance. It may be valuable information, a unique point of view, a vivid description, an interesting character sketch, a bit of humor, or the musical effects produced through the choice and arrangement of words. Without a compelling motive, oral reading rarely rises above the commonplace.

In the second place, a good oral reader knows his audience and adapts his interpretation to their interests and needs. He is aware, for example, that they are receptive and eager for the message or that their interest must be aroused, favorable attitudes developed, and desirable responses elicited. In the light of such facts, he plans his approach to the reading and develops the kind of presentation that will arouse maximum interest and convey effectively the ideas and feeling intended.

In the third place, the good reader has mastered the basic skills of perception so well that he recognizes words quickly and accurately and pronounces them clearly and distinctly. Equally important is ability to group words together in thought units and to read aloud smoothly and without evidence of effort or difficulty. To achieve the level of mastery desired, long periods of basic training in reading are often necessary. Not infrequently the help of a speech specialist is desirable in overcoming specific difficulties.

In helping his listeners grasp the author's meaning, the good reader uses various devices. He highlights, through the use of emphasis, new or important ideas; he makes clear the transition from one idea to another; he indicates by proper phrasing the units of thought within a sentence; he relates the ideas of a series by keeping his voice up until the end is reached; he indicates climax by the force and vigor of expression; he brings out similarities and contrasts by emphasizing the items compared. He varies his rate of reading, modulates his voice, and uses facial and bodily expressions in the effort to convey meanings.

The training of pupils to convey meanings effectively is an insightful but subtle art. The teacher should have a good understanding of the techniques or skills involved. However, he does not center attention upon them as such. If, for example, a pupil emphasizes the wrong word in reading, the teacher helps him to identify the right one. If a pupil fails to bring out a difference, the teacher directs his attention to the things to be contrasted and suggests that he re-read the passage to make clear the difference between them. The teacher relies far more on helping the child to grasp clearly the idea to be presented than on formal directions concerning modes of expression. On occasion, however, he may read a pas-

sage to help the pupil identify an improved way of expressing an idea, or he may ask other pupils to do so.

The imparting of mood and feeling is an equally challenging task. If it is achieved effectively, it greatly heightens interest and appreciation on the part of the listeners. As indicated earlier, a first requisite of a good reader in this connection is a vivid sensing of the mood and feeling intended by the author. The techniques for helping the listener acquire the mood and feeling are many and varied. For example, changes in rate of reading often reveal action or excitement. A rising inflection indicates doubt; a falling inflection, certainty; a rising and falling inflection, indecision. The spontaneous use of facial expressions and bodily activity aids materially in imparting mood, such as joy, sorrow, excitement. The belief prevails, however, that, if the reader senses mood and feeling vividly and appropriately and is eager to read to others, he will need little guidance in these techniques. When he is unsuccessful, the teacher attempts to aid him, primarily through a discussion of the meanings and feelings he wishes to convey.

The comments thus far have related chiefly to oral reading as a useful art. One of the most valuable sources of help now available for teachers is Ogilvie's chapter on oral reading in her recent book entitled *Speech in the Elementary School.*[9] Other chapters give needed help in related fields, such as informal speaking, speech, voice, diction, dramatics, and choral speaking.

[9] Mardel Ogilvie, *Speech in the Elementary School* (New York: McGraw-Hill Book Co., Inc., 1954).

The authors [10] of textbooks on speech and expression for use at the high-school and college levels think of oral reading much more largely as a fine art. Accordingly, they analyze in great detail the basic elements of expression, the various aspects of voice, and the nature of the various speech sounds. Independent of the level for which a textbook is intended, the suggestions made are concerned with the four major tasks in oral reading, to which reference was made earlier. The chief differences, as far as age groups are concerned, relates to choice of materials, the specific methods used, and the intensity of the training provided.

Concluding Statement

As an appropriate conclusion to this discussion, may I summarize briefly six characteristics of effective oral reading as currently conceived:

1. It is motivated by a keen desire on the part of the reader to share with others something to which he attaches real significance.

[10] a) Argus Tresidder, *Reading to Others* (Chicago: Scott, Foresman & Co., 1940).

  b) W. M. Parrish, *Reading Aloud* (New York: Ronald Press Co., 1953).

  c) Charles Woolbert and Severina E. Nelson, *The Art of Interpretative Speech* (revised ed.; New York: F. S. Crofts & Co., 1946).

2. It is prepared and presented in the light of a careful study of the purposes to be achieved and the interests, needs, and probable attitudes of the listeners.

3. It is based on both a penetrating grasp of the meaning and a vivid sensing of the mood and feeling intended by the author. The great importance attached to this requirement is one of the distinguishing features of the current effort to improve oral reading.

4. Effective oral reading is preceded by such a thorough mastering of word recognition that the reader, while reading to others, is free to focus attention entirely on the act of transmitting the author's message to them.

5. A good oral reader makes use of varied techniques in conveying both meaning and feeling to his audience. The prevailing view today is that this should be done within the framework of the reader's natural modes of expression and his normal pattern of conversation. As pupils advance, however, increasing attention should be given to the more technical aspects of expression and speech.

6. A good measure of the quality of oral reading is its effectiveness in conveying the desired understandings and in producing the intended effects on the listener.

R E A D I N G   F O R
T H E   G I F T E D

88. THE IMPROVEMENT OF READING IN GIFTED

CHILDREN*

J. C. Gowan and R. W. Scheibel

EVERYONE recognizes that able adults, embarked on an intellectual life, need skills for wide, quick, and effective reading if they are to enlarge their arena of cognition and function effectively in a complex culture. Too often, however, the fact that any particularly able student reads at or above his grade placement level is taken as sufficient proof that his reading is satisfactory. Reading competence which may be satisfactory for the average person may be quite unsatisfactory for the gifted student. One of the ways in which it may be defective is that the rate of reading is too slow to allow the able person to acquire quickly all the knowledge and information which he needs to feed and orient his mental processes. Good decisions cannot be made on the basis of insufficient data or information. In our increasingly complicated civilization, the need to keep up in a number of fields by the sheer intake of large amounts of reading becomes more onerous each year. The plight of a person insufficiently nourished in this regard may be compared to that of an electronic computer whose input is bottlenecked by some inadequate design which permits less than high speed feeding of data for processing. While it is obvious that there may be many other facets to reading than mere speed, we shall assume that speed is a necessary (but not a sufficient) condition for reading adequacy on the part of a superior student. We may then pose the main

* From J. C. Gowan and R. W. Scheibel, "The Improvement of Reading in Gifted Children," *Educational Administration and Supervision,* XLVI, No. 1 (January, 1960), 35–40. Reprinted by permission of the authors and Mrs. Harry Buchholz.

issue of this paper which is: How and to what extent can speed be improved in the reading of gifted children?

Brief mention may be made at this juncture of the literature. It is surely unnecessary in an article of this type to do more than cite the pioneer work of Hollingsworth,[11] or Witty,[21] since their research is basic in the field. Summary notice may be made of some of the later investigations into the reading ability of gifted students. Among these are the following:

Barbe[1] found that gifted children learn to read earlier than average, read about five hours per week, but use the library less than had been expected. Bliesmer[2] found that when bright children are compared with dull children of the same mental age, but different chronological age, the bright ones are superior in comprehension, memory for details, and relationships, but are similar in reading rate, word recognition, and word meaning. Carroll[3] indicated that the superiority of the bright in spelling is due to superiority in phonetic generalization. Danielson[4] found that intellectually superior children reached a higher level of achievement if a more varied and extensive reading program is substituted for the conventional study course. Strang[17] recognized that the gifted child at grade placement may be a remedial reading problem and offered suggestions for his improvement. She also[18] explored satisfactions which come to gifted children as needs in reading are met.

Specific programs for the reading progress of able students have been widely reported. Robinson,[16] in an ambitious work, has indicated the extensive efforts at all levels to improve reading for able students. Deason[5] gave details of a traveling science library for gifted students. Gearhart and Foster[8] supplied annotated lists of books. Thurber[19] described honors work. Examples of specific reading programs for gifted students in California school districts run the gamut of types which may be useful for study. A "Great-Books" seminar-type program in the Ontario Schools was described by Flory.[6] Lazarus[12] has detailed a similar program in the schools of Santa Monica. In Ventura County, the use of a tape recorder and earphones has been found helpful in permitting gifted students individual attention and directing them to individual projects involving the use of the library.* Palo Alto and San Diego may be mentioned as other communities which have developed special reading programs for gifted students. The use of extensive reading programs for the gifted in connection with studies other than English, such as social science, natural science, and "general" reading has been described by Flynn,[7] elsewhere,[10] and in various summaries.[13, 15]

Reference may be made here to a study reported elsewhere,[9] comparing the relative weights of intelligence, interests, and reading ability in relation to achievement. Intelligence was measured by the American Council on Education Examination, reading ability by the Iowa, achievement by the Coöperative Culture Test, and interests by the Kuder Preference Record. The subjects were one hundred college juniors. Reading ability correlated .54 with achievement under these circumstances, and showed a partial correlation of .45

* Personal communication.

with achievement even with intelligence held constant. The study, after finding negligible correlations between interests and achievement, concluded that reading ability, even apart from its intelligence component, occupies a central position in the determination of achievement.

Raubicheck [14] in another study of the reading ability of high school pupils of superior ability presents extensive results of the amount and quality of their reading. He concludes: "It is a fatal mistake in dealing with superior pupils not to press them at every stage to the limit of their capabilities. When this condition is achieved, the aspiring pupil will soon set the pace for the perspiring teacher."

Other investigators, such as the Wheelers,[20] note after a summary of their investigations into the reading ability of gifted students: "The most seriously retarded readers in our schools are the mentally superior students."

As a result of the foregoing analysis of the literature, the following propositions are emergent:

1. Reading is central in the determination of achievement in students.
2. The reading of gifted children is often seriously behind their potential: i.e., most gifted children are hidden remedial reading candidates.
3. Special programs of various kinds can improve this reading adequacy, which, for the gifted child is often merely a matter of increasing the reading rate.

To indicate the extent to which the reading rate of gifted children may be improved by remedial reading techniques, the following experiment was conducted by the junior author. The subjects were two classes of gifted A10 honor English students in a large suburban high school. The students were selected for the honors class on the basis of teacher recommendation, scholastic achievement at B+ or better, and performance on the Iowa test of general knowledge at the 80th percentile or above in the five areas of correctness of writing, interpretation of literature, background in literature, general vocabulary, and composite score. A class of 27 such students served as the controls in the conventional English program. A class of 34 such students served as the experimental subjects. Each group was tested before and after the program with the Iowa Silent Reading Test. In addition, the experimental group took the SRA Reading Book Two speed tests before and after the program. The program for the experimental subjects consisted of a six-week intensive training on remedial reading techniques with emphasis on speed, consisting of lectures, reading materials, individual help, drill, tests, and the use of the tachistoscope and slides.

Results showed that while the control group gained two percentile points (from a composite score at the 83rd to the 85th percentile), the experimentals gained eleven percentile points (from a composite score at the 83rd percentile to the 94th percentile). The experimentals moreover increased in reading rate from a mean of 284 words per minute (with a sigma of 96) to a mean of 896 words per minute (with a sigma of 459), while gaining in comprehension. At the beginning no student had a rate over 576 words per minute. At the end, two students were reading over 2000 words per minute, eleven were over 1000 words per minute, and all but nine were over 600 words per minute. The critical ratios for improvement in both tests on the part of the experimentals were well beyond the .01 level, and the critical ratio for the excess of improvement of the experimentals over the controls was at the .01 level of confidence. The experiment constituted a graphic illustration of how much can be accomplished in improving the reading rate and hence the reading adequacy of gifted children by intensive remedial methods.

In conclusion, educators have not been enough aware of the demonstrated possibilities of large gains in reading rate on the part of all gifted students when remedial methods suited to their ability and interests are employed. Since comprehension presents but a minor problem for these readers, the rate of reading intake constitutes a serious bottleneck which needs to be adjusted. Much of this improvement in reading efficiency can come as a result of understanding techniques to change of pace in reading procedures—when to skim and how, when to read for close detail. Remedial reading procedures are effective for the gifted not only in allowing them larger quantities of intake, but in the smaller time required by the reading improvement techniques to produce significant results. As the urgency of this problem becomes better understood, and as it is more widely realized that remedial reading for the gifted is an important service from which most of them can greatly profit, we may expect continued expansion of high school and college programs for the improvement of reading effectiveness of superior students. It will be found that this is one of the easiest and most effective ways to improve the achievement of these students and to retain more of them through the college program.

REFERENCES

1. BARBE, W. B. "A Study of the Reading of Gifted High School Students," *Educational Administration and Supervision*, 38, 1952, pp. 148–54.
2. BLIESMER, E. P. "Reading Abilities of Bright and Dull Children of Comparable Mental Age," *Journal of Educational Psychology*, 45, 1954, pp. 321–24.
3. CARROLL, H. A. *Generalization of Bright and Dull Children*, Teachers College Contributions #439, New York: Columbia University, 1930.
4. DANIELSON, C. L. "A Study of the Effect of a Definite Course of Reading in General Literature upon Achievement in Content Subjects with Children of Superior Mental Ability," *Journal of Educational Psychology*, 20, 1929, pp. 610–21.
5. DEASON, H. J. "A Challenge for the Scientifically Talented," *American Library Association Bulletin*, 52, 1958, p. 108.
6. FLORY, VERA. "A Working Program for the Gifted," *Bulletin of the National Association of Secondary School Principals*, 40:221, September, 1956, pp. 82–85.
7. FLYNN, E. L. "For the Superior Learner," *Library Journal*, 79, 1954, pp. 492–95.
8. GEARHART, G. K. and FOSTER, R. L. "Library Materials for the Gifted," *American Library Association Bulletin*, 52, February, 1958, pp. 107–8.
9. GOWAN, J. C. "Intelligence, Interests,

and Reading Ability in Relation to Achievement," *Psychological Newsletter,* 8:4, March, 1957, pp. 85–88.

10. GOWAN, J. C. and WILBAR, MILDRED. "Santa Monica High School Evaluates a Program for Gifted Children," *California Journal of Secondary Education,* 30:4, April, 1955, pp. 218–22.

11. HOLLINGSWORTH, LETA. *Children above 180 IQ: Origin and Development.* Yonkers on Hudson, New York: World Book Company, 1942.

12. LAZARUS, A. L. "Grouping Based on High Interest versus General Ability," *California Journal of Secondary Education,* 30, 1955, pp. 38–41.

13. NATIONAL ASSOCIATION OF SECONDARY SCHOOL PRINCIPALS. "Teaching Reading for the Gifted in Secondary Schools," *Bulletin* of the Association, October, 1955, pp. 13–28.

14. RAUBICHECK, C. W. "The Reading of Superior High School Pupils," *English Journal,* 29, September, 1940, pp. 522–50.

15. *The Reading Teacher.* Symposium Issue on the Gifted, 9:4, April, 1956.

16. ROBINSON, HELEN. *Promoting Maximal Growth among Able Learners,* University of Chicago, 1954.

17. STRANG, R. "Gifted Children Need Help in Reading," *Reading Teacher,* 6, 1953, pp. 23–27.

18. ———. "Insights of Gifted Students about Reading," *Reading Teacher,* 9:4, 1956, pp. 204–8.

19. THURBER, G. "Honors in History Require Library Use," *American Library Association Bulletin,* 52, February, 1958, p. 106.

20. WHEELER, L. R. and WHEELER, V. D. "Relationship between Reading Ability and Intelligence among University Freshmen," *Journal of Educational Psychology,* 40, April, 1949, pp. 230–31.

21. WITTY, P. and LEHMAN, H. C. "A Study of the Reading and Reading Interests of Gifted Children," *Pedagogical Seminary and Journal of Genetic Psychology,* 40, June, 1932, pp. 473–85.

89. SOME FIELD OBSERVATIONS ON EARLY-GRADE PROGRESS IN READING*

Earl K. Stock

FROM observation of school reading instruction over a period of years, two conclusions seem to be justified: that pupils capable of fast learning are being moved too slowly and that slow-learning pupils are being moved too rapidly in their developmental reading programs. In considering whether the pupils are being moved rapidly or slowly, we take account of the degree of accomplishment, both qualitative and quantitative, in reading skills, interests, and abilities.

Fast-learning pupils may be thought of as those ranking in the upper third or fourth of a class which follows reasonably well the normal distribution curve on a general intelligence test. Slow-learning pupils may be thought of as those who fall in the lower third or fourth of the class distribution.

As we analyze the reading situation, we are likely to find one or more of several factors operating to produce the results referred to above.

Fast-Learning Pupils

Misapplication of readiness principle. In the fast-learning group the first fac-

* From Earl K. Stock, "Some Field Observations on Early-Grade Progress in Reading," *Elementary School Journal,* LV (May, 1955), 517–20. Reprinted by permission of the author and The University of Chicago Press.

tor operating to affect pupil progress is a commonly misunderstood or misapplied conception of the principle of readiness. "Reading readiness" may be defined as the presence of those conditions that make it possible for pupils to attack the acquisition of skill in reading with success and satisfaction.

Teachers are well inoculated with the idea that there should be a readiness program before actual reading instruction begins. The difficulty seems to be that there is not an equal understanding of the great differences in kind and amount of readiness preparation needed for different pupils. This misunderstanding is enhanced by the plethora of available commercial materials to develop readiness and by the slavish devotion to them in the form and extent in which they are published.

Briefly, these are the major, commonly accepted bases for judging a child ready to begin actual reading:

1. Sufficient mental maturity
2. Good background of information
3. Ability to see likenesses and differences in forms
4. Auditory discrimination
5. Oral-language facility
6. Memory span of ideas
7. Attention span
8. Social maturity sufficient to make satisfactory adjustment to the school situation

9. Freedom from extensive auditory, visual, and nutritional defects and physical defects of other types

10. A strong desire and urge for reading

In any average first-grade class there will be a group of children who meet these conditions fully and who are filled with the desire and urge to get at the business of reading. Their readiness needs consist mainly in adjusting to the school situation, to the teacher and other pupils, and to several technical requirements, such as following lines from left to right, associating the spoken word with the printed form, and recognizing likenesses and differences in word forms. For them, acquiring these specialized abilities is not a long or tedious task if the teacher approaches it with vigor and directness and utilizes well the higher abilities, maturity, and eagerness of this group.

Here is where a common fault enters. Too often the teacher feels obligated to wade through the full reading-readiness publication purchased for the grade, as well as all the "suggested activities" of the accompanying manual —these to the last picture, the last game, the last routine. This malpractice is not confined to teachers who use commercially prepared readiness materials. There are others who indulge in various kindergarten-type activities, picked up at reading conferences, summer school, or elsewhere. Many of these activities are commendable in kindergarten or for immature and slow-learning pupils, but their use is not defensible for those pupils who are ready, or nearly ready, for reading.

Several results are fairly certain to follow prolonged, unnecessary use of readiness materials. First, little addi-tional readiness is gained; a pupil can only be "ready," not doubly or trebly ready. Second, a considerable period of time is lost. Third, much of the eagerness of the child is dissipated, and the sharp edge of desire is dulled.

Thus the first step in retardation has taken place; the second step is like unto it. An increasing amount of time is utilized in carrying out all the word drills, workbook exercises, and suggested activities supplied with the textbook in reading, whether they are needed or not. The fault is not necessarily with the materials but with the lack of choice, discrimination, or emphasis exercised by the teacher. Hence pupils who can and should be engaged in actual reading, to their joy and profit, are often engaged in some activity which is related to reading but is not reading. They are doing something which is not valuable to them but which may, in fact, be destructive to their best reading progress.

The net result may be retardation of the pupil, often amounting to as much as four to eight weeks in Grade I. Nor is this statement of the result merely a matter of observation; measurement of reading progress by the best available testing techniques produces ample evidence of this condition.

Though this result does not necessarily accompany one type of reading program more than another, it is perhaps more readily described for groups making use of a basal reading series. A group of fast learners should readily show a reading development evidenced by completion of the average first reader with high-level achievement and a considerable number of supplemental books. In many instances—an appalling number of instances—this level is not reached by the end of Grade I.

Prolonged review. At the beginning of both Grades II and III, certain review activities are desirable. Here again, however, valuable time is frequently lost through unnecessary and unproductive attenuation of the review procedure. It is not uncommon to find that the brighter pupils have gained reading skill over the summer vacation rather than lost it; they have continued their maturation, increased their information, interests, and experiences, and usually have carried on their home reading habits. Certainly, only a short period of time is necessary to renew school habits, regain lost vocabulary, and acquire new interest and enthusiasm for school tasks. Challenging reading material should be made available quickly in order that the pupils' increased maturation and whetted interest shall be utilized as motivating forces for rapid attack and development of new levels.

Slow pace. Another cause for subnormal advance in Grades II and III is the frequent failure to realize and understand the speed with which fast learners expand and advance their reading activities during these years. Word-recognition skills accelerate rapidly. Comprehension stretches far ahead, often to surprising lengths. Abilities in drawing conclusions and in forming judgments and generalizations blossom and bloom. Curiosity, imagination, and creativeness burst forth if given opportunity and encouragement.

Yet, in spite of this psychological background, classroom teachers too often maintain a studied pace from day to day, month to month, year to year. There is but one result—retardation. By the end of Grade III, it is not uncommon to find retardation of a half-year to a full year and, for the brightest pupils, several years.

Neglect of the fast-learning. A third factor contributing to the retardation of fast-learning pupils is the general failure among school leaders and teachers to assume proper responsibility for this group. These pupils do very well and "get along," and that is regarded as sufficient for them. It is not a cause of alarm, or even concern, if they are not making the best progress possible for them. To a large extent they are a neglected group. Their educational opportunities are not in proportion to their abilities or to their potential value to society.

This philosophy and practice operates in various phases of the educational program, and no less in the field of reading. In recent years there has been a tendency to place more emphasis on the importance and needs of "the gifted child," but action has been slow and largely restricted to the very brightest. Consequently, to the aforementioned bad instructional practices we must add a poor educational philosophy as an influence affecting the reading retardation of our better pupils.

It is not the purpose here to consider retardation in fields other than reading. Obviously, they will be coexistent, especially in personality development, interest in the over-all school program, and in habits of work, attention, and study. General retardation is an almost certain accompaniment of reading retardation.

90. HELPING THE SUPERIOR READER *

Gretchen Wulfing

"TEACHING would be simple if all children could learn as easily as those in the advanced reading group," is doubtless a thought of most teachers. Not only do these children master the skills of reading with little effort, but they are likely to become independent readers and enthusiastic users of books at an early age.

Good readers, however, are apt to be left to their own devices in a crowded school schedule. Indeed, many of them are actually retarded in reading because they fail to achieve the skill of which they are capable. Good readers need guidance, as do all children, although it may be a different kind of guidance from that required by the slow or average learners.

American schools are committed to the policy of helping each child attain the maximum development of which he is capable. There is considerable evidence to indicate that many schools, in their zeal to make all children literate, have done better in helping slow learners reach their maximum level of development than in challenging bright children. Society needs the abilities of all, but it expects from the most intelligent and best educated segment of the population the exploration of new

frontiers of knowledge for the benefit of all. Bright children must be discovered early and given the guidance necessary to develop their potentialities, both for their own growth as individuals and for the continued progress of society.

This monograph is concerned with the pupils who acquire reading and language skills more rapidly than the average. It points out to teachers some ways of identifying these boys and girls and offers suggestions for a program of reading instruction which will meet their needs.

Who Are the Superior Readers?

Soon after school opened in September the children in Miss Walker's sixth grade were given a standardized test in reading. The teacher had already studied the pupils' cumulative records and had observed their choices of library and reference books during the first few days. Now she wished to study the test records carefully as a guide to organizing groups for reading instruction and planning the year's program.

The individual scores ranged from 8 years and 6 months to 15 years and 4 months, typical for the grade. One group of eleven children scored considerably above sixth-grade level. Miss Walker decided that, for a few weeks at least, these children would form the advanced group in reading.

---

* From Gretchen Wulfing, "Helping the Superior Reader," in *Contributions in Reading,* No. 14, pp. 1–4. Reprinted by permission of the author and Ginn and Company, Boston, Mass.

Comparison of reading achievement with the ages of these eleven pupils revealed that all but one were younger than the average sixth grader. Indeed, Roger and Pauline, who attained the highest scores in reading, were the youngest pupils in the class. Pauline had been given an individual test of intelligence the preceding year, and was found to have an IQ of 143 which indicated that she was intellectually gifted. Group mental test scores were available for the other ten children, of whom four fell within the normal range of 90 to 110, three between 110 and 120, and three above 120, Roger being in this last group.

Patty and Don, whose mental test scores were not above normal, scored rather high on the reading test. They seemed tense and over-anxious to succeed. Was this achievement in reading due to high expectations at home? The teacher made a mental note to find out more about Patty and Don and to do what she could to ease the pressures on them.

Bill and Tony seemed to shine in reading and in discussions, but they found arithmetic and written expression difficult. Bill, the oldest pupil in this group, was a poor speller. The mental ability of these boys on the group test was average, yet they scored high in reading achievement.

The other five pupils, all slightly younger than the average sixth grader, with IQ's ranging from 116 to 125, were also good readers who seemed to have no outstanding personal or learning problems.

Miss Walker will discover many other facts about the abilities and interests, even certain weaknesses, of these eleven children as she works with them during the year. Her preliminary appraisal, however, has revealed certain general information about the superior readers in her class:

1. Some good readers, such as Pauline and Roger, are children of high intellectual ability who are likely to do well in most school subjects, and who may have been accelerated one or more years by the time they reach the sixth grade.
2. Some good readers—Patty and Don, for example—may have struggled to gain success at considerable cost in order to meet standards set by their families. Such children are likely to show the strain of their efforts.
3. Some good readers, such as Tony and Bill, have verbal skills considerably above their level of performance in other fields.

How Can a Teacher Recognize the Advanced Readers?

The true ability of many superior readers is never recognized. These children go through school condemned to a routinized program of reading, seldom challenged by the kind of reading experiences suited to their needs. In surveying a class to discover the good readers a teacher will look for children who—

1. Are younger than the average pupil in the grade and who may have been accelerated in school.
2. Are interested in words, use wide vocabularies, have accurate concepts of word meanings.
3. Use reference books to gain information, organize the ideas thus

gained, and give excellent reports to the class.

4. Are voracious readers.
5. Show initiative in exploring new fields of learning, often delving deeply into some field in which they are interested.
6. Have intellectual ability above average as measured by standardized tests of mental ability.
7. Score one, two, or more years above grade level on standardized tests of reading achievement.

How Can a Teacher Adapt Reading Instruction to the Needs of Superior Readers?

Children who work easily with the symbols of language, like all children, need good instruction in all types of reading. The teacher must plan for them as carefully as for any other group in her classroom, although she will vary the emphasis, the timing of new learnings, the amount of independent work, and the standards of performance in keeping with their abilities and needs.

These children have a flair for words and word meanings. They remember them easily, associate words of similar or opposite meanings, and frequently work out their own methods of attacking unfamiliar words with a minimum of teacher direction. While they require guidance in these aspects of reading, they do not profit from the prolonged drill which may be needed by slower learners.

Superior readers are capable of getting the meaning quickly from the printed page, of reflecting about what they read, and of using the ideas gained in solving problems or carrying on various projects. These creative aspects of reading should be emphasized.

Certain children may have difficulty with some phases of reading. A high score on a reading achievement test does not necessarily indicate equal competence in word meaning, reading for the main idea, reading for detail, and the like. By analyzing each child's performance on reading tests and in classroom activities, the teacher must discover the skills which each child needs to master and must provide the necessary instruction.

Important aspects of a good reading program for superior readers are as follows:

Provide for all-round development of each child. All children need to be accepted by their classmates, to have friends, and to engage in normal work and play activities. All children need experiences which help them learn about the world in which they live. All children need to express themselves creatively in some way such as speaking, writing, music, art, or the dance. All children need to develop feeling for others and skills of working together for the common good. Children who learn rapidly are no exception. There is danger in exploiting their facility in reading to the exclusion of other activities.

The child's placement in school is important if he is to be a well-rounded individual. He should be a member of a group comparable in physical and social development, even though he is able to read at a level considerably higher. If he is well developed physically, mentally, and socially, he may work well with children a year or two older, but he is likely to suffer social maladjustment if he is accelerated more than this.

If the entire class is working with large centers of interest in which many subjects are integrated, there will be countless opportunities for the superior readers to function as group members and exercise leadership in group activities: participating in committee work, doing extra research and reporting findings to the class, and carrying on various creative enterprises with other members of the group. In a classroom in which there is democratic give-and-take, the less capable readers learn to appreciate the contributions of those who read fluently, and they in turn learn to value other children who have different abilities.

Provide a wide range of materials. It is a major responsibility of the teacher to see that superior readers have access to reading materials of many kinds. Some of these materials will be available in the school; some will be found in the public library to which these children should be introduced early; some will be provided by the home; some may be obtained from interested adults or other children in the community who have similar interests and hobbies. Since these children show initiative in seeking information, they should be introduced to reference books of all kinds and taught how to use them. Without an adequate supply of materials, no program for superior readers can be effective.

Some types of materials needed are

1. A good basal reader and supplementary reading textbooks for learning the skills of reading. These may be a grade or two above the actual grade placement of the children in the reading

group, provided the concepts expressed in the stories are not too mature for the children, or that the children do not move from a very easy book directly to one much more difficult, with the resulting danger of leaving large gaps in their learning. For instance, advanced children in the primary grades can often read a third- or fourth-grade reader without meeting concepts too difficult for them, whereas fifth-grade children might have the skill to read at high-school level but would encounter interests and ideas which are suitable for adolescents and which they had not lived long enough to understand.

Reading textbooks can often be used flexibly to the advantage of superior readers. A group of stories in a reader may arouse interest in a specific topic such as folklore, hero stories, family life in different countries, or humor, and the group may wish to pursue that topic by reading related stories in supplementary readers or in individual library books.

2. Books for free reading, suited to their ability and interests, including everyday life stories, biography, poetry, folklore, science, life in other lands and times, puzzles, riddles, and humor. The teacher will wish to see that guidance is provided, partly by herself, partly by the public library, and partly by the home (a) to encourage the children to read widely in many fields and (b) to help them develop taste in selecting books which are well written and true to life.

The Horn Book Magazine [1] will

[1] Published six times a year by the Horn Book, Incorporated, 585 Boylston Street, Boston 16.

prove invaluable to both teacher and pupils in keeping abreast of current publications for children and young people.

3. Informational materials in social studies, science, mathematics, health, and the like, which are suited to their ability and which help them explore more deeply topics on which the whole class is working. A wise teacher, so far as possible, provides reading materials of easy, average, and difficult levels in order that all pupils may secure and pool information. For the superior readers such materials would include textbooks, reference books, newspaper clippings, pamphlets, and free materials obtained from a variety of sources. Indeed, the securing, classifying, and filing of non-textbook materials related to the current class interest may well be the responsibility of the more capable readers.

4. Reference materials, including picture dictionaries for young children and elementary and unabridged dictionaries for those in intermediate and upper grades, encyclopedias such as *Compton's Pictured Encyclopedia* [2] or the *World Book Encyclopedia*,[3] a good atlas, Eloise Rue's *Subject Index to Books for Primary Grades* [4] and *Subject Index to Books for Intermediate Grades*,[5] Stanley Kunitz's *Junior Book of Authors*,[6] the *World Almanac and Book of Facts*,[7] *Information Please Almanac*,[8] and *Readers' Guide to Periodical Literature*. The *Children's Book on How to Use Books and Libraries* [9] by Carolyn Mott and Leo B. Baisden is an excellent guide for children in learning to use libraries and basic reference books.

Help children acquire specific study techniques. The basal reading program with its accompanying teachers' manuals and workbooks provides for the introduction of these skills at appropriate levels of development. During the primary years pupils learn to use a table of contents, to read for the main idea or for details, to follow directions and the like, in connection with their regular reading instruction if the teacher is careful to make use of the suggested lessons in the manual and workbook. Pupils can then be helped to apply their skills to reading simple social-studies, science, or other materials.

In the intermediate and upper grades superior readers should devote approximately one period a week to the learning and practice of study skills, using the basal reader or textbooks in some other field which lend themselves to this purpose. Skills in taking notes or in outlining, for instance, may be learned by using science or social-studies materials as well as from the reading textbook; skills in reading graphs or tables may be learned from

[2] F. E. Compton & Company, Chicago, new edition annually.

[3] Field Enterprises, Inc., Chicago, new edition annually.

[4] American Library Association, Chicago, 1943. First Supplement, 1946.

[5] American Library Association, Chicago, 1940. First Supplement, 1943. Second Edition, 1950.

[6] The H. W. Wilson Company, New York, Second Edition, Revised, 1951.

[7] Edited by Harry Hansen, New York World-Telegram, New York, published annually.

[8] John Kieran, Editor. The Macmillan Company, New York, published annually.

[9] Carolyn Mott and Leo B. Baisden, *The Children's Book on How to Use Books and Libraries* (New York: Scribner's Sons, 1955).

the arithmetic book or encyclopedia.

Once children have learned the skills demanded in work-type reading they should be encouraged to apply them as they seek and use information for class projects or in the pursuit of their own hobbies.

91. ACCELERATING THE READING SPEED OF SIXTH-GRADE GIFTED CHILDREN *

Robert A. McCracken

Purpose

IN determining the reading needs of two sixth-grade classes by the use of an informal reading inventory, it became apparent that silent reading skills were underdeveloped. Of the 56 pupils examined in the two classes only one pupil exceeded the speed of 250 words per minute when reading silently. The purpose of this study is to evaluate a three-week training program for eight gifted children who performed well in all areas of reading except silent speed.

The Subjects

Pupils were selected by three criteria:
1. They rated above 120 IQ on the *California Test of Mental Matu-*

* From Robert A. McCracken, "Accelerating the Reading Speed of Sixth-Grade Gifted Children," *Exceptional Children,* XXVII (Spring, 1960), 27–28. Reprinted by permission of the author and *Exceptional Children.*

rity, Elementary S-Form, given six months earlier.
2. They rated above sixth grade level in both reading vocabulary and comprehension on the *Iowa Test of Basic Skills, Form I,* administered two weeks prior to the beginning of the reading instruction.
3. They exhibited no reading deficiency on the informal reading inventory except the inability to read rapidly silently.

The eight pupils who met these criteria were girls. Table 1 presents their chronological ages, the mental ages, the CTMM IQ scores, and the ITBS grade level scores for reading comprehension and vocabulary.

The Teaching Procedures

The procedures were similar to those used in adult and college reading programs. No mechanical devices were used. The pupils met for nine lessons of 45 minutes each.

TABLE 1.

*Identifying Data for Girls Receiving
Reading Instruction*

Pupil	Chronological age	CTMM MA	IQ	ITBS grade levels comprehension	vocabulary
A	11-9	15-2	129	8.2	8.7
B	11-1	14-6	131	8.0	8.2
C	11-4	15-0	133	9.0	8.1
D	11-8	14-2	121	10.6	9.0
E	11-0	16-5	149	10.6	absent
F	11-2	16-6	148	8.0	8.5
G	10-9	15-4	143	7.9	8.6
H	11-5	14-6	127	7.5	9.0

During each session at least one practice exercise was read, speed measured, and comprehension checked. All comprehension was done without reference to the text. The *Reader's Digest Skill Builder* for grade four, part one,[1] was used at the beginning of the program and the *Skill Builder* for grade six, part two,[1] was used for the last two sessions.

The following ideas were discussed with the group:

1. Speed is related to the difficulty of the material being read.
2. Speed should be shifted to suit the reader's purpose.
3. Rapid reading is an active search for answers (answering the purpose).
4. Rapid reading depends upon what the reader brings to the text.
5. Formulating questions from text clues, recalling known information stimulated by the title and

[1] *The Reader's Digest Reading Skill Builders,* education division, Reader's Digest Services, Inc., Pleasantville, N. Y., 1958.

text clues, and reading questions before reading the text speed comprehension.
6. The paragraph is the basic unit of thought.
7. Most paragraphs contain a topic sentence.

The Results

Table 2 gives the results of the rate exercises.

TABLE 2.

*Mean, Minimum, and Maximum Words
per Minute, and Average Percentage
Comprehension for Representative
Lessons*

Lesson	1	3	5	8	9
Maximum	244	414	540	1260	1200
Mean	202	280	450	966	792
Minimum	160	210	360	470	524
Comprehension	89	92	96	81	95

Several reactions were noted as the pupils participated:

1. They were reluctant to accept the belief that word meanings and ideas come from within the reader, that the reader rearranges his understandings from the stimulus of an author's words.

2. On essay questions the pupils did not like to consider more than one answer correct, even when different answers could both be supported by the text.

3. At first they were reluctant to accept reading as the getting of meaning. They said, "I answered all the questions, but I really didn't read it."

4. At the end they were worried about going too fast. They wanted to know how fast they should read.

5. At the beginning they did not feel that they could read much more rapidly, and at the end they did not understand why they had ever read so slowly.

Discussion

The author inferred that these pupils did not want to accept the responsibility required of a mature reader, the responsibility for determining what is worth reading, why it should be read, how it should be read, and when it has been read satisfactorily. This may be a result of their educational environment which does not encourage greater independence.

The nine lessons possibly did little except disinter the latent achievement of these pupils. Probably much latent achievement is still buried. Even these gifted children could benefit from instruction directed to this end.

Generally the concern for speed reading and mature reading-study habits is reserved for college reading classes or high school classes for college bound students. Apparently these skills could be taught much earlier; the gifted children in this study were well ready at the beginning of sixth grade. It seems a tremendous waste to wait until college to help these pupils to exploit themselves. The increased amount of reading that sixth-grade pupils could be freed to do in junior and senior high school is yet to be realized.

92. READING MATERIALS FOR SUPERIOR READERS*

Paul Witty

SUPERIOR readers will be found at every grade level. Among 518 eighth-grade graduates in Springfield, Illinois, 154 exhibited ninth-grade

* From Paul Witty, "Reading Materials for Superior Readers," in *Materials for Reading*, Supplementary Education Monographs, No. 86, compiled and edited by Helen M. Robinson (December, 1957), pp. 19–24. Reprinted by permission of the author and The University of Chicago Press.

reading attainment, and 171 reached or exceeded the tenth-grade norm.[1] These eighth-grade pupils may be considered superior readers. Included in this group there may be some pupils who are gifted mentally. There will be perhaps others somewhat above

[1] Glenn Myers Blair, *Diagnostic and Remedial Teaching* (revised ed.; New York: Macmillan Co., 1956), p. 5.

average in ability—pupils who are exceedingly industrious and diligent in their efforts to reach high academic goals. And children of average mental ability will sometimes be found, too, in the group of superior readers.

To offer superior readers the kinds of materials that they require to make steady, commendable progress, the teacher will need to obtain data concerning the mental ability and the educational attainment of each pupil. In addition, rather extensive information is needed concerning each pupil's home background, his interests, and his personal and social needs.

The Gifted Pupil Who Is a Superior Reader

Gifted pupils often require special attention since their reading ability may be far in excess of the norm for the grades in which they are enrolled. However, they need guidance and encouragement to develop well-balanced and individually appropriate patterns of reading. It is imperative that the gifted child who is a superior reader have challenging experiences in reading from the first. Terman reported that half of one group of pupils with intelligence quotients of 135 and higher were able to read upon entering first grade.[2] Such children sometimes develop indifference or antagonism toward reading if they are obliged to follow the routine and repetitious procedures and materials used in typical pre-primer and primer programs. Of course the problem of providing for

[2] Lewis M. Terman and Margaret Lima, *Children's Reading: A Guide for Parents and Teachers* (New York: D. Appleton & Co., 1926).

the superior reader exists throughout the elementary and the secondary school. Materials which make possible the continuous development of the superior reader are required at every instructional level.

Multiple-Track Materials for Basal Instruction

To care for the superior reader, multiple-track materials are now being developed for basal instruction. One textbook company has developed a two-track program for basal instruction. Thus the basal readers include identical subject matter in two textbooks for a single grade level, and the text of one book is distinctly easier than the other. For the high school, another publishing company has produced materials of instruction on different levels of reading difficulty.

Perhaps the most ingenious development of such multiple-level materials is to be found in the "SRA Reading Laboratory" (Science Research Associates, 1956). This comprehensive compilation of materials includes fifteen teaching units for each of the grades from third to twelfth. Each unit is presented in a four-page booklet, which is designated by color rather than by a grade marking. A preliminary reading test is used to establish each pupil's reading level. Upon completion of each unit, a test is given to reveal the pupil's status or growth in vocabulary and in ability to comprehend the printed materials. Thus through the use of these materials, the superior reader might be enabled to progress rapidly in mastering reading skills.

Various adaptations of textbook materials to challenge the superior reader are found in our classrooms. According to one plan, several textbooks, published by different companies, are employed in each class. Sometimes the textbooks are chosen from three grade levels of difficulty, when the abilities of children are found to vary widely. Thus for a fifth grade, one third of the textbooks might be at the fourth-grade level, another third at the fifth, and still another third at the sixth-grade level. This procedure makes it possible for the superior reader to have access to a variety of basal reading materials which are more appropriate and challenging than are the typical materials of his grade.

Materials for the Primary Grades

Considerable criticism has been voiced recently over the sterility of some pre-primers and primers and their lack of suitability for superior readers. There is urgent need for additional challenging reading experiences from magazines, newspapers, and children's books of many kinds on many topics. For the first-grade pupil who is a superior reader, primer material should be employed that is challenging in vocabulary and meaningful in concept content. Among such pamphlet materials are "Our Animal Story Books" (Heath, 1941); "The True Book Series" (Children's Press), which are timely for first-grade pupils of superior ability; and the "I Want To Be Series" (Children's Press), which offer primary-grade children interesting information about types of work they admire.

The primary-grade child who is a superior reader should have access to story material that is well written, stimulating, and closely related to the child's firsthand experience. Imaginative materials, too, form part of a balanced reading program for such children. These children are particularly attracted to humorous and imaginative writing. They may read *The Cat in the Hat* (Random, 1957) again and again and also find special joy in Ludwig Bemelmans' *Madeline* (Simon & Schuster, 1939). These children enjoy, too, some of the stories in the "Little Golden Books" (Simon & Schuster) and the "Book-Elf Series" (Rand McNally). Some superior readers in the first grade develop their own libraries at home by accumulating books found in inexpensive series. Such children may soon add attractive longer books, such as McCloskey's *Make Way for Ducklings* (Viking, 1941) and Lynd Ward's *The Biggest Bear* (Houghton, 1952). A child who has a shelf for books related to television may include volumes from the "Disney Series" (Heath) when interests are awakened or enriched through a Disney presentation. Pride of ownership of books is often a factor in causing a child to develop a lifelong interest in reading.

Biography is popular with some superior readers. An introduction to George Washington, Abraham Lincoln, and Benjamin Franklin, such as is given in the books by the d'Aulaires, is especially appropriate for the primary-grade child. The original and effective illustrations in the volume entitled *Abraham Lincoln* (Doubleday, 1939) are an inspiration to superior pupils, who, through books of this kind, are sometimes led not only to read more widely but also to experiment in the making of illustrations. The teacher should be zealous to see that the superior reader is also introduced to materials in the field of science. Special interests may be discovered by discussion of television programs such as "Zoo Parade" or "Mr. Wizard."

An early introduction to books on many subjects is particularly desirable in helping the superior reader cultivate his taste and improve his skills. The book table in the primary classroom is a good place to display groups of books on various topics. Simple source materials and dictionaries should be available for the superior reader to use at this time.

Superior Readers in the Middle Grades

It is desirable for the middle-grade teacher to consult the results of standard tests to ascertain the frequency of superior readers and their needs in each grade. On occasions, it is appropriate to group the pupils in a class according to interest or ability.

Superior readers in a regular class may often profit from membership in a group that is reading according to a center of interest. The teacher should encourage the superior readers to contribute to each topic from their reading of stories classified one or more grades above their own. The teacher will be helped by using Rue's *Subject Indexes* (American Library Association) to assist pupils in finding appropriate and challenging short episodes or stories. In these guides, stories for the middle grades are conveniently classified according to topic and grade level. Similarly children who are superior readers may be expected to contribute to centers of interest from the field of children's literature. To aid the teacher in finding such books, the *Cadmus Catalog* (E. M. Hale) will be especially helpful, since it contains short annotations of many excellent and well-liked children's books and the titles are classified by grade and by topic. Of distinct help to the teacher in quest of the right book for the right child will be the *Combined Book Exhibit* (950 University Ave., New York), an annual catalogue of children's books.

Some of the recently published series books are helpful in meeting the needs of the superior reader. "The First Book Series" (Watts) is designed to provide introductory books to guide children in their explorations in fields they find or "discover" to be of interest to them.

One of the objectives of instruction for the superior reader is to lead him to become independent and resourceful in using the library to satisfy his own needs. He should be encouraged to follow his interests and to develop a balanced and varied reading program. He should have guidance in the use of source materials and should be encouraged to make extensive use of dictionaries, maps, encyclopedias, and other reference materials. The use of magazines, too, should be encouraged.

The superior reader often needs help

in satisfying his personal needs. The teacher who is thoroughly acquainted with children's books may give substantial help to such pupils by directing them to appropriate books.

The reading of well-written and well-documented biographies, such as Genevieve Foster's *Abraham Lincoln's World* (Scribner, 1944), affords the superior reader an opportunity for examining the authenticity of various presentations about national heroes. Again, series books, such as "The Landmark" and "The World Landmark" books (Random), may be used to advantage if their contents are examined critically.

One of the responsibilities of the teacher is to become acquainted with children's literature and with other materials in order to suggest individually suitable and beneficial reading for the superior reader. Helpful professional books are now available to aid teachers in gaining this information, for example, May Hill Arbuthnot's *Children and Books* (Scott, Foresman, 1947) and *Time for Poetry* (Scott, Foresman, 1952). Among others are Annis Duff's *Bequest of Wings* (Viking, 1944) and Anne Eaton's *Reading with Children* (Viking, 1940), and *Treasure for the Taking* (Viking, 1946). Another provocative book about children's literature is Josette Frank's *Your Child's Reading Today* (Doubleday, 1954).

The teacher will find help in obtaining recently published books for pupils by examining annotated lists. In selecting books, the teacher will work closely with the librarian. Together they may consult the excellent reviews of children's books in periodicals.

Role of Poetry, Dramatization, and Story-Telling

Poetry is very personal expression, and the reading of poetry may evoke an intense personal response when it recreates an individual's experience. Through poetry, many pupils can be led to a deeper appreciation of words and their meaning. Appreciation for the word that is most appropriate or most exact in describing an experience may transpire from the study of poetry, since some poetry certainly fulfils the definition given by Coleridge: "Poetry —the best words in the best order." Story-telling and dramatization should form important parts of the superior reader's experience. The entire March, 1957, issue of *Elementary English* is devoted to creative writing and storytelling, and a useful bibliography is included.

The superior reader will profit greatly from experiences which combine the language arts and provide occasions for written and oral expression as well as for reading.

The Superior Reader in Junior and Senior High School

Case studies suggest that most high-school students who are generally good readers still need guidance. Some are inclined to read all materials in about the same way. Others are lacking in the development of specialized vocabularies. Others need to become skilled in critical reading ability. Still others read little independently and lack the ability to find and use source materials effectively.

Nearly all junior and senior high

school pupils need to develop some of the more subtle reading skills, such as determining the nature of proof and examining the validity of basic assumptions implied in different presentations. The book *How to Improve Your Reading* (Science Research Associates, 1956) contains many suggestions for the development of such skills, so frequently neglected or little stressed at the high-school level.

Reading to Satisfy Personal and Social Needs

Each teacher should study his group carefully and then try to provide diversified reading to satisfy worthwhile interests of individuals and groups. The methods referred to earlier may be utilized for the superior reader, and the following books may be consulted as sources of materials: *By Way of Introduction* (American Library Association, 1949), Roos's *Patterns in Reading* (American Library Association, 1954), and *Books for You* (National Council of Teachers of English).

The teacher should try to see that the best of the old books, the classics, are introduced when pupils are ready to read them. Many of these books can be related to pupils' interests. One of the best sources for guidance in the use of books, old and new, to meet developmental needs is Lenrow's *Reader's Guide to Prose Fiction* (Appleton, 1940). This type of guidance should be associated with experiences in the reading of recently published books of immediate interest and significance.

In the building of an ideal of self, books may help the superior reader

greatly. Several writers, according to Russell and Shrodes, "agree that bibliotherapy provides opportunity for catharsis and greater insight into one's own motivation and the behavior of others. They agree that in bibliotherapy some sort of integration of intellectual perception and emotional drive takes place." [3]

To engage successfully in the guidance of reading, the teacher needs reliable information concerning the reading ability of each pupil and information pertaining to each pupil's personal and social adjustment. Some helpful procedures are now being used to obtain such data. Through various approaches the teacher may acquire a somewhat valid basis for suggesting experiences in reading that will be especially valuable in fostering personal and social adjustment of the superior reader. Books, of course, will not be "prescribed," nor will reading be the sole method through which improved adjustment will be sought. Varied experience, discussion, and investigation will also be significant aspects of the process.[4] In order to participate successfully in guiding the superior reader, the teacher will need to be acquainted with many books, as well as with reliable sources for other information.

Concluding Statement

Our schools have been severely criticized for their failure to teach reading

[3] David H. Russell and Caroline Shrodes, "Contributions of Research in Bibliotherapy to the Language-Arts Program. I," *School Review*, LVIII (September, 1950), 335.
[4] Spencer Brown, *They See for Themselves* (New York: Harper & Bros., 1945).

skills effectively to all pupils. Despite the commendable work of good schools in this respect, it has become clear that there is a great neglect of exceptionally able pupils. Unfortunately the commendable efforts are widely scattered. Moreover, they constitute only a beginning in meeting a great need. It is hoped that the future will bring a greater appreciation of our responsibility and a widespread tendency to provide adequate materials and curriculums for the superior reader.

H E L P   F O R
T H E   R E T A R D E D   R E A D E R

93. WHAT WE KNOW AND CAN DO ABOUT THE
POOR READER*

Arthur I. Gates

LIKE susceptibility to colds and other common bodily ailments, reading disabilities and failure have always been with us. The statements of certain journalists to the contrary notwithstanding, retardation in reading is not a development of the last two or three decades. What has developed during this period is a vigorous program of study designed to correct and prevent reading difficulties. This intensive research enterprise was the result of the recognition of the extent and seriousness of difficulty and failure in reading which prevailed in 1920 and earlier. At that time, during the heyday of phonics and "meaty" pri-

mary material, one child in every five or six, as shown by Percival's study,[2] was required to repeat one or both of the first two grades primarily because of retardation or failure in reading. Difficulty in learning to read plagues the teachers and children of all nations, even those in which the relationship of letters and sounds is not so distressingly inconsistent and bewildering as it is in English.[1]

Learning to Read Is Hazardous

It is important that parents and inexperienced teachers realize that learning to read is one of the most critical and difficult tests of a person's lifetime. For many it represents as serious a problem in adjustment as leaving home for the first time, going into the armed services, or getting married. The seri-

* From Arthui I. Gates, "What We Know and Can Do about the Poor Reader," *Education,* LXXVII (May, 1957), 528–33. Reprinted by permission of the author and The Bobbs-Merrill Co., Inc., Indianapolis, Ind.

ousness of the task results from the fact that learning to read is for many a very difficult and subtle task. It comes at a time when the child is so young and inexperienced in learning in a new and often confusing group situation and one which demands so many other new adjustments. Difficulty springs, too, from the fact that his success or failure in learning to read is fraught with serious social consequences. If he learns to read well, all is well; if he does poorly or fails, the respect of his parents and acquaintances and his own self-esteem are threatened. When the test of learning to read becomes a test of a child's status as a total person, it becomes an ominous source of anxiety, which increases the difficulty of learning and subtly induces many children to seek some sort of "escape" from the test. Unfortunately for the youngster, there is no satisfactory escape from learning to read, as there are from most of his other activities. If a child doesn't get on well in hopscotch or baseball or singing, he could turn to something else and save face. But, there is in school and elsewhere today, no satisfactory substitute for reading. The difficulty and cruciality of the learning-to-read period combine to make it a cauldron of anxiety and trouble, perplexing to child, parent, and teacher. And herein lie the major "causes" of retardation and failure in reading.

After little more than three decades of study of the processes involved in learning to read in school, studies carried on by many specialists—teachers, educational diagnosticians, psychologists, neurologists, psychiatrists, oculists, anatomists, and others—it is recognized that to learn to read successfully a child must be pretty well equipped with aptitude for this type of symbolic learning; he must enjoy quite good health and vigor; he must be well taught; he must be well adjusted to the teaching mentally and emotionally, and he needs to be pretty lucky. Conversely, it is recognized that a deficiency in any of these areas may cause trouble in learning. There is nothing startling in this view. Every good physician knows that a similar situation exists in relation to keeping a person "in the pink" of physical condition, especially during a period of new and crucial adjustment. Whether a child's health and vigor are excellent, average, or poor depends upon his general physical equipment, how he is nurtured and taught, the nature of his mental and emotional adjustment, the kind of habits he forms, and, to some extent, on his luck.

Prevention and Correction

Efforts to improve the program for securing better development of reading interests and ability, of preventing difficulties, and diagnosing and correcting those which appear are substantially the same in character as the corresponding approaches of medicine. All phases of the work depend upon achieving an understanding of all the factors which help and hinder improvement and of discovering and controlling their role in the case of each individual.

To prevent or cure reading difficulty, a teacher or reading specialist must determine the role of many factors quite as a physician must consider the effects of many influences if he is to prevent or cure indigestion, headaches, or insomnia. Among the former are intelligence, or general aptitude for scholastic, especially symbolic learning, which may be gauged by using a "general intelligence" test. The reading specialist may use several tests of special abilities such as ability to perceive and recall word-like symbols; and ability to perceive similarity and difference in word-like sounds. Such tests are similar in character to the physician's tests of blood pressure, pulse rate, and temperature. A physician's or specialist's diagnosis of vision, hearing, and general physical condition are also often needed. The reading specialists, like the physician, will take a careful case history, giving the same attention to the psychological and educational factors that the physician gives to the physical, and both would take account of the character of the child's activities and relationships in the home, the neighborhood, and the school.

Emotionality

Reading difficulties, like indigestion, may be produced or aggravated by emotional factors existing in the home or playmate groups or the school. Indeed, both may arise from the same conditions—from such influences as overprotection, or overly severe discipline, or indifference of the parents or other older members of the family. The child who is "babied" too much may resent the inability of the teacher to lift him individually over every hurdle in learning to read and lack the initiative to learn by himself. Indeed, many children are dismayed to find

that one cannot learn to read without effort. They may expect the story to come to them from the printed page as easily as it does from the movie or the television screen, and when it does not, they may become so discouraged or resentful as to seek to escape responsibility by refusing to try to learn or so jittery or apprehensive as to be unable to learn. Overanxiety of the parents or siblings or teacher may have the distracting effect that severe stage fright has for an adult. In such cases, urging the child to try harder or even trying inexpertly to help him learn may tighten rather than loosen the child's straitjacket of doubt and tension. In all such cases—and they take many other forms—some sort of psychotherapy is essential.

By "psychotherapy" is not here meant special treatment by a psychologist or psychiatrist, although on rare occasions the help of such a specialist is indicated, nor is a separate period or provision of therapy necessarily required. What is suggested is that once the existence and nature of unfavorable emotional conditions and misleading personal relations are discovered, steps should be taken to relieve them. This may often be accomplished best by a shrewd teacher or reading specialist— who is or should be an exceptionally insightful teacher—in the course of normal classroom activities and often combined with suggested modifications of the pattern of family life. Usually, however, the demand for this type of therapeutic re-education of the child and his family or both calls for a considerable amount of extra time for diagnosis and individual counseling by the teacher. One of the tragedies is that a teacher who possesses the ability and desire to grapple successfully with such subtle problems simply does not have the time. She has many other problems, many other subjects, and many other phases of instruction in reading to attend to.

Reading Skills

Reading is probably the most difficult and subtle of all the scholastic abilities and skills to teach and the critical period comes at the very beginning of school life when the children are least experienced and most readily bewildered. It is very difficult to show a child, for example, all the tricks of working out the recognition and pronunciation of the weirdly artificial little hieroglyphics which printed words are. To be successful a child must catch on to good techniques. What is good for one word is often poor for another. To learn to recognize, sound, and blend the sounds of the letters may suffice for *hat* or *bag* but be utterly confounding for *haughty* or *hippopotamus,* the former because of phonetic inconsistence and the latter because the number of letters exceeds the child's immediate memory span. (The adult reader might try to blend the letter sounds of *zhljrpaufiom* from memory—it should be less puzzling because of his many years of experience with letters and their sounds.)

The child must learn much by trial and error, and inappropriate techniques await at every hand to lead him astray quite as they do the adult who tries to learn to play golf or bridge or the violin without continual, expert, and individual instruction. Here is where "luck" enters. In learning to read, many children have the bad luck to hit off on faulty techniques which handicap them seriously. If a child, for example, begins to look first at the *end* or the *middle* of the word, rather than the beginning—a technique that works perfectly well in recognizing coins, insects, earrings, faces, and almost every object on earth except printed words—he is in for trouble. The woods of beginning reading are full of such treacherous pitfalls. Hence the need of a careful diagnostic inventory of the skill, insights, techniques, and devices used by each learner.

Skill in using some one or a combination of several such diagnostic inventories now available is part of the equipment of every good reading specialist and an increasing number of teachers. They help the diagnostician discern the good and poor techniques used by a youngster. Using them gives no automatic insight; much depends upon the shrewdness of the teacher as, of course, it does in the case of the physician or music or golf instructor. The insightful diagnostician in all these fields uses the data from the diagnosis as a basis for planning a program of therapy or instruction tailored to fit the needs of the individual. This is called "corrective reading" or "remedial reading" but it differs in no important respect from the best types of everyday instruction. Indeed, the work of the reading specialist at its best differs from that of the regular classroom teacher only in being more expertly conceived, more skillfully conducted and precisely adjusted to the needs of each child.

To teach such a subtle skill as reading to thirty to forty children is a formidable task for the best teacher and, of course, not all teachers are perfect. Some children are unlucky enough to get a relatively poor one—one who is so easy going or unsympathetic that children become passive or aimlessly active, or one who is so autocratic as to make them jittery or fearful or angry, or one who is so uninspiring or inept, or one who is so blind to individual difficulties and needs as to leave children groping in uncertainty and confusion. Some children, moreover, are so unlucky as to miss school or change schools or teachers or encounter shifts in teaching methods or stumble into a change of interpersonal relationship in school or home at critical periods, and any gap not skillfully and individually bridged or any change not adequately guided may plunge the youngster into trouble. Emotionally unsettling events such as illness or misfortune or anger occurring to a member of the family or to the teacher or a playmate may be sufficient to reduce greatly the child's learning. The reaction of the teacher or pupils to a youngster on an "off day" may have a persistingly destructive effect. The writer recalls the occasion when one of the world's outstanding actors, who specializes in oral reading, made four or five "slips of speech" in each of a half dozen brief introductions of the artists participating in a program. If the most experienced and expert performers have such conspicuously bad spells, it is to be expected that a rank beginner will often have pathetically bad days. To offer crude, unsympathetic treatment at such a time is to sow the seeds of rebellion or failure.

Panaceas

The considerations just presented should convince the parent that there can be no panacea for the troubled reader. There are unfortunately many panacea peddlers for poor reading, as there are for all sorts of physical ailments. Popular among them are various systems of formal phonics, most of which have appeared and reappeared for more than a century. Certain forms of psychiatric or psychoanalytic procedures have been advocated as sufficient for all cases. Recently popular are various mechanical gadgets such as rapid exposure apparatus, motion picture materials, and various pacing machines. There are also a number of highly artificial and therefore novel forms of practice methods such as the kinesthetic method (tracing the outline of letters, etc.), flash card methods, experience story methods, reverse image exercises, visualization and other methods. None of these is good for all cases; to use any one in certain cases would be to add oil to the fire. Some of them are valuable for limited uses with certain cases. One should be suspicious of all panaceas, especially any rigid scheme of formal or freakish drills or mechanical gadgets.

Parents and Reading

Parents often ask whether there is anything they can do to help a child learn to read or to improve his reading ability and interests. There are, indeed, many things parents can do. There is evidence that much of the basal equipment for reading is learned at mother's knee. Mother and father may contribute richly during all the pre-school years by helping the child engage abundantly and enjoyably in language activities. Answer the child's questions as fully and meaningfully as possible. Talk to him, tell him stories, report your daily experiences, and encourage him to talk to you—the more the better. Take him on tours to the local stores, museums, factories, plants, and other places and while doing so engage him in conversation, read the signs, placards, advertisements, and talk about them. Provide him at home with reading matter, signs, ads, picture cards, magazines, and books—alphabet books, picture books, story, and other books. Read them to him, observe the pictures and diagrams together.

Television programs, wisely selected, provide excellent opportunities for family enjoyment of great value. In using all these materials, read the words and text to the youngster, look at the pictures and talk about them together and *answer the child's questions,* listen to his comments, and respond as helpfully to them as you can. If he asks the name of a letter or a printed word, tell him. Run your finger along under the line of words you are reading as he observes. Put words and phrases on objects and pictures in his room and answer the questions he asks about them. Play word sound games. "What words begin with the same sound as *cat;* or end with the same sound as *sing?*" Should you teach him? No, not in a formal sense. Try, rather, to help him enjoy and engage at length in all kinds of verbal activ-

ity. If you can do that, you will have introduced a superior type of teaching. You will have helped your child enormously to make learning to read in school more certain and easy. If he learns to read before entering school, as many children with special aptitude will, so much the better. But don't undertake to teach him a heavy, formal system of phonics. This is a job for an experienced teacher.

The child will be helped enormously by the same pattern of family activity all through school, even into college. Let there be, at the appropriate level and in the proper areas, lots of conversation, reading aloud, reporting experiences, and problems in which every person's contributions are welcomed and respected. Let there be a daily reading period, observed with the same regularity and conducted with the same spirit of enjoyment as the evening meal. Let each person read what he likes and feel free to talk about it to others.

Before a parent implies that his children's questions and comments are too silly and childish to merit respectful consideration, he might remind himself that in a few years his comments will seem equally naive and ignorant to the son or daughter who comes in fresh from study of up-to-the-minute knowledge in high school and college. The parent may expect to get, and deserves, the same treatment from his grown-up son or daughter as he gave them when they were children. Good readers, good students, and good citizens tend to develop in homes in which good reading and good talk are a regular and enjoyable part of family life.

A good reading specialist can spot in a few minutes a child who has suffered linguistic malnutrition in the home. And let no teacher or parent believe that a heavy dose of formal phonetics, or any other similar panacea, whether administered in the home or school, is a substitute for a wholesome diet of verbal food.

REFERENCES

1. KARLSEN, BJORN. "We have Remedial Reading in Europe, Too," *California Teachers Journal,* May, 1955.
2. PERCIVAL, WALTER E. *A Study of the Causes and Subjects of School Failure,* Unpublished Doctor's Dissertation, Teachers College, Columbia University, New York, 1926.

94. READING DISABILITY AND THE ROLE OF THE TEACHER*

Jeanne S. Chall

THROUGH the years there has been a growing recognition of the fact that learning difficulties, especially reading difficulties, are not a simple matter. Extensive clinical diagnoses of reading disability cases have again and again shown the pervasiveness of psychological problems among poor readers. In fact, emotional factors are so prevalent that it is rare to find a child without such problems among those treated in reading clinics.

What may we infer from this? Only that some relationship between emotional adjustment and reading exists.

* From Jeanne S. Chall, "Reading Disability and the Role of the Teacher," *Elementary English,* XXXV, No. 5 (May, 1958), 297–98. Reprinted by permission of the author and the National Council of Teachers of English.

The nature of the relationship, however, is not always clear. Emotional difficulties may develop first and interfere with the child's learning. The reading problem may develop first, and bring out emotional reactions which further inhibit learning. Or it may be that emotional problems exist side by side with the reading difficulty. They may both stem from a common cause, or from different causes. *In short, the presence of an emotional problem in reading disability cases does not imply a necessary causal connection.* For individual cases, it is usually difficult and time-consuming to disentangle the causal relationship.

Because of the complexity of the problem, teachers have begun to question their role. Should they teach the child to read, or should they get at the basic cause of his reading difficulty?

Many teachers who have come to consult us at the Educational Clinic have expressed their perplexity this way: If Frank has a reading problem, then there is probably a psychological cause. How can I cope with this? I have neither the time nor the training to get at the psychological problem.

If the teacher is conscientious and tries to help Frank with his reading, she often feels frustrated because she is treating a "mere symptom." Should Frank's mother show her concern with his reading and offer to help him, it is often interpreted as probably the root of his reading problem: pressure from "mother." It may well be that Frank's mother is pressuring him to achieve higher standards than he is able to reach. But it may just as well be a sincere concern and desire to help. Even if the teacher's assessment of Frank's problem is correct, she is limited in carrying out the necessary treatment, for this is the function of a specialist.

In our contacts with children, parents, and teachers at the City College Educational Clinic, we have begun to wonder whether teachers' confusion about their role might not stem from an over-interpretation of the facts of psychological causation. True, many children have difficulty with reading because of emotional problems. Though the teacher might be able to detect the presence of an emotional difficulty, she cannot diagnose its nature. At our clinic it takes a team of specialists—a clinical psychologist, a psychiatrist, pediatrician, social worker, and educational specialist—at least ten hours of testing, interviewing, and conferring to make such a diagnosis. Even then the conclusions are often tentative. There may be a psychological base for the child's learning difficulty, but often other problems exist simultaneously, such as slow maturation, visual and auditory difficulties, long absences from school in the early grades, and poor teaching.

In view of the complexity of the causal picture, and our relatively limited knowledge of the dynamic relationship between psychological factors and learning, it appears that the teacher's role might best be performed by being an understanding, competent teacher. She need not feel called upon to identify, describe, and treat the "basic" cause of the reading difficulty. Instead, she can accept the child's difficulty in learning to read and work with it. Here are a few suggestions.

First, the teacher should reorient her attitude. Reading is a serious business for the child, perhaps the most important business in his young life. Any help that a teacher can give a child with this central aspect of his life should not be underestimated as the treatment of a "mere symptom." It should be given its full weight of importance. It is important not only for his learning, but for his total adjustment. When the teacher helps a child succeed in an area where he has met consistent failure, the result can only be beneficial, no matter what the initial cause of the failure may be.

Second, the teacher should make use of all available tools to identify pupils who are below par in reading, and to use the best techniques for helping them overcome their handicaps. If all methods prove ineffective, a reading consultant, remedial reading teacher, or a child guidance agency should be consulted.

Is the teacher, then, to ignore the child's emotional difficulties? No. She cannot, even if she tried. If the child's emotional problems are serious, they need treatment as such, and the proper referral should be made. The child's emotional problems will also show up in his learning. He will need more acceptance and encouragement than those who make normal progress. His learning progress will usually fluctuate markedly. A month may pass by when he does very well. Then he seems to "forget everything." It is then that the teacher needs to practice fully the art of good teaching, to de-emphasize the child's present failure and remind him of his past success. Her confidence in his ability to learn and her patience in helping him cannot be overestimated. The child is thus helped not only with his reading, but learns to accept himself as a worthwhile human being who can succeed in spite of his difficulties.

Probably one of the most important factors overlooked in helping children with reading difficulties is the teacher. With the recent emphasis on psychological factors in learning, many teachers have underestimated their role as teachers, and have, in fact, been almost afraid to teach. Yet, they can contribute most, not by delving into the child's deeper problems, but by teaching him to read.

95. SUCCESS LEVELS FOR RETARDED READERS*

Emmett Albert Betts

WHEN would-be athletes turn out for high-jumping practice, the track coach conducts try-outs. By means of these try-outs, or tests, he finds out how high each boy can

* From Emmett Albert Betts, "Success Levels for Retarted Readers," *Education,* LXXVII (March, 1957), 398–403. Reprinted by permission of the author and The Bobbs-Merrill Co., Inc., Indianapolis, Ind.

jump. From past experience, he knows that many boys can clear a bar set four feet high and that a few boys can clear a bar at five and one-half feet. In short, the coach expects boys of about the same age to vary considerably in their beginning records.

This track coach has a point of view which we need to understand: he expects *differences* in ability. There are big differences in what individuals of the same age can do in sports, music, art, reading, or any other activity.

There are big differences in the ages when children learn to talk. For example, Karen began to use words at eight months; Virginia, at twelve months; and Billy, at forty-eight months.

Consequently, there are differences in the ages at which children learn to read. At three years of age Charlie was reading street signs and easy-to-read letters from his aunt. At four years of age, Sally was enjoying third readers. These exceptional children begin to read early.

Between their sixth and seventh birthdays most children take some interest in reading. However, George was not ready to learn to read until he was nine years of age. Because he was generally slow in growing up, Paul learned to read only street signs, road markers, and the like when he was twelve years old.

Yes, the track coach is aware of the differences in ability because he has learned to see them. Differences in ages at which children learn to walk are obvious to parents who keep records of their children's growth. Likewise, differences in readiness for learning to read and in reading abilities stand out clearly for teachers and psychologists. Being aware of these differences is the starting point for parents and teachers who give the right help when it is needed.

How High Can He Jump?

The track coach knows all too well one of the fundamentals of teaching:
set the bar at a height where the athlete can clear it. He knows that if he sets the bar so high that an athlete cannot clear it, he not only discourages him but also creates an impossible learning situation. So the coach knows that he must begin where the learner is—at a level where the boy can clear the bar.

By using the coach's idea, we can help our children with their reading problems. Since readers and other school books are graded in difficulty, each succeeding book calls for more and more skill. For this reason, Tommy cannot be expected to read a fourth-grade book if he cannot read a primer. Likewise, Jane cannot read a ninth-grade book if she stumbles in reading a fifth-grade book. Therefore, finding out how high one can jump in reading seems to be a sensible idea.

Reading Levels

Perhaps this idea of estimating reading levels can be best illustrated by Donald's case. Donald was ten years old when he came to us for help. Like many retarded readers, he was in the depths of despair. He hated school, disliked his teacher, and thought his parents were unfair. He felt that everyone was against him because he couldn't read and didn't like to read. He wasn't even sure that he could learn to read— maybe he was hopeless!

In one way, Donald may have had a fortunate school situation. He was not considered for demotion to a lower grade. He was not held back with younger children. Instead, he was permitted to stay in the class with his age mates. He was now in the fifth grade, but was unable to read with any group in the class.

Remembering the example of the track coach, we decided to find out how high Donald could jump in reading. For this purpose, we used a set of school readers, graded in difficulty.

Donald's Independent Reading Level

At the pre-primer, or beginning, level, Donald had no difficulty. This was his independent reading level. He read orally at sight without hesitation and with good expression. He read silently without lip movement, finger pointing, or other signs of difficulty. His comprehension was excellent. Even more important, Donald was amazed that he could read anything so well.

First Signs of Difficulty

The primer—the second book of the series—had more words, longer sentences, and other elements which posed additional problems for Donald. At this primer level, the first symptoms of his difficulty appeared.

Donald could recognize twenty-six out of twenty-seven words in his oral reading at sight of the first page. But his oral reading at sight was not smooth or rhythmical.

On the second page, he read silently to answer our questions. Here, there was a slight indication of lip movement when he came to unknown words. Donald reread orally parts of this page to answer our questions. Using the help he had gotten from his preparation through silent reading, he read orally with rhythm and expression.

Up to this point, Donald had proved to himself two things. First, he could read *on his own* at the beginning, or pre-primer, level. While it was true that interesting books at this level were not available, nevertheless he could read something—even though it was only a pre-primer! Second, he could read a primer under teacher guidance, without practicing bad reading habits, such as lip movement. That is, he could do it if he had a chance to read silently first, and if he learned how to use phonics and other word recognition skills as he progressed.

With a sigh of relief, Donald commented, "I didn't know I could do it. Maybe I'm not hopeless."

More Signs of Difficulty

With some misgivings, Donald attempted to read the next book—a first reader. At this level he was up against two-line sentences, longer words, more kinds of punctuation marks, and other elements which made the going rough.

Donald tried to read the first page orally. He made two starts on the first sentence. He could not recognize *stopped, climbed,* or *picked.* He substituted *dogs* for *puppies.* He didn't know what to do about a comma which he interpreted as a period. He did word-by-word, unrhythmical reading in a high pitched voice. Donald summarized his situation with one remark, "This *is* getting tough."

After we reminded him of how his oral reading in the preceding book had smoothed out following silent reading, Donald read the second page silently.

He began to run his finger under each word, whispering to himself. He asked for help on the recognition of two out of thirty-seven words. He had to reread the selection twice in order to answer one of our questions.

Following the silent reading of the second page, Donald read parts of it aloud to answer our questions. His oral rereading was much smoother than when he read the first page aloud at sight. But he was still bothered by the difficulty of the written language.

Donald's recovery of his ability to read rhythmically and with a conversational tone following silent reading was good news. His ability in this respect meant that he was a run-of-the-mine retarded reader. He could be taught by traditional methods IF his teacher used beginner's books.

Frustration

When we gave Donald the second reader, he squirmed in his seat and frowned at the page. The first word and the last three words of the first sentence were blanks for him. On the next sentence he fared no better. He could not begin to understand the story because the words were so much black ink to him. He was stopped cold. Donald was completely frustrated!

Donald had his own way of describing his situation. "This is hopeless!"

There are some people who will say, "Donald couldn't read a first reader, but I bet that he could read the fourth-grade book he had in school last year!" Well, we gave Donald this chance. He was a realist—skeptical of the outlook —but willing to try.

When shown the fourth reader used in his class the year before, however, Donald became tense and exclaimed, "I hate that book! I hate the stories. Why, I even hate the color of it!" We were unable to persuade him to attempt reading the book. Donald knew when he had both shoulders on the mat— when he was counted out by the referee!

Number of Symptoms

Donald's case illustrates an important point: signs of trouble multiply at each succeeding level.

Remember that Donald read the pre-primer with excellent comprehension and without the use of crutches, such as finger pointing and lip movement. At the primer level, he could not recognize all the words. Furthermore, he used lip movement, which was a symptom of his word-pronouncing problem.

At the first reader level, Donald's number of symptoms jumped from two to five. He resorted to finger pointing in order to keep his place on a line of unknown print. He repeated a part of a sentence to pick up the thought. He could not pronounce some words and made substitutions for others. He read in a high-pitched voice because he was under emotional pressure. Worse still, his comprehension dropped because he was bogged down with printed words he could not identify.

Word-by-word reading, frowning, tenseness, lip movement, finger pointing, errors in word pronunciation, low comprehension, a high-pitched voice, lack of interest—all these and other types of behavior are symptoms of reading difficulty. When Donald, Tommy, or any other person is required to read material which produces these symptoms, they drill bad habits into their nervous systems. Even worse they learn to dislike—or to hate!—reading.

Intensity of Symptoms

Donald's case illustrates another point: each symptom becomes worse as the reading material becomes more difficult.

Donald had no lip movement when he read the pre-primer. He began to make use of silent lip movement at the primer level. He began to whisper the words to himself at the first-reader level. He was muttering the words to himself when he tried to read silently the second reader. In short, this sign of trouble became worse from one reader level to another.

Donald's voice gave another clue to his reading level. When he was at ease, he read in a conversational tone. As he began to meet unfamiliar problems, he became tense and raised his voice. As he met more new situations, his voice became shrill, high-pitched.

Word pronunciation errors offer another good example of how a symptom can become worse at each level of difficulty. Donald asked for some help at the primer level. At the first-reader level, he both mispronounced and substituted words. However, his substitutions (for example, *dogs* for *puppies*) made sense; they were meaningful. When he made an unsuccessful attempt to read at the second-reader level, his substitutions (for example, *boy* for *deep*) did not make sense. He could not get enough of the story to help him with the meaning of a word.

Donald knew when he was reading

at par. He was very much aware of the need for more skills as he read at higher levels. He needed no expert to tell him he was mired down. The symptoms stood out for him like beads of sweat on his forehead.

A Clear Statement of Truth

Estimating a child's reading level is king's business. Because we believe this, we always demonstrate for parents and teachers how it is done. For one of our demonstrations, nine-year-old Debbie volunteered. After Debbie was introduced to the audience, we explained that we were going to find how high she could go in reading a set of books. Since Debbie was confident and at ease, she was eager to try the idea.

Debbie had the reputation for being an excellent pupil in her fourth-grade class, so we gave her a running start with a third reader. While she seemed to enjoy the story, she was not having to use all of her ability. Neither did she with the fourth-reader story!

At the fifth-reader level, Debbie did not break her stride, but she was finding the selection a challenge. She appeared to be reading at her level of ability.

Debbie was having a good time, entering into the reading and discussion with enthusiasm and poise. When we occasionally commented to the audience on points in the demonstration, she listened earnestly.

At the sixth-reader level, Debbie began to show signs of trouble. Her reading rate fell off sharply and she was unable to grasp all the ideas. She mispronounced *smugglers* because she did not know the meaning of the word.

Even Debbie, a superior reader, was beyond her reading level.

Debbie reacted nobly. She had understood the purpose of the demonstration, modestly volunteering to read the books for ten- and eleven-year-olds. Sensing the main idea of finding reading levels, Debbie brought the meeting to a dramatic point with this straight-forward explanation to the audience: "If you can't do it low, you can't do it high!"

If Debbie's clear statement of truth could be put into practice, there would be much more happiness in schools and homes.

96. A CHALLENGE: I CAN'T READ*

Hazel S. Rench and
Frances M. Moroney

"YOU know I can't read!" This statement came emphatically from Bob on the first day of September. Such a remark did not startle Miss Moroney for she usually had at least one retarded reader in her fifth grade at the beginning of the year. Looking at Bob she saw the same defiance in every feature of his handsome, sullen face and in every line of his well-built body that said, without words, "Teach me. I dare you to!" He shrugged off her welcoming smile and brushed past her to a seat as far away as possible from the chatting groups of fifth graders.

In the next few days, Miss Moroney's

* From Hazel S. Rench and Frances M. Moroney, "A Challenge: I Can't Read," *Elementary English*, XXXII, No. 7 (November, 1955), 455–58. Reprinted by permission of the authors and the National Council of Teachers of English.

first move was to find out something about Bob's background. A conference with his mother revealed that he had transferred from a nearby school mainly because the children made fun of his lack of reading ability. He was a child of older parents with six married brothers and sisters who had children of their own. His mother's over-protection made Bob rebel against family rules and regulations and most other human contacts. His meager records had no reading test score, and any attempt to find his reading level by a standardized test failed because of his lack of cooperation. However, a Stanford-Binet Intelligence Test, administered by a specialist, showed that he had average intelligence and should be able to master the necessary reading skills. His health record was perfect.

With this information, Miss Moroney planned her approach to another reading problem. She knew that she must find his interests, gain his trust, improve his social relations with the group, and build up his self-confidence in order to teach him to read.

During the beginning weeks of school, Bob proved to be an interesting contradiction. Miss Moroney's first step was to help him find a friend. That friend turned out to be Joel, a happy boy, already popular with this group of fifth graders. Fortunately, the boys liked each other almost immediately. Joel proved an able ally because it was through him that she heard about Bob's tame pigeons at home. By her own observations she had discovered Bob's interests in sports and all mechanical gadgets. Now his love of animals should provide an entering wedge to reading.

He accepted the daily school activities indifferently except when the discussion touched upon one of his special interests. There was one exception to this indifference—he loved to listen to stories—any kind—and he was always the first to be ready for story time and the last to want it to come to an end. These bits of information kindled Miss Moroney's hopes even though his response to any effort to teach him reading was always the same, "I can't read, I told you," or "I'll read only two pages," or "I'm tired now, I don't want to read any more."

Her efforts were rewarded one day when Bob asked if he might bring his pet pigeons to class. This necessitated a temporary cage and offered Bob the opportunity of visiting the maintenance room where he found another friend in the janitor. The day the pigeons arrived Bob proudly displayed his pets, answered questions asked by the group, and for a time was the star of the fifth grade. But, as always, with these inquisitive fact finders, there were questions Bob could not answer. One interested questioner came to the rescue with, "I'll look it up, Bob; I'll help you." The two boys were off to the library where, with the help of the librarian, they searched books to find the missing information. Urged on by common interest they gathered their facts, organized them, and returned to share their findings with the rest of the class. For the first time this year Bob was beginning to see a personal need for reading skills.

Additional help came from an unexpected source. The first graders who were studying about pets invited Bob to bring his pigeons to their room. This opportunity to do a job he liked, alone, brought to light hidden talents. Bob showed amazing poise before this younger group, gave an interesting, well-organized talk, and demonstrated his innate love for animals in the manner in which he handled his pets.

After this episode he was willing to accept the books Miss Moroney suggested. These were books of high interest for readers with a limited recognition vocabulary ranging in difficulty from primer to third grade reading level. Among these were:

"The Cowboy Sam Series"

Cowboy Sam
Cowboy Sam and Porky
Cowboy Sam and Freddy
Cowboy Sam and Shorty
Cowboy Sam and the Rodeo
Cowboy Sam and the Fair
Cowboy Sam and the Rustlers

Cowboy Sam and the Indians
"The Blaze Series"
  Blaze and the Gypsies
  Billy and Blaze
  Blaze Finds the Trail
  Blaze and the Forest Fire
"The Core-Vocabulary Readers"
  The Ranch Book
  Rusty Wants a Dog
  Smoky the Crow
"The Air Age Readers" and some of "The First Book Series" by Watts.

Miss Moroney felt that now she could begin a carefully planned reading program to build the necessary reading vocabulary. Words were selected from his reading, brush-penned on slips of paper, studied, and kept in a shoe box. This list grew as each evening Bob studied the newspaper and circled such words as "by," "good," "it," etc. The Dolch list of 220 basic sight words were mastered in this way.

Miss Moroney observed that Bob had one chronic reversal. When he did writing, he made b's for d's. Also his left-to-right eye movements consisted of many jerks and repetitions, and he pointed to every word as he labored slowly along each line. But as Bob mastered sight words he gained interest. He willingly started his personal dictionary and worked industriously in a phonics workbook at primer level.

The "Blaze" books followed the "Cowboy Sam" books. During his first hour with *Cowboy Sam,* how surprised he was to discover that he had read not one chapter (stories to him) but three. "I didn't know I had read so many pages," was his amazed comment. What a different attitude from September when he was saying, "I don't want to read—I'll do only two pages."

As the year progressed, Bob entered into the activities of the class. At one point a tape recording of his oral reading from *Billy and Blaze* was made. When Bob read his paragraph, he stumbled over the word, "seemed." In the play-back, he supplied the missing word instantly, from memory. Miss Moroney noted Bob's immediate interest in the mechanical operation of the recorder. After one explanation, he could use it. From that time on Bob became the operator as various tape recordings were made of reading activities and reports from science and social studies. He responded quickly to anything mechanical and showed others how to operate the recorder and filmstrip projector.

A unit on photography really captured his interest completely. In order to make his pin-hole camera, he had to read and follow directions accurately and make measurements carefully. His camera was the first one finished and ready to take pictures. The directions for making prints from these negatives were given orally. Bob listened intently to the explanations and at the end could repeat every step of the process more clearly than anyone in the class.

Bob arrived early on the morning set for converting the storeroom into a darkroom for printing the negatives. No one worked more enthusiastically than he, as he tied on his rubber apron, put the trays of water and hypo in the proper places, and helped the boys and girls with their printing. Bob had accepted responsibility as well as human companionship.

A week later Bob's mother arrived at school for the purpose of finding out what equipment was needed for this darkroom. Bob was so enthusiastic that he had begged for one at home. In a few days he was in business for himself printing negatives for all his older brothers, sisters, and nephews.

But it wasn't until he started reading *Tim and the Tool Chest* by Beim that he asked to take a book home. How long Miss Moroney had waited for just such an expression of interest! So at the year's end Bob was beginning to enjoy reading—beginning to want to read.

Miss Moroney had found Bob's interests and given him an opportunity to pursue them; she had helped him to improve his social relations and as a result gained his trust and built up his self-confidence. Because of these things it was possible for her to teach him the skills he needed in order to find some measure of satisfaction in reading. Rebellion against his past failures was not completely overcome. Any attempt to give him a reading test aroused all of his old antagonisms. Miss Moroney wisely concluded that testing was not that important. Since Bob had read about twenty-five books during the year, she felt that she had succeeded in helping him to accept the fact that he could read, that he needed to read for information, and that he could read for fun.

With Bob well on the road to successful reading, it is essential that the program of work started with him be continued. To make sure that no time be lost Miss Moroney took Bob's records, a list of books read by him, and a summary of his individual program to his sixth grade teacher. There she found an understanding, sympathetic listener and left the conference confident that Bob would be given the opportunities and the necessary guidance to grow in his ability to read.

97. SHOULD PARENTS CODDLE THEIR RETARDED READERS?*

Mary H. B. Wollner

A GASP went up at a meeting of parents of one hundred retarded readers in a summer reading clinic when it was suggested to them that they could help their children best by relaxing all pressures related to reading at home and by establishing firm, consistent general discipline.

This surprise is understandable when we realize the confusion that exists in the minds of the public about what goes into re-educating children who have failed to learn to read up to their mental capacity. Tests and interviews with children who show a true pattern of reading and spelling retardation and talks with their parents reveal both turmoil and tragedy. These children and adults have experienced the hurt of failure, and they are looking for ways and means of turning the tide of learning into a positive direction.

Removing Parental Pressure

Our first request of parents who bring children into summer reading classes for tutoring is that they do not carry on any coaching or teaching activities at home. "Please have fun

* From Mary H. B. Wollner, "Should Parents Coddle Their Retarded Readers?" *Education*, LXXX (March, 1960), 430–32. Reprinted by permission of the author and The Bobbs-Merrill Co., Inc., Indianapolis, Ind.

with your child this summer," we advise, "and leave the teaching to the clinic."

Release from home pressure in the very sore area which surrounds the subject of reading is one factor essential to the progress of each pupil. Parents, understandably anxious to cooperate in what they hope will be rapid progress, often ask: "Should we hear our child's words? Have you any drills we could do together at home? How can we help to speed up our child's learning, so he'll be up to grade level in the fall?"

It often is helpful to explain that the request for removal of pressure of teaching by parents is a protective measure; that is, it is intended to protect and preserve the essential qualities of the parent-child relationship. A growing child is so dependent upon the love and approval of the adults in his home that every time one of them corrects his pronunciation of a word, or corrects his spelling, or supplies a word in his reading which he cannot remember, there is implied criticism, which may cause the child to experience unduly strong fear—fear that he will lose parental love and approval.

Sensitive parents are torn between their desire to help the child and their impatience to see him progress. We feel that, whenever a parent attempts to teach in a subject in which the child has chronic difficulty, there is great danger that the child will absorb the impatience of the parent, become impatient with himself, and lose all courage to proceed.

One father asked, "How can we get across to our children the idea of the importance of learning to read?" The answer sounds simple, but it is difficult to arrange. The poor reader must be presented with tasks related to reading, which he can master, so that he takes note of his own progress and, thereby, gradually gains a sense of confidence in his powers to learn something on his own.

A growing child, by virtue of his youth and inexperience, cannot grasp the whole significance of education, nor estimate the importance to himself of mastering reading for self-development. Even a child who progresses normally or rapidly in learning to read has to wait for a period of two to six years before his mastery of the mechanics of reading opens the door for him to independent, voluntary reading. Therefore, when we tell a child, "You ought to hurry up and learn this well, so you can enjoy reading and study more efficiently," we are talking from the standpoint of adult wisdom and experience. But the child figuratively is deaf to this argument, not because he is naughty, or stubborn, or lazy, but because he hasn't lived long enough to comprehend its truth. The only language a youngster understands is the firsthand experience of specific learning success.

Parental Example

What can parents do at home to help? They can set examples of good reading habits. A father who regularly reads good literature aloud, for his own pleasure, helps his whole family, including the retarded reader. He provides the children with a vital aspect of reading—the listening, attending, and comprehending aspect.

On the other hand, a parent who sits down and tries to share the reading of a primer or basic reader with his child is running the risk of showing up and "rubbing in" the child's chronic difficulties and errors. The child, of course, finds it difficult to pay attention, feels no enjoyment, and is unable to prevent himself from making errors. In spite of his conscious efforts, even the compliant child will continue to fall into the same errors over and over again—when he reads to a parent.

Reading Teacher

All reading, then, should be banned from the home and left to a reading specialist or remedial teacher. Such a teacher is trained to vary the exercises and procedures in such a skillful way that the youngster is not forced to fail repeatedly.

Another thing about the reading teacher which makes her different from parents is her attitude of objectivity, which helps to boost the morale of the retarded reader. When a child has to be corrected by a stranger, self-respect is not destroyed, as it often is when the child is corrected by a blood relative. Even the regular classroom teacher sometimes becomes so emotionally involved with a child's reading problem that she cannot help him.

We now understand enough about the emotionality of most children who are experiencing reading failure that we can state that they progress best in an atmosphere of friendly impersonality. This means that the teacher or tutor must be able to establish himself as a person who likes children and who is able to accept the reader just as he is. The tutor's training, then, enables him to offer a carefully selected series of tasks and challenges to the child, which will encourage the child's growth in independence and confidence.

The fact that reading cannot be taught but must be learned is not obvious to the general public, but it is exceedingly obvious to those of us who work in reading clinics. Our job is to set up the lessons so that the child will succeed, presently will acknowledge his own success, and, then, will begin to pull himself up by his own bootstraps. Parents, when they try to be teachers, tend to focus their main attention on the outcome and to view the errors as stumbling blocks. Reading clinicians focus their main attention on the learner and his individual way of learning; they view the errors as signposts to help them to design corrective instruction.

Discipline

Still parents may ask, "What can we do?" Then they show surprise if we say, "Don't nag, punish, or deprive the child. But be sure you have a firmness and consistency in home discipline."

There is evidence that improvement in home discipline results in improvement in reading for some retarded readers. By discipline, however, we do not mean punishment or deprivation. A child deprived of a camp experience, a game with his friends, a friendship, or the privilege of watching television because of his lag in reading development, will be likely to translate this to mean, "They don't love me because I'm dumb. So, what's the use of trying?"

Too often, a child who experiences trouble in reading also has trouble growing in responsibility and self-discipline. Such a child comes from an atmosphere which confuses him because it alternately punishes and coddles.

The kind of discipline which is meant here is the kind calculated to bolster the child's feelings that somebody cares. It should include consistency in the routines of eating and sleeping. Parents should insist, in a friendly but unyielding manner, that the youngsters go to bed at the time set by the parents. Firmness implies that the parents do not give in to the child against their own better judgment. For example, if television poses a problem, a parent may find it helpful to get the child to "star" his favorite programs—one star for pretty good, two stars for good, three stars for very good, and so on. Parents may then permit the child to watch the five-star programs but not the others. A child scarcely can be expected to develop critical powers and good taste, unless the parents guide him.

In addition, parents may look for signs of the child's growing up and may encourage him to assume responsibilities in and around the home. If the child wishes to take care of a garden or a pet, or if he wishes to do some independent shopping or trading, he should be allowed to do so. These experiences can be valuable in permitting the child to feel needed, grown-up, and capable.

A tightening of home discipline will aid a child in growing up, relinquishing his baby habits, and feeling that someone cares about his character development. The "growing up" feeling is closely related to an improvement in ability to read. Coddling, oversympathizing, nagging, blowing hot and cold —i.e., now indulgent, now strict—all hinder the growth process because they leave the child feeling helpless.

98. MEETING INDIVIDUAL READING NEEDS*

Ruth V. McCreary

MEETING the individual needs of every child so that he can learn to read according to his potential ability is the philosophy of the reading program which began at Wooster, Ohio in the fall of 1950.

While children of to-day are reading more and better than ever before, the changing times demand constant improvement in reading skills.

Child studies over the past thirty years furnish evidence that the main causes of reading difficulties are: immaturity at the beginning stage, emotional disturbances, low intelligence, physical defects, absenteeism, changing schools, mass education, lack of up-to-date books as well as other instructional aids, and faulty teaching.

* From Ruth V. McCreary, "Meeting Individual Reading Needs," *Elementary English*, XXXVI, No. 5 (May, 1959), 294–97. Reprinted by permission of the author and the National Council of Teachers of English.

The initial step toward reading improvement in the Wooster schools was the administering of a survey reading test,[1] to all pupils in grades two through six. The results of this test brought out the fact that while the majority of the pupils were average and above in ability, there were many reading problems among the approximately 1,500 children enrolled at that time. Some were retarded from two to four years.

In order to reach as many children as possible, individual remedial instruction was started in the sixth grade, so that these pupils would have a better foundation before going on to junior high school. There was no instruction provided on that level at the beginning of the program. In 1957, a full-time reading improvement teacher was added to the junior high school staff.

[1] California Reading Test, California Test Bureau, 5916 Hollywood Blvd., Los Angeles 28, California.

Since there were so many children in need of help when the program began, the pupils with the highest I.Q.'s were considered first. We felt that they would profit most and the length of instruction would be shorter than for those who learned more slowly.

During the first year of the program in grades three through five, the pupils receiving remedial instruction were divided into small groups of five or six each. These children had three half-hour periods of group teaching each week while those having individual help were given two half-hour periods every week. Pupils were excused from their classroom for this special work. The remedial teacher travels between buildings.

Various remedial techniques and materials were tried out. Pupils receiving individual teaching were given the Gates Reading Diagnostic Test.[2] With the help of this test, reading difficulties were diagnosed, the instructional level was found, and a special program was worked out for each child.

After experimenting with many materials, the following have been found to be effective: a 7 x 8½ spiral notebook for recording examples of the letter sounds,[3] words missed on the Dolch Basic Sight Word list,[4] the Webster Word Wheels,[5] words that the child confuses, such as "went" and "want" and new words to be learned. "Eye and Ear Fun" phonics series,[6] by Clarence Stone and "Spelling Magic," [7] by William Kottmeyer, are used by each pupil according to his reading level and special needs. "Functional Phonetics," [8] a series of three books by Dr. Anna D. Cordts, are used by all pupils. Each child has a reader on his instructional level and a library book on his independent reading level for pleasure reading.

As soon as the pupil has mastered the Dolch list and has developed some independent word attack ability he is ready to enjoy the Dolch "Basic Vocabulary Series," [9] the "Cowboy Sam," and "Buttons" books.[10] The "I Want to Be" books,[11] by Carla Greene, encourage independent reading at beginner's level. Supplementary primers from various reading series also furnish good practice material at this stage.

With the average and above average pupil, the remedial course of instruction is continued until the classroom teacher feels that the pupil is ready to go on his own at his grade level. Children often show a gain of two or three levels with a few months' teaching.

If the pupil is slow-learning and his I.Q. is such that he may never bridge the gap between his reading achievement and grade placement as he advances through school, the individual instruction may continue on through junior high school or until he is old enough to obtain a working permit.

[2] Bureau of Publications, Teacher's College, Columbia University, 525 West 120th Street, New York 27, New York.
[3] Phonic Talking Letters, #262, Ideal School Supply Company, Harry M. Ward, Bryan, Ohio.
[4] The Garrard Press, Champaign, Illinois.
[5] Webster Publishing Company, St. Louis, Missouri.
[6] Webster Publishing Company, St. Louis, Missouri.
[7] Webster Publishing Company, St. Louis, Missouri.
[8] Benefic Press, Chicago, Illinois.
[9] The Garrard Press, Champaign, Illinois.
[10] Benefic Press, Chicago, Illinois.
[11] Children's Press, Chicago, Illinois.

Since the reading program has been extended into the junior high school, we are taking care of the type of pupil who will not be able to do the scholastic work in the senior high school; but he is having the enriching experience of working with pupils of his own age with differing abilities. This will help him to understand and adjust to the individual differences that exist among all children and adults. A great deal can be learned by listening, observing, and participating even if there is a wide range of abilities in the group.

In the junior high school reading improvement program some teaching is done in small groups in addition to the individual help. The type of instruction depends upon the special needs of each pupil. In the elementary grades all special reading instruction outside the regular classroom is done individually.

We have no special classes but we have special reading teachers to help the classroom teacher take care of the individual needs of the pupils. We have found that the needs of all types of children can best be met through partial segregation from the regular classroom.

Programs explaining how reading is being taught and how children learn to read are given for clubs and PTA groups.

A fall and spring "Book Fair" is held annually.

Classroom libraries have been established. New books are added each year. The importance of children's literature was stressed through a series of radio quiz programs, "Books are Fun." It was given each spring for three years, beginning in 1952. The manager of the local radio station was master of cere-

monies. Members of the American Association of University Women assisted with this program by acting as judges and helping with transportation.

Supplementary books with a wide range of reading levels have been added to every classroom.

Teachers are encouraged to study the special needs of their pupils and to take care of individual differences by grouping and projects in addition to individual attention and referral to the reading supervisor for help with special problems.

The above average pupil is not neglected. He, too, is provided with reading material at his particular level.

A summer school was conducted for the first three years of the program in order to reach some of those who could not be included in the regular school schedule. This type of group instruction is no longer necessary. However, individual instruction is available at a nominal fee during the summer for those children who seem to need additional work.

Our reading problems continue to diminish each year. All children in the special reading program, which includes grades three through eight and a few senior high school pupils, receive instruction in small groups or have individual help. We take care of about two hundred cases during the school term and about thirty additional pupils during the summer. Since there are now over 2000 children enrolled, we feel that the number of reading problems is low in proportion to the normal expectancy for an enrollment of this size.

We find that pupils are upgrading each year. The majority are well above the norm on the California Achievement Test which is given every spring.

Children coming from other schools who have been labeled non-readers, all learn to read when given our special reading course. While many examples could be cited, one of the most recent cases is that of a boy who entered one of our sixth grades in 1956, with an all "F" report card. He was thirteen years old and had just been transferred from grade to grade as the family moved about the country. A Stanford-Binet test showed that he had average ability. We knew that he could learn to read, so an individual program was worked out for him. Tommy had to start at pre-primer level, but he was eager to learn. He was accepted by the sixth graders and the teacher gave him as much individual attention as he could. He had two half-hour lessons with the special reading teacher every week. He was very restless and nervous at first but soon overcame his fear. Tommy wanted to read and in a short time was asking for a library book to take home. By the end of the term, tests showed that he had gone from pre-primer to third grade level. He was retained in the sixth grade to help him build vocabulary and to get a better foundation in reading. He had individual instruction during the summer and made satisfactory progress in the sixth grade the following year. He is now making pass-

ing grades in the junior high school. He will continue to receive reading instruction with the junior high school reading improvement teacher.

This boy took part in the summer recreation program and was co-builder of a "silver nosed rocket ship" for stunt night. If the school had not taken an interest in Tommy, he could have developed a bitter feeling toward all school activities. We feel that delinquency in the form of vandalism and other acts of law breaking can best be combated by reaching children before they become problems.

Truancy has been reduced to a minimum. We try not to neglect anyone and to make everyone feel that he belongs.

A half-time special reading teacher was assigned to the program in 1954. Because of the expanding enrollment this was increased to a full-time teacher in 1955. The enrollment continues to grow and adjoining school districts are being added to the system, so two full-time elementary teachers and a junior high school teacher in addition to the reading supervisor are a part of the reading program for 1958 and 1959.

Many examples can be given of pupils who were greatly retarded at the beginning of the program, but with individualized instruction have shown great improvement. These former pupils are now earning their living as useful law-abiding citizens.

99. READING CLINICS*

Albert J. Harris

A READING clinic is an organized group of people whose primary function or purpose is helping individuals become better readers. Because reading clinics vary greatly in their specific objectives, their organization, and in their modes of functioning, it is impossible to give a generalized description of how reading clinics work. It is, rather, necessary to describe a number of different kinds of reading clinics, and to indicate the points of differences as well as the elements there may be in common.

The most numerous reading clinics are those sponsored by colleges and universities. A listing published in 1960 † gives information about more than 120 college and university reading clinics. Of these, twenty-seven provided services only to the students of the institution; the rest provided some kinds of service to other clients.

The objectives and purposes of typical university clinics often include the following: (1) training of graduate students in the techniques of reading diagnosis and remedial reading instruction, (2) conducting research on various problems in reading, (3) providing developmental reading programs or courses in which competent undergraduate readers can raise their reading skills to higher levels, (4) providing remedial reading programs for undergraduate students whose reading ability is poor, (5) providing remedial reading services for elementary and secondary school pupils, (6) providing developmental or "speed reading" courses for adults, (7) providing consultant services to schools or school systems.

Because a major responsibility of universities which provide doctoral programs in reading (or in a specialization such as educational psychology, in which reading may be emphasized) is to train graduate students, both the remedial program and the research program in reading are likely to be closely integrated with this training function. In such institutions the person in charge may be a senior professor. The remedial teaching is done largely by graduate students taking courses in diagnosis and remediation, or by advanced graduate students working full or part time as members of the clinic staff. The clinic's case load is likely to be governed by the training needs, and the number of clients accepted is largely determined by the number of graduate students for whom supervised experience is necessary. Among the best known of the university clinics are those located at the University of Chicago, Boston Uni-

* From Albert J. Harris, "Reading Clinics," *The Reading Teacher,* XIV, No. 4 (March, 1961), 232–35. Reprinted by permission of *The Reading Teacher.*

† *Directory of Reading Clinics,* EDL Research and Information Bulletin No. 4 (Huntington, N.Y.: Educational Developmental Laboratories, 1960).

versity, Columbia University, New York University, Syracuse University, Temple University, University of Florida, and University of Minnesota.

Reading clinics which are located in undergraduate colleges usually give top priority to service for their own students, with both developmental and remedial programs. In addition, many of them offer remedial reading services to the community. Usually this work is done by members of the clinic's paid professional staff, although sometimes undergraduates taking courses in the teaching of reading are used as tutors for children.

Clinics located in colleges and universities usually have related clinical services so that special examinations can be arranged as needed. Thus in a large university, a reading clinic may be able to refer its clients to other units within the university, such as a psychological clinic, a speech clinic, or the ophthalmological, pediatric, neurological and psychiatric clinics of the university hospital. Specialized resources within the community, such as medical clinics, child guidance clinics and social service agencies, are also used by many college and university clinics as needed. Special services of these types are more likely to be available in large cities than in smaller communities.

College and university reading clinics are usually expected to be at least partially self-supporting. They usually charge low or moderate fees, but not enough to cover the full cost of the services provided. A few do not charge any fees, and some are completely self-supporting. They are vitally important, not primarily for the number of clients helped, although this service is a useful

one, but rather in training reading specialists for many different kinds of positions.

Second in number are the reading clinics organized as independent units. Some of these are sponsored by one or more civic or charitable organizations and obtain only part of their income, or none at all, from fees. Examples of these are the Northside Center for Child Development in New York City, and the Junior League Reading Center in Chattanooga, Tennessee. Some are independent nonprofit organizations with a board of directors to whom the professional staff is responsible. Most of the independent clinics, however, are private enterprises operated on a profit-making basis. They vary greatly in size, services offered, and competence and professional outlook of staff. Some of them are directed by people with good professional training and experience, and provide service of high quality. A few, unfortunately, utilize high pressure advertising methods, and provide service of mediocre quality.

Reading clinics not associated with schools or charitable organizations are, in most states, not subject to any kind of governmental supervision other than that over private business ventures in general. Before utilizing the services of such a clinic, therefore, it is desirable to make careful inquiries concerning the professional background of the staff and the organization's repute among local educators.

Least numerous, but increasing in number, are reading clinics which are organized within public school systems. The pioneer city in developing school reading clinics was St. Louis. Other large cities which have school reading clinics are Philadelphia and New York. New York City started with one clinic unit in 1955, and has been adding one or two units a year, so that in September, 1960 there were nine units in operation. Each unit has a staff of three or four "reading counselors," a full-time psychologist, a full-time psychiatric social worker, a part-time psychiatrist, and a clerk; all units are supervised by an administrator who in turn is responsible to an associate superintendent of schools. A description of this program has been published in this journal.*

The reading clinic as an organized group of professional people working together in a cooperative fashion has possibilities of action which are beyond the capabilities of the remedial teacher or reading specialist working in a schoolroom setting. Psychological examinations, social work with parents, and psychiatric evaluations and recommendations are available as needed. The clinic remedial teacher encountering difficulty with a child can consult with colleagues and with professionals trained in other disciplines. A clinic can conduct more thorough diagnostic studies than most remedial teachers, and can sometimes succeed with difficult cases that are not responsive to the usual kinds of remedial help.

One should not overlook remedial

* Stella S. Cohn, "The Special Reading Services of the New York City Board of Education, Part I—An Overview of the Program." *The Reading Teacher,* XII, No. 2 (December, 1958), 107–14. Margaretta W. Fite and Margaret M. Mosher, "The Special Reading Services of the New York City Board of Education, Part II—The Clinical Program." *Ibid.,* No. 3 (February, 1959), 181–86.

reading clinics which are part of larger clinical organizations, and clinics which carry on remedial reading programs as part of a total program of services for children. In New York City, for example, two general hospitals have small remedial reading clinics, related to their pediatric and psychiatric clinics. In America there are several hundred psychoeducational clinics, child guidance clinics, and mental hygiene clinics which find children with reading disabilities among their clients. Many of these clinics diagnose and treat reading problems. Often in such a clinic the educational, emotional, and social problems of a child receive simultaneous help, so that the child may be getting remedial teaching from one staff member, psychotherapy from another, and his mother may be seeing a third staff member. This kind of coordinated effort is particularly helpful with cases in which the emotional and social problems seem to be blocking progress in learning.

In many reading clinics there are facilities for both individual tutoring and small group work. Relatively few clinics provide individual help only; some see clients only in small groups. Groups generally vary in size from two to five or six children. In a few so-called clinics, teaching is done with groups of ten or more; these are really schools with small classes rather than clinics. When student groups are that large, it is unlikely that either in diagnosis or in instruction there can be the careful consideration of individual problems and needs, and the frequent consultations among staff members, which are characteristic of a properly functioning clinic.

There are, then, many kinds of reading clinics. Many of them are widely known, some are little known, even in their own communities. Collectively they form an excellent resource for the teacher or parent trying to find help beyond what the school can give. Those which train reading specialists and serve as research centers fulfill a vital role which is unique and indispensable.

INDEX

463